TRAVELING
Europe's
TRAINS

FIFTH EDITION

JAY BRUNHOUSE

PELICAN PUBLISHING COMPANY
Gretna 2001

First edition, 1989
Second edition, 1991
Third edition, 1994
Fourth edition, 1997
Fifth edition, 2001

This book is a revised edition of *Adventuring on Eurail* © 1989, 1991.

*The word "Pelican" and the depiction of a pelican are trademarks
of Pelican Publishing Company, Inc., and are registered in the
U.S. Patent and Trademark Office.*

Library of Congress Cataloging-in-Publication Data

Brunhouse, Jay.
    Traveling Europe's trains / Jay Brunhouse.—5th ed.
        p. cm.
    Includes index.
    ISBN 1-56554-854-X (pbk)
        1. Europe—Guidebooks. 2. Railroad travel—Europe—Guidebooks. I. Title.

D909 .B779 2001
914.04'56—dc21

                                                                2001032741

Maps by Brian Clarke and Jay Brunhouse

*Information in this guidebook is based on authoritative data available at the time of
printing. Prices and hours of operation of businesses listed are subject to change without notice. Readers are asked to take this into account when consulting this guide.*

Printed in Canada

Published by Pelican Publishing Company, Inc.
1000 Burmaster Street, Gretna, Louisiana 70053

Contents

Preface

Train travel in Europe is catering to your needs. The railroads want to get you from place to place as fast, as comfortably, and as conveniently as possible lest other passengers defect to auto and air. Europeans drive their cars to points less than an hour away and fly to points more than four hours away. It is in the one- to four-hour trip range that railroads shine.

The new high speed doesn't peril the traditional scenic routes that delight visitors. These routes have been protected. Their costs are underwritten by government and local authorities on the grounds that they attract tourists and/or provide service for the communities. These routes remain to charm you.

Throughout all of Western Europe, trains are convenient, comfortable, and economical highways of travel, free of gridlock. Europeans prefer them and, once aboard, you learn why. They give you the opportunity to dart from one city center to another. With insight, you see and enjoy Europe's beautiful rivers, lakes, Alps, and hillside chateaux from panoramic windows. Travelers on Europe's trains save money, learn from Europeans in congenial, give-and-take surroundings, explore corners of Europe where scenery dazzles their eyes, eat and sleep well and soundly, and arrive fully ready to go. They enjoy more than just a trip. They create a memory.

This book tips travelers on Europe's trains about how to get from here to there in the most efficient, convenient, comfortable, and fastest ways while saving money in the act. Pleasure-lovers discover thrilling scenery and wild and secret corners aboard exciting, offbeat trains—comfortable and dazzling—for little money, little hassle, and maximum delight.

Trains steal into hidden corners uncorrupted by automobile exhaust. Those who have traveled in the past are thrilled to discover European trains' time-warp speed, efficient infrastructure, and old-fashioned ambience.

Traveling Europe's Trains gives insight into the art of moving yourself here and there free of stress. Train travelers have perfected this art to its finest form. Take your pencil in hand. This guide tells you how to use Europe's trains and how to discover Europe from Wales to Russia. Highlight the information you'll use and put this book in your travel bag.

New and remodeled stations, subway links, and airport connections make trains easier to use. Sparkling, new stations, like Lisbon's Oriente and Berlin's Alexanderplatz and Friedrichstrasse, convenient new stations like Frankfurt Airport's new high-speed *Fernbahnhof* and those remodeled so thoroughly that they look like new, including Zurich, Leipzig, Mainz, and Rome main train stations. You use escalators and ramps instead of steps, read electronic and digital signboards, and use tourist offices located in the stations to help you see the city and book hotels for you. And of course, you can wear mouse ears to the new Disneyland Paris TGV station.

Narrow-gauge, cogwheel trains take you to the North Face of the Eiger; lonely lines reach the Midnight Sun at the most northerly station of Western Europe; rickety trams teeter along the cliffs of the Isle of Man, through the feudal highlands of Sardinia, and down Alpine ridges to the French Riviera.

You find that Europe's trains give you more time to enjoy yourself, smoother and more social travel, flexible and simple planning, and—with one of the new crop of cheap rail passes—your best value in Europe.

Acknowledgments

Thank you to those who helped me gather and confirm information, making this edition current and complete. Thank you Veronique Amato, David Boyce, Dave Beal, Lisa Brainin, Helga Brenner-Khan, Eric Buhlmann, Orla Carey, Cece Drummond, Maebeth Fenton, Cyril Ferris, Nils Flo, Hugo Furrer, Guirec Grand-Clement, Pat Gudel, Bruce C. Haxthausen, Jean Heger, Robert Jenkins, Helmut Klee, Andy Lazarus, Chris Lazarus, Erika Lieben, Alexander Loidl, Benson Leung, Joe Lustenberger, Gerhard Markus, Dominique Martin, Silvia Mayr-Pranzeneder, Evelyne Mock, Jan Nijboer, Armond Noble, Alan F. Reekie, Ingrid Rowe, Nathan Sawyer, Dag Scher, Barbara Schmidt, Jayne Shackleford, Cynthia Smith, Patricia Titley, Richard Tretten, Elke van Dommelen, Pilar Vico, and Alan C. Wissenberg. Flowery bouquets to expert editor Nina Kooij.

TRAVELING
Europe's
TRAINS

Introduction

There is feeling and thrill in traveling Europe's trains. Eurostar under the English Channel, across the Oresund Fixed Link to Sweden, TGVs, ICEs and gracefully tilting Pendolinos ignite travelers' sense of imagination with their thundering "whooshes," space-age speed, and sci-fi interiors. At the beginning of each chapter, read the Smart Traveling tips about how to get from here to there in the most efficient and economical ways. The first chapter helps you plan and takes you to Europe, well coached, with the right rail pass in your hand. You are guided aboard your train, to your destination, and back onto your train again so carefully a first-time traveler will have no worries. It steers veteran travelers toward overlooked scenery and wild and secret corners aboard exciting trains—the most comfortable and the most dazzling—for little money, little hassle, and maximum delight. You choose the scenic trains to enjoy. It makes traveling Europe's trains a snap.

You won't have to wave your passports at border guards or be disturbed during the night for passport checks when traveling between countries participating in the Schengen agreement. These include Austria, Italy, France, Germany, Spain, Portugal and the Benelux countries. Switzerland has not participated—no surprise.

Experienced travelers know all national train systems have their

quirks and secrets. Chapters revealing the fascination and operation of
traveling through the Eurotunnel by train, taking you aboard Europe's
trains from Dublin to Moscow, through the Alps, and from the
Midnight Sun to the Mediterranean beaches show you how to use trains
to your advantage. Trips taking you everywhere a train ticket goes—
West Europe, Britain, and East Europe, too—are described in careful
detail to simplify your traveling and your planning so you return home
happy, filled with memories, and still with money in your bank.

Timetables follow each trip to give you the latest schedules.
Remember that summer and winter timetables change yearly. Times
are shown using the same twenty-four-hour clock you see in Europe.
Major cities and connections are capitalized, and indications in a time
column show you when the train does not stop at that station. Notes
indicate special restrictions and tell you what you will find aboard your
train. Here is your first tip: when you can punch up a twenty-four-hour
clock on your digital watch, use this mode when reading timetables.

Other travel books tell you where to stay and what to see. This one
tells you how. It gives you tips to make your travel time exciting, social,
and offbeat—every moment a pleasure.

For simplicity, this book has dropped all the umlauts, accents, and
other pronunciation marks you see as you travel. The Thomas Cook
timetable retains all local spellings.

Will you have language troubles in Western Europe? None. Most of
the words you need to know to travel by train are obvious. Pictographs
(illustrated in the free rail pass reference materials you send for) are
used throughout Europe—and you won't need them in Britain. You
have found already most of the important word translations in this book.

City names are generally the same as in English. Just a few baffle:
Copenhagen is Kobenhavn; Florence is Firenze; Venice is Venezia in
Italian, Venedig in German; Antwerp is Anvers in French, Antwerpen
in Dutch; Geneva is Geneve in French, Genf in German; Munich is
Munchen in German, Monaco in Italian (the state of Monaco is Monte
Carlo to the Europeans); Vienna is Wien; Helsinki is Helsingfors in
Swedish; Athens is Athinai; Prague is Praha; Warsaw is Warszawa;
Moscow is Moskva; the Danube is the Donau; Hauptbahnhof is
German for main train station and Bahnhof refers to any train station.

It's advisable always to travel as though you were trekking through
New York's Times Square, but it is never so dangerous. Except for
areas of high drug activity and unemployment, such as in Eastern

Europe, most travelers report smooth and safe travel. Paranoia is not worth your mental effort, but caution is. (One publicized incident where travelers on a night train were reputedly gassed and robbed sounds as likely as flying saucers.) Carry little cash, preferably in a hanging pouch, rely on ATMs, and keep separate a photocopy of your passport and credit cards.

Smart Traveling on the Trains of Europe

Arranging Your Itinerary

Study guidebooks—Milk tourist offices—Get free train information—Use the Thomas Cook European Timetable—Plot your train travel strategies craftily—Let travel agents fill in the blanks

Study Guidebooks

You can gather all your general and specific information about packing, hotel and hostel accommodations, air transportation, food, shopping, and sightseeing from guidebooks in your library and bookshops. Tailored for train travelers with flexibility are the *Let's Go* guides, edited by the Harvard Student Agencies (St. Martin's Press, 175 Fifth Avenue, New York, NY 10010). Pelican also has a complete line of destination guides that you should consult (Pelican Publishing Company, P.O. Box 3110, Gretna, LA 70054-3110).

Milk Tourist Offices

After you have a general idea of your plans, check the Internet and contact the national tourist office of every country you think you might possibly visit. Their addresses and websites are in Appendix A. Don't simply ask for "information" or you will receive broad-brush brochures with pretty pictures. Ask specifically for details about your special interests, e.g., discount programs for hotels, subway savings and maps, castles to see, scenic bicycle routes, city "keys" or discount programs for museum admissions and city tours, regional maps and sightseeing in specific cities and areas.

Get Free Train information

Even when you are not considering buying a Eurailpass, its distributors provide you with excellent, free information (see below, and Appendix A for addresses). Ask for all the following:

• The Eurail/InterRail eighty-nine-page timetable (with map) for the best European InterCity trains.

• "Eurail Map & Traveler's Guide," an indispensable large foldout Eurail train map of Europe with excellent "how to" text on the back filled with wise tips on all aspects of train travel in Europe.

• "Europe on Track" (from Rail Europe, *www.raileurope.com*), "Europe Rail" (from DER Tours, *www.dertravel.com*), "Discover Europe by Train" (from CIT Tours, *www.cit-tours.com*), "Britain Secrets" (from BritRail, *www.BritRail.net* or *www.britainsecrets.com*), giving you Eurail and other rail-pass prices and rules.

Rail Europe has a fast and convenient tool for you to obtain train schedules and prices between city pairs by fax-back. Dial either 1-888-382-7245 or 1-800-EUROSTAR and select from a menu of four options: information on rail passes, hotels, air, and rental cars; information on specific countries; information on train fares and schedules between more than 3,000 European cities; or a brochure. When you enter on your telephone keypad your arrival and departure cities you receive fare and schedule information for train travel between them, and when you then enter your fax number, almost immediately your fax machine receives the printout, which you can use for your planning.

The web is overflowing with travel information. Almost every railroad has a web page. To save cataloging the many sites, you can access the GermanRail site at *www.bahn.de* and then click on "virtual railways" for links to every site.

Use the Thomas Cook European Timetable

Check to see whether the reference desk of your public library has a copy of the Thomas Cook European Timetable, which is updated monthly. Should your library fail you, look for it in bookstores specializing in travel literature. If there is no travel bookstore near you, order the timetable from Forsyth Travel Library, (1-800-FORSYTH). June and subsequent summer issues have the complete summer timetables. Cost is $27.95 plus $4.95 priority shipping.

The Thomas Cook European Timetable helps you with detailed advance planning. When you buy one, carry it with you, or tear out the pages covering the countries you are visiting and take them with you, but in many train carriages filled with travelers in Europe you will see one or more copies of the bright, orange-colored timetable, and the owner will be more than happy to let you browse through it.

All European railroads publish complete timetables, but they are generally too bulky to carry around. In some countries they run into many volumes. Agents in the information offices will check their computers for you, but most railroads also publish pocket-sized timetables for their most heavily traveled routes and place on racks leaflets listing connections between popular city pairs or regions. These are available, free for the asking, in the information offices of the railroads (not the tourist office) in train stations.

Plot Your Train Travel Strategies Craftily

Consider several travel strategies depending on where you decide to go and what you want to do. Travelers covering long distances prefer the circular trip plan. Start and end your train travel at your airline's European gateway and cover your stops with a circular plan that brings you back to your gateway city. (You can sometimes arrange an "open-jaw" airline ticket that allows you to return from a different city than the one in which you arrived.) When you want to see Europe extensively, you can see more using this plan.

You have best results when you plan at least one overnight following your arrival at your airline gateway city to allow for jet lag and familiarization, and at least two when you return there. This gives you flexibility to change your plans or cope with any unexpected delays during your trip.

Before you leave home, make a working itinerary. Using your timetables, select the best trains. Outline your day, city, and train connections. Carefully note the days of the week because some trains do not run on weekends or local holidays.

Make your itinerary loose enough so you can vary it depending on circumstances. Keep backup and alternative plans in the back of your mind. You can usually count on reliable train connections, but strikes and natural disasters such as washouts can (and do) devastate split-second plans.

Some travelers save money by alternating nights in hotels and aboard trains. They travel on an overnight train, check into their hotel in the morning, shower, etc., do their sightseeing in the afternoon, and see the city by night. On the following day, they check out of their hotel, leave their luggage with the concierge, top off their daylight sightseeing, dine, pick up their luggage, and leave on the late-evening overnight train for their next destination. This plan works either with a consecutive-day rail pass or a flexible rail pass allowing you to validate a single box for overnight trains departing after 7 P.M. (see below).

The second strategy involves locating in one city and taking day trips to nearby places of interest. This fits well with a flexible rail pass because you can conserve your day boxes for long distances. You double your time on the train and return to your bed at the mercy of the train schedule, but you won't waste time packing, unpacking, and checking in and out of hotels. When you want to see an area intensively, this is the plan you follow.

Let Travel Agents Fill in the Blanks

The right travel agent will save you a lot of time and effort and surprise you with good advice. Their computers handle rail passes. Let them buy for you your Eurail, regional, and national rail-pass products, hotel packages, and airline tickets. They also can make reservations (up to two months in advance) for seats, overnight sleeping cars, and couchettes in the trains. Make your sleeping reservations at the same time you buy your rail pass, as soon as you can, to avoid electronic glitches. You must pay a service charge for seat reservations, making them more expensive than when you make them in Europe, so unless it is essential to secure them early, you are generally wiser to wait until you arrive in Europe and visit your first train station to make reservations.

In conjunction with rail passes, Rail Europe and DER Tours offer "Go as you please" hotel voucher plans for use throughout Europe (see "Locating a hotel room," below) and Hilton International Hotels offer discounts.

It's not worth agents' time to write your letters for inexpensive hotels or pensions, and you are better off handling this yourself before you leave or, even easier, arranging accommodations at the tourist office when you get there. Most travelers like to have a confirmed place to stay for the day they arrive and then make their subsequent arrangements as they travel along.

Choosing the Right Pass

*Eurailpass—Pass Protection—Eurail Flexipass—Eurail Saverpass—
Eurail Youthpass—Europass—Eurail Selectpass—National and
regional rail passes—Rail/Drive passes*

Eurailpass

Eurailpasses are airline-style tickets covering unlimited travel on the national train networks of seventeen countries: Austria, Belgium, Denmark, Finland, France, Germany, Greece, Hungary, Republic of Ireland, Italy, Luxembourg, the Netherlands, Norway, Portugal, Spain, Sweden, and Switzerland. Eurailpasses come in two versions: consecutive-day passes for continuous use for a given time period and flexible passes making it possible to choose the days you wish to travel within a reasonable time.

BritRail, Eastern European countries (except Hungary), and some private lines are not affiliated with Eurailpass.

It is true that when you pay for all your transportation in one lump sum, Eurailpasses seem like a lot of money, but nothing approaches their value when you take total advantage of them.

• It is convenient. By buying rail passes before leaving home, you avoid standing in lines at counters you sometimes can't find to purchase tickets or surcharge coupons in unfamiliar currencies from foreign agents who often do not speak English (this problem is acute in Eastern Europe). This frees you to board almost any train you choose, thus making it easier for you to travel on impulse, especially on the more popular lines with trains departing hourly.

• It is easy to use. You don't have to sort through stapled and loose tickets and coupons to show the conductor. Just flash your pass.

• You can change your mind. When an acquaintance convinces you to go to Rome instead of Vienna, just board the next train. When it's flooding in Venice, get off the train in sunny Salzburg.

• It's cheap. You pay in low-inflation dollars. Fixed prices reflect last year's exchange rate and protect you from creeping dollar devaluation.

• You pay at home and know in advance to the cent exactly how much your transportation will cost. When crises rack the European currency markets, you are secure in having locked in dollar prices before departure. If the dollar sags, wheezes, or does a loop the loop, you have no worry.

• Free train travel information gives you a planning edge. Maps and pocket timetables guide you through Europe.

Eurailpasses cover fast-train surcharges with only a few exceptions. You sit in first-class sections of the best trains of Europe without having to go to the trouble and expense of buying a supplement coupon. Further, you have access to the handful of elite trains that are limited to buyers of first-class tickets only, such as the Crystal Panoramic Express in Switzerland and the panoramic dome cars of the Swiss railroads.

Your travel agent provides your Eurailpass with the line blank where your passport number is to be entered. Before you board your first train, you must have staff at the train station (any train station in Europe) validate the pass by entering your passport number and hand-stamping it or validating it with the agent's validator. When traveling, you should keep your passport handy so the conductor can check it against the passport number on the Eurailpass. In practice this happens very rarely, except in the Netherlands where rumor has it that forgeries have been found.

Reservation fees, special business train supplements for meals or deluxe seats, the Flam line supplement (see "Scandinavia" chapter), and charges for sleeping accommodations on trains or aboard ships are not covered by the pass.

Treat a consecutive-day Eurailpass like a cow. Milk it every day. Eurailpass gives you free the kinds of things you would want to do even if you had no other reason to buy the pass itself. The bonuses cover thirty-seven column inches of fine print on the back of the free Eurailpass map. Read how best to use them in each section of this book.

When you choose a Eurail Flexipass, Europass (see below) or national flexipass that you can use at your discretion, it makes sense to conserve the days for long-haul travel and buy local tickets for inexpensive, short excursions.

The Eurail Executive Committee authorizes four European railroads to distribute Eurailpasses in North America: French, Swiss, German, and Italian. These are represented by Rail Europe (FrenchRail owns the majority interest, SwissRail the minority), DER

Tours (GermanRail owns the majority interest), and CIT Tours (Italian Railroads). Each of the companies' programs will offer slight variations. Each of the companies also market national and regional passes associated with their interests and, in addition, thanks to FrenchRail, Rail Europe markets a stable of passes for travel in Eastern European countries.

Buy your pass through your travel agent or directly through the distributors. Their addresses are listed in Appendix A.

Travelers planning to visit Europe in the spring (through June) can compound their savings by buying at the last tick of the old year's clock, when rail pass prices may increase. When you buy before the turn of the calendar, you have six months to validate your rail pass in Europe before boarding your first train. This makes it particularly convenient for travelers planning to use passes valid for longer periods of time, such as one or two months, because you can validate your pass before your deadline in June, and travel during the summer at the previous year's prices (which were set even the year before that).

Eurailpasses are most easily purchased from your nearby travel agent at home. But—contrary to popular notion—they may also be purchased in Britain and Eurailpass countries at any of the fifty-six Eurail Aid offices listed in Appendix B by permanent residents of North and South America, Australia, New Zealand, most of Africa, and Asia excluding the C.I.S. who have been in Europe less than six months. In addition to being less available in Europe, they are sold at a ten percent premium over the price you pay at home and you must pay in local currencies. This latter restriction is less onerous than you would think because most Eurail Aid offices accept MasterCard and Visa. The price is pegged to the U.S. dollar price plus ten percent, so no matter whether the dollar is weak or strong relative to the currency of the country where you make your purchase, you will always pay 10 percent more than at home.

Pass Protection

The European Railroads' policy is that no pass is refundable or replaceable if lost or stolen, but North American distributors have come up with plans that protect you against this. If you sign up for their plan, at a cost of $12 per pass, they will compensate you for the unused portion of a lost of stolen pass. To qualify for reimbursement, you need to file a police report, and then you must purchase a replacement rail pass or rail ticket and complete your train travel. You will be reimbursed for the unused value of the pass. The procedure and conditions for obtaining a reimbursement are listed in a flyer that you receive with you pass.

BritRail Passes are never refunded or replaced. Refunds are limited to completely unused, unvalidated passes returned within six months to one year of date of issue and subject to cancellation charges of 15 percent.

Eurail Flexipass

Travelers do best buying consecutive first-class Eurailpasses when traveling extensively across Europe, but those visiting only a few international destinations save money buying Eurail Flexipasses or Eurail Youth Flexipasses. These provide travel for the specific number of days required, and allow a reasonable time in which to use them.

There was a time when European trains were blooming with flower children holding Eurailpasses and knocking about carefree from Narvik to Naples. Those days are long gone. Modern rail pass purchasers are known to be more likely to stop longer at a single destination.

Eurail Flexipasses gives you new options in planning. You stay as long as you want in one place without squandering money you invest in a pass. Concentrate your time in fewer locations and range less far afield with your travel adventures. Break your train traveling to rent a car, spend some time with relatives in the old country, sunbathe on a Greek isle, ski in Switzerland, or even take time to visit England or Eastern European countries that don't honor Eurailpasses.

Flexipasses are do-it-yourself passes. Your airline-style pass includes spaces to date in ink on the days you travel. Enter the date when you decide to board the train—or aboard the train quickly when the conductor ("controlleur") starts to pass through—but enter it carefully with the correct date because the conductor is not allowed to accept cross-outs and you will waste a date. Then you travel that entire day as much as you want until midnight.

When you start your trip between 7 P.M. and midnight, date the box with the following day so your validation continues until the following midnight. Some travelers ride overnight and use up only one validation date while avoiding the cost of lodging.

Traveling on one of the overnight international sea crossings covered by Eurailpass uses up only one validation date because you enter either the date of departure or the next day's date to take advantage of connecting trains at both ends.

Eurail Saverpass

Eurail gives a fifteen percent discount for groups of two or more travelers traveling together on a first-class consecutive or Flexipass basis. The problem is traveling together. Your group can't break up and go traveling off in separate directions and still qualify for the discount. However, children aged four to eleven pay only half price but count fully as part of your group.

When you tailor your traveling to these restrictions, you qualify for the good deal.

Eurail Youthpass

When you are younger than 26 on your first day of travel, you qualify for a 30 percent discount for a second-class Youthpass. You can buy consecutive-day Eurail Youthpasses in increments of 15 or 21 days or one, two, or three months. You can opt for Eurail Youth Flexipasses valid for ten or fifteen days of travel within two months. You save money of course, and you find it easier to meet Europeans of your same age, who almost always will be traveling at the lower fares. Second-class travel is more crowded, more social, and every bit as scenic as first-class travel.

You get even more value from Youth Flexipasses when you combine them with inexpensive second-class national and regional passes according to your travel plans. Eurail Youthpasses give you the same benefits and bonuses as first-class Eurailpasses, except that you must pay to upgrade to first-class-only trains and express steamers on the Rhine River. You would only ride these anyway when you travel with parents or older adults (especially when they need you to qualify for a Eurail Saverpass) or when you want extra comfort and greater flexibility with a full-fare Eurailpass.

Europass

Europasses, introduced in December 1993, outsold Eurailpasses for the first time in 1996. Europasses allow you to specify and purchase in advance close to the exact number of days between five and 15 that you wish to travel by train.

You can consider Europasses as regional flexipasses covering five base countries: France, Germany, Italy, Spain, and Switzerland. In addition to the five base countries, there are associate countries, called "zones." With an eight-day or longer Europass you can add zones to your Europass, in which case it is called a "Europass Plus." There are four zones: Belgium/Netherlands/Luxembourg, Austria/Hungary, Portugal, and Greece (including the ferry crossing from Italy). They all cost the same. When you add one zone, you pay $60 extra, adult; $45, youth. You can add a second zone of your choice for $40 more, adult, $33, youth. Adding these zones does not increase your days of validity, only the range where you may travel.

Europass offers a companion discount like the Eurail Saverpass discussed above. Two persons traveling together at all times receive a 15 percent discount on the price of a Europass. Travelers under twenty-six traveling second-class receive a one-third discount for a Youth Europass.

Europasses offer all the advantages of Eurail Flexipasses but you do not have to pay for the 10-day minimum unless you need to, and they are cheaper. In essence you pay only for the countries used by most Eurailpass purchasers without having to pay for the privilege of possibly traveling through the entire 17 covered by Eurailpass.

When you further want to travel in a country or area that is not a core or associate country, you have a generous two months to complete your travels, so the flexipass feature of the Europass makes it possible for you to use a national rail pass for the country of your desire and wrap your Europass dates around your dates there. Compare the price of this combination with a Eurail Flexipass.

Europass fills the gap between national passes and the nearly continent-wide Eurailpass. When you plan to travel in one or maybe two countries, national passes are more economical. Look to a combination of national rail passes by consulting brochures available free from Rail Europe, DER, CIT (see Appendix A). When you are ranging far afield, a Eurailpass is your vehicle. When you are traveling aboard the five networks sponsoring this pass, Europass fills the bill.

Eurail Selectpass

On January 1, 2001, a new Eurail railpass was offered to appeal to those planning shorter and more geographically limited European travel. The Eurail Selectpass allows you to travel among any three adjoining Eurailpass countries (17 in total), whether they are adjoined

by land or water. You select the countries you know you will visit.
Examples include Germany-France-Ireland, Germany-Denmark-
Finland, Switzerland-Italy-Greece, and because Benelux is counted as
one country for Selectpass purposes, Netherlands-Belgium-Luxembourg-
Germany-Austria.

The Eurail Selectpass is a flexipass available for five, six, eight, and
10 days within two months. Prices are five to 10 percent less than a
Europass of the same validity period, so a Selectpass is more economical for you if you only plan to travel in three countries, and it is especially advantageous if you are going to travel in a country not covered
by Europass, such as traveling between Germany and Italy through
Austria.

You can by the Eurail Selectpass in its standard flexipass version, or
you can save 15 percent using a Eurail Select Saverpass for two to five
persons traveling together at all times, or 30 percent for a Eurail Youth
Selectpass for travelers ages 12 to 25. You may validate your Eurail
Selectpass in any of the 17 countries covered by Eurailpass.

National and Regional Rail Passes

So many American travelers use Eurailpasses on long European
express trains that conductors' eyes sometimes blur checking the
passes. When a conductor sees you flashing the colorful rail pass of his
homeland, he knows you have an interest in his country. He adjusts his
eyeglasses, smiles, and mentally snaps to attention.

Most national railroads of Europe have their own all-purpose rail
passes valid for unlimited travel within their borders. Some are good
deals you buy in advance in U.S. dollars. The most popular ways to save
money—and have lots of fun—are the best-selling passes of Britain,
Finland, France, Germany, Italy, the Netherlands, Norway, Spain,
Sweden, Switzerland, and the Eastern countries. regional passes for
Scandinavia, Iberia, Benelux, Britain + Ireland, and European East
(Austria, Hungary, Poland, the Czech Republic, and Slovakia) combine travel on several networks and extend the coverage you receive
with a Eurailpass.

Such passes save you money in several ways. You pay less per day,
adults can travel second-class at lower prices, you take juniors with you
and pay as little as half for their tickets (free with a Swiss Pass), and
sometimes you receive useful side benefits that are more generous
than Eurailpass' bonuses.

National rail passes and regional rail passes do not let you travel across unlimited national boundaries like the continent-wide Eurailpass, but when you plan to travel in a single country or region these passes will save you money compared to a Eurailpass. Residents have their own promotional pass programs for which you are ineligible.

Travelers buying a single country or regional pass use the same reasoning to decide whether to buy consecutive-day or flexible rail passes when both are available. When you want to travel extensively, you choose consecutive rail passes. When you want to travel selectively, you take flexipasses.

Rail/Drive Passes

A Rail/Drive pass can be an ideal marriage, but leave the driving to your spouse.

Some of your friends report good results driving through Europe in rented cars. They argue fiercely with others who advocate train travel. Both cite the relative convenience, cost, and ability to learn about and appreciate Europe while traveling by their favorite means.

Rental auto advocates insist that you can visit villages not served by trains, and thus take advantage of cheaper lodging; that you can Drive to the front door of your destination and make detours on a whim.

The most common reason that you hear for not traveling by train is that train travel doesn't let you see the countryside or reach remote areas. Renting a car, just like at home, seems to be a solution, but Europe is different than home. Visiting Europe gives you the additional, and better, viable option of traveling by train—an option you don't have at home.

Annually, you see four times as many fatal accidents on European roads as on North American ones. Your chance of having an accident in Europe is 125 times greater on a highway than on a train. Each year, nearly 60,000 people are killed on the roads in western Europe, but the railroads have managed to improve their safety record, year in and year out. Twenty years ago there was 1.0 passenger fatality per billion train passenger miles, but today this figure has fallen to 0.3. Renting a car means cursing gridlock, fighting congestion and watching the road ahead. Is this why you visit Europe? The cost can also be higher than expected, considering the high cost of gasoline, taxes of 6 to 33 percent, and highway and bridge tolls.

Local trains carry visitors to remote towns just as easily as rental cars. Unlike the train system in North America, the European rail system not only spreads out like a series of high-speed connecting webs between major cities, but connecting local trains take you from the closest hub to the tiniest village. When you visit friends, they expect to meet you in front of the station. Otherwise use the taxi, streetcar or subway in front of the station.

Everyone who has traveled by train will tell you that you get on and off easily. With a train, you don't isolate yourself, you get the feeling of the country, you learn information you can use, and you gain insights from the Europeans you meet in your train compartment. You cut the red tape, insurance headaches, and difficulties of picking up and returning cars. You see more than when you are behind a wheel cursing crazy drivers or buried in a road map sorting out lines that don't seem to exist. You don't have to stuff the back seats of small automobiles with your luggage or worry about it or the car getting ripped off. You don't suffer the quirks of foreign automobiles or strange, and sometimes dangerous, obscure rules of the road. You don't have to search out parking places, figure out the parking fee system, and walk even greater distances through pedestrian malls from a parking place than from the train station. Combination Rail'n Drive passes are available in Britain, Britain plus Ireland, France, Germany, Spain, Scandinavia and Switzerland and with Eurailpasses and Europasses.

The EurailDrive Pass gives you three individual days' unlimited use of a Hertz or Avis rental car in the 17 Eurailpass countries added to the features of a four-day Eurail Flexipass, the option of buying at a preferential rate up to five additional train travel days and as many car days as you like, and free drop-off within the country where you take possession. It allows you to choose between three car categories with manual transmission.

The eight-day Europass Drive plan is similar to the Eurailpass Drive. It is less expensive but you must follow the country restrictions of the Europass described above.

Whether these will save you money depends on your travel plans. When you Drive the cars here and there along your route you save considerably over expensive one-day car rentals. But when you break your travels and drive a car from one location for an extended time, a weekly rate may save you money.

Rail passes give you the freedom to travel easily over long distances. Your car gives you local transportation, delivers you to doorsteps of relatives, and takes you to special, secluded hideaways.

Rail 'n Drive Avis and Hertz plans in connection with national rail passes work similarly. The car rental companies have locations throughout Europe (and on the Greek islands), many in or near train stations. On average their European fleets are less than six months old and English-speaking personnel are on call 24 hours a day.

Hertz offers a special plan to Eurailpass holders who are 26 years and older. The rate includes unlimited mileage, collision damage waiver, and local taxes. You can reserved through a Hertz reservation center in Europe or directly in Europe at the nearest Hertz office.

Boarding Your Train

Using subway and rapid-transit services—Finding your departure platform—Locating your proper carriage—Dining on wheels

Using Subway and Rapid-transit Services

All of Europe's major cities have either a subway or a rapid-transit connection to their principal train stations—and usually both. Subways save you steps by bringing you directly into the platform areas in many stations ("Bahnhof," "Estacion," "Gare," "Pu," "Stazione"). Rapid-transit trains from the suburbs (which in all cases you ride free with a Eurailpass except for Paris's rapid-transit electric trains, the RERs) sometimes let you off on platforms parallel to the one from which you leave.

Almost all major cities have two or more train stations. Be absolutely certain you go to the correct one. You don't want to carry your luggage into Paris's Gare d'Austerlitz only to find out your train is boarding at the Gare de Lyon.

Finding Your Departure Platform

When you arrive, especially when you are in a hurry, immediately look for departure information. This could be in the form of numeric signs, clacking digital signs, huge electronic displays, or old-fashioned, yellow posters—"Abfahrt," "Avgaende," "Avgang," "Depart," "Lahtevat," "Partenze," "Salida," "Vertrek" (not the white ones, nor the ones printed in red in the Netherlands; those are for train arrivals). They confirm your departure time and tell you the number of the departure platform or track ("Arden," "Bahnsteig," "Binario," "Gleis," "Linho," "Plattaforma," "Quai," "Raide," "Spar," "Spoor," "Spor," "Via," "Voie").

Locating Your Proper Carriage

While you are walking to your platform, look for posters (sometimes on blue paper) or glassed-in bulletin boards ("Composition des Trains," "Composizione Principali Treni," "Indulo Vonatok," "Kaukojunien Vaunujarjestys," "Nemzetzoki Vonatok Osszeallitasa," "Placement des Voitures," "Stand van de Rijtvtgen," "Var i Taget gar Vagnen," "Vognanviser," "Vognenes Placering i Perron Afsnit," "Wagenstandanzeiger") with color-coded cutouts of lined-up locomotives and train carriages (couchettes, dining, first- and second-class, etc.). You may see these anywhere, but most often right in the center of the departure platform when you get there. It is easiest to pick out your train by its departure time.

On these posters you identify the carriage in which you have a reservation by its destination and carriage number. Often, vertical lines or strings are superimposed to form a grid. A "sector" (repere, secteur, Sektor, vagnlage) letter (*A, B, C,* etc.) indicates where your carriage now stands or will stand when it arrives. These letters are prominently hung above the respective platform locations. Walk to the stopping sector for your carriage to avoid having to rush down the platform when your long train pulls in and makes ready to depart. When you have no reservation and are traveling by rail pass—and don't care which carriage you board—still determine where the carriage you prefer to your specific destination comes to a stop.

While you are looking at the train make-up, look to see whether your train is carrying a buffet or restaurant car and where it is located relative to your carriage.

In Swiss stations, in addition to composition boards, the digital departure signs above the platforms give you the entire train make-up at the bottom: an arrow indicates the direction the train travels, a "1" indicates each first-class carriage, a knife-and-fork dining symbol indicates the restaurant car, and a "2" indicates each second-class carriage. Below this shorthand is a note telling at which sector the car for children will arrive. (These carriages are marked with a teddy bear and a "Kinderwagen" sign.) Zurich's Hauptbahnhof's digital signs contain lists of destinations, type of train, departure time, and digits showing how the carriages stand in sectors *A, B,* and *C.*

A yellow stripe (blue dashes on some Dutch trains) indicates first class although most high-speed trains have abandoned this convention in favor of using more distinguished liveries. When your train slows to a stop, you should be standing beside your carriage, but be sure to check that your destination matches the signboard fixed to the outside of the carriage (some new trains have LED displays on the outside showing destinations and times of arrival). Another signboard is usually posted in the vestibule. French TGV, Thalys, Spanish AVE, and German ICE trains have LED displays in the vestibule showing their destination, train number, and carriage number, so it is difficult to go wrong.

When you are carrying heavy luggage, leave it in the space usually provided at the entryways of salon carriages, but guard it carefully at station stops. When it is light, hoist it onto the overhead rack above your seat or slide it into a space between back-to-back seats.

When you sit in a compartment, you have overhead privileges. Etiquette requires that you pile your suitcases in the space in the overhead rack directly above your seat and not distribute them randomly. This makes it easy to see that your seat is occupied even when you leave it for a moment.

With a reservation, you have an assigned seat. Without one, you must be careful not to sit in one already reserved. These are marked electronically or with paper or plastic strips (usually yellow) inserted in seat backs or on hallway doors. On the other hand, when there is no slip or it says "non reserve" or "nicht reserviert," it is available. When the seat is reserved from Hamburg to Cologne, for example, you are welcome to sit in it between Mainz and Basel.

In a compartment, try to sit next to the window facing forward. In a salon car, you can appreciate the scenery better by sitting next to a window at the back of the carriage.

Dining on Wheels

Europe's newest and fastest trains generally position dining cars in the center of the trains, effectively separating first- and second-class carriages. The dining spaces are divided functionally into two sections. The half facing the first-class carriages has tables set with white tablecloths, a complete menu, and waiters standing ready. The adjacent half facing the second-class carriages has a bistro, pub, or cafeteria selling snacks and refreshments or (in Britain) a take-away counter. Dining cars vary from train to train depending on the market served and customs of the country. You are guaranteed meal service on all international trains, except Thalys on weekends, ICE, Eurostar Italia,

EuroCity, most InterCity trains, and all the new night trains, e.g., Tren Hotel, InterCity Night, and CityNightLine.

You find exemplary dining cars on the best EuroCity trains, Switzerland's Glacier Expresses, Germany's InterCity Expresses, Cisalpino, and InterCity trains in Germany, Austria, Italy, and Switzerland. Waiters bring meals to your seat on Eurostar, British InterCities, French TGVs, Spanish Talgos, Norwegian ICEs, Swedish X2000s, and Finnish InterCities. Wheeled refreshment trolleys (called "mini-bars") overflowing with local specialties, sandwiches, pastries, and refreshments clatter through the aisles on most long-distance trains.

As you would expect, prices are higher aboard trains than in stations and higher in stations than in local supermarkets. Large train stations have some sort of travelers provisions, supermarket, or grocery store you should visit. One of the more important things to buy for long trips is a liter or two-liter plastic bottle of mineral water with a twist-on cap. Some travelers bring canteens with them. A Swiss army knife with a bottle opener and corkscrew is even handier.

Arriving in Your City

Luggage carts—Changing your money—Locating a hotel room—
Reserving your train connection—Getting to your hotel

When you arrive in a new city, get money, a hotel, and your onward reservation before leaving the station. Public transportation to your hotel is usually a snap.

Luggage carts

Luggage carts are usually available on the platform, and sometimes free for you to use, but in most large stations they are linked together so that to release one you must have a coin of the proper denomination. These annoying mechanisms refund your coin when you lock up your cart. Using the cart costs you nothing, but it means you must have a correct coin when you arrive.

Big spenders will be pleased to hear that porter services are making a comeback. You can find them in just a few of the largest stations such as Paris Nord, in Italy, and main train stations in Germany. They are not cheap.

When you leave your train you often pass into an underground passageway. The direction toward platform one leads you to the main hall. Here you usually find a change bank, ATMs, train information office, and—in most countries—a tourist office nearby.

Changing Your Money

The very first thing to do upon arrival is to change for local currency. ATMs are your best bet for favorable exchange rates and they are open after the banks close. Every traveler will benefit from carrying a bank credit card or ATM card for withdrawals or instant cash. These friendly devices will accept your Visa or MasterCard or "Plus" or "Cirrus" network ATM card, depending on whether the machine's bank is affiliated with your home bank. It helps to carry two cards from different banks to increase your chances that one will be accepted. Some machines will read your card as being issued in the United States and automatically give you directions in English. Some call you by name, and then refuse the card you carry. Most require you to press the "English" button. Often there are also change machines with directions in English that change currencies twenty-four hours a day. You simply insert bank notes from any hard-currency country and receive bills in the local currency. Beware of any change office that is not a bank. You can expect poorer rates and/or a heavy service charge no matter what the large posters claim. Avoid getting caught with very high denomination coins by changing them into paper before you leave. Spend the lower-denomination coins for provisions.

Locating a Hotel Room

Your second order of business is locating a room for the night. Some tourists scrupulously follow hotel recommendations in travel guides, but the rule is simple: the more you pay the more you get, and vice versa. Competing hotels on the same block with equal amenities charge virtually the same. In fact, ones recommended in best-selling guides may be able to charge slightly more because of their popularity with guidebook-reading disciples. Beware of hotels that guidebooks describe as "clean." When writers say nothing more positive, look elsewhere.

It's often worth a few minutes after your arrival just to go outside the train station and look around. Frequently you see an attractive or suitable hotel nearby. There are sparkling Frantours Hotels in Paris' Gare de l'Est and Gare de Lyon. There are hotels right in Madrid's

Chamartin and Barcelona's Sants train stations. Glasgow's two stations have hotels in the station. In Cologne and Zurich, you will see clusters of hotels outside the back entrances. GermanRail has an affiliated string of InterCityHotels that you can book right at GermanRail reservation counters. Most of them are located adjacent to the train stations. Find them in Augsburg, Berlin Ostbahnhof, Frankfurt/Main, Hamburg, Magdeburg, Nuremburg, Stuttgart and Ulm. The InterCityHotel in Munich is not affiliated.

In many large train stations there are two information offices—one operated by the railroads ("Auskunft," "Information," "Inlichtingen," "Neuvonta," "Oplysninger," "Reise Zentrum," "Renseignements," "Travel Centre") and one by the city tourist office. The personnel in the train information office usually will politely refuse to answer your questions about hotel rooms. Those in the city tourist office send you across the station for train information.

You often find the city tourist office ("Bureau de Turisme," "Tourist Information Centre," "Turismo," "Syndicat d'Initiative," "Verkehrsverein," "Verkehrsburo," "VVV") by looking for the information sign: "i." You may see it adjacent to the train information office, a few doors down the street from the exit of the train station, across the street, in a kiosk in the plaza in front of the train station, or nearby, but indicated by an arrow. When the city tourist office does not have a location at the train station, often a commercial, profit-making organization performs the function of finding you a room. In many Swiss and German train stations you find electronic consoles with photos of hotels, their prices, indications of whether they are filled, a city map showing you their locations, and—in Switzerland—automatic, free telephone connections with their room clerks to make reservations.

The best time to arrive at the tourist office for a hotel booking is about 10 A.M. When you arrive at popular or convention destinations late in the afternoon or in the evening, you will find it very difficult or impossible to find a good room unless you have made reservations in advance. You may have to reboard a train just to find a soft place to sleep.

At the tourist office counter, specify how much you want to pay and the area you want to stay in. Staying near the train station is often convenient, but sometimes an off-color neighborhood is also nearby. The tourist office personnel advise you. You are usually charged a nominal service fee. Sometimes you must also leave a reasonable deposit, which is later deducted from your hotel bill, and are told to check into your assigned hotel within a specified period of time. This time is negotiable when you have errands to accomplish first.

This plan usually gets you a suitable hotel, but in some cities you can't find a tourist office. In any event, you lose time you would rather be spending seeing your new destination.

Rail Europe offers Best Western Hotel, Frantour, Sofitel, Mercure, and SRS Worldhotel vouchers. Hotels can be either reserved in advance or through toll-free telephone numbers as you go. Sofitel Hotels are usually well-located, modernistic, gleaming business hotels. Mercure offers Spartan, budget rooms in brand-new, efficient settings, sometimes near train stations. Best Western has 1,000 hotels throughout Europe. Frantours has train-station locations in 22 cities in France and 25 cities in 9 other countries. SRS properties tend to be upscale and located in downtown locations.

Pre-purchased vouchers let independent travelers do the following:
• budget exactly how much they are spending in U.S. dollars before they leave,
• know beforehand where they are going to stay so that they won't have to rush to locate a hotel before the sun sets,
• eliminate time wasted standing in line at the tourist office or otherwise locating a hotel, and
• retain their flexibility.

You already have heard how well rail passes work. You will be delighted to find vouchers also work marvelously well for train travelers in hotels geared more for independent travelers than business travelers. Careful analysis of the hotel rack rates compared with the price of vouchers shows that vouchers come out price winners, but not by much.

Hotel ratings are of little or no use to independent travelers. Obviously, ratings by an official or quasi-official organization cannot take into account subjective factors such as friendliness, hospitality, and coziness, where smaller hotels excel. Facilities such as a gymnasium or health club may be important to a traveler tired from business negotiations and earn a five-star rating. Independent travelers want to see the sights instead of spending their time within tour walls.

During the summer, many of the larger hotel chains try to fill their rooms when business travel slackens by offering discounts. A little telephone research can save you up to 50 percent. During July and August, and on weekends only throughout the rest of the year, from

Belfast to Bucharest, Hilton International gives 30 to 40 percent off to holders of Eurailpasses. Quote code RR.

Reserving Your Train Connection

Before you leave the train station, go back to make your reservation for your next train. Rail-pass holders do not pay fast-train surcharges but must pay for seat reservations where required. A reservation will cost you several dollars, and if you change your plans you will have to throw it away, but it will save you time and reassure you to make it now.

Reservations are one of the most arbitrary factors in train travel. Each country has its own rules. Modern trends in European train travel seem to be copied from airline experience: speed, at-seat meal service, and unfortunately, also complicated reservation requirements. High-speed trains, which were on the drawing boards a few years ago, demand a reservation.

Which trains require reservations? While you are in the train station, look at the electronic bulletin boards and the yellow departure sheets. The national timetables and the Thomas Cook European Timetable are otherwise your definitive sources. As a reasonable rule of thumb, here is an outline:

In every Western European country, the highest-speed and premium trains require reservations. Obligatory reservations are shown in the timetables by an *R* surrounded by a box.

On some trains you can make reservations, which are not obligatory, but are recommended reservations. These are shown by a white-on-black *R*, or (in Italy) *PG*. For your own peace of mind, you should reserve seats on EuroCity (EC) and international express trains during busy travel seasons on Fridays, Sundays, and local holidays. Couchettes and sleeping compartments always require reservations. Regional and local trains are not reservable.

You can make prior reservations up to two months in advance through a travel agent in North America, but it is generally easier and less expensive to make them after you arrive in Europe, at any large train station.

• In France, seat reservations are available for a small fee on most long-distance trains and are obligatory for all TGV trains within France and Thalys between Paris and Amsterdam. You can book them as late as the same day you depart. Look for the reservations window marked "Jour."

• Benelux is a reservation-free zone, but even here reservations are required for international Thalys trains.

• GermanRail uses a complex fare system whereby point-to-point ticket purchasers pay more for faster trains to compensate for their saved time. Besides the Metropolitan train, which is not a DB train, the only trains which require reservations are ICE Sprinter trains, but all ICEs are reservable and those buying point-to-point tickets usually reserve their seat. Board any GermanRail train without a reservation, but be sure not to sit in a seat reserved for someone else.

• In Switzerland, reservations are not required on most trains, except that they are compulsory on the Crystal Panoramic, Golden Panoramic, Glacier, William Tell, and some Bernina express trains. The ETR 470 Cisalpino tilting trains also require reservations when you travel to Italy.

Seat reservations may be made on all Swiss EC and IC trains. On EC trains between Switzerland and Austria and Italy, the Swiss Railroads runs a number of first-class-only observation cars. When you travel first class on these routes, be sure to use these trains and reserve seats in the Panoramawagen.

• In Austria, seat reservations are not required, but you may make them on all EC, National EC, IC, and Fast (D) trains.

• In Italy, seat reservations are compulsory on all Eurostar Italia/Pendolino trains. Check the timetables. Reservation requirements are strictly enforced in Italy. If you board and find an unreserved seat in a train requiring reservations, the conductor will charge you for the seat, plus a penalty!

• The Spanish Railroads' (RENFE) long-distance trains can be very crowded at peak hours. Reservations are compulsory. AVEs and Talgo 200 trains using Spain's high-speed corridor fall into a special category. They are not covered by rail passes without payment of a substantial supplement. The special fare structure depends on the class of travel and the time of day. Reservations are required.

• In Portugal, seat tourist offices are compulsory on international, IC, and Alfa Pendular trains. You may make them on InterRegional (IR) trains.

• In Britain, you can reserve seats in advance on all InterCity trains (except Gatwick Express) and on certain Regional Railways and Network SouthEast trains. It is essential for you to reserve on certain services at peak periods (Friday afternoon/evening, bank holiday, and

Christmas periods), and to and from Scotland. You can normally reserve from about two months in advance up to about two hours before departure (for early morning trains, up to the previous evening). Reservations are obligatory on trains marked in the timetable with a white R in a black box. Those marked with an R in a white box are often crowded, and reservations are recommended.

• Reservations are not required in either the Republic of Ireland or in Northern Ireland except for the deluxe Gold service between Dublin and Cork.

• All Nordic countries burden their prestige trains with mandatory reservations requirements.

• Denmark's trains to Germany require a reservation.

• Norwegian Railroads (NSB) requires reservations on their "Signatur" tilting trains (their fastest trains on long routes). If you board without a reservation, the fee will be collected by the conductor. NSB also requires reservations on their ICE trains from Oslo. Their cost depends on destination and class of service booked.

• In Sweden, you need reservations on all X2000, IR, and IC trains except on local segments of less than 100 miles. Travelers north to Kiruna/Narvik require a seat, couchette, or sleeping reservation as far as Kiruna. Be sure to reserve trains running above Arctic Circle in Sweden far in advance.

• Finland requires that you reserve on IC, S 220 Pendolino, and trains indicated in the timetable.

Not all booking agents can or want to be bothered speaking or mis-understanding English. You save yourself many headaches by giving to the reservations agent a piece of paper showing your date of travel (numerals for the day, month, and year, in that order), the time you want to leave (using the twenty-four-hour clock), departure city with arrow pointing to destination city, whether you prefer a smoking or a nonsmoking ("Nicht Raucher," "Niet rokers," "Non-fumar," "Non-fumeurs," "Non fumatori") compartment or section.

Smoking is prohibited on many local and regional trains, but most long-distance trains (which will require reservations) such as FrenchRail's TGVs, GermanRail's ICEs, and Swedish X2000s have placed single, separate carriages front and rear, for first- and second-class smoking passengers respectively, so that nonsmoking passengers will not have to walk through smoke-filled areas to and from the dining or bistro car located in the center of the train.

Present your reservations request simultaneously with your Eurailpass and—if you wish—your bank credit card. (To conserve cash, consider using your bank credit cards to make as many Europe-wide advance reservations as possible.) Present all three at once. In many countries there is a minimum credit-card charge.

In larger stations in Germany and in Stockholm's Central station, you find computerized timetable information machines, which print out train connections. You can take the printouts to the reservations counter to show exactly on which train you wish to reserve a seat or couchette.

Usually reservations counters are separated into domestic ("Binnenland, "Inland," "Inrikes," "Interieur," "Paikkalippuja") and international ("Ausland," "Buitenland," "Matkapalvelu," "Utrikes") reservations. Make sure you don't stand in a long line at the wrong counter.

Getting to Your Hotel

Many large train stations are served by rapid-transit trains and/or subways. There are almost always discounts available on the subways ("Metro," "Metron/Metroon," "Metropolitano," "Underground," "U-Bahn," "T-Bana") including multiple-ride, magnetically encoded tickets, strip-tickets, and passes for a day, a week, or longer.

Rapid-transit (except Paris' RERs) but not subway trains are covered by your rail pass. In the Munich Hauptbahnhof you find parallel "S-Bahn" and "U-Bahn" lines. Rail passes cover only the former.

International

Smart Traveling on International Trains

Eurostar under the English Channel—Le Shuttle-Taking your car along—Thalys-Red and rapid—Cisalpino Italy-Switzerland-Germany—Artesia takes you between France and Italy—Zurich-Paris on the Heart Line—EuroCity-The European standard

Eurostar Under the English Channel

Eurostar, the twentieth century's most dramatic train, is waiting for you in London's Waterloo International terminal.

The already warmed-up supertrain is ready to take you through the English Channel Tunnel and, at 186 mph, over FrenchRail's TGV Nord Europe and Belgian high-speed lines to Paris or Brussels.

Eurostar has a complicated pricing structure involving three classes of ticket. "First Premium" gives you first-class seating, meals and business services, including access to Eurostar Lounges in London, Paris, and Ashford. "First Class" seats you in first-class reclining seats, gives you a meal at your seat and a complimentary newspaper. "Standard Class" provides seats in second-class carriages and allows you to walk to the bar car to purchase food.

43

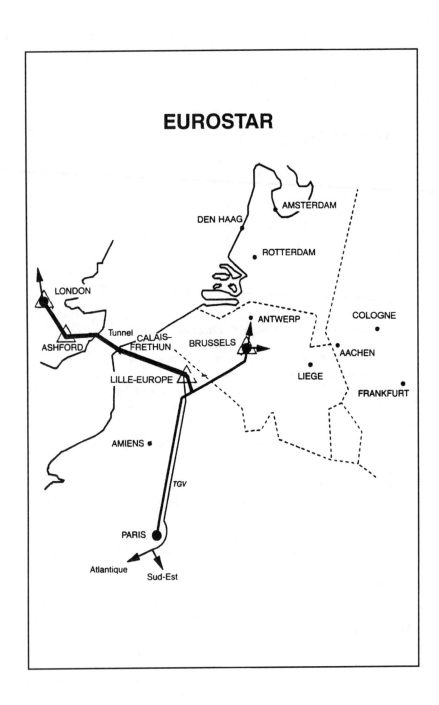

Within the "First Class" and "Standard Class" categories, discounts are given for senior (over 60) travelers, leisure travelers (advance purchase, round trip, minimum two-night stay), and pass holders. The Youth Open Voucher allows those under 26 to travel without advance reservations and provides second-class tickets from 45 minutes to two months before departure. Occasional sales are offered. Check *www.raileurope.com* or telephone 1-800-EUROSTAR.

Those with a Eurailpass, Europass, Europe Selectpass or BritRail Pass receive a 30 to 35 percent discount when buying first- or second-class Eurostar tickets. Those with second-class Eurail Youthpasses qualify for the discount even when buying first-class Eurostar tickets. You must validate your pass before your trip on Eurostar. When you have a France Railpass you receive the same discount on Eurostar tickets between France and England. Purchasers of Benelux Tourrail rail passes receive the same discount between Brussels and England. Seniors receive 27 percent off.

Since commercial service began on November 14, 1994, 32 million passengers traveled Eurostar trains through 2000. Of these, more than three percent were from North America. There are 19 round trips daily on the three-hour London-Paris route (16 on Fridays, 24 in summer), and 10 on the two-hour, 36-minute London-Brussels route.

Past, Present, and Future

July 29, 1987—Anglo French Fixed Link Treaty signed by Prime Minister Margaret Thatcher and President Francois Mitterand.

1988—Tunnel boring started from English and French coasts.

October 30, 1990—Pilot bore established contact between tunnels from Britain and France.

December 1, 1990—Service tunnels connected.

May 17, 1993—Waterloo International terminal completed.

May 24, 1993—First running of TGV-R over TGV Nord Europe high-speed line.

June 20, 1993—First Eurostar train transported through tunnel for intensive trials and testing.

September 24, 1993—First scheduled TGV-R services on the Nord Europe high-speed line between Paris and Calais, via Lille Flandres station.

March 7, 1994—First running of freight trains through Channel Tunnel.

May 6, 1994—Official inauguration of Channel Tunnel by French President Mitterand and Queen Elizabeth, who traveled through it one direction aboard Eurostar and the opposite by car-carrying train.

May 19, 1994—First scheduled operation of truck-carrying trains through the Channel Tunnel.

May 29, 1994—TGV interconnection between TGV Nord Europe and TGV Southeast opened. Disneyland Paris TGV station opened.

November 13, 1994—Charles de Gaulle TGV station opened.

November 14, 1994—Commercial Eurostar train service inaugurated.

December 22, 1994—Start of scheduled public operation of "Le Shuttle" double-decked, auto-carrying trains.

January 23, 1995—Calais Frethun station opens to Eurostar traffic.

May 23, 1995—One millionth passenger travels on Eurostar.

January 8, 1996—Ashford International station opens.

June 2, 1996—Opening of first segment of high-speed line between Lille and Brussels cuts travel time between London and Brussels (with stop in Lille) to three hours, 12 minutes; Thalys trains link Amsterdam and Paris via Brussels in four hours, 46 minutes.

June 2, 1996—Opening of Jonction Sud allows direct connections for Eurostar passengers at Lille TGV station to Brittany and the southwest of France.

December 14, 1997—King Albert II and the president of France open the Belgian high-speed line to link the 186-mph TGV Nord French line to the Belgian capital, cutting journey time between London and Brussels to two hours, 45 minutes.

October 5, 1998—Construction contracts signed for the Channel Tunnel Rail Link (CTRL). Construction begins on CRTL segment from the tunnel to Ebbsfleet.

2002—High-speed line between Brussels and Cologne will open via Liege.

2003—The CTRL will be completed from the Channel Tunnel to Ebbsfleet.

2007—CRTL through Kent from the tunnel to St. Pancras Station will cut travel time between London and Paris to two hours, 25 minutes; two hours, 10 minutes, to Brussels.

2005—High-speed line will open from Brussels via Antwerp and Rotterdam to Amsterdam, cutting travel time between Paris and Amsterdam to three hours, 10 minutes.

London to Paris in Three Hours

Time Zero—Waterloo

Scripted bilingual announcements are made at 15, eight, and three minutes before departure. English is used first when in England, and French in France.

When your yellow-and-white train purrs out of London's Waterloo International station, you feel as though you are embarking on a momentous trip instead of a quick, three-hour dash to Paris.

All cliches aside, the articulated train named Eurostar is the culmination of twentieth-century land travel. This is, after all, a new era in European train travel. You venture where no passenger has gone before. You glide at 100 mph through a $15 billion undersea tunnel beneath the expanse of water that separated Britain from the European continent since the Pleistocene or Ice Age. Although the complexities and ramifications of one of history's largest and most expensive land-travel engineering projects were enormous, planners worked to make it simpler than flying.

In several competitions, two travelers left a common location (usually a hotel) in London (or Paris) at the same time. One traveled to Paris (or London) via Eurostar; one by scheduled airline.

Usually the one traveling by Eurostar arrived at the common destination in downtown Paris (or London) only a few minutes earlier than his partner who had traveled via Heathrow and Charles de Gaulle Airports. Eurostar is on time, or within 15 minutes, 87 percent of the time, compared with 70 percent for the airlines.

So, the time differential is not significant. What the competing travelers did with their time is more important.

The air passenger had about 60 minutes in the air to do his or her work, relax with friends, or skim a good book. The Eurostar traveler had up to three hours.

When the racers arrived at their destination, it is safe to say that one was groggy. The other was relaxed and ready to go. No wonder Eurostar has a 62 percent market share and become the premier carrier on the London-Paris route.

Your trip is less scenic than taking a narrow-gauge train through Switzerland and less adventurous than the Arctic trip to Narvik,

Norway. Even passing through the tunnel is a nonevent. But certainly it's less frustrating than taking the guff you get from airlines.

No matter how much and how often you have traveled aboard the trains of Europe, there's a good chance that your trip aboard will break your own personal records.

- It will be the fastest you have ever traveled on land (186 mph), and
- the lowest below sea level (157 feet) some 140 feet under the seabed, and
- through the longest tunnel (31 miles), and probably
- aboard the longest train (a quarter mile), and
- the first time you have had to change your watch on a train unless you have traveled between Spain and Portugal or eastward from Western Europe.

Your first-class seat is grand, located by itself beside the window. The couple on the opposite side of the aisle seems just as interested in the train as you. In summer about 85 percent of the travelers are leisure travelers, but across the aisle, regular business commuters confide they have switched to Eurostar. "Planes are maddening. They sit forever on the tarmac waiting for takeoff."

First class is configured 2+1, but even the passengers seated 2+2 in the second-class carriages feel the freedom of the train despite no empty seats. The train's seats are like an airplane's except that they face in two directions, forward and back, so the train won't have to turn around at the end of its run. But passengers feel as though they have more room, even in second class. It is no illusion. If they had a tape measure they would find their second-class seats are on a 33.3-inch pitch. Airlines' B-767s' seven-across seats from London to Paris are configured 2-3-2 with a 32-inch pitch. Your first-class seat has a 36.4-inch pitch, giving you all the legroom you deserve.

The reclining, plush seats are comfortable and firm. An interesting design detail is the bilevel overhead rack. You can use a small lower shelf for items like umbrellas, etc., which can get lost at the back of a full-depth shelf, and a full-size upper rack for your luggage.

First class is usually respectably full, but farther down the train there is often plenty of room. Tip: Traveling Eurostar second class can be a steal. Until everyone catches on, and second class becomes more popular, you will be able to spread your belongings across empty, albeit narrower, seats.

London's Underground takes you from your hotel as you choose the most convenient of the Jubilee, Northern, Bakerloo, or Waterloo & City Line from Bank station directly to Waterloo International station on the south side of the Thames River. Modern trains, which first ran in 1997, began taking you to Waterloo on the Jubilee Line's extension, which opened in 1998. The extension was the largest construction project in Europe at that time and the largest addition to the London Underground network in 25 years.

A friendly host helps you run the magnetic stripe on the back of your Eurostar ticket through the automatic entry gate. Then you pass through a metal detector. Most passengers are waved past the X-ray unit. Only a selected fraction of passengers are checked. If you are "it," violent protests won't prevent guards from X-raying your film.

Guards allow passengers onto the platform only 20 minutes before departure. Check-in time is eight minutes before departure. You need very few minutes to wheel your no-charge luggage carts onto the platform and to find your right seat before Eurostar's doors swish shut.

The departure lounge has a west wall of glass, so you see the trains through the west side wall. On the north side, the wall of glass gives you a view of the new train shed and platforms of the domestic concourse. You find electronic signboards, an information counter, telephones, shops, a cafeteria, and a bar. There are separate departure lounges for holders of first- and second-class tickets, and an exclusive full-service lounge for First Premium ticket purchasers. An information system directed you to the escalator or ramp nearest your seat on Eurostar and you climbed to the departure platform.

Waterloo International was designed "appropriate to the 1990s, but in keeping with the great tradition of British Railway architecture." Much of the new terminal replaces side tracks used for storing trains at the former domestic Waterloo station. A soaring, 437-yard glass roof was grafted onto the existing station and five quarter-mile-long platforms constructed atop the new four-level international terminal to handle efficiently the crush of 15 million international travelers a year. The terminal shines from two and a half acres of glass, two acres of stainless steel cladding, and 1,000 tons of steel. Construction wasn't easy. The former station had been constructed on brick arches with Waterloo & City line's ticket halls and two more London Underground lines below—not to mention four banks of escalators. And the Jubilee Line's construction under Waterloo had to be taken into account.

Eurostar is the brand name of your train. Marketing consultants devised a stylized *e* logo with three wavy strokes to represent the British, French, and Belgian railroads working together and a gold star to indicate the future.

Taking the up-only escalator to the platform area you see arriving passengers descending on down-only escalators to the arrivals area below. The arrivals area, with a customs hall and baggage checking, is on the ground floor, and on the same level as an enlarged London Underground ticket hall, taxis, and buses outside. At basement level is a parking garage (including short-term parking). Waterloo International resembles an airport.

On signal, you board your Eurostar at one of Waterloo International's five platforms, and your quarter-mile-long train rumbles over a familiar path out of Waterloo and turns to climb across the new double-tracked overpass viaduct known as the Stewarts Lane chord. Eurostar crosses above the other tracks from Waterloo and onto the electrified mainline tracks of the boat train (which has been discontinued) which lead away from London's Victoria station to the mouth of the Channel Tunnel. It was unthinkable to use Victoria station as a terminal for Eurostar. Already jammed Victoria station would be swamped by the heavy additional passenger load upwards of three to six million passengers a year initially. The taxpayers using Southeast England's train network and already crowding Victoria would be outraged; travelers arriving in Gatwick Airport and using the Gatwick Airport Express to Victoria would be delayed; the Victoria subway station would be overwhelmed; and taxis and buses using the awkward street access outside Victoria station would be grid locked.

Once Eurostar passes Tonbridge on the line from Victoria to the English Channel you finally pick up speed approaching 100 mph if necessary to maintain schedule. Eurostar is sluggish over the British third-rail network, but flies once it hits the overhead catenary wire. BritRail installed continuously welded rails and strengthened the power supplies to accommodate the long Eurostar trains. You rather enjoy the slowest part of your trip through Kent where you look at the green fields and melancholy cows in the "Garden of England."

The Kent folk fought a successful delaying battle against a high-speed line through their fields. They couldn't see any benefit to them in a train that wouldn't stop and would shave only 20 minutes off a three-hour trip. Moreover, they said, it would risk damage to the fragile pastoral peace of the wealthy and influential county. But finally progress prevailed and contracts have been let to a consortium that includes Virgin (which also runs an airline) and Bechtel, based in San Francisco, to build a 68-mile, 167-mph, dedicated line between the tunnel and London's St. Pancras station. But it won't be ready until the next millennium and its justification is not speed, but capacity.

While you approach the tunnel, as a first-class passenger, you are served a stylish meal at your seat by your steward. The surprisingly well-done morning meal consists of orange juice; poached apple; English breakfast of sausage, bacon, omelet, tomatoes, and mushrooms; breakfast rolls and croissants; tea or coffee. A cold plate is offered in lieu of the English breakfast.

On evening passage, stewards serve grilled fillet of beef, potatoes, vegetables, cheese, and a sugared fruit dessert, plus tea or coffee. The alternative is halibut.

Second-class passengers can use the food trolley and bar services for cash—British, French, and Belgian as well as Euro currencies are accepted. All products are the same regardless of where you boarded.

Meal services are provided by a consortium named Momentum, formed by British company Granada Food Services and Italian company Cremonini. All staff wear the same uniforms, receive the training, and speak functional English and French. Half are based in London, and a quarter each in Paris and Brussels. British passengers are astonished at the excellent service. The English rarely make good waiters. They seem to think that waiting is a menial job rather than a professional service. They are used to restaurant cars where waiters rush diners and give the impression that they are doing the passengers a great favor. Eurostar is different. Nothing is too much trouble and nobody is closing up while you are still eating.

1:00 Hour—Ashford

The first chance for Eurostar to stop is at Ashford International station, 13 miles from the tunnel entrance. It was officially opened on Monday, January 8, 1996. Passengers aboard a 7:19 A.M. departure to Paris were the first to make the two-hour trip. Thirteen Eurostar trains call on the international platform on weekdays, six to Paris and seven to Brussels. The new station cost about $150 million, including new platforms, tracks, and signaling, as well as a new domestic ticket office. The parking lot has space for 2,000 cars and opens up a large swath of

the South East for park-and-ride passengers. The new domestic platform at Ashford is served also by frequent trains from many parts of
Kent and East Sussex.

The new Ashford International station is on two levels with the
ground floor consisting of immigrations and arrivals halls, ticket
office, and entrance concourse. The upper level has a departure
lounge for 800 travelers, shops, a cafe, and security control. Flows of
arriving and departing international travelers are separated by an
underpass and footbridge connecting the station building and international platforms. The new domestic station is north of the railroad
and linked to the domestic platforms by an underpass.

It is a curious fact that the fastest start-to-stop service in Europe
begins at Ashford. Ashford to Paris in two hours is 125 mph start to
stop.

1:10 Hours: Enter Channel Tunnel

Past Ashford you coast through the changeover between British third-
rail power supply and overhead tunnel power supply at the point indicated by lineside signs near the junction with the original line to/from
Folkestone. At Cheriton you slow for the "UK Terminal," where you
glimpse the car park, tollbooths (payment by cash, credit card, or pre-
paid ticket), frontier offices, and a food and shopping center resembling a highway service stop. Cars, buses, and trucks are moving up
and down the eight loading and unloading platforms (each 0.6 miles
long) for loading onto and off of Le Shuttle.

It's curious that Cheriton is policed by the Kent Constabulary, who
have jurisdiction on the Channel Tunnel-operated shuttle trains, while
Eurostar International passenger trains fall within the jurisdiction of
the British Transport Police in the U.K. The dividing line between
French and British law is fixed at a point halfway through the tunnel.

Eurostar enters the tunnel complex without stopping, Running
down the one in 90 gradient, you have no trouble reaching 100 mph
in a very short time. There's just a kind of humming; a slight increase
in sound level. The windows are pitch black, and all you see for the
next 25 or so minutes is a procession of green lights flying past every
four seconds. Channel Tunnel is the longest undersea tunnel ever
built, but your Eurostar crossing itself is a short part of your journey.
Passengers timing the passage report differences of 27 minutes (69
mph) to 23.5 minutes (80 mph).

For enthusiasts who wish to time their run, from Waterloo station it is 58.1 miles to Ashford, England; 71.3 miles to the north (English) portal; 102.7 to the south (French) portal; 104.7 to Calais; 168.1 to Lille and 307.7 to Paris.

The Channel Tunnel consists of three separate tunnels. The two train tunnels are known as Running Tunnel North (RTN) and Running Tunnel South (RTS). Between them, and linked to them, is the Service Tunnel (ST). Each of these tunnels is just over 31 miles long. To prevent rabid foxes and rats from racing through the tunnel and infecting England, electrical barriers on the floor stun wayward animals so that they can be repatriated.

You exit near Calais at "Terminal France," the Coquelles complex's loading point (La Cite de l'Europe), which is similar to the British one, but more than four times larger. The unloading of the automobiles reminds you that the French and English normally drive on different sides of the road and you wonder how easily British visitors will adapt—a frightening thought—to the French style of right-hand-side, aggressive driving.

1:33 Hours—Calais-Frethun

Don't forget to adjust your watch for the one-hour time change. Four Paris-bound Eurostar trains call at FrenchRail's first station, Calais-Frethun, two miles after you leave the Channel Tunnel. Passengers from London are allowed to disembark, but passengers coming from Paris are not, on the theory that terrorists might leave a bomb on Eurostar before it enters the Channel Tunnel.

From here you follow the lines of TGV Nord Europe to Paris. Although the Channel Tunnel and TGV Nord Europe are separate enterprises, the two projects are economically interdependent. The Channel Tunnel is only viable if it is enhanced by TGV Nord and TGV Nord is only viable if it can carry the traffic from England generated by the tunnel. Together they are a cornerstone of the coming European High-Speed Network.

Now as Eurostar accelerates effortlessly to 186 mph, drivers are required to tell the train captain when the train reaches that speed so that he may announce it to the passengers. Sometimes drivers never need to reach 186 mph, but they lie, so that you can go home with a smile on your face and tell your friends. Your ride is smooth, and you admire the green countryside. The land is flat, so that the occasional vertical steeples become very distinct, but you can only focus on distant structures because those nearby flash past too quickly. Nord-Pas de Calais is a fascinating frontier region embracing land and sea with a rich history and a blend of French and Flemish culture that exists nowhere else.

Now it's quiet and your ride is astonishingly smooth as you skim along at 186 mph. The ride quality throughout the train is truly amazing. At 186 mph it seems like 120 mph (except when passing another Eurostar). In Britain 90 mph seemed like 40. Running at 186 mph in France is about as smooth as 90 mph on British rails. One traveler did a coin test of Eurostar. He balanced a pound sterling coin on its edge atop his Eurostar's fold-down table. The coin nestled, most stable, in a groove in the table and remained upright. Try that on a standard British train and you will be chasing your money faster than inflation.

You have a chance to look at your 20-carriage-long (1,291 feet) train. You think of Eurostar as a train. It is also a computer network on wheels. Each carriage has its own computer; the power cars have 11 at each end. Each computer interacts and exchanges information. The 18-carriage train is divided into two mirror-image segments, each with three first-class carriages, five second-class carriages, and a bar car (plus a power car for each segment). This feature allows the train to be separated for removal from the tunnel, if necessary, and also allows the train to split for eventual destinations beyond London or Paris. Each first-class car seats 39; each second-class car seats 60. A fully loaded train carries 210 first-class and 584 second-class passengers. Two of the three first-class cars are nonsmoking; four of the five second-class cars are nonsmoking. Smoking is permitted in the bar car that separates the first- and second-class cars.

Your Eurostar train is one of 38 Class 373 trains fabricated under contract to a consortium that has changed composition several times and developed into an Anglo-French private-sector company including British Airways. The original British share of the contract was 46.67 percent, which is equivalent to 16 of the 38 basic trainsets, with 18 for FrenchRail and four for the Belgian Railroads. Eurostar's 38 Class 373 trains are interchangeable, but the trainsets are separately owned, maintained, and berthed. You can tell who owns a particular Eurostar trainset and where it is based by the first two numerals of the four-digit identification numbers stenciled on the power cars. Those 16 beginning with "30" are owned by Eurostar UK, and based at North Pole International. Belgian Railroads' four, the "31" series, are based at

Forest Midi, Brussels. FrenchRail's 18 trainsets are the "32" series at Le Landy, Paris.

Eurostar seems at home running over TGV rails, which is only logical because Eurostar is a sensible progression of French TGV (Trains a Grande Vitesse) engineering. The first highly successful TGV Southeast line connected Paris and Lyon in two segments during September 1981 and September 1983. It introduced France to 167-mph shark-snouted trains, destroyed air competition, and deferred growth of highway traffic. The second-generation TGV Atlantique accelerated to 186 mph along a western branch to Brittany in September 1989, and southwest to Bordeaux and the Spanish border in September 1990. It showed that comfortable high-speed travel also can be smooth as silk. The TGV-R (*R* for "reseau," or "network") third-generation high-speed train modified TGV-A's design for high-speed running on TGV Nord Europe Line as far as the entrance to the Channel Tunnel. Extensions added the capability of running through interconnections onto FrenchRail's Southeast network in 1994 and then onto the Atlantique network in 1996, thus unifying the TGV lines and creating a network interconnecting high-speed travel throughout most of France (see "France" chapter). Mechanical, electrical, and aerodynamic design and much of the interior architecture of Eurostar resembles these advanced French TGVs.

2:00 Hours—Lille

Your Eurostar slows at the new Eurostar station named Lille Europe. It stops only if it is bound for Brussels. Aboard your Paris-bound Eurostar, you see Lille Europe only as a long tunnel while you travel over the central tracks bypassing the four platform lines.

Lille Europe TGV station not only is used by Eurostar trains between Brussels and London, but it anchors TGV trains to Paris and TGV trains running along the new TGV Paris bypass corridor to the Southeast and Atlantic networks.

For those passengers changing trains in Gare Lille Europe, the station introduced a new way of finding your carriage. Because the system is new, it is confusing, but it couldn't be simpler. The departure boards show you the acces (access) letter, *A* to *L,* for your train. When you find your platform you are directed by video screen to your boarding sector depending on the carriage ("voiture") number shown on your reservation coupon.

Gare Lille Europe is massive. Escalators zig-zag between levels and *acces* areas. The connecting Lille Metro station adds to the bustle. The enormous oval building is called the "Lille Grand Palais." It is Lille's new exhibition hall. On your left is the soaring business center complex "EuraLille," which consists of geometric high-rise offices; a four-star, 200-bedroom hotel; and businesses including the World Trade Center Tower, the Credit Lyonnais Tower, and the Hotel and Office Tower.

Lille, capital of Nord-Pas de Calais, is one of France's major cities and railroad hubs. Lille Europe station is located on the edge of the city's center, but only a quarter-mile from the existing classical dead-end terminal, which was renamed Lille Flandres to prevent confusion. Lille Flandres was France's busiest outside Paris. You can count on a 10-minute walk between Lille-Europe and Lille-Flandres stations.

Lille Europe is the new terminus of the VAL fully automatic (driverless) Metro line 2 North, a 2.36-mile-long, eight-station, VAL section extending to Roubaix and Tourcoing. Like the trains of VAL line 2, modern streetcars on the meter-gauge Lille-Roubaix/Tourcoing line, underground here, stop near both Lille stations.

Eurostar's initial route was planned to bypass Lille to the west, but intense political action by Pierre Mauroy, former prime minister and mayor of Lille, swayed the decision in favor of a station in Lille. Because of the decision to serve Lille and the economies of keeping the tunnel short (!), Eurostar's London-Paris route is not direct. London to Paris is 210 miles as the crow flies, but 280 miles by highway and the tunnel, and the routing via Lille adds 25 miles to that (though only about eight minutes at 186 mph).

Lille's urban area includes 1.1 million residents—more if you count adjoining Belgian communities associated in a Euro-metropolis. Take a walk through Lille's old town to be dazzled by a kaleidoscope of rich architectural styles, colorful facades, and stucco decorations.

2:02 Hours—Fretin Triangle

About seven miles out of Lille Europe station, Eurostars bound for Paris and Brussels diverge. They each take the appropriate side of the triangular junction near Fretin to join the main Brussels-Paris high-speed line. You may see a Burgundy-livery, Amsterdam-Brussels-Paris train curving around the opposite arc.

South of the Fretin triangle, Eurostars for Paris pass through the former coal-mining country. Now that the pits have closed, all is lush and green — a paradise for cattle.

2:21 Hours—Arras Cutoff

About three miles south from the point where you see Arras on the west, you pass the junction of the spur to Arras. This spur is bypassed by Eurostar but allows use of the high-speed track for 187-mph TGV service between Paris and Arras. Arras is worth a detour to see the Old Town ("Les Places") dating from the eleventh century. The splendid Grand Place, Place des Heros, and Rue de la Taillerie boast dazzling seventeenth- and eighteenth-century Flemish-baroque facades. TGVs cut the travel time from Paris to 50 minutes from one hour, 30 minutes.

This Eurostar experience is so great, you reflect, why hasn't it been done earlier? The idea isn't new. To commemorate the Peace of Armiens in 1803, Napoleon approved a concept—a tunnel for horse-drawn trolleys between France and England—proposed by a French engineer in 1802. It was not until 1881 that British and French companies actually undertook preliminary tunneling near Dover and at Sangatte, near Calais. However, for fear that a tunnel would expose Britain to a military invasion, the British government ordered the companies to stop work after only one year. Other schemes were proposed before the First World War, but they too were quashed by the British military. In the late 1920s, a study group reported favorably on such a project, but again British politicians opposed it.

Interest in a Channel Tunnel reappeared after World War II, but more than 40 years passed before a viable project gained British government support. Against the backdrop of Britain's entry into the common market, the political climate turned favorable. Nevertheless the 1974 elections delayed ratification of a treaty and the British government rejected the project—to the dismay of the French.

By 1985 privatization was proceeding apace in Britain and the British government approved a plan to be funded entirely by private capital. The 1987 Channel Tunnel Act specifically precludes the use of any British government funds or guarantees for the tunnel system. Further, it specifies that no funding should be allowed for international railroad services, meaning that Britain's international services have to be financially self-sufficient.

2:29 Hours—TGV Haute Picardie Station

The small Picardy TGV station was the last detail of the TGV Nord Europe to be settled. It is located at a road crossing near the new superhighway between Amiens and St. Quentin. Part of the reason for the delay in this choice was civil disobedience by supporters of an alternate route for the high-speed line to the Channel Tunnel via Amiens, the capital of Picardy. This second line has been promised "when the line via Lille is saturated." This may be a long way off.

You notice Eurostar coasting now, and realize that it is slowing to rejoin conventional tracks at Gonesse, 9.8 miles north of the rejuvenated Paris Gare du Nord. As Eurostar enters Paris you see a nice view of Sacre Coeur, high atop its hill, dominating the skyline.

3:00 hours—Paris Gare du Nord

At Paris's Gare du Nord, you arrive on a dedicated track, formerly number three, now the "Quai du Talent," celebrating leading French and English film, music, sports, and media personalities. In the station you find one of the most amazing thing of your entire trip: signs in the English language! The entire station has been remodeled for the arrival of Eurostar and TGV Nord Europe trains. The departure lounge opened May 12, 1998, accommodates 1,000 travelers. For First Premium passengers, the Salon Eurostar provides newspapers, beverages, phones, copiers, and Internet access, as well as direct access to the train through a new passageway. You would know the station is old only because the 1865-69 facade and clock have been preserved. Platforms were lengthened and the suburban trains that formerly used the center platforms were diverted. The new, 1,300-car subterranean parking garage and facilities to provide meal service to the TGVs were installed. Departing taxis are lined up outside on the level below your arrival. Porters meet the trains. Use the elevators for luggage carts; otherwise you can ride the down escalator. Mainline (international) services are grouped in an office ("Espace Grandes Lignes") across the arriving taxi right-of-way to the west of the building next to track number one. Ticketing machines give instructions in English when you rub the British flag in the upper right corner of the screen, but they are so limited that they are rarely programmed to provide the service you need. Several fast-food franchises are across the street. The tourist office (open daily, 8 A.M. to 9 P.M.) will make hotel reservations for you. A money change office is available, but since you shouldn't expect bank rates, you may prefer to use a teller machine that will take American MasterCard or Visa cards or a bank note changing machine that converts pounds sterling and U.S. dollars into French currency at advantageous rates. Escalators carry visitors to the mezzanine and to the Paris metro below. The RER (rapid-transit) station for Charles de Gaulle Airport and greater Paris is on the same level—to the left as you leave your Eurostar (see "Getting around Paris" in the "France" chapter).

The exterior of the Gare du Nord has been cleaned and preserved. If you have a chance to go outside before taking the metro, do so. Stand back a little; the facade is considered one of the masterpieces of railroad architecture. It was built between 1861 and 1865 by the same architect who redesigned Paris's Place de la Concorde. The facade has three arches. The nine statues represent the capitals and leading cities of Europe: Paris (in the middle), London, Vienna, Berlin, Cologne, Brussels, Warsaw, Amsterdam, and Frankfurt. The statues above the ground floor represent Lille and other cities of northern France.

London-Netherlands

There are no direct day services between London and the Netherlands, but you make connections from Eurostar at Brussels' South station to Thalys, the Benelux train, or to the cross-Belgium train to Maastricht, depending on your destination. When Eurostar passengers connect to the Thalys train, they don't need to pay the Thalys surcharge, so it is convenient for them to use Thalys without extra charge to Rotterdam, The Hague, Amsterdam Airport, and Amsterdam Central Station. The additional fare to the Netherlands is the same wherever you travel, making Eurostar's fares to the Netherlands among the best Eurostar bargains. The cost per mile from London to Rotterdam is lower than that to Paris, even lower to Amsterdam, and dirt cheap when you change trains and continue without extra cost to the northern city of Groningen.

The Dutch Railroads reasons that you should not be penalized for the extra journey time to the north of the low country.

Hourly train service between the three Brussels stations and midsize Dutch cities consists of the Benelux train (see "Benelux" chapter) via Antwerp Central. You have 26 minutes between your Eurostar arrival and the Benelux train departure, making a trip time of about six and a half hours between London and Amsterdam, which realistically is not competitive with air travel, although many business travelers prefer it because of curiosity and the chance to work aboard the trains.

Changing between Eurostar and the Benelux train or other conventional train at Brussels' South station is very easy. You don't have to change train stations. The permanent, airport-style, dedicated high-speed train terminal, which is located on the west side of Brussels' South station at street level below the platforms off to the right (as you depart) at the Rue de France end of the concourse, includes an enclosed departure area, bar, shops, and toilet facilities. In addition to the two platforms for London Eurostar, it has four platforms (which are not controlled) for Thalys to Amsterdam. It is ultra-modern—which means it is out of step with the rest of the station, which needs a tip-to-toe refurbishing. Platform one is used for Eurostar arrivals from London; platform two for departures.

Passengers coming from the Netherlands changing at Brussels South station are subject to the required security check before boarding Eurostar trains for London. Modern escalators and elevators have been installed. Rolling beltways simplify baggage movement. New luggage lockers, 370 of them, accept British one-pound coins as well as Belgian and French currencies.

The Benelux trains to the Netherlands run without border delays on both Dutch and Belgian tracks. As a result of the large number of stops, the average speed is modest—about 112 miles in three hours. Outside the rush hours, a car journey is as quick. In addition to the hourly Benelux trains, four Thalys trains originating in Paris run via Brussels' South station to the Randstad cities. Although these Thalys trains get you to Amsterdam faster than the Benelux trains because they make fewer stops, their connections with Eurostar arrivals are poor.

In 2005, your travel time will be cut to one hour, 40 minutes (54 minutes between Antwerp and Amsterdam, down from roughly two hours), when the new, dedicated high-speed line is completed in Belgium and the Netherlands. Platforms 15 and 16 are earmarked for this service in Amsterdam's Central station. The underground Schiphol station has been enlarged from three to six tracks. The three island platforms are long enough to serve doubled TGV trains equipped to run on Dutch power supplies.

Le Shuttle—Taking Your Car Along

Le Shuttle is the rail service that allows passengers to travel with their vehicles through the Channel Tunnel. When service started on December 22, 1994, reservations were required and train ran hourly. Now Le Shuttle is operated as a true shuttle: turn-up-and-go with trains departing every 20 minutes around the clock. It's a free-flow system, with no reservations. Passengers show up and wait their turn to cross.

All types of vehicles make the undersea crossing, including cars, vans, trucks, motorcoaches, motorcycles, and bicycles. Le Shuttle offers a Short Break fare, which is a round-trip ticket that requires a return within five days.

Hertz, Le Shuttle's preferred car rental supplier, offers a plan called Le Swap where you rent a left- or right-hand-drive car and exchange it at the Hertz office at the entrance/exit to the Channel Tunnel for another with the steering wheel on the opposite side. For example, you might rent a left-hand-drive car in London, drive through Britain, ending in Folkestone, take your car on the train though the tunnel, swap it for a right-hand-drive car at the Hertz office at Coquelles and continue driving through France. Rates include the transportation through the tunnel.

The Le Shuttle consortium bought 126 single-deck vehicles for carrying trucks and buses, 126 double-deck ("tourist") vehicles for carrying automobiles, 33 loaders, and 38 locomotives. These are arranged into two separate segments that are coupled together to form a 2,600-foot-long, 30-vehicle train capable of carrying about 120 automobiles and 12 buses per shuttle train. Each two-level tourist vehicle (built by Bombardier of Canada) has room for five average-size family cars per deck. The single-deck shuttles carry one bus or four or five cars. Shuttles measure 85.3 feet long. Their 18.4-foot height is sufficient to transport 13.8-foot-high buses and their internal width of 12.3 feet leaves room for walking on both sides.

Although the tunnel infrastructure has been designed for a possible maximum speed of 125 mph, Channel Tunnel's shuttles run at a maximum speed of 80.8 mph so that it takes 35 minutes for the Channel Tunnel shuttle to deliver cars and passengers from platform to platform (and only eight minutes to load or unload).

Channel Tunnel's revenue comes from two sources: its own dedicated shuttle trains ferrying cars, coaches, trucks, and passengers between Cheriton and Coquelles and from tolls paid by European Passenger Services for the passage of Eurostar.

Thalys—Red and Rapid

You gotta love a train whose name means exactly nothing. Thalys is not the goddess of transportation. The train's operating company

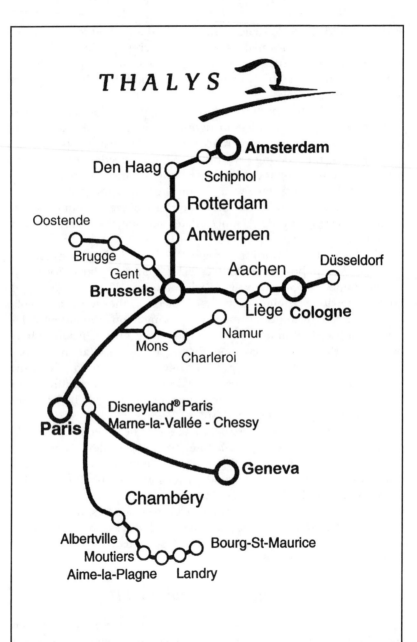

formed by the Dutch, Belgian, French, and German railroads hired a consulting firm to create a name that would be acceptable to both the French- and Flemish-speaking regions of Belgium. The contractors field-tested names that both Dutch- and French-speaking passengers could pronounce easily. They didn't check with English speakers. Say "tha-LEES."

The managers wanted a distinctive name they could trademark and avoid the cross-channel Eurostar's embarrassment over the appearance of Italian Railroads' Eurostar Italia, Eurostar-named pubs, kiosks, shops, restaurants, and general rip-offs. The name Thalys was selected by committee.

Thalys (*www.Thalys.com*) is a network of high-speed trains connecting the Netherlands, Belgium, France, and Germany, and is jointly owned by the railroads of those countries. It allows you to make high-speed connections Paris-Brussels-Amsterdam, Paris-Brussels-Cologne-Dusseldorf, Paris to seven Belgian cities via Brussels, Brussels-Disneyland Paris-Charles de Gaulle Airport-Geneva, and Brussels to sex French ski resorts during the winter.

Two different types of power cars are used, but the carriages are all the same (like TGV-Rs) for all routes, except for adaptation of the bar/buffet carriages. The locomotive of the PBKA Thalys—**P**aris-**B**russels-**K**oln (Cologne)-**A**msterdam)—has a rounded, red nose and one big square windshield, with the driver positioned in the middle as with Eurostar. The PBKA was built especially to run into Germany using 15,000 volts A.C. In Belgium, it works with 3,000 volts D.C., in the Netherlands with 1,500 volts D.C., and on the high-speed lines in France it Belgium, it uses 25,000 volts A.C. The PBKA was the first train that could handle four different voltages.

The locomotive of the PBA Thalys (**P**aris-**B**russels-**A**msterdam) has a shark-like snout, identical with a TGV-R, and two smaller, square windshields. This Thalys runs in France, Belgium (except Liege) and the Netherlands, but not in Germany, because it is not suitable for the German voltage.

Both PBA and PBKA consist of eight passenger carriages with one power car at each end, seat 377 passengers (120 in first class, 257 in second) and reach 186 mph on the high-speed lines.

In coming years, Thalys will be extended to run on new high-speed lines in France to Marseille and in Germany to Frankfurt/Main. It also will be diverted between Brussels and Amsterdam to run over the new high-speed line.

Thalys service personnel are employees of the Thalys operating company, not the national railroads. They welcome you at the doors and stamp your ticket as you board. There are no passport checks or customs inspections between any of these Schengen Treaty signatory countries.

Reservations and payment of a supplement are obligatory to ride a Thalys. Discounts are given to rail pass holders, but even when you hold a valid rail pass you are required to pay a variable supplement in the range of $25 for first class and $13 for second class (which includes reservation,) but it depends on your class of travel, itinerary, and type of rail pass.

The supplement covers the cost of the meal, which is served only on weekdays. On weekends, no meal is served, and you do not pay the supplement.

Amsterdam-Brussels-Paris

At Amsterdam's nineteenth-century, neorenaissance Central train station, follow the Thalys Bordeaux-red markers to platform 14b, where station workers have set out numbered Bordeaux-red flags marking the Thalys carriage numbers.

When your Thalys train glides into boarding position, you see it is massive and bold. It is basically a French TGV-R train painted Thalys red—which is the same shade as the Belgian Railroads' Bordeaux red—and gray, which is universal.

When you board you find the Thalys' first-class interiors feature orange-red seats arranged 2+1. They recline electrically with a touch of the control. The finish is gray, with gray carpeting. Unfortunate decorations rise above the tables in first class like hooded cobras ready to strike. These ill-conceived fixtures are lights, but are usually switched off.

Second class is decorated similarly, even with gray carpeting, which is unusually ritzy for second class, and the narrower seats are arranged 2+2. Between first- and second-class sections, most of one carriage is devoted to a bar arranged similarly to FrenchRail's TGV-Rs. In the vestibules you can read routing and train numbers on the LCD display screens. One carriage has a conference room at the end.

The train manager greets you in Dutch, French, and English. "The doors will be closing in a few minutes." They do, and off you go without further warning - on the dot.

You reach the Schiphol Airport stop almost before you get settled.

You zoom underground, with lights zipping by you like lasers in a special-effects space movie. Schiphol train station has modern digital signs, marble flooring, a moving walkway going up, and abundant, conventional luggage carts (because walkways are used instead of escalators, special luggage carts are not needed). Again, flags mark Thalys' carriage numbers. Luckily, there are large luggage spaces at the ends of the carriages to accommodate the air travelers boarding here. NS has an agreement with KLM for the sale of combined tickets covering KLM flights and journeys by Thalys on the Amsterdam-Paris route.

A hostess pushes a refreshment trolley down the aisle and offers you free coffee and orange juice. Refreshments in the Netherlands plus the snack served between Brussels and Paris are included in the Thalys supplement you paid.

You next stop is the Netherlands' seat of parliament, The Hague's HS station (do not confuse with The Hague's Central Station). HS was built by the Hollandsche Yzeren Spoorweg railroad, damaged by fire in 1989, had new fittings installed, arches replaced, and the whole refined to achieve a well-functioning new station completed in 1993. The original red-brick Romanesque facades were braced and preserved and the yellow-stained windows retained. In 1996, escalators to the platforms were installed.

At Rotterdam's Central Station, more passengers board but no one gets off. Amsterdam-Rotterdam passengers will have taken a Dutch InterCity train. Again, flags mark Thalys carriage boarding locations.

Passengers boarding here hurry up the stairs from Rotterdam's Metro station. The streetcar and bus circle is on the plaza in front. (Your national strip-tickets are valid.) The bank and train information office ("NS Inlichtingen Bureau") can be found in the entrance hall.

Rotterdam Central is a bright, airy station. Buses to North Sea ferries depart from the side door. City information (VVV) and train information share a yellow kiosk in the main hall. Cut flowers usually sold in Dutch stations brightly overflow an entire corner of the main hall.

Your ride is smooth, considering the age of the tracks. TGVs are the smoothest riding high-speed trains in Europe. You slow at Roosendaal station where you pass parked Dog's Head and Regiorunner NS trains.

No sooner do you cross the Belgian border than you are slowing slightly through brown brick villages and traversing stations of the greater Antwerp local network. Past Antwerpen Dam halt you speed past the automobiles on the major motorways, and the train supervisor announced "Antwerp Berchem," where you arrive at freshly paved platform number one.

Your suburban Berchem stop is a shortcut to slice travel time and avoid having to change direction at Antwerp's downtown Central Station. Whenever Antwerp center is your destination, you are better off taking the Benelux train (see Benelux chapter) from Amsterdam in order to arrive in Antwerp's attractive midtown. On the other hand, Berchem is a prestigious suburb.

Approaching Brussels, you pass through Schaerbeck station into the tunnel connecting Brussels' three main train stations. Surfacing at Brussels Kappelbrucke station you coast into Brussels South (*Midi/Zuid*) platform number five for a five-minute break. There are no flags here, but the platform is located in the freshly tiled annex and looks spiffy compared to the older, run-down, local-train platforms that need similar treatment. Up and down escalators take you to the station hall and the Eurostar trains standing nearby, on platforms number one and two, which are separated by a cyclone fence.

Eurostar passengers are able to use Thalys trains to and from the Netherlands without paying the Thalys supplement. Further, their additional fare is not based on the distance they travel which means that they can reach distant Groningen for the same price as Amsterdam or Rotterdam.

A new, French-speaking announcer now greets the new arrivals on Thalys. He struggles through the Dutch greeting, but relaxes speaking English.

On December 14, 1997, King Albert II and the president of France opened the Belgian high-speed line that links into the 186 mph TGV Nord French line. You can feel your train accelerate. A Thalys TGV on routine test set a new Belgian speed record on April 10, 1996, by reaching 167 mph on this stretch.

Lunch served at your seat is very skimpy. A hearty eater will need to supplement the meal with food from the bar car, but you can choose a beverage and it is followed by coffee or tea.

Running west across a plain in a shallow cutting designed to minimize the impact on the environment, your Thalys curves through one of the rounding sides of the Fretin triangle, about seven miles down from Lille Europe train station to the west and about 134 miles north of Paris. This marks your entrance to the TGV Nord-Europe line and the 186 mph speed limit.

The scenery along the high-speed line is almost nonexistent. You speed south through fields of grain and leafy, green vegetables that you can't make out. You are traveling so fast they appear a blur. You can't pick out the names of the towns or the TGV station you pass, although you know it is little-used TGV Picardie.

Somewhere along here is where a French TGV-R, very much like your Thalys, fell into a World War I tunnel at 183 mph on December 21, 1993. The train remained upright and traveled 7,447 feet before coming to rest. This unmapped area had been undermined by tunnels that the armies had burrowed under no man's land in order to lay mines beneath enemy trenches. After the accident, the TGV line was rigorously inspected for additional subsidence and liquid concrete inserted at suspicious locations.

Finally, just as on a Eurostar train, your driver cuts power and you coast into Paris' Gare du Nord (see "Paris train stations" and "Getting around Paris.")

Thalys has enlisted travel partners who give discounts to Thalys passengers. These include Avis; Galeries Lafayette, Paris; de Bijenkorf, Amsterdam; plus Hilton Hotels and Holiday Inns in Paris, Brussels, Antwerp, Schiphol Airport, The Hague, Rotterdam and Amsterdam.

Thalys Service
Paris-Brussels-Amsterdam

0719 0919 1419 1719	dep.	AMSTERDAM (CS)	arr. 1228 1528 1928 2228
0735 0935 1435 1735	dep.	Amsterdam (Air)	arr. 1210 1510 1910 2210
0800 1000 1500 1800	dep.	Den Haag (HS)	arr. 1144 1444 1844 2144
0818 1018 1518 1818	dep.	Rotterdam (CS)	arr. 1127 1427 1827 2127
0917 1117 1617 1917	dep.	Antwerp (Berch.)	dep. 1027 1327 1727 2027
0957 1157 1617 2017	arr.	BRUSSELS (Midi)	dep. 0945 1245 1645 1945
1007 1207 1707 2007	dep.	Brussels (Midi)	arr. 0938 1238 1638 1938
1205 1405 1905 2205	arr.	PARIS (Nord)	dep. 0740 1040 1440 1740

Brussels-Charles de Gaulle Airport-Disneyland Paris-Geneva

The daily Thalys train, introduced on May 28, 2000, is the first-ever direct service between Brussels and Geneva. It saves you changing trains and train stations in Paris, and cuts your travel time from more than seven hours to just five hours and 15 minutes. The longer route through Germany and Switzerland takes up to 10 hours.

Board your Thalys at the Thalys platform located in the annex of Brussels South (*Midi/Zuid*) station. You run south on the Belgian and

TGV Nord high-speed lines blazing fast, and you branch on the TGV Bypass north of Paris. Your first stop is at Charles de Gaulle Airport's TGV station. Ten minutes later you stop at Marne-la-Vallee for visitors to Disneyland Paris.

Past the suburbs of the French capital, you joint the lines of the TGV Southeast network, and branch off along the same scenic route followed by TGVs from Paris' Gare de Lyon to Geneva (see TGV Genevois chapter).

Brussels-Geneva Thalys

#386				#382
1619	dep.	BRUSSELS (South)	arr.	1157
1742	dep.	Paris (Roissy/CDG)	arr.	1034
1759	dep.	Marne-la-Vallee	arr.	1018
1953	arr.	Bourg en Bresse	dep.	0820
2106	arr.	Bellegarde	dep.	0707
2135	arr.	GENEVA (Cornavin)	dep.	0641

Paris-Brussels-Cologne-Dusseldorf

Your Thalys from Cologne undergoes a transformation on its way to Paris. Riders board in Cologne Hauptbahnhof, having changed from trains from Dusseldorf, the Ruhr, Hamburg, and as far as Berlin. Passing through Aachen, Thalys feels and sounds like a German train. German is the language of choice.

Arriving in Brussels Midi/Zuid station, there is a complete change of crew and language. The Germans hurry to other appointments, possibly to the Eurostar to London on the next track, and new passengers board. Your Thalys becomes a French train on its 186-mph way to Paris' Gare du Nord.

Four-voltage Thalys commenced service on September 29, 1997, and now you may board seven daily departures from Cologne (Hbf) or Paris (Nord), with stops in Aachen (Hbf) and Liege (Guillemins), but only one, at 7:30 A.M., from Dusseldorf (Hbf). Other connections from Dusseldorf to Thalys require you to take an InterCity or EuroCity train to Cologne and change there.

Cisalpino Italy-Switzerland-Germany

When I boarded in Lugano, Cisalpino's first stop in Switzerland (say

Chees-alpino, like an Italian), for the over-and-through-the-Alps south-north trip across Switzerland, I was especially curious to see what would happen when the conductor found that I had boarded without a reservation. I had only my Eurailpass in hand.

Regular passengers know that reservations certainly are required for riding Cisalpino trains in Italy. It was my understanding that reservations are not required for riding Cisalpino within Switzerland or Germany, but I was not sure that also would be the conductor's understanding.

I soon found out. The first-class section was about half filled, so I had no difficulty choosing a seat without a yellow reservation card attached. The Swiss conductor came to my seat, looking very official in his full dark blue uniform with kepi and ticket punch, asking "Do you have a reservation?"

"No."

"No? No? Where did you board?"

"Lugano."

The conductor raised his eyebrows. He was not pleased. He looked at me like I was stealing from his piggy bank. He frowned, skeptically. "If you got on in Italy you must have a reservation."

I shrugged my shoulders.

He examined my Eurailpass very carefully and held it up to the light, maybe looking for an Italian conductor's punch hole.

My rail pass completely covered my trip. No reservation fee. No supplement.

The surprising blue-and-white ETR 470 Pendolino train is the sparkling, 1996 creation of Cisalpino (CIS), the operating company held by the Swiss Federal Railroads, the Bern-Lotschberg-Simplon Railroads, and the Italian State Railroads, which financed the $20 million fleet of tilting trains.

Derived from Italy's ETR 460 Pendolino (see "Italy" chapter), but capable of running also on the Swiss electrical power supplies, the dual-voltage 470s are equally as powerful in either country, but Cisalpino ETR 470 trains are geared lower than ETR 460s so that they reach a maximum speed of 125 mph rather than the 460's 155 mph, a trade-off necessary to give them higher traction for better climbing power over Swiss mountain routes. Remember how your automobile climbs hills better in low gear than in high.

When they began operation on June 2, 1996, between Geneva and Milano, they had the honor of becoming the world's first international tilting trains. On September 29, 1996, nine-carriage, first- and second-class Cisalpino trains augmented the Cisalpino network by carrying passengers over the Basel-Bern-Brig-Milan and Zurich-Lugano-Milan routes with nine, 475-passenger ETR 470 Fiat trainsets.

Cisalpino added service to Stuttgart in autumn 1997, just as soon as Fiat could modify nine trainsets (at a cost of $5.5 million). Cisalpino considered this an efficient deployment of its high-priced equipment because the line between Zurich and Stuttgart is so highly curved that the tilting trains very effectively reduce travel time. It shares this running with the tilting German ICE T trainsets (see "ICE Generation").

Now, you ride CIS Geneva-Lausanne-Brig-Milan-Venice, Basel-Bern-Brig-Milan, Stuttgart-Zurich-Lugano-Milan, and Zurich-Lugano-Milan-Florence.

Whoa! What's happening?

Some passengers don't realize they have boarded a tilting train when they take their seats aboard the high-speed Cisalpino.

It comes as a surprise, then, but they know it well and good when their smart-looking, white-and-royal-blue train serpentines upward from their station, ducking and diving round curves. You feel Cisalpino's tilting right from the start of your trip. Few stretches of railroad line are straight in Switzerland.

Tilting trains perform beautifully on C-curves, as in Italy. It's another matter when they execute S-curves on the Lotschberg and Gotthard routes through Switzerland.

Tilting is the now-well-developed system of rounding curves 20% faster without upsetting passengers and thus decreasing overall travel time. Sensors in Cisalpino's leading vehicle send messages to the Fiat tilt system, which tilts the carriages one after another per software instructions.

Tilting works so well on curving older tracks that it eliminates the need to build expensive new high-speed lines. There is not a European railroad network that does not have plans for tilt in its future.

On Italian routes, curve radii exceed 1,600 feet and intermediate straight stretches separate consecutive curves. Tilting trains have time to return to vertical before they attack a second curve, but Switzerland's Alpine Gotthard and Lotschberg lines are lined with curves as tight as 820 to 1,000 feet, often one following another. Tracks verge on sheer drops and you burst through a whole series of short tunnels, some of which open straight onto perilous viaducts. By the time the back carriages of your train are starting to tilt for a left-hand curve, the front carriages and tilt sensor are already entering a right-hand curve, and at times it seems like your train is tilting left at the front while your rear section is still tilting right. At one curve you look down on the receding valley floor; at the next, up at 8,000-foot Alpine summits.

It is not advisable to walk along the train.

The nine-carriage Cisalpino trains offer 496 seats. The $20 million trains are air-conditioned and air-tight in order to make travel through tunnels more comfortable. The interiors, designed by the Turin designer Giugiaro, sport seats separated by tables. Interiors are subdued, gray blue in first class, sea green in second. Earphone jacks for taped music are installed beside every seat. Long windows are equipped with sun screens that you control electrically, but this is the downside of the Cisalpino, the shape of the windows. They are long, but horizontal. They limit your vertical vision so severely you cannot see conveniently some of the mountain crests, which is a shame when traveling in a country as scenic as Switzerland.

The tilt system is located entirely beneath the carriages instead of taking up passenger space. Full pressure-sealing lets you pass through the many tunnels traversed by CIS at full speed without popping your ears.

Italian designers know how to do bar/restaurants right. They have provided only 25 seats for you in their intimate bar/restaurant car but positioned their dining space beneath a low, intimate, light-studded ceiling, to make it the most beautiful restaurant area on the rails.

The restaurant seems to want to grab at passers-through by their elbows, "Come. Sit down, join us for a meal." The brilliant, low-backed, bright blue, velour-covered seats are arranged around varnished, real-wood tables. An authentic Italian coffee machine dominates the bar.

The adjacent bar for take-away food, next to the second-class carriages, is nearly as elegant.

Cisalpino accepts customary tickets, rail passes, and half-fare cards. Seat reservations are obligatory within Italy, and include a supplement of about $8. In first class, drinks are served and newspapers are available.

Artesia Takes You Between France and Italy

SNCF and Italy's Railroads formed a unique collaboration in 1996 to cut travel time between the two countries by providing high-speed joint service between France and Italy, with each country's prestige trains running with new multivoltage locomotives into its neighbor's stations. Seat reservations are compulsory, and rail passes are honored.

Artesia (*www.Artesia-geie.com*) is the marketing name for the 1998 mininetwork of higher-speed trains connecting Milano, Italy, with Lyon, France, in less than six hours and between Milano and Paris, France, in less than seven hours.

Artesia is one of the enterprises of Grande Lignes International (GLI), the division of FrenchRail (SNCF), which has some 15 fingers in everything from Eurostar to BritRail Travel International. In the case of Artesia, GLI cooperates with the Italian State Railroads (FS).

FrenchRail's TGV-R (Reseau) trains are like those which first ran on the TGV Nord line, but are specially equipped to run on both 3 kV dc and 1.5 kV dc. Artesia's red-striped ETR480 is the latest generation of tilting Pendolino trains. ETR480 is special because its power car, with the FS logo on front, can handle both Italian and French power supplies so that you don't have to wait for a change of locomotives at the border.

Like its Cisalpino cousin, ETR480 has a wonderful full-length dining car and a good, sturdy ride made possible by the undercarriage Fiat tilting system.

At Chiomonte, you see the Italian Alps looming high to the south. On the north the pines lining the mountain crests give the serrated summits a fuzzy, tentative profile.

The mountainside houses look like they were snatched from Switzerland on a quiet day. Their aged wooden beams blend with white plaster and irregular windows, balconies, and dark tile roofs.

The Alps here are formidable, but Artesia trains trace their twisting ways through the towering mountains between France and Italy with all possible speed and good comfort.

Artesia's Frejus, an Italian ETR480 Pendolino train, takes you out of Milano Centrale station at 1:15 P.M. so you are not likely to see Artesia's French TGVs leaving for Paris at 9:15 A.M. and 4 P.M.

Your starting point, Milano Centrale, is the grand station of Europe. Allow yourself time to look around (see "Islands of Order" in the Italy chapter). Your Frejus ETR480 train, and its ETR480 running mate, the Mont Cenis, call first in Torino's (Turin) Porta Susa train station and then spend 10 minutes at Torino's downtown station, Porta Nuova, where a wave of new passengers boards.

From Torino your Frejus takes you below wine terraces that zigzag precariously up mountainsides so steep and so difficult to harvest that you marvel at the vines' clinging tenacity.

Soon, you realize you a riding a true mountain railroad. Wildly racing brooks, elevated motorways running next to your route, and camping sites crowded with camper vehicles bearing license plates from faraway countries mark your route.

Past Oulx-Cesana your Frejus begins to run in and out of tunnels. Alps to 11,500 feet tower high above with faces so chiseled and broken and made barren by landslides and erosion that your Frejus seems a tiny toy below these giants.

After a quick stop in the white plaster Bardonecchia station, which has a remarkable roof of a brown stone hewn like slate, you pass in and out of so many tunnels that every time you emerge from a tunnel, the new view seems more magnificent than the last.

Through the Tunnel de Frejus, you arrive at Modane, the border town in the Rhone-Alpes region of France, and your Artesia train changes from 3000 Volts dc to 1500 Volts dc. The historical 8.5-mile rail tunnel was order by the Sardinian monarch in 1872 to unite those parts of his domain lying to either side of the Alpine divide.

From the station, Modane with its steeply spired church on the Frejus Valley floor appears very small. On the crests above you see the crenelated walls of a medieval fortress.

Leaving Modane, you pass into still another tunnel, but now your Frejus always heads down, down 18 minutes along the long valley of the River Arc to St-Jean-de-Marienne at the division between the north and south French Alps.

In Modane and St-Jean-de-Marienne industry is more important than agriculture. You see metal-working and electro-chemical plants, but you also admire the rows of green grape vines haphazardly planted on startling white soil and the castles perched high on the mountainside.

The valley city of Chambery on the River Isere lies below high Chartreuse and Bauges Savoy Alps. Slices of the mountain look like they were cleaved with a chain saw.

From 1232 until 1562, Chambery was the capital city of Savoy at the strategic crossroads of the ancient trade to Italy. It will surely remind you of a quaint Italian city with its rosy facades, wrought-iron balconies, and grand arcades. The Sainte-Chapelle part of Chambery's Chateau of the Dukes of Savoy was built by Amadeus VIII to house the Holy

Shroud. When Savoy became part of France in 1860, Italians removed the shroud to Torino where it is now known as the Turin Shroud.

In Chambery you can change for trains in every direction. Chambery's tidy station is a major rail hub. Artesia's Milan-Paris TGVs take you from here via Dijon's Ville station over high-speed tracks. The departures board also shows connections to Annecy, Geneva, and Marseille.

From Chambery, your Frejus twists north along Lake du Bourget into the posh casino- and lakeside-promenade-resort town of Aix-les-Bains. Even the white swans and pleasure boats enjoy the lake below characteristic, high Alpine peaks. Le Bourget is a picture-book, idyllic Alpine lake with all the delight you associate with that magic description.

Past Aix-les-Bains your Frejus further descends to a stop in Culoz, where you leave the wild Alps behind you and enter rounded limestone mountains characteristic of the Jura chain.

Past Culoz, your descent becomes ever sharper through forests of firs. You see sweeping panoramas of both Jura and Alpine mountains as well as the distant valley of the Rhone River to the south.

The fortified town you see on the crown of hills overlooking the Ain Valley is Perouges, a medieval curiosity. It was founded by settlers from Perugia in central Italy long before Caesar came to Gaul, and its difficult location has allowed it to escape the sieges of the Middle Ages, time, and tourism.

Your Frejus' final spurt takes you into Lyon's Part Dieu train station. Part Dieu is the bright, modern through station that SNCF built for its first high-speed line, which was between Lyon and Paris. From Part Dieu, your Frejus makes the short trip into Perrache station. Perrache is an old-fashioned station transformed into a hodgepodge transportation center. Foot traffic crossing between mainline and regional train platforms, regional and airport bus stops, two Lyon metro lines, and a taxi stand make Perrache difficult to find your way around but, luckily, the station is decently marked. The signs up and down the escalators connecting the three levels will get where you want to go.

Agents in Perrache's City information office help you with hotel reservations. From Perrache's back entrance you catch the airport bus to Lyon's airport, newly renamed Saint-Exupery (formerly Satolas) for Antoine de Saint-Exupery (1900-1944).

Italian ETR 480 service
Lyon - Turin/Milan

EC136 Mont Cenis	EC140 Frejus				EC142 Frejus	EC138 Mont Cenis
0630	1315	dep.	MILAN (Centrale)	arr.	1245	2150
0704	1350	dep.	Novara	arr.	1209	2116
0752	1440	dep.	TURIN (Porta Susa)	arr.	1118	2024
0812	1458	dep.	TURIN (Porta Nuova)	arr.	1100	2007
0900	1547	dep.	Ouix	arr.	1005	1916
0930	1628	arr.	Modane	dep.	0938	1842
1052	1808	arr.	Chambery	dep.	0803	1739
1109	1822	arr.	Aix-les-Bains	dep.	0750	1725
1225	1935	arr.	LYON (Part Dieu)	dep.	0639	1614
1237	1946	arr.	LYON (Perrache)	dep.	|	|

French TGV-R service
Paris - Milan

EC17 Manzoni	EC19 Dumas				EC16 Dumas	EC18 Manzoni
0754	1054	dep.	PARIS (Lyon)	arr.	1611	2254
1059	1402	dep.	Chambery	arr.	1308	1953
1208	1508	dep.	Modane	arr.	1202	1849
1235	1535	arr.	Ouix	dep.	1132	1820
1327	1627	arr.	TURIN (Porta Susa)	dep.	1043	1726
1422	1722	arr.	Novara	dep.	0947	1631
1455	1755	arr.	MILAN (Centrale)	dep.	0915	1600

Zurich-Paris on the Heart Line

"What is this? Everybody knows that from Zurich you go through Basel to get to Paris. We've done it for years. Why would anyone go through Neuchatel?"

The *Neue Zurcher Zeitung*, Zurich's preeminent newspaper, sharply criticized the new Swiss Railroads' timetable when it was issued.

For years the only rational way between Paris and Zurich was via Basel. Suddenly, with the advent of high-speed French TGVs, you were able to use the new high-speed line from Paris' Lyon station to Frasne and make same-platform connections there through Neuchatel to Bern.

This new route offered crackerjack same-platform connections, good trains and the wonderful scenery of the Jura mountains, castles, distant Alps, and Lake Neuchatel.

Still, you had to make two changes of train and reservations were required for two of the three segments, so those with cumbersome luggage preferred the duller, direct trains from Paris' East station via Basel. Less encumbered passengers enjoyed the Frasne alternative.

It took many years of negotiations before Zurich was at last granted a no-change TGV connection with Paris' Gare de Lyon. Trivoltage, silver-and-blue TGVs were renovated and customized with the banner "la ligne de cour FRANCE SUISSE" and the red heart logo of the "Heart Line." You enjoy carriages with a new interior design containing only 110, more spacious seats in first class and 240 in second. Reservations are required and global fares apply.

Although the new service is no faster end-to-end, the new Heart Line train replaced the former EuroCity train Arbalete (meaning "crossbow") consisting of older, standard FrenchRail Corail carriages.

Heart Line Service

0741	1648	dep.	PARIS (Lyon)	arr.	1311	2150
0926	1835	dep.	Dijon	dep.	1131	2011
1053	1952	arr.	Frasne	dep.	1013	1850
1110	2006	arr.	Pontarlier	dep.	0949	1824
1154	2049	arr.	Neuchatel	dep.	0905	1740
1228	2122	arr.	BERN	dep.	0832	1703
1345	2242	arr.	ZURICH (Hbf)	dep.	0715	1545

EuroCity—The European Standard

For international travel, EuroCity (EC) trains are the work horses. About 160 EC trains of European standard connect 200 European cities directly. They promise you multilingual personnel to help you on the departure platform and serve you on the train; dining cars, cafeterias, or at least a refreshments trolley; usually a free timetable at your seat; minimal wasted time (less than three minutes) at intermediate stops and border crossings; modern carriages; and speeds up to 167 mph (57 mph minimum). Rail pass holders don't pay the EC surcharge. For your own peace of mind, you can reserve seats on ECs during busy travel seasons.

International
Night Trains

Smart Train Lodging

One of the great pleasures of train travel in Europe is waking up in a brand-new city, yawning, stretching, and peeking expectantly out of the train window at bright, quaint, and surprising surroundings that promise fresh new adventures. Feeling vigorous and eager after a good night's sleep, you feel charged to conquer exciting new worlds.

Travelers often choose overnight trains through Europe to save their travel time and see more during the day and to cut down on hotel expenses.

Throw out your preconceived ideas about overnight train travel. The new generation of high-tech, high-convenience, tilting and double-decked sleeper trains known collectively as hotel trains now provides pampered service or even economic seats on Europe's most popular overnight routes. Tren Hotel (SpanishRail) and CityNightLine (based in Switzerland) are fresh air. These trains have nudged aside the familiar, older generation of overnight trains that have long carried

77

seemingly endless strings of sit-up carriages, sleeping carriages, sleep-erettes, and couchettes throughout Western Europe.

The new hotel trains are targeted primarily for business travelers by traveling along the most appealing business routes, but they provide space for budget travelers using rail passes in new sleeperette seats and innovative couchette bunks costing $20 to $40. Visitors still rely on their old favorite overnight trains to take them to vacation destinations.

Even on holiday routes, vacationers can board trains with fully equipped sleeping carriages ("Bedplaats," "Bedrijtuig," "Makuuvannu," "Place-Lits," "Schlafwagen," "Sovvagn," "Sovewagn," "Voiture-Lits") which were designed for demanding business travelers. Traditional couchettes ("Cabina de literas," "Cuccetta," "Ligplaats," Ligrijtuig," "Liegeplatz," "Voiture-couchettes") and reclining seats (sleeperettes) give you your best value for your money. Couchettes tra-ditionally are minidormitories with four or six bunks attached to the walls of the compartments. Their popularity with travelers and European families is well deserved.

Sleeping compartments are more private and more expensive. Top of the line is the "Single" (S), available in first class. This is a twin-bed-ded first-class compartment with only the lower bunk used. A first-class "Special" (Sp) is a smaller one-bed-only compartment. The larger first-class compartment is also available as a "Double" (D), with the top bed folded down. When one travels on a second-class ticket, the Sp com-partments are called "Tourist 2" (T2) with two beds, either one above the other or two upper beds, across from each other, and "Tourist 3" (T3), with three beds in a tier, one above the other.

Nordic and British railroads offer only sleeping-car accommoda-tions instead of couchette accommodations, but the three-berth sleep-ing compartments in Nordic countries cost about the same as couchettes farther south. British sleeping-car prices are substantially higher but still save money compared to hotel prices.

Travelers who don't want to pay for either a couchette or sleeping compartment still sleep very well by riding one of the older trains whose seats recline partially or collapse together by pulling forward at the bottoms, but the number of these trains is declining. When you ride one, it takes no practice to make three beds side by side by pulling forward at the bottoms. This is so practical the whole passenger list does it, but it's a nuisance when the claustrophobic person nearest the window crawls over two sleeping people to get off the train at 3:30 A.M.

Wise overnight travelers sit nearest the corridor so they can step out to visit the washrooms or snack bar, or even get off to buy a sandwich from a platform vendor during a lingering, middle-of-the-night stop. Overnight trains are usually in no hurry.

When there are only two riding in a compartment overnight, it is more comfortable to fold up the arm rests, stretch full-length along the seats, use a parka or even unsnap the padded headrests for pillows, and sleep soundly until morning. However, when the train is crowded and the compartments filled, no one can stretch out. Travelers spend the night uncomfortably avoiding their companions' space. It's not pleasant trying to sleep on crowded trains; a couchette is a better bet.

Food may or may not be available on overnight trains, and if it is, it is expensive, so take aboard water and whatever refreshments you require. A good rule of thumb: travelers staying in five-star hotels should book a sleeping compartment; those staying in two- and three-star hotels should book a couchette; those staying in youth hostels make do in folded-together seats. Use the Thomas Cook European Timetable or the free Eurailpass pocket timetable to block out your overnight travels and apportion your travel time so you still have time to enjoy the cities you are visiting.

Traditional couchettes

All the various sleeping-car configurations are not always on a given train or even in every country. Even international couchettes can be a surprise. A couchette originating in Zurich, Switzerland, for Amsterdam, the Netherlands, runs mostly through Germany, but may use an Italian Railroads' carriage staffed with a Danish porter.

You sleep two to a side in first-class couchettes and three to a side in second-class couchettes. The lodging cost is the same in both classes. The difference is the train fare. You receive more room in first class because you pay more for your ticket (or pass).

When you board carriages fitted with traditional couchettes, depending on the time of night, the standard bench seats usually have already been converted into bunks. Otherwise, passengers agree when it is time to convert them. All Europeans know how. Bright and (too) early in the morning, train employees clear the bedding and reconvert the couchettes to regular seating for daylight arrival.

Porters leave plastic-wrapped packages containing blankets, sheet-bags, and a pillow for every bunk. The sheet-bags, sometimes made of a soft, porous, synthetic fiber—they are disposable—are partially fitted like bottom sheets to keep them from slipping, but there is no way to tuck in the blanket. It is always a tug of war between you and gravity to keep the blanket from dropping to the floor. Sleepers stretch out quite comfortably, but undressing is discretionary in mixed company as there is no gender distinction when assigning bunks.

There is a surprising difference in comfort between four-person, air-conditioned, first-class couchettes, and six-person, second-class ones (which may or may not be air-conditioned). The extra space created by removing two bunks and two people is astonishing, but only French and Italian trains offer first-class couchettes and then only on domestic trips. When day compartments are not crowded many travelers find it more comfortable to sleep in an air-conditioned first-class sit-up compartment than a second-class, six-passenger, natural-ventilation couchette.

Sometimes couchette porters (who hold the passports to show at frontier crossings so sleepers need not be disturbed) often have a case or two of cold beer and soft drinks they are happy to sell when the journey begins. Many make their private compartments available for a pickup party of talkative international travelers. Couchettes can be reserved and paid for up to two months in advance through a travel agent in America, but it is easier and less expensive to reserve them in Europe at any large train station. All Western railroads but Portugal's and Greece's have connected, computerized reservations systems, but the Nordic system interfaces only with the German one. When couchettes are not completely sold in advance, you usually see a railroad agent selling couchettes at a portable reservations counter set up next to the train to accommodate last-minute arrivals.

When making a couchette reservation, specify which level bunk you prefer. Some travelers prefer top bunks because they are most private and give them space for their carry-ons. A ladder is provided to reach the higher bunks. Some prefer bottom bunks because they are most convenient. You find storage space beneath the bottom bunk and next to the top bunk. No one prefers middle bunks.

EuroNight—European Quality Trains

The glamorous Wagons-Lits sleeping-car system is a thing of the past, although you occasionally see a sleeping carriage still carrying an old Wagons-Lits logo. These have more or less been replaced by nationally owned trains running international routes. The 1993 train classification EuroNight (EN) is applied to international night trains of high standard. EuroNight trains are available for boarding in the starting train station a half-hour before departure and do not stop anywhere between midnight and 5 A.M. Porters speak at least one foreign language (usually English). Men and women have separate wash and WC facilities.

EuroNight trains consist exclusively of sleeping carriages, couchettes, and in some cases reclining-seat sleeperette cars. Sleeping-car and some couchette passengers receive breakfast packs and other travel accessories without extra charge, depending on the amount they have paid for their berths. Second-class passengers receive mineral water before retiring and a basic Continental breakfast. Couchette as well as sleeper customers receive a towel, soap, and a cup of drinking water. First-class passengers are greeted with a glass of Champagne, kir, or other alcoholic beverage as well as mineral water, a basket of fruit, a morning newspaper, and a more elaborate breakfast including muesli, cheese, etc. Disposable razors and toothbrushes are available from the conductor, who accepts credit cards for the purchase of extra drinks or snacks.

The Austrian EN Wiener Walzer takes you between Zurich and the Austrian capital. The EN Spree-Donau Kurier from Berlin (Ostbf.) via Leipzig, and Passau, to Vienna (Wbf.) carries blue and white Austrian sleeping carriages that were rebuilt in 2000 with 11 triple-berth compartments. The EN Hans Christian Andersen takes you from Copenhagen and splits for three destinations: Bonn, Stuttgart, or Innsbruck via Munich. Good EN trains also include the EN San Marco between Vienna and Venice; the EN Gottardo linking Lugano and Zurich with Florence and Rome; the EN Zurichsee connecting Basel via Zurich and Graz; the EN Remus between Vienna and Rome and the EN West-Kurier between Vienna and Bregenz. They all carry one- and two-bedded sleeping compartments and four- and six-bunk couchette compartments.

German ENs include the Donauwalzer between Brussels and Vienna/Munich via Cologne, Koblenz, and Nuremberg; the EN Jan Kiepura, running Cologne-Dortmund-Hanover-Frankfurt/Oder-Warsaw; and the EN Hans Albers between Hamburg and Vienna via Hanover, Fulda, Nuremberg, and Linz.

Tren Hotel

Tren Hotel (TH) is the Spanish brand of overnight train. Low-slung, tilting, Talgo Pendular trains (see "Iberia" chapter) fitted with two- and four-person rooms take you in comfort on international trunk routes between Spain and Portugal, France, Italy and Switzerland as well as within Spain on the Barcelona-Madrid-Seville/Malaga route. Their Gran Clase compartments even have a shower stall.

Trens Hotel are priced using a "Global" chart in which special prices are applied in regard to the category of class, the passenger type, the length of stay, and the purchase, refund, and exchange conditions. It excludes the normal use of rail passes, but rail-pass holders receive a discount, which varies between 30 and 50 percent depending on class of accommodation. The global prices include the night accommodation and a complimentary breakfast served in the dining car for those booked in single or double accommodation (even rail pass holders). You may make your reservations in the U.S. or in Europe, but travelers report that agents in cities not served by Trens Hotel are not familiar with booking procedures.

The TH Pablo (Pau) Casals from Barcelona (Sants) to Geneva, Lausanne, Bern, and Zurich (Hauptbahnhof); the EN Lusitania between Madrid (Chamartin) and Lisbon (Santa Apolonia); and the Antonio Machado between Barcelona (Sants) and Seville/Malaga carry "Gran Clase" sleeping carriages which can be used for single or double occupancy and contain private toilets and showers. Four-berth compartments on these trains are known as Turista class. You can also choose to ride in sleeperette seats to economize.

The EC Joan Miro between Paris (Austerlitz) and Barcelona (Sants), the EC Francisco de Goya between Paris (Austerlitz) and Madrid (Chamartin), and the EC Salvador Dali between Barcelona (Sants) and Milan (Centrale) complete your choice of upscale Talgo Pendular Trens Hotel traveling north from Spain.

Trens Hotel feature numerous people-friendly touches. Compartments are not roomy, but designers exploited every inch of space. You have a full-length mirror and a stepladder that drops out of the wall, providing easy access to the top bunks. You sleep under bright plaid blankets on comfy mattresses that make for a good night's sleep. You lock your compartment with a security-card key, and the Talgo's platform-level floor makes it easy to move you luggage on and off.

A spartan breakfast is included and is served in the dining car, which features white tablecloths, silverware, and good service. The Salvador Dali and Pau Casals also carry carriages with second-class sleeperette seats costing about $40, while the Lusitania also carries carriages with first-class seats costing $11 and second-class seats for $8, but these receive no breakfast.

CityNightLine from Berlin, Hamburg, Vienna and Zurich

The giant yellow letters on the $2.6 million, dark blue, double-decked carriages shout "CityNightLine," the marketing name of CityNightLine AG (*www.CityNightLine.ch*), wholly owned by GermanRail. CNL's fleet consists of high-quality, double-deck overnight hotel train carriages, single-level sleeperette carriages, and couchette carriages.

The Donaukurier CNL train takes you overnight between Vienna's Westbahnhof and Cologne/Dortmund, serving also Frankfurt/Main and Salzburg. Ride the CNL Komet between Zurich and Hamburg with service to Hanover, Dortmund, Freiburg, and Basel, and the CNL train named Berliner between Berlin's Zoo station and Zurich, stopping at Frankfurt/Main, Freiburg, and Basel. A portion of this train is split at Halle to serve Dresden via Leipzig instead of Berlin, and this portion is known as the CNL Semper.

CNL's air-conditioned trains give you three choices, all with breakfast included. When you choose "Deluxe" category *A,* you ride on the upper deck so that the additional panoramic windows expose the skyline; also, you have one or two wide beds, plus your own stall shower and private WC.

At 11.4 feet long, the Deluxe compartments are twice the length of the "Economy" compartments so that you can use a table and two armchairs. First-class rail pass holders pay slightly over half for a Deluxe accommodation. Europass holders need to buy the Austria add-on for CNL travel to Vienna.

When you choose lower-cost, "Economy" category *B* compartments, you have one or two beds—one above the other—and a wash basin. Stewards can connect two "B2" cabins together for four-person, family travel ("B4"). Rail pass holders and second-class, youth rail pass holders pay about 42 percent.

Budget category "C" passengers sleep in reclining, giant-sized seats designed to give you a feeling of seclusion by incorporating a canopy containing a personal reading lamp. Deposit your backpack and luggage in the storage space above you or between the seats. Your small continental breakfast is served on the fold-down table at your seat by a host. Rail pass holders, first or second class, pay $15, which is about 18 percent of the normal fare.

CNL trains between Dortmund and Vienna also carry refurbished couchettes, which are owned by GermanRail. They carry the same dark blue livery as other CNL stock and carry CNL logos, but you will also spot the GermanRail DB insignia. The air-conditioned compartments have either four or six berths each.

Until midnight, you can party in CNL's nearly carriage-length "Thousand-Stars Bar" beneath a lighting panel made possible by the use of fiber-optic cabling. Or you can dine in the small, white-table-cloth restaurant area of the lounge car designed by GermanRail's supplier of Bistro Cafes. Nearby you can patronize the souvenir shop and/or use the reception desk with telephone and fax connections.

Artesia de Nuit

Artesia's scenic daylight trains through the Alps are a delight, but if you need to save time and hotel expense, in 1999, SNCF and FS branded the extensive system of four Paris-Italy overnight trains with the Artesia mininetwork label, taking into its fleet the famous name trains from Paris: the Stendhal to Milano, the Palatino to Roma, the Rialto to Venezia (Venice), and the Galilei to Firenza (Florence), which depart nightly from Paris' Gare de Lyon between 7:30 and 10 P.M., and serve also Turin, Genoa, Pisa, Verona, Padova, and Bologna.

Artesia de Nuit includes an upmarket hotel carriage, known as "Excelsior," introduced on September 26, 1999. The refurbished coaches were completely gutted and new interiors designed by Giugiaro were installed at a cost of $1.5 million. Each carriage has seven "classic" compartments for two, as well as one "matrimonial" compartment with a double bed. Every compartment has its own shower and toilet, plus enough room for one child to join the couple. Every carriage has a small reception desk where you can take your own room key. The manager can lock doors centrally and observe corridors with closed-circuit television.

All have first-class sleeping carriages and second-class couchettes. The French couchette compartments are superior because they are occupied by only four travelers instead of six.

Artesia de Nuit uses global pricing, but rail passes are accepted for travel, plus of course you must pay for sleeping accommodations. First-class sleeping-car passengers can avail themselves of the Club Eurostar lounges in the major Italian train stations.

GermanRail International

In addition to the domestic night trains (NZ) described in the "Germany" chapter, GermanRail operates night trains between Amsterdam and Berlin, Paris and Berlin, Paris and Hamburg, and Bonn and Prague. These carry conventional five- or six-person couchettes, three-person sleeping carriages, compartments seating six, and bistro service. You can take your bicycle, except to Paris.

France

Smart Traveling on the Trains of France

Paris train stations—Getting around Paris—Airport trains—Versailles—Disneyland Paris—Overnight trains—Rail pass bonuses

More than two million passengers and 400,000 tons of freight are conveyed daily over the 21,100 miles of line operated by the French National Railroads ("Societe Nationale des Chemins de Fer Francais," or SNCF, *www.sncf.fr*). If they were put together to form a single train, the 15,300 passenger coaches and 153,000 wagons of the fleet would form a train almost 4,000 miles long and stretch from Paris to New York.

France is known for comfortable, convenient, and the world's fastest trains. Its "Train a Grande Vitesse" (TGV, *www.tgv.com*) put train travel back on the map of France. When the TGV Southeast went into service in 1981, it was the first new line to open since 1928. Originally a technical solution to the problem of saturation on the Paris-Lyon route, the TGV became a way of life. Taking two and a quarter hours to cover the 260 miles from city center to city center, it became easy for visitors to make a one-day round-trip excursion—no trek out to the airport, no delayed flights, no horror on the busiest toll highway in France. TGV ridership on the Paris-Lyon line started at 6.4 million a year. It now surpasses 21 million.

TGV Atlantique is the world's speed record holder at 320 mph, but the point is that TGV trains are a joy to ride, and well-planned station modifications make them easy to use. There are six TGV networks: TGV Southeast, Rhone-Alps (the Lyon bypass), TGV Atlantique, TGV Nord, the Paris bypass opened in 1996, and the TGV Mediterranee set to open on June 10, 2001.

The lines of the 186-mph TGV Nord Europe system are in part used by Eurostar cross-channel services described earlier. They are also used for travel to and from Brussels and serve 16 French cities using TGV-R (*R* for "reseau," or "network") trains (sometimes supplemented by surplus French Eurostar trains). The first running of TGV-R trains was May 24, 1993, when they cut the travel time from Paris to Lille's Flandres station from two and a quarter hours to one hour, twenty minutes, using the high-speed route only to Arras. When they traveled over the entire high-speed line between Paris and Lille, they cut the travel time to one hour flat on September 26, 1993.

The third-generation TGV-R trains are a refinement of the TGV-A (Atlantique) trains (see below). They are blue and silver and look at a glance like TGV-As, but they are slightly roomier—each carriage has one row of seats less—and have been shortened by dropping the carriages fitted with "Club Atlantique" semicompartments and shrinking the buffet-bar to only two-thirds of a carriage. The shortening permits them to cross the TGV Interconnection (serving Charles de Gaulle Airport and Disneyland Paris) and run on the TGV Southeast network, where the platforms are shorter. They are also pressure sealed (like German ICE trains) to allow running through tunnels without popping passengers' ears.

TGV-R power cars also incorporate a more powerful transformer and motors of higher capacity than TGV-A power cars. The profiles of the power cars make them look like sharks with backpacks. These changes allow their high-speed running on the steeper stretches of the new TGV Southeast line extension south of Valence and have been incorporated in the TGV Duplex trains.

You can ride TGVs from the Nord to the Southeast network from Brussels as far away as Nice (a staggering 485 miles), which is an amazing nine-hour trip. It takes less time than ever because TGVs bypass Marseille's St. Charles station and make their first stop at St. Raphael.

TGV Southeast's 167-mph network stretches from Paris' Gare de Lyon terminus throughout 50 cities in southeastern France to the

Italian border. TGV Southeast trains take you directly to five cities in Switzerland, two in Italy, French ski country, and the Riviera. TGV Southeast's 1981 carriages have been refitted on a program known as "Renovation 2," which pushed speed up to 186 mph, increased seat spacing so capacity fell from 384 to 345 passengers, and repainted to match the rest of SNCF's TGV fleet.

When FrenchRail introduced its towering blue-and-silver trains on December 19, 1996, FrenchRail's managers argued among themselves whether to call their new train a "double-decker," which sounds like a Dagwood sandwich/Vegas card-dealing policy, or "bilevel," which sounds like a house in the suburbs.

They compromised on the French "Duplex."

The name Duplex suggests to French thinking an apartment boasting a lively reception area (the train's upper deck) plus a private and calmer area on a different level (lower deck).

Lively or not, FrenchRail's new high-speed TGV Duplex train between Paris and Lyon solves the more pressing problem of saturation. The TGV line is a victim of its own success—too many passengers, not enough space.

The French solution was inevitable. Engineers couldn't lengthen the trains because lengthening the platforms in some stations would be enormously expensive. They couldn't make their trains wider because of international standards, but by relying on TGV technology that had been advancing ever since 1981, FrenchRail could seat passengers on two levels, one above the other.

FrenchRail engineers spent eight years perfecting the design for the first double-decked train to carry passengers at high speeds. They were limited by stringent total weight track limitations. The air-conditioning had to extend to two levels, something that had never been done before, especially within the weight package.

Engineers relied on the successful power equipment of earlier TGVs, but rearranged the drivers' compartments with the driver positioned in the center like Eurostar's. With no sacrifice of speed, they configured their trains to carry 545 passengers in three first-class carriages, four second-class carriages, and bar car. This is 45% more than a single-decked TGV unit.

You find ample space to set your luggage beside the larger-than-usual doors and face a circular flight of stairs. Bold, striped fabrics and basic colors attract you to the seats in the upper and lower decks. Your leg space is comfortable; seat pitch is 36.2 inches vs. 33.5 inches in the second-generation TGV. Everyone, even those in second class, can recline his or her seats.

"Personally, I'd rather ride on a Duplex carriage that is 60% full than a standard carriage that is packed," said a spokesman.

Headspace is so generous on the livelier upper level that you never consider that designing it might have been a problem. It is airy and not the least claustrophobic. From the upper windows you have good views and you can really see how high you are. "Cool," said one traveler, peeking at a regular TGV passing below.

Head clearance is less on the calmer lower level, where it is better to read a book or take a quick nap. The two smoking rooms (one each in first- and second-class) are on the lower levels only.

Unlike some other railroads' double-deck designs, the carriages are so well constructed that you feel almost no rocking or vibration even on the upper level. Engineers used long aluminum-welded sections and aluminum honeycombs.

The stairway is wide and so convenient that some passengers prefer to sit on the carpeted stairs than in their seats. Nevertheless, trudging up the stairs to the upper level is a nuisance for those with children and luggage.

Regardless of how safe it is to sit upstairs and to leave your luggage below, travelers feel more comfortable with their luggage nearby. They don't want to leave it out of sight. Getting small children up and down the stairs is sometimes a struggle.

Another drawback of a Duplex design is that there is only one corridor through the train, and to the bar car, and it is on the upper level. Passengers sitting downstairs must climb the curved staircases to walk through the train.

When you get to the bar car you probably won't realize that its floor level is lower than in the carriages with seats. It was designed to give you more height to stand—a nod to taller passengers. You can sit only at supremely uncomfortable stools at Formica-topped, sculpted places facing the windows, but the windows are larger than in the rest of the train and give you a better view of the passing scenery.

Avoid the upstairs WCs. They are so tiny that one can hardly avoid inadvertently stepping on the floor button that releases a torrent of water into the wash basin and splashes the occupant. The downstairs WCs are, by comparison, mansions.

TGV Atlantique takes you at 186 mph from Paris' Gare

Montparnasse terminus to Brittany; the Atlantique/Aquitaine branch takes you through Bordeaux to the Spanish border. Taking the afternoon Atlantique/Aquitaine to Irun shaves three hours off your travel time to Portugal. You change at Irun onto the Portuguese Sud Express, which continues overnight to Lisbon/Porto.

With the opening of the Paris TGV bypass on May 29, 1996, through Massy TGV station, 18 miles from the center of Paris in the southern suburbs, you make high-speed TGV connections from one area of France to another without having to go into Paris and transfer to a second train station with the French capital. You don't have to transfer between stations in Paris to travel from London or northern France to western or southwestern France by using Eurostar's stop at Lille Europ Station. Instead of three hours and thirty minutes, the trip between Lille and Le Mans takes two hours and thirty minutes; between Tours and Arras only two hours and twenty minutes, rather than three hours. Similarly, the last link in the Paris bypass reduces your travel time between the southeast or west of France and Normandy. Traveling from Lyon to Le Mans takes you three hours and five minutes (previously four hours); from Lyon to Rouen, three hours and thirty-five minutes (previously four hours and thirty minutes).

Brutally modern Massy TGV station is served by RER line *B* and provides you an interchange with RER line *C* at the adjacent Massy-Palaiseau station, so that you may board or leave the TGV network without traveling into downtown Paris.

TGV Mediterranee, opening on June 10, 2001, allows you to travel between Lyon and Marseille at 155 mph, and allows more frequent departures from Marseille to destinations as Brussels in five hours, twenty minutes; Lille in four hours, twenty minutes; Lyon in one hour, forty minute; Nantes in six hours, thirty-one minutes; and Paris in three hours flat.

In the main train stations, pick up small, free pocket timetables ("Le Fiches Horaires") between 180 cities served by the main lines and free brochures ("Guides TGV") giving the timetables together with the price for six TGV regions: Atlantique Ouest, Atlantique Sud-Ouest, Sud-Est, Midi-Mediterranee, Nord-Europe, and Province-Province. Similarly, there are six brochures ("Guides") for historic routes: Est, Paris-Limoges-Toulouse, Normandie, Paris-Clermont-Ferrand, Paris-Saint-Quentin-Maubeuge-Namur, and Paris-Brussels-Amsterdam. Even if your French is faulty, you can puzzle them out.

Eurostar takes you to London (see "Eurostar" chapter), Thalys takes you to Amsterdam and Brussels (see "Thalys" chapter), multivoltage TGVs and Italian ETR 480 trains take you to Italy (see "Artesia"), and Heartland TGVs take you to Switzerland ("Heartland"). EuroCity trains take you into all the other neighboring countries. Choose between EC Gustav Eiffel or EC Goethe for Frankfurt/Main, EC Maurice Ravel for Munich, and EC Mozart for Vienna, Munich, or Graz.

SNCF requires advance seat reservations on all TGVs. They are available up to 60 days in advance, but same-day reservations are no problem. Go to the reservations window marked "Jour," sometimes with a moving red-dot sign. Specify first (with or without TGV at-seat meal service) or second class, smoking or nonsmoking, and aisle or window seat. TGV tickets are not based on distance of travel, but TER trains still maintain distance-related pricing. There are two price levels for second-class TGV tickets. The higher applies to the most-used peak services.

The reservations/ticketing machines you see in the stations are not very useful for visitors with rail passes, but accept coins totaling up to 100 francs and credit cards for sums more than 30 francs.

Finally, validate the tickets you buy in France in the orange, automatic ticket punchers ("composteur") at the entrances to platforms. These validate the tickets based on an honor system, as conductors do not always check the tickets on board, and are required for insurance reasons. However, all tickets and reservations obtained in North America are exempt from this requirement. When you travel on a rail pass purchased before you leave and use a reservation made in France, you only need punch your reservation coupon.

You can browse through the magazine Grandes Lignes that you find free at the seats of the first-class sections of TGVs. When you read French, it is a colorful magazine with a minimum of SNCF propaganda.

Bicycles are for rent at the Gare de l'Est in front of track No.12 and in front of Gare Montparnasse near the merry-go-round. They are permitted on trains on weekdays between 9:30 A.M. and 4:30 P.M. and after 7 P.M. and without restriction on weekends, except on the Paris metro and on three stretches of RER line. Disassembled bicycles in transportation bags are permitted on Corail and TGV trains without additional charge.

FrenchRail is in the process of "regionalizing" regional networks, meaning that France's 22 regional councils will be responsible for their respective networks, and FrenchRail will simply provide train service.

France's regions almost ran out of lively colors for distinctive liveries and logos on their modern diesel or electrified railcars or trains comprising a network of practical, regional TER trains ("Trains Express Regionaux") until SNCF introduced a blue/silver gray livery. Largely unknown by foreigners, they provide you with local connections in 19 regions of France (all but the Ile de France, which has its own organization). TER timetables, which you can pick up free at the local stations, have been coordinated with the high-speed TGV lines, so that 20 percent of all long-distance travelers begin or finish their trips on the TER network.

TER trains are operated under agreements between SNCF and the respective regions. They are usually lighter than mainline trains and designed with commuter seating. You won't find them in timetables available in the United States, but their frequent departures will take you from city to city in the provinces, allowing you to visit by train cities off the beaten tourist paths. Be sure to pick up "Guide Regional des Transports" at regional SNCF stations.

The regions of Nord-Pas-de-Calais and Provence-Alpes-Cote d'Azur sport electric, double-decked, 85-mph TERs that differ from the double-decker Parisien RERs because of their air conditioning, larger windows and additional legroom.

Provence-Alpes-Cote d'Azur also runs sky-blue and stainless-steel railcars, while those of the Languedoc-Roussillon region are yellow railcars with first- and second-class seating. Metralsace, red with stainless-steel sides and the red-and-yellow Alsatian coat of arms on entry doors, is a 125-mph locomotive-pulled Corail train for the long, straight, level stretches between Strasbourg and Mulhouse.

The first TER, established in 1970, "TER Metrolor," runs through the departments of Moselle and Meurtheet-Moselle. TER Pays-de-la-Loire, white striped in green with blue piping, takes you through that department. Red-and-white "TER Limousin" and "TER Aquitaine" trains serve those areas.

Paris Train Stations

Base your travel in Paris, the hub of the French train system. Be sure to double-check from which train station your train departs. Each of Paris' six stations serves a sector of France and areas beyond. The stations are all terminuses, which means your train ends and does not continue through Paris. You must use suburban Paris stations to connect between lines.

You can say without exaggeration that all Paris train stations are good and big. All but perhaps Austerlitz and Montparnasse give a grand feeling and a sense of nostalgia. They have complete facilities. Tourist information offices (open Mon. to Sat., 8 A.M. to 9 P.M., May to October) will make hotel arrangements for you in the Gare du Nord (also open Sun., 1 to 8 P.M.), Gare d'Austerlitz (open to 3 P.M. only), Gare de l'Est, Gare de Lyon, and Gare Montparnasse. Look for the frequent "Point Argent" kiosks, which are ATMs.

As you might guess, Paris' stations do not use the arrival and departure time sheets standard in most of Europe. In some cases departures are shown on green sheets (not yellow), but more often you are treated to large overhead electronic arrival and departure boards giving your departure time and track number. Unfortunately, the track number may be posted so close to departure time that you must rush to the platform.

All stations have pushcarts for your luggage, but you must have a 10-French-franc coin to unlock them (which is released when you return the cart), and the carts are usually hard to find.

Electronic lockers, which remain closed for 72 hours, operate as follows: put your bag(s) inside a locker with door ajar, close door, deposit coins, receive a sealed slip of paper with instructions in French and English. Inside is your "secret" code. When you are ready to leave, you punch in your secret numeric code and the door pops open.

Paris' Montparnasse station on five levels, all connected with escalators, is headquarters for your TGV service to Brittany, Bordeaux, Lourdes, and Spain via Hendaye. It's the newest and snazziest of Paris' stations. The present station was built from the ground up in 1989 for the Atlantique and Aquitaine 186-mph TGV trains. You rise on escalators from one of the Paris metro stations on the bottom level; through the second level, a commercial gallery, to the middle level, street level. You then pass the consigne level to finally reach the top, platform level, with tracks 1 to 24. Buffets, fast food, shops, and essential services such as reservations and ticketing are scattered everywhere. In the rear of the track level your find Vaugirard station, with tracks 25-28. Montparnasse is Paris' busiest station—and it can handle all traffic within its vast glass and precast concrete shell.

Across from the station you can easily visit the Tour ("tower") Montparnasse, which many Parisiens criticize because it is the tallest skyscraper in Paris and too close, they feel, to the city center. It weighs

1.43 million tons, is 686 feet tall, and from the top you can see planes departing from both airports on opposite sides of Paris. The elevator to the Panoramic Tower lookout on the 59th floor takes 38 seconds. There is an entrance fee. At the open rooftop lookout, telescopes will show you all the detail of Paris. It is Paris' best panoramic viewing spot. On the 56th floor is the glassed-in, elegant "Ciel de Paris" restaurant.

The large area was created by demolishing smaller streets in Montparnasse (meaning "muses"), which was named for the hill. It used to be the artistic quarter of Paris, associated with such names as Edith Piaf, Ernest Hemingway, F. Scott Fitzgerald, James Joyce, and Oscar Wilde, who congregated in bars—some length of time after Marx and Lenin had completed their outlines.

Trains from Paris' Gare d'Austerlitz also serve the south of France and Iberia, but with deluxe Spanish Hotel trains. Austerlitz is the terminal for the RER line to Orly Airport. It contains a tourist office counter and a separate desk for youth hostel information (Avis is in the same room). Included in its services are the EC Francisco de Goya and the EC Joan Miro.

Gare du Norr is the terminus of the TGV Nord Europ network and the most user-friendly of the Paris stations to make it as simple as possible for English-speaking visitors and arrivals on Eurostar.

The ground level is divided into three sections:
• a fenced-off security area for Eurostar arrivals and departures (with mezzanine departure lounge);
• mainline trains (Grande Lignes) such as Thalys to Amsterdam, TGV-Rs to Brussels and Lille, conventional trains, and overnight trains north; and
• regional trains (Banlieue) in a separate fenced-off area with turnstile entry.

Below ground level are Paris metro stations on two lines, the RER stations for lines *B* and *D*, and a tunnel to Magenta RER station for line *E*. The line *B* station is your terminal for the RER line to Charles de Gaulle Airport.

Trains from Paris' tidy Gare de l'Est serve Strasbourg, Luxembourg, Frankfurt/Main, and German points south, and German-speaking Switzerland through Basel. The reserved waiting room for Venice Simplon Orient Express passengers is located opposite track 2. There are many inexpensive hotels across the street. Via elevator, the three-star Frantours Paris-Est hotel occupies the second and third floors above one wing of the station. There is also a room of coin-operated no-key lockers.

Gare de Lyon, the origin of the TGV Southeast network, takes you to Lyon, the Riviera, Italy, and Switzerland. It was rebuilt top to bottom for the first TGV Southeast network in 1981. At that time the dowdy terminus was transformed into a sprawling, multilevel jumble of a megastation with more trains, more tracks, more platforms, and boarding areas. They preserved the classic clock tower and added TGV tracks and access to the RER rapid-transit network below. It features the Belle Epoque Le Train Bleu restaurant (open noon to 2:30 P.M. and 7 to 10:30 P.M.) dedicated in 1900 at the time of the World's Fair. The adjacent, modern, two-star, 315-room Hotel Frantour Paris-Lyon is convenient—and a good value—for overnighters just passing through Paris.

Gare Saint-Lazare serves conventional trains to Normandy (including Dieppe harbor for ferries to Britain and London), Le Havre, and Cherbourg for ferry crossings to the Republic of Ireland. TGVs to Normandy depart from Gare du Nord. The attractive square in front of the station is the site of the tunnel to the Paris metro line known as "Meteor" and the RER station named Haussman, which dates from 2000.

Getting around Paris

The Paris metro system is so good, it's contagious. You get around easily aboard the ever-increasing and more-useful Paris metro and RER (rapid-transit) systems. Opened by President Jacques Chirac on October 15, 1998, the Paris metro's 14th cross-city line, known as Meteor, is driverless (it is controlled from a computer screen). The absence of a driver means that passengers can look ahead, into the tunnel. Transparent passenger doors on the platforms control access to the Meteor and safeguard against accidents. RER line E, known as EOLE ("Est-Ouest Liaison Express"), takes you into the outskirts with segments opened on July 14 and August 30, 1999.

It's a shame that Paris has perhaps the most convenient, efficient, and surely the least expensive public transportation system of any capital, because it discourages you from walking and really seeing the city. Looking at the metro map makes distances seem longer than they are. It's just as easy to walk two or three stops as to take the metro because you don't have to wind your way through corridors and climb stairs. For longer distances, riding Paris metro's 13 subway lines is a given.

Even better, there's RER, a second, independent underground train system. Tickets on one are valid on the other within city limits. With two overlapping/complementary underground transportation systems available to you in Paris, it is natural to ask which is better. Plan to use both. RER rapid-transit trains are larger (some are double-decked), less crowded, faster, cleaner, and make fewer stops. Their stations are spacious with the latest in electronic signing and interconnect with the metro at key locations. RER trains are better than the metro trains, but there are far fewer stations (the metro has 368 stations) and therefore less chance to use them.

Stop at the Paris Tourist Office at metro stop Charles de Gaulle Etoile (127, avenue des Champs-Elysees, open daily, 9 A.M. to 8 P.M.) for details on public transportation, system maps, and purchase of tourist tickets. Neither metro nor RER trains are covered by Eurailpass or France Railpass.

The Paris metro is usually the easiest and cheapest way to change between train stations. All six Paris train stations are connected to the subway net with metro stations below, but to connect between train stations you must usually change subway lines and this often requires considerable time and—if you are carrying luggage—effort. Here are the best ways:

• Paris-Nord to Paris-Lyon: Take RER line *D* south in the direction of Melun and Malesherbes. Get off at Paris-Lyon, the second stop.

• Paris-Lyon to Paris-Nord: Take RER line *D* north in the direction of Orry-la-Ville. Get off at Paris-Nord, the second stop.

• Paris-Nord or Paris-Est to Paris-Montparnasse: Take metro line No. 4 in the direction of Porte d'Orleans. Get off at Montparnasse-Bienvenue.

• Paris-Nord to Paris-Est: Walk (10 minutes). You can walk through a tunnel to Magenta RER station and then rise to street level to complete your exercise.

• Paris-Montparnasse to Paris-Nord or Paris-Est: Take metro line No. 4 in the direction of Porte de Clignancourt. Get off at station.

• Paris-Nord or Paris-Est to Paris-Austerlitz: Take metro line No. 5 in the direction of Place d'Italie. Get off at Gare d'Austerlitz station.

• Paris-Est to Paris-Nord: Walk on surface streets to Magenta RER station, descend, and reach Paris-Nord through a tunnel.

• Paris-Austerlitz to Paris-Nord or Paris-Est: Take metro line No. 5 in the direction of Bobigny. Get off at station.

• Paris-Nord to Paris-Saint-Lazare: Take RER line *E* from Magenta RER station to Haussman RER station. Both RER stations are connected to their respective terminuses by tunnels.

• Paris-Est to Paris-Saint-Lazare: Take metro line No. 7 in the direction of Mairie d'Ivry. Get off at Opera. Opera metro station is connected by tunnel to Haussman RER station by tunnel. Haussman is, in turn, connected to Paris-Saint-Lazare by tunnel. Don't get lost.

• Paris-Saint-Lazare to Paris-Nord: Use tunnel to Haussman RER station, get off at Magenta RER station, connect by tunnel to Paris-Nord.

• Paris-Saint-Lazare to Paris-Est: Walk via tunnel to Opera metro station. Board metro line No.7 in the direction of La Courneuve. Get off at Gare d'Est station.

You don't have to use stairs within Paris' train stations, but once you enter the metro system below, you encounter endless flights of stairs and long corridors in addition to escalators that usually work, but not always. The metro stations are not luggage friendly, especially when you try to pass items through the gates. Tip: Push or shove your baggage ahead of you when you insert your ticket into the gate-opening slot.

Riding Paris' 2,000 buses shows more of Paris and gives you a feeling for the relationships between major sights, but this is not as easy as it sounds because it requires a grasp of the surface streets, something riding the metro does not.

Each metro line takes its name from the end stops. For example, line 1 is called "La Defense/Chateau de Vincennes." When you take line 1 in the direction of La Defense you will travel west until you reach the end stop of the same name. Think in terms of directions. The orange signs in stations marked "Correspondence" mean you can change lines at that station to go in another direction. Just follow the signs. Trains run from 5:30 A.M. to about 12:30 A.M. In the night there are night buses.

RER criss-crosses Paris in the center and branches into the suburbs, to the airports, Versailles, and Disneyland Paris. There are five RER lines: *A, B, C, D,* and *E. A* and *B* are run jointly by RATP and SNCF, while *C, D,* and *E* are run by SNCF on its own. Line *A* shifts more than 50,000 passengers per hour per direction at the peak—and ridership continues to grow. B3 connects to Charles de Gaulle Airport, C2 and B4 to Orly Airport, C5 to Versailles, and A4 to Disneyland Paris. Metro tickets and passes are valid on RER within the city center.

The best way to ride the Paris metro is to use one of the metro passes designed for voters of the city rather than tourists. These are issued for calendar weeks beginning Monday (Coupon jaune—meaning "yellow") and for calendar months beginning on the first (Carte orange). There is also a pass valid for a year. Their disadvantage is that you need to supply a small passport-type photo (which the agent will affix). You may buy one at a quick-photo machine in Paris but will save aggravation by bringing it with you.

The average visitor, who doesn't stay long enough to take advantage of these passes, can best buy 10 tickets at once (called a "carnet") from a machine (press *E* for English) or an agent, or use two kinds of wallet-sized passes designed for tourists: the one-day "Formule Une" or the "Paris Visite," valid for either two, three, or five days. Neither the Formule Une nor the Paris Visite cards require a photo. The Paris Visite also gives significant discounts at many sights, including 20 percent off admission to the Cite des Sciences et de l'Industrie, and 35 percent off Canauxama cruises on Canal St-Martin.

The prices for all the passes mentioned above provide unlimited second-class travel on the metro, RER, and buses in zones 1 and 2 (also zone 3 for the "Paris Visite"), which is all that the usual visitor uses, but for higher costs you can extend these passes to increased zones or first-class RER and include RER transportation to Versailles, Charles de Gaulle Airport (zone 5) and Orly Airport (zone 4). In most cases it is cheaper to buy tickets for these longer distances separately.

In addition consider the "Carte Musees et Monuments" available from the Paris Tourist Office and metro ticket counters. They are available for one, three, or five consecutive days in 65 Paris museums including the Louvre and Musee d'Orsay. The cost savings can be significant. Additionally, with such a card you don't have to stand in line—and the time you save may make it worthwhile to you. You go straight to the head of the line.

Airport Trains

There are two train stations located underground near Charles de Gaulle Airport's terminal 2C (Air France's terminal). Free, yellow-striped, "ADP" shuttle buses circling the airport connect both of CDG's two terminals ("Aerogare") to them. The RER station takes you to Paris; the TGV station leads to Lyon, Bordeaux, Marseille, Nice, Lille, Poitiers, London, Brussels, Geneva, and other cities without a time-consuming trip into Paris. Thirty-six high-speed TGVs, all covered by rail passes, serve the airport's TGV train station. You can board a TGV train at CDG and arrive in Lyon two hours later, in Bordeaux about four hours later, or in Lille, to connect with a Eurostar train to London, in less than an hour. In other words, if Pierre takes a TGV from Lille and Paul takes a cab from Paris, they just may arrive at CDG at the same time.

RER trains use the 1994 RER station. Prices vary with distance (not covered by rail passes), but when you purchase a single ticket you have access to more than a hundred RER stations in the Paris area. RER line B3 trains depart every seven minutes, taking 30 minutes to Gare du Nord and then continuing to Chatelet-Les Halles, St.-Michel-Notre-Dame, Luxembourg, and Denfert-Rochereau stations between 5:05 A.M. and 11:50 P.M. In Chatelet-Les Halles, you can change to RER line D for Paris' Gare du Lyon.

The Air France bus (costing about the same as first-class rail) takes about an hour (barring gridlock on the motorway) from the Porte Maillot bus terminus near the Arc de Triomphe or Place Charles-de-Gaulle-Etoile (avenue Carot) with departures about every 12 minutes between 6 A.M. and 11 P.M. Roissybus, the transit authority's bus to the square in front of the Opera, where there is a metro stop, departs from Charles de Gaulle Airport every 15 minutes from 5:45 A.M. to 8 P.M. and every 20 minutes from 8 P.M. to 11 P.M. It takes about 45 minutes, barring gridlock. A special KLM bus takes longer because the driver must wait for the last passenger off the plane to clear customs.

From Orly Airport, board the Orly-Rail shuttle from Orly to the SNCF Orly-Rail station at Pont de Rungis station on RER line C. RER line C runs every 15 minutes to Austerlitz train station, St. Michel/Notre Dame, Musee d'Orsay, Invalides, Pont de l'Alma, and Eiffel Tower between 5:50 A.M. and 11:30 P.M.

The 1991 Orlyval automated, light-rail minimetro links Orly West and Orly South terminals with RER line B at Antony-Orly station in seven minutes, with departures every five to seven minutes. RER line B is your connection to St. Michael/Notre Dame, Chatelet-Les Halles, Gare du Nord, and Charles de Gaulle Airport stations. Your Orlyval ticket is also valid on metro and RER lines as needed to your destination.

Orlybus, the transit authority's bus, runs between Orly East terminal and Orly South to Denfert-Rochereau every 13 minutes (peak) and takes 30 minutes on average. At Denfert-Rochereau you find Paris Metro lines No. 4 and No. 6. Orlybus service runs from 5:35 A.M. to 11 P.M. from Orly South. The Air France buses leave Orly every 12 minutes daily between 5:50 A.M. and 11 P.M. for Montparnasse. A second stop takes you to the Invalides air terminal. Allow 30 minutes.

Formula One and Paris-Visite tickets (see above) are valid on Orlyval provided they includes zones 1-5. They provide discounts on Orlybus and Roissybus as well.

Before returning to Orly on your RER *B* train, make sure that Antony-Orly station is illuminated on the station billboard. Sit toward the rear of the RER train to make changing to Orlyval easier. Similarly, when taking line *B* to Charles de Gaulle Airport from one of the stations mentioned above, be sure the electronic sign or video monitor states "Roissy Rail," for this is just one of the two branches of the northbound RER, and you want to be on the correct train.

TGVs between FrenchRail's CDG airport train station and the train station at Lyon's airport, which has been renamed Saint-Exupery (formerly Satolas) for Antoine de Saint-Exupery, aviator and author of *The Little Prince*, whisk passengers hither and yon, but contrary to logic, TGV trains connect the Lyon airport train station to downtown Paris and the Paris airport train station to downtown Lyon. This is the kind of stuff that makes travelers scratch their heads and rail fans chortle.

Stunning is not too strong a word to describe the architecturally inspiring 1994 TGV train station at Lyon's airport. Dramatic fan-shaped arches of steel-supported glass soar like a bird with out-stretched wings above a central overpass. A schematic electric sign-board directs you to one of two gates leading to two island platforms, each served by four tracks. Your gate depends on your carriage number. Porte Rhone leads you to five sectors (repere) and Porte Alpes leads you to four.

While air arrivals use RER rapid transit trains from Charles de Gaulle Airport to central Paris, bus is their connection from Saint-Exupery airport to central Lyon. Buses depart from Lyon's Perrache train station every 20 minutes from 5 A.M. to 9 P.M. (except Saturdays 1 P.M. to Sundays 9 P.M. and French holidays, when it runs every 30 minutes). The travel time is about 45 minutes, depending on highway traffic.

Versailles

There are three train routes from downtown Paris to Versailles, taking 20 to 30 minutes. Of these, RER line C5 route to Versailles Rive-Gauche station takes you closest to the chateau.

You will have to pay for the RER even if you have a rail pass, so if you have a consecutive-day rail pass, you may prefer to take a train from Gare Saint Lazare to Versailles Rive-Gauche or from Gare Montparnasse to Versailles-Chantiers in order to save money.

The 1991 opening of Massy TGV station gives you a fourth route to Versailles. TGV trains between Lyon and Rouen pass through Massy TGV in the southern outskirts of Paris (use RER lines *B* or *C*), taking 10 minutes from Massy-Palaiseau to Versailles.

Alternately you can take bus line 171 from above Trocadero metro station to the last stop. For the bus you need either three metro tickets, a Formule Une valid for zones 1-4, or a Paris Visite valid for zones 1-2-3-Airport.

The chateau is open Tuesday-Sunday 9:45 A.M. to 5 P.M.; the Grand Trianon, Tuesday-Sunday 9:45 A.M. to noon and 2 to 5 P.M.

Disneyland Paris

Paris RER line A4 takes you to the "Disneyland Paris" complex, which is situated 12.4 miles to the east of Paris. Good places to board include the Chatelet-Les Halles interconnect with RER lines *B* and *D*, Gare de Lyon, and Vincennes.

In 1994 Disneyland Paris took on a new life when long-distance TGVs began calling at the Marne-la-Vallee station on the Interconnection Link between the Southeast and Nord Europe TGV networks, so that now you can wear your mouse ears on the TGVs from Brussels, Geneva, Lille, Lyon, and Dijon and nobody will think it is odd.

Overnight trains

SNCF's overnight equipment is so good it is exported. You can hardly resist riding overnight on the long routes from Paris because with a first-class rail pass you pay no more to sleep in a domestic couchette with four bunks than second-class passengers pay for six-bunk couchettes.

"Service Nuit" trains are entirely composed of Corail couchette carriages and Corail reclining-seat carriages. In the center of each train, you find a staffed service coach with vending machines selling drinks and snacks. You check in before departure to ensure no unwelcome visitors are aboard. For security, trains do not stop between 12:30 and 5:30 A.M. Women may request same-sex couchettes positioned close to the conductor's compartment. Couchette passengers use a fixed duvet instead of blankets and a sheet sleeping bag, and receive a welcome kit including a bottle of mineral water.

Budget travelers may also investigate the Cabines-8 found only on SNCF routes Paris-Quimper and Paris-Brest. These diabolically config-ured sleeping carriages are designed for young people who prefer not to pay for sleeping accommodations. Each carriage contains 12 com-partments with eight semireclining contoured bunks, four per side.

The bunks are treated as seats for reservations purposes so you pay no supplement. If the threat of claustrophobia does not faze you, these second-class bunks carry the right price. You pay only for a sim-ple space reservation, as you would for a seat on any long-distance train.

Rail Pass Bonuses

SNCF honors Eurailpass, Europass, Eurail Selectpass, and France Railpass on all lines. In addition, you receive discounted fares on Eurostar to England and Artesia to Italy. The Chemins de Fer de la Provence (CFP) gives holders 25 percent off (50 percent with a France Railpass), Chemins de Fer de la Corse on the island of Corsica gives 50 percent off, and the ferries between France and Corsica give a dis-count of 25 percent.

A France Railpass is as flexible as a Parisien tart's affections and as thrifty as a Gascon goatherd. With a three-day France Railpass, you can travel anywhere you choose on SNCF for a month for less than the round-trip fare on TGV between Paris and Lyon. Moreover, you can tailor your pass to your exact needs by buying the precise number of days you need (up to six extra days). All passes must be validated at any French train station (which may be done up to six months after issuance in the U.S.). Fast-train surcharges are covered but you must pay for the required reservations.

When you travel with a companion you can obtain a special price. Two persons together pay about three-quarters of what they would pay buying individual passes.

First-class prices cost about 80 percent of a Europass; buying sec-ond-class travel gives you an additional 20 percent savings. Children four to eleven pay half the adult fare. Those under four ride free.

Enter your name and passport number and have it validated at an SNCF station (at an "Orientation" kiosk or ticket window) where the agent will enter the first and last day of validity. If the agent asks you when you will start travel, tell a fib. Say "Today." You have one full month to travel. Otherwise the agent will ask you to come back and stand in line again. Personally complete the day boxes in ink in numerical sequence on the days you travel. When you start your trip after 7 P.M., enter the next day's date and travel overnight using up only one validation day.

A France Weekender Pass, introduced in 2000, lets you turn your trip from London aboard Eurostar into a minitour of France. It allows four consecutive days of unlimited train travel when Saturday and Sunday are included, and is only available for travel October to March. First day of travel must take place within three months of the purchase date. Travelers with a France Weekender Pass receive the discounted passholder fares on Eurostar, Artesia, Talgo overnight trains to Spain, Artesia Nuit, and international TGVs to Brussels, Geneva, Lausanne, and Zurich.

SNCF provides a series of Decouverte tickets, which are "social" discounts for travel at nonpeak travel times. The "periode bleue" generally includes all trains departing Monday noon to Friday noon and Saturday noon to 3 P.M. on Sunday. A "Decouverte 12-25" is the youth discount, "Decouverte Senior" is for those over 60, "Decouverte a Deux" is for couples traveling together, and "Decouverte Sejour" is for trips exceeding 125 miles with a Saturday night stay. Variable reductions are granted with "Decouverte J8" for reservations made eight days to two months in advance, and a greater discount is allowed with "Decouverte J30" for reservations made 30 days to two months in advance.

The France Rail'n Drive program allows you to combine the France Railpass with an Avis car rental. Avis has 520 locations throughout France including more than 200 in train stations. SNCF/Avis' basic one-month package gives you three days of unlimited train travel in France (plus the free airport transfer coupons and discounts) and two days of Avis car rental with unlimited mileage, VAT (value-added tax), and basic insurance included. (Gasoline is extra.) You can purchase extra days of train travel and auto rental. Third and fourth persons sharing the car need only buy a France Railpass.

To sample France's rail speed and adventure to offbeat corners, travel on the 186-mph TGV Atlantique to Brittany, the TGV Genevois from Paris to Geneva, the Chemins de Fer de Provence from Nice to Digne, and Metro Basque from Bayonne to St. Jean-Pied-de-Port described here.

TGV Atlantique
Into Brittany by 186-mph Supertrain

Blasting through Brittany at 186 mph, passengers use the white-striped, hinged vinyl tables separating their seats to write postcards as smoothly as if they were writing from their nearest library. You accept the well-known fact that TGV-A ("A" for "Atlantique") is fast. It comes as a surprise that TGV-A's innovative concept in pneumatic suspension makes its ride as calm as a Breton cow.

Atlantique is a victim of its own success. It moves so effortlessly, without shimmy or shake, that passengers can't appreciate that it holds the world's speed record of 320 mph set on May 18, 1990. Ten-carriage-long return trains take 2.9 seconds to flick past your window. Atlantique pulverizes rain into nuclei so microscopic that the 186-mph wind wipes them from the windows even before they wet it.

TGV-A impresses you with its substance and power. These trains differ from the other blue and silver streaks you see in France. They are longer and carry a full-length bar car and special club cars with small, four-person compartments down one side of the aisle with electronically controlled seats. Many travelers prefer this seating. Pairs occupying the facing seats along the window chat intimately.

Climb TGV-A's shiny aluminum steps from a platform on the top level of the five-level, bright glass, metal, and red granite Paris Montparnasse station, your high-rise "Ocean Gateway" to the Atlantic network. Your TGV-A takes you to Brittany along dedicated high-speed track that branches into three routes. The 386-mile North Brittany line takes you to Rennes, St. Brieuc, and Brest with a further branch from Rennes to the south coast of Brittany through Lorient to Quimper, Brittany's ceramic and pottery center. The 304-mile South Brittany line takes you to Nantes, St. Nazaire, and Le Croisic.

The southern fork of the high-speed stretch to St. Pierre des Corps opened in September 1990. It takes travelers via the TGV station in Vendome from Paris to Bordeaux in less than three hours, reaching the Spanish border in just over five hours.

Your blue-and-silver Atlantic supertrain's livery was designed to reflect the sun, sea, and sand of Brittany and the Atlantic coast. It was so successful that the livery was then applied to SNCF's entire fleet of TGVs. Instead of yellow roof-line striping to mark first-class sections,

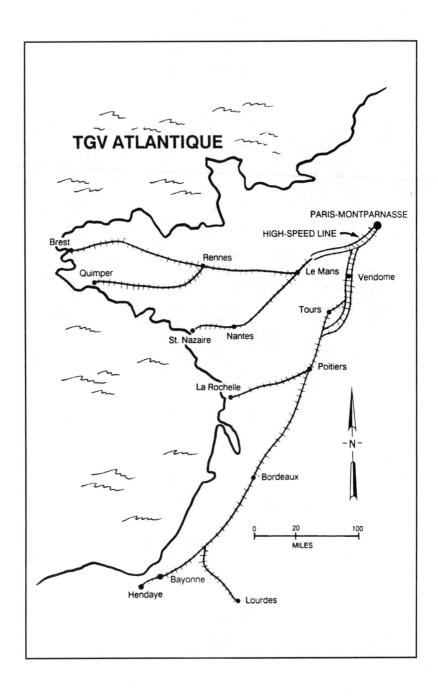

TGV ATLANTIQUE

PARIS-MONTPARNASSE

HIGH-SPEED LINE

Brest

Rennes

Quimper

Le Mans

Vendome

Tours

St. Nazaire

Nantes

Poitiers

La Rochelle

- N -

Bordeaux

0   20   100
MILES

Bayonne

Hendaye

Lourdes

TGV-A's doors are color coded (ocean blue-green for second class, cherry red for first, and yellow for the bar), but you may not even notice this. It is easier for you to rely on the easy-to-see numerals indicating class of carriage.

Check your seat reservation coupon in the vestibule before making your way to your seat. Above the compartments' entrances, LCD signs blink destination, train number, and carriage number.

A horn sounds and TGV-A's doors slide shut. In an instant, you leave Paris so quickly that when you enter tunnels you feel depressurization of your carriage. In the tunnel you enter the new high-speed line. While your TGV is coasting, the DC pantograph goes down and the AC pantograph goes up for high-speed travel. Above, environmentalists have created playgrounds, open spaces, and a cycle path. In open space, you are already passing the outskirts of Paris along land lucky enough to have been already reserved for a railroad line. This land included a roadbed that had been nearly completed before work was abandoned in 1934—a highly prized right of way, which came close to accommodating a motorway 30 years after the railroad, was abandoned. On return, when your ears pop, you know they are signaling your approach to Paris.

It doesn't take long for your TGV-A to run quickly up to speed: 186 mph like a stopwatch. Your speed is programmed by computer.

In first class, passengers read newspapers and fashion magazines and pound laptop computers on the tabletops.

Outside, the land is flat, spotted with woods along the high-speed track, but: think frogs. You see some of the ponds where environmentalists spent years relocating endangered species away from the train route and protecting them from hungry herons.

When you leave the high-speed railbed, past Le Mans, your train takes on a new feel. You hear the familiar clickety-clack of standard rails and slow down enough to appreciate the Gothic spires marking every village. You see why Brittany is famous for its characteristic, small black-and white prolific milk producers, "Pie Noire" cows, which sometimes mingle with brown "Salers" from Auvergne, in the mountains of France's Central Massif.

When you leave Angers' St. Laud train station (made attractive by tufa stone quarried in the Loire Valley), you see greenhouses, artichokes in the fields, and parasitic mistletoe richly infesting many of the trees. Brittany is the only region in France in which mistletoe grows.

Soon you are running along the right bank of the Loire River, wide and quiet. Magnolia trees and camellia bushes were brought from the French settlements in Louisiana before its sale to the United States in 1803.

You recognize Nantes from a distance by its tall buildings. Nantes train station has two accesses. The South access, added in 1989 with the introduction of TGVs, is modern, and has all amenities, ramps instead of stairs, a small restaurant, and an elevator to the passageways below the tracks. The North access echoes from the sixties, but is well marked and easily accessible. The new waiting room is called "Salon Jules Verne," named after a local boy made good.

The rafters of Nantes's St. Peter and Paul Cathedral, destroyed by a devastating fire in the 1970s, have been rebuilt. Beige tufa pillars soar higher than Westminster Abbey's to make this the brightest and warmest large cathedral in Europe.

In Nantes, among its many balconied mansions and its busy port, take time to visit Passage Pommeraye, an original three-level stepped galeria, and the predecessor of today's malls. Completed in 1843, the ancient faces, mice, and snails carved in stair risers and cheerful sculptures scattered throughout lend a feeling of fun.

Nearby, visitors are lucky when they come across the delightfully decorated La Cigale (meaning "cicada") tearoom. Try a pastry and a cup of coffee (or dinner) just to enjoy the atmosphere. It first opened at 4, place Greslin (facing the Opera) in April 1895.

After your train's three-minute halt in Nantes, new passengers board to join your entrance to traditional Brittany, a rough and tumble land of Celts, bagpipes, and the Breton tongue. In Brittany's center you find evocative regions where followers of King Arthur come to see "The Land of the Round Table" and the enchanted Broceliande forest charred by fire in 1990 where the wizard Merlin met the fairy Viviane and love inflamed them both. (To make sure of keeping Merlin, Viviane enclosed him in a magic circle. It would have been easy for him to escape, but he joyfully accepted his romantic captivity forever.) You see Merlin's seat and Viviane's bed. From here Sir Lancelot of the Lake set out for England and his seduction of Gweniviere, King Arthur's wife.

Past Nantes you run through fertile farming country where farmers harvest melons, cabbage, and onions. To the south tower the major harbor and industrial zone facilities of St. Nazaire on the Loire estuary.

St. Nazaire grew to a great shipbuilding center when, in 1856, large ships found it difficult to reach Nantes. During the Second World War St. Nazaire was a major German submarine base and the center of strategic fighting, blockades, bombardment, and, ultimately, massive destruction.

St. Nazaire train station is the final destination for many passengers. They carry their baggage up the apple-green stairwell.

Past St. Nazaire you enter the well-named Cote d'Amour. Even the sun gets brighter as you approach what many French vacationers to La Baule consider the finest beach in Europe—and they frolic here in July and August.

You stop at La Baule's Escourlac Breton-style station house on the northern tip of the diving, soling (the Olympic sport), and wind-surfing resort, and then you cross the canal to Le Croisic peninsula, traveling close above the salt marshes which identify this region. Women scrape crystals off the surface of the salt flats to obtain the finest quality white sea salt in Europe.

Sea birds watch your train riding bumpily onto a siding at Le Croisic's small station, the end of the line. Its continuation is blocked by Mont-Espirit, the curious 98-foot double-corkscrew mound, built from ships' ballast. From the summit you see the salt marshes to the east, the landmark belfry of Batz-sur-mer to the west, and the Atlantic Ocean in the distance.

Even while you are stepping down TGV-A's aluminum stairs, a cleaner is plugging in a vacuum cleaner to make your Atlantique spotless for its return trip.

Your TGV-A has a whole array of features for you to use throughout its 10 carriages, including telephone booths and a special diaper room in second class for parents with distressed babies. Probably your biggest surprise is that the mechanism adjusting seats in first class makes them rise or sink at the touch of a button just as in a luxury automobile.

Each first-class table has an individual light. Reading lights are behind the passengers and they control a fluorescent overhead lamp by button.

Walking through the carpeted first-class sections, you start behind a power car with the elevated nine-passenger, horseshoe-shaped "Le Salon" with video monitors, and then cross the standard "La Coach," half with 2+1 seats facing forward, half with seats facing backward.

FrenchRail calls the next two cars "Club Cars." "Le Club Duo" pairs gray-and-white striped plush seats facing one another beside the aisle across from "Le Club Quatre," four seats upholstered with black-and-white striped plush within partially closed, tinted-glass minisalons.

Atlantique's social whole-carriage bar car provides passengers with staggered rows of vinyl-topped snack counters. Across its stainless-steel sales counter, service personnel wearing SNCF badges heat microwave sandwiches and sell magazines, candy, coffee, wine, and minibottles of liquor. Low vinyl counters at the windows are equipped with small swivel stools to give you a fine place to eat, drink, and watch the scenery flashing past. Be sure to drop in. It's a great place to hang out and socialize.

The crowd in second class is definitely younger. They are sleeping and listening to earphones. Second-class is divided 2+1, some smoking, some nonsmoking. The equivalent of club in second class provides facing seats with partial tinted-glass partitions above the seats. Regular salons where half the seats face forward, half backward, have no need for these sound barriers.

Second class features rubber-mat flooring, fold-down footrests, rough-wearing fabric upholstery, and tables that fold down from seat backs. Only in the center, where passengers face one another, are there tables similar to those in first class. Up a few steps at the end brings you to "Le Kiosque," the second-class lounge arranged with two tables and second-class seats designated for single children.

Doubled TGV-A trains on the North Brittany line race from Paris' Montparnasse to Rennes, where its multilevel station is part of the district development plan that provided a shopping street above the tracks, a sweeping access hall to the platforms, elevators, and escalators. North of Rennes, visit one of the world's foremost pilgrim's shrines, Mont St. Michel. Rennes is your changing point for the local train to Pontorson, the closest railhead to Mont St. Michel. Six miles by bus, taxi, or bicycle rented at Pontorson, STN buses leave six times daily for the abbey. Follow the crowds. Bypassing the train connection, tour buses (air-conditioning, video, toilet) of Les Courriers Bretons leave directly from Rennes.

At Rennes, your doubled TGV is divided. One section continues on the North Brittany line to Brest's Art Deco, end-of-the-line, centrally located train station, allowing you to make the 386-mile trip from Paris in about something over four hours (including stops). Brest's station offers a splendid view overlooking enormous shipyards from the train station terrace. Brest's bus station is located in front of the train station.

The second TGV travels from Rennes along the completely electrified southern Brittany coast line to Quimper, the prosperous city still distinctly Breton in character and full of intriguing churches (including the cathedral of St. Corentin, the city's patron saint).

You need reservations for all TGV Atlantique runs. In first class, you can reserve seats "Club Quatre" in the minisalons or beside the window "solo" for intimate conversations. A "couloir" is an aisle seat, and "compartiment" is compartment.

TGV Atlantique timetables are among the most complicated in Europe. You find different schedules for Fridays, Saturdays, Sundays, Mondays, and Tuesdays-Thursdays. Fares and supplements, which vary with times of day in addition to days of the week, make it necessary to plan in advance. Rail passes save you from this torture. Pick up a free pocket timetable or "Guide TGV Atlantique Ouest" and just tell the reservation agent approximately what time and on what day you want to leave. With the opening of the southern bypass of Paris in 1996, you can ride some trains from Brittany straight through to Charles de Gaulle Airport via Massy TGV station.

TGV Genevois
Computer-Age Anachronism

The inquisitive ticketing machine inside the Gare de Lyon quizzes you with electronic questions. "Where are you going? First or second class? How many people? Do you accept the supplement?"

You answer, "No supplement," when you are traveling with a rail pass. The surcharge for the high-tech train to Geneva, the EuroCity TGV Genevois, is covered by your pass, but the Gallic machine seems reluctant to accept "No supplement" for an answer. Still, you must reserve a seat. You may not stand in the aisle.

The Genevois was one of the first group of TGV trains included in the select EuroCity network. It carries you on one of EC's most fascinating routes, linking Paris with Switzerland's cosmopolitan city through mountainous regions and past villages still anchored in the nineteenth century.

Until the TGV Atlantique's new railbed opened in fall 1989, your

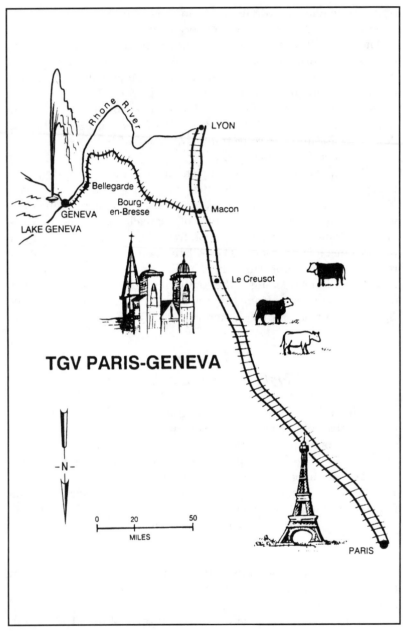

TGV PARIS-GENEVA

TGV Southeast train was the fastest in the world—but even if it were merely a speedy way of getting from one place to another, you would still find it fun, smooth, and exciting to ride. As it is, you get a scenic eyeful as well.

By using either the Paris metro's Gare de Lyon stop or RER station and climbing the escalator to ground level, you reach the station's TGV platform without ever seeing the light of morning. When you arrive at the platform, you step into the future. Purring, shark-snouted, Trains a Grande Vitesse surround you as far as you can see.

The TGVs are screamers. They sound like they are growling as their engines warm for fast getaways. Speeding at 167 mph much of the way, your TGV Genevois cuts your travel time to Geneva by more than two hours, to just over three and a half hours. Introduction of TGVs butchered air service and delayed congestion of toll roads on this route. It provided excitement for your trip.

TGVs on the Southeast network are single, articulated units of eight air-conditioned cars with engines at both ends. Usually SNCF couples two units together to double the seating to 772 (222 in first class, 550 in second). Still, trains are totally filled on busy days.

You purchase coffee, Parisian croissants, and reading materials in the bar car. In some carriages, you can order a continental breakfast served on the tray in front of you.

The EC TGV Genevois, followed later in the day by the EC Voltaire, the EC Versailles, the EC Henry Dunant, and the EC Jean-Jacques Rousseau, whisks you away promptly at 7:12 A.M. It doesn't immediately leap forward. While toiling through the suburbs of Paris, it vibrates with restrained energy. If you feel some disappointment, it is because you don't feel a jolt when your Genevois enters the high-speed corridor and accelerates to 167 mph. There is no speedometer to fascinate you.

Past the suburbs of the capital, your high-speed trip to Macon is pastoral. You study spotted cows grazing in the fields and ponder the speed of the train. There are no highways paralleling the tracks so you can't accurately gauge your speed, but the buttercups beside the tracks become a mustard-colored blur and you hear no clickety-clack from segmented rails. You know you must be at maximum speed.

You branch from the high-speed line at the modern Macon Loche TGV's stone stationhouse. The platforms are covered, but there are no luggage carts. The clickety-clack reminds you that you have returned to old-fashioned—and slower—railbeds.

Past the Bourg-en-Bresse station, two hours from Paris, you enter the Jura region of France. Green woods roll up the impressive heights above the train line. Old villages of monochrome stone houses center around churches that seem to belong on old sepia-tone postcards.

The passing scenery becomes so eye-catching that French travelers around you fold up the magazines that had interested them before and put away their attache cases and laptop computers.

Your attention focuses on the mountains taking shape in the distance. The French word "grandeur" says it all.

You can't escape the anachronism: speeding through ageless Jura mountains and time-forgotten villages in a computer-age bullet.

You see individual farmers tending little fields. Tiny vineyards spot the hillsides. You notice details that date from quieter times: a river with lily pads, a fisherman in a leaky rowboat, old towns pressed defensively against high mountains, churches of stone, an outcropping with a statue of an unknown hero on its summit.

Finally your Genevois passes the first of many tunnels. You aren't in the tunnel long, but it breaks the scenery. You continue at a brisk pace—no longer at 167 mph, but still very fast.

You finally slow when a broad river, the Rhone, appears on your right. Battlements of once-powerful castles dot the mountainsides overlooking the Rhone. A modern bridge spans the chasm.

At Bellegarde-sur-Valserine, an industrial city at the meeting of the Valserine and Rhone rivers, the only thing level is the huge rail yard. The city trails down the hillside toward the Rhone.

Here you can change for the French Lake Geneva resort of Evian-les-Bains by connecting railcar. It stands across the platform below the patina eaves of the weathered train station. "Evian" mineral water is served aboard the TGV Genevois.

From Bellegarde, a long tunnel brings your TGV to a route that twists miraculously through mountain valleys on embankments braced by stone. Mountains tower around the train. You follow the Rhone River below.

Finally your train levels off. TGV chimes sound. Passengers take Swiss bank notes from envelopes and you approach Geneva's Cornavin station along a level route surrounded by endless vineyards.

You arrive at the French/International TGV terminal at Geneva's Cornavin station. Tracks ("Voie") 7 and 8 are separated from Swiss national train traffic by glass doors kept closed except at arrival and departure times. Border guards check your passport as you enter Switzerland. Ramps allow you to wheel your luggage cart to Geneva's Tourist Office, which occupies a gleaming suite in the train station.

When you leave Geneva through the SNCF terminal for France, don't arrive more than a half-hour before departure time. You must linger in the modest waiting room until guards open the doors pneumatically.

Daily EuroCity TGV Service between Paris and Geneva

	EC971	EC973	EC975	EC977	EC979
dep. PARIS (Lyon)	0712	1018	1434	1718	1912
dep. Macon (TGV)	0850	1157			1857	2051
dep. Bourg-en-Bresse	0915		1634	1922	2118
arr. Culoz					2204
arr. Bellegarde	1023	1325	1744	2028	2224
arr. GENEVA	1054	1357	1814	2057	2253

	EC972	EC974	EC976	EC978	EC980
dep. GENEVA	0745	0959	1241	1641	1921
dep. Bellegarde	0812	1028	1309	1709	1950
dep. Culoz					
dep. Bourg-en-Bresse	0922	1140		1818	
dep. Macon (TGV)			1437	1838	
arr. PARIS (Lyon)	1122	1340	1619	2022	2300

EC971	EC	Genevois
EC973	EC	Voltaire
EC975	EC	Versailles
EC977	EC	Henry Dunant
EC979	EC	J-Jacques Rousseau

Chemins de Fer de Provence
Scenic Gateway to the Riviera

You climb to your second summit at St. Andre-les-Alpes station overlooking the stone houses of the village and prominent stone church. A fine, long view of snow-covered Alps opens before you to the south. Climbing higher, you see the weirdly scalloped shores of Le Verdon Lake below to the west, with water so calm ducks scarcely bob on the surface.

The little-known Chemins de Fer de Provence (CFP) narrow-gauge

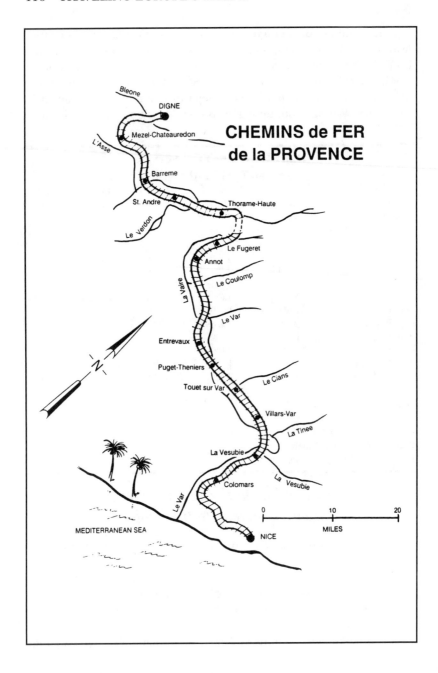

CHEMINS de FER de la PROVENCE

private railroad takes you 103 miles between Digne and Nice through Cote d'Azur's 103-mile-long back door, a bright, crisp ride through sunshine and mountain air, gorges, pre-Alps, and river valleys. The "Train des Pignes" on "Ligne Digne" is a little trip, an off-the-beaten-track secret. CFP allows a 25 percent discount with your European rail pass and gives you half off when you show your France Railpass. Those over 55 also receive 25 percent off.

CFP's blue-and-white diesel railcar is so intimate and open that you look over the engineer's shoulder at the rails ahead while your train skirts the edges of deep precipices and climbs steeply over the last range of Alps between the French interior and the Mediterranean.

More rock canyons than you will find in any other part of France, some as deep as 700 or 900 feet, mark your path. Your railcar teeters precariously on mountain rims and rocks from side to side along a roadbed that chatters your teeth. It is well known that this trip is wash-board rough.

You travel down again, past level fields of wheat and mountainsides covered with pine to the Asse River, where you cross into Barreme (pop. 435).

Between Barreme and Digne-les-Bains, the capital of the high country in Provence, you roughly trace the route of former mule paths Napoleon and his handful of supporters took returning from Elba in 1815. "The eagle will fly from steeple to steeple until he reaches the towers of Notre Dame." Villages boast commemorative plaques and monuments bear the flying eagle symbol inspired by Napoleon's remark. A house near Barreme's town square carries the inscription that Napoleon slept there on March 3, 1815.

Nice, in the Riviera, attracts visitors like a sunny magnet. Holiday makers enjoy frolicking along the beaches and feeling the charm of the Riviera while sipping coffee on the busy, four-mile-long Promenade des Anglais that borders the Mediterranean and represents the heart of the delightful Queen of the Riviera. Monte Carlo, a destination Americans enjoy visiting for its casino and princely flavor, is 24 minutes away by train from SNCF's Nice Ville station. The Nice station is pleasant, although you may not agree if you arrive at a platform accessible only by climbing and descending flights of stairs. Visit the Nice Tourist Office outside, adjacent to the station, for hotel reservations and information. It is open 8 A.M. to 12:30 P.M. and 2 to 6 P.M., Monday to Saturday, during the summer.

When you enter the modern, but lightweight, three-track 1992 CFP terminus at 4bis, Rue Alfred Bihet (Tel. 93-82-10-17), look behind you. CFP's former Gare du Sud has been completely transformed. Sud was a four-track station, the oldest in Nice, built in 1892, and the Place de Gaulle outside an was an enchantment with sidewalk fruit-and-fish markets and flower stalls and kiosks selling snack items ranging from excellent pizza to extraordinary, odd pastries.

CFP's Nice station is about a 20-minute stroll from SNCF's Nice Ville station. In the CFP station, ask for a map of your route to Digne at the ticket counter below the bright wall mural of the route.

The driver shifts your railcar's large diesel engine into low gear and accelerates sharply through Nice's city streets. You not only cross traffic intersections, but you have to stop for red lights when you meet them. You pass stop signals and cross boulevards bumper-to-bumper with automobiles before entering a black tunnel that takes you out of the city center.

You watch the surroundings through panoramic windows. The driver maneuvers jerkily. The orange seats and maroon leatherette headrests do not recline but are thickly padded. It is a very wide carriage for a narrow-gauge railcar. The rubber-mat floor still shows mop marks.

In 1994 floods closed the line at numerous points and washed out whole sections. Buses bypassing the destroyed sections were used for nearly two years and it wasn't until April 1996 that the CFP railcars were able to run the entire length once more without interruption when the replacement Gueydan bridge was opened. This last major piece of work was carried out by the French army. Total cost of repair was $6.6 million, of which the region paid $2.1 million.

Running rockily along the river Le Var, you begin to notice strange secluded hilltop chateaux. At St. Martin-du-Var station house, you see tulips and other flowers blooming under the trees in back.

You are traveling parallel to highway N202 on the east and the river on the west. Orient yourself by the names shown on road signs.

After stopping at La Vesubie-Plan-du-Var, you cross La Vesubie River on a gray steel-girder bridge to run counter to the racing river while the highway continues high on the mountainside. The Vesubie, a tributary of the Var, is fed by Alpine snows. Its valley reaches up to your right through gorges cut into vertical walls, a popular area for French tourists. You are entering the mountains and it becomes more fun. A tunnel takes you to the left bank of the cottonwood-lined Var. As you pass, you see a woman cranking up the red-and-white highway barrier to let road traffic resume.

Past Touet-sur-Var station house and the Cians bridge, a small road breaks away to your right for the Cians gorges, some of the finest in the Alps.

Puget-Theniers, the largest village along this route (pop. 2,000), is a southern town at the meeting of the Roudoule and Var rivers. You leave the Maritime Alps district and enter Alps de Haute Provence—at one and the same time the High Mountains and Provence.

You see high chateaux on the hillside before entering Entrevaux, a surprising fortified town (pop. 1,040) surmounted by its citadel. A short walk takes you to the west bank of the Var at the foot of a curious rocky spur.

When you leave Entrevaux, rocks take on strange, worn shapes. You first see distant snow at the time you enter your first snow tunnel. Streams in the Var Valley become wilder. Horses—grown mares and brownish-gray yearlings—romp in the fields.

You leave the Var to the east, flowing from the Daluis gorges, and continue up the Coulomp valley below landslide-scarred slopes to the Var's tributary, the Vaire, and then follow the Vaire Valley.

Rising above Annot's church steeple and red-tile roofs surmounting high facades in the medieval "old town," you gain your first true Alpine sensation. The mountainside is terraced in rock. Above Le Fugeret, your railcar wanders freely, through tunnels and loops, to gain altitude. Snow remains on the ground until April.

Passengers peer from the windows and take an interest in the jagged rocks to the east and the curious birds flapping as you pass through a jagged gorge. Everything looks greener.

You cross the Vaire River and pass through a black tunnel onto a second bridge across the Verdon River, a tributary of the Durance, which forms magnificent gorges in the limestone of the Haute-Provence. The fresh pine-scented air has a mountainous feeling to it.

You reach the first summit of your mountain railroad. Thorame-Haute's newly built mountain stone church looks handsome beside the flower-decorated station house.

Now you travel downhill through the upper valley of the Verdon in the same direction as the rushing river to the east. The hills are covered with trees of many different shades of green. You receive a hint of the Alps by forests of beech, pine, and larch. The crisp air and bright sky make this a summer tourist destination for the people of Provence.

Geologists recognize the name Barreme for the name "Barremian," given to part of the lower cretaceous layer.

Past Barreme, your railcar seems to be speeding downhill, but it can't be going too fast, because new Renaults on highway N85 outdistance you with little trouble. Children in the autos' back seats fan the air with their waving at you.

Past the stone Chaudon-Norante station house, you enter the pre-Alps of Digne, climbing through tunnels and along a creek to that capital of the Lavender Alps—a mountain city looking onto Alps nearby.

Lavender is characteristic of Haute-Provence. In the 1930s, farmers began cultivating plantations of this wild-growing mountain flower on higher slopes. Breathe deeply in July, when mauve flowers scent the air.

In Digne, a pleasant spa town, the CFP and SNCF stations share the same building. The SNCF rails are still there, side-by-side with CFP's, and although Digne has been abandoned by SNCF and you must take a bus, local authorities are determined to reopen the line to St. Auban, and are trying to determine whether they should simply refurbish the existing standard-gauge line, or alternatively lay a third rail on the standard-gauge track to allow CFP to extend to St. Auban.

A 20-minute bus ride to St. Auban (centre) or a one and a half hour bus ride to Veynes allows you to connect with the regular SNCF system. Because the Digne train station is outside the city, you won't find hotels, facilities, restaurants, or snack bars nearby. Walking into the city takes 15 to 20 minutes, but usually you can ride into town by a bus waiting for your train (not covered by rail pass).

Chemins de Fer de Provence
Summer Service between Nice and Digne

0642 0900 1243 1700	dep.	NICE (CFP)	arr. 1018 1349 1715 2035
0657 0915 1258 1717	dep.	Lingostiere	arr. 1004 1335 1659 2021
0705 0922 1306 1724	dep.	Colomars	dep. 0956 1327 1652 2014
0714 0931 1317 1733	dep.	St.-Martin-Var	dep. 0947 1318 1642 2005
0717 0934 1321 1736	dep.	Pont-Charles-Albert	dep. 0944 1314 1637 2002
0721 0939 1326 1740	dep. La Vesubie		dep. 0940 1310 1633 1958
0737 0955 1342 1756	dep.	Malaussene	dep. 0921 1252 1615 1941

0742 1000 1347 1801	dep.	Villars-sur-Var	dep. 0917 1248 1611 1937
0752 1010 1357 1811	dep.	Touet-sur-Var	dep. 0907 1238 1601 1926
0804 1022 1410 1823	dep.	Puget-Theniers	dep. 0855 1226 1549 1914
0812 1030 1418 1831	dep.	Entrevaux	dep. 0847 1218 1541 1906
0828 1046 1434 1847	arr.	Annot	dep. 0830 1201 1524 1849
0832 1050 1440 1852	dep.	Annot	arr. 0823 1155 1521 1846
0838 1056 1446 1858	dep.	Le Fugeret	dep. 0817 1149 1515 1840
0843 1101 1451 1903	dep.	Meailles	dep. 0812 1144 1510 1835
0853 1111 1502 1913	dep.	Thorame-Gare	dep. 0803 1135 1501 1826
0904 1123 1513 1924	dep.	Saint-Andre	dep. 0751 1124 1448 1815
0910 1129 1519 1930	dep.	Moriez	dep. 0745 1117 1442 1809
0920 1139 1529 1940	dep.	Barreme	dep. 0735 1107 1432 1759
0927 1146 1536 1947	dep.	Chaudon-Norante	dep. 0727 1059 1424 1751
0939 1158 1548 1959	dep.	Mezel	dep. 0715 1047 1412 1739
0953 1212 1602 2013	arr.	DIGNE	dep. 0700 1033 1358 1725
N/A 1407 1800 N/A	dep.	DIGNE (bus)	arr. N/A 1010 1102 1559
N/A 1439 1835 N/A	arr.	St. Auban	dep. N/A 0935 1027 1525

Metro Basque
Heart and Soul of Basque Country

Local Basque leaders call the railcar that takes you to the heart and soul of French Basque country "Metro Basque." It runs between Bayonne, the northern limit of the Basque coast in France, and St. Jean-Pied-de-Port, a different world, thirty-one miles, one hour, and 515 feet above it. St. Jean-Pied-de-Port, as its name suggests, sits at the foot of the pass of Roncevalles in the Atlantic Pyrenees, the gateway to Spain only five miles above.

Breaking your journey here on a trip between Madrid and Paris is an adventure, a diversion, and a prerequisite when you are interested in Basque culture.

Many Americans of Basque descent return every two or three years to visit their relatives. St. Jean's busy season is July and August, when French, German, English, and American visitors (no one counts Spanish Basques, who are not considered tourists) swell the population of St. Jean's 3,000 permanent inhabitants to 12,000 to 15,000. You enjoy the many summer festivities such as jai alai (which is as important to the Basque as the church), folkloric dancing, and serenades of choral groups.

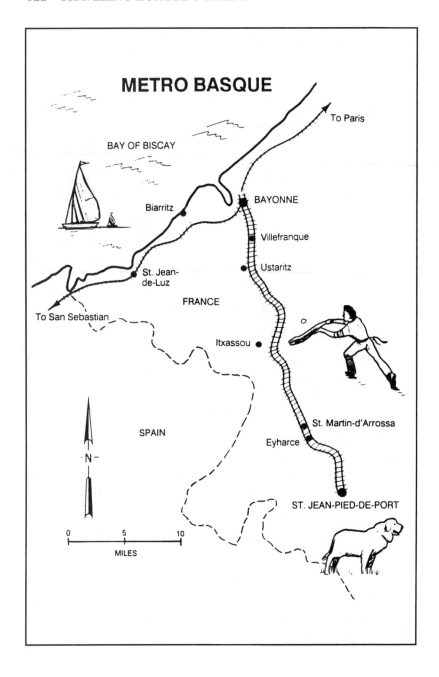

METRO BASQUE

BAY OF BISCAY

To Paris

Biarritz

BAYONNE

Villefranque

Ustaritz

St. Jean-
de-Luz

FRANCE

To San Sebastian

Itxassou

SPAIN

-N-

St. Martin-d'Arrossa

Eyharce

0   5   10

MILES

ST. JEAN-PIED-DE-PORT

Many young Basques came to the New World because at home only the oldest sons inherit their parents' farms and properties. Without property, younger sons tended to immigrate to the New World to make their fame and fortune. Many did, and became prosperous. Because Paul Laxhault is of Basque origin, many Basques have a keen interest in American politics and a fondness for American visitors.

Even now the population is not increasing.

Bayonne's station, where you begin your climb, is remodeled to accommodate TGVs from Paris. It is grand, distinguished by the preserved clock tower on the outside, and efficient inside. You snack in the adjacent modern buffet. Look for the departure times posted prominently above the information office and ticketing windows.

You see waiting on track No. 1 a pair of red-and-white railcars, which are part of the TER Aquitaine regional train system. The first-class section contains seats for nonsmokers and fewer, through an automatically opening glass door, for "fumeurs."

It's a comfortable, modern, pleasing train, no doubt completed by the same interior designers who won awards for the Corail trains.

Both cars have seats arranged like salons. First class has 2+2 maroon bucket-type seats facing each other. Second class, through another glass door that you open with a push on a lever (like Corail), is configured similarly with slightly less distance between brown leatherette seats. There is almost no difference between first and second class except for the blue carpeting in first and nonskid rubber flooring in second. Both are modern, spotless, and decorated with tidy, plaited curtains.

A few minutes late for departure, and concluding his gossip with the driver, the white-capped dispatcher waves his white-and-green paddle. The driver scampers aboard, closes the doors, and starts your electrified railcar on its single track away through a tunnel.

While your conductor checks the tickets and nods at your rail pass, you cross the Nive, a broad, brown river, and enter a second, long tunnel. Woods and fruit trees surround your line. Thorny berry thickets flourish on the slopes of the elevated railbed while you pass through flat farm country, with cornstalks thriving in the fields.

Your conductor announces your first stop, Ustaritz, on the speaker system. Ustaritz's station house is brown stucco with brown trim. All stations on this line are clearly marked even when the signs are covered with climbing, green vines.

You still travel on the level, running parallel to the slow-flowing Nive, to your second stop, Cambo-les-Bains, where white postwar homes are roofed with tiles.

Not all trains halt at the next stop, Itxassou, where villagers still don curious costumes and perform their annual, elaborate Corpus Christi procession.

Now you are beginning to climb modestly past whitewashed farm-houses with sagging tile roofs. Many Basques drive up the parallel two-lane blacktop highway, but still prefer the train occasionally to relish the scenery.

You feel the temperature cool when you slow for the station house serving St. Martin-d'Arrossa and the nearby villages of Eyharce and Osses. This is the junction of two rivers which form the now-raging Nive. You see large white Basque houses with cornerstones and brown or green shutters and trim. A few passengers change here for buses to Saint Etienne de Baigorny.

Finally you see black-faced sheep for the first time, happily munching the long green grass on the slopes. Some sheepherders own them; some rent. You see merinos with long, fine, silky wool, and the Basque sheep, manech, which are black and white with curved horns. But if you visit during the summer, you must go to the peaks of the Pyrenees to find them. The sheep are kept in the cities for six months until May 1, and then they spend six months in the high mountains.

On every side of the wide valley, trim Basque villages nestle amid manicured pasture lands. Each is centered on a church with a clock tower—the local custom is to toll the hour twice. Everything is green, casual, pastoral, and the epitome of quiet.

High above the ridges, hawks cry and immense golden vultures soar on the breeze, eyeing the flocks of long-wooled sheep below. Herds of sleek, blonde Basque cattle graze beside shaggy dark ponies called "pottoks," which are horses unchanged in appearance since they were portrayed on the walls of the Paleolithic limestone caves not far away.

At last you see St. Jean-Pied-de-Port, the former capital of Lower Navarre, built by Garcia Ximenes in 716. It became a French town as a result of the Treaty of the Pyrenees in 1659. Louis XIV had it fortified by Vauban and you can still see its ramparts, its walls, and its citadel dominating the town and the Pyrenees. When Wellington crossed the Pyrenees in 1813, he entered France via St. Jean-Pied-de-Port.

You are on the pilgrim's route through northern Spain to Santiago de Compostela. (Refer to this book's section on the Talgo Pendular to Santiago de Compostela.)

Bracken fern, green in spring, reddish brown in the fall, cover the steep slopes of the surrounding mountains, which dwarf the wooded hill above the town. Farmers scythe fern into tall, conical stacks for fodder, or simply burn it, turning the air blue with pleasant-smelling smoke.

Disembark at St. Jean-Pied-de-Port and walk from the train station to the city center along streets clearly posted with signs. The Syndicat d'Initiative in the center (on the left as you approach) is located in a modern building.

Inspecting the seven Gothic gates in the wall that used to surround the whole town (which were formerly locked at night) gives you an excellent grasp of the complex angles and divisions of this curiously exciting village.

St. Jean consists of shops and stone houses, each with two or three apartments, scattered along cobblestone streets fronted with steps instead of sidewalks. The crosspieces over the doors proudly proclaim who built them and when. Like all Basque houses, town and country, these are sturdy, half-timbered with stone and whitewashed stucco facades. Green or red-brown shutters are obligatory, for they are the Basque colors, but "Basque red" comes in many shades these days, depending on where the owner buys his or her paint.

The citadel you see brooding over the rooftops is used as a high school in winter and a museum in summer. Sheep graze in its moat.

The church's clock tower set into the city wall contains a small room that served as the city hall in medieval times. From the gate in the base of the tower, you cross a graceful stone bridge arching over the Nive.

Monday is market day all year long, all day long, in St. Jean, as it has been for centuries. You can buy berets (black only) from traveling peddlers, rope-soled canvas Basque slippers, Citroen tractors, Apple computers, fresh-killed wild doves, and ripe cheeses. Two thousand lambs are bought here every Monday.

During the summer, trains climb from Bayonne at 9:03 A.M., 11:40 A.M., 3:04 P.M., 7:48 P.M., and 9:05 P.M. From St. Jean-Pied-de-Port, you can return at 6:07 A.M. (except Sundays), 10:11 A.M., 1:31 P.M., 4:33 P.M., and 6:38 P.M.

Britain and Ireland

Smart Traveling on the Trains of Britain and Ireland

British trains—White Rose between London and York—Irish trains—London train stations—City Gold between Dublin and Cork—Enterprise between Belfast and Dublin—The London Underground—Airport trains—Caledonian Sleeper—Glasgow stations—BritRail Passes—Crossing the Channel by ship—Stena Line to Ireland—BritRail Pass + Ireland—Using Eurailpass bonuses in Ireland

British Trains

Railtrack IPO (Initial Public Offering) on the London Stock Exchange on May 20, 1996, marked a milestone for the British government in their rail privatization program. They raised close to $2.9 million on their ongoing program to break former BritRail into pieces and put every piece into private hands. In all, 25 train operating companies were sold separately, plus all ancillary assets and infrastructure. Buyers came from the U.S., Britain, and France.

Travelers to Britain find a patchwork of Train Operating Companies

(TOCs). Trips of any length at all mean you will use the services and see the gleaming new logos and liveries of two or more companies. Signs tell you that Railtrack (*www.railtrack.co.uk*) owns the infrastructure, including stations, and its website provides up-to-date and emergency information.

Alphabetically, the operating companies have matured into: Anglia Railways Train Services (AR, *angliarailways.co.uk*), c2c (*www.c2c-online.co.uk*), Central Trains (CT, *www.centraltrains.co.uk*), Chiltern Railways (CR, *chilternrailways.co.uk*), Connex (*www.connex.co.uk*), First Great Eastern Railway (GER, *www.ger.co.uk*), First Great Western Trains (GW, *www.greatwesterntrains.co.uk*), First North Western (FNW, *www.firstnorthwestern.co.uk*), Gatwick Express (GE, *gatwickexpress.co.uk*), GoVia, Great North Eastern Railway (GNER, *www.gner.co.uk*), Hull Trains (HT, *www.hulltrains.co.uk*), Island Line (IL, *www.island-line.co.uk*), Merseyrail Electrics (ME), Midland Mainline (MM, *www.midlandmainline.com*), NorthernSpirit (NS, *northern-spirit.co.uk*), ScotRail Railways (SRR, *www.scotrail.co.uk*), Silverlink Train Services, South West Trains (SWT, *www.swtrains.co.uk*), Thames Trains (TT, *thamestrains.co.uk*), Thameslink Rail (TR, *thameslink.co.uk*), Valley Lines (VL, *www.rail.co.uk/cardiff/home.htm*), Virgin Trains (Cross Country) and Virgin West Coast Trains (VT, *www.virgin.com/trains*), Wales & West Passenger Trains (WW, *walesandwest.co.uk*), and West Anglia Great Northern Railway (WAGN, *www.wagnrail.co.uk*).

And no two of the TOCs that BritRail has been broken into have the same ticketing scheme. Coping with the different tariffs makes a BritRail Pass just as convenient in Britain as a Eurailpass on the continent, but fortunately, in 2000, the Association of Train Operating Companies began marketing passenger services as "National Rail," with an excellent and nearly indispensable website, *www.nationalrail.co.uk*, to try to make train travel as seamless as possible for the general public. Their "National Rail Guide" includes sections on how to get information, and explains their ticketing schemes and how to buy tickets and plan journeys. It includes a network map.

Altogether, Britain has more track per square mile than any other country. More than 15,000 trains a day traveling over the 8,887 mile combined passenger network take you to more than 2,400 stations throughout England, Scotland, and Wales. London has eight mainline stations accessible by Underground. The Heathrow Express takes you from Heathrow Airport to Paddington Station, while London's

Underground takes you to and from Heathrow Airport to all the stops and interchanges on the Piccadilly Line. Gatwick Express trains speed you to and from Gatwick Airport to Victoria Station.

Travel in Britain centers on the electrified West (served by VT) and East Coast (served by GNER) lines taking you from London to Glasgow and to Edinburgh. Given a choice, travel on the 140-mph East Coast mainline. It is the pride of Britain (see "Flying Scotsman" section below). It has been almost 35 years since the West Coast Mainline, the 550-mile stretch linking London and Glasgow through many of Britain's main industrial areas, was the showpiece of the railroad. It had been electrified with what then appeared exotic continental-style overhead wires. Now speed restrictions rarely permit trains to reach the 110-mph maximum speed once achieved. Moreover, the West Coast carriages, in need of extensive renovation, will be replaced by tilting trains in 2002.

All name and InterCity trains carry first-class and standard-class (the British railroads call their second class "standard class") carriages. Most of the local trains consist of standard-class carriages only.

You can reserve seats in advance on all InterCity trains (except Gatwick Express) and on certain Regional Railways and South Eastern trains. It is essential to reserve on certain services at peak periods (Friday afternoon/evening, bank holiday periods), and to and from Scotland. You can normally reserve from about two months in advance up to about two hours before departure (for early morning trains, up to the previous evening).

Trainphones are common on IC and regional "Express" trains. You pay for your calls, national and international, by using a "Phonecard," which you buy in advance at train stations and elsewhere.

White Rose between London and York

GNER launched Britain's most prestigious train service between London Kings Cross and York on May 30, 2000, using two Eurostar trains leased from Eurostar UK.

Billed as "White Rose" service for the traditional emblem of York shire, the electric trains help provide two million extra seats a year to reduce the overcrowding of GNER's route between London and Scotland. GNER operates the busiest mainline fleet in Europe and offers 125 services a day during the summer.

The two Class 373/2 trains, now sporting GNER's dark blue and red livery, were originally built in 1994-5 for Eurostar service to Paris, but had not entered commercial service. The leased train are integrated with GNER's timetable to provide nine addition services each weekday and six extra on Sundays. Each of the 14-carriage trains can carry 558 passengers. They have two power cars, four first-class carriages, two cafe-bar coaches, and eight for second-class passengers, including a cellular-telephone-free carriage and a family carriage.

Weekday White Rose Service

0555 1234 1434 2100	dep.	London	arr.	1144 1319 2015 2111
0646 1322 2154	arr.	Peterborough	arr.	1046 1221 1911 2015
0716 1352 1550 2224	arr.	Newark	dep.	1013 1149 1827 1944
0743 1419 2249	arr.	Doncaster	dep.	0950 1126 1804 1920
0814 1454 1638 2318	arr.	York	dep.	0923 1103 1743 1857

Irish Trains

With a Eurailpass, it is not expensive to make Ireland your gateway to Europe because IrishRail (IR, *www.irishrail.ie*), which honors the Eurailpass, allows holders free use of their entire network, including DART (Dublin's state-of-the-art electric regional transportation system). Irish Ferries gives 50 percent off for passage from Rosslare, Ireland, to Cherbourg/Roscoff, France.

Irish trains run upon a nonstandard track gauge of five feet, three inches (1600 mm). Clearly it was never considered that a link to the European mainland would ever take place. Still, IrishRail is the most convenient way to see the green countryside for rail-pass holders. The black-and-orange IR trains are mainly standard class and many are standard class only. Some trains also have "super standard" class available for a supplement of $5, or $8 if meal service is offered. "City Gold" Pullman-style service is also offered on certain Dublin-Cork services (see below).

Make Dublin your rail hub to reach all popular tourist centers. Dublin has three main train stations: Connolly, Pearse, and Heuston. Heuston and Connolly were redeveloped in 1998 to make these flagship stations the symbol of twenty-first century train travel. New entrances and retail shops make the stations bright and convenient. Connolly and Pearse are connected by DART, which is free with your Eurailpass, IrishRail, or Eurail Selectpass. Hop on bus line No. 90 for express service between Heuston and Connolly stations.

Travel times are short on IrishRail's modern diesel trains. Train journeys never take more than four hours—which is about the time it takes you to get from Dublin in the east to Tralee in the southwest. On mainline service you relax in comfort and watch the green Irish countryside.

To see completely the Republic of Ireland, supplement your train travel with the red-and-yellow Irish Bus buses. They link every city and hamlet with mainline trains from stops usually in front of the train stations. Like IrishRail, Irish Bus is an arm of the national Irish Transport Company, "Coras Iompair Eireann" (CIE), and you receive a reduced price on a Bus Eireann Rover Ticket when you hold a rail pass.

London Train Stations

London has some 14 train stations, depending on how you count them, and the best way between them is by Underground. The ones you will be most likely to use are Waterloo International, for Eurostar to France; Kings Cross and Euston, for Virgin and GNER trains to Scotland; Paddington, for the Heathrow Express and travel to Wales; and Victoria, for the Gatwick Express and Southeast England.

All London's train stations are different, but feature lots of shops, "Cash Point" ATMs, newsstands, separated ticketing rooms, Thomas Cook hotel reservations offices, and usually a pub and Burger King restaurant. They also have one or more large digital departure time displays with hordes of passengers standing beneath them waiting for their train's platform number to be announced.

The pleasant Virgin Trains first-class lounge on the mezzanine on the east side of Kings Cross Station is available to holders of first-class BritRail Passes. It is complete with office equipment, deep-cushion chairs and sofas, and complimentary refreshments.

City Gold between Dublin and Cork

IrishRail is proudest of its first-class-only "City Gold" service. Holders of Eurailpasses and first-class BritRail Passes + Ireland are welcomed with Irish warmth. Those with second-class passes are treated equally royally after they pay a supplement of about $25, Dublin-Cork ($6.50 on Sundays). You join gregarious white-collar commuters with bulging briefcases who relax as they travel back and forth between Dublin and Cork in upgraded, first-class IC carriages attached to the front of IrishRail's best IC trains. You can identify the carriages by the City Gold logo.

City Gold passengers are greeted by a host and shown to their seats. Seating is 2+1, divided by a table with an elaborate lighting console/telephone jack. Free earphones connect to a Blaupunkt console for popular or classical music or news. The highlight is the meal service served at your seat by a waiter with a sense of humor.

The meal is not free to rail-pass holders. Including Salmon Supreme, Linguine Primavera, Baked Limerick Ham, Platform Grill, and the Station Master Special (an Irish beefsteak with vegetables and farmhouse French fries), dinner runs $10-$20. Prices include taxes, tip, and coffee or tea. Credit cards are accepted.

City Gold leaves from Dublin's Heuston station. The locomotive at the head is shining in IrishRail's orange and black livery. Look to see if it is the "Abhainn na Sionainne" ("The River Shannon"), the first diesel locomotive given a name by IrishRail.

The River Shannon 201-class locomotive was shipped by air from London (Ontario) to Dublin airport aboard a Ukrainian Antonov 124-100 airplane. The 112-ton locomotive was the second heaviest air cargo in history (the first was an electrical generator).

Traveling eastward into County Kildare you pass through deep-green pasturelands and past hedge-lined roads through Droichead Nuc (Newbridge) to Kildare city. The horses roaming the fields belong to the dozens of stud farms that make up the heart of Ireland's famous racing industry.

Turning southeast at Portarlington where the River Barrow divides the town into two counties (Laois and Offaly), you reach the county town of Portlaoise. Continuing into the natural charm of eastern Tipperary's landscape through Ballybrophy (where there are branch-line connections via Nenach to Limerick), Templemore, and Thurles, you halt in Limerick Junction so that, if you wish, you can change to or from the primary train to Limerick and Ennis, where the Irish government has spent $17 million to link most households and businesses to the Internet.

Your IC makes good time to Charleville (Rathluirc), the point where you enter County Cork. This northwest corner of County Cork is a region of stone, hills, and country estates of studding and riding stables set in parkland. You can make out the slopes of the Boggeragh mountains rising to the south.

Mallow, where the horse is king, is the center for processing sugar beets, fishing, hunting, and changing passengers to and from Killarney and Tralee.

Through the slopes of the Nagles mountains to the east, fertile land and thickly wooded valleys, your IC reaches vine-covered, end-of-the-line Cork train station. Nearby Blarney Castle is a magnet for visitors to Ireland who hope to win the gift of eloquence by kissing the Blarney Stone. To kiss this rough limestone block, lie on your back and lean out over a sheer drop. Make sure a pair of strong hands holds your shins. The stone is scrubbed with disinfectant four times a day.

Although IR's locomotives are capable of higher speeds, and the Cork line has already received substantial investment to bring the maximum line speed up to 90 mph, IR is cautious about changing the timetables so as not to upset the routines of regular travelers. Presently the best train takes you over the 165 miles in two hours, thirty minutes, making two stops, and averaging 66 mph.

Enterprise between Belfast and Dublin

There was a good deal of speculation about the color of the new Enterprise cross-border express trains between Dublin and Belfast which began service late in 1996. Because it is a joint operation between Northern Ireland Railroads (NIR, (*www.nirailways.co.uk*) and IrishRail, the color question was sensitive.

When the first of the 28 new carriages for the Dublin-Belfast service arrived from Zeebrugge at Dublin Port, reporters marveled at the handsome light-gray/dark-gray livery which didn't seem to antagonize anyone.

Eight daily departures (five on Sundays) take you between Dublin's Connolly station and Belfast's Central station over upgraded tracks in about two hours, depending on the number of stops. The trip exposes the essence of beautiful Ireland and contrasts Belfast, the capital of Northern Ireland, with its historic Troubles, and peaceful Dublin, the metropolis of the Republic of Ireland.

At Droghede you begin one of the most colorful stretches of train travel you will find in Europe.

The church tower of Droghede lies on your right. The brick and tile-roofed residential quarter is on your left. The river is wide and crammed with ships. The dockside is very quiet this day, a bank holiday. Orange-and-black "Arrow" IrishRail trains wait on adjoining platforms.

Passengers are mostly reading newspapers and dozing aboard your Enterprise train heading south, but some do business on their cellular telephones now that you have entered the Republic of Ireland from the north.

At Laytown Station, where you do not stop, you meet the Irish Sea full on, as it stretches quietly toward Wales. A few large, white ships dot the horizon, and you wonder whether they are the ferries connecting Wales and Ireland. Seagulls perch on the brown sand and waves roll in quietly. On the side of a cliff dropping to the sea, there appears to be a military firing range. A golf course can't be far away.

In the distance, across the green waters, you make out the peninsula of Howth.

Beside the sea, hay is arranged in yellow bales and rolls and the sheep and cattle grazing in on the green slopes are oblivious to the grand view. From your Enterprise train window, it is a glorious panorama, as you race past a fishing village. This is one of the most scenic stretches you will find in Europe.

Finally your spectacle ends as you pass the prim and proper townhouses and windmills at Skerries, north of Howth, but still, before you arrive in Dublin's Connolly Station, you see instances of dramatic beauty in the waters and green fields heading south, such as the massive shipping and fishing fleet and marina at Malahide (no stop) with the white fishing vessels lined up side by side.

It would be a sensitive issue in the pubs of Northern Ireland whether North Ireland trains were included in the British section or the Irish section of this guidebook, but because the international train from Belfast runs to Dublin, and not to London, it makes more sense to include it in the Ireland section.

In Belfast (*www.gotoBelfast.com*), The Troubles is spelled with a capital *T* because it refers specifically to the Nationalist-Unionist fighting which hauled Belfast into newspaper headlines. But since the 1995 ceasefire, Belfast is booming. The city center is alive with new shops, pubs, restaurants, and discos, and because central Belfast is now an attractive place to live, both property prices and tourism have tripled.

The Troubles has the same historic fascination for visitors as the Berlin Wall had after the German *Wende*. Since the 1995 ceasefire, the number of hotel beds has quintupled. Residents of Belfast brag about living in a special city with two cultures—both British and Irish.

In today's much-changed atmosphere, Loyalist and Republican wall murals have become popular tourist attractions in West Belfast. These political paintings are among the few remaining symbols of The Troubles, while there are hundreds of buildings, such as opulent Georgian, Victorian, and Edwardian edifices around Donegall Square, that prove Belfast's industrial and cultural strength over the past 200 years, when Belfast claimed the world's largest weaving and tobacco factories, the most extensive ropeworks built, and the world's greatest shipyard.

If you choose to take a rail 'n drive pass or simply to rent an automobile, you can make a day excursion from Belfast to the mysterious and beautiful Giants Causeway (*www.giantscausewayofficialguide.com*), so named because when it was discovered it was believed to have been built prehistorically by giants. It is Ireland's number two visitor attraction (after the Book of Kells in Dublin) and a World Heritage Site of exceptional interest and universal value, accessible by the coast road via Larne.

Nearby the Giants Causeway, most everyone visits the Old Bushmills Distillery of Irish malt whiskey for the free tour and educational sampling.

IrishRail refers to the Enterprise trains as their "Eurostar," claiming that they were modeled on the cross-channel train, and pointing out that they connect two capital cities and were built by the French company, De Dietrich, which built the end passenger carriages for the TGV and Eurostar trains. Half are owned by IR; half by NIR. Like the Dublin-Cork service (above), the trains are pulled by new GM class 201 diesels, but in this case, half are owned by NIR. First-class carriages seat 47 travelers, sitting 2+1, separated by tables. You can use the radio/tape/CD unit. Meals are served at your seat in first class. Second-class passengers, seated 2+2, patronize the cafe/bar carriage, where they buy sandwiches and drinks to eat there or take to their seats.

Eurailpasses are valid only in the Republic of Ireland, and not in Northern Ireland (which also does not honor BritRail Passes), so Eurailpass holders will need to buy a ticket between Belfast and Dundalk, which costs exactly half of the Belfast-Dublin fare of about $50, first-class, and $30, second-class.

The London Underground

London's train stations, and Heathrow Airport too, are connected by London's busy subway system known as the Underground, or "Tube." When you buy individual tickets, remember to keep them to operate the automatic turnstiles when you exit.

It's convenient to buy day or longer-term London Travelcards for the Underground. They are reasonably priced. When you buy them by the day, no photograph is required. You can even buy them from the vending machines located in Underground stations for unlimited travel over a 650-square-mile area, but with a catch: you can't buy day Travelcards before 9:30 A.M., Mondays to Fridays. This is fine for late-rising visitors, but makes them unsuitable for business travelers.

Travelcards are valid for unlimited travel by the Underground, Docklands Light Railway, London-area trains, and on most of London's buses (not the Airbus). For slightly less, you buy a Travelcard valid for a day only in central London, which is usually sufficient.

You can buy longer-term Travelcards for seven or more days for the exact number of days you require. Generally, when you will be traveling in London for four or more days, it is cheaper to buy a seven-day Travelcard than single one-day Travelcards. For these, in London you will need to obtain a free photocard, requiring a passport-type photograph either brought with you or bought from a machine. These make it economical to take buses for very short distances, transfer from bus to bus, and from Underground to bus and vice versa—which is a great travel advantage.

When you want the convenience of paying in dollars, the security of having a Travelcard voucher in hand before you leave, and the ability to exchange the voucher at Heathrow Airport for your trip to central London, buy either an "All Zone" or "Central Zone" London Visitor Travelcard valid for three, four, or seven consecutive days of unlimited travel. Central Zone covers zones 1 and 2 of London's Underground. All Zone also includes transportation between Heathrow airport and central London (but not on the Heathrow Express Train) and the Docklands Light Railway.

Airport Trains

London's Gatwick and Heathrow airports take about the same time to reach from central London, but the cost of the least expensive ground transportation from London to Heathrow is about a quarter that of getting to Gatwick.

The January 19, 1998, Heathrow Express train speeds nonstop at 100 mph between Heathrow Airport and Paddington Station, in central London, in 15 minutes, every 15 minutes. You board at two brand-new stations at the airport: Heathrow Central for terminals 1, 2, and 3, and a second at terminal 4, which adds five or six minutes to your travel time. The Heathrow Express is spiffy, but long, with first-class carriages at each end of the train. When you arrive at Heathrow Airport holding a first-class BritRail Pass, have it validated at the ticketing office, and then proceed to the first class carriage at the head of the train. The air-conditioned interiors are comfortable, with two-opposite-two seating in second class and one-opposite-two in first class, with generous leg room and abundant luggage and overhead space.

Incidentally, you can use the train, free, to transfer between terminal 4 and the other terminals.

Heathrow Express trains depart from Paddington Station, platforms 6 and 7, between 5:10 A.M. and 11:40 P.M. daily. Second class costs about $15 each way; first class costs about $30. BritRail Passes are accepted.

Paddington train station has 27 desks served by most airlines, including Air Canada, American Airlines, British Airways, Canadian Airlines, Qantas, and United Airlines. You can check in your luggage any time on the day you fly, up to two hours before your flight time, collect your boarding card at Paddington, ride the Heathrow Express to your terminal, and go straight through passport control to your departure gate.

The Piccadilly Line on London's Underground serves Heathrow Airport, and using it has the advantage that you can reach an Underground stop near your final destination either directly, or by changing to another of London Underground's 11 lines. The downside is that it is slower, can be crowded, is not luggage friendly, and changing lines with luggage is a bother. Trains run every few minutes, from early morning until after midnight.

The Piccadilly Line has two stops at Heathrow Airport: use the first stop for Heathrow terminus 4, the second for terminals 1, 2, and 3 (make sure you know which terminal your flight departs from). Allow at least 50 minutes between the airport and Piccadilly Circus; 58 minutes from King's Cross/St. Pancras. When you must change from one subway line to another, your trip will take much, much longer, especially on Sundays when service is less frequent.

At London's Heathrow terminals 1, 2 and 3, you wheel your suitcases right up the gates of the Underground. Fare is about $5, which seems a lot for a subway ticket, but compared to airport transportation in other cities, it is cheap. Heathrow lies in London Underground's outer tariff zone, zone 6.

Arriving passengers should use the information desk as they leave the airport and enter the Underground station. Agents will give you directions to your destination, an Underground map, and sell you your ticket (which you will keep to exit the system).

Departing passengers with only hand luggage can check in with British Airways in Heathrow's Underground station and go straight to their departure lounge for their flight.

Gatwick Airport has its own train station right in the heart of the airport with direct train services to many parts of England. To reach Gatwick Airport from London, board the Gatwick Express (*www.gatwickexpress.co.uk*) at Victoria station's modern Rail/Air check-in facilities on platforms 13 and 14. This area is equipped with elevator, escalator, and special escalator-friendly luggage carts. British Airways maintains a passenger lounge above the platform.

The gray-and-white, red-striped aging Gatwick Express train, specifically designed for air travelers, is being replaced by a red, yellow, and white "Darth Vader" eight-carriage electric railcar. You ride in carpeted, air-conditioned carriages, enter through wide doors, store your luggage on convenient shelves, and walk between compartments through automatically opening doors. You may telephone from the train and charge it to your credit card.

The Gatwick Express carries you nonstop at speeds up to 90 mph, cutting your travel time between Gatwick and Victoria station to 30 minutes. Quarter-hourly service runs from 5:50 A.M. from Victoria until 12:50 A.M. During the night, standard train service (taking 52 minutes) continues hourly. Second class costs about $18 one-way; first class, about $28. BritRail Passes are accepted.

The Gatwick Express takes you to Victoria station. When you wish to go to other spots in London, or beyond, it may be more convenient to take Thameslink Rail (*www.thameslink.co.uk*), which serves 11 stops from Gatwick as far as Bedford, and makes a stop at Kings Cross Thameslink train station, about 1,000 feet from the main Kings Cross train terminus where you board the GNER trains to York and Scotland.

Boarding your flight at Gatwick Airport, TR drops you about 10 minutes from the South Terminal, and 15 minutes from the North Terminal. Air arrivals follow the train symbols to the TR stations. TR tickets are available from the ticket desks in the North and South terminals between passport control and baggage reclaim, South Terminal arrivals hall, and opposite check-in zone H for London tickets only. Ask for Thameslink when buying your ticket. There are about four departures per hour, and the trip takes about 46 minutes between Gatwick Airport and Kings Cross.

Stansted Airport, 33 miles from London's Liverpool Street station, has its own train station right in the heart of the user-friendly, 1991 airport terminal building. It knocks spots off Heathrow for convenience. It is the only airport in Britain where you can wheel baggage carts right onto train station platforms. The shining Stansted Express operated by WAGN is a dedicated train with departures every 15 minutes between 8 A.M. and 4 P.M. on weekdays, and half hourly from 5 A.M. to 11 P.M. on all days. It takes you to London's Liverpool Street station in 42 minutes, with an intermediate stop at Tottenham Hale which you can use to transfer to the Victoria Line of the London Underground for a direct route to the West End (Oxford Circus) as well as Euston and Victoria stations. First-class gives you a free hot drink, newspaper, and laptop connection. BritRail Passes are accepted. Taxis are about five times more expensive and take longer. There is also hourly service to Cambridge and Peterborough continuing to Liverpool or Birmingham.

When Manchester Airport train station was opened in 1993, Manchester Piccadilly station express trains were extended to the airport, calling at Stalybridge and the airport-branch junction station, Heald Green. Manchester airport train station is right in the heart of the airport complex, linked to Terminal One by a covered escalator and Terminal Two by a 24-hour a day shuttle bus service. There are up to six trains per hour (three trains per hour on Sundays; hourly during the night) between Manchester's Piccadilly station and Manchester Airport, taking 15 to 23 minutes, operated by electric railcars with blue Manchester Airport "airexpress" regional railways logo. You find increased luggage space. There are regular through trains connecting the airport with Preston, Lancaster, Liverpool, Sheffield, Leeds, York, Glasgow, and Edinburgh. You have good mainline connections to London's Euston station.

Birmingham Airport is beside Birmingham International train station, which is served by direct trains to principal towns and cities. Frequent Tyne and Wear Metro service runs between Newcastle Central train station and Newcastle Airport, linking the north's Regional Railways and InterCity networks directly with the airport.

Southampton Parkway train station is adjacent to Southampton/ Eastleigh Airport—a three-minute walk. Direct InterCity services link Southampton Parkway with Midlands, northwest and northeast England,

and Scotland. London Luton and Glasgow airports still lack rail links, so you rely on frequent bus connections to the nearby cities.

Caledonian Sleeper

ScotRail has assumed control of Britain's Caledonian Sleeper train between London's Euston Station, North West England, and Scotland aboard refurbished Mark III carriages. First-class sleepers accommodate one passenger; second-class cabins accommodate two in an upper and a lower berth. Each cabin is equipped with blankets, cotton sheets, air-conditioning, bedside lighting, wash basin with electrical shaver outlet, and hand towel. All berths are nonsmoking.

There is also a nonsmoking carriage fitted with reclining seats, footrests, tray tables, individual reading lights and access to buffet facilities. Advance reservations are compulsory.

ScotRail provides Caledonian Sleeper departures from London Euston at 11:55 P.M. for Edinburgh and Glasgow, and at 9:30 P.M. for Aberdeen, Fort William, and Inverness. Reservations are required. BritRail Passes cover the transportation, but you must pay supplements for the cabin facilities.

Travelers joining at the starting point of the train may occupy cabins one hour before departure time. At end stations, you may remain in your cabin until 8 A.M. Your porter asks you whether you wish to be awakened early for arrival or after sleeping late. He awakens first-class passengers by delivering a newspaper and complimentary orange juice, hot croissant, jelly, and coffee or English tea freshly loaded aboard en route. Second-class passengers receive cookies in lieu of croissants.

Special Caledonian Sleeper reception lounges are available for complimentary coffee or tea and cookies before boarding at London Euston (access via platform 16), Inverness (station concourse), Aberdeen (station concourse), Carlisle (in the Lakes Court Hotel), and Edinburgh Waverley (adjacent to platforms 11/14). At Glasgow Central, passengers can board the sleeper at 9:40 P.M. where the on-board lounge car will be open.

The on-board lounge service is provided primarily for first-class passengers although second-class passengers are welcome during slack periods. The lounges are first-class salon cars converted into pubs with bars, 26 lounge seats, and a public telephone. Located midtrain, this is where first-class passengers buy drinks, light meals, and snacks before turning in and after awakening.

Glasgow Stations

Glasgow is not only a good jumping-off place for the West Highland line (see section following), it is an interesting city to visit in its own right. Rail fans should not miss visiting the Glasgow Museum of Transport (free admission and free guide service), which is one of the happy surprises of Scotland.

Glasgow has two stations. Both of them are very good, with adjacent hotel and all facilities. The Station Hotel is located right in Glasgow Central Station, which is the terminus of the electrified trains to London on both the East Coast and West Coast mainlines and your jumping-off station for your trip through Burns country to Stranraer and Stena Line's HSS fast ferry service to Belfast, taking 90 minutes. The station is one of the best organized in Britain and certainly one of the most comfortable in all Europe.

Glasgow Queen Street Station is the terminus for the diesel railcars on the West Highland line and the excellent Class 158 Express Trains which shuttle to and from Edinburgh on the hour and half-hour from both cities. The Copthorne Hotel (owned by Aer Lingus) fronts on George Square. It has its entrance a few feet from the Queen Street Station exit. (For advance reservations phone Aer Lingus, 1-800-223-6537, or Utell Int'l, 1-800-448-8355).

There is a quarter-hourly shuttle bus between the two train stations, but if you are not burdened with luggage and the weather is good, it will be more pleasant and faster to walk the five blocks. For directions, look for Strathclyde Transport Central Area maps posted in both stations.

BritRail Passes

Eurailpasses are not valid in Britain, but you can choose from such an array of tempting train values that your head begins to swim. Check the websites and write for the free color brochures from BritRail and Rail Europe (see Appendix A), take it slow, and find the right combination for you.

BritRail Passes are your basic go-everywhere, see-everything travel convenience. One of the beauties of the passes is precisely that they are valid throughout Britain. You have no concern about which rail company you are traveling on. They are your ideal way to adventure in Britain by train. You travel free on every train in England, Scotland, and Wales (but not North Ireland), save Eurostar (where you receive a discount); Tyne and Wear Metro trains (Newcastle area); Glasgow Underground trains; London Regional Transport Underground trains; buses, ships, hovercraft, and jetfoils; the narrow-gauge private railroads in Wales; the Isle of Man trains; and the steam locomotive in Scotland.

You can buy consecutive and flexipass first- and second-class passes. Second-class passes ("standard-class") are sold for more than one-fourth off the prices of the first-class passes. Buy consecutive passes for eight, 15, or 22 days or one month.

The passes are especially attractive to those over 60 and those between 15 and 26. Seniors pay about 15 percent less for a first-class Senior Pass and youths pay about 46 percent less for a second-class Youth Pass. There are no first-class Youth Passes or second-class Senior Passes. When you buy an adult or Senior Pass, one accompanying child (age five to 15) gets a free pass of the same type and duration. You must ask for the BritRail Family Pass when booking. Additional children purchase the appropriate pass at half the price of a regular adult pass. Children under five travel free.

BritRail Flexipasses allow you leisure time, like Eurail Flexipasses. You pay a premium of about 28 percent to be able to stretch your travel days over a two-month time period. This would give you a chance to settle in one spot or take excursions such as Eurostar to the Continent. BritRail Flexipasses are available for four, eight, and 15 days. Senior and Youth BritRail Passes are also available with the same Flexipass option.

Travel for any flexipass day ends at midnight, but you can continue past midnight to the destination or intermediate stops on trains that have commenced their journeys before midnight without using the following day's validation. For example, a pass whose day of use is May 14, may be used on a train departing at 11 P.M. that does not reach its destination until 8 A.M. on May 15, without writing in "May 15."

BritRail has a special deal called the BritRail Party Pass for groups of three or four, where the third and fourth passengers receive a 50 percent discount. It applies to first-class BritRail consecutive-day and flexipasses. Passengers must travel together at all times and passes must be of the same type and validity/duration.

There is also a BritRail Weekender Pass valid for four consecutive days (which must include a Saturday night).

You buy BritRail Passes on the Continent, in Germany and France, for example, and in the Republic of Ireland, but you pay in local currencies, so it is more convenient to buy them before leaving America.

The BritRail Southeast Pass allows you to save big if you will be traveling solely in southeastern England. Network Southeast offers special flexipasses for the large swath surrounding London between Exeter and Kings Lynn, which includes the famous Kent resorts and major port cities. You have access to beautiful countryside, the rolling South Downs, and some of the most fascinating cities in England, such as Oxford, Salisbury, Cambridge and Brighton. You can visit East Anglia to the northeast, or go as far west as Exeter on the edge of Dartmoor. These make refreshing day trips from London.

Southeast Passes are available for three or four travel days in eight, or seven days in 15. You have a choice of first- or second-class passes, but you will have to pay supplements to reach cities outside Network Southeast's service area such as Bath or use InterCity trains via Reading. Those five to 15 years old pay one-third or less, depending on the length of the pass's validity.

The Freedom of Scotland Travelpass gives you unlimited travel on all ScotRail services north of the cities of Berwick-on-Tweed on the east coast and Carlisle on the west, as well as transportation on most Caledonian MacBrayne ferry services and discounts on all P&O ferries to Orkney and Shetland.

To gain the greatest benefit from your Freedom of Scotland Travelpass, timetables and a map are essential. These are included in the complimentary pack issued to all purchasers. The pack also contains a free "Scotland Discount" 40-page booklet and plastic countdown card valid in more than 400 stores and services where the Scottish Tourist Board has negotiated at least a 10 percent discount and a 10-50 percent discount in more than 200 restaurants, night spots, and sightseeing attractions.

You can buy the Freedom of Scotland Travelpass for four days travel within eight, or eight or 12 days within 15. It is available only in "standard class." In Scotland all trains are second class only, except for the InterCity trains running south to England and the blue-livery, Class 158 Express which runs along the Glasgow-Edinburgh flagship route—and to Inverness and Aberdeen through Stirling, Perth, and Dundee. It is smooth-riding luxury for a two-car unit, with indirect lighting and storage space between seat backs.

The tourist routes are operated with lighter-weight Sprinter and Super Sprinter railcars, in bright new liveries. These cars are sized and panoramic-designed for the scenic routes. They have, incidentally, the best-designed loos of any train running, but don't forget to push the "lock" button or the next customer will be as startled as you.

The Freedom of Scotland Travelpass sold in Britain is identical to the Freedom of Scotland Travelpass sold here, but it is priced in pounds sterling. Normally it is cheaper to buy a Freedom of Scotland Travelpass before you leave.

None of the passes or tickets is valid on special excursion trains, privately owned railroads, Fort William to Mallaig steam services, or the Strathclyde PTE Underground. You must pay supplements for seat reservations and sleeper accommodations.

The Freedom of Wales Flexi Pass is an economical travel option for visiting the principality of Wales. There are two standard-class options available. The shorter duration Flexi Pass gives you any four days of train and bus travel within eight days. The longer alternative gives you eight days of train and bus travel within 15 days. You don't have to travel on consecutive days, but you must begin travel after 9 A.M. on weekdays. Connecting service from major cities in England, like Crewe, Chester and Shrewsbury, is complimentary.

Discount coupons for popular attractions, such as castles and museums, are supplied with the pass. In addition, when you validate the Flexi Pass in Britain, you receive a comprehensive travel pack of maps, guides, travel information, and the discount vouchers.

The BritRail Pass 'n Drive plan combines a two-month BritRail Flexipass with three days' train travel and a Hertz rental automobile with unlimited mileage for two days within a month. For long hauls, you use the train, and for short hauls and exploring the countryside, you have a car from some 100 pickup stations at major train stations, at 11 airports, or 89 more at practically any place you might venture.

Before leaving home, you obtain your travel documents from your travel agent. Each car rental voucher is valid for 24 hours and includes unlimited mileage, so you keep the car for blocks of 24-hour periods. You pay no drop-off charge, so you can pick up a car in one station and drop it off in another. You may choose to use the vouchers individually or in multiples at locations along the way. You pay for the package in dollars and receive all instructions before you leave, making it very easy to use. Minimum age for rental is 25.

Crossing the Channel by Ship

The ships of the Stena Line (*www.stenaline.com*) have been hit hard by competition from the Eurotunnel on its choice English Channel link, but the Gothenburg-based line, which took over Sealink British Ferries in 1990, operates more ships to more places from Britain than any other company. The *Stena HSS* is the world's largest, smoothest, fast ferry, with the world's only floating McDonald's, a children's play area, and on-board shopping. Stena Line's fast Lynx catamaran on the Dover-Calais route can carry 700 passengers and 180 vehicles and can complete the crossing in 45 minutes. In 1996 Stena put the Stena Emperor into service, which with a capacity of 550 cars and 2,300 passengers, is the biggest on the route.

Although designated boat trains have been eliminated, traditional surface crossings between London and Paris still exist in the form of SeaTrain Express carried by deluxe SeaCat catamarans.

Why would you consider traveling from London to Paris by connecting train, catamaran, and French train link, when you can do it in just under three hours in one train? The answer is price and flexibility. With one ticket, you can break your journey anywhere within England or France. For example, you can travel to Boulogne, stay a few nights, and use the rest of your ticket to travel to Paris, perhaps with a stop in Amiens.

The crossings between Dover, England, and Calais, France, are carried both by Stena Line ships with a crossing time of 90 minutes and Lynx catamarans, which take 45 minutes.

For its Newhaven-Dieppe route, Stena Line refurbished two ships— the *Stena Londoner* (formerly the *Versailles*) with a British crew and the *Stena Parisien* (formerly the *Champs Elysees*) with a French crew. They make the crossing in four hours. Stena's Lynx catamarans take two hours and 15 minutes on the same route. Rail connections operate both day and night.

Discounts are given on Stena Line crossings between Calais-Dover, Dieppe-Newhaven, and Cherbourg-Southampton to holders of Eurailpasses, Europasses, and France Railpasses.

To Belgium, you have a choice of either Oostende Lines' Jetfoil or ships across the English Channel from London's Victoria station via Dover to Ostend. The train/Jetfoil typically takes 5 1/4 hours; the train/ship, 7 3/4 (for more information refer to Benelux chapter and also for sailings to the Netherlands).

Scandinavian Seaways offers crossings from Harwich, England, to Esbjerg, Denmark Gothenburg, Sweden; and Hamburg, Germany.

Board the train from London's Liverpool station. Buses take you from Hamburg and Gothenburg ports to city centers.

Stena Line to Ireland

Crossing the Irish Sea for Dublin (*www.ukireland-fastlinks.com*)? Leave London's Euston station for Holyhead, where you board Stena Line's HSS fast ferry service taking 99 minutes to Dun Laoghaire. There you connect for a short trip to Dublin by bus or DART train (see section following). The HSS makes five round trips through the day and night, timed to connect with British trains.

Visiting southern Ireland? Leave London's Paddington station on an InterCity train for Fishguard, where you board Stena Line's *Lynx III* for Rosslare in just 99 minutes.

For Northern Ireland, take ScotRail from Glasgow to Stranraer. Stena Line's HSS fast ferry service from Stranraer West Pier to Belfast Donegall Quay (covered by the BritRail Pass + Ireland, see below), with five crossings each way in summer, takes one and a half hours. The HSSs alternate with Stena Line ships departing every two to three hours and take three hours for the crossing. Hoverspeed's SeaCat catamarans sail five times daily and take one and a half hours.

BritRail Pass + Ireland

The BritRail Pass + Ireland combines Stena Line sea crossings with train travel in Britain, Northern Ireland, and the Republic of Ireland. You combine visits to England, Scotland, and Wales with Dublin's pubs, museums, and cathedrals; or the scenic beauty of Cork with London's history; or Northern Ireland's mountains and glens with Scotland's remote Highlands.

You travel round trip on Stena Line ships, HSS fast ferries or catamarans across the Irish Sea between Dun Laoghaire and Holyhead, Fishguard and Rosslare, and Belfast and Stranraer. The flexipasses are sold only in the U.S. for any five or 10 days within one month.

You may buy Ireland Rail & Bus Cards through CIE in the U.S. (see Appendix A) or wait until arrival in the Republic of Ireland. (Passes that are valid in Northern Ireland also may be bought there, but you pay in the Irish Republic's currency.) Ireland Rail & Bus Cards give you four choices of travel throughout Ireland by either IrishRail or Irish Bus's network of frequent, modern coaches that covers the Republic via major highways between large centers, and via local roads between smaller towns and villages.

The Irish Explorer Pass (Rail Only) gives you unlimited travel in standard class on IR service throughout the Republic of Ireland, including DART and Suburban Rail services in Dublin. It is valid for five travel days out of 15. When you add a bus option for 50 percent extra, your number of days increases to eight, and you can use also unlimited Irish Bus services and city bus services in Cork, Limerick, Galway, and Waterford.

The Irish Rover Pass is valid for train travel in both Northern Ireland and the Republic, and includes IrishRail, Northern Ireland Rail, DART, Suburban Rail services in Dublin, and suburban services in Northern Ireland.

The Emerald Card provides unlimited intercity and city travel through both the Republic of Ireland and Northern Ireland using the services of Irish Bus, IrishRail, Northern Ireland Rail, Ulsterbus, and city bus services in Dublin, Belfast, Cork, Limerick, Galway, and Waterford. You buy the flexipass for either eight days' travel in 15 or 15 days in 30. It is available in the U.S., the Irish Republic, and Northern Ireland. Children under 12 travel for half-fare.

The Freedom of Northern Ireland Ticket, costing about $50, allows seven days' unlimited travel on NIR and Ulsterbus (*www.ulsterbus.co.uk*). On Sundays you can take as many NIR train journeys as you wish for about $4.50. A family of four pays $11. Buy these offers in Northern Ireland.

Using Eurailpass Bonuses in Ireland

Eurailpass gives you a bonus that is essential for Eurailpass purchasers. It allows you to connect with the trains on the Continent at half price plus port taxes. Irish Ferries gives Eurailpass holders 50 percent off and Irish hospitality on its two large and comfortable car ferries, the *M.V. Saint Patrick II* (7,940 tons) and the *M.V. Saint Killian II* (10,256 tons) serving the Irish port of Rosslare and the French port of Cherbourg/Roscoff. Irish Ferries' Rosslare-Cherbourg sailings (17 hours) take you twice weekly from early April to late September.

You will compare Irish Ferries' sailings with minicruises. You dine in a dining room or cafeteria, shop duty-free, gamble, go to the movies, and socialize in the bar-lounge and disco. You must pay extra for cabin accommodations, but by the time your Eurailpass credit is deducted from the overall charge, your costs for these are quite reasonable. For prices and reservations, contact CIE Tours (see Appendix A). Advance reservation is compulsory if cabin accommodation is requested. For the months of July and August reservation is compulsory whether or not cabins are requested.

Irish Bus offers Eurailpass holders a reduction on the price of its three-day Rover ticket, which is valid on Irish Bus Expressway and Provincial Services in the Republic and on city services in Cork, Limerick, Galway, and Waterford. The ticket is valid for three days travel within eight days.

Britain and Ireland's great trains take you speeding from London to Edinburgh aboard InterCity supertrains, aboard ScotRail's scenic North Highland and West Highland lines, across the Isle of Man, along the coast of Wales and through slate-mining Welsh countryside, and on an electric odyssey along the Bay of Dublin.

Flying Scotsman
The Plum of Britain

Your InterCity 225 is six miles out of London's King's Cross station accelerating past 100 mph when you see the light at the end of Wood Green tunnel. You feel the sensation of top speed and a kaleidoscope of impressions. At milepost 8, you are at 115 mph. Running level, Great North Eastern Railway's supertrain romps. Wooden picket fences divide green fields. The first 140-mph marker board zips past your window.

InterCity 225, racing up the electrified East Coast line, makes Edinburgh accessible from London in four hours and cuts your travel time between London and Leeds to two.

Great North Eastern Railway (GNER, *www.gner.co.uk*) is considered the winner of the plum of the train operating franchises, with Britain's best route and Britain's best trains. InterCity 225 is aptly named, because it runs at 225 kilometers an hour (140 mph) through rolling green British countryside.

You ride aboard Britain's best equipment, save the White Rose Eurostar train, sitting in stunning "Mark 4" passenger carriages and riding behind Britain's powerful locomotives, Electra power units, with driving vans/trailers.

Everywhere that InterCity 225's Electras with class 91 serial numbers stop, you see towheaded youngsters crowding platforms, pursuing their peculiarly British hobby: "train spotting." Everyone in Britain seems to be a "Griser," named after Sir Alfred Griser's steam engine. The instant observers recognize a never-before-seen Electra coming into view, they add it to their lists by jotting into their copybooks its serial number, date, and where they spotted it.

On the nameplate of one Electra, they see a mouse. Having long since exhausted the roster of benevolent kings, queens, and major royalty to christen their locomotives, railroad executives honored Terence Cuneo, their artist celebrated for illustrating 40 years of British train history, who always marks his art with a small mouse.

GNER introduced a somber navy blue livery, with gold GNER logos, a broad orange band in the middle of the body sides and the legend "The Route of the Flying Scotsman." The head-turning Mark 4 carriages stand apart because their sleek walls cant aerodynamically inward.

When you press the push buttons to slide open the external doors and board, the first thing you observe is "Metro-Cammell" milled into the serrated aluminum steps. These Mark 4 carriages were the first to be designed and built outside former BritRail's workshops by competitive bidders.

Mark 4's spacious interiors surprise you with their radical departure from the standard look you expect from trains in Britain. Designers created a restful ambience with decorative shiny chrome-plate tubing, soothing gray fabrics, diffused ceiling lighting, indirect light spilling down the wall, pink linen gardenias and Dudson china set upon permanently anchored gray tabletops, and overlapping black-and-white box designs in the woven carpet. Staff looks efficient wearing company-issue red ties, gray vests, red-striped white shirts, and black skirts or trousers.

Variations in seating layout and full-height tinted glass screens disguise the length of the salon and create an intimate first-class interior. In the middle of the carriage, files of 1+2 seats change to 2+1, offsetting the aisle and creating an interesting focal point, or key.

Tip: For individuals or pairs, the roomiest seats are those facing pairs at the key: numbers 12F and 12B and 13F and 13B. (*F* for front-facing and *B* for back-facing.)

The gray plush seats recline a few inches with a tug on the black release. Put your soft-sided luggage in the overhead racks; store your hard suitcases and backpacks in the ample space near the entryways.

The bar/buffet (say "buffey") section is situated between first- and second-class sections. You find pay telephones in both.

GNER's first-class Pullman service gives you a choice of reservations either in a normal salon with at-seat meal service or in the dining room where, mornings, a complete English breakfast is served. Because of Pullman's departures timed for business travelers, few stops, high velocity, and two catering cars for meals, Pullman's passenger carriages are usually crammed with briefcases.

The decor in the second-class carriage is rosier, not gray. Travelers sit 2+2 throughout, which prevented designers from staggering the files. Decorators instead staggered tinted glass partitions and inserted occasional tables to achieve a social atmosphere with denser seating.

In second class, service personnel push snack trolleys through carpeted aisles (what a surprise to find rough-wearing synthetic tweed carpeting in second class!). Passengers use tables folding down from seat backs.

North of Stevenage, your 225 settles into a steady 125-mph warmup. It feels as if it wants to go faster as it skims quickly atop elevated trestles. You stop first at small, brick Peterborough station, already 76 miles up the line in 44 minutes (averaging 104 mph). On departure the conductor announces over the intercom, "We would like to welcome those passengers who have just set atrain at Peterborough."

North of Peterborough, track and overhead wiring run arrowstraight to the perspective's vanishing point. Toward Grantham you glide through countryside populated by nibbling, black-faced sheep and snug, tile-roofed brick row houses nestled far away from motorways peppered with commerce. Above Grantham's Georgian houses, you see one of Britain's noblest church spires. This miracle of medieval achievement, built just before 1300, towers 300 feet with its sculptures intact.

Up the East Coast line, golden fields of rapeseed (Canola) grown for monounsaturated oil brighten one side and bored-looking, brownand-white dairy cows opposite make a striking contrast to the occasional industrial site.

Past Newark, your train begins to feel as though it is hurrying. It rocks through a complex of curves. The driver is obviously pushing the limits of existing track. You worry that your coffee cup will bounce into your lap. "It's time to wake passengers getting off at Doncaster," the conductor jokes.

York, the best-preserved medieval city in Britain, provides your Flying Scotsman's second stop. In 1840, the city fathers knocked two holes in the city wall to provide access to their new train station. The present site was Europe's largest station when it was built in 1870-77. It still has the longest platform in England. The Royal York Hotel in the station was splendidly rejuvenated in 1991. Guy Fawkes, the folk hero who tried to blow up Parliament, came from York. Try to visit York's famous Railway Museum (open daily), which was recently expanded. It houses a history of the railroad.

Approaching Durham, 18 minutes after your stop in Darlington, you are treated to one of the most memorable views on your journey north as Durham Cathedral and Castle, jointly designated as a World Heritage Site, come into view.

After four hours you run through a cutting into Edinburgh's Waverley station (the conductor announces: "Weaver-ly"). From above, the cutting's banks look so similar to a river's that passers-by are astonished to see rails below.

Edinburgh's Waverley station's location places it amidst visible highlights of Scotland and below Edinburgh Castle. In front you see the memorial erected by the queen's own Cameron Highlanders to their comrades fallen in Egypt. It shows a Highlander in a kilt. The Gothic Sir Walter Scott Memorial is across the street.

Waverley is a rambling affair, with tracks on four sides of the covered middle area that is bisected by auto, bus, and taxi traffic. The area in front of the station contains an amazing multilevel atrium shopping center opened July 4, 1988, by Her Majesty the Queen. Up the escalators and past the modern sculptures, the Edinburgh Tourist Board's Information Center (open 8 A.M. to 11 P.M., Monday to Saturday; from 9 A.M. on Sunday) offers a hotel accommodations desk and an Internet Cafe. The Information Center is always a busy place, with guidebooks and souvenirs for sale, a Bureau de Change, a wealth of free tourist brochures, and computerized information on the Edinburgh Festival in season.

In the station it is easy to find the buffet, Railbar, City Transport Information, Festival Office (for the Edinburgh Festival), and the Travel Centre. You also find a "Shopping Parade" of kiosks. Waverley's smooth floors are ideal for suitcases with wheels because you must walk long distances. Look for pushcarts hidden away in the corners.

Above the station, the Balmoral, extravagantly remodeled, is the former North British Hotel. As it was once, it is again considered by some as the best in Edinburgh. The black hands of the clock atop are set two minutes fast so travelers won't miss their trains.

London-Leeds

Travelers have to admit that compared with some of the views they see through the window of a train, their approach to Leeds is not that arresting. But as your Intercity 225 approaches Leeds station, the familiar preamble to virtually any northern industrial city becomes more interesting.

In the midst of railroad cuttings and warehouses, passengers note an extraordinary tower. During West Yorkshire's heyday a Victorian industrialist modeled a factory chimney after Giotto's campanile for Florence Cathedral—in brick, not marble—and his industrial folly still stands.

From what you hear about Leeds these days, it is, according to its champions, the new capital of England's revived and assertive North. Its magnetism is expected to increase now that business travelers commute to Leeds from London aboard GNER's Intercity 225 in two hours. But it comes as something of a disappointment to stroll down its main business streets. Buildings like the magnificent Town Hall and the Corn Exchange show an undeniable grandeur, but Leeds also has more than its fair share of bleak office blocks.

Leeds station, in the center of town, is a covered, efficient, medium-sized station. The station's best feature, facing City Square, is the 1937 Queens Hotel with its art deco Portland stone facade. On the concourse to your left when you arrive, you find telephones, luggage checking, ticketing, and train information. Arrows point to city information nearby outside.

Weekday Pullman Service, London to Edinburgh/Glasgow

	LONDON (Kings Cross) dep.	Peter-borough dep.	YORK dep.	Dar-ling-ton dep.	New-castle dep.	EDIN-BURGH arr.	GLAS-GOW (Cent) arr.
(SP)	0800	0845	0952	1020	1051	1218	1319
(FS)	1000	1045	1153	. . . .	1247	1412	1519
(NL)	1030	1115	1226	. . . .	1321	1451	. . . .

(HC)	1200	1245	1356	....	1456	1625	....
(SP)	1500	....	1647	....	1741	1907	2015
(TS)	1700	....	1847	1915	1946	2114	....
(TP)	1730	1815	1924	1951	2026	2216	....

Weekday Pullman Service, Edinburgh/Glasgow to London

	GLASGOW (Cent.) dep.	EDIN-BURGH dep.	New-castle dep.	Darling-ton dep.	YORK dep.	LONDON Peter-borough dep.	(Kings Cross) arr.
(SP)	....	0600	0730	....	0825	....	1012
(HC)	....	1130	1300	....	1355	....	1557
(NL)	....	1230	1400	....	1455	....	1651
(FS)	1200	1300	1430	1501	1532	1558	1740
(SP)	1400	1500	1627	....	1721	....	1910

FS = The Flying Scotsman
HC = The Highland Chieftain (to Inverness)
NL = The Northern Lights
SP = The Scottish Pullman
TP = The Tees-Tyne Pullman

The Gutsy Kyle Line Wild and Romantic

While your Kyle train's ScotRail (*www.scotrail.co.uk*) diesel railcar in its flashy new purple, green, red, and white livery, its face painted safety-yellow, climbs steeply into the sparsely settled northwest corner of Scotland, your fellow passengers prepare for the wildest and most romantic passage in all of Great Britain. For best results, sit on the right.

The Highlands' wild landscape and sparse population make building difficult and expensive, yet Kyle was ultimately served. Riding the North Highland Kyle line from Inverness to Kyle of Lochalsh reveals the essence of Scotland, exposing tough new images every moment. Your 82-mile run shows peaks, headlands, forlorn islands and skerries, lochs and glens—and yet cries of protest from the local people were needed in 1974 to save this line much admired by train-lovers and adventurers.

When your train pulls in at one of the 14 lonely stations along the line, villagers climb aboard, marvel at the train, and greet friends.

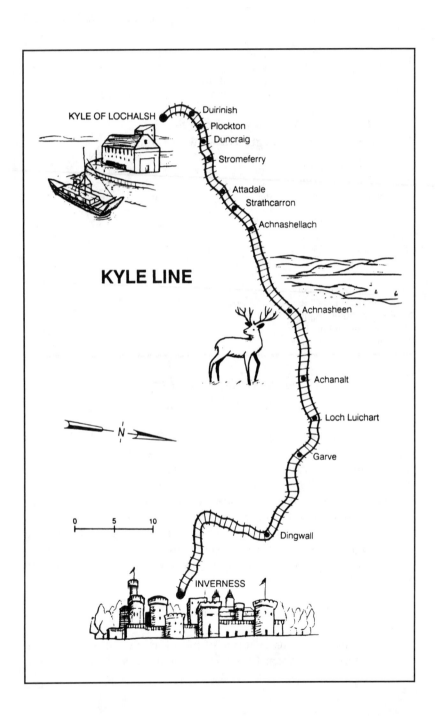

KYLE OF LOCHALSH

Duirinish
Plockton
Duncraig
Stromeferry

Attadale
Strathcarron

Achnashellach

KYLE LINE

Achnasheen

Achanalt

Loch Luichart

Garve

N

0   5   10

Dingwall

INVERNESS

Postal workers collect the mail while passengers board from creaky wooden footstools still used because there are few boarding platforms. Your Kyle train is designed for longer-distance, cross-country journeys. Five sets of panoramic windows, each with about six feet of antiglare, tinted, and double-glazed glass, show you a changing picture of Scotland's Highlands.

You never lose sight of the views. The line twists so tightly that you see both the driver ahead and the carriages trailing you as you round the many curves.

Kyle line trains run every day of the week from the brightly remodeled Inverness station. BritRail and Freedom of Scotland Travelpasses are welcome. Be sure to pick up a free Kyle line color brochure at the Travel Centre. Maps and cameras are required equipment on this line.

Passing over the nine arches of the 1990-rebuilt stone viaduct over the river Ness, you travel half an hour to Dingwall. In the green fields past Dingwall, try to picture one of the bloodiest clan battles in history, pitting the Mackenzies against the MacDonalds in 1429. It took place on Knockfarril (579 feet), near the vitrified fort built by King Brude of the Picts.

Now you climb steeply past Raven Rock, hunching 250 feet over the line to your left. At the summit of your first climb you see the dramatic contrast between the quieter green countryside dotted with cattle that stretches back below your train to Dingwall and the harsh Highlands ahead. Over the crest you approach brown, lifeless hills, wild woodlands, and rocky landscapes. Until the beginning of June, snow hugs mountains you see on your right.

Your ScotRail train picks up speed on the downhill slope, crosses the Blackwater, and races beside Loch Garve on your right. Loch Garve, which means "Rough Lake," is mirror-smooth on calm days, and you see the reflection in the lake of pine-covered Little Wyvis (2,497 feet). The greater bulk of Ben Wyvis (3,297 feet) hulks behind it.

Your diesel coasts to a stop at Garve beside the tiny, tan, plaster station house surrounded in summer by cut wheat cropped in the fields. You see the pink Garve Hotel nearby. Garve, in the mountains of Wester Ross, is a camping center during the summer.

From Garve you pass through rolling countryside and past reforesting plantations. Passing over the Corriemoillie Summit (429 feet), you see heather-clad Loch Luichart with birches lined along its shores. The sky is incandescent with blue. The six miles of Loch Luichart join the weather systems east and west.

Loch Luichart was the first lake in the Highlands used to generate electricity in 1952. The hydroelectric project lifted the water 20 feet and submerged two miles of land, including the former track and station. Your train has been rerouted to the hastily built stone station house replacing the one sitting underwater.

You enter Strath Bran on the south side of Loch a Chuilinn, then cross quickly to the north side of sparkling Loch Achanalt (the two lakes are practically continuous) past marshy fields to Achanalt station.

Continuing along Strath Bran through wet, green grasslands, with desolate mountains in the distance, the scenery hardens.

When you approach the tiny village of Achnasheen, meaning "Field of Rain," you have reached the bleakest bit of the line.

Your train comes to a stop. Post-office workers unload mail. Then your car climbs again. The treeless and rocky hills are especially attractive to a certain breed of mountaineer. Looking westward toward Glen Docherty you see the Torridon Mountains, old even in geologic terms. Liathach is the great barrel peak to the left, banded with hoops of sandstone and rising shear. To its right you see high-ridged Ben Eighe, looking white as snow but really covered with pale quartzite fragments for much of its height.

The summit of the line, Luib summit, lies only 700 feet above sea level between Loch Scaven and Loch Gowen, which drain into different seas. It is not high, but wild. You hear the crying of curlews and the loud, fluting calls of European sandpipers. Sometimes you see herds of deer, and golden eagles soaring on broad wings. In September, you may well hear great stags roaring at one another.

You almost hear your heated diesel sighing with relief as it heads downhill. At the Glencarron halt, some of the passengers with packs, ropes, and pickaxes climb off, planning to scale the cleft peak of Fuar Tholl (2,968 feet) on your right.

You then enter the deer-haunted Achnashellach Forest, thick with spruce, willow, birch, and holly. Watch for the splendid view of Glen Carron on your left before you glide into Achnashellach station.

Out of Achnashellach you pass Loch Dhugaill, surrounded with spruce. This is the country of the oldest rocks in the world, Archean gneiss forming its floor and Cambrian quartzite its walls, so that the predominant colors are pinks and grays.

At Strathcarron, the second double-tracked station, a warm burst of air prompts you to remove your parka. You leave behind cold hills and enter the softer Gulf Stream climate.

Across the lake to your right, you see the whitewashed cottages of Loch Carron village gaily bedecked with roses. Loch Carron had good herring and salmon fishing before fishing failed about 1850, too early for the Kyle line to be of any help.

Loch Carron widens on your right, and the pressing question of the moment, as you look back at Fuar Tholl, is whether you really make out the famous profile of George Washington in the outline of the mountain.

You stop next at Attadale, meaning "Valley of the Fight." Here you try to imagine Vikings dueling and sporting. You run side by side with the highway between Attadale and Stromeferry through tall spruce forests on dangerously steep slopes.

Stromeferry, at the narrowest part of Loch Carron, was a short-lived terminus of ships to the Hebridean Islands, but piracy and shipwrecks abruptly terminated trading.

This last part of the Kyle line, past Duncraig, is the most spectacular. Look sharply, for the scenery dashes by faster than words. On level ground you race below Duncraig Castle past the village of Plockton before finally slowing for Plockton's train station on the western outskirts. Duncraig Castle, dating from 1886, is hardly visible from your train, but in 2001 it became a hostel for 100 youthful backpackers.

Plockton is the gem of the Kyle line. Your train curves along the shore of saltwater Loch Carron, revealing gleaming white cottages across azure water with silver-gray Harbor seals frolicking and playing in the sunny waters. The striking, pink-rock Applecross peaks rise in the background. Plockton owes its size to the days when its schooners traded as far away as the Baltic. It looks like an island from your view but is actually on a thin promontory.

You see it best from across the water, a classic picture with wonderful changeable light and palm trees. You see paintings of this scene, complete with romantic yachts decorating the foreground, hanging in parlors and pubs throughout Britain.

When you run along the lakeside between tall mountains past Plockton, you become more excited than during any other section of the line. You see the western shore. You had not imagined such enchanting colors. Clouds, seaweed, and waterfalls suffuse in a soft, bluish light. Dozens of rivulets dash down. In the water, granite chunks lie pink, freckled with bright gold algae. Glorious views glow in changing shades of watercolor.

Past Duirinish, you travel inland through the Drumbuie crofting area. You realize your trip has to end soon when you cross the wild coast colored with orange lichen-daubed rocks, tide pools alive with sea creatures, and magnificent vistas of islands with pig-Latin names: Rassay, Scalpay, Loggay, Pabay, and the Crowlin Islands.

Breathe deeply the salty air when you step off in the Kyle of Lochalsh station. The terminus, whose site was blasted from solid rock, is right on water's edge. Fishing boats, cottages, the old hotel, the ferry, and the incomparable scenery make Kyle one of the best-placed stations in Britain. Photographers immediately scurry up the hill behind the Railway Terrace next to the Tourist Information Centre to capture on film the big, sweeping picture of mountains, islands, and the houses that look like white miniatures ready to tumble into the sea.

Kyle is Gaelic meaning "strait" or "narrows." It was simply "Kyle," population 600, until it took on its elegant new name on that historic day in November 1897, when dignitaries from all over Scotland came to declare the railroad officially open.

It is by no means the end of your travels. A Scottish Citylink Coach will take you across the 1995 balanced-cantilever Skye Bridge, which was the first link to the island since glacial times, to Kyleakin on the Isle of Skye. The bridge is a political football because of tolls that the locals consider exorbitant. The Bank of America owns it. From here, travel by bus across Skye to Armadale for the Caledonian MacBrayne ferry back to Mallaig and the return West Highland line connection to Fort William (see the following section).

Some adventurers plan their Kyle visit for Friday, in order to connect with one the weekly Caledonian MacBrayne sailing to Mallaig.

The Lochalsh Hotel, the old-fashioned resort hotel opposite the train station at water's edge, offers overnighters magnificent views across the sound of the Isle of Skye, except of course when the famous Skye mist descends.

Kyle Line Winter Service
Monday-Saturday*

0855	1053	1800	dep.	INVERNESS	arr.	0948	1420	1948
0911	1109	1824	dep.	Muir of Ord	dep.	0930	1400	1928
0921	1119	1833	dep.	Dingwall	dep.	0922	1351	1920
0942	1140	1855	dep.	Garve	dep.	0857	1328	1856
0950	1148	1904	dep.	Lochluichart	dep.	0848	1317	1843
0956	1154	1910	dep.	Achanalt	dep.	0842	1311	1837
1007	1206	1921	dep.	Achnasheen	dep.	0832	1301	1827

1025	1224	1938	dep.	Achnashellach	dep.	0813	1243	1808
1035	1236	1948	dep.	Strathcarron	dep.	0805	1235	1800
1040	1241	1953	dep.	Attadale	dep.	0759	1228	1754
1053	1254	2006	dep.	Stromeferry	dep.	0748	1216	1743
1101	1302	2014	dep.	Duncraig	dep.	0739	1208	1734
1105	1306	2018	dep.	Plockton	dep.	0736	1205	1731
1108	1309	2021	dep.	Duirinish	dep.	0732	1201	1727
1117	1318	2030	arr.	KYLE	dep.	0723	1152	1748
1220	1525	....	dep.	Kyle**	arr.	....	1120	1615
1335	1655	....	arr.	Uig (Skye)	dep.	....	0930	1445

No Sunday trains.
** Bus connection via Kyleakin, Isle of Skye.

West Highland Line
Bonnie Banks and Bonnie Braes

"Is the gradient very steep?" you wonder.

"Steep?" roars the conductor. "It's vertical!"

He does not exaggerate all that much. After Ben Nevis, your view narrows into a rock defile shared with brawling Highland streams. Rock strata line the faces right and left. Then suddenly you face Loch Treig, an intensely dramatic lagoon stretched like a vast silvered pane of glass below the great green hump of Stob Coire Easain, 3,658 feet up.

There is no road. Your train wobbles giddily along a ledge hacked from the mountainside. Reflections shine from below through gaps in the bracken. Details float by in slow motion. A Cheviot sheep stares you in the eye. A tiny scintillation of mica catches the evening sun.

From Corrour summit you descend along Loch Treig and curve westward to Tulloch. Now your one-class, flashy ScotRail (*www.sco-trail.co.uk/scotrwhl.htm*) diesel train runs west along Glen Spean into the wild Monessie Gorge. Water rushes and foams through the tortuous, rocky gully. You feel the influence of the great commanding presences of Nevis, Dorain, Vorlich, and Vain and the breathtaking vistas opening up from among these giants.

Thundering on a narrow ledge along the vertical rock walls, you suddenly see the valley opening again to Roy Bridge.

Dramatic engineering makes traveling along Scotland's 164-mile West Highland Line between Glasgow and Mallaig exhilarating. You make more than a train trip to Mallaig through pretty countryside. It is a dramatic experience. Your train rumbles through laborious cuttings hewn through rock, crosses 11 tunnels, climbs gradients as high as 1 in 48, and threads its way atop remarkable bridges and magnificent viaducts mastering the most tortuous terrain in Britain. The West Highland Line was not meant to be a tourist attraction, but to open up parts of Scotland nearly impossible to reach and to carry the cargo of the profitable west coast fish trade.

Departing from Glasgow's Queen Street Station, your train purrs though the steep Cowlairs tunnel also used by Glasgow's electrified commuter trains and begins the West Highland Line proper at Helensburgh Central Station.

Past Craigendoran you climb through the woods above Gare Loch to Garelochhead, the first of the stations noted for their wooden shingles and two-tone green decor. Like a postcard below is the Faslane naval base, where Winston Churchill departed on his voyage to North Africa during World War II. The large, amphibious shed anchored above the waves recently sheltered American Polaris nuclear submarines.

Now you cross to Loch Long and climb above it. At the head, the bulk of "The Cobbler" mountain (2,891 feet) makes you feel insignificant. While crossing the mile-wide neck of land separating Loch Long from the fresh water of Loch Lomond, wonderful views of the loch appear. Then you climb high above the loch through woods and above waterfalls to Ardlui. On the far side of the loch, Ben Lomond towers 3,192 feet. The lochs disappear while you climb steadily up Glen Falloch and curve across the Dubh Eas water on Glen Falloch viaduct.

Oban and Mallaig trains are usually connected together until Crianlarich except when heavy passenger traffic demands running separate trains. Platform lengths limit train length to six carriages. So when your Scots conductor announces, "We are approaching Crianlarich station where the train will 'splat,'" loud guffaws resound through your carriage from the Londoners riding in back.

Mallaig Line

Your train for Mallaig climbs above the Strath Fillan river to the south. Clinging to the hillside, you cross the great watershed of Scotland where the rivers flow to the Atlantic instead of the North Sea.

Ahead appear two large steel viaducts standing on tall masonry piers. This is called the Horseshoe Curve, the most spectacular of the line. The line doubles back on itself in the form of a horseshoe as you round Ben Odhar, crossing the viaduct to the foot of Beinn A Chaistel, and then continuing by the second viaduct to the mighty Ben Dorain.

From Bridge of Orchy, high above Loch Tulla, you swing eastward and enter the wild Rannoch Moor, 20 miles long and 20 miles wide. Sunlight glitters on pools and summer colors blaze from the yellow Scotch broom, purplish-pink heather, and emerald Highland grasses. Railroad engineers defeated this vast, desolate stretch of treacherous peat bogs by piling thousands of tons of ash and earth upon a mattress of tree roots and brushwood.

At the heart of the moor, the remote, chalet-style Rannoch station with Swiss birch shingles is the exodus for hikers with metal-tipped walking sticks, knickers, and heavy woolen sweaters so thick a sheep would sweat.

Then you cross a large viaduct to climb steadily north through the only snowshed in Britain to the 1,350-foot summit at Corrour, another mountaineer haven. Expect to see deer in winter and spring. From this forsaken, windswept station you look down towards Loch Ossian (1,269 feet—the highest in Scotland) at the foot of Beinn na Lap mountain (3,066 feet).

Past Roy Bridge at the mouth of Glen Roy, you see on the left Keppoch House, the ancient seat of the McDonalds. Your last lap to Fort William takes you past Inverlochy Castle and the Lochaber Mountains.

The only substantial town on the Mallaig Line, busy Fort William is also the terminus of the West Highland sleeper train to/from London's Euston station. The station occupies the shore of Loch Linnhe, cutting off the sea from the main street. Ben Nevis mountain, Britain's highest, fills the horizon.

During the summer, the "Jacobite" steam train operated by West Coast Railway Company, Carnforth (Tel. 01463-239026, *www.mallaigheritage.org.uk*), conveys passengers between Fort William and Mallaig, departing Fort William at 10:25 A.M. Rail passes are not honored. Locomotives sometimes include the ex LMSR Class 5 "Black Five" No. 5407 and ex LNER Class K1 No. 2005.

Leaving Fort William, your train reverses direction to cross the River Lochy past the old Inverlochy Castle ruins (the "fort" from which the town takes its name; the "William" is from King William of Orange) and continues along the 1901 stretch of track taking you to Mallaig.

After Banavie, your next stop is Corpach, with its huge paper mill, and then you travel along the shore of Loch Eil. Look back to see a wonderful view of Ben Nevis. You pass through stations overlooking the long stretch of water and then climb steeply through rocks to Glenfinnan. This is probably the most delightful stretch of your entire journey.

The curving, concrete Glenfinnan viaduct is one of the most photographed scenes in Scotland. It was a mighty challenge to build out of concrete, a new engineering material, because it meant carrying the railroad over 416 yards across the valley on 100-foot stilts supporting 21, 50-foot spans. You see on your left a magnificent view of silvery Loch Shiel and the Bonnie Prince Charlie Monument below where the prince rallied the clans and began his ill-fated rebellion. His forlorn, kilted statue faces up the glen, with Loch Shiel shimmering behind him.

Your head swirls as you wind through rock cuttings and above exquisite Loch Eil with delightful islets and tall silver ilex and beech. The hint of lonely, uninhabited country that you have felt from the beginning becomes overwhelming.

Following the rushing river Ailort to Lochailort, you see, on the left again, the delightful view of Loch Ailort feeding toward the Atlantic. Then you pass through a series of short tunnels with Loch Dubh on the right, clatter over Loch Dubh by viaduct, and see another spellbinding view on the left over Loch Nan Uamh.

Now you are on the edge of an exciting stretch. Your train plunges from the viaduct into a tunnel, emerges, and disappears into a second. Borrodale Bridge appears at the end of the 349-yard tunnel as you break into daylight only 86 feet above the glen on a single span of 127.5 feet.

Through more short tunnels to Arisaig, everything now looks westward to the Atlantic. Look over Loch Nan Ceall to see the weird mountain shapes of the islands of Rum and Eigg floating on the sea. You can identify Eigg, the notched island with its flat top and the molar-tooth Scour of Eigg rising 1,289 feet.

Past the sandy bays of the Morar estuary, with Loch Morar (the deepest in Britain, home of the Morag monster) to the east, you run along the Sound of Sleat opposite Skye before descending peacefully toward Mallaig, still looking to the offshore islands.

Pass a miniature blizzard of the wings of white gulls and auks. Scarlet and tawny fishing trawlers crowd the harbor. With seals and glinting sea, Mallaig, one of Europe's major herring ports, is a prosperous place with white houses running up around the bay.

Crowds watch trawlers unloading though the night, bathed in hectic orange from the fish-pier lights. Cranes dip and swing their dangling fish through darkness. Mackerels crunch underfoot; ice crashes, slung by men in grotesque orange overalls.

From Mallaig station, 650 feet away, the pier for Caledonian MacBrayne berths ferries for the 30-minute crossings to Armadale on the Isle of Skye, and for Rum, Muck, and Eigg. Follow the arrow, "Skye Ferry," on your right. Don't hurry; the Caledonian MacBrayne office is locked until shortly before departure.

As you exit the Mallaig train station, the small tourist office (for hotel reservations) is at the end of the street on the right.

Oban Spur

Blooming orange nasturtiums and red roses amongst grass so green it could only be in Scotland surround remote Crianlarich's 1880 stucco station. From here a delightful spur of the West Highland Line, also dating from 1880, takes you through wild scenery to Oban terminus, the old port where you can board Caledonian MacBrayne steamers to Scottish islands. The mountains of Scotland surround you. To the east towers Ben More (3,843 feet). In the west rise Ben Oss (3,374 feet), Ben Dhu Craig (3,024 feet), and Ben Lui (3,708 feet). Look for the remains of the Callendar & Oban eastern branch north of Crianlarich station.

You run northwest along Strath Fillan. Along this stretch you watch the Mallaig Line piercing the flat spread north across the river. Entering woods, you reach Tyndrum Lower station and then swing west through hills into Argyll along beautiful Glen Lochy. You have to be an expert to keep track of the breeds of sheep you see in the Highlands. There are more than 30. The ones you see here each have a black face with a white spot and horns.

You drop though hills overlooked by peaks to the south and then reach the glazed canopy of the red stone Dalmally station at the southern end of Glen Orchy. The line came to an end here until money raised in the 1870s allowed construction to Oban.

Sweeping around the head of Loch Awe you see the ruin of Kilchurn Castle, the ancient stronghold of the Clan Campbell, and the loch beyond. Loch Awe station has a small pier for steamer trips on the loch.

You curve along the edge of the lake, passing the hydroelectric power station near Cruachan. When the loch narrows sharply, you enter the skinny, rock-walled Pass of Brander. This is a memorable stretch linking Loch Awe and Loch Etive. You skirt mighty Ben Cruachan (3,689 feet) to the north and landslide-marked slopes to the south. Note the wire landscape fencing protecting the track.

You cross River Awe on the bridge that was the setting for Sir Walter Scott's romance, *The Highland Widow*. Past white Inverawe House, you turn west to Taynuilt, a delightful village on the shores of Loch Etive, then run through woods and rock cuttings beside the lake through the region known locally as "Australia" because of its bushlike character. Look across the water to Benderloch and then ahead to the great 1903 steel cantilever bridge at Connel Ferry. Near Connel Ferry you see the Falls of Lorc, where the tidal waters flow over a ledge of rock at the narrow entrance to Loch Etive.

You now climb through Glen Cruitten across hills and around Oban to descend with splendid views of the town and its harbor. Ferries berth below its handsome Victorian stone buildings and the strange circular coliseum ruin known as McCaig's Folly perches high above.

Oban is a sheltered, coastal resort, famous for its single-malt Oban whisky. The town and its picturesque bay are nearly landlocked. Hotels lining the promenade cater to thousands of visitors making this their base.

Oban is the main port for Mull, Ionc, and all the Inner Hebrides and Outer Hebrides islands via Caledonian MacBrayne ferries. "The Earth belongs unto the Lord and all that it contains. That is, except, the Western Isles, which are Caledonian MacBrayne's." Railfans visiting the Isle of Mull will find that their ship is equipped with everything suitable for the 40-minute crossing. Upon landing at Mull, walk seven minutes left along the coast rather than along the highway to reach the MullRail train, which doesn't leave until the last passenger off the ship has arrived.

MullRail is a delight for five-year-olds and railfans. This happy train runs on a straight line following the coast on 10 1/4-inch gauge using Mull-grown timber sleepers over peat bogs through pristine forests alive with pheasants. Fallen trees are covered with lush green moss. Freedom of Scotland Travelpass holders receive a 15 percent discount on tickets.

Mull managed without a railroad for over 150 years. When the 1858 Torosay Castle, a Scots Baronial Mansion, and its beautiful Italian gardens were opened to the public in 1975, visitors were reluctant to walk the best part of over two miles from the pier at Craignure to the castle. Thus, the Mull Railroad, the first island passenger railroad ever to be built in Scotland, was opened in June 1984. MullRail is open at Easter, then from early May to mid-October.

West Highland Line Summer Service
Glasgow-Mallaig

(1)	(2)	(2)				(3)	(3)	(4)
0812	1240	1810	dep.	GLASGOW (Queen St.)	arr.	1113	1544	2114
0829	1300	1828	dep.	Dalmuir	dep.	1053	1527	2045
0837	1307	1835	dep.	Dumbarton Central	dep.	1045	1514	2032
0855	1323	1853	dep.	Helensburgh Upper	dep.	1031	1458	2020
0906	1334	1905	dep.	Garelochhead	dep.	1019	1446	2001
0926	1357	1925	dep.	Arrochar & Tarbet	dep.	1000	1427	1947
0945	1412	1948	dep.	Ardlui	dep.	0946	1413	1929
1001	1427	2003	arr.	CRIANLARICH	dep.	0929	1353	1923
1005	1439	2015	dep.	CRIANLARICH	arr.	0923	1347	1917
1015	1454	2026	dep.	Tyndrum Upper	dep.	0911	1339	1912
1030	1504	2040	dep.	Bridge of Orchy	dep.	0857	1320	1859
1051	1525	2106	dep.	Rannoch	dep.	0837	1301	1840
1103	1537	2118	dep.	Corrour	dep.	0824	1250	1828
1120	1554	2134	dep.	Tulloch	dep.	0809	1233	1812
1130	1603	2144	dep.	Roy Bridge	dep.	0754	1222	1801
1138	1609	2150	dep.	Spean Bridge	dep.	0748	1216	1755
1149	1622	2205	arr.	FORT WILLIAM	dep.	0735	1203	1742
1200	1627	2210	dep.	FORT WILLIAM	arr.	0730	1152	1737
1206	1633	2216	dep.	Banavie	dep.	0724	1145	1731
1212	1638	2221	dep.	Corpach	dep.	0721	1140	1726
1218	1644	2227	dep.	Loch Eil (outward)	dep.	0715	1134	1720
1223	1650	2232	dep.	Locheilside	dep.	0708	1128	1713
1234	1702	2242	dep.	Glenfinnan	dep.	0658	1118	1703
1249	1718	2258	dep.	Lochailort	dep.	0642	1103	1645
1258	1727	2308	dep.	Beasdale	dep.	0632	1052	1635
1306	1734	2315	dep.	Arisaig	dep.	0626	1046	1626
1315	1742	2323	dep.	Morar	dep.	0617	1037	1617
1322	1743	2330	arr.	MALLAIG	dep.	0610	1030	1610

West Highland Line Summer Service
Glasgow-Oban

(1)	(2)	(2)				(3)	(3)	(4)
0842	1240	1810	dep.	GLASGOW (Queen St.)	arr.	1113	1614	2114
0858	1258	1826	dep.	Dalmuir	dep.	1055	1555	2055
0907	1307	1835	dep.	Dumbarton Central	dep.	1045	1545	2045
0925	1323	1853	dep.	Helensburgh Upper	dep.	1031	1533	2032

0936 1334 1905	dep.	Garelochhead	dep.	1019 1521 2020
1000 1357 1925	dep.	Arrochar & Tarbet	dep.	1000 1501 2001
1014 1412 1948	dep.	Ardlui	dep.	0946 1447 1947
1030 1427 2003	arr.	CRIANLARICH	dep.	0929 1432 1929
1034 1433 2009	dep.	CRIANLARICH	arr.	0922 1428 1922
1040 1440 2016	dep.	Tyndrum Lower	dep.	0911 1421 1916
1056 1457 2033	dep.	Dalmally	dep.	0852 1402 1852
1101 1501 2038	dep.	Loch Awe	dep.	0847 1356 1846
1106 1506 2043	dep.	Falls of Cruachan	dep.	0841 1351 1839
1117 1516 2052	dep.	Taynuilt	dep.	0832 1342 1832
1126 1527 2102	dep.	Connel Ferry	dep.	0821 1331 1820
1140 1539 2115	arr.	OBAN	dep.	0810 1320 1810

(1) Mondays to Saturdays, runs separately
(2) Daily, separates at Crianlarich
(3) Mondays to Saturdays, combines at Crianlarich
(4) Daily, combines at Crianlarich

Isle of Man
Train-Lover's Paradise

Your coastal car swings out to Laxey Head. A splendid view opens beneath you of Douglas' Victorian promenade, its pink-and-green horse trams, and the Irish Sea breaking on its strand. When your climb toughens and your frail car tilts upward more steeply to climb one foot in every 24 instead of one in 38, you see the rugged coastline stretching out to far Maughold Head.

Your car labors at its effort. It vibrates, shakes, and rumbles. Wood rubbing on wood sings of excellent maintenance.

Your cautious pace gives you time to appreciate the view as you near Ballaragh, meaning "Place of the Rocks." You could not find a better name. Cliffs rise to more than 600 feet. While you run along the cliffside more than 500 feet above the frothy breaking waves of Bulgham Bay, you are traveling on one of the most spectacular railroad stretches anywhere in the British Isles.

When you near the end of your dramatic climb beside the cliff, you reach the highest point of Isle of Man's coastline, 588 feet above the crashing surf. Turning inland, your car descends more or less continuously through lush green countryside to Ramsey.

Manx Electric Railroad's (MER) charming electric streetcars trundle through glens and atop cliffs. Aboard its cars you see some of the

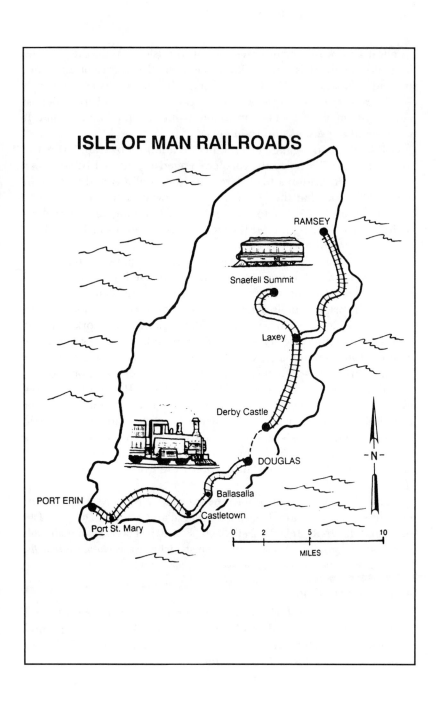

ISLE OF MAN RAILROADS

RAMSEY

Snaefell Summit

Laxey

Derby Castle

DOUGLAS

PORT ERIN

Ballasalla

Castletown

Port St. Mary

-N-

| 0 | 2 | 5 | | 10 |

MILES

loveliest and most romantic scenery on the Isle of Man, the 32-mile-long dot in the Irish Sea midway between the coasts of England, Ireland, Scotland, and Wales. It is served by Manx Airways and Irish Sea Ferries' (*www.steam-packet.com*) Seacat ferries to and from Belfast and Heysham and Superseacats to and from Liverpool and Dublin. It is an island of railways and tramways.

MER's three-foot-gauge electric fleet is admired by train-lovers the world around. Their pleasing cars have waged a continual 100-year war against modernization and closure since their delivery and first use in 1893-1906. Now that they earn their keep by attracting visitors, they receive funding adequate to ensure their safe running and meticulous maintenance. During the MER Centenary celebrations in 1999, Manx from the whole island turned out.

The Isle of Man has been heavily hit by changes in vacation patterns. The railroads and the unspoiled environment used to attract workers from the industrial north of England (Birmingham, Manchester, and Liverpool). Brightly polished steam locomotives, colorful additions to the countryside, took them to deep Manx glens, patchwork quilts of fields, the breathtaking sea—places their friends in smoke-filled cities could hardly contemplate. Now, "sun holidays" on the Mediterranean lure away its visitors with cheap airfares and mass air transportation.

From 500,000 annual visitors after World War II, Isle of Man now welcomes only 200,000. The result is that you can take advantage of tremendous overcapacity and remarkable, well-maintained electric and mountain railroads and steam trains. With the drying-up of Man's traditional tourist market, a new breed of visitor has discovered this anachronism. The Isle of Man is known the world over as a vintage transport paradise.

For information visit or contact the Isle of Man Railways, Department of Tourism, Leisure and Transport, Strathallan Crescent, Douglas, Isle of Man IM2 4NR, Tel. 01624-663366, Fax 01624-663637, e-mail rail-info@bus-rail.gov.im. Websites of interest include *www.tramway.com/fts*, *easyweb.easynet.co.uk/-iomvc/*, and *www.gov.im/tourism*.

Manx Electric Railroad

You board the MER within reach of the salt spray at the north end of the Douglas promenade and climb to almost 600 feet along a precipitous ledge before returning almost level with the Irish Sea in Ramsey, 17 3/4 miles and 75 minutes to the north.

Derby Castle station lies at the northern end of Douglas's Victorian promenade. (The unique steam locomotive trip to Port Erin, from the Douglas Bank Hill station, is described later in this section.) Purchase your tickets at the whimsical ticket house designed with lacquered branches to resemble an illustration in a child's fairy-tale book. BritRail Passes are not honored on the Isle of Man.

One glance around the car reveals meticulous attention to preservation and detail. MER still operates its original rolling stock—the newest dating from 1906, and original tramcars 1 and 2 dating back to the opening in 1893. Your lacquered car shines with such a gloss that you can make out your reflection in the walnut paneling. Seats covered with flowery maroon plush have reversible backs for travel in either direction.

Leaving Douglas's promenade, anchored on the opposite end by the bright Gaiety Playhouse, your car crawls and squeaks up the persistent rise. Squealing wheels rounding the curves excite remarks from many of the younger passengers. Passing the ungated level crossings, your motorman sounds his air whistle or gongs loudly to tell automobile drivers that he is insisting on his right-of-way.

Soon after departure comes the spectacular stretch along the cliffs high above Bulgham Bay. When you near the stone-covered Howstrake station, look down at the splendid panorama of Douglas Bay to the east. To the west, the hedge-lined green fields are filled with grazing sturdy Frisian cows standing like plaster statues ignoring the rain. Black-faced sheep cluster together in the fields; none are the curious four-horned Loaghtans native to the island.

Your car levels and the motorman eases back on his brass handle before swinging sharply inland and starting his descent, one foot in 24, along the wooded approach to Groudle, the terminus of the 1893 line. Groudle Glen was created by the Victorians as a pleasure park complete with waterwheel. Two-foot gauge tracks linked the glen with a clifftop zoo. After falling into disuse, the line has now been lovingly restored by enthusiasts and, by 1992, extended to its original length. Built in 1896, the line climbs from the seclusion of a wooded glen before bursting onto the clifftops with magnificent views out to sea. Services are normally hauled by the original steam loco "Sea Lion," which is supplemented on occasion by diesel.

The long descent of your MER past Groudle into Laxey opens the lovely panorama of the Laxey bay and beach, the tiny harbor with its neat, white-painted lighthouses, and the headlands beyond.

At Fairy Cottage and South Cape stops you see the signs, "Alight here for the beach." In summer there is a minibus return.

MER shares the brown Laxey station house with the 1895 Snaefell Mountain Railroad, which runs daily during the summer (subject to weather). Their terminus lies in a romantic wooded glen in the center of the village, decorated by nearby Christ Church.

While in Laxey, walk down the convenient, well-marked path through the green, gorse-clad valley of Agneash to visit Lady Isabella. She's not a member of the British aristocracy but the name given to the celebrated Laxey Wheel, the largest waterwheel in the world at 72 feet in diameter. Built in 1854, the red-and-white wheel pumped the Laxey lead and silver mines until the 1920s. Now it is primarily a well-manicured tourist attraction.

Your car scrapes the white paint of the Mines Tavern leaving Laxey. It is a wonderful, old-fashioned British pub with needlepoint-covered chairs, gleaming brass, shining glasses, darts, and an open fire.

You run parallel to the six original tramcars of the Snaefell Mountain Railroad until they turn up the mountain and begin to climb at a gradient of one in 12 feet on their 30-minute journey. In 1996, No. 7 "Maria"—the only freight tram on the railroad—was reinaugurated.

When you climb to the summit of Snaefell (2,036 feet—the highest point on the Isle of Man) in that train, sit on the left side so you can see the rail of the Fell brake mounted on its side between the running rails. From the summit you can see England, Scotland, and Ireland on a good day.

The hardest part of your trip aboard the MER is over. Your MER car seems to fly past farms—sheep, cows, and green- and straw-colored meadows ringed with stone walls harboring scores of cats, not the tail-less Manx breed, husbanded in Douglas's cattery, but the common alley variety.

About a mile past the green hut beside the Cornea halt, you pass Ballafayle, the residence of Sir Charles Kerruish. He is the Speaker of the House of Keys, the ancient parliament that celebrated its 1,000th anniversary in 1979. Look for his Manx "Three Legs" flag fluttering in the breeze.

Descending steadily toward Ramsey Bay, you see the Victorian hotels lining the Ramsey waterfront, a smaller echo of Douglas, and you find this symmetry most satisfying. Your car formerly ran out on the 2,000-foot Ramsey Pier but now you complete your electric railroad run not far from the city center. At Ramsey, a small museum recounts the history of the railroad with a fascinating collection of old photographs.

Isle of Man Steam Railroad

The Port Erin line, the longest narrow-gauge steam railroad line in the British Isles, uses historic carriages pulled by one of the 2-4-0 engines—Loch (1874), Maitland (1905), Hutchinson (1908), or Kissock (1910)—from Douglas Bank Hill station in the Isle's capital city, to the southwestern hamlet of Port Erin.

The 15 1/2-mile stretch opened August 1, 1874. It is built now much as it was then. The train's story is one of evolution, with change sometimes for the better, often for the worse, but with a spirit of continuity for over a century.

The four steam locomotives still used are a fraction of the 16 original ones. They are lovingly maintained and professionally cared for. Two are red, one is blue, and one is green, and they are named for original directors of the railroad. They look chubby because of the side tanks holding cold water, and they don't need a tender for supplemental fuel.

Buy your ticket for Port Erin at Douglas's redbrick train station at the head of the harbor. Arched ornamental gates sparkle with domes and pinnacles still glittering with the gold leaf applied in the railroad's more optimistic days.

You depart Douglas with a climb of one foot in 65. You can feel your blue No. 12 engine, the Hutchinson (1908), working hard. Sitting in one of the original wooden carriages, you really know you are traveling by steam. Even the Hutchinson's modest climb produces loud puffing, smoke, soot, and flying cinders, leaving you little doubt that there is a steam engine up front.

You cross the Douglas River on the 1979 girder-span Nunnery Bridge. Past the Nunnery on your left, one of the Isle's "Stately Homes," you enter a narrow rock cutting where engines are prone to lose traction in autumn due to fallen leaves.

After a half-mile, you see spectacular cliff views opening out toward Santon Head in the south, and toward Little Ness in the Douglas direction.

Past Port Soderick station (3 1/8 miles, 13 minutes), you run through the wooded Crogga valley—a treat in bluebell time. In season, dazzling displays of rhododendrons open up beside the line. Children reach from windows to catch wild flowers and leaves brushing gently against your train as it passes.

Beyond Santon (5 5/8 miles, 24 minutes), the main highway runs below the track on your left but climbs up and passes over the train at the Blackboards. You don't see any black boards now, but when the road traffic was drawn by horse, a wooden screen was erected between the train and the highway to prevent horses from taking flight at smoke-belching monsters.

The airport you see on your left is Ronaldsway, site of the celebrated battle in Manx history. From here, Manx Airlines serves London, Liverpool, and Dublin.

Break your trip at Castletown (9 7/8 miles, 42 minutes), the capital of the Isle until the 1860s, to explore Castle Rushen, one of the finest preserved medieval castles in Europe. Its Elizabethan clock with only the hour hand is still in use. You also see the Nautical Museum, the harbor, the beach, and King Williams College where Bragg, the Nobel-prize-winning physicist, was educated.

When the Hutchinson pulls you past Port St. Mary (15 3/4 miles, 62 minutes), you see Port Erin in the distance, nestling between ground rising to the south toward the Sound, which separates the Island from the Calf of Man, and the high ground of Bradda Head to the north. Crowned by Milners Tower, Bradda Head makes a popular subject for amateur photographers.

When you arrive at the award-winning red-brick terminus at Port Erin (15 5/8 miles, 65 minutes), head for the beach or train museum. You will see there the locomotive that hauled the first train of 1873, a great sampling of historic locomotives, the coaches used by Queen Elizabeth in 1972, and those used by the Duke of Sutherland on opening day, 1873.

After the electric trams, mountain railroads, and steam locomotives, your four-ring entertainment is completed by returning to Douglas and riding one of its 23 famous horse trams along the promenade. After being pulled by one of the nineteenth-century iron horses, you wonder which is more temperamental, the four-footed white trotters or the red, blue, and green steam locomotives.

Douglas is served by traditional ferry service with four-hour crossings from Belfast, Dublin, Liverpool, Fleetwood, and Heysham and an eight-hour sailing from Ardrossen in Scotland.

BritRail Passes are not honored on the Isle of Man, but you may purchase a one-day Rail Rover, a three-day Rail Rover allowing you unlimited travel within a week on scheduled Steam, Snaefell Mountain, and Manx Electric railroads or a seven-consecutive-day Island Freedom pass.

MER trains run half-hourly during the summer from 10 A.M. to 5:30 P.M. The Steam Railway runs six departures on Mondays to Thursdays beginning at 10:10 A.M. and finishing at 6:20 P.M. On Fridays to Sundays, there are four departures, concluding an hour earlier.

Gwynedd
Sea, Steam, and Slate

Hold on to your tongue. You struggle and stutter on the Welsh consonants of Blaenau Ffestiniog, Tan-y-bwlch, Betws-y-coed, and Llyn Ystradau.

Your adventure in Gwynedd, Wales' north county, is a wild, dramatic trip beside the crashing waves of the Irish Sea, below soaring thirteenth-century castles, and through green valleys on a narrow-gauge, Victorian steam train.

You first follow the Cambrian Coast of Wales. A classic steam locomotive of the Ffestiniog slate railroad takes you on a volunteer-restored narrow-gauge line. Finally, you sweep down the Conwy Valley line past Conwy Castle.

Cambrian Coast Line

Entering Wales at Machynlleth station on the Cambrian mainline from Shrewsbury (covered by the Freedom of Wales Rail Pass) aboard Central Trains (*centraltrains.co.uk*), take a second to glance at the classic stone station house. Its restoration was completed in 1996. It looks like a million dollars, and it should, for that was the cost of its restoration. Guards split your train, so be sure you are in the correct segment. Sit on the left. Once past Machynlleth you have a new feeling—less cultivation and more wilderness. The river pours into the bay. You run past vast tidelands. Waterfowl of all feather are stalking the mud flats for food; boats are aground waiting for the return of the sea. Your train runs along an embankment, through cuttings and tunnels on high ground where the sea thunders against cliffs.

Your train is slow. Welsh claim they have proof that Superman is

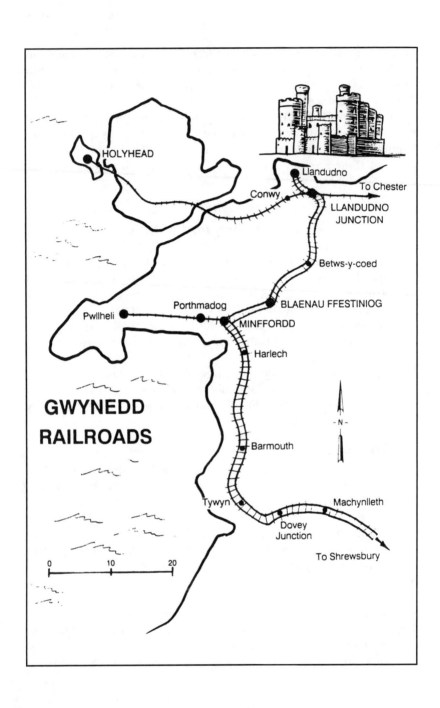

HOLYHEAD

Llandudno

Conwy

To Chester

LLANDUDNO
JUNCTION

Betws-y-coed

Porthmadog

BLAENAU FFESTINIOG

Pwllheli

MINFFORDD

Harlech

GWYNEDD
RAILROADS

- N -

Barmouth

Tywyn

Machynlleth

Dovey
Junction

To Shrewsbury

0   10   20

Welsh. "It is well known," they say, "that Superman can outrun a speeding train, and only in Wales is that possible." The panorama is great—over salt marsh and fine brown sand marked only with the footprints of fowl. Fishing boats have found the deep water channel close to shore. High stone breakwaters show how violent the sea becomes.

Just short of Tywyn station, you pass the Talyllyn Railroad Museum (*www.talylln.co.uk*). The sign reads: "Tywyn for the Talyllyn Railway." Golden Jubilee celebrations are set for 2001.

Curving high on the cliff, you swing for a memorable vast panorama of the village of Fairbourne (for the railroad of the same name). Steep rocky hills push the track right to the water's edge; you feel the power and beauty of the sea.

Stone walls, none of them straight, divide the green fields below the mountains into jigsaw pieces filled with sheep of different markings. Rhododendrons bloom profusely.

Cross Barmouth Bridge, which was restored as part of the $25 million, 1996 modernization of the Cambrian Line. Soon you see Harlech Castle, formidable on a crag 200 feet above sea level. Look back after passing Harlech for another view of this mighty thirteenth-century fortress.

Rheilffordd Ffestiniog Railroad

You debark at the two-level Minffordd station and climb steps up the narrow path to board the world's oldest railroad company, the private, steam-hauled Rheilffordd Ffestiniog Railroad (FR, *www.festrail.co.uk*), the greatest of the "Great Little Trains" (*www.whr.co.uk/gltw/*) that steam-train-lovers and adventurers use to explore Wales' normally inaccessible rich, green countryside.

When you have time to spare, board at FR's larger Harbor Station Porthmadog terminus. This gives you a chance to admire the Welsh Pony, beautifully painted and lined in the style of the 1920s atop a slate plinth, stroll along Porthmadog's sandy beaches, dine or snack in FR's station restaurant, shop in the large souvenir and model store, and enjoy FR's small museum—but the FR station is about a 15-minute walk at the opposite end of the town's main street from the town's Cambrian Coast Line station.

FR's Minffordd station is unstaffed and lonesome. It has a locked stone station house with green shutters, lonesome green benches, and that's all.

Incorporated in 1832 and operated almost continuously since 1836, the slim-gauge (one foot, 11 1/2 inches) FR stands in the record books as the oldest surviving company in the train transportation business. Now that the volunteers have renewed the operation and restored its antique steam locomotives to their original shine and vigor, FR is a point of pride for everyone of Welsh origin.

BritRail Passes are not accepted on FR, but FR honors the Freedom of Wales Pass and the North & Mid-Wales Rover valid for three days in seven, which you can buy in Britain.

You sit in first-class observation cars, with high-backed upholstered seats, or third-class 2+1 seats. FR won't let you be a second-class traveler here. (First-class tickets cost about 25 percent more.)

Your coach is small but your fellow passengers and the friendly staff give it a happy feeling. The best place to sit to see the rugged scenery is on the east, the same side as the platform at Minffordd. Elbow room is tight, but your interest is fun, not transportation, even while traveling from one end of Wales to the other by using the northern interchange with the main lines.

Your antique locomotive hisses steam and begins its 65-minute trip at Porthmadog's harbor. It runs across the "Cob," an embankment for the toll highway and the railroad across the wide estuary. Its first request stop, Boston Lodge, fenced by original FR ironwork, is the location of the foundry works responsible for maintaining—and in some cases actually building—the rolling stock.

You see the panorama of Snowdonia opening on your left. On the right, you duck your head to see Harlech Castle. Now your rattling carriage begins to tilt upwards for a narrow, tottering, almost continuous climb of one foot in every 70 you pass, sheer above the Vale of Ffestiniog and through the green Snowdonia mountain range with the Dwyryd River meandering below. You look for the pointed summit of Mount Snowdon (3,650 feet), the highest in England and Wales, barely visible in the distance. The valley below Snowdon was known as Cum Hetiau (Hat Valley) in the nineteenth century because so many train passengers lost their hats in the open carriages.

Past Minffordd, your hissing locomotive pauses to take water beside the creeper-covered stationmaster's stone house in Tan-y-bwlch, 7 1/2 miles from Porthmadog. Tracks run around three sides of the parklike bowl in the mountains.

In a few minutes your train puffs through Dduallt and then you begin a spiral—the only one in Britain. A distant nuclear power station appears on your right, on your left, and then on your right again.

Engineers abandoned the original line and built the spiral to gain elevation when the reservoir of the coming Tanygrisiau pumped-storage hydroelectric power station flooded their first tunnel. You pass through a more recent tunnel in a spur of the Moelyn Mountains before you reach the shores of the new man-made lake. Below, you see the former roadbed looking like a grass-topped wall running beside the reservoir (now a gravel highway and perfect for a hiking trail).

From the reservoir, you descend to the Tanygrisiau station, crossing first a road to the parking lot and then Wales' highest road, leading to the top dam of the power station. The automatic traffic lights flash red, the bells clang, and traffic backs up 15 car lengths, more or less. Some of the motorists take their children from the backseats to have a good view of your classic steam engine hissing past.

In Tanygrisiau look back to a mountain still covered with a shower of chips of slate. It seems more significant to you when you realize this slate is the reason for your train's existence.

It's downhill now. You pass a waterfall and wind between two-story, slate-roof houses built of the same stone as the craggy peaks around you. The calliope-like sound of your train's steam whistle announces your arrival in the joint terminus in Blaenau Ffestiniog, the slate capital of the world. It was opened virtually on FR's 150th anniversary in 1982.

The Ffestiniog steam operation dates from the grimy times when handcrafted blue-gray slates were exported around the world for fancy roofing, paving, and fencing. The Welsh slate industry employed 16,000 workers—a quarter of them in the Llechwedd mines in Blaenau Ffestiniog.

Transporting large loads of finished slates became an acute problem by the 1820s. The roads were so rocky that slate had to be first carried in wicker baskets slung over the backs of mules and then transferred to horse-drawn wagons rented from local farmers at rates the slate entrepreneurs considered exorbitant.

After the horses pulled the slates down the Vale of Ffestiniog, the slate was reloaded into small sailing boats, each manned by two men known as Philistines and dressed in tall felt hats like the gamekeepers of the day.

In 1836, management began a simple rail operation. Tracks were laid and gravity-drawn trams loaded with slate were rolled down from the quarries to a new port facility. Horses hauled the empty cars back up (and then returned by riding down in so-called "dandy cars"). Passenger transportation began in 1865, two years after the horses had been replaced by steam locomotives.

On the FR's celebration of 150 years of service in 1986, a gravity slate train was run for the first time in nearly 50 years—and stole the show.

To save the railroad, in severe disrepair in 1954, most of its shares were transferred to a charitable trust. More than 6,500 dedicated volunteers and an accomplished salaried staff turned it from near ruin into a top pleasure railroad. Any profit is returned for expansion and improvement.

There are six steam locomotives (the "Merddin Emrys" was returned in 1988 to Victorian-style service), including strange-looking "double" engines known as Fairlie Articulated. These pieces of machinery are polished, buffed, and lubricated to peak efficiency and luster. "Prince," one of the original six locomotives, restored again to a vivid recreation of an early FR livery, is again in regular passenger service. Prince's twin locomotive is the highlight of FR's museum in Porthmadog.

Today FR carries only passengers on its 13 1/2-mile route, giving you an excellent way to see the wooded Welsh countryside once ripped apart by the Industrial Revolution. A bus from the train station takes you to the Llechwedd slate caverns, Wales' largest working slate mine.

Conwy Valley Line

At Blaenau Ffestiniog interchange, cross a crooked concrete footbridge above the rail lines rather than simply changing platforms. First North Western Trains' (*www.firstnorthwestern.co.uk*) Conwy Valley Line takes you on your final segment through industrial history because of the stone quarries. You travel from the mountainous heart of the country, following the Conwy River to its estuary.

Leaving Blaenau Ffestiniog you travel through a long tunnel through the mountains. Then you follow the twisting route of the River Lledr, winding downward through rocky cuttings and under rough stone bridges.

Be sure to sit up front, behind the driver, for the excellent view down the Conwy Valley. You meet the North Wales scenic line at Llandudno Junction where you see a splendid view of the magnificent thirteenth-century Conwy Castle, which England's King Edward I built to subdue the Welsh. With walls and towers almost complete, it is one of the most spectacular examples of medieval military architecture in Britain. It was named a World Heritage Site by UNESCO in 1988.

In Llandudno, diesel InterCity high-speed First North Western and Virgin Trains will whisk you along the beautiful North Wales Coast Mainline west to Holyhead (for ferries to Ireland) or east to Chester (for London). Farther up the line, Llandudno was built to become North Wales' premier seaside resort.

Peak Ffestiniog Railway
Summer Service

Porthmadog	dep.	1025	1100	1135	1245	1345	1425	1455	1600
Minffordd	dep.	1035	1110	1145	1255	1355	1435	1505	1610
Penrhyn	dep.	1040	1115	1150	1300	1400	1440	1510	1615
Tan-y-Bwlch	dep.	1105	1140	1220	1325	1425	1500	1635	1640
Blaenau Ffestiniog	arr.	1135	....	1250	1350	1455	....	1605	1705
Blaenau Ffestiniog	dep.	1155	....	1300	1400	1510	....	1615	1730
Tan-y-Bwlch	dep.	1220	1250	1325	1425	1540	1605	1640	1755
Penrhyn	dep.	1235	1310	1340	1445	1555	1625	1700	1810
Minffordd	dep.	1250	1315	1355	1450	1610	1635	1710	1820
Porthmadog	arr.	1310	1330	1405	1510	1620	1645	1730	1835

Frequencies vary month to month, on weekends, and on holidays. Trains also call at Boston Lodge, Plas Halt, Dduallt and Tanygrisiau on request. Inform the guard when boarding. To board, signal the driver by hand.

Weekday Service
Machynlleth—Minffordd-Pwllheli

1019	..	1417	..	dep.	Birmingham	arr.	1226	1421	1623	..
1125	..	1525	..	dep.	Shrewsbury	arr.	1122	1320	1520	..
1246	..	1643	..	arr.	MACHYNLLETH	dep.	1005	1159	1404	..

1252	1427	1706	2112	dep.	MACHYNLLETH	arr.	1001	1142	1342	1659
1259	1434	1713	2119	dep.	Dovey Jct.	dep.	0955	1136	1336	1653
1311	1446	1726	2131	dep.	Aberdovey	dep.	0941	1122	1324	1639
1318	1453	1731	2137	dep.	Tywyn	dep.	0935	1116	1318	1633
1337	1511	1748	2156	dep.	Fairbourne	dep.	0915	1057	1255	1615
1346	1518	1758	2204	arr.	Barmouth	dep.	0907	1049	1247	1607
1347	1519	1759	2204	dep.	Barmouth	arr.	0906	1048	1245	1606
1410	1545	1822	2227	dep.	Harlech	dep.	0844	1027	1223	1544
1424	1559	1839	2242	dep.	MINFFORDD	dep.	0828	1010	1205	1527
1430	1604	1841	2246	dep.	Porthmadog	dep.	0824	1018	1201	1523
1453	1626	1904	2309	arr.	PWLLHELI	dep.	0800	0942	1137	1459

Dublin's Electric Odyssey
A Nice Bit of an Outin'

The Irish know that Howth is a seaside place for fishermen, Dun Laoghaire for gentry, Dalkey for artists, Killiney for lovers, and Bray for all of the above.

Visiting adventurers may not be familiar with these distinctions, but the Dublin Area Regional Transit (DART) trains make it convenient for you to explore the area around Dublin for yourself, free on an IrishRail or Eurailpass, but it is so inexpensive you will not want to use a Eurail Flexipass box. DART takes you north to Malahide and the picture-book fishing village of Howth and south along one of the most scenic stretches of coastline to Bray and Greystones. You hop on and off to visit pretty coastal towns and yacht harbors, museums, and restaurants.

Dubliners, among the most critical of people, criticized DART when it was proposed. Now that the electrified system is running flawlessly, they have taken it to their hearts and are looking forward to its extension. They discovered that it is much more than a boon to commuters or a vast technological improvement; it is an indispensable part of Dublin's transportation infrastructure and more—it has taken on the character of a leisure pursuit, giving to Dubliners and visitors "a nice bit of an outin'."

Howth (say "Hooth"; the name comes from the Scandinavian "hoved," meaning "head") is a mixture historic village, busy fishing port, and Dublin suburb. The sea gulls in Howth are the fattest in the northern hemisphere. One step out from Howth station and you smell the aroma of fresh salmon, which sells extremely reasonably.

From the summit of the Hill of Howth, 567 feet above the station at sea level, you can see Bay of Dublin, the Wicklow Mountains, and, on a clear day, the top of Mount Snowdon in Wales.

Stone buildings line the pier facing the station. Drydocked green-and-white, blue-and-brown fishing vessels are propped above the pier, workers scraping and repairing their hulls.

DART electric railcar, appropriately green, leaves Howth past heather-covered islands to the west, across mud flats busy with sea gulls, and past shacks and fishing craft in dry dock. After you glide smoothly south past the rear of Parson's steel-fabrication works, you see across the main road to the east, on the high ground, the spire of St. Mary's Church of Ireland emerging above the trees, and below, almost in the shadow of the spire, the entrance gate to Howth Castle.

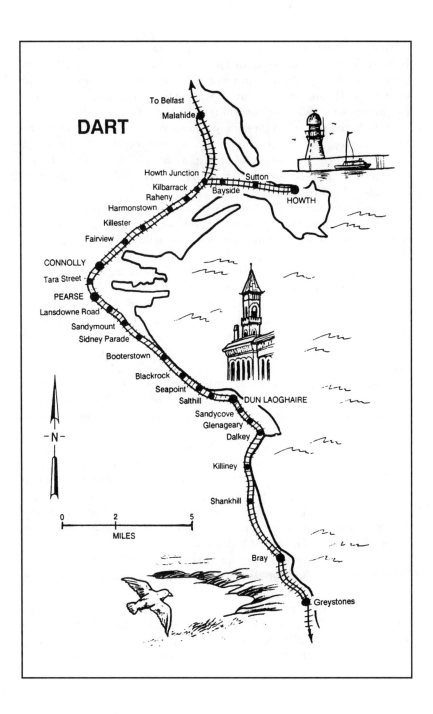

DART

To Belfast
Malahide

Howth Junction
Kilbarrack
Raheny
Harmonstown
Killester
Fairview

CONNOLLY
Tara Street
PEARSE
Lansdowne Road
Sandymount
Sidney Parade
Booterstown
Blackrock
Seapoint
Salthill
Sandycove
Glenageary
Dalkey
Killiney
Shankhill

Sutton
Bayside
HOWTH

DUN LAOGHAIRE

Bray
Greystones

- N -

0   2   5
MILES

You pass the first of at least three golf courses—just as green as all Ireland in spring. Just south of Howth, Sutton station lies at the narrowest part of the isthmus connecting Howth with the mainland. Your next stop, Howth Junction, is the joining of mainline trains from Dublin to the DART corridor south to Dublin's Connolly Station.

At Killester, you reach the famous "Skew Bridge." Built in 1843, the bridge was regarded as a triumph of engineering at the time. From here you run on the original embankment, which was entirely surrounded by water a century ago but now is all but lost amidst the ever-expanding land reclamation.

From Killester you glide south past row houses and parks. You see red-sweatered men struggling with bad weather on the golf course to the west, and shipping cranes and storage facilities in the distance to the east.

Dublin's Connolly Station, formerly known as Amiens Street Station, is Dublin's major terminus in size but not in number of passengers served. It has been transformed into a bright, functional station, with Oslo restaurant, newsstand, and ATM ("Cash Point") down the escalator. You have access to the Mainline Booking Office, the Information Bureau, the cloakroom, the cafeteria, the central bus station, and a taxi pickup in front.

DART platform 6 takes you north; platform 7 takes you south to Greystones. Enter through the gate to platform 4. Check the departure times on the standard railroad departure sheet in the Connelly ticketing hall.

When your southbound DART leaves Connolly, you glide almost noiselessly out onto the beginning of the Loop Line over Amiens Street. Take a look at the Italianate tower of the mainline terminal building facing Talbot Street and the fine old grimy and faded red-brick Victorian railroad offices with yellow brick window arches and dull-blue brick band. Inside, workers pilot the entire "space-age" computerized Central Control of today's rail system.

You pass through the rooftops past the new Irish Life Assurance building complex with golden windows. In front you see the Chariot of Life sculpture, "Look Ma, no reins!"

You travel on the elevated railroad to the stop at Tara Street Bridge over the Liffey River, but Tara Street station has no exit or entrance on Tara Street. The station opens onto George's Quay.

The stretch of the Loop Line between the Tara Street station and

Pearse Station (formerly Westland Row) is the shortest distance between any two DART stations, yet for so short a stretch you see much: the notable spire of City Quay Parish Church, the more ponderous roofline of St. Mark's, Hawkins House, the darkly tinted glass of the Irish Press newspaper office, and the distinctive 130-foot watchtower of the Tara Street fire station. Finally you pass through Trinity College. Yours may be the only train actually to run through part of a university. The Loop Line viaduct curves gently across the Botany Bay area of the university, giving you a close-up of Trinity's Parade Ground and science buildings.

You arrive on the green ironwork bridge in red-brick Pearse station with antique girders and a glass arch overhead.

From Pearse Station you reach the interesting three-span skew bridge over the Grand Canal. To the west is the tall, gaunt Guinness malt store. Originally, in 1834, planners sketched a single bridge here, but engineering problems necessitated building two, the first almost square on, and the second a genuine "skew" bridge of 33 degrees— and both so low that in later years no double-decked streetcar or bus could pass under them.

At Landsdowne Road station, sports fans depart almost beneath a modern two-tier sports stadium straddling the station and the railroad line. This is the mecca of Irish rugby and a regular site for international and European Cup soccer matches.

The annual fair in Donnybrook nearby gave a new word to the English language. Established by King John in 1204, the fair was finally abolished in 1855 because more fistfights broke out outside the bareknuckle prizefighters' rings than within.

The new DART station in the pleasant seaside village of Sandymount, one of the line's most attractive stops, stands on the site of stations dating back to 1835.

Just after Sandymount, and before you stop at Sydney Parade, you see a fine view of Gothic St. John's Church across the green grass of Monkstown Rugby Club. On a late summer evening the church's warm sand-colored stones and its ornamental windows catch the last glow of the setting sun.

Past Sydney Parade, the setting for James Joyce's short story "A Painful Case," you spring suddenly into a panoramic scene of the bay. The vista opens across the bay that Dubliners claim is lovelier than the Bay of Naples and your senses dance an Irish jig. Your railcar, like a child dashing eagerly to water's edge, runs along the sands and as close to the seabirds fishing in the waves as prudent.

Past Blackrock, you watch clammers shoveling through the mud flats, filling their red plastic buckets to the limit. The coastline is alive with windsurfers steering their colorful craft and assembling their bright-as-buttons equipment in parking lots from Blackrock to Dun Laoghaire. Yachts dance in the harbor and seawalls protect oceangoing ferries.

Passengers on the overnight Irish Mail train/boat route from London get their first taste of the DART system at Dun Laoghaire (say "Dunleary"). Buses to and from Dublin's Heuston station are also available.

Dun Laoghaire, which was first called "Dunleary" and then "Kingstown" in honor of the visit of King George IV, is primarily a sea town, the only Irish port directly administered by the government and not by locally elected officials. Between the harbor and the DART station, look for the tiny brick office marked by the green *i*, which combines the tourist information office, the "Bureau de Change," and the Stena office. New berthing facilities and passenger terminal building were constructed in 1994-95 for the arrival of the Stena HSS, the world's largest high-speed ferry.

DARTing south from Dun Laoghaire to Sandycove takes you beneath seven overpasses including three major road crossings. To complete DART, these either had to be lifted, rebuilt, and the highway approaches altered, or your train's roadbed had to be lowered by about 20 inches. As a result, you now pass over a one-mile stretch of continuously paved concrete railbed, the first in Ireland.

From your stop at Sandycove you see teams of windsurfers, canoeists, and water-skiers in Scotsman's Bay immediately outside Dun Laoghaire's east pier. Walk 15 minutes from the station to Sandycove's premier attraction, the Martello Tower, built in 1804 to withstand the Napoleonic invasion that never came.

From Dalkey's green cement station house, you, like George Bernard Shaw, see beautiful seascapes. Dogs play in waves. Anglers cast into the surf. The great playwright spent the happiest days of his youth here on Torca Hill, overlooking the splendid sweep of Bay of Dublin.

South of Dalkey, you travel on cliffs overhanging the sea. Mountains rise in the distance. At Killiney you have a chance to walk parallel to the DART line for breathtaking views, or to climb the steep lane opposite the station and in 10 minutes reach a charming district distinguished by early Irish Christian architecture. Past Killiney and Shankhill you journey inland; white row houses separate you from the ocean. You pass through the middle of a golf course. All Ireland looks like a golf course in springtime, but this is probably the only golf course with a commuter hazard.

You now approach Bray, one of Ireland's premier seaside resorts. The welcoming promontory of Bray Head stands high above the sea and Bray crowns the southern shore of Bay of Dublin.

At Bray station you see the original iron pillars bearing the logo, "Irish Engineering Co., Seville Works, 1853." "David's Diner and Market" sells fresh fruit and soft ice cream.

Bray, in County Wicklow, the only city outside County Dublin to be served by DART, is a fishing harbor, a holiday resort, a town of handsome urban architecture, an important shopping area, ... and the honeymoon capital of Ireland.

DART continues to update and enlarge its train fleet. The latest, the May 2000 delivery from the Alstom works in Barcelona, Spain, added five two-carriage railcars seating 40, and with standing room for 185. The August 2000 delivery from Tokyo in Japan added four, four-carriage electric railcars, with each carriage seating 40.

Dublin Commuter Tickets are sold for one, four, and seven days, a month, and a year. The one- and four-day tickets do not require a photocard, but have various restrictions. Seven-day tickets commence on Sundays; monthly tickets on the first of the month. Short Hop tickets are available for zone *A* and zone *B*. Medium, Long, and Giant Hop tickets extend the Short Hop tickets in three consecutively larger zones.

Benelux

Smart Traveling on the Trains of the Netherlands, Belgium, and Luxembourg

Dutch trains—Belgian trains—Luxembourgois trains—Airport trains—Getting around Amsterdam—Getting around Brussels—Railroad museums—Flower Train circuit—Channel ferry service—Using Eurailpass bonuses—Rail passes

The well-developed national railroads of the three Benelux countries make it easy for you to travel from city to city. Over "Nederlandse Spoorwegen" (NS, *www.ns.nl*) network, 1,760 miles, NS runs some 2,288 coaches (including multiple units) providing more than 135,000 seats on more than 4,300 passenger trains from 360 stations. About 1,300 of these units consist of electric railcar units (or EMUs) made up of two, three, or four carriages. Ninety-five percent are on time.

The "Societe Nationale des Chemins de Fer belge" (SNCB, *b-rail.be*), which is called "Belgische Spoorwegen" in Flemish, and the "Societe Nationale des Chemins de Fer Luxembourgois" (CFL, *www.cfl.lu*) are nearly as busy and punctual.

Nowhere do the trains run so often and so efficiently. When GermanRail officials visited the Netherlands, they said, "It is impossible to run a train system this way." The Dutch turn the trick by running primarily short, busy railcars that combine and split frequently. Their platforms are long to serve two or even three trains one after another on one track.

The Belgian railroads similarly offer frequent services on a dense network. Luxembourg, because of its size, offers inexpensive service over a nominal railroad infrastructure supplemented with buses.

Flat countrysides, dense train networks, frequent services, and short distances make it easy for you to see the Benelux nations by train. You can see any of these countries easily from wherever you make your base. You don't have to pack or unpack here.

Dutch Trains: "No Train, No Gain"

NS is an autonomous and financially independent body; however, the Dutch government finances track maintenance and construction including the Amsterdam-Antwerp high-speed line expected to be completed in 2003, and pays subsidies to NS to compensate for reduced fares for certain categories of traveler.

The Dutch railroads' network operates like one efficient rapid-transit area with international services superimposed upon it. Only trains to Germany and Belgium and InterCity Plus trains have separate locomotives. The Thalys trains described in the International chapter have matched power cars inseparable from the passenger carriages. The rest are sets of electric railcars plus a few diesel railcars connected together in twos and threes to provide high capacity, frequent service, and great flexibility. Domestic trains do not require reservations, so don't even try to make them.

You find all kinds of services listed in the NS timetable, which is for sale in the station bookstores, and the "Intercityboekje" (InterCity Summary) available free, although a timetable is scarcely necessary because of the frequent running of trains. These are:

• InterCity trains (IC) serve some 30 large and middle-sized cities. For longer stretches they are very comfortable and very fast. They run almost always half-hourly between IC stations and offer food-trolley service.

• InterRegio trains (IR) are fast trains serving some 80 stations.

• Stoptreinen (no abbreviation) stop at every windmill.

• Night train (N) carry you during the early morning hours on the crescent between Utrecht (Centraal Station) and Rotterdam (Centraal Station) with stops in Amsterdam (Centraal Station), Schiphol Airport, Leiden, The Hague (HS), and Delft.

• International trains include Thalys (abstract symbol), described in the International section; cross-border night train such as the EN Donauwalzer between Amsterdam and Vienna; and the 125-mph, OverNight Express between Amsterdam and Milan (which dates from 2000); and the German IR trains between Amsterdam and Berlin and the four ICE 3 trains between Amsterdam and Cologne, which began service in October 2000 and will be extended to Frankfurt/Main in 2002.

All bets are off during rush hours when everyone wants to get home as soon as possible. High-density trains take charge on the busiest commute corridors. Depending on the region, these trains are called "City Pendel, "Spits Pendel," or "Star Net," and replace stoptreins for this time only. These local trains carry no first-class and run eight times an hour instead of four. Passengers are not surprised to have to stand. IC and sneltreins continue business as usual.

You can travel anywhere in the Netherlands speedily by combining trains. The yellow departure timetables posted in the train stations are your key to finding your way about easily and quickly. There are usually four domestic sheets and one international sheet. Find the sheet showing your destination. The simple schematic route diagrams showing you the order of stations on your route make your planning easy.

The departure time and platform number followed by an *a* or *b* are printed beside every train's destination. Pay special attention to these letters, which refer to portions of the platform where your train boards. NS platforms are extraordinarily long in order to accommodate two or more trains at the same time. The train you want will be at the portion indicated on the timetable.

Dutch stations are generally quite easy to navigate, except that some, like Utrecht Centraal Station, The Hague Centraal Station, and Schiphol Airport Station, have attached shopping complexes which overwhelm you with an array of too many shops and too much fast food. The bright, newer stations, built in a flurry of construction, use an economical but sound construction technique—tinker-toy modern. You always find up escalators. If there are no down escalators, look for the elevator to help you get your luggage to street level. Most stations have a GWK Bank for changing money and an ATM ("Geldautomat") not far away.

Transporting one million Dutch travelers a day, it is no wonder NS is converting to double-decked trains with all deliberate speed, and with good results. The double-deckers have double the comfort of the first build of Dog's Head trains they replaced.

The Dutch used imagination creating a lexicon for their trains:

• The sentimental favorite of the NS fleet is the blue-and-yellow railcar called "Dog's Head." Its distinctive profile says it all. Most of the older build of Dog's Head trains dating from 1954(!) have been already demolished.

• Another representative animal is the "Buffel" (Buffalo), a popular new diesel railcar with 2+2 seating in first- and second-class. Its name comes from its distinctive profile.

• The pride of the NS fleet is the air-conditioned "Regiorunner," a 1995 double-decked railcar with a distinctive nose, tapered sides, striped very attractively in blue and yellow. First-class sections, above and below, are fitted with plush seats, 2+1, which recline grudgingly a few inches. Second-class sections are 2+2, and have uncommonly comfortable vinyl upholstery. You will like the good headroom, even upstairs. Incidental tables are located below the windows. All sections have linoleum flooring. A feature of the Regiorunner is the food-trolley elevator that allows the Service One catering vendor to serve both levels.

There is a second double-decker of older make, which you can identify by its flat sides and unimaginative yellow-and-blue markings, which is much less comfortable. The seats don't recline. You sit in 2+2, worsted-fabric seats, even in first class, or second-class seats that are vinyl, but more primitive than the newer double-deckers. Ventilators in the roof of the upper level provide air circulation.

• NS's IC-3 "Koploper" railcar was introduced in 1977. You recognize it miles away by its raised driver's cabin, which allows the driver a better view and ingeniously permits passengers to cross from one independent unit to another when IC-3s are coupled together. It is the 747 of the train world. You ride this 100-mph train between the Randstad (the high-population-density area stretching from Rotterdam to Amsterdam to Utrecht) and the east and north of the country.

• You can tell the Sprinter train by its beveled profile. This electric railcar set was introduced in 1975 for fast acceleration and braking so it could decrease the travel time between nearby stations.

• The 1994 electric "Railhopper" two-carriage Stoptrein with hooked nose, bulges outward in the center in order to allow five people across in second class (four in first) for short trips, but Dutch travelers, larger than the European average, protested so vigorously that the train was reseated 2+2. It is usually run in multiples connected together.

• The "Wadloper" single and two-carriage diesel railcars are second-class only and have large open areas at the ends marked for bicycles. Completely new plush seats were installed in 1997. On the exterior, units have a dark gray panel around the cab windows and a "cow-catcher."

Round-trip tickets ("Retour") are less than twice the single fare ("Enkele reis"), but valid on the day of issue only. Children under four travel free; those four to 11 for about U.S. $1.50 when accompanied by an adult over 19—limit three children per adult.

Your train ticket enables you to hire a taxi in 111 cities for a flat rate. The "Train Tax," is a clearly marked normal taxi that you share with other passengers. Its driver will transfer you from the train station to anywhere within the city limits. About 230,000 passengers a month use the service and the subsidized program, begun in 1990, now is self-sufficient. You must buy your ticket at the ticket office in the station you depart. With a rail pass, just show it when buying your train taxi ticket. When you arrive at you destination, take your computer-printed train taxi ticket to the clearly marked taxi stand. It couldn't be easier, and a bargain, too. Train taxis operate from 7 A.M. on weekdays and Saturdays and from 8 A.M. on Sundays and holidays until the last train has arrived at the station. This special service is not available in Amsterdam, Rotterdam, or The Hague because of violent hostility from the cab driver establishment.

With a train ticket or pass, you can rent a bicycle at a discount. You must provide identification and you are usually required to put down a substantial deposit. Not all stations have this service, but you bike well in the Netherlands, where there are more bicyclists than voters, bike lanes are common, and the land is flat.

Belgian Trains

The four-mile-long, six-track tunnel linking Brussels North (Nord/Noord) and South (Midi/Zuid) stations, which now forms the backbone of the almost completely electrified Belgian Railroad network, was opened in 1953, almost half a century after work on it began. International trains do not stop at Brussels Central Station, located roughly halfway along the tunnel, because Central's platforms are too short, but you can reach it easily. It is only a few minutes away by local train.

When you arrive in Belgium, get a free copy of the pocket-sized brochure "IC/IR—Treinwijs." SNCB's timetable is arranged for departures at fixed intervals, i.e., the same minute after the hour, every hour. SNCB publishes a full timetable with excellent directions in English for sale in all stations and post offices.

Belgian trains come in several different liveries, all bearing the network's distinctive B logo. You ride four categories of SNCB domestic trains. InterCity and InterRegio (IR) trains usually run hourly. IC lines are designated A through N. IR lines are labeled a through p. InterCity trains give you fast connections between major centers of Belgium and foreign terminuses. IR trains take you to more intermediate stops. Local (L) trains stop everywhere except stations where only peak trains (P-trains) stop. Peak trains are often double-deckers running at busy travel hours.

Heavy investment by SNCB is bearing fruit. You ride in the latest in electric InterCity railcars and carriages. These 100-mph railcars and coaches have individual, comfortable seats arranged 2+1 in first class and 2+2 in second. They have air-conditioning, heating, telephones, and retention toilets. SNCB claims they are the quietest in Europe. Derived from the Danish IC3s, you can recognize them by the same thick rubber seal around the whole of the front and a driver's area that can be folded sideways when two units are coupled together. The digital passenger information system is displayed both at the corridor ends inside and by doors outside.

From Brussels South station you can ride the Eurostar to London, Thalys and the Benelux train to Amsterdam, Thalys TGV-R trains to Paris, and the three-voltage Thalys to Cologne. Eurostar arrivals are timed to give good connections to the Thalys for Cologne. The EuroNight Donauwalzer takes you from Ostend through Brussels to Vienna.

When you buy an ordinary one-way or round-trip domestic ticket (including those to the airport), remember that both directions must be used on the day you buy your ticket. You may buy a ticket five days in advance, but be sure to say on what date you plan to travel. Train tickets issued to or from the "Brussels Agglomeration" are valid for connecting train travel to or from any of the 28 stations in the Brussels Capital Region. As a rule, tickets are not sold on trains, except to those who board at an unmanned train stop. If you are unable to buy a ticket, you can buy one on board, but be sure to tell the conductor before boarding that you have no ticket. If you fail to do so, a conductor may fine you 1,000 Belgian francs. A fee of 50 Belgian francs is added when a ticket is bought on the train.

Luxembourgois Trains

Luxembourg City, the Grand Duchy of Luxembourg's enchanting capital, is so well connected to the rest of Europe by train that the tourist board is tempted to call it the "Green Heart of Europe." Once there you easily explore Luxembourg's gracious mountains and valleys by CFL's extensive bus network.

Luxembourg City's modest train station is one of the few with leaded glass windows and a striking, green patina steeple. A modern wing leads to a fourth, functional east platform, completed in 1990, with bright, friendly colors and a weather-resistant Plexiglas cover. Free luggage carts stand on platforms and elevators are available to take you between platforms.

The modern leaded-glass windows picturing the profile of Luxembourg Castle dominate the interior and cast colored southern lights on the central hall. Train information is in a modern office; money change and a pleasant pub/cafeteria are opposite. Use the coin-operated lockers in the main hall. When they are filled, check your luggage with the "Consigne des Bagages" down the hall. You orient yourself with city and regional maps protected in a glass case in front of the station.

Hotels and banks for changing your money surround the Place De la Gare. Turn to your right as you exit for the bus stands where you board both the Luxair airport bus and the city buses to the airport. Past the bus stands, the Luxair terminus accommodates the information office of the Luxembourg Tourist Board. They give you a hotel brochure with prices, photos, addresses, and a map (most hotels are in a circle around the train station). "We do not make hotel recommendations, but we will telephone for you." They do, at no cost, according to your selection from the brochure, but everything closes tightly from noon to 2 P.M. for lunch.

Make Luxembourg City your base. Like a star, five lines with two electrical systems converge here. Luxembourg lies on the mainline of the Swiss Brussels-Namur-Luxembourg-Metz-Strasbourg-Basel route, which carries the EC Vauban on to Milan. You travel by EC Le Mosellan and EC Victor Hugo to Paris's Est station, and you can board in Luxembourg the overnight train between Cologne and the south of France and Spain.

Electrification of the "Ligne du Nord" or "Nord-Streck," the Northern line, was completed in 1993, completing electrification of CFL's 171-mile network (except for two short stretches), and with the completion of the electrification of Belgium's Liege-Luxembourg line in summer 2000, you ride trains formed of CFL electric locomotives and SNCB carriages between Liege and Luxembourg.

As Luxembourg is such a small country, international traffic is of great importance. The most frequent service is to and from Brussels, usually hourly semifast trains integrated into the Belgian InterCity network. Travelers to France pass through Thionville to Metz and then onward to Paris' Gare de l'Est or Basel via Strasbourg. InterRegio trains take you along the Wasserbillig route to Trier, Germany, and then Koblenz. In addition, two-carriage Regional Express railcars operate hourly to Trier. While you are in Wasserbillig, note the Mosel River flowing behind the station. You can see German trains on the opposite bank.

Airport Trains

When you arrive by air in Benelux, you have it easy.

Schiphol is one of the two best train airports in Europe because of its mainline connections completed in 1986. Schiphol station was extended from three to six platform tracks in 2000 to cope with traffic growth. InterCity and EuroCity trains take you from Amsterdam's airport without change to Berlin, Germany, and Groningen and Leeuwarden in northern Netherlands. Thalys takes you without change to Brussels and Paris, and with a change to Eurostar in Brussels, all the way to London, thus giving you a way to reach all of northern Europe.

Seven train an hour whiz you north to Amsterdam's Central station, so you won't have to wait over 13 minutes and might need to wait only six. Travel time is 19 minutes. Trains south to Leiden take 19 minutes; to The Hague's Centraal station take 29-40 minutes, and 45 minutes to Rotterdam Centraal.

Schiphol Airport has been enlarged and transformed into something of a shopping mall, but follow the signs showing the profile of a train that does not much resemble a train at all. You must use your imagination. These signs lead you to the train station hall. In the large hall (past the Burger King) devoted to railroad functions, you see the NS Reisburo (travel bureau) and clearly marked counters for international and domestic (Netherlands/Belgium) ticketing. "Vertrek/Aankomst Departures/Arrivals" directions are printed on backlit yellow posters and country maps. Current departures are shown on video displays. Moving walkways lead you to the platforms below.

SNCB's three-carriage electric trains with the large red-and-blue "Brussels Airport Express" letters on the sides take you between Belgium's National Airport at Zaventem and Brussels' three downtown train stations. They are covered by rail passes. Between 5:24 A.M. and 11:46 P.M., three trains an hour connect the airport with Brussels' North, Central, and South stations and hourly with Schaerbeck station. Allow 12 minutes to reach Schaerbeck, 17 to North, 22 to Central and 25 to South stations. Hourly trains travel to Ghent.

Riders going to Brussels' airport find departure times and platform numbers on the large departure signs. From the Central Station, look for the signs "Bruxelles National-Aeroport/Brussel Nationaal-Luchthaven" and an airplane pictograph pointing to Track A, across the subterranean station from all the rest.

The Brussels Airport Express's stop at South station allows you to make rapid connections for Paris, Amsterdam, and Cologne. Sabena buses run hourly from National Airport to Antwerp (Crest Hotel and Centrum) and Ghent (Kouter and St. Pieters station).

You can validate your rail pass, buy tickets to major Belgian cities— as well as Paris—and make international reservations at the Belgian Railroads' ticket office in the customs hall at the airport. To get from the customs hall to train platforms, simply follow the signs, "Airport City Express."

You have two choices for travel between Luxembourg's Findel Airport and train station. Most take the blue-and-white Luxair bus leaving every 30 minutes from the front of the airport terminal. Others walk across the airport's small parking lot to the yellow sign marking the bus stop for Luxembourg city bus line 9, which departs every 15 minutes during the week, hourly on Sundays and costs about one-fifth that of the airport bus. The city bus takes about 10 minutes longer to the train station but you can get off near many hotels and the youth hostel.

Getting around Amsterdam

There are four offices of the Amsterdam tourist office ("VVV") to help you with hotel reservations for the day you arrive and coming days, in Amsterdam and for the rest of the Netherlands. They are located:
- on Stationsplein, the square facing Amsterdam Central Station (open daily 9 A.M. to 5 P.M.),
- near Leidseplein, the popular gathering point reached by street-cars 1, 2 and 5 (open daily 8:30 A.M. to 8 P.M.),
- on Stadionsplein, near the Olympic Stadium in Amsterdam's out-skirts (open Mon.-Sat. 9 A.M. to 5 P.M. and Sun. 9 A.M. to noon), and
- in the Central Station itself, track two.

The Holland Tourist Information Board has an office at Schiphol Airport (open daily 9 A.M. to 10 P.M.).

The tourist office personnel also will give you information on every sort of activity, including visiting museums, shopping, dining, making excursions, and attending the theater, opera or ballet.

You are fortunate that Amsterdam has an excellent public transportation system. Bigger and better, Belgian-built, blue-and-white streetcars with padded seats forge farther and farther into the suburbs. There are 17 streetcar lines (five originate in front of Central station), 30 bus lines, and four metro lines plus eight night bus lines. The new red, white, and blue Sneltrams (fast streetcars) of metro Line 51 run between Central, Amstel, Duivendrecht, RAI, South, and Amstelveen stations, which are equipped with twin-level platforms.

Circle tram 20 is just what the name indicates. Tram 20 makes a round-trip through Amsterdam in both directions, and its route was chosen to take you past almost all tourist attractions. You don't have to change streetcars, you can stay seated until you come to the museum, square, or monument you want to visit, or you can use Circle-tram for a minisightseeing trip. The streetcar rides every 10 minutes from 9 A.M. to 7 P.M. The last streetcar leaves from Central Station at 6 P.M.

Streetcars on most lines require you to enter the back door, where there may or may not be a seated inspector to check your ticket. Strip-tickets are the cheapest and most convenient way to ride streetcars and buses, rather than day or multiday passes, because you can use strip-tickets whenever you need to over a period of days. A strip-ticket is just what it says—a long card divided into horizontal strips. You are permitted to travel on one validation throughout the entire central city—the large zone that includes everywhere you are likely to go—for an hour including transfers between streetcar lines, buses, and the metro. Thus you can make a short trip and return all within an hour using only one validation. If there is an inspector aboard, he or she will stamp your strip card according to your destination. If not, for your first trip, fold the card on the line between strips one and two. Stamp strip number two by pushing it (strip side down) into the slot of one of the squat yellow stamping machines inside the streetcar. Wait for the "ping!" sound.

You can buy 15-box tickets (two boxes equal one trip in one zone) at machines in the train stations ("Nationale Strippen Kaart"). The correct code to order strip cards is "2-2-2-2." You can also buy them at the white "GVB" transport office opposite Amsterdam's Central Station, at a city information (VVV) office, or at any post office. Streetcar drivers are allowed to sell day tickets, one-hour tickets, and two-, three- and eight-strip strip tickets, except on Line 5, where there are ticketing machines (with directions in English) located in the middle. You won't have any trouble with these machines so long as you pick your zone before putting in your money.

Unless you plan to spend a day riding public transportation or traveling to and from Amsterdam's suburbs, strip-tickets are cheaper and more flexible than the Circle-Amsterdam ticket, which is valid day and night for up to nine days. Consider strip-tickets as national currency. Use them for transportation not only on Amsterdam's public transportation, but for transportation in all of the Netherlands' major cities and even on NS trains for local transportation.

Getting around Brussels

Use Central Station (Gare Centrale/Centraal Station, Brussels is bilingual French/Flemish) as your entrance to Brussels because of its location. Remodeled in 1991, it is bright and airy with metro connections. Walk five minutes downhill past convenient hotels toward the town hall's spire to the Grande Place. Belgium's tourist information office, for hotel bookings and abundant information, is one block north, at 61, rue du Marche aux Herbes (open 9 A.M. to 8 P.M. June-September and to 6 P.M. in winter) or use the smaller tourist information office located in the city hall (the magnificent building dominating the west side—open 9 A.M. to 6 P.M.; closed Sunday during the winter).

You can get around Brussels using the integrated network of metro, streetcar and bus lines on a single ticket (or validation of a multiride card), which allows you an hour's unlimited travel. Several companies that use letters to identify their routes provide inter-urban bus service. You will need to refer to the network maps and schedules displayed in metro stations and at most stops. Pick up a free pocket map and ("Transports Publics/Openbaar Vervoeror") schedule booklet at the transit authority's information offices in the South train station, Rogier, and Porte de Nemur metro stations. The green line (Line 3) connects the North and South train stations. At the stop "De Brouckere," you change to the red line (Line 1) for the Central and Schuman stations.

Brussels' Central station is most used as a commuter station serving downtown Brussels and the Grand Place. A statue of a train worker represents the 3,012 workers killed for the fatherland during the wars of 1914-18 and 1940-44. The "Vertrek/Depart" electronic departures board is next to the "Consigne/Bewaring" luggage check counter.

The train information office in the North train station (Gare du Nord/Noordstation) is located in the departures hall. Nearby is a change bank and pubs where beer flows freely, but the brightest is the "Taverne Edelweiss" in the subway section, where food is presentably served. There is also a waiting room in the underground passage between the entrances to tracks 9 and 10. You also board railcars to Brussels' Zavendem Airport here from various platforms shown on the yellow departure signs.

Brussels' South station (Gare du Midi/Zuidstation) consists of one long departure hall with escalators to and from the platforms above. Most passengers enter and leave the station via the connecting Brussels metro station (with both orange and green lines) where they pass the money exchange (Change/Wissel) office. SNCB's "Travel Centre" (open 6 A.M. to 10 P.M.) begins at the escalator leading to platform 10. Their agents accept bank credit cards for payment.

For hotel and tourist information and reservations, look for the hotel *i* sign. Electronic departure signs above the track entrances ensure that you board the correct train. Be aware that two sets of train arrival and departure sheets are posted. One set provides the times for Monday to Friday departures and arrivals. The second set is valid on Saturdays, Sundays and holidays (read: "Zaterdag, zondag/Samedi, dimanche"). The post office is next door.

South station's new, enclosed Eurostar arena stretches off to the right (as you depart). It is modern. Changing between Eurostar, Thalys, or conventional trains at Brussels' South station is very easy. Platform one is used for Eurostar arrivals from London; platform two for departures. Brussels South has sparkling, improved Thalys platforms, but the domestic platforms need work.

Railroad Museums

The Netherlands Railroad Museum in Utrecht was remodeled for the 150th anniversary celebrations of NS in 1989. The train Expo has gone, but the museum remains, much the richer for the anniversary. It inherited some of the specially refurbished equipment and one of the most entertaining train films you will see, called Cadans, for "cadence," the rhythmic clickety-clack that trains make, but the museum's rolling stock has been stored away from climatic influences that night cause rusting, until the museum's upgrading is completed in 2004.

You can reach it by a short walk to the south from the exit of Utrecht's modern, innovative Central Station.

SNCB's Railroad Museum is a much smaller version, admission free, that train enthusiasts will enjoy despite explanations in Flemish and French only. It is clearly marked by arrows in the railroad (not the metro) portion of Brussels' Gare du Nord. Its central feature is the astonishing "Land of Wales," built 1842-47 in Brussels, a narrow-gauge steam train that ran between Antwerp and Ghent. Visitors see exhibits of every sort including signaling, types of rail, sleepers, etc.

The Railroad Museum in Schepdaal, Belgium (open 2-6 P.M., Sundays and holidays from April to mid-October and on Saturdays in July and August), about 10 miles from Brussels, is housed in an old tram depot, which opened in 1887 for steam trains on the Brussels-Schepdaal route. It features steam locomotives, a fuel tram, two-axled electric trams and postwar vehicles.

Flower Train Circuit

NS devised a one-day Flower Train itinerary for the many visitors to the Netherlands enchanted with the floral beauty brightening the low country. It begins and ends in Amsterdam's Central station, but you have the freedom to join at any point along NS's dense network.

From Amsterdam Central the stretch to Haarlem takes you over the oldest railroad section of the Netherlands (1839), and you see vivid contrasts between old and new. You pass old warehouses and the seventeenth-century harbor area; on your right, a bird preserve. Parallel to the track on the left runs the Haarlemmer Trekwaart, a commercial canal dug in the seventeenth century.

Past the lake to your south, Haarlemmermeer, the railroad and canal suddenly come close together. The last of a medieval peat polder unfolds on the north. Past the highway you see the Roman church towers of Spaarnwoude, situated on the most easterly part of an old beach wall. A little farther you cross the water of De Liede, and farther on you pass an elegant series of windmills. Entering Haarlem, you see on your left the somber nineteenth-century prison and the medieval Amsterdamse Poort. Haarlem's 1908 station is a showcase of Art Nouveau. Look at the tile tableaus or visit the first-class restaurant.

The train from Haarlem takes you down the length of the bulb-growing area. The most beautiful time to visit here is April and May, when the view of the bulb fields is absolutely breathtaking with unexpected combinations of bright colors. You enter the bulb-growing area at the village of Vogelenzang, which is situated exactly on the edge of the inner sand dune and the geest (the sandy soil between the dunes and the polder). About three miles farther is the former station of Lisse on the left and the world-famous De Keukenhof, the greatest tulip and bulb show in the world during the spring. You can reach it by bus from Haarlem and Leiden stations. (A NS day trip covers this excursion; see "Doing Your Own Thing," below.) Flower lovers will visit the Hortus Botanicus in Leiden.

Entering The Hague, capital of the Netherlands, a long strip of private market gardens and sports fields extends along both sides of the track deep into the city. Flower lovers will take a walk to the Clingendael.

After changing trains in Hague Central Station (CS) (do not confuse with Hague NS station) you zigzag easterly through the green heart of Holland where narrow, straight fields lie parallel to silver lines of canals. Just before Zoetermeer you see on your right the site of the 1991 Floriade exhibition. Past Zoetermeer Oost station, you cross the Rotte River, which is high above surrounding land. On your right you see a line of four fine windmills constructed in the eighteenth century to reclaim a peat bog. The Tweemanspolder is almost 15 feet below sea level.

At Gouda station change to the train taking you through

Waddinxveen station and past Boskoop, the nursery center of Dutch trees. Immediately after leaving the station you see a view of the tree nurseries.

At Alphen aan de Rijn change to the train up the Oude Rijn to Utrecht, crossing the river about a mile past Woerden. Farther on the left the towers of the nineteenth-century castle "De Haar" rise above the forest.

Returning from Utrecht to Amsterdam you pass through woods, hills, and the forested area of "Het Gooi" southeast of Amsterdam.

Channel Ferry Service

With cross-channel traffic siphoned away by the Eurotunnel, ferry crossings of the English Channel have been decelerated. Still, times are competitive with Eurostar from the Netherlands and if you find yourself near a port, you may avoid the roundabout trip by using the ferries between Hook of Holland and Harwich, Vlissingen and Sheerness, or Ostend and Dover.

Crossing the English Channel by steamship is certainly one of the most pleasant, or miserable, events of your European vacation. You avoid the roundabout train trip and airport terminuses but face possible boredom or foul weather. It can be great fun or a horror best forgotten. Look for special, all-inclusive, bargain offers at the train and tourism offices when you visit Amsterdam, Brussels, or London.

To reach London from Amsterdam, ride Stena Line's SeaCat catamaran service via Hook of Holland to Harwich, where you can take the train to London's Liverpool Street station. The transfer at Hook of Holland is easy because moving walkways and luggage carts help you from train to boat. There are four crossings per day which take four hours and carry up to 1,000 passengers. Eurailpass and Europass holders receive a 30 percent discount.

Using Eurailpass Bonuses

Eurailpasses and Europasses with the Benelux add-on cover not only unlimited train transportation over the three networks, but on NS' sea-green, cross-country "Interline" buses in the Netherlands and railroad buses in Belgium and Luxembourg. Simply show your pass to the driver.

You can make a number of excursions through Luxembourg's delightful countryside into quaint villages aboard CFL's tan coaches striped with burgundy red. Because you use your rail pass, you visit the same sights as the tour buses without cost. Your bus calls at all small villages, enabling you to see the detail of the landscape and get on and off as you wish to explore.

You receive a 30 percent reduction on the full fares of the Stena Line crossing between Hoek van Holland and Harwich.

Rail Passes

The railroads of Benelux cooperate on a regional rail pass called the Benelux Tourrail. This gives you unlimited travel on the trains of SNCB, NS, CFL, and the bus lines in Luxembourg. You also receive more than a 25 percent discount on Panorama-Tours' city tour in Brussels and at the Antwerp Zoo, which is located next to Antwerp's Central station. It is also a good buy because you can use it to buy discounted tickets on Eurostar trains between Brussels and London. Holders pay about 75 percent for first-class Eurostar tickets and about 65 percent for second class, but have to validate their Benelux Tourrail before the trip.

A flexipass, the Benelux Tourrail is valid for travel on any five days of your choosing within a month. The Tourrail is a single coupon, computer-printed on ticket stock with spaces for five travel days ("Reisdag"). Date the spaces as you travel.

Buy them in the U.S. before departure, or in Europe at the larger train stations and many travel agencies in the Benelux countries. When two adults travel together, the second person pays only half. Second-class passes are about one-third less expensive than first-class ones. Those between four and 25 buy a second-class Benelux Junior Tourrail for another one-third off.

You save a lot of green with passes on the yellow NS trains, especially during June, July, and August with the "Summer Tour" described below.

The Holland Rail Pass is available for three or five travel days within a month, either first or second class for unlimited travel on the entire NS network and on specially marked Interliner buses saving time between stations. A second adult pays half the adult fare. Travelers over 60 receive a 20 percent discount either first or second class, and those under 26 receive a 20 percent discount on second-class passes only.

For a single day's unlimited travel, you can buy a "Dagkaart." In conjunction with this pass you do well buying an "OV Dagkaart," Public Transport Link, to give yourself unlimited travel on all the public streetcars, city and regional buses throughout the Netherlands and on the Amsterdam subway—a convenient and economical advantage. NS saves its best bargains for sale in the Netherlands only during July and August. A special version of Holland Rail Pass called "Summer Tour Rover" ("Zomertoer") allows one or two persons traveling together to travel three days within 10, second class only. Single travelers save about one-third compared to a normal three-day Holland Rail Pass and two traveling together save half. You can upgrade these tickets to include a linked, "Zomertoer Plus," ticket for buses, metros and trams.

Finally, in the Netherlands, there is a "Maandnetkaart" which allows you to travel for a month on NS.

SNCB offers first- and second-class B-Tourrail passer similar to Benelux Tourrail, but valid for travel five days in one month in Belgium only. You buy these in Belgian francs at Belgian train stations for about 60 percent of the cost of a comparable Benelux Tourrail. They are not available in the U.S.

In Luxembourg you can buy a day pass for unlimited first-class travel on CFL for about $3.50. You can cover the entire CFL network in 12 hours with proper planning. Ask for an "Oeko-Billjee Letzebuerg." A booklet of five tickets is available for the price of four. The ticket is also valid on all bus services including CFL, Luxembourg city buses (AVL), TICE, and RGTR, which is a grouping of CFL buses and about 20 private operators. Don't forget to validate your tickets using the validating machine on the platform.

The Luxembourg Card is available for one, two, or three days, covering travel as above, but adding free admission to 32 tourist attractions and providing reduced admission fees on others. The Luxembourg Card costs about $7.50 for one day. Families receive reductions.

Travel through the Benelux countries by boat across the Netherlands' Zuider Zee, aboard the Benelux Train between Amsterdam and Brussels, aboard Europe's lowest train, spend a day in the Ardennes, and discover the low countries with discounted Dutch and Belgian day trips.

Around the Zuider Zee
Tamed Sea and Steam

Have you ever wanted to sail across the Netherlands' Zuider Zee (nowadays known as the Ijsselmeer)? Crossing this inland sea is

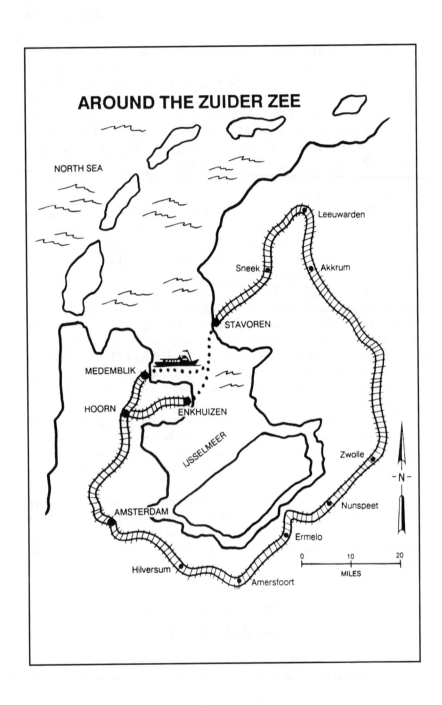

AROUND THE ZUIDER ZEE

NORTH SEA

Leeuwarden

Sneek

Akkrum

STAVOREN

MEDEMBLIK

HOORN

ENKHUIZEN

IJSSELMEER

Zwolle

Nunspeet

AMSTERDAM

Ermelo

Hilversum

Amersfoort

- N -

0   10   20

MILES

smooth as Dutch peanut butter. When your train arrives in Stavoren, the *Bep Glasius* is unloading passengers and a line of bicyclists is forming to wheel their "feetsers" onto its deck. The full fare is only about $6. Ask for your rail pass discount.

The *Bep Glasius* is primarily a pleasure boat. Those without bicycles have backpacks.

The Netherlands has no rugged Alps or ragged fjords. Its charm lies in its tamed sea and in the fertile, flat farmlands crisscrossed with canals.

A one-day round trip through the north of the Netherlands, across the Ijsselmeer, and south through West Friesland, samples the pleasing scenery of this low country. Plan your departure from Amsterdam for an early hour so you have time to cross the Ijsselmeer and browse leisurely through the open-air Zuider Zee Museum in Enkhuizen.

Tamed Sea

Be sure you board the appropriate segment of your yellow-and-blue InterCity train at Amsterdam's Central station. It divides in Zwolle. One half goes to Groningen. You want to be in the half marked "Leeuwarden."

On its run to Leeuwarden your train makes very few stops. Your first, after 20 minutes, is in the 1992 station in Hilversum, the headquarters for Dutch radio. Your second (after another 12 minutes) is in Amersfoort, the junction for trains coming from Hook of Holland and Rotterdam. By the time you stop in Zwolle, where your train splits, you are entering Friesland, the land of cows, cheese, and tall, blond people.

Your train proceeds as a local. By the time you approach Akkrum, the land is appealing. Broad fields are peppered with black-and-white cows. You pass ribbonlike, calm canals busy with pleasure motor yachts, sailboats, and barges.

After waiting almost a half-hour in the white-brick Leeuwarden station (you can lunch in the station restaurant or hire a bicycle), you board a second-class-only, lime green-livery "Wadloper" diesel train for a 49-minute run to Stavoren. NS does not operate this train. It is operated by NoordNed (meaning Network North), one of the regional train operating companies that assumed money-losing routes of NS in 1999. The driver revs its motor like an old Ford, and—clickety-clack—off you go down the single-track line, past sheep, cows, and horses.

Some farms have black, glazed-tile roofs. This is a region of intensive farming. Of course, one of the hazards of traveling by train

206 TRAVELING EUROPE'S TRAINS

through farm country is that the windows will be lowered and farmers will be fertilizing.

Herons stand sentry in stagnant, water-filled ditches. Most passengers get off at Sneek. The farmhouses have acre-size red-tile roofs enveloping everything down to the first floor.

The canal running adjacent to your train is packed with small pleasure boats when you reach Workum. You often see curious sights along the tracks. Here you see a stack of bundled thatches for thatching roofs.

From the end of the line at Stavoren, cross the bricked plaza to the VVV office to buy your ticket, and show your rail pass for a discount. The 12-mph *Bep Glasius*, a 300-passenger ship built by Peters' Scheepsbouw in 1966, crosses the Ijsselmeer only in summer. Aboard, you buy sandwiches and fabulous Dutch fast food such as French-fried potatoes and split pea soup in the luncheon area below deck.

From the deck you see a crazy, kaleidoscopic world of fantasy sails and ships: sailboats, cabin cruisers, schooners, very daring windsurfers, huge barges, Chinese junks, Singaporean bum boats with eyes painted on them, and dark masted fishing vessels that look like they might be manned by pirates. About halfway, you are met by a fleet of kayaks.

The afterdeck becomes one huge parking place for fully laden bicycles. After an hour, you finally view the profile of Enkhuizen—the city hall and church.

When you land at one of Rederij NACO's three slips (the others take you to Urk and Medemblik) after your one and three-quarter hour crossing, you are greeted with the rare contrasting scene of the train station with a train and boat unloading passengers at the same time. Have your camera ready.

This area of West Friesland is interesting for its seafaring tradition. West Friesian ships sailed the world's oceans from Enkhuizen, Medemblik, and Hoorn (say "Hoor'n") to trade with faraway countries.

Enkhuizen is lined with the old seawall that used to protect the city from storms on the former Zuider Zee, ending at the Old Harbor where you see traditional sailing vessels, the fishing fleet, and numerous yachts. Beyond the seawall is the "living" Zuider Zee Museum, showcasing preserved fishing village homes, and giving you a remarkable picture of the life and work of the people of the region who depended on this inland sea until 1932 when the Barrier Dam sealed the Zuider Zee from the North Sea.

From your landing near the train station, walk five minutes to the boat quay for your boat ride to the Zuider Zee showcase.

Leave the open-air museum on foot, pass through the town proper, and walk back to the train station in order to see the West Church and the South Church and to photograph the old fortified tower named "Drommedaris."

At the brick Enkhuizen station house you rejoin the electrified lines of NS. It takes you slightly less than an hour to reach Amsterdam Central station by half-hourly double-decker Stoptrein—but while you're here, travel the Historic Triangle.

Typical Round Trip
Crossing Zuider Zee

1106	arr.	Amersfoort	arr.	1724
1034	dep.	Amsterdam (CS)	arr.	1759
1146	arr.	Zwolle	arr.	1640
1208	arr.	Meppel	arr.	1623
1256	arr.	Leeuwarden	dep.	1536
1322	dep.	Leeuwarden	arr.	1507
1342	arr.	Sneek	arr.	1443
1411	arr.	Stavoren	dep.	1414
1415	dep.	Stavoren	arr.	1405
1600	arr.	Enkhuizen	dep.	1245
1607	dep.	Enkhuizen	arr.	1223
1714	arr.	Amsterdam (CS)	dep.	1119

Daily Rederij NACO Service
May to September

0845 1245 1645	dep.	Enkhuizen	arr.	1200 1600 1935
| | |	arr.	Zuider Zee Museum	arr.	1130 | |
1005 1405 1805	arr.	Stavoren	dep.	1015 1415 1815

Historic Triangle

Steam-enthusiast volunteers come from all over the Netherlands to donate their time freely so you can travel on the 12-mile, 1887 line from Medemblik to Hoorn (the namesake for Africa's Cape Horn). The restored steam locomotive "Bello," built in 1914, and the blue loco "Sluiskil" pull an excursion train comprised of classic Austrian-built coaches.

This is the same Rail Idee as an NS day tour (see the "Doing Your Own Thing" section below), but with a rail pass you save money because you don't pay for the NS transportation to and from Enkhuizen and Hoorn.

• Begin your excursion in Enkhuizen by boarding the boat for Medemblik at the quay.

• When you would rather begin in Hoorn, take the IC train from Amsterdam to Hoorn's 1991 brick NS station house. Immediately cross the metal overpass to the small "Stoom Trein" building. The red-brick station house, with yellow-brick striping and a Spanish tile roof, is a museum in itself—filled with train memorabilia. Beds of flowers (tulips in the spring) surround the "P + R" (park and ride) parking lot. At trackside is the entrance to the museum workshop.

At Medemblik, you can visit the Dutch Steam Engine Museum (admission: about $2, adults; $1, children; plus a $1 surcharge on dates when the engines are working).

Most of your train trip back to Amsterdam from Hoorn takes you through lovely farmland: lovely because it is flat and fertile; lovely because colorful flowers are grown for sale. Shortly after Zaandam's bright, new station you see the shipping and shipbuilding on Amsterdam Harbor. Your final stop before Amsterdam's Central Station, at Amsterdam's futuristic 1986 Sloterdijk station, is interesting because it serves cross traffic in two directions from two levels. The train to Schiphol Airport leaves at right angles from the upper platform.

Volunteer Steam Train and Boat Services
Early April to Late October

(2)	(4)	(6)	(8)			(1)	(3)	(5)	(7)
1045			1430	dep. Enkhuizen	arr.	1400			1745
			1445	dep. Zuider Zee	arr.	1345			
1200			1600	arr. Medemblik	dep.	1230			1630
1245	1420	1525	1615	dep. Medemblik	arr.	1205	1325	1440	1520
1255	1430	1535	1625	dep. Opperdoes	dep.	1155	1315	1430	1510
1300	1450	1540	1630	dep. Twisk	dep.	1150	1310	1425	1505
1305	1500	1545	1635	dep. Midwoud	dep.	1150	1305	1415	1500
1325	1520	1605	1655	dep. Wognum	dep.	1145	1240	1350	1440
1335	1530	1615	1705	dep. Zwang	dep.	1115	1230	1340	1430
1340	1535	1620	1710	dep. Wester blocker	dep.	1110	1225	1325	1425
1345	1540	1625	1715	arr. Hoorn	dep.	1105	1220	1320	1420

All services do not run daily. Generally, services 1 and 2 run daily. Services 7 and 8 run daily except Tue.-Fri. during May, June, and Sept. During July and August, services 3 and 4 run Tue.-Thurs. and 5 and 6 run Wed. and Sun.

Amsterdam-Brussels-Paris
High Speed in the Low Lands

You travel at the highest possible speed to and from the Netherlands and Belgium aboard the version of the French TGV named "Thalys." You stop at only the main stations between Amsterdam and Paris, and you pay a significant supplement to ride it. When you want to get off or on at one of the midsize stations bypassed by Thalys between Amsterdam and Brussels, and save money at the same time, use the International Benelux train that supplements travel between these popular cities and takes 18 minutes longer. The Benelux train is available, without supplement or reservation, to rail pass holders. Thalys is your choice to Paris.

Benelux Train

From Amsterdam Central, you depart, not pulled by a locomotive in front, but pushed, by the locomotive in back. The driver controls from a special compartment in the front of the train.

Between Amsterdam's Central station, Schiphol Airport, Rotterdam, The Hague, Antwerp, and Brussels, you ride the Benelux Train—the namesake of the Benelux countries. The Belgian locomotives and Dutch carriages are painted in a shared, single livery—a combination of the NS yellow and the Bordeaux red of the Belgian railroads.

It is an impressive train: no-nonsense, comfortable, and most convenient for you to ride. It departs hourly, free without supplement to holders of Eurailpasses, Europasses with the Benelux add-on, and Benelux Tourrail passes. Reservations are not required.

You sit in orange-plush 2+1 first-class seats that recline a few inches when you press the orange armrest release; they have sturdy, fold-down tables in their backs. You look through panoramic windows that partially roll down—something you appreciate after riding sealed, high-speed trains. A clouded-glass partition separates smoking and

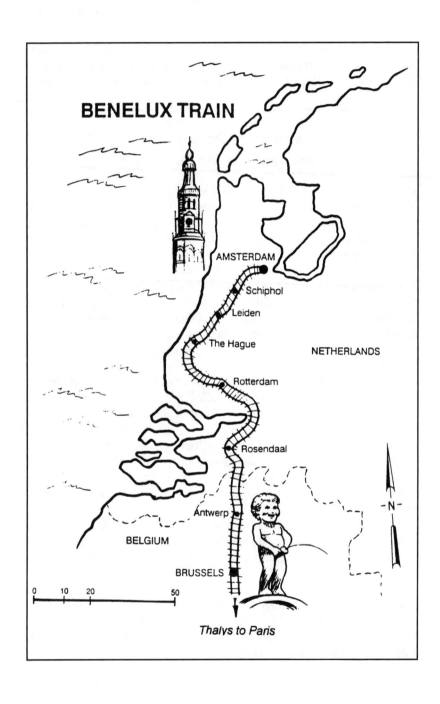

BENELUX TRAIN

AMSTERDAM
Schiphol
Leiden
The Hague
NETHERLANDS
Rotterdam

Rosendaal

Antwerp
BELGIUM
-N-

BRUSSELS

0 10 20   50

Thalys to Paris

nonsmoking sections. The interior doors open with a press of the lever. One first-class car is half compartments, half salon style; one contains a telephone booth; and one has a special compartment for bicycles. Linoleum floors and jet-type blowers for ventilation are used throughout.

Take a good look at the doors on this train. They are of a special Dutch design that quickly flies open into two halves to make it easier for you to get on and off faster—and are a boon to all those Dutch travelers bringing their bicycles with them.

Leaving Amsterdam's Central station (CS), you travel first over old track, then over new—past the futuristic elevated stop at Amsterdam-Sloterdijk. After a quick stop at the new Amsterdam-Lelylaan station (accessible by city streetcar line No. 1), you hear the announcement booming over the loudspeaker: "Next station: Schiphol." Out of Schiphol, employees of Service One, an enthusiastic Dutch firm, push refreshment trolleys down your train's aisle. They wear Bordeaux-red jackets to match their train's livery.

About half an hour south of Amsterdam you pull to a stop beside Leiden's brick station house. In 1989 President George Bush visited this university city and cited Leiden as a special city, a place where Americans trace their origins—where the pilgrims came to escape persecution and Rembrandt lived and worked.

Between Leiden and The Hague you see the changeover from dunes to peat polders while your train passes through one of the most densely populated areas of the Netherlands. Just out of Leiden, you cross the Oude Rijn ("Old Rhine"), which is now a branch of the Rhine, but in the Roman and early-medieval ages, it was the main current. Past Leiden-De Vink station, the broad polder unfolds on your right.

Out of Rotterdam CS you pass the Rotterdam Blaak station opened by Her Majesty the Queen Beatrix on September 15, 1993, wearing an NS-blue-and-yellow dress. Then you enter the new 1.74-mile Willemspoor Tunnel under the Meuse River that replaced the Meuse Bridge, part of which has been preserved as a monument to Rotterdam's World War II survivors. The tunnel consists of eight parts, each weighing 25,000 tons. At its lowest point you are 50 feet below the water level of Amsterdam.

In Dordrecht, a charming center on the Merwede River with canals and spectacularly preserved facades, you will enjoy visiting the Great Church or Church of Our Lady and climbing the tower (Tuesday to

212 TRAVELING EUROPE'S TRAINS

Saturday, 10:30 A.M. to 4:30 P.M., during the summer). The station was fitted with escalators in 1996. From Dordrecht, you cross the steel-girder Moerdijk bridge, the longest rail bridge in the Netherlands. At the red-brick Roosendaal station house, the border crossing, you see a whole carnival of NS equipment, including double-deckers—some blue-painted—on different tracks.

It is a shame you bypass Antwerp's 1905 grand Centraal Station, which was nicely spruced up for visitors to Antwerp's 1993 Cultural Capital of Europe celebrations. Antwerpians ("Signors") call Centraal Station the "Railway Cathedral." The ornaments and crests were regilded and the marble polished, but now your Benelux train has been diverted and you can expect dirt and dislocation while a third subterranean level is being added to permit through running of high-speed trains between Paris and Amsterdam. It's a large, ornate, beau-tifully classic station with direct access to the Zoo next door. Adjacent to Centraal is an access to Antwerp's efficient streetcar network, "Station Diamant," named for the gem quarter nearby.

Your first stop in Belgium, Berchem, is used by Thalys trains that must bypass Centraal because, until the new platforms are opened, it is not a through station and costs time. Although Berchem lies in Antwerp's sub-urbs, this is where you alight for Antwerp until Centraal is reopened.

When you enter the Belgian capital city's environs, before reaching Brussels' North station, you see to the west the giant aluminum Atomium representing a molecule of iron magnified 200 million times, symbol of the 1958 Brussels' World's Fair. In the same glimpse you see the first of Brussels' many Gothic churches.

Brussels' North station is a remodeled and expanded CCN ("Communication Center North") combining train, metro, bus, and airport connections. It's Brussels' biggest, and includes the Belgian Railroad's Train Museum as well.

When the Benelux Train leaves the North station, it tunnels under-ground to Brussels' Central station, an underground station built on the side of a hill so that its entrance is at street level. It is quite like a busy subway stop, and likely your best bet to alight in the Belgian capital.

Continuing south from Brussels' Central station, your Benelux Train emerges into the sunlight at Brussels' Chapelle station, bypassed by express trains, and you see Brussels' Palais de Justice to the east before the driver brakes your Benelux Train for the end of the line, Brussels' South station, and your connection for Eurostar to London or Thalys to Cologne.

Sample Benelux Train Service

1025	dep.	AMSTERDAM (CS)	arr.	1438
1041	arr.	Schiphol Airp.	arr.	1422
1058	arr.	Leiden	arr.	1405
1103	arr.	The Hague (HS)	arr.	1358
1121	arr.	Rotterdam (CS)	arr.	1339
1138	arr.	Dordrecht	arr.	1323
1203	arr.	Roosendaal	arr.	1253
1223	arr.	Berchem	arr.	1235
1250	arr.	Mechelen	arr.	1208
1309	arr.	BRUSSELS (N)	arr.	1149
1314	arr.	BRUSSELS (C)	arr.	1145
1318	arr.	BRUSSELS (S)	dep.	1143

Benelux trains depart daily, hourly, at the same minute after the hour from Amsterdam Central Station from 6:25 a.m. to 8:25 p.m. and from Brussels South Station from 6:43 a.m. to 9:43 p.m.

Amsterdam-Flevoland
Europe's Lowest Train

Weesp is your last chance to admire a traditional Dutch village in the old land. You leave Weesp's needlelike church spires and traditional drawbridge and head into the Netherlands' new land. You have no feeling you are traveling 20 feet below sea level on Europe's lowest open-air train line (the Channel Tunnel, of course, is even lower).

You would be thrilled to look up and see an oceangoing ship passing on the way up the Rhine River, but everything you see is perfectly natural. Fish swim in sub-sea-level canals. Rabbits scamper in negative-elevation fields. Unconcerned cows amble with full udders. And new cities grow larger brick by brick as you travel through the Flevoland, the reclaimed plot of land which once lay below the Zuider Zee.

This is an interesting discovery not because of the scenery, but because it shows you the magnitude of Dutch determination, and success, in reclaiming fertile land from the sea.

Of the 30-mile Flevoline, you travel over 25 miles of land newly reclaimed from the sea and descend from a high point of 50 feet above sea level to 20 feet below. Between Amsterdam and Almere, your first stop in the Flevoland, you cross more than 100 bridges.

The Dutch have been winning battles over the sea for centuries. It is a part of their history and an essential element in their country's security and prosperity. Their story's crowning glory is the Zuider Zee project—the draining of more than 616,730 acres of sea; the creation of land in five polders. Three of these—the North East Polder (the oldest, dry for 55 years), East Flevoland, and South Flevoland (the newest, dry for 30 years)—now make up the new province of Flevoland, northeast of Amsterdam. The provincial capital, Lelystad, is only some 63 miles by train from Amsterdam.

You have a great deal of luxury choosing your train through the Flevoland. From Amsterdam, take a streetcar to Amsterdam's Central Station, look on the yellow departure billboards for "Lelystad C," and ride an escalator to your correct platform. Sneltreins leave every 30 minutes, and in addition, twice-hourly sneltrein departures take you to Weesp where you can change to a stoptrein to Lelystad. The trains of NS' choice are the older, less comfortable double-deckers.

From Amsterdam's CS, your sneltrein first passes Amsterdam's Muiderpoort station, one of the many satellite stations still in Amsterdam city, which in fact you also can reach easily by streetcar. From Muiderpoort, you pass a small part of Amsterdam's harbor sheltering many small Dutch naval vessels, industry, and then a private marina.

Before your train slows for your stoptrein's next stop, you see cows of all colors: brown, black-and-white, fawn. The fields are broad and green and the superhighways you pass have eight or more lanes and are blacktopped.

Shortly before Weesp, you cross over a canal with heavy shipping. Below, a red Belgian fishing vessel cuts under the bridge. On one side of the train you see the black needlelike church spire of Weesp and modern apartment blocks of brown brick which are so common in the Netherlands, and on the other, across from the village, grazing land for more cows. Alternate sneltreins stop at Weesp's open-air station for passengers for villages along the line to change to a stoptrein. On departure you pass on your right the only windmills you will see. They aren't large and they aren't rotating, but they are adjoined by several thatched-roof houses.

In Weesp, you also leave the main rail line leading on toward Amersfoort and then to Germany. Traveling on the diverging rails you see IC trains and a GermanRail train connecting Amsterdam's Schiphol Airport with Hanover.

On May 21, 1993, Queen Beatrix inaugurated Amsterdam's southern ring connection between Amsterdam's RAI convention hall station and Weesp, which created a short-cut between Lelystad and Schiphol Airport and is now served by half-hourly trains. You just as easily board a train to Lelystad at the RAI station as at Amsterdam Centraal, whichever is more convenient. These trains connect with the Lelystad-Amsterdam CS trains at Weesp.

Your train enters Flevoland when water opens on your left and then your right and you cross a causeway parallel to the main highway. This is part of the ring of water left circling the Flevoland, connected to the Markermeer, the remaining southern body of water from the pre-existing Zuider Zee ("Meer" means "lake," "Zee" means "sea").

Flevoland is very grassy and flat, with farmers furrowing their fields with tractors. Past Almere Muziekwijk station you can read "1987" embedded in the concrete.

While your conductor is announcing Almere Centrum station you see an ultramodern steeple to your right, apartment blocks everywhere, and canals. This is the new land.

Almere Centrum, a stop for both stoptreins and sneltreins, is covered with red tinker-toy struts to support the plastic and plaster covering. You realize the extent to which this is a planned city. Everything you see is modern, blocky, and space-saving, but not crowded. From all appearances, it is a comfortable place to live.

You stop at Almere Buiten station, where a city is still abuilding. The station is already in place. Your train skims above the flat furrowed fields and rows of trees acting as windbreaks. You see no windmills. In fact, you travel a long way with no distinctive feature except for green acres and fields checkered with golden cylinders of rolled-up hay and the brown leavings of the wheat harvest.

Past Almere, woods of fast-growing trees have already appeared. At last, you see Lelystad in the distance, not so much as a soaring Oz at the end of a yellow brick road, but as a low accumulation of efficient three- and four-story apartment buildings mixed with industrial buildings of so many Dutch and international companies that it appears there has been a financial incentive to build here.

Lelystad Centrum's surprisingly spacious, spick-and-span, and uncluttered train station has a "Het Station Petit Restaurant." Inside is a brass plaque marking its opening in 1988 by the queen, a GWK bank and ATM machine, ticketing, bookstore, secure bicycle stand, and bright flower shop—all the amenities that the Dutch consider necessary for a full-service station.

End-of-the-line Lelystad Centrum is like all the new NS stations circling Amsterdam. They feature bright blues, reds, greens, and yellows. These flamboyant colors make the architecturally exciting stations fresh.

Sample Sneltrein Timetable
Amsterdam-Flevoland

1007	dep.	AMSTERDAM (Centraal)	arr.	1456
1027	dep.	Almere (Centrum)	dep.	1434
1033	dep.	Almere Buiten	dep.	1429
1045	arr.	Lelystad (Centrum)	dep.	1417

Through Sneltreins depart Amsterdam (CS) daily, half-hourly, at the same time past the hour from 7:07 a.m. to 12:17 a.m.; from Lelystad (Centrum) through Sneltreins depart daily from 5:56 a.m. to 12:17 a.m.

A Day in the Ardennes
Battle of the Bulge

An excursion through the back rails of the Ardennes forest, where the Battle of the Bulge raged, to Bastogne takes you on so many changes of train that it seems like a relay marathon. It is not for those with heavy luggage, just for those seeking pleasure.

Begin your train relay by pushing the button to open the door of the InterCity train on the route Brussels-Namur-Luxembourg. Your InterCity train originates in Ghent, arrives in Brussels' South station at 40 minutes past the hour, every hour, and then calls at Brussels-Central, Brussels-Nord with its outdoors platforms, Brussels-Schuman, and then Brussels-Luxembourg, which corresponds to the district where it is situated.

A woman conductor wearing a bulky blue sweater and meter-maid cap with SNCB insignia checks your train ticket, Benelux or Belgian Tourrail Pass, or Eurailpass.

Speeding along the mainline, you reach Namur, known to Flemish speakers as Namen, via Ottignies and Gembloux on the River Orneau. Namur, the largest city of your route, is the capital of Wallonia at the confluence of the Rivers Sambre and Meuse. Dominating Namur is the Citadel, which houses a Weapons and a Forest Museum. There are beautiful churches in the center, the famous Rue des Brasseurs pedestrian area, and the museum Felicien Rops.

Continuing, shift to the right side of the train to admire the coming stretch of idyllic scenery. After only 10 minutes, your IC leaves and takes you along the banks of the Meuse to Dinant parallel to the river on the right. Nowhere is the Meuse more beautiful and better suited to visitors than in the Namur region, where it is joined by numerous rivers and streams. Abbeys are almost as commonplace as castles. The old brick-and-stone villages, the rocks, and the fortresses all form a permanent pageant on the banks of a river that continues peacefully and romantically on its way.

You see wonderful luxurious landscapes with views of the Meuse on the right. You see tiled-roof vacation homes mixed with ancient stone buildings that are worn and still sturdy after resisting centuries.

You pass Godinne standing on a meander of the Meuse. Its old center dates from the seventeenth century, and you see old farms, half-timbered houses, and a Spanish-style castle. The area is soft and amiable. You pass frequent locks on the Meuse, which is channeled and controlled.

Yvoir is perhaps the most charming of all the Meuse region summer resorts, set among woods and rocks, with its island accessible by ferry. The ruins of Poilvache Castle, one of the largest in the county, overlook the Meuse.

Dinant is the prettiest of all the Meuse's daughters according to Victor Hugo. It's the queen of tourism for the region. Its modern train station is happily sited just across the Meuse from the formidable Citadel fortress 325 feet above the river (besieged 17 times) and the riverbank Collegiate Church with an onion dome. The fortress flies a yellow, red, and black Belgian flag at full mast.

Now you have a choice. You can either take the return IC train to Namur and continue by IC train to Libramont for Bastogne, or you can board the SNCB bus to Bertrix for a pastoral bus ride following highways to Libramont. Although it is a bus, it is assigned an SNCB train number and is free on your rail pass. Boarding the bus, sit on the left for views of the Meuse and fantastic rock formations.

Your route leaves the Meuse at Anseremme to follow the smaller, wilder Lesse. The most popular stop is Houyet, which is a busy trailer and camping site. You know you are in wild, vacation country when you see kayakers splashing along the eight-mile segment from Houyet to Anseremme on the River Lesse. The Lesse is tip-to-toe with blue, yellow, and red plastic kayaks.

Past Houyet your bus takes you through quiet farmland toward Beauraing, known to Christians by the frequent appearance of the Virgin Mary between 1932 and 1933. It is now a place of pilgrimage with a museum dedicated to the Virgin.

After Pondrome's brick station house, you reach the River Wimbe and the country becomes hilly and wooded. On the upper plateau of Orchimote, villages become widely scattered and less important. You pass relatively obscure Voneche, which shows evidence of Ardennes logging by the spruce logs piled high, but neatly. Gedinne is a large, characteristic village with church and nearby ski slopes. After Gedinne the trees thin, the land becomes flatter, farming takes over, and cows become conspicuously fat.

Through this remote district, at Paliseul, you cross the major highway with trucks hauling much lumber along the main route south to France. Approaching Bertrix, the houses become stone, two stories tall, and surrounded by fields of corn.

From Bertrix continue by bus seven miles to Libramont. Libramont is a larger station lying on the mainline between Luxembourg and Brussels so that international trains come screaming through without stop. When you chose to take the easier way, you will arrive in Libramont by IC train after returning to Namur.

At Libramont, around July 21, there is the largest agricultural show in Belgium with more than 100,000 visitors. It features demonstrations and trials of the last Ardennes cart horses, which are exported worldwide and were used by Julius Caesar's legionnaires and during Napoleon's Russian campaign.

For your final segment, from Libramont to Bastogne, you must board a bus. Again, this is an SNCB bus, so your driver accepts your rail pass without question. The farming country becomes mixed with increasingly dense woods: the Ardennes.

Bastogne has two train stations: north and south. Bastogne-Sud is brownstone with red brick piping. Bastogne-Nord is relatively new. Both are about equidistant from the city center, but Sud may be more convenient, and is the first stop for your bus.

Bastogne has gone down in history as the center of the terrible Von Rundstedt offensive in the winter of 1944-45, which marked the start of the Allies' final advance. It was during the Battle of the Bulge that General McAuliffe pronounced the resounding "Nuts!" to the call for his surrender.

Standing at the crossroads of the Ardennes, Bastogne still bears vivid reminders of this bloody episode. The most moving place is Mardasson Hill and its memorial to the 77,000 American soldiers killed during the battle.

Mosaics by Fernand Leger decorate the crypt containing three places of worship (Catholic, Protestant, and Jewish).

Illustrating the battle, the Bastogne Historical Center on the same hill is built in the shape of a five-pointed star. Everywhere in the town and its vicinity are memorials to the terrible winter: a Sherman tank and monument, a bust of McAuliffe on McAuliffe Square (where the tourist office is located), and one of the "freedom milestones" along the way taken by American troops from Normandy.

Because of the constant hustle and bustle (there are 300 shops open every Sunday), Bastogne was nicknamed "Paris in Ardennes" as far back as the seventeenth century. Other sights worth seeing include St. Peter's Church and Trier's Gate, and the Mathelin House (open 10 A.M. to noon, and 1 to 5 P.M., Tue.-Sun. during July and August).

From Bastogne, return by bus to Libramont and change to one of the hourly, fast InterCity trains back to Brussels (two hours to Brussels South), or travel east to Luxembourg.

A Day in the Ardennes

0944	dep.	BRUSSELS (South)	arr.	2121
0948	dep.	Brussels (Central)	arr.	2117
0951	arr.	Brussels (North)	arr.	2113
0953	dep.	Brussels (North)	arr.	2112
1001	dep.	Brussels (Schuman)	arr.	2104
1005	dep.	Brussels (Luxembourg)	arr.	2100
1021	dep.	Ottignies	dep.	2046
1031	dep.	Gembloux	dep.	2035
1042	arr.	NAMUR	dep.	2022
1047	dep.	NAMUR	arr.	2017
1051	dep.	Jambes			
1100	dep.	Lustin			
1103	dep.	Godinne			
1108	dep.	Yvoir			
1115	arr.	DINANT			
1027	dep.	DINANT (train)			
1155	arr.	Namur			

| 1224 | dep. | Namur (train) | | \| |
| 1324 | arr. | Libramont | dep. | 1917 |

| 1330 | dep. | Libramont (bus) | arr. | 1912 |
| 1405 | arr. | Bastogne (Sud) | dep. | 1837 |

\| = Does not travel this route

Doing Your Own Thing
Dutch Treats and Belgian Bargains

Netherlands by day. Amsterdam by night. Both NS and SNCB have arranged for you to maximize your pleasure and minimize your cost.

Netherlands is world famous for friendly, gregarious people, windmills, tulips and wooden shoes. Amsterdam is famous for great museums and above all, party time. Almost every visitor chooses Amsterdam. Does this tell you something about the average tourist? You can use Amsterdam as a base for exploring the Netherlands or you can use the Netherlands as a base for exploring Amsterdam. It's as easy either way with the NS' "Er op Uit!" (*www.ns.nl/er-op-uit!/*) discount tickets that apply in either direction so that you can stay in such delightful cities as Leiden and Utrecht and still see Amsterdam's museums and other attractions.

The two railroads offer you well-conceived, economical, independent day trips to let you see their small, exciting countries by train, learn about their complex customs and history, and come to understand their ways of life. All-inclusive tickets cover all the best things to see in the Netherlands and Belgium. You go sightseeing for a low all-inclusive price and save in three ways. You receive reductions on train trips, you pay reduced fares for bus and streetcar connections, and you get discounted entrance fees.

Buy individual day-trip tickets (called "Rail Idee" in the Netherlands, these are not the same as the day cards described earlier) at any train station ticket office. These include your round-trip train journey (originating where you wish), the price of the attraction, connecting bus or streetcar fare, and sometimes coffee and cake. You travel independently, receive a substantial discount, know the total cost in advance, and determine your departure times yourself.

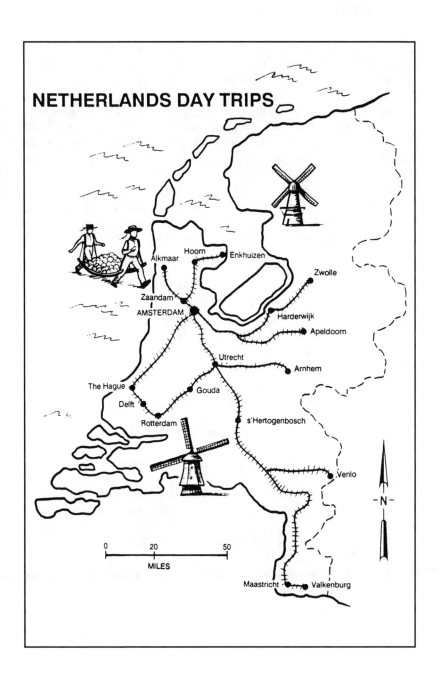

NETHERLANDS DAY TRIPS

Alkmaar
Hoorn
Enkhuizen
Zwolle
Zaandam
AMSTERDAM
Harderwijk
Apeldoorn
Utrecht
Arnhem
The Hague
Gouda
Delft
Rotterdam
s'Hertogenbosch
Venlo
Maastricht
Valkenburg

- N -

0   20   50

MILES

If you already have a special train ticket such as a Benelux Tourrail or Eurailpass, use it for the train journey and buy an "Attraction Ticket" ("Attracktiekaartje") at your departure or arrival station. An Attraction Ticket gives you the benefit of the railroads' planning and discount and lets you see the same day trip you select but without paying for the train. The money you save on day-trip tickets won't in itself justify buying a Eurailpass or using up a flexipass box, however. To spend as little as possible, plan your itinerary to take these day trips before you validate your rail pass or after it expires.

NS's program of more than a hundred Rail Idees is set out in the Dutch-language booklet, "Er op Uit," which is sold at ticket offices at stations and from NS's information offices. Selected Rail Idees are given in some of NS's free literature such as the brochure, "Exploring Holland by Train." The complete collection of Belgian day trips is presented in free brochures available in Belgian stations. Ask for "B-Excursions" (in French) or "B-Dagtrips" (in Flemish).

To gain a thorough impression of the Dutch way of life, modern and past, take day trips to Rotterdam, Arnhem, Enkhuizen, The Hague, Volendam and Marken, Zaandam, and Maastricht. Rail fans enjoy Utrecht's Railroad Museum and enthralling music box and barrel organ museum (as who wouldn't?) and the volunteer steam train between Hoorn and Medemblik.

The day trips offered by the Belgian Railroads include city sightseeing, zoos, museums, leisure parks, boat excursions, gastronomic meals, and lots more. Visit Antwerp, Brussels, Brugge, Ghent, the Belgian Coast and the Ardennes Forest, Liege, the River Lesse, Bastogne, and the Mariembourg "Three Valleys" steam train and use the day-trip scheme as a vehicle to make excursions into adjacent countries as well.

You buy domestic Belgian day-trip tickets in every Belgian station— at every ticket counter. The agent simply enters the code number in a computer. Day-trip tickets to international destinations are sold at international stations (North, South, and Central, in Brussels).

In Rotterdam, you sail in a motor launch from Willemsplein Quay for a round trip through the city's large, modern port complex. You climb the "Space Tower" in a glass-enclosed lift winding slowly up and around Euromast's steel extension to the very top of the television tower. Your ticket includes the train ride to Rotterdam, the round trip of the harbor, admission to the Euromast and Space Tower, and a day Rail Ranger ticket for the subway, bus, and tram.

In Enkhuizen, visit the preserved Zuider Zee houses and travel by ferry from Enkhuizen's train station to the Zuider Zee Museum and return. Your ticket includes the train, the ferry, and admission to the museum.

At Monnickendam, board the "Marken Express" boat to the Island of Marken, see the cottages built on piles in the IJssel lake, dams, dikes, and fishing boats with colored sails, and then continue by boat to Volendam. Your ticket includes the train, bus, and Marken Express boat.

The scale-model town of the new Madurodam in The Hague shows you how classic Dutch architecture looks to birds with broad wings. Then you visit Scheveningen, one of the Dutch people's favorite seaside resorts with a pier and sea pool. Your ticket includes the train, admissions to Madurodam and Scheveningen Pier, and a day Rail Ranger ticket.

Curators of Arnhem's Open-Air Museum carefully gathered, rebuilt, furnished, and preserved a magnificent collection of complete farms, houses, cottages, and windmills so you can appreciate how the Dutch used to live. Your ticket includes the train, the museum bus, admission, and a Dutch pancake with coffee.

In Zaandam you see the 1948 village called Zaanse Schans, an open-air museum of seventeenth-century houses and windmills. You visit the Windmill Museum to see how windmills work and cruise on the river Zaan. Your ticket includes the train, a brochure, admission to the Windmill Museum, the river cruise, and a Dutch pancake with coffee.

Another day trip is a walking tour of Maastricht to magnificent churches, historic public buildings, city walls, period houses, and Roman ruins. You cruise on the river Meuse (Maas). Your ticket includes the train, the river cruise, a grotto tour, admission to St. Servaas Church, and coffee with a Limburg open fruit pie.

When you have determined what dates you are going to be in the Netherlands, take out your pencil and note some of the following attractions. Seasonal events are some of the most interesting.

• Keukenhof Lisse—Between the end of March and the end of May tulips are in full bloom.

• Kaasmarkt Alkmaar—On Fridays only from the middle of April until the middle of September, board the "Kaasmarkt Express" from Amsterdam to Alkmaar for the colorful cheese market.

• Westfriese Markten—On Thursdays only from the end of June

until the end of August, in Schagen's market you can enjoy a folkloric color pageant with dancing and music.

• Hoornsemarkt—On Wednesdays only from the beginning of July until the end of August, ride to Hoorn to see the 600-year-old town present the famous old-time Dutch market and bring the medieval guilds of trade and artisans back to life. Don't miss visiting also the Friesian Museum in front of the market.

• Kaasmarkt Gouda—On Thursday mornings only from the end of June to the end of August, take the train to the Gouda cheese market in the interesting city that gave the cheese its name.

Selected Schedule of NS Day Trips

• Amsterdam, city exploration
• Amsterdam, Jewish Historical Museum
• Amsterdam, Rijksmuseum and canal cruise
• Apeldoorn Paleis Het Loo, House of Orange royal palace
• Arnhem Open-Air Museum
• Burgers Zoo and Safari Park
• Delft, city exploration
• Efteling, country's top amusement park
• Enkhuizen, Zuider Zee Museum
• Historic triangle by steam train and boat
• Kroller-Muller Museum, De Hoge Veluwe nature reserve
• Maastricht, boat trip and grottoes
• Rotterdam, city exploration or boat tour
• Scheveningen Sea Life Center
• Stavoren-Enkhuizen boat trip plus Zuider Zee Museum
• The Hague, city exploration
• The Hague, Madurodam
• Utrecht Railroad Museum
• Valkenburg
• Zaanse Schans open-air museum

Selected Schedule of SNCB Day Trips

• Antwerp, Zoo
• Antwerp, round trip of the port
• Antwerp, boat excursion on the Schelde River
• Bokrijk open-air museum
• Brugge, boat trip through the canals

- Brugge, boat trip on the Damme River
- Brugge, visit to York, England
- Brussels, Atomium
- Eupen tourist train
- Ghent, city and museum explorations
- Ghent, boat trip
- Han-sur-Lesse, grottoes
- Hasselt, city tour
- Knokke, butterfly garden
- Lesse River, kayak trip
- Liege, city tour
- Meuse River, Dinant, with Citadel
- Meuse River, Namur
- Meuse River, boat trip Dinant-Namur
- Maredsous, abbey visit
- Ostend, boat trip
- Yvoir, butterfly center and nature oasis
- Zeebrugge, round trip of the port

Switzerland

Smart Traveling on the Trains of Switzerland

Swiss tilting—Airport trains—Zurich S-Bahn—Swiss Pass— Using Eurailpass and Europass bonuses—Regional passes

In 1847, the Spanisch-Brotli-Bahn (Spanish bread-roll railroad— Spanish Brotli are an old pastry specialty of Baden) began the history of the Swiss Federal Railroads (SBB) by puffing from Baden to Zurich for the first time. In the four-language confederation, the railroad has Web pages in four languages, *www.rail.ch* for English, although English is not one of the four Swiss languages, *www.sbb.ch* in German, *www.cff.ch* in French, and *www.ffs.ch* in Italian.

In 2000, SBB completed, for the most part, its extensive and expensive commitment to introduce new rolling stock, including tilting and double-decked trains, improve travel time with new track and tunnels, and provide on-time, regular-interval departures as often as quarter-hourly on the most heavily traveled routes.

The Swiss are proud of their train network. Their trains are best, according to travelers' votes. The trains give you unsurpassed views of the Alpine country and take you places automobiles can't. The trains' punctuality, impeccable maintenance, helpful personnel (who often speak English), comfort and cleanliness, and service to the tiniest and most colorful villages make Switzerland come close to being a train travelers' kingdom and certainly Swiss travelers are kings. It's said that you can get anywhere in Switzerland by train. That's quite untrue. Switzerland has 3,600 incorporated communities but only 1,900 train stations. Yet, buses, ships, cable cars, and trams make Switzerland so accessible that half of all Swiss households live within a kilometer (0.6 miles) of a train station, and 97 percent of all Swiss households live within a kilometer of public transportation. Every Swiss makes 48 train trips a year and covers more than 1,100 miles on average over the 9,000 miles of train, boat, and postal bus routes comprising the Swiss Travel System. This high usage is due not only to ecological considerations, but to the proximity of stations. It makes the Swiss the European leaders in train travel.

Keeping track of the Swiss train companies is like tabulating a can of alphabet soup. The Swiss Federal Railroads has nine initials and four Web sites—three initials for each of the three largest language groups: SBB (Schweizerische Bundesbahnen) for the German-speaking region, CFF (Chemins de Fer Federaux Suisses) for the French, FFS (Ferrovie Federali Svizzere) for the Italian, and Web sites for each, plus English. Coaches carry all three designations but you'll see "SBB" in this book. Nearly a hundred additional companies operating private railroad lines, funiculars, ships, and cable cars with their particular initials in one or more languages are combined into the integrated Swiss Travel System with dovetailed timetables and coordinated connections. All schedules are posted for you to see in every station, posted on the Web, and grouped into a single official timetable ("Indicateur," "Kursbuch," "Orario"), which for your convenience is revised only once a year at the beginning of June in two volumes, one for trains (with summer and winter supplements for international connections) and one for buses.

SBB has three kinds of domestic trains: InterCity (IC), InterRegio (IR), and Regio Express (RX). New class 2000 locomotives pull SBB's IC train fleet at the fastest speed on the Swiss network, 143 mph, over the seven-mile stretch between Martigny and Riddes. When you ride them you find they are utilitarian but not flashy. New double-decked ("bilevel") ICs carry you on the route between Zurich and Lucerne. Every IC carries a "silent compartment" where cellular telephones and portable stereos are banned.

InterCity trains carry sit-down restaurant carriages with white linens, tables for two or four, waiters in white jackets, and excellent cuisine catered by local companies. "Le Buffet Suisse" carriages characterized by a band of violet around the windows and a diagonal swathe across the kitchen area specialize in cafe grills and dishes such as spaghetti. The Glacier Express has a particularly famous dining car, but more of that below. In the "Fromage Express," a dining car made up to look like Gruyere cheese traveling daily on the Basel-Bern-Lotschberg-Brig line, you can enjoy fondue, raclette, or cheese plates in cooperation with the Switzerland Cheese Association (reservations free through Minibuffet AG, Bern, Tel. 031-22-21-91). The splashy, red-and-white McDonald's dining cars (with no exterior arches) have been converted into shops run by Coop-Railshop and are used on the Zurich-Bern route.

EuroCity trains take you to and across Switzerland, which, because of its location, is a crossroads of Europe and, because of its beauty, is a popular destination. EuroCity trains include SBB air-conditioned salon carriages built in 1990-91 for use on 125-mph routes to Munich, Paris, Prague, Stuttgart, Milan, Brussels, Ventimiglia, and the Netherlands.

On EuroCity trains to and from Switzerland, SBB runs a number of first-class-only panoramic cars with raised floors and deep windows that curve to shrink the roof to about four feet across. It is possible for you to ride in these "Panoramawagen" between Switzerland and Austria or Italy on the EC Canaletto between Zurich and Venice, the EC Transalpin between Basel and Vienna, and to France on the IC Riviera dei Fiori between Basel and Nice via Milano. When you travel first class on these routes, be sure to use these trains and specify reservations in the Panoramawagen.

Switzerland is the only country where you see so many kinds of high-speed trains. French TGVs from Paris arrive in Bern, Lausanne, Geneva, and Zurich. Two GermanRail ICE trains from Hamburg via Frankfurt/Main pass through Basel, and run right into Zurich's Hauptbahnhof. The ICE Thunersee runs between Kiel and Interlaken's East station. Cisalpino ETR 470 tilting trains connect Geneva, Basel and Zurich with Milan. Both Cisalpino and GermanRail ICE T trains cruise between Stuttgart and Zurich, and the two night trains, CityNightLine and EuroNight (see "International" section) both serve Zurich.

Except for the scenic express trains and international Cisalpino trains to Milan, reservations are not obligatory in Switzerland, but they are available on most Swiss InterCity trains. When you reserve on these trains, one of the first-class carriages may be marked *R* where the reserved seats are located. Unmarked first-class carriages are open to all first-class ticket holders.

When you trace the outline of Switzerland on a map, it's all bulges and squeezed-out extrusions. Vertically, it's even tougher. You find few straightaways because the Swiss network through the Alps is built to circumvent the high Alpine peaks. This makes it ideal terrain for tilting trains. In addition to sampling the five routes described here, you'll enjoy riding the Cisalpino trains described in the International chapter on the Gotthard route between Zurich and Lugano. Slow-train attractions include the 1994 Panorama car on the Brunig line (*www.breunig.ch*) between Lucerne and Interlaken (which is SBB's only narrow-gauge line); the narrow-gauge Rhaetian Railroads, (RhB, *www.rhb.ch*) connections to Arosa, Scuol, and other mountain resorts; the 1996 Mont Blanc Express between Martigny in Switzerland and St-Gervais in France; and the modern blue-and-white electric railcars of the Centovalli line between Locarno and Domodossola, mostly on Italian soil but covered by the Swiss Pass described below. At 11 major stations of RhB in the mountainous canton of Graubunden, you can rent scooters (*Trottinett*), ride them downhill over country paths and quiet roads, and return them at the next RhB station. Cost is $7 per half day.

Swiss Tilting

Switzerland's Intercity-Neigezug (ICNs, Intercity Tilting Trains) introduced on May 28, 2000, are named in honor of famous Swiss citizens. Le Corbusier was an architect, Germaine de Stael, an author, and Heinrich Pestalozzi an educator and founder of the Red Cross.

At maximum speed of 137 mph, these trains take the curves very smartly. With the timetable change in 2001, tilting trains began cutting travel times by 15 minutes between eastern and western Switzerland via Biel on the so-called Jura Foot line, which carries you along the route St. Gallen, Zurich Hauptbahnhof, Biel (called Bienne in French), Lausanne, and Geneva. Future service between Geneva and Basel is on the drawing boards.

Each of the 24 ICNs is composed of seven comfortable but uninspired carriages equipped with air-conditioning, passenger information systems, wheelchair spaces, and retention toilets. They have 113 seats in first class plus 12 in first-class business, 326 seats in second class, and 23 in the dining carriage. In addition to the restaurant, first-class passengers can enjoy at-seat service. Reservations are not possible except in first-class business.

New Tilting Train Service

0843 1043 1743 1943	dep.	St. Gallen	arr.	0819 1019 1719 1919
1006 1206 1906 2106	dep.	Zurich (Hbf)	arr.	0710 0854 1610 1754
1140 —— 2040 ——	dep.	Biel/Bienne	dep.	0520 —— 1427 ——
1249 1449 2149 2349	arr.	Lausanne	dep.	—— 0610 1310 1510

Airport Trains

You find it very convenient to use SBB's excellent airport trains in Zurich and Geneva. Stations at both airports are integrated into the Swiss railroad network by long-distance IC trains not only to city centers but also directly to international destinations. At Zurich and Geneva airports, first stop by train information *i* to have your Swiss Pass, Europass, or Eurailpass validated. Arriving at Zurich's Kloten Airport, proceed via escalators (direction: "Bahn/Railway") using the escalator-friendly luggage carts. At Geneva, you merely push your cart across to the adjacent train terminus to catch your train.

The Zurich Tourist Office in Kloten airport is located in terminal B for tourist information, hotel reservations and streetcar tickets (open daily from 10 A.M. to 7 P.M.).

Departing Zurich Hauptbahnhof, look for the airplane symbol for the trains serving Kloten. Some are ICs, some are express trains, and some are double-decked S-Bahn (rapid-transit) trains. The through trains make getting to Zurich airport from long distances easy. The S-Bahn trains make getting to Zurich airport from anywhere in canton Zurich as easy as conceivable because you don't have to go through Zurich Hauptbahnhof.

Because of the convenience of the air/train connections, most airlines (excepting U.S. carriers) allow you to check in with your luggage and receive your boarding pass in advance at 24 Swiss railroad stations. When you reach Zurich or Geneva airport, just go directly to the gate. In reverse, you can send your luggage from the U.S. directly to your Swiss destination's train station so that you don't have to pick it up from the airport carousel and carry it onto the train. Economy-class passengers pay about $17 per piece.

Basel-bound visitors should consider using the Basel/Mulhouse airport (which is in France) served by Air France and Swissair.

Zurich S-Bahn

The entrance to the Zurich Tourist Office is located in the cavernous main train station hall, which after reconstruction, is the largest in Switzerland. The tourist office is an excellent place to pick up free tourist information and make hotel reservations. In summer it is open from 8:30 A.M. to 8:30 P.M. on weekdays; to 6:30 P.M. on weekends.

Opposite you find Cybergate, "the Ultimate Internet Bar," open 11:30 A.M.-11 P.M. daily; on the first lower level you find ATMs open 24 hours.

The escalators you find in the direction of the Limmat river on the east side of Zurich's main train station take you to platforms 20-24, the underground center of Zurich's environmentally friendly S-Bahn system, which opened in May 1990, and accepts Eurailpasses, Europasses, and Swiss Passes. Use them to travel to every village in canton Zurich and many excellent places in the greater Zurich region in a reasonable time at hourly or half-hourly intervals.

These trains consist of double-decker carriages with first-class sections tucked away on the lower level. They are shorter, so you must use the middle of the platform to board. The S-Bahn's main corridor takes you from Winterthur, through Effretikon (with a branch to the Zurich airport), to Zurich's main station, and along the west bank of Lake Zurich through Thalwil and Wadenswil. On Lake Zurich's east bank, S-Bahn's "Gold Coast Express" runs to Rapperswil.

Some of the other scenic places to visit easily by S-Bahn include Stein am Rhein, Schaffhausen, Bremgarten, Zug, Einsiedeln, Baden, and Brugg. Travelers without rail passes encounter a patchwork of price zones. Single tickets are priced by destination keyed to postal (Zip) codes. The color-keyed maps on the automatic ticketing machines give you your destination number and the machines in the stations do the calculations for you. Twelve-trip strip cards and six-day S-Bahn Flexipasses give travelers a 16 percent discount.

Swiss Pass

Swiss Passes are versatile. You receive travel on the SBB; most of Switzerland's privately owned railroads (more than Eurailpass/Europass); lake steamers on the lakes of Geneva, Lucerne, Thun, Brienz, Zurich, Neuchatel, Biel, and Murten; on the Rhine between Schaffhausen and Kreuzlingen; on the Aare river between Biel and

Solothurn; and all of the Swiss postal buses. In addition, you may purchase as you please tickets on mountain funiculars and private lines at reductions up to 25 percent. Further, you may ride public transportation (streetcars and buses) in 30 cities including Basel, Bern, Geneva, Biel, Zurich, Winterthur, Baden/Wettingen, Lausanne (including the funicular to Ouchy), La Chaux-de-Fonds, Fribourg, Lugano, Locarno, Neuchatel, Olten, St. Gallen, Schaffhausen, Solothurn, Aarau, Thun, Lucerne, Zug, and Montreux/Vevey.

You buy Swiss Passes for four, eight, 15 or 21 days' or a month's consecutive travel or a Swiss Flexipass valid for any three up to nine travel days in one month, either for first- or second-class travel. First class costs about 60 percent of a Eurailpass. You save still more because you can buy Swiss Passes for shorter periods and second-class travel, which is still quality travel in Switzerland.

Two or more companions traveling together are eligible to buy a sharply reduced-price Swiss Saverpass or Swiss Saver Flexipass. This reduces their total cost dramatically, but limits their ability to travel separately.

When you buy a Swiss Pass or Swiss Card, ask for and fill out the free Swiss Family Card, which allows a parent to take along children under age 16 at no charge. Children six-15 pay half for second-class passes and receive 40 percent off first-class passes. Those under six travel free.

Swiss Passes and Flexipasses are available only to those residing outside Switzerland and Leichtenstein, but they may be purchased in Switzerland and at most European train stations, although of course it is more convenient to purchase them before you leave the U.S. They are valid beginning at midnight on the date you choose and end at 1 A.M. on the day following the last date of validity.

All lines covered are shown on a map supplied with your pass. You pay a supplement on certain TGVs, Bernina Expresses, Glacier Expresses, and some touristic postal coach routes.

You can receive a refund only by returning your pass to the issuing office before the first day of validity or in case of documented illness or accident. It will not be replaced if lost or stolen.

You often see yellow-and-white buses with bold red stripes and posthorns front and side parked in front of train stations. These are the famous Swiss postal buses that you ride free with a Swiss Pass. Of the thousand or so routes you may wish to use, the most exciting include the transit of Italy from Lugano/Menaggio/Chiavenna/St. Moritz and the dazzling routes over the Susten, Furka, Neufenen, and Gotthard passes from Meiringen and Andermatt.

Using only one day of a Swiss Pass you can ride free over the ingenious combination of postal bus/trains between St. Moritz and Zermatt. Postal buses take you over the Maloja Pass and through the Italian lake region between St. Moritz and Locarno's new train station, where you board the Centovalli train to Domodossola, Italy; transfer to postal bus over the Simplon Pass to Brig; and then ride the Brig-Visp-Zermatt (BVZ) railroad to Zermatt. Integrated timetables allow you to leave St. Moritz at 8 A.M., arriving in Zermatt at 7:45 P.M., or depart Zermatt at 8:10 A.M., arriving in St. Moritz at 7:50 P.M. Seat reservations on the postal buses are compulsory, but free of charge.

You may also take free cruises on Lakes Geneva, Constance, Zurich, Lucerne, Thun, Brienz, Neuchatel, Biel, and Murten, on the Untersee segment of the Rhine River between Schaffhausen and Kreuzlingen, and on the Aare River between Biel and Solothurn. You will find it very enjoyable to break your travels with restful day outings on these big white steamers. The most beautiful way to enter Geneva is by lake steamer.

A Swiss Pass or Swiss Card allows you a 10 percent discount on the total rental cost of skis, poles, and snowboards in more than 30 Swiss ski resorts. Wherever you see the sign "Swiss Rent-A-Ski" outside a sporting goods store, you can rent material in perfect condition for downhill or cross-country skiing.

Finally, show your Swiss Pass or Swiss Card for a 35 percent discount to the Transportation Museum in Lucerne (*www.verkehrshaus.ch*), which you can reach by streetcar or ship from the main train station. This is one of the best technical museums in Europe.

SBB offers the Swiss Card valid for half-fare travel on all public transportation (including city buses and streetcars—simply press the "1/2" button on the ticket vending machine). One in three Swiss adults owns one. One version combines a rail card with a bank credit card. You buy them, valid for one month, in U.S. dollars. Your children under 16 traveling with you are free.

Although you pay half-fare for many trips that Eurailpass or Swiss Pass holders ride free, you frequently come out ahead when:

• Your travel is lighter than it would take for a Swiss Pass to pay for itself, or

• When you travel on routes not fully covered by the Swiss Pass such as to the Jungfraujoch, Schilthorn, and Gornergrat.

When you buy them in the U.S., Swiss Cards include a one-day trip from a Swiss airport or border station to your destination in Switzerland and return. You are allowed to use different Swiss airports or border crossings arriving and departing.

Swiss Cards cannot be purchased in Switzerland. You buy in Switzerland the "Swiss Half-Fare Card," which costs about two-thirds of the Swiss Card and gives you all the advantages of a Swiss Card except that the transfer is not included. When you plan to fly to Zurich or Geneva and base your first and last days near those cities, you won't need the transfer and can save a few dollars buying a Swiss Half-Fare Card in Switzerland. Normally you save money buying your card in North America and using the transfer ticket to your destination in Switzerland.

You may also buy the Swiss Transfer Ticket separately. It is valid for your first and last day in Switzerland, but nothing else.

For longer stays or multiple visits to Switzerland, buy a Swiss Half-Fare Card in Switzerland valid for a year. Analyze your itinerary before making a purchase, but it is a good bet that a half-fare card will save you money.

Using Eurailpass and Europass bonuses

Most of the railroads and all of the same lake and river steamers listed for Swiss Pass (although half-fare must be paid for crossings of Lake Constance) honor Eurail and Europasses, but with significant exceptions. Not participating in these programs (but in the Swiss Pass arrangement) are the Furka-Oberalp Railroad (FO) and the BVZ Railroad, which you need to use on the Brig-Disentis and the Brig-Zermatt segments, respectively, of the Glacier Express, the Goschenen/Andermatt connection with the Gotthard line. Nor are Eurailpass holders eligible to use the Swiss "Family Card" for their children.

Eurailpass and Europass holders are not allowed to ride free the private Railroads of the Jungfrau Region, or the Rigi Railways, but you receive a 25 percent reduction by showing your pass when you buy your tickets. You don't have to validate a day box of a flexipass to receive this discount, which is a major savings.

In addition, you receive a 35 percent reduction to the top of Mt. Pilatus near Lucerne, so you can ride by funicular from Alpnachstad (which you can reach by included lake ferry) and by cable car from Kriens (35 percent off). You also receive a 35 percent reduction on admission to the Transportation Museum in Lucerne, a must-see for anyone interested in transportation, and a 50 percent reduction on the Burgenstock funicular.

Regional Passes

When you are interested in traveling intensively in only one particular region, you may be able to save money by buying a summer-season only regional pass which blankets all sorts of transportation within your region of interest. In the Bernese Oberland and Central Switzerland (where it is called the "Tell-Pass") you can buy passes valid for 15 days, of which you choose five for unlimited travel and the remaining days for travel at half-fare. Passes valid for two or three days' free travel in seven (the rest are at half-price) are also available in these regions and for the Lake Geneva, Lausanne/Montreux, and Oberwallis regions, as well. In Graubunden, you can buy passes for three, five, seven, or 10 free days within 10. The Lugano region offers you passes for second-class-only travel in either three or seven days out of seven. The Appenzell card is valid for one, three, or five consecutive days.

Regional passes vary in price between $45 and $150, and you can choose them for first- or second-class travel except in the Lugano region. You receive a 20 percent discount on their purchase when you already hold a Swiss Pass or Swiss Card. Unmarried children aged 16 to 25 receive half off when traveling with parents. Purchase them at train stations of the regions you are visiting.

Now that you have your travel pass or ticket in hand, discover five great Swiss trips: the Glacier Express from Zermatt, the Bernina Express, the William Tell Express, the railroads of the Jungfrau Region, and the Panoramic Express from Montreux.

Glacier Express
Alpine Discovery

Glacier Express train service between Zermatt and Chur or St. Moritz has flowered since tourism officials realized, with surprise, that a glamorous trip in a spectacular train 169 miles across the top of the Alps could attract visitors without trampling the landscape or forcing taxpayers to invest additional Swiss francs.

One train a day since 1930 was good enough until visitors discovered the excitement of traveling above the Rhone and Rhine rivers along their valleys to their sources at the Furka Pass. The route atop

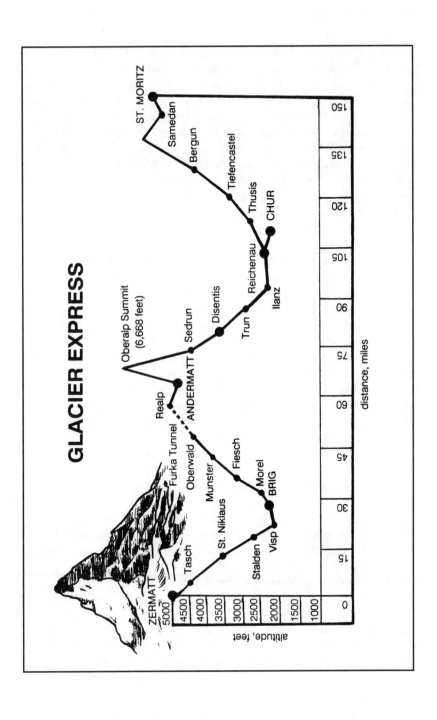

GLACIER EXPRESS

the Alps that carried 20,000 passengers during 1980 ballooned to 250,000. The newest timetable shows four Glacier Expresses a day in each direction. They feature especially built first-class panoramic dome cars similar to the ones on the Panoramic Express (see chapter on the Golden Pass Panoramic, below) and famous dining carriages.

This train curiously has always been named "Glacier Express," in English and French, although you pass through three language regions (French, German, and Romansch). When the Furka tunnel was opened in 1982, the Glacier Express moved from summer-only service to a year-round delight.

Glacier Express' Swiss-built panorama cars are designed to satisfy the demands of tourists who come from far away to experience Switzerland's Alpine scenery. The panorama cars, with red interiors, are first-class only. Passengers sit 2+2, separated by white tables.

The expansive windows measure about 6 1/4 feet high and almost 4 feet across. They open the carriage to the outdoors so greatly that it seems like you can pick the wildflowers beside the tracks. They make the carriages seem enormous—as they say, "as big as all outdoors." They turn your trip from an adventure into an unforgettable experience. It hardly seems like you are aboard a train, which is, of course, most unfortunate for confirmed train lovers.

The windows of the air-conditioned carriages are crystal clean, but still, you can't open them and lean out—something that is so disappointing to photographers that they would be well served to avoid Glacier Express trains which convey *only* panorama cars.

Because the top windows are canted to show mountaintops there are no overhead racks; instead, the seat arrangement allows you to stow your luggage between the seat backs or in the luggage areas at both ends (one end has coat hangers).

Make reservations in advance unless you only use the segments east of Disentis carried by the Rhaetian Railroads (RhB, *www.rhb.ch*). Obligatory seat reservations cost nine Swiss francs. They may be made in most large train stations throughout Europe.

The belle époque Glacier Express dining carriages are all walnut pan eled with heavy brass fixtures and yellow-brown petit point upholstery (the newest one seats 60). White-jacketed waiters serve lunch, but you should make dining reservations in advance. There are never enough seats to accommodate all travelers. The conversation piece is the Glacier Express wineglass (for sale) with a stem bent so that, in theory, you face it one way uphill and reverse it downhill. In fact, you worry more about your wine sloshing over when you are traveling horizontally.

When you arrive at the Zermatt train station, you are immediately drawn into that magical square in front of it that bubbles with enchantment and leads to the fairy-tale main street lined with hotels and shops designed in the characteristic architecture made fashionable by the Seilers, the family of hoteliers who established Zermatt in 1855. The Bahnhofplatz is dominated by horse-drawn carts and is filled with charm. You are welcomed by parties of bell captains and drivers in black hotel caps, ready to lead you in a horse-drawn carriage to your nearby hotel. In winter, riding in horse-drawn sleighs gives you the feeling of being in a winter wonderland.

When you clear the sparkle from your eyes, you see that Zermatt's modern Gornergratbahn station stands opposite the train station on one side of the Bahnhofplatz and a Swiss chalet housing the tourist bureau stands on the other. The tourist office is open 8 A.M. to 8 P.M., Monday to Saturday, and 4 to 8 P.M. on Sundays.

While you are in Zermatt, take a journey up the world's first electrified rack railroad, the Gornergratbahn, for one of the most rewarding mountain train adventures in Switzerland. The Matterhorn (and there is no competition) is one of the world's most-photographed natural wonders. It dominates the scene throughout most of your journey and you see increasingly magnificent views of the surrounding peaks as you climb.

From the Gornergrat (10,132 feet), extend your excursion still more by climbing farther to the east on the 2.8-mile cable line to Stockhorn (11,588 feet) on the highest open-air transport in the Swiss Alps.

Leaving Zermatt, the Glacier Express retraces your cogwheel train's ascent, because there is no other way to Zermatt, but you still enjoy revisiting the 1 1/2 hours of smashing scenery. You pass cataracts, rushing waters, and tall, wooden Valais houses and storage barns, or Spychers, protected from rats by stones.

The powerful red Brig-Visp-Zermatt Railroad (BVZ, *www.bvz.ch*) railcar, required for the steep upward climb, engages the cogwheels and pulls your Glacier Express train out of Zermatt. (The BVZ accepts Swiss Passes, but not Eurailpasses.) Red carriages are narrow, because of the slim gauge, but still offer ample space to first-class passengers riding 2+1.

You follow your path on diagrams inserted in the utility table below your window showing altitude relative to distance to St. Moritz. St. Moritz (5,822 feet) and Zermatt (5,261 feet) surmount each end, but on the way you climb to 6,668 feet at the summit, Oberalp Passhohe, cross 291 bridges and viaducts, and pass through 91 tunnels.

When your train stops in Tasch, the point closest to Zermatt accessible by car, you look out on the parking lot. It is said that this is the largest parking lot in Europe. Since 1965, the BVZ has maintained hourly bus service between St. Niklaus and Visp and even runs a school bus between Stalden and Visp.

The BVZ lives in mortal fear of road building. Rail travel is profitable here. The BVZ is one of the few narrow-gauge railroads turning a profit. Renewals and reconstructions were undertaken on guarantees from federal and cantonal authorities that no road would be built up the Visp Valley above Stalden, but this promise lapsed in 1952. A highway from Tasch to St. Niklaus was authorized in July 1961.

The cogs reengage at Randa, seven miles down the Glacier Express route, where you see the Dom rising up one side and the Weisshorn up the other. These are the highest peaks in the Alps after Mont Blanc and Monte Rosa. Descending another eight miles, you pass through Brattbach tunnel, 428 feet long, and a series of concrete avalanche shelters. Officials realized these were necessary to maintain Zermatt as a winter sports center when the winter avalanche of 1931-32 buried the line.

In Visp, your BVZ train stops in the street in front of the SBB station. Your final 5 1/4 miles of the meter-gauge BVZ parallel the tracks of the SBB. The BVZ segment makes it possible for you to travel by meter-gauge lines from the top of the Gornergrat 211 miles to Tirano in Italy, with only two changes, at Zermatt and St. Moritz.

The junction at Brig allows you to connect to or from north-south and east-west trains. Your BVZ train runs into the south side of an island platform in front of the SBB station with road traffic rushing past on both sides. This is a good point to connect from the narrow-gauge BVZ from Zermatt and the Furka-Oberalp (FO, *www.fo-bahn.ch*) trains from Andermatt with the standard-gauge SBB and Bern-Lotschberg-Simplon Railroad (BLS, *www.bls.ch*) line to and from Italy.

The SBB station has both stairs and ramps to the platforms. The higher-numbered platforms refer to the FO station on the open square in front of the SBB station. Glacier Expresses eastbound usually depart from platform 14, westbound from platform 13.

A red FO locomotive takes command of the Glacier Express in Brig, but you don't change trains. While it departs over FO tracks through the scenic and broad upper Rhone Valley at 3,300 to 4,300 feet, you hear the first of the frequent, recorded descriptions in English, French, and German that add so much to the enjoyment of your trip that you are scarcely tempted to doze.

The valley supports farms and farmhouses on both sides of the line. You can always see one snowcapped peak at the end of your line of sight, which in turn dissolves into another when you reach there. Dense pine forests clothe the lower slopes of the mountains. Above, you make out high Alpine pastures and still higher summits covered with snow the year around.

Your train climbs steadily from Brig except for abrupt steps typical of glacial valleys, at Grengiols, above Fiesch, and below Gletsch. Above Grengiols, the valley is known as the Goms. At these steps, the valley also narrows, forcing your train to use loops, spirals, or a rack, or even all three, to overcome the height.

After you pass through the chestnut forests surrounding the village of Morel, you reach Betten, where you feel the cogwheels chattering as you climb. Past Grengiols, you cross the viaduct of the same name (102 feet high, the highest bridge of the FO) and enter a tunnel looped to correct an altitude difference of 505 feet.

Leaving behind the Rhone Valley's picturesque villages, you reach the reddish-brown Oberwald station (4,480 feet) where your train swings into the all-weather, 9.59-mile Furka tunnel, the longest narrow-gauge train tunnel in the world, which permits the Glacier Express to operate all year round. However, it deprives you of views of the Rhone glacier that awed early travelers. You must now take the postal coach over the Furka Pass to approach this azure glacier.

Special flatcars transport automobiles through the Furka tunnel in winter, when the Furka Pass is closed—a great convenience for skiers—but unfortunately corrosion of the rails in the humid tunnel is proceeding twice as fast as expected. This is partially due to salt-containing snow melting from the automobiles onto the rails. Engineers watch the rails closely, prevent galvanic corrosion, and wash them regularly.

After 17 minutes, you emerge from the tunnel at Realp (5,045 feet). From here you serpentine downward through six U-turns with a view down on Andermatt (4,701 feet), the famous ski resort, which bristles even more in summer with Swiss soldiers on their compulsory annual military service maneuvers. Andermatt's depot and spacious, modern station also connect to FO's 2.3-mile-long, double-rack railroad which gives you the option of descending the mountainside in 15 minutes to Goschenen on the north side of the Gotthard tunnel to change to trains of the Gottard line.

Past Andermatt, you begin climbing sharply to the Oberalp Pass, the highest point on the line (6,670 feet), but you feel the cogwheels under the train chattering, so you know your climb is under total control. When you leave, Andermatt appears almost vertically below your train, first on one side and then on the other. You trace out your train's path ahead by the ribbon of rail zigzagging above you. These curves on the Glacier Express are nearly right-angle turns.

Beyond the Oberalp Pass, you have some fine views over the Outer Rhine Valley as you descend to Sedrun on a ledge high above the river. It is said that Sedrun is where the Rhine spends its vacation.

Nineteen minutes later you come to a stop in Disentis-Muster (3,707 feet), but don't look for inspiration in the eye-catching onion-shaped dome of the baroque church on the valley floor. Look up to the left (north) to the imposing Benedictine Abbey on the mountainside, which is the place of prayer for the rich folks. The poorer folk attend the church on the valley floor. Disentis used to be divided into two villages: one by the Abbey, one by the river.

Disentis is the geographic center of the Alps. On the north (Germanic culture), the mountains have German and Romansch names; on the south (Italian culture), they have Italian and Romansch names.

In Disentis, your Glacier Express train joins the Rhaetian Railroads (RhB, www.rhb.ch) system (which accepts Eurailpasses and Europasses). Your first segment, to Ilanz, was laid specifically to connect the RhB with the FO. This is the least challenging of all the narrow-gauge sections, although you pass over the lofty Val Rusein and Val Lumpegna viaducts shortly out of Disentis.

You descend steadily all the way from Disentis to Ilanz, with good views of the valley in the first four miles as you run high above the left bank of the Outer Rhine on a rock ledge. As you approach Ilanz, the lower slopes of the valley are thickly wooded with conifers. The typical farmhouses you see on the mountainsides, in the Valais style, are quite a change from the Engadine houses you will soon see.

Ilanz (2,289 feet) is the first town on the Rhine, and is the beginning of Switzerland's Romansch-speaking region. Yellow and red postal buses stand by ready to take passengers up the twisting Vals Valley to the health resort of Vals, where the mineral water, Valser, is bottled. (You might also see a tanker car labeled "Valser" transporting the water.)

Past Ilanz, on the Ilanz line opened in 1903, you see spectacular limestone scenery. The major obstacle to construction was the deep gorge that the Outer Rhine had carved through prehistoric landslides of rubble more than 2,000 feet deep. A second handicap was that high villages along the route were remote and inaccessible. Steeply graded roads had to be built between the stations and the villages.

In Reichenau, where the Outer Rhine and the Inner Rhine converge right next to the imposing railroad bridge, you meet the Albula line. From here, Glacier Express trains scramble. Some continue north to Chur, some head south to St. Moritz through the Albula tunnel, and some do both by being divided in Reichenau into two sections. Please follow these paths in the section below describing the Bernina Express, which departs from Chur.

Connections between Zurich and Chur are convenient, so that you can begin or end your trip in the Swiss metropolis.

Summer Glacier Express Service

A900	B902	C904	D906				F901	G903	H905	K907
0810	0852	0932	1010	dep.	ZERMATT	arr.	1443	1643	1702	1743
0821	. . .	. . .	. . .	dep.	Tasch	dep.	1432	. . .	. . .	. . .
0957	1020	1109	1146	dep.	Brig	arr.	1313	1513	1541	1613
1130	1150	1255	1335	dep.	Andermatt	arr.	1123	1323	1404	1442
1238	1256	1400	1442	arr.	Disentis	dep.	1018	1218	1255	1345
1315	1315	1415	1452	dep.	Disentis	arr.	1008	1208	1222	1335
1357	1357	1449	1530	arr.	Ilanz	dep.	0936	1132		1258
1430	1430	1532	1559	arr.	CHUR	dep.	0857	1057		1220
	1655	1755		arr.	ST. MORITZ	dep.			0930	1000
			1723	arr.	Klosters	dep.		0937		
			1748	arr.	Davos Dorf	dep.		0913		
			1752	arr.	Davos Platz	dep.		0909		

| = does not run on this route

Bernina Express
The Impossible Takes a Little Longer

You roar into the cliff of the black Landwasser tunnel, your Bernina Express throttled wide open, soaring high above the stream and over the treetops, riding the summit of an unseen viaduct without guard railings. It is like flying—or falling.

This high point of the 6 1/2-mile section from Tiefencastel to Filisur follows your crossing of two famous viaducts. First you pass the Schmittentobel viaduct, 6.1 miles out of Tiefencastel. Its seven arches rise 118 feet. Then, out of a 164-foot tunnel, you quickly glimpse ahead the five classic arches of the elegant 1903 Landwasser viaduct curving to the right over the river far below. The viaduct's 400-foot span rests on 213-foot piers, and its celebrated southern arch plunges you directly into the Landwasser tunnel.

The Albula line is a triumph of creative railroad engineering. Your powerful, red, electric locomotive climbs through so many extraordinary spirals and tunnels up the Albula Valley that it resembles a model engine racing through every complicated loop, tunnel, bridge, cloverleaf, and dramatic overpass that an ingenious toy shop display can conjure.

Your locomotive's speed of 30 to 35 mph seems heady, given the acrobatics, but your narrow-gauge coach swings around tight corners so smoothly that you don't feel frightened—even at the edges of sheer cliffs. You are too preoccupied watching the extraordinary views.

Classic Bernina Express

The Rhaetian Railroads (RhB, *www.rhb.ch*) introduced the best train on this line, your classic Bernina Express, in 1973, for a one-day excursion through a rarely visited corner of Switzerland. With the introduction of a postal bus connection in 1992, it became possible for you to make a round trip. In 2000, the addition of panoramic carriages made it an irresistible trip.

Passengers must pay a surcharge of seven Swiss francs which includes a seat reservation and covers the explanation of the scenery and route on the loudspeaker system and the colored Bernina Express certificate you receive. Make your reservation in advance at any train station in Switzerland, Germany, or Austria.

Your red carriage departs from track six of Chur's award-winning 1994 train station with a 165-foot, fully glazed arched roof soaring over the high-level postal bus station (RhB trains for Arosa leave from the square in front of the station) down a broad flat valley with forested mountains on both sides. You see corn; cows; big, busy factories; and churches with onion-shaped steeples. On the first stretch from the mountain capital of Graubunden canton, you will be traveling on the

Albula line. Between Pontresina and the Swiss border across from Tirano, Italy, you will be riding on the Bernina line.

RhB is a private company serving the largest, mountainous canton of eastern Switzerland. It celebrated its 100th birthday in 1989. Your seats in its first-class panoramic carriages give you astonishing views. The spic-and-span 1983 salon cars were refurbished in 1992 with maroon plush upholstery and matching carpets. These carriages remind you of SBB's InterCity trains and seem just as spacious, and when you lean out their windows, you hear cowbells. You feel nature and the excitement of historic railroad engineering and nearly miraculous construction.

Hikers push the windows down from the top to admit fresh mountain air. Photographers lean out, snapping photos nearly the whole length of the trip. In winter, skiers and beautiful people traveling to St. Moritz are warmly dressed. The train passes through the most agreeable summer and winter mountain climate in Europe.

During your 2 1/4-hour, 55-mile trip from Chur to Pontresina, you pass through 42 well-engineered tunnels or galleries totaling more than 10 miles (well over a quarter of the mountain segment). The line's 108 bridges and towering viaducts of arched rock and stone come to nearly two miles.

You first follow the Rhine Valley to Reichenau where the Inner Rhine (Hinterrhein) comes from the south to join the Outer Rhine (Vorderrhein) beneath the Castle of Reichenau. The two rapid rivers churn together, mixing their chalky blues and cloudy whites of melted snow and glacier runoff.

You pass steep and thickly wooded slopes with villages and ruins of feudal fortresses secluded in green foliage. Bends are so sharp that you can see both the locomotive and the end of the train. Past 1994's aluminum-and-glass Thusis station house you travel eight miles through the Schyn gorges to Tiefencastel, one-third in tunnels and one mile over early twentieth-century viaducts. The sturdy, hand-built stone bridges complement the wonderful scenery rather than cheapen it.

The view here is very good from the left side, but the back seats of the carriage give a better panorama of the unfolding landscape outside. The murky tints of the blue-white waters of the Albula River run far below your train twisting on the mountainside.

The valley widens again and you see the Tinzerhorn mountain group ahead. Change to the right side for better views of the breathtaking scenes you are approaching. Past Tiefencastel, the Albula River runs fast and the valley becomes more and more wooded with fir trees, larches, and arolla pines. At this point you cross the Schmittentobel viaduct and roar into the Landwasser tunnel, as described at the beginning of this section.

Like many admirers of the Landwasser viaduct, break your journey at Filisur station (boarding a local train later on) to walk down the footpath and inspect the dramatic structure from below.

It is at Filisur (3,556 feet) that the route of the Heidi Express (see below) from Landquart joins the core route and enters the Albula line south into the Engadine region.

The most difficult terrain of your trip is on the 5.8-mile segment from Filisur to Bergun. You climb one foot for every 28 traveled. The Albula Valley becomes narrower and your route becomes more steeply walled-in. In this short section, you pass through fourteen tunnels and over eight viaducts.

The 1903 section past Bergun to Preda is technically the most interesting and one you will always remember. "Slow but sure" is the watchword you appreciate during this stretch. The direct distance to Preda from Bergun is four miles, but surveyors have bent your line into such extraordinary contortions of loops and spirals that you actually travel 7.6 miles, including 1.7 miles through seven tunnels. If you climbed directly, you would climb one foot for every 16, but the expensive spirals and reversals of direction safely reduce your grade to one in 30.

Plan to change from side to side to watch the elegant contortions. Look back for at least three extraordinary sights of the pleasing village of Bergun while your train climbs higher and higher. The noted "Rail Trail" alongside this segment attracts many hikers.

You enter the Engadine region. Engadine architecture is so unique and bright that it sets the region off from the rest of Switzerland more distinctly than if you had crossed a frontier. The houses you see are white and thick-walled, with small, irregularly spaced windows widening outwards. Their most distinctive feature is their "sgraffito" (now you know where the word "graffiti" came from). Masons covered rough, gray plaster with coats of white limewash and then artfully scraped away the wash to bring out charming gray scrolls, interesting geometries, and fascinating embroideries.

From Preda, your Bernina Express picks up speed through the 3.6-mile Albula tunnel. It seems to go on forever. It is the highest (6,242 feet) principal tunnel through the Alps and the most expensive and difficult engineering work of the RhB.

When you emerge from the Albula tunnel at Spinas, clumps of larch have reappeared and your train is pointed downwards. You cross and recross the Beverin River at Bever, where you see beautiful examples of Engadine architecture on your west side. Then you run down the flat floor of the Inn Valley above the Inn River. The colors of the glorious peaks of the Bernina massif ahead through the Pontresina Gap are vivid. The air is electrified with natural radiation.

Both St. Moritz and Pontresina—all the villages of the Engadine region, in fact—welcome tourists. The inhabitants speak Romansch, Switzerland's fourth national language, but the area is so international that English is widely understood. Bring extra money if you can, for a champagne summer in St. Moritz or the mountaineering center of Pontresina, but if you can't, come anyway. Inexpensive lodging catering to clever travelers is easy to find.

Besides more aerial acrobatics, the Bernina line presents you with another distinction: it is a joy to photograph. You are able to focus on the magnificent scenery through pulled-down windows of conventional carriages while traveling along at only a snail's pace. Trains south of Pontresina average only 20.5 mph, including stops, making your train even slower than the Glacier Express.

Beyond Pontresina, the valley becomes wider with every mile. Panoramas open on every side while your train runs high on the mountainside on tracks that were laid to avoid spoiling the beauty of the Taiser Forest. Past the Berninabach Falls bubbling with froth in early summer, you turn your lens to the right for a splendid picture of the magnificent Morteratsch glacier and the most glorious peaks of the Bernina range, especially Piz Bernina itself, a double rocky summit of 13,261 feet.

High above the timberline, you reach the summit at Bernina Hospiz (7,403 feet), where winter lasts seven months. You have climbed 5,973 feet by simple adhesion—even more than any Swiss rack railroad with cogs—and reached the highest station in Switzerland served by adhesion railroad.

Lago Bianco to your right, covered by ice until late May, was originally four lakes but it was dammed to form a reservoir for the Brusio power station, forcing the railroad to be moved some 30 feet higher. Look for the former path running along the edge of the lake. From here you descend through the 630-foot Scala tunnel, the Pozzo del Drago tunnel (the dragon is rumored to lurk in the nearby lake), and an avalanche gallery to reach Alp Grum (6,858 feet).

It is time for lunch. Your Bernina Express carries a refreshments trolley where most passengers buy snacks, but travelers have a chance to disembark at the brownstone Alp Grum station, which is a popular jumping-off place for Alpine hiking and an amazing place for lunch, and then continue on a later train. You enjoy vast views over the Palu glacier and its surrounding peaks. There is also an Alpine garden. Most thrilling of all is the view from above the tracks on the terrace of the Bellavista cafe with a view across to the Palu Glacier and down the Poschiavo Valley to blue Lake Poschiavo, 4,231 feet below and only 6.8 miles away. The trains calling at the toylike Puschlav station below look like those on a scale-model railroad.

Climbing from Pontresina has been relatively easy. Descending follows a route that required surveyors to perform near miracles. To reach Poschiavo, your train has to drop 4,034 feet through larch and spruce forests in a horizontal distance of only 4.7 miles. Engineers solved this problem by designing a series of cautious, cascading cuts, circular tunnels, sharp zigzags, and astonishing loops.

First you descend to the right in a semicircle, your train's wheels screeching, below Alp Grum station to the 833-foot Palu tunnel, in which you make a three-quarter turn and emerge down the mountain. For a second time you pass below the Bellavista terrace into the 948-foot Stabline tunnel, emerging on the back slope of Alp Grum before doubling back through the 745-foot Pila tunnel and returning below the terrace for a third time.

In less than 10 minutes, you look up from Cavaglia (5,553 feet) to see the restaurant at Alp Grum, now 1,305 feet above you. The forests have turned to deciduous trees: hazel, aspen, alder, and birch.

Your final approach to Poschiavo is the most miraculous of all. Your train makes four more zigzags and tunnel turnarounds. You see Poschiavo first on the left and then four more times on the right while your train loops above the towers of the city. Photographers race back and forth across the carriage in order to capture all of the kaleidoscopic scenery, exclaiming "Why am I always on the wrong side?"

Past Mira Lago (whose name, "Look at the Lake," refers to your view), you again descend steeply. After passing Brusio your train makes one of the world's most amazing loops across a raised, corkscrew stone viaduct having a radius of only 164 feet. Nearby highway traffic comes to a standstill while drivers and passengers watch you descend.

Then your Bernina Express continues effortlessly down the valley past vineyards, fig trees, and former tobacco fields which now yield herbs for healthful teas, across a steel bridge over the pressure pipes of the Brusio power station (which generate electricity powering the line), and past the Renaissance pilgrim's church of the Madonna di Tirano to the Italian frontier at Tirano.

Pick up your free colored Bernina Express certificate by showing your ticket at the Swiss train station, before you walk the few feet into Italy and border guards check your passport. Tirano is a pleasant little town of mountain houses and terraced vineyards where you will have time for lunch at one of the outdoor cafes on the city's main street.

Heidi Express

> *"You mount a narrow-gauge train and as the small but very powerful engine gets under way, there begins the thrilling part of the journey, a steep and steady climb that seems never to come to an end. For the station of Landquart lies at a relatively low altitude, but now the wild and rocky route pushes grimly onward into the Alps themselves."*   Thomas Mann, *The Magic Mountain*

The Bernina Express' 1995 sibling follows a slightly different route. Named the Heidi Express, this time Heidi isn't leaving her grandfather to travel northwards to Klara and Fraulein Rottenmeier, but southwards. And what a lot there is for her to see: colorful, flower-dotted meadows, Davos, Engadine, and mountains that grow taller by the moment. The goats and cows look much the same as at home, but the friendly local farmers at the end of her trip greet her in Italian: "*Ciao, Heidi Come stai?*" Like the classic Bernina Express from Chur, this train, too, is on its way to the Mediterranean-like valley of Veltlin with its olive trees, oleanders, and vineyards.

The children's book, *Heidi*, by Johanna Spyri, made the village of Maienfeld into something of a tourist attraction and gave the region, and the train, its nickname "Heidi."

RhB's new train leaves not from Chur, but Landquart, close to the original Heidi's home, up the Rhine Valley 1,715 feet high. When you board the Heidi Express, you follow the foaming River Landquart upstream through the steep rock walls of the Chlus gorge and reach the luscious green meadows and woodlands of the mountain valley Prattigau with its capital, Klosters (3,870 feet). After you cross the summit of the Wolfgang pass (5,350 feet) using loop tunnels to cope with the rise in altitude, your Heidi Express cruises down the Landwasser Valley beside Davos lake to Davos-Platz.

Your path from Landquart to Klosters covered the origins of the RhB lines. It was opened on October 9, 1889, and at the time was the highest adhesion line in Europe and one of the steepest. Its extension to Davos was opened on July 20, 1890.

Davos, at 5,118 feet, lies in the Landwasser Valley. Sheltered from the north and east winds by high wooded mountains and exposed to the full sun, it became famous for its curative climate. The numerous sanatoriums built to cure tuberculosis, the scourge at the beginning of the century, became the forerunners of the present-day hotel industry.

From Davos your Heidi Express rolls over the 1909 stretch across bridges and through tunnels to the RhB's longest bridge, the 688-foot-long Wiesner Viaduct, 288 feet above the River Landwasser.

In Filisur (3,556 feet) your Heidi Express merges with the route of the classic Bernina Express from Chur and you begin the Albula line south into the Engadine region.

The introduction of the Heidi Express gives you a choice of premium trains on a thrilling route. Which to take? Take one going down, the other coming back. It's a day not to be missed.

Bernina Express Bus

The Swiss Travel System added a whole new dimension to scenic train experience when they introduced in 1992 postal bus service between Tirano and two stops in Lugano, Via S. Balestre stop in the center of the city and Lugano train station.

The blue-and-white, Italian-plated Giuliani e Laudi Bernina Express buses leave from the square on the Italian side. The buses run during the summer only. It obligatory that you make advance reservations costing 12 Swiss francs at any Swiss train station or from your travel agent before departure. Diretto trains leave approximately every two hours over the lines of the Italian State Railroads to Milano's Centrale station.

Lugano is a satisfying vacation destination because of its mild weather, excellent tourist facilities, and its site on beautiful Lake Lugano with funicular to Monte San Salvatore and cogwheel railroad to Monte

Generoso. When you step out of your train at Lugano's hillside train station you are face to face with the funicular to the center of the lovely city. The official language here is Italian, but in season you hear more English and German.

Now you have a great, convenient goal and a sensational way to get there. Just as exciting, you can make your trip aboard the Bernina Express in the opposite direction, by starting at Lugano. All segments—including mainline connections, the narrow-gauge Rhaetian Railroads, and the new postal bus—are covered by Swiss Passes, Swiss Cards, Europasses and Eurailpasses. Reservations are possible on the Heidi Express, but are not obligatory. Only Bernina Express trains require reservations.

Should you want only to make a day trip from Zurich, you can use the Bernina bus connection to make a 6:30 A.M.-9 P.M. round trip along this spectacular route. Every visitor interested in the outdoors, however, will prefer to break his or her trip to stay in one of the charming mountain villages in the spectacular Engadine region of Graubunden and in Lugano beside the lake.

Summer Bernina Express Service

F417	G503	A501				H502	D500	F478
|	|	0848	dep.	CHUR	arr.	|	1853	|
|	|	0930	dep.	Tiefencastel	arr.	|	1758	|
|	0745	|	dep.	Landquart	arr.	1901	|	|
|	0827	|	dep.	Davos Platz	arr.	1743	|	|
0930	|	|	dep.	ST. MORITZ	dep.	|	|	1739
0943	1015	1050	dep.	PONTRESINA	arr.	1620	1637	1726
1022	....	1128	arr.	Alp Grum	dep.	1526	....	1640
1103	1140	1202	arr.	Poschiavo	dep.	1450	1525	1552
1111	1150	1211	arr.	Le Prese	dep.	1438	1516	1540
1146	1224	1240	arr.	TIRANO	dep.	1405	1445	1505
		1415	dep.	TIRANO (bus*)	arr.		1315	
		1715	arr.	LUGANO (FFS)	dep.		1030	

A501 & D500 = BERNINA EXPRESS with panoramic carriages, reservations costing CHF 7 are required.

G503 & H502 = HEIDI EXPRESS, reservations costing CHF 5 are recommended.

E417 & F478 = Local Bernina Express train, reservations costing CHF 5 are recommended.

* Bernina Express Bus, reservations costing CHF 12 are required.

The Route of William Tell
The Cradle of Switzerland

"Swear we the oath of our confederacy! We swear we will be free and sooner die than live in slavery."   F. Schiller, William Tell

One of the great Alpine journeys for tourists of the 1880s was the William Tell Express by paddle steamer from Lucerne to Fluelen at the far southeastern corner of Lake Lucerne, where visitors joined a steam train for the run through the St. Gotthard tunnel (completed in 1882). The trip through the beautiful cradle of Swiss freedom and independence was revived in 1988, still using an authentic paddle steamer, but with passengers transferring to mainline electric train to Lugano.

In Lucerne you begin the first of two integrated laps of the Swiss Travel System: "Across lake; over mountains." You steam across Lake Lucerne with romantic Alps of every shape rising about you and climb by train through the heart of the Alps via the high St. Gotthard pass, but to your pleasure you travel along a route singing with memories of William Tell, the storied Swiss folk hero credited with rallying the Forest Cantons from the Hapsburgs' grasp and creating independent Switzerland.

You can follow the route of William Tell independently with a Eurailpass, Europass, Swiss Pass, or Central Switzerland's regional "Tell-Pass," or trace it with the help of an escort on the arranged Will Tell Express trip. You relive the birth of independence on Lake Lucerne in the core of the confederation.

The 800-passenger paddle steamer *Unterwalden* sets its red-and-white Swiss flag waving smartly when you set out on Lake Lucerne. *Unterwalden*, built in 1902, was returned to service in 1985, meticulously restored with $1.2 million donated by those you see listed in a scroll aboard the ship as "Friends of the Steamship Association."

Unterwalden's first-class salon shines with parquet floors, inlaid furniture, wooden scrolls, white-tablecloth tables, and frilly curtains designed to highlight the delicate carvings surrounding the windows and covering the sills.

While enjoying a typically Swiss meal in the first-class salon and cruising to Fluelen, the Forest Cantons of Central Switzerland spread out around you. To the east you see Mount Rigi (5,800 feet), looking to the south you see the Burgenstock (2,700 feet), while to the west, Pilatus (6,985 feet), surmounted by the world's steepest cogwheel railroad, is fading in the distance.

Across the lake you approach Weggis, the queen of the resorts on Lake Lucerne. An aerial gondola here leads to the crest of the Rigi mountain above. In 1870, some 40,000 travelers (including Mark Twain) visited the summit by foot, horseback, or sedan chair to witness the magical sunrise and hear for themselves Alpine yodeling. The Vitznau-Rigi railroad, at the next landing on the lake, opened the following year, making it the oldest cogwheel railroad in Europe. It celebrated its 125th anniversary in 1996. The Vitznau-Rigi railroad and the gondola from Weggis meet in Rigi Kaltbad, 3,290 feet above Lake Lucerne.

The lake steamer's premier stop on Lake Lucerne is the resort of Brunnen in canton Schwyz. The people of Schwyz gave Switzerland its name as well as its flag when, two years before the oath of freedom, as a result of an uprising, they were awarded a banner showing, on a red field, a white cross representing the Lake of Lucerne.

In town lies the "Square of the Swiss Abroad," the end of the "Swiss Path" opened in 1991 celebrating the 700th anniversary of Swiss independence. It should attract everyone fond of the outdoors and Alpine air. A footpath leads around Lake Uri from the Ruetli meadow to the square. Each of Switzerland's cantons was responsible for freely designing a length of the 20-mile trail proportional to the number of its inhabitants in a sequence determined by the canton's date of entry into the confederation. Thus canton Uri takes pride of responsibility of the first stretch and leads hikers into a chronology of the confederation superimposed upon nature. Walkers will tread through seven centuries of history presented by the cantons according to their concepts.

Aboard the *Unterwalden*, from Brunnen you steam past the Schiller Stone, rising from the lake like a gleaming monolith, which is a memorial to the author of Switzerland's national epic. The inscription reads: "To him who sang Tell's glory, Friedrich Schiller—the Original Cantons, 1859."

> *"Right against the Mytenstein, deep-hidden in the wood, a meadow lies, by shepherds called the Ruetli because the wood has been uprooted there. Tis where our canton boundaries merge."*

You coast past the Ruetli landing decorated with hand-carved insignia of the three original cantons. On this almost inaccessible stretch of meadow every Swiss child knows that 33 representatives of the founding cantons (Schwyz, Uri, and Unterwalden) pledged to defend themselves against all forms of foreign domination.

You may get off and on the ship at the Ruetli landing—a spot where every Swiss heart beats faster, but a better way is to get off the boat earlier at Treib (1:47 P.M.), take the red TSB funicular up the mountain to Seilisberg and follow the last stretch of the Swiss Path down the mountain through the sectors maintained by cantons Unterwalden and Schwyz to the foot at the Ruetli meadow where you board the next Lake Lucerne ferry. The funicular is not covered by rail pass. Figure about 50 minutes for the easy downhill walk along the well-maintained gravel path. The TSB is timed to accommodate every ship landing.

"The cantons three are to each other pledged to hunt the tyrants from the land. The league has been concluded and a sacred oath confirms our union."

At the landing at Tellsplatte, the Chapel of William Tell (Tellskapelle) commemorates the point where William Tell, a prisoner, leaped to freedom from Viceroy Gessler's ship on hurricane-ripped Lake Uri. It lies at water level accessible only by a narrow path along the shoreline.

"And when I had descried a shelving crag that jutted, smooth atop, into the lake, with a bound I swung myself upon the flattened shelf and thrust off the puny bark into the hell of waters."

By the time you have finished your three-course meal, Lake Uri has narrowed and the Urirotstock Alp rises vertically from the water in the west while you cruise to your landing in Fluelen below the gilded points of the church's steeples. On the escorted trip, English-speaking guides take you a few hundred feet more to the blue-and-white William Tell Express signboard where the William Tell Express train is already waiting. It couldn't be more convenient, but walking on your own is no more difficult.

Almost before you settle in your seat, your train speeds through the deep ravines and precipitous cliffs of the Reuss Valley and takes you past Altdorf, the capital of canton Uri and the key to the St. Gotthard Pass.

"This cap will be set upon a lofty pole in Altdorf, in the market place, and this is the Lord Governor's good-will and pleasure, the cap shall have like honor as himself and all shall reverence it with bended knee and head uncovered."

In Altdorf's main square the statue of the storied archer, his hand resting on his son's shoulder against a primitively painted mountainside panorama, stands at the spot where, according to local folklore, vicious Viceroy Gessler ordered his hat, as a symbol of subjugation, flown from a flagpole. Passers-by bowed in submission, but Tell ignored it, and was ordered to *"take thy bow and make thee ready to shoot an apple from the stripling's head."*

About a half-hour past Altdorf everyone begins looking for the well-known three views of the village of Wassen (population 900, altitude 3,051 feet). The line climbs more than 600 feet in a huge S-bend, three times crossing the Meienreuss waters cascading down from the Susten Pass. You watch while three successive views of the Wassen church float past your window from different sides and different inclinations. Some refuse to believe it is the same structure, so ask them to fix their eyes on the flagpole in front, which usually flies the canton Uri flag.

The St. Gotthard line carries you from 1,540 feet to 3,628 feet at the entrance to the 9.3-mile St. Gotthard tunnel at Goschenen. Engineers required seven years to complete the tunnel. On June 1, 1882, the inaugural train reached Airolo, replacing the stagecoach that had required a whole day between Goschenen and Airolo.

If one thing is certain about the weather, it is that it will be different north and south of the Alps. After 10 minutes, you emerge from the tunnel at Airolo, see palm trees, and feel the milder climate of Ticino, Switzerland's Italian-speaking canton.

Crossing Levintina Valley, your William Tell train zips past Biasca, crosses cantilevered bridges, and delivers you to Bellinzona, Ticino's capital city. Some travelers change trains for Locarno, but most remain aboard for Lugano.

From Bellinzona, you tunnel below Montebello Castle's crenelated walls and enter the fruitful Lombard plain of Italy, taking another 27 minutes to Lugano. After a stay in Lugano, you might like to take the Bernina Express postal bus to Tirano to take the Bernina Express train north (see preceding trip).

When you choose to take the William Tell Express package, you should make advance reservations at any train station or with the Lake Lucerne Navigation Company (*www.lake-lucerne.ch*), Werftstrasse 5, P.O. Box 4265, 6002 Lucerne (Tel. 041-367-66-66). You receive meals, transportation on a Lake Lucerne paddle steamer, train travel aboard customized first-class carriages, and a gift package including a folder containing timetable, map, and description of itinerary plus a small souvenir (such as a key chain) for only a small surcharge over the normal fare. When you already hold a Swiss Pass or Eurailpass, you just pay a supplement amounting to about 28 percent of a standard fare. A travel agent will be able to combine this trip with other excursions.

When you choose to travel on your own totally free with a Eurailpass, Europass or Swiss Pass, take an earlier Lake Lucerne Navigation steamer from the landing in Lucerne across from the train station. In Fluelen board any of the hourly trains to Lugano or back to Lucerne or Zurich (going north you may have to change trains in Arth-Goldau).

Summer William Tell Express Service
Boat, Lucern to Fluelen and
Train, Fluelen to Lugano/Locarno

Lucerne	dep. 120		Fluelen	dep. 1516
Fluelen	arr. 1457		Lugano	arr. 1723
			Locarno*	arr. 1730

* Change trains in Bellinzona

Railroads of the Jungfrau Region
Top of Europe

The North Face of the Eiger

After burrowing through the solid rock of the Eiger for several miles, Eigerwand station is startling. You hear "Ahs" as your train passes portals glowing with reflected white light. Folk music plays on the platform. It gives you an eerie feeling to be at this treacherous location where climber after climber tried and failed to scale the out-side wall until finally, in 1938, the sheer face was conquered for the first time.

Passengers surge from the train to a set of 12 plate-glass picture windows—enough for everyone—revealing an amazing view of the Grindelwald valley, some 6,000 feet below. From the portals you look out onto the very center of the Eiger North Face.

The Railroads of the Jungfrau Region (www.jungfraubahn.ch) carry you to lands of snow and ice you cannot possibly reach otherwise unless you are a competent Alpine climber accompanied by guides.

Interlaken Ost (for "east") train station is your stepping stone to the

RAILROADS OF THE JUNGFRAU REGION

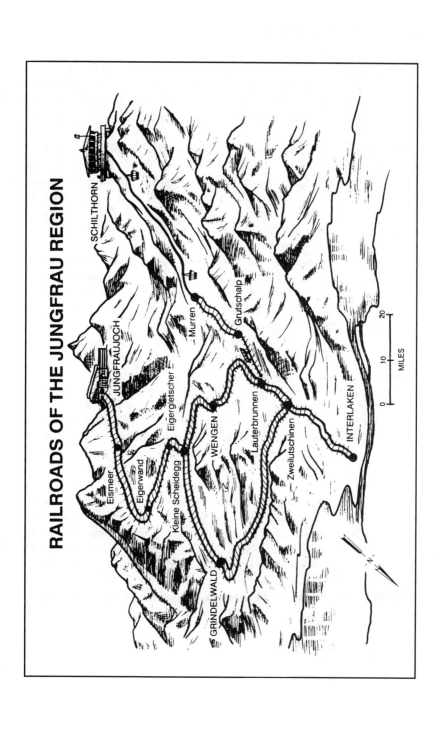

SCHILTHORN

JUNGFRAUJOCH

Eismeer

Eigerwand

Eigergletscher

Murren

Kleine Scheidegg

Grutschalp

WENGEN

Lauterbrunnen

GRINDELWALD

Zweilutschinen

INTERLAKEN

MILES

0   10   20

258 TRAVELING EUROPE'S TRAINS

Jungfrau Region. Narrow-gauge BOB (Bernese Oberland Bahn) trains departing from platform 2 take you to the region famous for the highest train station in Europe, a score of great mountaineering centers, and the spot where James Bond confronted his archenemy in *On Her Majesty's Secret Service.*

When you travel from Interlaken Ost to the Jungfraujoch, BOB's route takes you through Grindelwald to Kleine Scheidegg, where you board the yellow-striped maroon carriages of the Jungfrau Railroads, new in 1992. When you return to Interlaken Ost, take the western arc descending from Kleine Scheidegg on the Wengernalp Railroad (WAB) to Wengen's train station. WAB celebrated its centenary in 1993.

Your second option from Interlaken Ost station takes you to the Schilthorn (of James Bond's Piz Gloria notoriety). It treats you to four spectacular modes of travel. Leave the WAB at Lauterbrunnen, board the funicular to Grutschalp, transfer to the mountain Murren Railroad, and top your ascent with a dramatic gondola ride to the mountain-top restaurant crowning the Schilthorn (9,748 feet).

When you have taken both the Schilthorn and the Jungfraujoch trips, you judge the question: "Which is better?" The Jungfraujoch is more famous and gives you things to do at the top—a museum, ice palace, "Toporama," and more. The Schilthorn gives you a stunning panorama, a thrilling ascent, and Bond's Piz Gloria. Try both.

Your climb to the Jungfraujoch is expensive (the Schilthorn adventure is less expensive). Eurailpasses and Europasses get you only a 25 percent reduction, but without using a day of your Eurail Flexipass, past Interlaken Ost and Swiss Passes take you free only as far as Grindelwald (although the cards come in handy again during the Schilthorn trip). Although trains are second class only, do not invest in this trip when it is cloudy at the summit. The tourist office next to the extravagant Grand Hotel Victoria Jungfrau, a 10-minute walk from Ost station about halfway to the West station, will give you reliable advice before you set out, and you hotel may be connected to the rotating video camera at the summit, so that you can see for yourself. At the same time, check to see if there is an early-morning departure (before the connecting trains from Zurich and Geneva arrive) at reduced prices.

To the Jungfraujoch

Your 1990, brown-and-tan BOB car marked for Grindelwald (those in front marked for "Lauterbrunnen" travel up the Lauterbrunnen valley for Wengen, Lauterbrunnen, and the funicular to Grutschalp) stops first in Wilderswil. Several Swiss with walking boots and Alpine walking sticks get off for the rack-and-pinion railroad to Schynige Platte.

Shortly before making your second stop, you get your first teasing view of the great white Alps in the distance. You feel a surge of anticipation as you cross the first frolicking branch of two Lutschinen torrents, the White Lutschine and the Black Lutschine, and you arrive in Zweilutschinen, where the rivers meet. Railroad workers separate the two sections of your train.

Your car to Grindelwald climbs along the raging Black Lutschine, carefully banked with flagstones on the left. Contrary to its name, it is white with melted glacial runoff.

Through the Grindelwald valley, you see tall chalets scattered on the left. On the right you hear bell-tolling cows. Outside your pulled-down window you can almost pick a dazzling horticultural bouquet of delicate white wild flowers. A river on your right charges down over huge boulders and the waterfall dropping from above makes a rainbow arc from the sun.

Now you come round a bend, revealing a vision. The magnificent Eiger towers like a giant wall, its peak hidden in flying clouds. You look to the left and there is the Schweizerhof hotel with its red shutters. Now your train coasts to a stop in the brown-shuttered Grindelwald station (3,392 feet).

On an unforgettable site, Grindelwald, the "Glacier Village," is the center of the eastern Jungfrau Region, and looks like a Swiss village should look. Each chalet is neatly arranged and tucked under a tree, balconies are swept, geraniums are in full bloom and fuchsias flower from every window box. Firewood is corded neatly and stored symmetrically under the eaves. In the fields, hay is carefully stacked.

Grindelwald has changed with the times by adding a few key hotels and a modern indoor swimming pool, but it has not lost its essential mountaineering charm or its good mountain air. The tourist office (open 8 A.M. to noon and 2 to 5 P.M., closed Sunday) is three to four minutes to the right up the main highway from the station.

You quickly change to the waiting, 31-inch-gauge, green-and-yellow striped, 1993 WAB train carriage which starts out down the mountainside past gardens filled with fruit and great dahlias of all colors before stopping at Grund station, the WAB train depot. Then you zigzag up the opposite mountain slope for your approach to Kleine Scheidegg.

This is a playground for long camera lenses. You see model farms, summerhouses, hotels, chalets, churches, and cows with bells swinging on their necks.

At the Brandegg stop (4,272 feet), your ears pop. The clang of cowbells wafts through the lowered windows. The animals look uncomfortable on the steep mountainside as they take the last clumps of green grass.

Past Alpiglen (5,252 feet), your train enters a snow shed and then clanks through a double-tracked passing-point. The landscape has scattered trees, stubborn shrubs, and a marshy look. You pass through more snow sheds with extruded steel uprights for strength.

Kleine Scheidegg (6,762 feet) comes into view. From a distance, the big hotels look like those found on a game board. A lilting alphorn serenades you as you climb off into a semicircle of hotels and restaurants. On this ledge connecting the Lauterbrunnen and Grindelwald valleys, you can cross to one of several large restaurants facing the station. Crowds of adventurers bask in the sun and enjoy the outdoor service on sunny days. Usually you will see a man in full Swiss folk costume playing an alphorn. You can order a nice lunch, a pair of sausages with potato salad, or just a beer while you listen to the melodious sounds of the alphorn and relish the incredible view of the Eiger, immense before you like a wall.

Kleine Scheidegg's shingled train station faces the waiting carriages of the 39-inch-gauge, Jungfrau Railroads (JB) for your trip to the summit. In addition to their 1993 maroon-and-yellow carriages, JB is proud of their "Rowan" carriages with natural rowan-wood sidings.

So formidable were the difficulties of working at this great altitude that 16 years were required to complete the 5 3/4 miles upward from Kleine Scheidegg. Even then, the track ended at the Jungfraujoch, 1 1/4 miles and more than 2,000 feet below the summit of the Jungfrau, its intended goal.

Over the first half-mile, which is flat, your train reaches its maximum speed, 15 mph, but slows perceptibly when you start to climb. Immediately you have wonderful views back on Kleine Scheidegg and the Eiger glacier close on the right glaring brightly at you. When you near the glacier you see its detail, the scalloping and furrows caused by runoff, and you appreciate the vastness of it even more.

Your climb is so steep that those facing forward are thrown against their seat backs and those facing backwards brace themselves to keep from sliding out of their seats. Be sure to choose a forward-facing seat on the right side.

Your first stop is the Eigergletscher (Eiger glacier) station (7,612 feet), which was faced with granite in 1990. This is where the construction crew in 1898 established a colony of 150 workers just below the perpendicular North Face. Now you see the repair shop for the Jungfrau Railroad just below the entry to the long tunnel ahead.

Surging ahead, you enter the 4.4-mile tunnel gallery where you will spend some 41 minutes in darkness. Travelers exclaim and push up the windows because of cold air suddenly blasting on them. Heat percolates from under the seats. You sit 2+2 in one-class, fancy seats more spacious than the other narrow-gauge trains of the Jungfrau Region.

You climb so steeply that when you pass the horizontal sign "Open all year round," it appears cocked at an angle. The maximum gradient would be one foot in four on a direct route, so a corkscrew tunnel had to be constructed. The curved course allows you to stop at two intermediate stations with extraordinary views.

A gong sounds. Now you hear yodeling. Then an impersonal, recorded greeting in German and then French and English announces a five-minute stop at Eigerwand, the "Face of the Eiger" (9,400 feet).

From Eigerwand your train curves slightly more than 90 degrees in order to continue its climb. It runs through a tunnel scarcely big enough for one train only. You wouldn't dare walk alongside.

Less than a mile farther, now below the southeastern face of the Eiger and 10,368 feet high (a job that took the tunnelers two years to excavate), you reach the Eismeer (Sea of Ice) station. A hollow has been carved out of the rock big enough to hold a double track, so that ascending and descending trains pass one another. Once again you hear yodel music and an announcement for a five-minute stop. Here you see a view over the ragged surface of the glacier toward the Wetterhorn, the Schreckhorn, the Fiescherhorner, and the great crevasse under the Monchsjoch.

Your final segment lifts you only 970 feet, so the designers flattened the gradient from one in four to one in 16 feet (except for the last l,640 feet). For many years this stretch was carried by ordinary adhesion, at just more than 11 miles an hour, but now the line is rack-and-pinion throughout.

The Alpine world of the Jungfraujoch (11,336 feet) is on view at the "Top of Europe" complex, where five levels of modern architecture blend harmoniously with the surroundings. Take the elevator to the Sphinx Terrace overlooking the Aletsch Glacier; see the ice sculptures in the Ice Palace; visit the scientific exhibit. When you get hungry, dine in a restaurant or cafe. This is a wonderful complex of mountain restaurants, panoramas, activities, husky dogs, mountaineering, and the "Toporama" slide show.

Departures are half-hourly during the summer. If you miss one there is always another carriage waiting for you. You will be warm and satisfied after your magnificent day, and you won't be alone dozing on your way down.

To the Schilthorn

For the Schilthorn (*www.Schilthorn.ch*), be sure to board a BOB car at Interlaken Ost station marked for Lauterbrunnen (alternately, you can descend via WAB to Lauterbrunnen from the Jungfraujoch). In Lauterbrunnen, you can either scramble across the tracks or use the underpass to the blue building, the lower terminus of the "Bergbahn Lauterbrunnen-Murren." Your climb in the stepped, 60-passenger funicular will surprise you with its steep incline and length.

When you reach the upper terminus you immediately board the waiting Murren Railroad, a one- to four-car, brown-and-tan electric tram which takes you 2 3/4 miles horizontally to Murren (5,373 feet).

You will see one of the grandest views of the world here. The magnificent presence of the Jungfrau seems only a stone's throw away across a precipitous chasm. On your return, a casual walk from Murren to Grutschalp will long remain one of your fondest memories.

When your tram reaches Murren, disembark and walk through the village 15 minutes to the Schilthornbahn—there is only one street through Murren so you can't get lost. You pass every shop conceivable for a small village and carefully tended, flower-covered chalets as pleasant as any. Benches along the way offer places to break your walk.

You join the Schilthornbahn at its second stage. The first stage brings riders from the valley floor (free with the Swiss Pass) in 100-passenger gondolas from the Stechelberg Valley terminus at Gimmelwald (4,484 feet), with free parking for 1,500 automobiles and served by postal bus from Lauterbrunnen.

Your second-stage, swinging, 80-passenger red gondola with white "Schilthorn Bahn" lettered in front (reduction with a Swiss Pass) glides over the spacious Blumental ("Flower Valley") in a cable span of 3,038 yards supported by only two intermediate pylons. You appear simply to glide up a threatening rock face to a stop at the top of a towering bastion. First you look down on unbelievable rock formations sculpted by snow and glaciers. Then you look down on the glaciers.

At Birg, you change gondolas. Birg (8,781 feet) has a restaurant and sun terrace. Your second gondola is a single-cabin for 100 persons. Between Birg and the summit, you see the scenery unfolding in all directions until you see Mont Blanc and Germany's Black Forest appearing in the distance and the Jungfrau Alps face you. This span is 1,931 yards long—the longest unsupported span in the country. You notice even the gondola operators look exposed and weathered and wear dark glasses and sun creams. Finally you see some venturesome, hearty Swiss outside clambering down the snow. Your gondola swings to a final stop and you feel as daring as James Bond himself when he took those last few steps here to meet his archenemy in *On Her Majesty's Secret Service.*

Piz Gloria has been enlarged after that film. It is still a round building, but now with a two-level restaurant and an open sun terrace. The solar-powered restaurant revolves in 50-minute cycles past a continuous circle of picture windows that show off sectors of the 360-degree panorama. There are revolving restaurants and other revolving restaurants, but none have prepared you for the sense of the Swiss Alps rotating around you while you enjoy hearty Swiss specialties to the melodies of a mountain accordionist. Below, there is a self-service cafeteria with modest prices.

On the sun terrace, deck chairs are especially valued by travelers who have trouble with the high altitude. The red-and-white Swiss flag fluttering overhead seems planted as a backdrop for your photographs. If you err and come when Piz Gloria is shrouded in clouds, there is a panoramic vision show called "Touristorama."

Railroads of the Jungfrau Region
Typical Service
Interlaken—Grindelwald—Kl. Scheidegg-Jungfraujoch

0932	dep.	INTERLAKEN OST	arr.	1627
0937	dep.	Wilderswil	dep.	1622
0946	dep.	Zweilutschinen	dep.	1615
0952	dep.	Lutschental	dep.	1606
0959	dep.	Burglauenen	dep.	1559

1002	dep.	Schwendi	dep.	1556
1008	arr.	GRINDELWALD	dep.	1550
1019	dep.	GRINDELWALD	arr.	1545
1026	dep.	Grindelwald Grund	dep.	1541
1054	arr.	KLEINE SCHEIDEGG	dep.	1502
1102	dep.	KLEINE SCHEIDEGG	dep.	1449
1112	dep.	Eigergletscher	dep.	1440
1153	arr.	JUNGFRAUJOCH	dep.	1400

Interlaken—Lauterbrunnen—Wengen—Kl. Scheidegg-Jungfraujoch

0932	dep.	INTERLAKEN OST	arr.	1627
0937	dep.	Wilderswil	dep.	1622
0945	dep.	Zweilutschinen	dep.	1615
0954	arr.	LAUTERBRUNNEN	dep.	1605
1010	dep.	LAUTERBRUNNEN	arr.	1600
1024	arr.	WENGEN	dep.	1543
1030	dep.	WENGEN	arr.	1535
1046	dep.	Wengernalp	dep.	1511
1055	arr.	KLEINE SCHEIDEGG	dep.	1502
1102	dep.	KLEINE SCHEIDEGG	arr.	1449
1112	dep.	Eigergletscher	dep.	1440
1158	arr.	JUNGFRAUJOCH	dep.	1400

Interlaken—Lauterbrunnen—Murren-Schilthorn

1032	dep.	INTERLAKEN OST	arr.	1527
1037	dep.	Wilderswil	dep.	1522
1045	dep.	Zweilutschinen	dep.	1515
1054	arr.	LAUTERBRUNNEN	dep.	1505
1102	dep.	LAUTERBRUNNEN	arr.	1458
1113	dep.	Grutschalp	dep.	1447
1130	arr.	MURREN	dep.	1430
1140	dep.	MURREN	arr.	1420
1155	dep.	Birg	dep.	1410
1159	arr.	SCHILTHORN	dep.	1401

Golden Pass Panoramic Designer Train by Pininfarina

Your cream-and-night-blue designer train curls back and forth, up through terrace after terrace of lush vineyards. Your stiff climb takes you up a gradient of one in 15.4 over the six miles between Montreux and Chamby as you zigzag upward from 1,300 feet to 2,500 feet.

You look down on Montreux's freshly whitewashed hotels, patina-green copper roofs, and brown wooden chalets getting smaller and smaller. The little strip of town set upon the only place the Swiss could

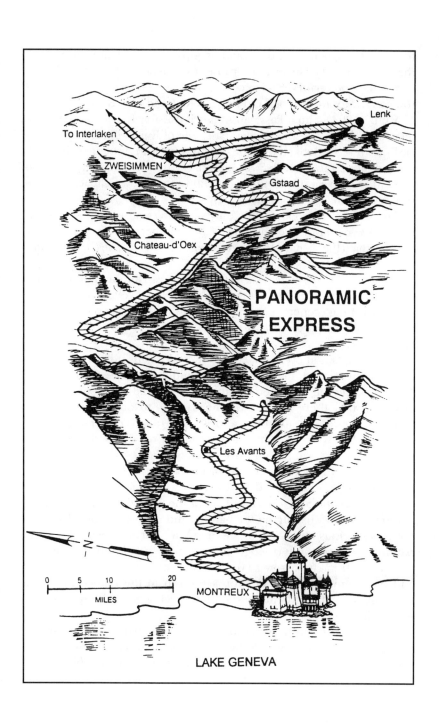

Lenk

To Interlaken

ZWEISIMMEN

Gstaad

Chateau-d'Oex

PANORAMIC
EXPRESS

Les Avants

N

0   5   10   20
MILES

MONTREUX

LAKE GENEVA

find for it between the steep Vaudois Alps and the "Vaud Riviera" on the shores of Lake Geneva never loses its charm.

You have powerful views from the Golden Pass Panoramic of the narrow-gauge Montreux-Oberland Bernois Railroad (MOB, *www.mob.ch*).

MOB's 1993 Golden Pass Panoramic is possibly Europe's most striking train running on the Golden Pass, one of Europe's most spectacular lines. It is overlooked by many North American passengers because of its great popularity with Swiss nationals (first-class traffic was up 480 percent in 10 years) and the reputation and greater capacity of the roughly parallel Glacier Express trains.

The Golden Pass Panoramic only seats 160—all in first class—but what seats you have! The end cars—front and back—were designed by Pininfarina (the celebrated "couturier des carrosseries") and built near Florence, Italy.

Twelve lucky passengers sit in Grandes vues Panoramic, which are three rows in front of and below the driver, where you sit nose-to-nose with onrushing scenery, because you have nothing between you and the view but wraparound glass. The experience is the only one of its kind in Europe.

The driver sits above, isolated and locked for his privacy and safety, and you store your luggage in the middle carriage—which is the "Saanen" electric locomotive cunningly tucked away inconspicuously—so that there are not overhead racks to obscure your views through the dome windows above. His raised driver's cabin is cramped, but your train has video cameras on the body sides and above the buffer beam to improve visibility.

The Golden Pass Panoramic is divided into two first-class sections, front and back, each served by a hostess who welcomes you aboard. Catering is by the SSG, the subsidiary of the Swiss Federal Railroads.

Doors open with a tug on the handle, and close automatically. Even the very spacious number two, "Grande Vue," carriages excel for their panoramas. The window ledge is lower than usual and the window posts are extremely narrow, so you not only look through the overhead and panoramic windows, but you see down to the railbed below. It gives you a feeling of being outdoors yourself among the spectacular mountain scenery.

The front seats are reserved on a first-come, first-reserved basis, so you may not be able to secure one, but be sure to reserve a window seat. All you see from the plush blue seats is the panorama of the mountains.

Travel is free on a Eurailpass, Europass, or first-class Swiss Pass. All you need is a reservation costing six Swiss francs, which makes this one of the great finds of European train travel.

The end carriages contain a bar and a lounge with divans, which are not reserved, so that you can move around to enjoy the freedom and watch different perspectives unfold of the changing panorama unfold. These glassed wonders show you beautiful scenery in a way no other carriage can.

The Golden Pass Panoramic makes three departures daily in each direction over the 55-mile length between Montreux and Zweisimmen. When you can't fit the Golden Pass Panoramic into your timetable try to reserve the Inter Regio Panoramic, bright in its golden livery to match the Golden Pass Panoramic, which carries both first- and second-class ticket and pass holders.

You can board the Panoramic in Zweisimmen, but the shimmering glare off Lake Geneva during a westward afternoon descent to lakeside blinds your view, so it is always more scenic to make this trip going east-ward from Montreux.

There is no better place to stay before beginning or after ending your Panoramic Express trip than Montreux. The flower-scented prom-enade here is one of Europe's most beautiful. Montreux occupies a lovely site sheltered from the wind on the eastern end of Lake Geneva and known for the mildest climate north of the Alps. Tourists enjoy excursions, water sports, tennis, and just strolling along the prome-nade. Snow in winter falls only a few hundred feet above the town.

Montreux's train station, one of the few in Europe with three track gauges, is arranged awkwardly on the side of a mountain but the recently installed escalators and elevator make it easy to get from one level to the other.

The MOB office is next to platform No. 5, where you leave your nar-row-gauge Crystal Panoramic train. Platform No. 1 is used for the Swiss Federal Railroads' standard-gauge line to Lausanne/Geneva/Geneva Airport. Swissair check-in for Geneva Airport is directly below at the street-level entrance.

Montreux's tourist office is beside the lake down the flight of stairs across the street from the train station. Go to the promenade and 1,000 feet to the left (south). Agents at the tourist office will give you a free Golden Pass Panoramic color brochure and map. Of course, they will also make hotel arrangements.

The steamers circling the Lake of Geneva dock nearby before pro-ceeding around Chillon Castle. (They, too, are free on Eurail and

Swiss passes—even for landings in France, and an excursion to Yvoire is recommended.) To reach the train station from the lake steamers, walk left and up the steps.

As your Golden Pass Panoramic leaves Montreux and weaves farther up the mountainside, Lake Geneva shrinks and becomes dwarfed by gray, snow-streaked French Alps towering in the background. With a view like a satellite in the sky, you can pick out the casino and the red-and-white Swiss flag over the Montreux Palace Hotel. The tall building you see near the lake was built in 1964, when high-rises were the rage. It is a condominium boasting a 26th-floor restaurant. The Eurotel to its right was built the same year. It is the second-tallest in town. You see the lake hamlets Vevey and Lausanne to the north, and the Rhone River valley to the south disappearing toward the Simplon Pass.

You can choose to sit either first- or second-class in the panoramic carriages of the Inter Regio Panoramic and Mixed Panoramic trains. Traveling first class, you sit 2+2 with nine rows per carriage. Second-class passengers sit the same in 14 rows per car. The difference is the amount of legroom and the comfort of the upholstery.

The hillside above Montreux is famous for its trees and flowers. You pass through grape arbors to an altitude of nearly 2,000 feet, past walnut trees to 2,300 feet, and among fruit trees to the summit. Wild narcissus sparkle in springtime. Chernex is the site of MOB's workshop, where MOB's dedicated crew is passionate about making the Golden Pass Panoramic the best train running.

On your left you see the first of the charming chalets like those in the Bernese Oberland; they give you a warm first impression of the celebrated Golden Pass route, which rivals the Glacier Express for the most spectacular east-west route in Switzerland. Looking up through the oblique windows reveals the crests of the Alps and gives you great depth of perspective. You feel inspired by the devastating height of the Alps above you. Because about 90 percent of your car is glass, be thankful for the air-conditioning which overcomes the greenhouse heating.

Climbing through the stiffest gradient of the line, you cross the crest. You final memory is your long view down the valley to Chillon Castle, with a white Lake Geneva steamer gliding into dock.

Through the 8,000-foot-long Jaman tunnel you enter the wholly different Sarine valley. Your Panoramic picks up speed through a series of reverse curves on the single, narrow-gauge track. The Saanen locomotive set the MOB's speed record: almost 70 mph. The conductor with a blue-and-white MOB winged emblem pinned to his black cap (patent leather visor) accepts your Eurailpass, Europass, or Swiss Pass with a smile.

Now you are riding through cuts in the limestone mountainsides past Les Scieres. Brown-and-white contented-looking cows graze in the tall, green grass. Families harvesting hay wave at you with green handkerchiefs, glad of an excuse to lean on their wooden rakes. Most passengers wave back. The brown-and-white cows shake their heavy bells and more or less ignore them.

The valley is wild and green, but above, the limestone Vaudois Alps form flat-topped ridges and throw long shadows you see through the oblique windows. You regret that your train seems to rush. You wish it would slow down so you could study the rugged mountain crests, the peaceful valleys, and the randomly scattered, typical houses with broad, graceful eaves, intricate woodwork, and flower boxes overflowing with bright yellow and blue blossoms.

Looking at the homes, the dress, and the work, you form an impression of the way of life of these mountain people who speak French, are generally Protestant, and decorate their farmhouses profusely. They live in tidier versions of those you will see only a half-hour ahead in the Bernese Oberland, the region that gave our language the word "chalet" and made this form of house synonymous with Switzerland the world over. They have low-pitched roofs and wide eaves on four sides.

Your Golden Pass Panoramic departs Switzerland's eastern canton, Vaud, at Chateau-d'Oex (say "Chateau Day"). You are halfway through your trip and halfway between the Bernese Oberland and the Lake of Geneva.

The mountain village set among towering Alps at 3,083 feet becomes in January the world's colorful capital of hot-air ballooning.

In winter, skiers race along the slopes and in summer, mountain bikers in competition tear through the trees.

Chateau-d'Oex's traditional architecture mixes chalets, farmhouses and hotels. Here you find the typical family resort of the Vaudois Alps, with public pool and skating rink and a high lift to La Braye on the summit above.

Guests congregate around the tables of mountain inns to enjoy the local fondue and raclette made from the tart l'Etivaz cheese produced in some 150 chalet dairies. Its flavor makes the regional cheese specialties the most renowned in Switzerland.

The ladies in the tourist office some three minutes down the hill-side from the train station are pleased to provide you information and hotel assistance. Before you leave you can read *www.chateau-doex.ch*. You pass through Rougemont station (3,254 feet), remarkable for its carved wood decorations. The huge sloping roof below the train that catches your eye covers an early Romanesque church built on the site of an eleventh-century, Cluniac priory. Swiss from all over the country travel here to visit the church and the adjacent sixteenth-century castle.

The quaint Saanen station (3,364 feet) marks the point where you leave the French-speaking Sarine valley and enter German-speaking Canton Bern. Some houses here, now adorned with climbing plants, date from the seventeenth century. Saanen's old-fashioned character makes a good contrast with that of its booming neighbor, pricey Gstaad, only three minutes ahead.

In Gstaad, buildings get bigger. The hotels do well here in this smart village, one of Switzerland's premier winter resorts and a quiet summer destination.

When your panoramic train winds up the 180-degree Reichenbach curve overlooking Gstaad, the view back is ideal for photographers. Passengers cluster to the windows to take advantage.

Saanenmoser's train station (4,043 feet, the highest point on the line), with green shutters and cutouts in the shape of hearts, must be the most filigreed in the world. The station's dark brown wood sets off the white detailing and lace curtains on the windows.

Picking up speed, you sweep down the Saanenmoser depression. Spike-tipped, 5,000-foot Alpine peaks stand in the distance and farm-houses defy the pull of gravity on both slopes of the valley.

Your trip is nearly over when you pass through a spiral tunnel to arrive on the valley floor at Zweisimmen (3,090 feet). This is your junction for Lenk and Spiez/Interlaken, the route known as the "Golden Pass" leading onto the Brunig Line (*www.breunig.ch*) to Lucerne. Tracks 1 and 2 (42-inch gauge) are devoted to your narrow-gauge train from Montreux. Tracks 3, 4, 11, and 13 (60 inches) lead SBB trains to Spiez/Interlaken.

Construction is planned to add a third rail for narrow-gauge trains to the standard-gauge line connecting Zweisimmen with Interlaken's East station and then over the Brunig line to Lucerne.

Almost everyone changes for the dark-blue-and-white carriages of the

Switzerland 271

Bern-Lotschberg-Simplon Railroad (BLS, *www.bls.ch*) for the 27-mile run to Spiez. This private line, which boasts the most powerful locomotives in Switzerland, also accepts Eurailpasses, Europasses, and Swiss Passes. Those travelers to Spiez are back on big rails, but how disappointed they must feel when they look up for the view and realize they no longer have windows to see the high scenery. You may change here for the connection to Lenk. After some minutes, the dispatcher waves his signal wand, and you go—but in a surprising direction: not back up the mountainside. You travel 12 miles laterally, up the Simmental ("Tal" meaning valley), and arrive 15 minutes later in Lenk at the foot of the 10,600-foot Wildstrubel.

The Simmen Valley is a showcase for beautiful farmhouses. Every year a panel of judges selects the most beautiful farmhouse in Switzerland and every year a farmhouse in the Simmental either wins or ranks high.

The village of Lenk (3,500 feet) is another of those wonderful summer and winter mountain resorts of which Switzerland seems to have no end. Whether you visit for lunch before continuing or take an extended vacation here, Lenk is a pleasant stay.

Golden Pass Panoramic Train Service

1028	1428	1628	dep.	MONTREUX	arr.	1228	1428	1828
1038	1439	1639	dep.	Chernex	dep.	1219	1419	1819
1053	1453	1653	dep.	Les Avants	dep.	1207	1407	1807
1113	1513	1713	dep.	Montbovon	dep.	1147	1347	1747
1127	1427	1727	arr.	Chateau-d'Oex	dep.	1130	1330	1730
1129	1429	1729	dep.	Chateau-d'Oex	arr.	1128	1328	1728
1139	1439	1739	dep.	Rougemont	dep.	1119	1319	1719
1144	1444	1744	dep.	Saanen	dep.	1114	1314	1714
1147	1447	1747	arr.	Gstaad	dep.	1110	1310	1710
1149	1449	1749	dep.	Gstaad	arr.	1108	1308	1708
1157	1457	1757	dep.	Schonreid	dep.	1101	1301	1701
1201	1501	1701	dep.	Saanenmoser	dep.	1057	1257	1657
1215	1515	1715	arr.	ZWEISIMMEN	dep.	1044	1244	1644
1249	..	1742	dep.	Zweisimmen	arr.	1008	1211	1526
1307	..	1801	arr.	LENK i. S.	dep.	0950	1153	1610

Inter Regio Panoramic trains depart Montreux at 12:28 and 6:28 P.M., and depart Zweisimmen at 9:44 A.M. and 2:44 P.M.

Iberia

Smart Traveling on the Trains of Spain and Portugal

Spanish trains—Madrid-Seville by AVE—Madrid-Cordoba-Seville—Barcelona-Valencia-Alicante with Euromed—Madrid-Valencia on Alaris—Riding RENFE's domestic overnight trains—Using Madrid's and Barcelona's train stations—Airport connections—Rail lounges—Portuguese railroads—Using Lisbon's public transportation—Rail pass travel

It's surprising that traveling between the two Iberian countries, Spain and Portugal, is so difficult. No mainline train connection between the two countries is available with rail pass and no through day train, at all, between Madrid and Lisbon. Your best connection between the two capital cities is the Tren Hotel Lusitania, and this uses "Global" pricing, which puts rail-pass holders at a disadvantage. The alternate way between Madrid and Lisbon for rail-pass holders is to take the afternoon Spanish Talgo train from Madrid to San Sebastian or Irun. In either station you can join the overnight Portuguese train, the legendary Sud Express, to Lisbon or Porto via Medina del Campo and cross the famous Eiffel Bridge en route. This option loses an afternoon from your trip.

If you want to travel to Portugal from France, and care to bypass Spain, take the TGV connection from Paris for the Sud Express and don't go through Madrid.

The alternatives for crossing between Spain and Portugal are to use the secondary lines in the north of Portugal connecting to Galicia or the DAMAS bus service (or ferry) in Andalusia crossing the Guadiana river to Portugal's Algarve. These options are described in the text below.

Travelers curious about visiting Andorra, Europe's newest republic (1993), should use the French overnight train carrying first- and second-class French couchettes and second-class compartments from Paris (Austerlitz) to L'Hospitalet, France, your bus gateway to the tiny republic. The bus service operated by Societe Franco-Andorrane de Transports makes immediate connections. From Andorra via bus to La Tour-de-Carol you connect with a second-class-only Spanish "Delta" train for Barcelona.

Spanish Trains

RENFE, the acronym for the Spanish Railroads, "Red Nacional de los Ferrocarriles Espanoles," (*www.renfe.es*) is in hot competition with deregulated air fares and automobile traffic. Their trains are innovative and comfortable to ride. AVE is *Alta Velocidad Espanola*, the 196-mph high-speed train between Madrid and Seville. Euromed (Em) indicates the 124-mph trains Barcelona-Alicante. Talgo 200 (T200) are Talgo trains equipped to run on both the high-speed line and the broad-gauge tracks. "Talgo" indicates quality express trains using light, articulated carriages. InterCity (IC) and Arco are quality day express trains. "Trenhotel" (hotel) are quality night trains, while "Estrella" (Estr) are night trains with sleeping cars, couchettes and seated carriages. "Alaris" are 124-mph tilting trains on the Madrid-Albacete-Valencia line. "Diurno" (*D*) trains are ordinary day trains.

RENFE's flagship train is the aging EC Catalan Talgo between Barcelona and Montpellier, with TGV connections to Geneva and Paris, the only one to use spacious "Internacional" carriages. Low-to-the-ground, tilting Talgo Pendular units are some of the most comfortable you ride in Europe. The premium, 186-mph AVE (for "Alta Velocidad Espanola," or "Spanish high-speed train") delights everyone and the high-speed Talgo 200 trains surprise everyone when they change gauge and branch off over the wide-gauge network to take you to Malaga, Cadiz, or Huelva. The newest improvement in service is the constant reduction in time between Barcelona and Valencia on Euromed TGVs taking you over Mediterranean Line Spanish wide-gauge tracks at 124 mph.

Unfortunately, the Spanish Railroads puts a lump in your travel plans by limiting the use of rail passes on AVEs, Talgo 200s and posh Trens Hotel. Pass holders do, however, receive discounts. RENFE's point-to-point ticket fares are not based on mileage traveled, but are set to reflect variations in seasonal demand and relative advantage over competing air and road transportation.

You use sparkling stations like Madrid's Puerta de Atocha, Seville's Santa Justa, and Barcelona's Estacio de Franca (Termino); you transit well-managed hubs such as Madrid's Chamartin station; and you relax in first-class lounges open free to all first-class rail-pass holders. Wagons-Lits personnel staff restaurant and sleeping cars. You agree that Spain is a great nation to visit by train.

RENFE requires reservations on its long-distance trains, but RENFE's computerized system makes them easy for you to obtain at any RENFE office or train station or even up to two months in advance from the U.S., from Rail Europe (see Appendix A). At Madrid's very convenient, downtown RENFE office at Alcala, 44 (open 9:30 A.M. to 8 P.M., use the Banco de Espana metro stop) agents can make your reservations for Spain, Italy, and to Portugal. They accept bank credit cards for payment, but not for reservations. Be sure to flash them in advance to alert the booking agent.

RENFE's trains run on wide-gauge (5 feet, 6 inches) rails, except for the AVEs and high-speed Talgo 200s, which zip along 1992's 295-mile European standard-gauge (4 feet, 8 1/2 inches) link between Madrid and Seville. You must change trains when you cross the French frontier or your train must be accommodated to the change of gauge. RENFE mechanics change gauge by adjusting the wheelsets on the go so smoothly that you can realize it only by the slowing of the train through the gauge-change station. Talgo trains such as the EN Jean Miro, EN Francisco de Goya, EN Pablo Casals, and EC Catalan Talgo are designed so mechanics in a work pit at the border widen or narrow their wheelsets while at night passengers remain sound asleep and during the day curi-ous passengers open the doors to watch. Similar arrangements allow Talgo 200 trains to enter and exit the standard-gauge high-speed line. The facility at Hendaye for swapping undercarriages was shuttered in 1996 when the last of conventional overnight trains was discontinued.

Travelers from northern Europe to Morocco frequently use the overnight Media Luna train between Irun and Algeciras. In Algeciras, they change to ferry, but this overnight service runs during the summer only. A Talgo 200 leaves Madrid Atocha Station in the morning, runs via the high-speed line to Cordoba, where it changes gauge, and reaches Algeciras in early afternoon, averaging about 68 mph over the 400-mile distance. South of Bobadilla you pass through superb mountain scenery, and climb some steep gradients, especially the S-shaped rise out of the Guadiaro Valley between La Indiana and Ronda.

Track laying began in spring 2000 on the 218-mph Madrid-Barcelona line. The Madrid-Lleida section is due to be in use by June 2002, while the line should completed in 2004, when it will take 2 1/2 hours between Madrid and Barcelona compared with 6 1/2 hours at present.

Many travelers are surprised to learn about the well-running secondary meter-gauge train network across the north of Spain because they don't see it on the Eurailpass train map—for the reason that FEVE does not accept Eurailpasses. FEVE, "Ferrocarriles de Via Estretcha," claims to be the longest continuous narrow-gauge network in Europe—a claim that is echoed by Switzerland's Rhaetian Railroads. Their "Mini-Apolo" diesel units were modernized in 1999 with Volvo engines, air-conditioning, digital passenger information displays, retention toilets and upholstered 2+2 seating.

Madrid-Seville by AVE

After considering 100 different names, Spain's 186-mph train between Madrid and Seville was dubbed AVE, which stands both for "Alta Velocidad Espanola" (Spanish high-speed) and "Ancho de Via Europeo" (European gauge), and also means "bird" in Castilian, which led to the design of the logo. After its debut, it suffered mechanical problems, causing the AVE to soon become known as the "Averias," which is Spanish for breakdowns. After the running in was completed, it became known to tens of thousands of visitors to Seville's Expo as Europe's best train.

The vice president of the Spanish government opened the high-speed line on April 14, 1992, and then traveled from Madrid to Seville in 2 hours, 55 minutes, with three publicity stops. Scheduled service began a week later, on April 21, 1992. A Spanish-built AVE established a new Spanish speed record of 221.6 mph on April 23, 1993.

Sadly, Eurailpasses or Spain Railpasses do not cover travel on AVEs, but pass holders do get a price break. AVE has three classes: "Turista,"

"Preferente," and "Club," which are shown on the exterior of the carriages. The fares are not calculated by distance traveled; the special fare structure depends on the class of travel and the time of day. (The monstrous "yield management" system used by airlines is at work.) Time division No. 1 (early; trains departing at 7 A.M.) has the lowest fares. Division No. 2 (normal) applies to trains departing all day and evening except peak. Division No. 3 (peak) applies to trains departing at 8 A.M., 2 P.M., and 7 P.M. When you buy your tickets in advance, and are holding your Eurailpass or Europass, you pay $20, $40, or $60, respectively for Turista, Preferente, or Club. In Europe you receive 15, 35, or 40 percent off the normal price. Holders of Eurail Youthpasses are accepted only in Turista class.

Reservations are required. In Spain you receive 25 percent off for one-day, round-trip tickets, 20 percent off for round trips within 15 days. The return trips may be made on Talgo 200 trains. Those 65 and over receive a 25 percent discount; children four to 11 pay 60 percent.

AVE's Tourist Class with 2+2 seating offers audio-video, a bar/cafeteria, a drink machine and telephones. Travelers in the open salons of Preferred Class sit 2+1 and also receive newspapers and magazines. Travelers in Club Class sit in the mixed compartment/aisle arrangement of the preferred TGV Atlantique-type (see "France" chapter) carriages. They additionally receive a very fine meal service at their seats. Again, the full-length bar car resembles TGV Atlantique's except for stand-up, wooden-topped islands for passengers to snack.

You depart from the ground level of Puerta de Atocha station. Departures ("salida") are shown on an electronic board in the departures hall and again over the platforms in the departure area. Show your ticket at the gate before entering the platform. South of Getafe, some 13 miles south of the Spanish capital, you follow the track bed of the former Madrid-Badajoz broad-gauge line whose track was torn up and parts of the bed straightened to allow you to reach 186 mph. After you pass Ciudad Real, you run parallel to the still-existing broad-gauge line to Brazatortas. Building the northern segment on the right-of-way of a prior secondary line broke all construction speed records. In one year the infrastructure was completed.

Your introduction to Andalusia is entirely olives. Olive trees, with their twisted trunks and stunted branches pruned to grow no higher than a man on a ladder can reach, define the arid hills and gorges and break into the crusty brick red soil. They *are* the landscape.

From Brazatortas you enter the challenging Sierra Morena mountains that provided the second segment of track construction. At Villanueva you slow along the difficult 17-mile section to Adamuz, climbing at a gradient of 1 in 80 and negotiating curves with a minimum radius of 7,500 feet. This segment built through difficult mountainous terrain required construction of 3.7 miles of long bridges and 9.4 miles of tunnel in the 69.6 miles to Cordoba. On two occasions an embankment collapsed on completed stretches of the line. You arrive on one of Cordoba's station's six AVE tracks. There are three more for broad-gauge trains, and parking for over 1,500 automobiles. King Juan Carlos inaugurated the station on September 9, 1994.

From Cordoba south to Seville you hug the existing broad-gauge line very closely. You arrive at the new Santa Justa station in Seville, although a short branch is available for access to the 1992 Expo site on the island of Cartuja. In all, you have passed through 17 tunnels, 9.8 miles in total length, and crossed 31 viaducts totaling 6.1 miles.

Seville's 860,000-square-foot permanent terminus called Santa Justa was inaugurated on May 2, 1991, on Avenida Kansas City (named for Seville's sister city) with both standard- and broad-gauge platforms, and with a new link to the line west to Huelva. If a new train station can be blocky—constructed of brick, concrete, and glass—and grand at the same time, it is due to the long, sweeping "travelators," or moving walkways rising and descending to track level from the mezzanine-level entrance hall. Above you find all the necessary train functions. The timetables are on posts scattered about this level. Luggage carts are available for a 100-peseta coin deposit.

Seville's magnificent, Eiffel-designed, neo-Mudejar Plaza de Armas station is locked up tight and sad to see. A modern hotel of the same name is adjacent. The beautiful station may be redeveloped into a leisure/retail complex.

AVEs depart nearly hourly. The nonstop trip from Madrid to Cordoba takes one hour, 38 minutes at 131 mph; nonstop trains to Seville take two hours, 15 minutes. Formerly, you needed about 6 1/2 hours to reach Seville from Madrid partially because the roundabout route followed by the old rails skirted the mountains.

Each of the AVE trainsets, which can be linked together to form a doubled train, comprises two power cars and eight carriages, and is 656 feet long overall. Weighing 392 tons empty and 421 tons fully booked, it will ordinarily stop in 6.8 miles from 186 mph, but can be stopped in 2.2 miles in an emergency. Only one of the two pantographs is used on the high-speed line, but both would be used to travel on broad-gauge lines.

The AVEs have cosmetically changed nose profiles midway between FrenchRail's Atlantique and GermanRail's ICE, designed to withstand a direct impact at 62 mph without collapsing. Their livery was modified to the white, blue, and gray colors adopted by RENFE for all their high-speed trains and high-performance locomotives.

Each AVE provides 329 seats—30 in Club class, which is laid out with four-person compartments on one side of the aisle and a single file of seats on the other; 78 seated 2+1 in Preferente; and 213 in Turista. There are another eight places in the conference room and 21 seats in the vestibules. Space between seats is very generous and several video screens are fitted in the ceiling of each carriage.

Catering on AVEs is performed by a subsidiary of Swissair. Preferente class passengers have access to at-seat meal service. Club-class travelers receive airline-style meals. In both classes, you have access to free newspapers, coffee, and soft drinks, included in your fare, but panoramic windows and pleasing counter arrangements make the bar/cafeteria, located between the Turista and Preferente classes, a popular place to visit for snacks and something to drink.

Madrid-Cordoba-Seville

The high-speed line for the AVEs brought broad implications for travel in all of Spain. A special unit of RENFE is using gauge-changing, high-speed Talgo 200 trains to take you over a peninsula-wide high-speed network. These trains, blue-and-white with yellow striping, leave from the same standard-gauge platforms of Puerta de Atocha as the AVE trains.

Simultaneously with the construction of the AVE trainsets, RENFE obtained gauge-changing, 124-mph Pendular sets from the Talgo company for Talgo 200 high-speed service beyond Seville over wide-gauge lines to Granada, Malaga, Cadiz, and Huelva, and gauge-changing, dual-electrical-system "Europa" locomotives built in Munich, Germany, by Krauss-Maffei capable of 125 mph (140 mph for short periods). These tall locomotives, painted in AVE livery, use one electrical system on the high-speed line, the second on the broad-gauge lines. Gauge-changing installations in Madrid, Cordoba, and Seville make it possible for the convertible-gauge trains to take you on and off the high-speed line.

Madrid-Malaga Talgo 200 trains via the high-speed corridor take four hours, 45 minutes, which saves you 20 minutes. Talgo 200 service between Madrid and Cadiz/Huelva using the new Majarabique gauge-changing installation near Seville reduces your travel time by 2 1/2 hours. The Torre del Oro train from Barcelona to Badajoz/Cadiz, composed of Talgo Pendular carriages, also takes advantage of the Madrid-Seville line over part of its route as does the overnight Antonio Machado hotel train between Barcelona and Seville/Malaga.

Barcelona-Valencia-Alicante with Euromed

At 7:42 A.M. the sun begins to reveal with weak light the rippling waves of the Mediterranean Sea. It is a delightful wake-up. Beside your Euromed train, white cubic buildings emerge like phantoms from the morning glimmer.

You may have made several times the trip by train between Barcelona and Valencia, but this trip is the speediest, this trip is the earliest (the sun may not come up until you reach Tarragona), and this trip is aboard the new Euromed TGV train.

The sunrise over the Mediterranean is the most stunning of all. The scattered clouds glowing red and rose-colored in morning sky over the sea are even more dramatic after the rains left in Barcelona.

This trip has many neckties. Early risers sit in posh Preferente (first class) with a rail pass plus substantial reservation fee. Turista class has fewer neckties and more backpacks.

The scrub-covered hills shine in the golden sunrise. They look magnificent, and the low angle of the sun casting long shadows makes them look much higher than they appear at midday.

Euromed trains are the world's only wide-gauge TGVs. Otherwise, the new wide-stance (1668-mm) trainsets are almost identical to AVE trains, which were derived from the French TGV Atlantique, the world speed record holder and generally considered the most successful TGV with the possible exception of Eurostar.

Upgraded Euromed passenger service between Barcelona and Alicante via Valencia was introduced on June 15, 1997, following extensive rebuilding of the "Mediterranean Corridor," the line which follows the coast from Barcelona via Tarragona to Valencia.

The major upgrade of the infrastructure on the 229-mile line included track renewal and doubling, new cutoffs, and level crossing eliminations. The work cost about U.S. $660 million, including a 0.6-mile-long viaduct over the Ebre delta in order to avoid a dogleg via

Tortosa. End-to-end train times were reduced from six hours, 10 minutes in 1992 to four hours, 40 minutes.

A second phase of work costing U.S. $330 million was completed in 1999 between Sagonte and Oropesa del Mar, cutting another half-hour off your travel time.

Here is an example of a line systematically upgraded to high speed, rather than a high-speed line completed whole, like that from Madrid to Seville. Spanish Railroads forecasted a traffic rise of 7.3% overall, including 10% on Barcelona-Valencia.

Confusingly, 186 mph on a new line is know as *alta velocidad* whereas 124-137 mph on an upgraded line is known as *velocidad alta*.

Joining Spain's AVE train, this was the second high-speed train to be introduced by RENFE. Euromed operates between Barcelona and Alicante, making stops only in Tarragona, Castellon, and Valencia. Five trains run daily between Barcelona and Valencia, three of which continue on to Alicante.

Each Euromed train consists of three Preferente, four Turista, and a cafeteria/bar carriage. First-class travel includes a food and beverage catering service by Wagons-Lits Spain, as well as access to the Euromed lounges at the train stations in Barcelona, Valencia, and Alicante.

Preferente carriages seat 39 passengers each and feature individual luggage lockers. You travel in grass-green interiors with 2+1 seating. At 7 A.M., Preferente is nearly 100% business. Turista class, with dark blue 2+2 seating, accommodates 56 passengers, with the exception of the one nearest the power car which contains a baggage compartment and seats only 45.

Carriage 4 is the "cafeteria," a very efficient full-length bar car similar in concept to the French TGV Atlantique but differently arranged. Telephones are available in carriages 4 and 5. Carriage 7 is designated for the use of cellular telephones.

When you descend in Barcelona's Sants train station by elevator, you find your Euromed purring beside a makeshift check-in desk where two English-speaking ladies cancel your ticket and direct you to your carriage ("coche"). Luggage carts are available here.

Your train is painted in white and blue livery with a large "Euromed" marked on the side of the power cars.

What do you get for your Preferente ticket? Pampering. First bright-as-a-button hostesses hand out in-ear earphones. You hear announcements in Spanish, Catalan, and English.

A video starts with a "Welcome to Euromed" introduction. You receive Spanish and English (sometimes) newspapers. You leave Barcelona's Sants station through a tunnel that seems to go on forever.

This is a good train for working—the ride is the smoothest in Europe (the equal of the TGV Atlantique that I have written postcards upon while traveling 186 mph), the service is uplifting, and the ambience is excellent.

You scan a breakfast menu. One's Spanish may not be good, but you can guess that you will receive scrambled eggs, cubes of potatoes, York ham, fruit of the season, bread, orange juice, butter, marmalade, and infusion coffee.

The TV has faded to a wild-animal film. Bears are rolling in the snow. Lambs are leaping.

Breakfast appears on a tray designed to neatly fit the fold-down seatback table, with white tablecloth and napkin. The eggs were scrambled, the ham was York, and the potatoes were little cubes, but the zucchini/carrot mixture was a surprise.

It is still dark outside, but the lights appearing in the windows of the blocky white buildings tell you that families are breakfasting and getting ready for work. In the harsh glare of afternoon you see that the beachfront cities here have the same washed-out, sun-bleached and hung-over look of beach cities throughout the world. Why do they all have tile roofs, white walls, and balconies?

Euromed arrives at Tarragona's blocky, modern station on track ("via") one. More attache cases board. Tarragona is a modern city of wide avenues and busy streets. The sea front rises in tiers up a cliffside brilliant with flowers.

The morning light has become bright enough for you to make out the deep red color of the earth. Artichoke plants are just beginning to make their way. There are olive trees and so many orange trees that one would think one was in the province of Valencia instead of Castellon. Valencia is famous for the export of oranges to England for the manufacture of marmalade.

Euromed's second stop, Castellon de la Planta, lies at the center of a "huerta" so unendingly flat that it is known locally as La Plana. In addition to oranges, Castellon exports painted tiles, furniture, and rope-soled shoes.

About 10 minutes before arrival in Valencia you enter a long submerged stretch with occasional cuttings leading you above ground to high-rise buildings and booming construction projects.

Valencia is the capital of the province of the same name and Spain's third-largest city. Valencia's Termino station was formerly known as Estacio del Nord. It is a bright, traditional station—as old-fashioned and pleasant as you can get. It has all services including baggage checking (lockers). The tourist office by track 1 is open 10 A.M. to 6:30 P.M. Arrival and departure times are displayed on electric signs identified in both Spanish and Catalan: Llegadas/Arribades and Salidas/Eixides. One notes that these Catalan words are closer to English.

First-class ticket- and pass-holders can well take advantage of Termino Station's quaint first-class lounge, called Sala Euromed, beside track 1. It contains antique floral glazed tiles, overstuffed seats and a refrigerator filled with free soft drinks, mineral water, and orange juice. The coffee machine is working well. The room might remind you of your grandmother's parlor.

Euromed Daily Service
Barcelona—Valencia/Alicante

BARCELONA (Sants)	dep.	0700 0900 1100 1600 1800 2030
Tarragona	dep.	0748 0949 1149 1649 1849 2119
Castellon de la Planta	arr.	0858 1102 1302 1802 2002 2232
Castellon de la Planta	dep.	0903 1104 1304 1804 2004 2234
VALENCIA (Nord)	arr.	0945 1149 1350 1850 2049 2319
VALENCIA (Nord)	arr.	1000 1200 1400 1900 2100 . . . .
Alicante (Terminal)	dep.	1135 1335 1535 2035 2235 . . . .

Valencia/Alicante - Barcelona

Alicante (Terminal)	dep.	. . . . 0655 0925 1425 1625 1825
VALENCIA (Nord)	arr.	. . . . 0829 1055 1555 1800 1958
VALENCIA (Nord)	dep.	0640 0840 1110 1610 1740 2010
Castellon de la Planta	arr.	0717 0917 . . . . 1647 1817 2047
Castellon de la Planta	dep.	0719 0919 . . . . 1649 1819 2049
Tarragona	dep.	0836 1037 1306 1807 2005 2205
BARCELONA (Sants)	arr.	0936 1133 1403 1903 2103 2303

The first departures each direction do not operate Sundays. The last departures each direction do not operate Saturdays.

Madrid-Valencia on Alaris

Alaris is the brand name for RENFE's first Italian-style tilting trains.

Inaugurated on February 16, 1999, Alaris takes you at up to 137 mph between Madrid and Valencia, via Albacete, over rebuilt line. Ten InterCity 2000 trains cut your travel time from three hours, 50 minutes to between three hours, five minutes, and two hours, 50 minutes, with seven daily departures plus three additional departures on most days. Alaris features a buffet/bar car located in the center of the train, plus a child chaperone, and each passenger has access to on-board audio and video entertainment.

Based on the ETR 460 Pendolino, Alaris is unique from other ETR 460 derivatives because up to three of the three-carriage sets can operate in multiple. Tilt operates to a maximum of eight degrees and allows Alaris to take curves 30 percent faster than normal.

Riding RENFE's Domestic Overnight Trains

RENFE's standard domestic overnight trains are called "Estrella," and provide you with adequate accommodations in conventional, second-class brown-and-white couchette carriages (French Corail equipment), in carriages with seats that do not recline, and in well-worn first- and second-class sleeping cars. Estrella Gibralfaro takes you between Barcelona and Malaga/Cadiz/Granada and the Estrella Bahia de Cadiz takes you between Barcelona and Granada/Almeira/Cadiz.

Using Madrid's and Barcelona's Train Stations

The 1992 Seville World Exposition and the 1992 Summer Olympic Games in Barcelona had a very positive fallout for train travelers. In addition to the new high-speed line between Madrid and Seville (see "AVEs," above) and the new Seville train station, you will be using bright new-from-the-ground-up stations in Madrid and Barcelona.

Madrid is the hub of Iberia's broad-gauge network. You will probably arrive or depart from Chamartin station, one of Europe's brightest, in the northern outskirts of the city. Here you find at least three banks offering to change money, a hotel reservation ("Reserva Hotelera") booth opposite tracks 7/8, a post office opposite tracks 9/10, train information counters between tracks 11/12, and the Sala Club Intercity between 13/14. Luggage lockers are across the driveway as is the check-in counter for the Hotel Chamartin.

In addition to the international Chamartin Station, you will probably use Madrid's large Atocha station where, at the Puerta de Atocha, AVEs and Talgo 200s leave for Andalusia with the determination of jet planes. This 1989, glass-and-cement station relies extensively upon unpretentious red brick, concrete, and matte-texture cast iron. It is really a transportation hub with three separate departure and arrival areas. Excellent direction sign posting simplifies getting around its confusion of many levels of activity. The direction for AVE departures is well marked as are the metro, the platforms for the Cerciana trains, and other station facilities. There is a dedicated AVE waiting room on the mezzanine which otherwise struts a long, glass wall fully overlooking the tracks and the waiting AVEs. On the ground level are eight standard-gauge platforms boarding the AVE and Talgo 200 departures for Andalusia. Suburban trains depart on the 10 tracks of the lower level which run across the city to Chamartin station.

The original Eiffel-designed Atocha station was not demolished. Incorporated into the new Atocha, it has been grandly remodeled and the interior humidified with water mist to create a tropical garden of palms, banana trees, and water lilies. It features an "outdoor" cafe on the same level as train departures. With the birds chirping, it doesn't take too much imagination to feel yourself in deepest Africa or an Amazon rain forest. All this still has every feature of a mainline station, including taxis, luggage checking, ticketing, money changing, LED departure boards, information counters. Reach the AVE club area on a moving sidewalk.

Madrid's Principe Pio (formerly "Norte" train station) has been redeveloped into an ungainly rapid transit and subway hub. The stylish former entrance has been abandoned and covered with rubbish and graffiti.

Reach these stations by underground metro. (Ask for a metro map—"Guia del Metro"—upon entering the system.) To reach Puerta de Atocha station use the metro stop called "Atocha RENFE" (do not confuse with "Atocha" stop).

A 10-ride magnetically encoded ticket costing about $5 gives you a substantial per-ride savings and eliminates the bother of buying separate tickets costing about $1 each for each metro trip. Metro cars are modern with upholstered seating. "Sol" metro stop below the Puerta del Sol, the center of Spain, is the hub of Madrid's metro.

Supporting RENFE's long-distance trains, you can ride a whole network of Cercanias throughout the Madrid area which you can board at a variety of stations, including Atocha, Chamartin, Principe Pio (also known as "Norte"), Nuevos Ministerios, Recoletos, and others. Madrid has 20 six-car double-deck units for use on routes where journey times exceed 30 minutes, where most of the demand is concentrated at the end of the line, and where there is more than 2.5 miles between stations. This enables RENFE to put to good use the enormous seating capacity of these units. You can ride Cercanias over lines stretching into the surrounding countryside as far as El Escorial (line C-8a) and Aranjuez (line C-3), which make worthwhile, interesting excursions.

Entering through the turnstiles demands a magnetically encoded ticket, so if you are traveling with a rail pass you must alert the guard that you want through so he or she can open the barrier for you. In Atocha station, look for the sign: "Billetes *sin* banda magnetica."

Along the underground train tunnel between Chamartin and Atocha stations, look for "Nuevos Ministerios" and "Recoletos," RENFE's two small stations resembling subway stops. Line C-2 rapid-transit "Cercanias" trains pass through these stops five times an hour from 5:08 A.M. to 11:38 P.M., taking you to El Escorial and Aranjuez (among others). Depending on where you stay in Madrid, it may be more convenient for you to board here than Chamartin or Atocha (check RENFE's timetable and posters on the walls). Automatic ticketing machines reduce the length of lines and congestion. You may find also that RENFE's frequent rapid-transit train service ("Cercanias") between Nuevos Ministerios/Recoletos and the big stations gives you more convenient access to long-distance trains originating at Chamartin and/or Atocha than by a long metro ride or surface transportation—and these Cercanias are covered by rail pass.

Reach Nuevos Ministerios RENFE station by metro lines 6 and 8. Follow the signs: "Accesos RENFE."

In Barcelona, a complex of three train terminuses and rambling subway lines that were completely rejuvenated for the Olympic Games is guaranteed to get you around town comfortably.

Barcelona's busiest station is the large Sants station (also called "Central"). It has everything. When it was new it was virtually empty. Now they have managed to create chaos out of order. It is a helter-skelter station, a busy transportation hub, handling as it does RENFE's long-distance trains to Madrid and Andalusia, regional trains, single- and double-deck local trains ("Cercanias/Rodalies"), "Delta" trains to La Tour de Carol and two metro lines. Each has its own separate departures board. Schedules are shown on the information posters. Here you board Talgo 200s to Madrid, Seville and Cadiz; Diurno trains to Cordoba and Seville over the old tracks; and Estrella trains to Malaga, Seville and Cadiz. Sants also is the terminus for the Tren Hotel Pablo Casals for Zurich, the Salvador Dali for Milan, and the through Barcelona-Seville/Malaga Antonio Machado gauge-convertible Talgo train that uses the high-speed line between Madrid and Seville.

In the station you find money change, hotel booking counters, an in-station hotel (the Hotel Barcelo-Sants, *http://www.hotelbook.com*), stairs and elevators to the tracks on subterranean level (choose the latter). Sala Euromed for first-class ticket holders and Tourist Information are both in the same row as the elevators. The Sala Euromed is open well before the first departure to Valencia at 7 A.M. Tourist Information sleeps late. In Sants station it is helpful to study the large, backlighted diagram of Barcelona's complex transportation systems all shown together. It includes RENFE stations, metro and provincial networks, and the "Ferrocarrils de la Generalitat de Catalunya" (FGC), which consists of a standard-gauge railroad from the Placa Catalunya that you can use for visiting Mount Montserrat and a meter-gauge railroad from the Placa Espanya running north and west from Barcelona. Both are accessible by metro and operated by the Catalan government.

The smaller, underground Passeig de Gracia station lies on the same line as Sants. Gracia, with an underground reception hall, is very likely the most convenient place for you to debark because its central location places you adjacent to Barcelona's subway and only four blocks north of the Placa de Catalunya. Be prepared to climb a modest flight of stairs.

Officially named "Estacio de Franca," the former Termino station was reopened in 1992 with marble, gilding and a good scrubbing after a four-year remodeling project that cost $80 million. The 1929 original ironwork and glass classic facade was retained—and the station's clock, which has seen much turmoil during its history. The ornamental, historical lamps positioned at the head of each track make a distinctive statement.

The totally renovated station includes a huge departures/arrivals hall with restaurant and cafeteria. Franca's platform area gives you a feeling of great spaciousness. Platforms 9 through 12 have been either covered with concrete or permanently covered so that the entire central area gives you a feeling of great spaciousness.

Barcelona's subway trains are modern. On lines L1 and L3 you ride 1992 Mitsubishi equipment, license-built in Spain. On lines L4 and L5, you ride refurbished 1970s trains with air-conditioning added. The metro stations require much walking. To reach Sants RENFE station, use Sants-Estacion on lines L3 and L5, not Praca de Sants on lines L1 and L5. Barceloneta (line L4) is the closest Metro station to Franca. Look at the area map when you come out of Barceloneta for directions to Franca around the corner. Passeig de Gracia station lies on lines L3 and L4.

The entire metropolitan area of Barcelona has a unified fare system for bus, RENFE's Cercanias, and FGC. The area is divided into six zones. If you buy a ticket for zone 1, it is valid throughout Barcelona and into neighboring towns on any operator for 75 minutes. Change from one mode of transportation to another as you please.

The 1929 funicular from Paral-lel metro stop to the top of Mount Montjuic was upgraded into a high-speed system for the Olympics to carry 8,000 travelers an hour at 33 feet per second, making it the world's highest-capacity funicular. You can reach Paral-lel on metro line L2 as well as metro line L3 thanks to the December 1995, extension.

Airport Connections

On June 14, 1999, Madrid's Barajas Airport was connected to the city's 1445-mm gauge metro system on Line 8, so that you may travel to or from nearly any destination in Madrid by boarding at the airport.

When the Madrid-Valladolid/Barcelona Y-shaped high-speed line is completed in 2002, you will be able to board European-gauge trains calling at Baranjas.

In Barcelona, board Cercanias/Rodalie local train line No. 1 trains for the airport at Barcelona's Sants station. The trip takes 18 minutes.

Malaga's airport is connected to the city and the Costa del Sol on the Malaga-Fuengirola line (see "Welcome Train" below.)

Rail Lounges

RENFE has taken a page from the airlines' attempts to build upper class travel. They offer a perk which is not often realized by rail pass holders: RENFE maintains "Sala Clubs" in all its main stations which are like are first-class airline lounges. They are oases of quiet and gentility featuring overstuffed furniture, magazines, and television, with free coffee and soft drinks, bottles of water, beer and orange juice free for the helping. For admission, the receptionist checks for a first-class reservation coupon ("Billette + Reserva") on an InterCity (first-class),

Estrella (sleeping compartment), Talgo (first-class or sleeping compartment) or AVE (Club or Preferente class). You must reserve these trains anyway, so all first-class passengers including rail pass holders should make a point of enjoying these havens.

For quiet before boarding, look for rail clubs at Madrid-Chamartin station (between the entrances to tracks 13 and 14), on the mezzanine of Madrid's Puerta de Atocha station, at Barcelona's Sants station (in the center island between elevators to tracks 10 and 11), in the Vigo terminal (brightly marked in the center), in Cordoba (up a flight of stairs), Valencia Terminus (by track 1), and Zaragoza.

Portuguese Railroads

The Portuguese Railroads ("Companha dos Caminhos de Ferro Portugueses," or "CP," *www.cp.pt*) suffered for decades from Portuguese economic difficulties and political uncertainties. CP has tried to maintain a comprehensive regional and InterCity network service for the country's citizens on little more than a shoestring budget. Ridership has decreased as the Portuguese gain in purchasing power, and road building outpaces rail network improvements, so that Portuguese turn more and more to using the family auto. Realizing this, it is surprising that CP's trains run as efficiently as they do and are as comfortable as they are.

Portuguese trains are classified as Alfa Pendular, Intercidade (IC), Interregional (IR), Regional, and Suburbano, in decreasing order of quality. The first two require reservations costing about $3.50 which are best made at the departure train station minutes before departure. When you want assurance of a seat, tickets and reservations for the Alfa Pendular trains and the IC trains Lisbon-Porto and Lisbon-Algarve can be made electronically 20 days in advance and the IC trains Algarve-Lisbon can be booked manually 10 days in advance.

CP's international train is the overnight Sud Express which connects from Lisbon and Porto not to Spain, but to France at the French/Spanish border. There you change to the connecting TGV Atlantique train to save four hours to Paris. Reservations are required.

CP's trains run on wide-gauge rails, the same as Spanish trains, so you won't be delayed by changing trains at the border. Since 1995 when the Schengen agreement took effect there are no passport checks or customs formalities.

In addition to the hotel train Lusitania between Lisbon and Madrid and the Sud Express, travelers use two other less-traveled routes for crossing the border between Spain and Portugal on secondary lines. In the north, railcars, with first- and second-class seating, take you between Vigo's 1988 station and Porto's Sao Bento station.

In the far south, the 2,185-foot, 1991 international bridge crosses the Guadiana River at Vila Real de Santo Antonio. Construction of the harp-shaped bridge, which had to be supported by pillars sunk in an artificial island because of marshland, took 15 years for the two governments to agree upon. Take the Algarve train (see section below) to Vila Real de Santo Antonio Station, about 5,000 feet from the bus station and ferry landing for the still-operating ferries to Ayamonte. DAMAS buses connect with train arrivals, departing at 11:15 A.M. and 2 P.M. for the 20-minute, 75 cents, ride across the bridge to Ayamonte. At Ayamonte, you change to DAMAS buses to Huelva, which takes 60 to 75 minutes, or to Seville, which takes about 2 hours, 30 minutes. You can save money with a rail pass by taking the bus to Huelva and then walking about three blocks (15 to 20 minutes) down Italia street to the Huelva train station where Talgo Pendular trains depart for Madrid and local trains depart for Seville. These are free with rail passes. Similarly, DAMAS buses from Huelva to Ayamonte connect immediately to the DAMAS buses across the bridge to Guadiana station, where you can board an Algarve train.

Using Lisbon's Public Transportation

Lisbon boasts a modern metro system which was extended in 1995-99 to double its track length, increase the number of carriages in its fleet from 245 to 361, and lengthen its trains from four to six carriages. Metropolitano de Lisboa, which carried 117 million passengers in 1997, predicted 200 million passengers in year 2000. You ride four metro lines, identified by color. These are red, with a compass rose insignia; yellow, with a sunflower ("girasol") insignia; green with a caravelle sailing ship ("caravela"); and blue, with a sea gull ("gaivota").

Luckily for train travelers, the metro planning commission gave priority to connections to and between Lisbon's dispersed train stations. The April 1998, extension was the green line between Rossio and Cais do Sodre train stations. The red line from Oriente train station to Alameda metro station was opened May 1998. Santa Apolonia and Terreiro do Paco train stations were connected on the blue line in late 1999.

The subway stations are beautifully decorated but rarely offer escalators or elevators, so be prepared to climb stairs. They are remarkable for their originality and ambience. Many are magnificent, elegantly adorned with "azulejos" (glazed, colored tiles). Entrances are indicated by large red "metro" plus a broken-letter *M* signs on the street. Convenient special tourist transportation tickets issued by Lisbon's bus and tram operator, Carris (*www.carris.pt*), allow unlimited travel on all of Lisbon's buses, trams, and funiculars for one day (about $2.25) or three days ($5). "Passe Turistico" tickets include travel also on the metro for four days ($8.50) and seven days ($12). They are sold Mondays through Fridays from 8 A.M. to 8 P.M. at Carris kiosks throughout Lisbon and at Alvalade, Areeiro, Campo Grande, Colegio Militar, Entre Campos, Pontinha, Marques de Pombal, and Jardim Zoologico metro stations. You will find them outside the Santa Apolonia station, in the so-called Eiffel elevator, and at the foot of the Park Eduardo VII near the Praca Marques Pombal.

You may also buy the Lisboa Card valid for 24 hours (about $8.75), 48 hours ($14.50), or 72 hours ($18.50), which provides not only free unlimited travel on Carris bus, trams and elevators and the metro, but offers free entrance to 25 museums and monuments and discounts on various services. You can purchase the Lisbon Card at the central office, 50 Rua Jardim do Regedor (Tel. 343-36-72/3), the Museu Nacional de Arte Antigua, the Mosteiro dos Jeronimos, and at the tourist office in the Lisboa Camping-Parque Municipal.

To use the metro, obtain a pocket map ("Guia do Metro") at a tourist office or subway station or check the posters in any subway station. A normal ticket is valid for one hour after being validated and costs $0.40. A 10-ticket "cademeta" is $3. You can buy tickets in every station at an automatic ticket vending machine or at a ticket office. You must keep them until the end of your journey. One-day ($1.25) and seven-day ($3.35) tickets are good buys. You board the train in the direction of the last station shown on the branch you wish to use.

Carris runs a fleet of single and articulated, orange Volvo buses throughout the city. Consult your Carris map for route information. Arriving and departing airline passengers can use the Aerobus between Portela Airport and Cais do Sodre train station with stops at Marques Pombal, Avenida Liberdade, Restauradores Square, and Rossio, among others. Buses leave every 20 minutes, from 7 A.M. to 9 P.M.

In an effort to ease commuting traffic congestion in Lisbon, where up to 450,000 vehicles enter every Monday morning, Prime Minister Antonio Guterres himself drove the first train on November 15, 1998, across the new rail line added onto 25 de Abril bridge.

Four-carriage, double-deck 87-mph electric rapid-transit trains built by Alstom/CAF in 1998-99 let you travel in air-conditioned comfort between central Lisbon and the south bank of the Tagus river in 25 minutes.

Safety engineers allow only one train in each direction on the bridge at any one time. You can board at stations in central Lisbon including Entre Campos (with an interchange to the yellow metro line), Sete Rios, Campolide, and Alvita.

Trains operate every 15 minutes, off-peak, and every seven minutes during rush hours. Planners figure to reduce gridlock traffic on the bridge by 11 percent from 140,000 vehicles a day. The extension of Lisbon's metro yellow line will relieve traffic over a second bottle-necked artery.

Rail Pass Travel

A Eurailpass will take you through both Spain and Portugal, but a Europass requires a Portugal add-on for that country. With a Eurail Selectpass, you can select Portugal, Spain, and France.

With an Iberic Railpass you may travel as you please within and between Spain and Portugal. You may purchase one for three to 10 days according to the exact number of days you plan to use them within two months. Alternately, you may opt for separate Spain or Portugal rail passes when you plan to spend more or less of your time in one or the other nation. The advantage of a rail pass covering both countries is that you will have to validate only one day box on the day you cross the border. With separate passes you must use up one day box on each pass. The disadvantage is that Iberic Railpasses are priced for first class only, while you can buy Spain Flexipasses for second-class travel and, also, although you can buy them only in multiples of four days, Portuguese Railpasses cost about half as much per day.

Like Iberic Railpasses, Spain Flexipasses for unlimited travel on RENFE are available for three to 10 days of travel within two months. You choose the number of days you will be traveling. The prices for first-class travel are 15 to 20 percent less than those of a Europass and you need buy one for only three days. Second-class Spain Flexipasses save you even more. Expressly excluded from both passes are Trens

Hotel, the AVE high-speed trains and Talgos operating on the high-speed line, and to ride these trains you will be required to pay hefty supplements. Supplements for your use of all other trains, including those normally requiring *A* supplements, are included, but not sleeping or eating surcharges. Neither FEVE nor the Al Andalus tourist train honor these passes.

The Portuguese Railpass available from Rail Europe in the U.S. allows travel in first class on any four days in 15. The price is very reasonable, but Portugal's small size limits your train traveling potential.

In Portugal you can buy Tourist Tickets ("Bilhete Turistico") giving you unlimited first- or second-class travel on CP trains and buses for seven, 14 or 21 consecutive days, but you must pay supplements and seat reservation costs to ride on Alfa Pendular and IC trains. The Terreiro do Paco-Barreiro ferry is not covered. Children 4 to 11 and adults over 65 receive about a 50 percent reduction on the Tourist Tickets. Similarly, adults over 65 years of age are granted by CP a 50 percent reduction simply by showing proof of age, such as, a passport, when you buy a point-to-point ticket. Such tickets are valid only for travel between 9:30 A.M. and 5 P.M. and after 8 P.M.

In conjunction with Spain Railpasses, you can also purchase a Spain Rail 'N Drive Pass. It is a very attractive combination in Iberia, where automobile drivers enjoy staying at Spain's paradors (for reservations, contact Marketing Ahead, Tel. 800-223-1356) and Portugal's pousadas. The Spain Rail 'N Drive combines three days of train travel in Spain with three days of Avis car rental.

The four train discoveries described in this chapter take you aboard the Talgo Pendular from Madrid to Santiago de Compostela, the time-saving ride along Spain's Costa del Sol, the terrifying trams through Lisbon's Alfama district, and trains tip to toe through Portugal.

Tilting Train Pilgrimage
Lazy Way to Santiago de Compostela

While you are lounging lazily on Spain's sparkling Talgo Pendular train, waiting for the television to blink on and wondering whether this posh train really tilts around curves as designed, you might consider reading chapter XIII, "Santiago de Compostela," of Michener's *Iberia*.

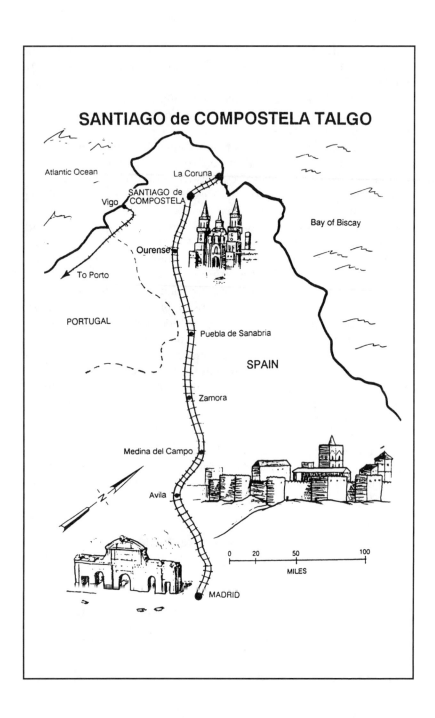

SANTIAGO de COMPOSTELA TALGO

Atlantic Ocean

La Coruna

SANTIAGO de
COMPOSTELA

Vigo

Bay of Biscay

Ourense

To Porto

PORTUGAL

Puebla de Sanabria

SPAIN

Zamora

Medina del Campo

Avila

0   20   50   100
MILES

MADRID

You are entering the Galicia region from Madrid and are still three hours from Santiago, your destination.

When one traveler made this trip, he came alive with Michener's sentence: "I was fortunate in reaching Compostela at the precise point in the year when I could best witness the significance of the town and its cathedral in Spanish life, for El dia de Santiago (the day of St. James) occurs each year on July 25, and is the occasion for a religious celebration of great dimension." The traveler looked at his watch. It was indeed July 24.

A pilgrimage to Santiago de Compostela is still important not only for the devoted, but for casual students of world history. In A.D. 812, a hermit saw in the heavens a bright star hovering over a vacant field where the body of St. James (Sant Iago), uncorrupted by the passage of time, was unearthed. The apostle, who became known as St. James Matamore, the Slayer of the Moors, was later seen riding a white horse and instilled the spirit for the reconquest of Spain from the infidels. Today Santiago de Compostela's cathedral stands where that vacant field presumably lay.

The last Compostelan Holy Year fell in 1993, a year when July 25 fell on a Sunday, but any pilgrimage aboard the Talgo Pendular, free on a Eurailpass, Europass, or Spain Flexipass, is a convenient, but lazy, way to visit Europe's No. 2 (after Rome) holy city and the site of one of Christendom's most venerated cathedrals. Santiago was named one of the "Cultural Capitals of Europe" for 2000.

During the eight-hour, 420-mile run, you are treated to the scenic contrasts of desiccated Old Castile and the twisting adventure of a mountain railroad into green Galicia.

Your train leaves from Chamartin station. Your slate-blue-and-white Talgo Pendular is among the most comfortable-riding and innovative in Europe. Talgo stands for "Tren Articulado Ligero Goicoechea y Oriol." The last two names are those of the inventors of the system and the first three words mean "lightweight articulated train." Because they are articulated units, the string of shorter, connected, low-profile parlors bends around curves like a rubber snake. The latest generation, called the Pendular, additionally tilts according to ingenious design. Suspension from above the center of gravity causes the bodies to swing centrifugally and round curves so smoothly you'll see scarcely a ripple in your coffee.

You stretch out in oversize, 2+1, deep bucket seats. They have folding tables in their backs, but when you recline, your seat's cushions slide forward so you don't disturb the person behind you. The 21-inch-wide seats have a 39-inch pitch in first class. Each first-class parlor holds 26 seats; the second-class parlors, four across, hold 36. First class is smoke free. Second-class has one parlor allotted to smokers. First-class smokers head to the bar to light up.

The Virgen del Pilar diesel locomotive pulls away from Madrid's Chamartin station exactly on time, with a rumble like thunder. You see a long, panoramic, industry-free view open back on the city through a forest of encina, or live oak, trees. Spanish children delight in eating these trees' nuts, which are similar to chestnuts and almonds.

Almost instantly the conductor comes through to check your reservation card and ticket or pass. Staff passes out the food price list and menu, plus earphones for the movie. About halfway to Avila (pop. 40,000), your Talgo enters the summer-parched high plateau known as Old Castile. Outside, the ground is rocky and not very rich, so you are hardly surprised when you come eye-to-eye with a black bull snorting angrily and pawing the yellow leavings of a wheat harvest.

Entering Avila, watch for Europe's most vivid enduring example of medieval fortification. When the station no longer blocks your view, your eyes rivet to the sight and you can trace out the cathedral and the crenelated walls and battlements not far to the south.

Past Avila, the rocks become more hostile and the live oaks juice-less. Your Talgo climbs relentlessly. It is uncompromising country.

You may have lunch, catered by the Wagons-Lits company, either at your seat or at the counter of the bar car located between first- and second-class sections. The daily special (veal) costs about $15.50. Combination plates, also veal, cost about $14 and $10. The chicken plate costs about $7.75. Wine and mineral water cost extra. Dinner is not served, but the bar car is available for snacks.

When, after nearly two hours, your Talgo reaches Medina del Campo, a busy agricultural market and major railroad junction, and pulls to a stop next to the Eiffel-designed canopy of the brick train station, you can't help but remark how green things are becoming. Sunflowers are tall, pines begin dotting the hills, and farmers are harvesting leafy vegetables.

Your Talgo makes a *V* turn when the Virgen del Pilar shuffles by on an adjacent track and the new Virgen de la Macarena diesel locomotive takes charge of your train and pulls away with passengers facing backward. You rotate your seat to look forward once more.

In about 40 minutes, your Talgo Pendular passes Toro, the fine-looking village with picture-book profiles of the Romanesque Collegiate and San Lorenzo churches. The Duero below, one of Spain's five major rivers, flows slowly but still looks fresh and blue. Wheat flourishes north of the river, grapes to the south. The light blossoms of almond trees dot the landscape in spring.

Irrigation takes hold outside. There is heavy cultivation. Stalks of corn line the fields, peach and pear trees droop with fruit, tractors ready the slopes for vegetables and, in the distance, sheepherders prod their flocks with crooked staves.

When the Virgen de la Macarena locomotive begins its serious climb into the Leon Mountains, it passes hay deposited in peaked piles. Burros and horses mill about. The land is now dry and soon changes into mountains.

Except for the handsome Romanesque facade of the train station, modernized to look very efficient, historic Zamora—three hours out of Madrid—now seems to be composed entirely of tall red-brick and white-brick apartment structures. The return Talgo arrives on the adjacent track. It left from Vigo/A Coruna 30 minutes earlier than you started.

With hardly a warning, the video lights up on four television sets suspended from the ceiling so that every passenger can see them easily without craning their necks. The train manager passes down the aisle renting out blue-and-yellow earphones that plug into the outlet in your armrest. If you don't appear to speak Spanish he will pass you by. The audio is all in Spanish. *Jaws* and *Dracula* are evergreens with RENFE.

About four hours away from Madrid, you first glimpse the mountain lake of Sanabria (3,280 feet), spotted with vacationers kayaking and windsurfers maneuvering their bright sails.

The mountain village of Puebla de Sanabria is a postcard-perfect picture of houses with granite roofs and white walls. It lies at the foot of the Sanabria valley, which is alive with streams rushing through its undergrowth. The black slate-covered station house with white lawn chairs overlooking the lake could be a model for a miniature railroad display.

You see the train is entering different countryside, wet and green and chock-full of granite. This is the isolated, rainy region at the northwestern corner of the Iberian peninsula called Galicia. There are no seductive Carmens or flamenco dancers here. Myrtles and camellias bloom. Beaches are empty and churches full. General Franco came from here.

Galicia is one of Spain's least affluent regions and also one of its most independent. Its language is half-Portuguese. Its wealth of granite sets it apart from the rest of Spain, as do its culture and Celtic heritage. Bagpipes are the native instrument.

Builders have turned their abundance of the gray-and-white stone into barns, corncribs, garages, homes, terraces, and fences that range across the countryside in elaborate mazes only goats understand.

By the time your Talgo reaches La Gudina, thoughts of dried Old Castile are replaced by the view to the north beckoning with charisma. An occasional flock of sheep meanders to the train line.

The Virgen de la Macarena curves in and out of tunnels. This is the true mark of a mountain railroad. Fields look like patchworks. Ferns flourish on embankments beside the windows. Pastoral fields of corn and vineyards spread below. The majestic Cantabrian Cordillera Mountains rise before you, almost blue in the distance, crisscrossed with brown firebreaks.

This corner of Spain is on the western fringe of the Middle European Time Zone. In summer, the sun is still high. Your carriage for Santiago dawdles at Ourense, while workers split the train. Passengers lug their suitcases up and down the aisle to get into the correct half. Some continue to the 1990 terminal at Vigo overlooking its busy, beautiful, natural harbor on the Atlantic coast north of Portugal. The segment taking you to Santiago continues farther to A Coruna, Galicia's principal port and city.

It is getting late. You are restless to arrive, but the vistas are some of the most idyllic in Spain. You see tiny, cone-shaped haystacks and grapevines trained on wooden trellises. The hills roll as far as the horizon.

The Virgen pulls steadily on a long, steady climb until finally, a few minutes late, it snakes through the crisscrossing pattern of rails to arrive at track No. 1 in Santiago de Compostela.

The five-track, canopied, through station is across town from the cathedral, but still it is the popular destination for throngs of modern-day pilgrims and students. You find train information (but no tourist information), ticketing, and an ATM machine in the lobby. Orange-and-white "Region Galicia" diesel railcars idle on adjacent tracks. Lockers are located in a stone satellite building. The guardrails are lined with blue-painted, cast-iron cockleshells. This symbol honors those who came, beginning in the eleventh century, not by tilting train, but by wearing out countless pairs of stout sandals.

Santiago de Compostela's Praza do Obradoiro, the square before the cathedral, is one of Europe's most magnificent. Across from the cathedral Santiago's splendid, five-star Hostal de los Reyes Catolicos is part of Spain's National System of Paradors. This national monument, commissioned by the monarchs to house the poor, the sick, and the pilgrims, dates from 1501. It is the most desirable hotel in Galicia. Like all paradors, it is represented in the U.S. by Marketing Ahead, 433 Fifth Avenue, New York, NY 10016 (Tel. 212-686-9213, Fax 212-686-0271).

Talgo Pendular Service
between Madrid and Santiago de Compostela

Mon.-Sat.		.		Fri.	Sun.-Sat.
1400	dep.	MADRID (Chamartin)	arr.	2130	1735
1521	dep.	Avila	dep.	2003	1605
1611	dep.	Medina del Campo	dep.	1920	1520
1700	dep.	Zamora	dep.	1820	1423
1816	dep.	Puebla de Sanabria	dep.	1704	1307
1955	dep.	Ourense-Empalme	dep.	1532	1135
2119	arr.	SANTIAGO DE COMPOSTELA	dep.	1446	0952
2220	arr.	A Coruna-San Cristobal	dep.	1255	0900

Talgo carries first- and second-class carriages and bar between Madrid and A Coruna.

The Welcome Train
Secret of the Costa del Sol

Jet lag is merciless. When the glass doors of Malaga's "Gateway to the Costa del Sol" airport snap shut behind you, you are newly arrived, glazed with jet lag, and too groggy to glance up to the tiny overhead sign pointing to the train: "Ferrocarril."

Lined-up taxis and standing buses offer you transportation to your beach apartment, condo, or hotel, but your best ride is the Costa del Sol train.

At first you may be chagrined at the tackiness and disrepair of the Costa del Sol, but after you get to know the convenience of the Costa del Sol train and the Portillo bus system you move around easily and discover a fascinating and very enjoyable experience.

The train runs 20 miles along the most popular stretch of Spain's

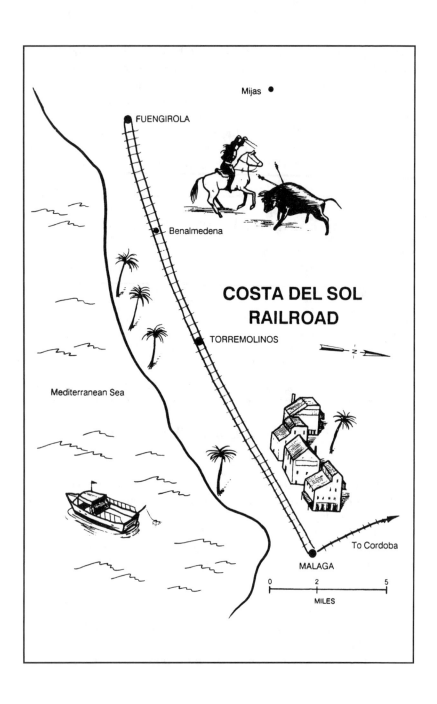

Mijas ●

● FUENGIROLA

● Benalmedena

COSTA DEL SOL
RAILROAD

TORREMOLINOS

Mediterranean Sea

To Cordoba

MALAGA

0   2   5
MILES

sunny strand, from Malaga to Fuengirola. The arrow at the airport points out a paved path (perfect for luggage with wheels) that leads for two minutes through the parking lot to the elevated train stop. RENFE's Costa del Sol train is kept the best secret in the south of Spain because it loses money. The national railroad makes no pesetas on this cheap service with a view that gives you a clever budget way to orient yourself to the fascinating jumble grown up along the warm-water beaches. An excursion on this cunning train shows off the many sights of the coast stretching west from Malaga. From the windows you get marvelous views of the quaint village of Mijas snuggled in the mountains, the blue Mediterranean lapping at the sand, rows of olive trees and eucalyptus groves, snow-covered Sierra Nevada mountains in the distance, artichokes, horses, and truck farming. Of course, you also see the endless houses, condos, and hotels embracing starkly modern, traditional Spanish, and elaborate Moorish styles, all distinguished by the identical color: blinding white.

Designers have modified the no-frills train carriage for airport service. They created floor space for suitcases at the entry doors and built overhead racks broad enough to support piles of luggage. The 2+2 maroon leatherette seats are in good condition despite heavy use, but the linoleum floor is scuffed from the dragging of countless suitcases.

Your efficient, self-propelled, electric train set, a workhorse of local and regional transportation throughout Spain, passes every 30 minutes between Malaga-Centro-Alameda and Fuengirola. Show your rail pass or buy a ticket on board. Tickets are inexpensive, so don't expend a day box of a flexipass. Only at the bigger, fully staffed stations do personnel sell tickets in ticket booths at the entrance.

Most of the line is above ground, but in Malaga, Torremolinos, and Fuengirola the stations are subterranean. The entrances to the underground Torremolinos and Fuengirola stations are difficult to see—even when you are standing next to them. Escalators take you to street level, but descend by stairs. There are 19 stops between Malaga and Fuengirola. Making the complete run takes 40 minutes.

This line gives you easy access to a series of communities, none far from the line, but most passengers board at Malaga-RENFE, Malaga airports (National and International), and Torremolinos. Note that there are two airport stops. The one closer to Torremolinos, which used to be called "Vuelos Charter," is for the International terminal.

The one closer to Malaga, "Aeropuerto," is for the National terminal. This is probably the one you will use, but be sure to check in advance. The underground Torremolinos station entering on the square between Avenida Santos Rein and Calle de Emilio Estaban is the most complete of the line. Decorated with blue, green, red, and yellow tiles and blue benches, there is a magazine stand, a few lockers, a ticket kiosk, and a public telephone.

A tunnel connects the Malaga-RENFE stop to the separate mainline Malaga train terminus, where rays of red and yellow gleam through Moorish colored-glass windows. Luggage lockers are on the far side. A second exit leads directly to the parking lot and taxi stand, the post office in back, and the bright snack bar/cafeteria and bank across the street.

High-speed Talgo 200 trains leave from Malaga's mainline station five times daily for Madrid by way of high-speed line between Cordoba and Madrid. Hotel trains run along the same route to Madrid and to Barcelona.

Spaced along the Costa del Sol's main arterial highway, parallel to the railroad, you will see Portillo bus stops. After you have stored your luggage, the Portillo bus company is an easy way to get around. Riding their relay system of long-distance, middle-distance, and local buses stretching from Malaga to Algeciras (for an excursion to Gibraltar) is actually more convenient than renting a car and finding a place to park it.

The Costa del Sol is now a string of "urbanizations" (real estate developments) rambling end-to-end along blue Mediterranean shores like suburbia overflowing—not entirely admirable, but agreeable and comfortable for everyone. After the initial surprise of the clutter, it becomes fascinating to discover its hidden pleasures.

You will soon find that this area is not typically Spanish. It is a unique international settlement that takes on a flavor of its own when all the Norwegian restaurants, Danish bakeries, Swedish smorgasbords, Irish pubs, and Finnish coffeehouses merge with German Bierstuben, English teahouses, Canadian beer bars and American hamburger cafes, shopping malls, golf courses, yacht harbors, and beaches.

The marvelous result of this conglomeration is that it works. The English tongue is the common denominator. Nationals of all ages from everywhere in Europe, America, and the British Commonwealth coexist in harmony and shared enthusiasm.

It is said that the Costa del Sol is not for everybody, but when it's a good place for gray-haired folks (tea rooms, short distances, warm weather), swinging singles (bars close at 6 A.M.), and families with children (activities, beach), you wonder exactly who wouldn't enjoy an inexpensive, warm-weather visit here.

Welcome Train Timetable

Distance in Miles	Station	Time in Minutes
0	Malaga-Centro-Alameda	0
1	Malaga-RENFE	2
2	San Andres	6
3	Los Prados	8
5	Vuelos Nacionales (Aeropuerto)	11
6	Vuelos Internacionales (Charter)	13
7	San Julian	14
8	Campo del Golf-Campamento	16*
9	Los Alamos	18
9	La Colina	19
11	Torremolinos	23
11	Montemar-Alto	25
12	El Pinello	26
13	Arroyo de la Miel	28
16	Torremuelle-Benalmedena	30
17	Carvajal	34
18	Torreblanca	35
19	Los Boliches	38
20	Fuengirola	42

*Service three times daily

Terror Trams of Alfama
Seeing Lisbon Cheaply and Easily

You swoop and rise through hills and drops that measure a good 500 feet. You clutch, white-knuckled, at the grips of the advertisement-pasted cars while rows of pastel houses whiz beside you and glimpses of churches flash at you from cobblestone alleyways.

You look up and see stairways leading toward blue skies. Automobile horns honk on streets above your head. On your electrico's grinding struggle to the summit, your trolley wheezes, jerks, creaks, and chatters so loudly that many passengers standing elbow-to-elbow wonder, "Can this wreck take it one more time or is its axle going to snap and take me with it?"

Circling through Alfama, Lisbon's Moorish neighborhood that survived the murderous earthquake of 1755, you ride the most infamous stretch of rail experience in Europe. Portugal's capital city can easily claim to have the most thrilling streetcar network built. Its tram system is widely held to be the most terrifying in the world.

Riding through Alfama on one of the rickety, two-axle trolley cars is an adventure that ages you prematurely, like a ride on a killer rollercoaster. Part of the excitement comes from riding on cars that groan from heavy use and seem to go back to shortly after Ulysses founded Lisbon. They climb the hills with the reckless drive of San Francisco's cable cars—but vehicles in Lisbon. advertising blue jeans, beer, and vacations in Paris have no strong cables to save them from breaking away and skidding into the Tagus River below.

Most of the little trams (not covered by rail pass) are only large enough for 14 sitting on the green leatherette seats and 20 hanging on the cracking leather straps or clutching at the chromium-plated poles. The floors are made of brown, abused wooden slats with dust accumulated in their crevices.

Riding downward, fascinating side scenes plunge past you and the rows of houses you glimpsed ahead seem to twirl around and fly past you on the opposite side.

Lisboans on the "electricos" (the name began in the early twentieth century when electric-powered trams replaced horse-drawn vehicles) gaze calmly at the passing sights. Mothers cradle their babies and hum lullabies while young boys stretch and rap the church windows alongside and smudge fingertips against the stuccoed walls sweeping past. Some alleys are so narrow that the streetcars fill the few feet separating houses. Pedestrians dodge nimbly into doorways to avoid the pushy, onrushing trams. Stop-and-go signals are essential on the narrowest curves to regulate traffic and reduce the number of head-on collisions.

Instead of the automatic, electric signal lights you expect to see, you sometimes find casually dressed guards still assigned to blind corners, directing traffic by hand with a signal baton and rickety box to sit on, coping with streetcars plummeting down the wrong direction of one-way streets and mad auto drivers sneaking behind them.

Electricos are an endangered species in rapidly changing Lisbon. The last and most daring of the lines climbing the Alfama hills is renegade electrico line No. 28. It is your ultimate test. It sometimes runs the wrong way—against auto traffic. Visiting Lisbon and not riding a No. 28 streetcar is like visiting San Francisco and not riding a cable car or visiting a theme park and not riding a roller-coaster.

So that the trams could maneuver through the claustrophobic maze of streets, engineers laid the tracks narrow-gauge (only 23.6 inches) with only one pair of thin rails. Luckily, just when an approaching tram seems ready to crash into another and panicky tourists realize the emergency brakes might not be working, the tracks part at the last instant and the cars veer sideways as if testing the riders' nerves and sanity.

In such a hodgepodge, the safe use of vehicles secured by tracks embedded in cobblestones is essential. Their limited freedom prevents reckless or annoyed tram drivers from nicking or scraping the already peeling whitewash on the house walls (or the advertising on the trams, for that matter).

Find your way using a free map from the tourist office on the Praca dos Restauradores next to the Eden theater. They also will secure hotel reservations and provide free information. Schedules and maps pinpointing the zig-zagging routes of trams and buses throughout Lisbon are posted on the walls of the glassed-in bus stops in the business district and timetables are posted at stops on cylindrical orange tubes. You can buy a thorough guide to the public transportation system of Lisbon and its environs (including an official map of bus and tram lines) in the booth at the foot of the Santa Justa elevator ("Eiffel Elevator").

The Lisbon streetcar system, which was formerly one of the largest, is still one of the creakiest in the world. It has retained those hill-hugging beauties that give Lisbon a special cachet and charm visitors. Running double trolley carriages through the narrow streets is out of the question. It would be indictable to try to pull passive passenger trailers around the curves. They are operated by Carris, the transit authority, using trams with bodies built between 1932 and 1937 in the Carris works at Santo Amaro on chassis built by Brill between 1899 and 1901. The youngest tram is older than the parents of most of today's straphangers. Rather than completely scrapping the antiquated remnants, in 1992 Carris sent number 270 electrico to Nuremberg, Germany, for refurbishment and subsequent return to the streets of Lisbon. The Germans installed a new chassis with new braking and improved suspension and electrical controls but didn't touch the original body. With this new know-how, the Carris shop in Lisbon modernized 44 more. In all fairness, in a city offering magnificent surprises to walkers, the trams are convenient, if unnerving, and inexpensive. Considering the hilly terrain and capricious nature of the streets, it is surprising the trams do as well as they do.

To sample the dashing of the remarkable trams through Alfama, take line No. 28 between Estrela and Graca terminal, which is more of a four-by-eight-foot orange-and-white kiosk than a terminal. Enter the front and exit from the back. Buy your ticket at any Carris kiosk.

Along your route you will find the excellent Miradouro (meaning "belvedere") Santa Luzia extending from the small church of Santa Luzia and built over the remains of old Arab fortifications. It is one of Lisbon's most attractive lookout points where you will see a splendid panorama of Lisbon and shipping on the Tagus River. The Belvedere of Santa Luzia is an oasis of trellises, benches, and blue-and-white-tiled murals. Under the vines' shade, local men play cards and checkers. This is the perfect place to begin a walking tour down through Alfama but first to see St. George Castle, where Portugal's first king, Alfonso Henriques, conquered the Moors in 1147. Cross the road and follow the yellow signs pointed uphill to "Castelo S. Jorge."

Line 28 is in danger of becoming a tourist route like San Francisco's cable cars. Even worse, Carris has discontinued many tram lines and is introducing (horrors!) long, articulated Star-Wars-yellow streetcars ("Electrico Articulado") in a city long resistant to fads.

Prime example of 1996's Electrico Articulado is tram line 15 between Praca da Figueira and Alges, which is a relatively level stretch, and therefore unfortunately susceptible to the garish articulados. Riders of the articulated streetcars without a ticket push the button to open the doors and buy the ticket (escudo coins only) using the automatic ticket machine inside the streetcar's center articulated unit. Those with prepurchased tickets punch their tickets at the validation units located at each door.

Leaving tram No. 28, and happy to be back to steady terra firma, you nod to your fellow passengers to say, "Well, we made It—this time at least. There won't be any articulados here."

The 1999 Museu da Carris (open Mon.-Sat. 10 A.M. to 4 P.M., Sun. 10 A.M. to 1 P.M. and 2 to 4:30 P.M.), located at the Lisbon Santo Amaro tram depot, displays practically every Lisbon tramcar type and many other rare and interesting exhibits.

Portugal Tip to Toe
The Porto Alfa Pendular, Algarve, Castles, Casinos, and Port Wine

"Under no circumstances should you take the train from the Algarve to Lisbon." Algarvian Senhor Jaoa Lima, graduate of the University of Wisconsin, was adamant. He waved his arms like a sea gull. "If you must, take a bus. They have videos."

"We didn't come all the way from California to the Algarve to watch a video in Portuguese. We want to see Portugal up close, the people, and how you live."

Lima looked discouraged. "The videos merely have Portuguese subtitles.

"We complain continuously to the government for better train service to our region," he confided. "If you want to ride an excellent train, take the train from Lisbon to Porto."

Contrary to Lima's expectations, the InterCity train taking you from Portugal's Algarve region is spacious and clean, often arrives in Lisbon seven minutes early, and is as quiet as a dormitory—except for the raucous noises you hear resounding from the bar two carriages away.

Many Portuguese are critical of their country's facilities, but even their secondary trains are decent, their food is never bad even in the bistros, and Lisbon's subway is convenient. On the other hand, when you say the facade of their magnificent neo-Manuelino Rossio train station is dirty, they say it is "discolored."

Because of the network structure in Portugal, you are virtually locked into using Lisbon as your base for train travel. There are no through trains passing through Lisbon. Lisbon has five stations and five lines.

Santa Apolonia Station

Conveniently near the foot of Alfama is the dark-rose-colored Santa Apolonia train station, your gateway to the trains of Europe and where you may have your rail pass first validated at door No. 47.

Santa Apolonia is literally the end of the line for international traffic. It is a tidy station, but small. Santa Apolonia faces out on a taxi loop and a modern sculpture honoring immigrants to Portugal. It is easy to reach by the newest (1999) station of the Lisbon metro system on the

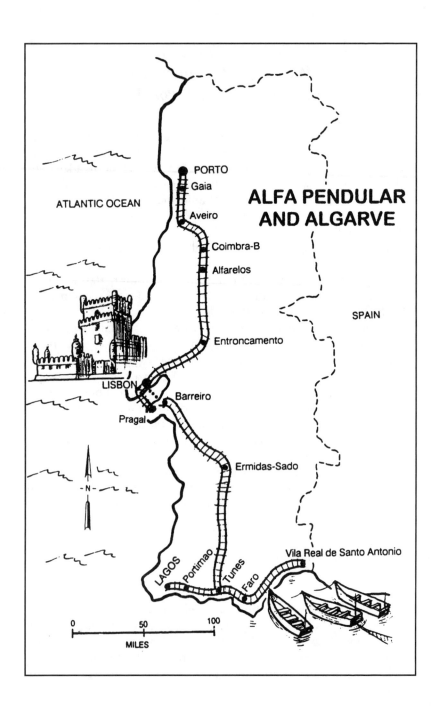

ATLANTIC OCEAN

PORTO
Gaia
Aveiro
Coimbra-B
Alfarelos
Entroncamento
LISBON
Barreiro
Pragal
Ermidas-Sado
LAGOS
Portimao
Tunes
Faro
Vila Real de Santo Antonio

ALFA PENDULAR
AND ALGARVE

SPAIN

N

0   50   100

MILES

blue line, or you walk not far from the city center or take buses 9, 12, 46, or 90. Buses 9 and 12 take you down Avenida Liberdade, the main artery, past the tourist office.

When you enter Santa Apolonia, you find the ticket windows 1 to 11 straight ahead. Although usually a formality, because the trains are rarely totally filled, CP requires you to make seat reservations for all CP's InterCity and Alfa Pendular trains from here to Porto. You can make them electronically up to 20 days in advance. CP merely recommends reservations for IRs.

Through the middle is the train gallery. Track No. 3, where the "Sud Express" leaves for Paris, is on the north and on the south is track No. 5. You must walk farther down the gallery to find tracks 1, 2, 6, and 7. There are no luggage carts, but porters are available.

Down the tracks on the south side next to track ("Linha") No. 5, you come to doorway No. 47, which is the international terminal office for validating your rail pass, changing money at the bank (open 8:30 A.M. to 1 P.M. and 2 to 5 P.M.) and making sleeping reservations for the Sud Express to France. Next door is the room with luggage lockers. The luggage checking counter is nearby. The currency change machine is next to track No. 5. There's an ATM for cash advances on the opposite side next to track No. 3.

The train information office is located around the corner on the far left north corridor (look for the "*i*" sign) together with the waiting room. English-speaking ladies give train information.

Oriente train station

Lisbon's stunning new train station, among concrete palm fronds, is Europe's most astonishing. The 1998 Oriente station was designed to serve the Lisbon Expo '98 site, but it continues to be favored by those in the area, and has a future as a terminus.

With this work, Barcelona-born Santiago Calatrava secured his reputation as the greatest railroad architect of the end of this century. Like his imaginative Lyon Airport's Satolas TGV station, Oriente is graceful with wide arches and sweeping curves.

The magnificent glass roof is supported by 15 50-foot "palm trees" that make you feel like you are passing through an Amazonian cathedral. Descend escalators below the train platforms and you find Oriente metro station, beautifully decorated with colorful, contemporary *azulejos* at the terminus of the red (compass rose) line.

The station is underused at present, serving as a stop for the Lisbon-Porto service, and in 2001, the terminus for the double-deck trains to Sintra on the Cintura line, but in 2003 it will become the terminus for the Algarve trains when the new rail-only Tagus bridge is completed.

Lisbon-Porto

The line between Portugal's two main cities deserves to be served by one of Europe's most technically advanced trains. It is. The route which links almost one-third of all Portugal's inhabitants (in a country of 10 million, 2.5 million call Lisbon home, and Porto is home to 800,000) is almost totally double tracked with tight curves served by Portugal's Alfa Pendular train. You ride in one of 10 six-carriage sets derived from the Italian Pendolino design. The introduction of the red, white, and blue tilting trains, a wide-gauge version of the Italian ETR 460 Pendolino, on the Portugal's main north-south line was terribly delayed. The 10 trains were originally expected for the 1996 Lisbon Expo. The units were actually delivered from 1998 to 2000. They operate four daily round-trip services between Lisbon and Porto. You can board the first train from Lisbon in the morning and alight from the last train from Porto at Pragal on the southern side of the Tagus bridge, but the remainder originate and terminate in Lisbon's Santa Apolonia Station. Fiat Ferroviaria designed and largely manufactured the 137-mph trains in its Savigliano plant near Turin, Italy, but ADtranz Portugal assembled them at Amadore in Lisbon's suburbs.

These trains differ from the Spanish tilting Talgo Pendular trains because these use Italian active tilting technology rather than Spanish passive tilting technology. At first glance, they look like the Italian Pendolino, but Portugal's trains (the work of Italian designer Guigiari, who also worked on Cisalpino's ETR470 liveries) are nearly five inches higher and five inches wider. They also differ from the Italian trains because they use German rather than Italian electrical equipment. Inside, you enjoy TV screens on the inside of every carriage.

Shortly out of Santa Apolonia terminal, your train makes a quick stop among the concrete palm fronds of the 1996 Oriente station. You may of course board here, as well, because of the station's convenient subway connection.

Before your second stop, in Coimbra, you pass the city of Caxarias, where an interchange between local trains and buses was opened in 2000 to give connections to the Sanctuary of Fatima, the center of pilgrimage.

Coimbra (say "Queem-bra") is a romantic city with the legendary landmark fountain of the Portuguese Romeo and Juliet. It boasts the oldest and most prestigious university in Portugal. Your Alfa Pendular stops in Coimbra-B station, which was built on the mainline when engineers couldn't figure a way to divert the tracks into the core of the city. In case you wonder, there is a Coimbra-A station still standing on the banks of the Mondego River and still connected to Coimbra-B by heavy-duty local trains, much to the annoyance of the city fathers who object to the intrusion of large trains into the city center.

At Aveiro stop, look to the west and the station's facade decorated with blue murals. This is one of Portugal's three great azulejo-decorated stations. (The others are Porto's Sao Bento and Pinhao in the Douro Valley.)

Before crossing the Douro River into Porto, you stop briefly at Vila Nova de Gaia on the south bank. The city is the home of the port wine companies. You then proceed along the south bank of the "Golden River," perhaps gasping as the best view of your trip comes into view as you cross the 1991 Sao Joao bridge over the Douro River and the panorama of the old stone city of Porto spreads on the right bank before you. You see the old town, topped by the towers of the cathedral and the Clerigos belfry, rising in tiers from the Douro. Overlapping series of hillside alleys are lined with architecturally dazzling houses decorated with corbels and (occasionally) tiled facades.

Some 186 yards to the west, and built 103 years earlier, you see the original Queen Marie Pia railroad bridge built entirely of steel girders by French engineer Gustav Eiffel while he lived in Porto for several years. The bridge is now a national monument. It had to be abandoned in 1991 because safety engineers imposed a speed restriction of 12.4 mph and created a terrible bottleneck. The new bridge carries a double track and may be crossed at 75 mph, which reduces your Lisbon-Porto travel time by a few minutes.

Sadly, you leave your view of Porto when your train enters the tunnel and comes to a stop in the mainline Campanha station, where there are special Alfa Pendular facilities. This gives you a chance to board one of the many connecting trains and continue to the downtown Sao Bento station just to the see the great display of artistic tiles, *azulejos*, which echo the skies and cover the walls of the reception hall. It is the pride of CP. Although in need of a good cleaning, they're a feast for the eyes.

Painted in 1930 by Jorge Colaco, these tile pictures include a full-color frieze of everyday life in Portugal and feature historic panoramas in blue: Joao's entry into Porto (top right) and his capture of Cueta (bottom right).

Across the Douro River from the lodges and showrooms of the wine producers, Porto is a veritable hive of activity and the capital of Portuguese baroque, epitomized in the church of Sao Francisco.

Porto has three train stations. The most important is Campanha. From here you will board the train up the Douro Valley or travel north across the border to Spain's Galicia or settle into a high-speed train racing south to Lisbon, but the Lisbon trains no longer cross the now-unused railroad bridge built in 1877 by Eiffel with a soaring arch span of 530 feet.

Trindade station is used to reach nearby villages, but Sao Bento terminus in the city center is special.

Lisbon-Porto Alfa Pendular Service

		(1)	(2)			(3)
LISBON (Apolonia)	dep.	N/A	0955	1355	1655	1855
Lisbon (Oriente)	dep.	0704	1004	1404	1704	1904
Coimbra-B	arr.	0859	1159	1559	1859	2059
Aveiro	arr.	0930	1230	1630	1930	2130
Vila Nova de Gaia	arr.	1005	1305	1705	2005	2205
PORTO (Campanha)	arr.	1010	1310	1710	2010	2210

		(4)	(2)			(5)
PORTO (Campanha)	dep.	0705	1005	1405	1705	1905
Vila Nova de Gaia	dep.	0711	1011	1411	1711	1911
Aveiro	dep.	0746	1046	1446	1746	1946
Coimbra-B	dep.	0818	1118	1518	1818	2018
Lisbon (Oriente)	arr.	1009	1309	1709	2009	2209
LISBON (Apolonia)	arr.	1020	1320	1720	2020	2220

(1) Originates in Lisbon Pragal Station, Mondays-Fridays
(2) Mondays-Saturdays
(3) Sundays-Fridays
(4) Mondays-Fridays
(5) Sundays, on other days terminates in Lisbon Pragal Station

Douro River Train

Your train from Porto, the northern capital of Portugal, running up the parched Douro Valley is not new, and not fast, and clatters somewhat, but it is in good condition and you have room to stretch out.

Just as your train gives you a sense of motion, the gritty landscape gives you a sense of being as you run east following the right bank of the Douro, the *Rio do Ouro*, or River of Gold, below. When the river rises deep among the summers' infernos of the Urbion Mountains north of Madrid it is called the Duero; in Portugal, the Douro.

Your train's whistle bellows like a conch horn or a call for a fox hunt. Terraced vineyards embrace both banks, but when you look from the north of the river to the south, the orderly rows of grapevines appear more picturesque. Your views are sweeping and you are charmed by the valley's varied Mediterranean appearance.

Romans planted vines here, but the port wine industry traces its history to two sons of an English merchant, who while visiting some remote monastery in about 1678, sipped the sweet wine mixed with brandy to stop its fermentation.

Generations of winemakers labored to tame the wild Douro Valley and turn it into the primary residence of port wine. "God created the earth, man the Douro," say inscriptions on the vineyards. Wine is the valley's pride and virtually its only pursuit.

You may relax knowing that your train into the rugged country beats hours driving down bumpy roads along the winding river into the heart of vineyard country, and that Portugal has the highest traffic fatality rate in Europe.

Out of Porto you first pass through the gentle green hills and villages nestling amidst almond and olive groves of the *Baizo Corgo* (lower Douro). This area's accessibility makes it the most productive and most visited zone but its wine is of lower quality than the higher and more difficult river regions.

The mountainside looks like hell to work, so it is surprising that the tenacious vines endure, struggle to survive, and even bear fruit in such a parched environment.

The secret is the stratum of highly permeable schist set in a sea of granite. The schist, rich in minerals, maintains the vines through the long, hot, arid summers and winters so bitter that "even the vines cry with cold," according to poet Maguel Torga.

In 1757 the Marquis of Pombal's bureaucrats turned the area into the world's first controlled appellation zone.

After about two hours your train brings you to Regua, a junction. Unless you happen to be aboard one of the two daily direct trains, you have some 10 minutes to change here. In Regua the wine is stored after harvest. On the riverbanks a few wine barges still depart for the lodges in the city of Vila Nova de Gaia across from Porto.

The transfer to the lodges down the Douro from the vineyards where men once trampled the grapes underfoot to the sound of the accordion, always singing, was formerly accomplished by great barges, with four oarsmen who guided the craft down the rushing river. Now transportation is largely by truck and rail and the wine press has replaced the men.

Though some producers age their ports in their *quintas*, the estates founded by the dynasties of the port trade, they send most barrels from Regua to the merchants' lodges in Vila Nova de Gaia, where since the 1700s, the sheds have clung to the steep banks of the Douro in a veritable maze of long buildings with the names of the shippers lettered on the roofs.

After the skins and juice ferment together the liquid is spiked with high-proof grape brandy to produce a red wine with 18% or 19% alcohol. Over 90% of the precious wine is exported. France is the biggest consumer, followed by Belgium, Luxembourg, and the United Kingdom.

You may change at Regua from your wide-gauge train to the narrow-gauge train for Vila Real, which will take you along a jolting but scenic route into the high, austere mountain range of Serra da Estrela. This nature preserve is a landscape of jagged boulders, pine and chestnut forests, and rich pastures that provide the source of Serra cheese.

In the higher elevation of *Cima Corgo*, the middle Douro region, you arrive at the jewel-box train station of Pinhao. It is famous for its *azulejos*, a national craft taken up from the Moors.

The *azulejos* on the Pinhao train station's exterior give you a vivid picture of valley life when producing port wines was not so mechanized. You see scenes of women plucking the blue grapes, laborers' backs bending under 125-pound basketfuls, *rabelo* barques used to transport the pressed fruit to the lodges in Gaia, oxen hauling the oaken casks filled with already fermenting juice, and of course panoramic scenes of the terraces and the Douro Valley and River.

The *Cima Corgo* is the center of the port-producing region where serious ports originate. Hillsides give way to steep slopes, green turns to brown, and terraces must be hewn out of sunbaked slopes.

Further upstream toward the Spanish frontier, your train continues. The river becomes crowded between steep mountains and the vines become more sparse. Although the schist here is easier to work because it is older, only the brave cultivate the land. For some this is a land rich in promise.

The Douro River train is covered by Portugal and Iberic rail passes, Eurailpasses, and Europasses, but it's not worth validating a day box of one of the flexible passes because using the train is cheap. Pay $19 one-way first class from Porto to Pinhao; $14 second class.

Six port wine cellars in Vila Nova de Gaia are open daily except Sunday for tours, sampling and selling at various hours, but you can expect reduced hours on Saturdays and during the winter. Ask at the Porto tourist offices at Rua Clube dos Fenianos, 25 (phone 312-740) or Rua Infante D. Henrique, 63 (phone 200-9770).

Reach the port wine cellars on buses No. 57 and No. 91 from Praca Almeida Garrett next to Sao Bento train station.

Lisbon-Algarve

The best trains to the Algarve, the "Portuguese Riviera" stretching along Portugal's sunny southern shores, are two crack diesel InterCity trains which whisk you in four hours, 20 minutes, from Lisbon's waterfront Terreiro do Paco station to Faro. The trains were cascaded from Porto duty when Alfa Pendular trains were introduced. Their exteriors were fabricated in Portugal of stainless steel but the interiors duplicate snappy French Corail materials and design. The only difference is the language of the newspapers the passengers read. The bar car features sandwiches, cakes, coffee, and bottles of liquor. Less expensive InterRegional trains take you along the same route in about five hours, 15 minutes, but don't require reservations.

The 1999 extension of the blue metro line to the new Terreiro do Paco metro station allows you easily to reach the spruced-up and now-exquisite Terreiro do Paco train station adjacent to the finest square in Lisbon, the Praca do Comercio, which is known to all as Terreiro do Paco, the "Palace Terrace." Past the train station decorated with tiles depicting Algarvian city crests, you board, through separate first- and second-class entrances, CP's half-hourly blue-and-white ferries across the Tagus River to the Barreiro station. Rail passes are accepted aboard. A direct link between Lisbon and the Algarve will not be completed until 2003.

After your ferry crossing to Barreiro, follow the crowd down a ramp past kiosks, shops, and a waiting room through a ticket-checking station onto your waiting train of French Corail design. Your carriage is pleasant and the French-design bar car is available.

Running 155 miles in three hours, 45 minutes, to Tunes, the junction for connecting trains to the western Algarve, your InterCity is not fast, but comfortable, and gives you just the right pace to distinguish the harvest years painted on the cork trees. You see sights you never see from the colorless, commercial highway. You absorb the feeling of the region as you observe casual cowherds with staff and cap and brown bulls with wicked-looking horns drinking from streams. You see olive trees, orange groves, pine and eucalyptus forests, and many small farms.

You cross what seems like an invisible line across Portugal. South of the line the villages consist of boxy, flat-roofed houses. North of it, they are all peaked with tile roofs.

InterCity Service between Lisbon and the Algarve

IC581	IC571				IC580	IC582
1330	1740	dep.	LISBON (T. do Paco)	arr.	1205	1850
1400	1810	arr.	Barreiro	dep.	1135	1820
1425	1825	dep.	Barreiro	arr.	1105	1805
N/A	1853	dep.	Setubal	dep.	1042	N/A
1715	2130	arr.	Tunes	dep.	0755	1501
1720*	2135*	dep.	Tunes	arr.	0747	1442
1757	2206	arr.	Portimao	dep.	0713	1403
1817	2222	arr.	LAGOS	dep.	0657	1345
1717	2132	dep.	Tunes	arr.	0752	1458
1723	2139	dep.	Albufeira	dep.	0747	1453
1750	2205	arr.	FARO	dep.	0720	1425
1815*	2210*	dep.	FARO	arr.	0624*	1408*
1926	2313	arr.	Vila Real de			
			Santo Antonio	dep.	0600	1245

*Change trains

Lisbon-Sintra

Your trip to Sintra to see the extravagant Palace of Pena begins at

Lisbon's Rossio brightly remodeled (1996) station. Terminus of the one of the heaviest trafficked lines in Europe, Rossio station is located in the heart of Lisbon across from the Teatro National (National Theater) and the metro station named Rossio (on the green line) on Rossio Square. You enter the station through one of the most astonishing facades of the European railroads. It is in the neo-Manuelino style of the nineteenth century (connected to the adjacent hotel so royalty could proceed directly), but discolored by the traffic exhaust from Rossio Square in front.

Its interior is also charming. You see tile pictures of local produce on the east side and saints on the west. Visit the information counter (English spoken) on the ground floor, but follow the stairs and several flights of escalators all the way past various shops to "Gare," where travelers without rail passes buy tickets. When you come via the steps ("calcada") leading down from the crest of the hill above, enter the side door on the top level (with taxi access).

The two-class, red-and-stainless-steel air-conditioned electric railcars built by Sorefame (now ADtranz Portugal) were introduced in 1998, although some 1992 units have been renovated and reintroduced. Four-carriage units, usually doubled, depart quarter-hourly from 5:08 A.M. to 10:08 P.M. through the long tunnel into Campolide station. In 2001, CP begins additional service to Sintra from the new Oriente Station using 12 of the same double-decked trains that cross the Tagus Bridge. This is the first use of double-decked trains on the Sintra Line.

As you travel along the line to Sintra, you pass a disorderly array of suburbs. Finally, you see to the left Ferdinand of Coburg's palace on the highest peak of the Sintra hills above the Portela de Sintra station.

On fast trains your trip takes 45 minutes; nearly 100 trains run on weekdays. Outside the end-of-the-line peeling-paint Sintra station, taxis stand offering to take you to the palace. You can change to or from the cross-Tagus rapid-transit trains at Campolide station or to or from the metro blue line at Sete Rios station.

Lisbon-Cascais

Take one of the frequent (73 daily from 5:30 A.M. to 2:30 A.M.), simple, one-class, stainless-steel Sorefame/Budd electric trains from Lisbon to Cascais along the so-called Estoril line departing from Cais do Sodre train station. Your 16-mile excursion along the Tagus River to the coast is covered by rail pass.

The trains date from between 1950 and 1979, although some of the units from 1959 were set on 1924 chassis from wooden-bodied units built in France. In 1999-2000 these units were refurbished—new fiberglass front ends, new doors, reflective window bands, new seating, modernized interiors, and air-conditioning—instead of being replaced, so that the 1924 chassis will continue service well into the millennium. Perhaps some will reach a century of service.

You easily reach (and find) the Cais do Sodre train station because it is the terminus of the green metro line opened on April 19, 1998. With a rail pass you ride up the escalators and walk through the open portals of the presentable, buff-colored station's gates to the boarding area, where video monitors inform you of your track number (according to destination) and departure time.

After the Alcantara station, your Estoril Railroad passes under the Ponte 25 de Abril suspension bridge—Portugal's "Golden Gate." Note the addition of the new, lower deck to support the electric rapid-transit trains linking the northern and southern portions of Lisbon. The River Tagus has always been a major barrier between the two sides of the river, but the problem became acute after the 1966 opening of the bridge facilitated explosive growth south of the river and automobile traffic became so heavy that 30-minute delays became normal. It took up to two hours to travel nine miles. Construction of the Cross-Tagus line was awarded to the same New York consulting engineering firm which originally designed that bridge and modeled it on San Francisco's famous landmark.

You run a block from the Tagus until you reach the Henry the Navigator Memorial, where you begin to travel alongside the sailboats and Tagus promenade. Your best view of the bridge is looking back immediately before you reach the Belem station—a superb view. The lighting effects at night are particularly spectacular.

The Belem station is a convenient place to debark to view Belem Tower, the great Jeronimos Monastery across the highway, and the Henry the Navigator Memorial.

Past the Alges stop, your train travels closer to the Tagus and you have a better view of the shipping, the breakwaters, and then the beaches. All along the stretch from Alges to Cruz Quebrada to Caxias, looking back toward Lisbon gives you a fine long view of the graceful suspension bridge.

You don't appreciate the splendor of the coast—the blue water and frothy waves breaking on the white sand—until just before your stop at S. Pedro do Estoril station, where you see a nice panorama of things to come. Estoril is your glamour stop, in front of the Casino. The tourist office is across the street. Past Estoril to Cascais, you pass beaches and luxury hotels. The bay and sandy beach for which Cascais is famous begins just before its unsheltered end-of-the-line train station.

There are departures for Estoril and Cascais about every 12 to 20 minutes from 5:30 A.M. until 2:30 A.M. Departures for stations as far as San Pedro alternately leave Lisbon every 12 to 20 minutes. On weekdays nearly 300 trains run daily in both directions. Your trip to Estoril takes 28 minutes. The faster trains make five stops along the way.

Scandinavia
and Finland

Smart Traveling on the Trains
of Scandinavia and Finland

Swedish trains—Norwegian trains—Danish trains—Finnish trains—Airport trains—Stations and subways—Midnight Sun travel—Your gateway to Russia—Using Eurailpass bonuses—ScanRail Pass—National rail passes—City travel cards

Hans Christian Andersen traveled by mail coach and sailing ship on his first trip from his home, Odense, on the island of Funen, to the Danish royal capital of Copenhagen in September 1819. You can make that trip now in two hours, 40 minutes by Danish IC3 InterCity train.

The great Scandinavian writer was the consummate adventurer: "To travel is to live." He realized travel meant meeting new people, visiting new surroundings, absorbing new impressions, discovering new joys in nature, and feeling vibrantly alive.

Traveling by train through Scandinavia is easy using the 1,250-mile network of the Danish State Railroads (DSB), the 2,500 miles of the Norwegian State Railroads (NSB), and the 7,000 combined miles of the Swedish State Railroads (SJ AB) and private train companies.

322 TRAVELING EUROPE'S TRAINS

Finnish State Railroads' (VR) 3,650 miles complete your Nordic adventuring. Ride them from where the storks nest in the chimneys of Denmark to the blue fjords and stark glaciers of Norway to where the Midnight Sun beats down on the land of the Lapps above the Arctic Circle in Sweden and Finland.

When Queen Margrethe of Denmark and King Carl Gustaf of Sweden opened the Oresund Fixed Link connecting the two countries by tunnel and bridge, road and rail, on July 1, 2000, they changed train travel in the Scandinavian countries. After 10 years' construction work, trains began regular departures from Malmo's Central Station at 6:09 A.M., and from Copenhagen's Central Station at 6:16 A.M., on July 2, cutting the travel time between these two cities to 35 minutes, compared with an hour (in good weather) aboard the ferry you took previously.

Engineers adapted 11 X2000 train sets to run on both Swedish and Danish electrical power supplies, and scheduled eight departures daily on weekdays—nearly every hour—to take you via the Fixed Link in high style between Copenhagen and Stockholm in about five and a half hours, with stops at Copenhagen's Kastrup Airport, and—combined with the Eurotunnel and Denmark's Great Belt bridge—the 10-mile Oresund Fixed Link makes it possible to travel without sea ferry from London to Narvik, Norway, above the Arctic Circle. It brings closer the island of Zealand (the eastern part of Denmark) and Scania (the southern part of Sweden with strong ties to Denmark), and their two cities, Copenhagen and Malmo, to form the Oresund Region. With 3.5 million inhabitants, the Oresund Region is the largest domestic market in northern Europe, and the eighth richest in Europe in terms of GNP. It is larger than Stockholm, and equal in size to Berlin, Hamburg, or Amsterdam.

For the seafaring Dane, bridges are awe-inspiring pieces of work, and they like to remember Bifrost, the magical bridge of Norse mythology, that linked the home of the gods to the world of mortals in a rainbow mixture of fire, water and air.

The $3 billion Oresund Fixed Link is the longest combined rail/road/tunnel crossing in the world. Accountants expect it to pay off construction costs and become a cash cow for the two governments after 24 years of its operation at an average of 10,000 vehicle crossings per day.

Trains depart every 20 minutes by day and hourly by night between Copenhagen and Malmo. Travel time is 35 minutes with three or four stops en route, including Kastrup International Airport. Fare is about $10, and discount tickets are offered for frequent travelers, compared with about $32 charged for automobiles crossing the Link. Charges to the trains are less than true cost because they are cross-subsidized from highway tolls in order to promote environmentally friendly train travel. You can use credit cards for both train and toll.

The 27 three-carriage Oresund electric trains, built in 2000, resemble Denmark's InterCity trains in many ways. They have the rubber ring front ends, which allow the driver's position to be folded away when two units are coupled together for multiple service, and up to five may be joined together.

The seats are also similar: 20 first class, 176 second class, and 41 jump seats for those who wish to sit near their luggage. However, the new units are not articulated and have wide central doors and smooth rather than ribbed sides. The wide doors and low floor design mean that you can load your luggage on and off easily.

You speed up to 112 mph in the new silver gray Oresund electric units. SJ owns 10 of the $180 million new units; DSB owns 17. You are able to reach Helsingor on the Danish side and Helsingborg and Kristianstad on the Swedish.

From Copenhagen's Kastrup International Airport, your train runs parallel to cars on the highway onto an artificial peninsula on the Danish coast before you enter the 2.2-mile tunnel, which is the world's largest immersed tunnel based on volume, with four parallel tunnel tubes, including two auto lanes.

The Link was a trade-off between tunnel and bridge. A tunnel below the whole waterway would have been more expensive. A total bridge would have been cheaper, but it was necessary to build a tunnel at the western side to provide a shipping channel through the Oresund.

Before the dredging vessel *Castor* could begin preparing a trench for the submerged tunnel, the area had to be swept with special equipment to detect World War II bombs littering the seabed. Ten unexploded bombs were found. Historians believe they originated from British planes that dumped loads of unwanted bombs and rockets off the Kastrup Peninsula to celebrate the end of war in 1945.

Surfacing on Peberholm, the artificial island 2.5 miles long, your train takes the lower deck of the 4.8-mile bridge. Automobiles climb on the top deck of the bridge and take 10 minutes to drive across the Fixed Link.

The bridge is the world's strongest cable stay bridge, built to carry the combined width of two auto lanes, plus a third emergency lane, and the dual track railroad. Environmental measures include noise barriers for trains although the highway above has no barriers.

DSB trains run on the right; SJ on the left. To solve this conflict, right hand running is used on the bridge and into the outskirts of Malmo.

You leave the bridge at Lernacken, just on Swedish soil, and your train changes from Danish power, 25 kV A.C. 50 Hz to Swedish 15 kV A.C. 16.7 Hz power supply while coasting. The changeover in the westbound direction is made at Kastrup.

You circle through the outskirts of Malmo, with a stop at Malmo Syd Station, which is built in the middle of nowhere but is well used by passengers arriving by car and traveling to and from Kastrup Airport. Your final stop is Malmo Central Station, which is a dead-end station.

The Oresund Fixed Link replaces the most heavily traveled international ferry route in the world. There was a ferry crossing every seven minutes, 4 train ferries an hour, 400 train carriages a day. Each crossing took 25 minutes.

For more information, access *www.oresundskonsortiet.com* and *www.oresundsbron.com* and view photos at *www.bridgephoto.dk.*

The most popular way to reach Copenhagen for jumping off to Norway and Sweden/Finland is aboard DSB's IC3 EuroCity trains from Hamburg, Germany, and now one train, the Hamlet, continues across the Fixed Link to Malmo as well. The EC Christian Morgenstern, the EC Thomas Mann, the EC Karen Blixen, and the EC Bertel Thorvaldsen terminate in Copenhagen. They take you to Scandinavia via the mainline from Hamburg, Germany, named for the migratory flight path of birds, cutting the former travel time between Hamburg and Copenhagen by nearly an hour to 4 1/2 hours. To accommodate the high-tech trains (see "Danish Trains" below), GermanRail increased track spacing at three critical locations and DSB modified the leaf doors of their trains to match the height of the German platforms.

Your EC train takes you right aboard alternating half-hourly DSB and GermanRail ferries from Puttgarden to Rodby and on to Copenhagen. Remain in your train while it is being shunted aboard the ferry to Rodby, then dine, shop, and return to your seat when it docks. Don't miss your chance to enjoy an open-faced sandwich,

Danish pastry (better on a DSB ferry than a German one), and Danish beer in the cafeteria. You buy cigarettes and liquor in the 24-hour duty-free shops aboard the ferries. Even at prices higher than at home, they are bargains here—something obvious by the long lines of Swedish shoppers struggling with fully loaded red plastic shopping baskets. Be sure to do enough duty-free shopping to last throughout your entire stay in Scandinavia.

The night crossing of Scandline's ship between Sassnitz (Germany) and Trelleborg (Sweden) connects with a fast train on the German side to Berlin's Lichtenberg station; the day crossing connects to an IR train to Berlin's Ostbahnhof and Zoo stations, and continues to Leipzig's main station. On the Swedish side the ships connect with trains to Malmo. Because all these connections, including the ship, are covered by Eurailpass, this is an attractive alternative to Sweden from Berlin or Leipzig.

In addition to SJ's mainline train up the Swedish West Coast to Oslo, you can also reach Norway by several ferries from Denmark or by train via Storlien, Sweden, to Trondheim. Reach Finland by Silja Line ship from Stockholm or by bus (covered by rail passes) north of the Gulf of Bothnia between Sweden and Finland. Tagkompaniet, North Sweden's private train operating company, reopened the line from Boden to Haparanda between mid-June and mid-August, but VR closed its rail connection from Kemi to the Swedish border in 1988.

Swedish Trains

Because of privatization, trains in Sweden are in a state of change. The Swedish parliament split SJ into four subsidiaries for sale to private interests. One of these is SJ AB, the passenger division, which is still 100 percent owned by the state. SJ AB operates only some 60 percent of the services in Sweden. The new company Svenska Tagkompaniet (literally, Swedish train company) operates 1,600 miles of long-distance train in the north of Sweden covering Stockholm-Narvik (Norway), Gothenburg-Gavle, Boden-Lulea, plus Boden-Tornio (Finland) and Vassas-Umea, which had no service. A company jointly owned by SJ and NSB operates the line between Stockholm and Oslo. Local traffic in Stockholm (SL) is also privatized. As a result SJ had to take down the SJ signs in stations serving the new railroads.

Swedish trains are designated X2000, InterCity, InterRegio, InterNord, and Nattaget (night trains). Ticket prices are based on relative advantage over competing forms of transportation, not on distance traveled, and thus are relatively arbitrary. Reservations are required on all journeys over 90 miles. Point-to-point fares include seat reservations.

Swedish trains are nonsmoking. This was necessary because Swedish cigarette smokers had been reserving seats in nonsmoking sections and then moving into the smoking section to light up. This meant some nonsmokers had to sit in the smoking section. Now smokers have to search out smoke ghettos in vestibules at each end of the train, spaces nonsmokers do not have to walk through.

X2000 trains are the tilting blue-and-white, four-headlight (required by law in Sweden), stainless-steel bullets you see speeding across the landscape between Stockholm, Gothenburg, and Malmo. They are Scandinavia's fastest (running at 125 mph), sleekest, and most innovative trains. They hold the Swedish speed record at 171 mph.

Lacking a large population base to support massive investment in megaspeed trains, yet threatened by loss of business to domestic air travel, SJ manufactured the X2000 to comfort visitors' rides around curves by tilting like the Italian Pendolino (see the chapter on Italy) except that the power car remains upright in order to simplify transmission of electricity.

Traffic analysts determined that hourly departures for X2000s were essential to attract business travelers. Because of their frequent runnings, X2000s are short trains consisting of single power cars, two first-class and two second-class intermediate passenger coaches (the second-class coach with 2+2 seating was not added until 1996), a bistro carriage, and a driving trailer incorporating second-class seating.

Building separate dedicated high-speed railbeds was not within SJ's financial means, so SJ took a cost-effective approach to upgrading existing lines. Travel times were continuously decreased as newly upgraded stretches were put into service segment by segment.

Following X2000's premier running on September 4, 1990, between Stockholm and Gothenburg (Karstad in 1992; Uppsala, Mjolby, and Jonkoping in 1993; Malmo in 1995; Sundsvall and the Gothenburg-Malmo connection in 1996), SJ gradually added train sets and departures to the timetable. Departures from Stockholm complement conventional InterCity trains (which make more stops) between city centers, and make the 280-mile trip to Gothenburg in close to three hours. Air passengers need two and three-quarters hours from city center to city center.

Motorists take about five hours to drive. In 1991, SJ carried 39 percent of the combined Stockholm/Gothenburg air/train traffic; in 1992, 42 percent; in 1993, almost half. By November 1994, X2000s carried 33 percent of the traffic; SAS carried 31 percent; a private airline, 17 percent; and InterCity trains, 19 percent.

The X2000 is a big, roomy, substantial train. You probably won't feel it tilting on its run between Stockholm and Gothenburg, but if you hear a hiss, it's tilting. You receive a high level of service on board, sitting 2+1 in two different classes named "X2000" and "X2000 budget." First-class passengers receive a first-class meal and plug-in earphones that you control by the console at the edge of your chair. The fidelity is good (much better than airlines). Second-class passengers must bring their own earphones (or rent), but they can use the earphone jacks.

You need reservations on all X2000 and InterCity trains. ScanRail Pass holders must pay a supplement to ride the X2000, either first or second class. This includes their seat reservation. Euailpass holders pay no supplement, but must make a reservation costing about $5.

SJ's two-class InterCity trains (which sometime carry Family Carriages with supervised children's playrooms) have some of the widest seats in Europe, and they recline more than those in other European trains. Seat backs and tables are high—to fit the tall Swedes.

First- and second-class carriages are divided into segments with differing seating innovations and pleasant arrangements. Sales kiosks divide their restaurant cars. Half is set for first-class service with white linen; half provides second-class cafeteria service.

Between Oslo's Sentral station and Stockholm Central station, SJ runs two direct InterNord (IN) trains a day. These consist of SJ IC carriages with a compartment set aside for selling coffee and snacks. In addition you may take Norwegian trains between Oslo (S) and Karlstad (C) to connect with SJ X2000 trains to Stockholm. The trips take about six hours.

Even in Sweden you'll see some of the Danish IC3 train sets on the Karlskrona-Kristianstad-Malmo "Coastal Arrow" line. In Sweden, the sets are known as Class Y2.

The Inland Railroad between Mora and Gallivare is a private railroad offering a 25 percent discount to holders of ScanRail passes, but no discount for Euailpass holders. Trains had been pulled by steam locomotives, but for environmental reasons Inlandsbanan AB now uses three diesel railcars with ethanol-fueled Volvo bus engines for

328 TRAVELING EUROPE'S TRAINS

daily departures during the summer between Mora and Ostersund and between Gallivare and Ostersund, which cost about $20 and $40, respectively. Reservations are required and must be made early at Tel. 498-20-33-80 or *www.inlandsbanan.se* or *www.ief.se.* The line is surrounded with trees, so "wild" is what you see on this scenic railroad— no mountains, which are distant, and few Lapps.

Norwegian Trains

NSB (*www.nsb.no*) operates day trains, Express trains, and Signatur trains as well as night trains to connect the larger cities, while InterCity trains serve the cities in southern Norway at intervals of one to two hours. Local trains connect Oslo, Bergen, and Trondheim with their suburbs and smaller towns.

Three electrified mainline routes run from Oslo: south and west to Stavanger (the Sorland line), due west to Bergen (the Bergen line), and north to Trondheim (the Dovre line). From Trondheim adventurers continue north to Bodo (the Nordland line) or cross into Sweden by diesel-hauled train (the Meraker line). The diesel-operated route north and east from Oslo (the Roros line) is protected by UNESCO because of its mining history.

During late 1999 NSB began to put into service the first of 16 gray and dark blue Class BM73 130-mph tilting trains with the brand name Signatur on routes between Oslo and Trondheim, Oslo and Stavanger, and Oslo and Bergen, cutting journey times by about one hour. The four-carriage Signatur trains are equipped with undercarriages adapted from the Swedish X2000 tilting train, but with steerable axles.

Signatur trains have interiors designed for long-distance travelers, with 56 passengers in first class and 151 in second. You can buy meals from the cafe/bistro car located in the center of the train or opt for at-seat service in Signatur Pluss (first) class. Comfortable seats and a table make it easy for business travelers to place their laptop computers and use the power connection. When you want to listen to music, you can buy a set of headphones at the coffee bar. Smokers utilize a separate smoking compartment. Young children use a play area with parents' seats alongside. Point-to-point tickets require paying a supplement that includes a seat reservation. Eurailpass holders are welcomed in Signatur (second) class and pay the normal reservations fee. For travel in Signatur Pluss, Eurailpass holders must pay a supplement. Holders of first-class Eurailpasses pay half supplement.

Aboard Express trains on the Bergen and Dovre lines, you ride in NSB's good-looking "B7" carriages, maroon with black detailing. They sparkle with good space, high-quality materials, and unexcelled ambience. Their panoramic windows, almost twice as wide as high, are safer and give you even broader views ahead. They were refurbished in 1995 when they added a stylish bistro car with Scandinavian-modern tables and cafeteria service. Staff in the new bistro cars offer snacks and beverages, a breakfast buffet, lunch, and dinner.

B7 carriages have smooth aerodynamic profiles, making them look different from other European trains. Longitudinal aluminum sections make them five to six tons lighter than steel cars, dynamic undercarriages send them around curves 10 percent faster, and air-filled rubber cushions dampen track noises and vibration.

Express trains have no first-class section. The nine-seat deluxe section is the "Salong," which requires a second-class ticket and a supplement costing about $31. These passengers sit in reclining seats and receive blankets, fresh fruit, coffee or tea, and one meal.

One carriage devoted to "Standard" seating offers coffee or tea and a newspaper. Travelers with first-class rail passes may sit in this preferred section without paying a supplement. Those with second-class tickets or passes pay a supplement of about $8.

"Economy" 2+2 seating makes up the balance of the train. The supplement costs about $3. You can bring your own food and let the scenery entertain you. There is also a "Barnetog" section for children and their parents, plus seats for the handicapped. The smoking section car is half of the last carriage on the train. Without pull-down windows, the smoking ghetto becomes so foul that some smokers are tempted to quit.

IC trains take you on three high-density routes in "Class 70" units. You ride them Oslo to Lillehammer, Oslo to Gothenburg, Sweden (with connections to Copenhagen), and Oslo to Larvik (for the ferry to Denmark) and Skien. Skien is a center with 50,000 population, but 300,000 live in the area between Skien and Oslo.

The IC trains are red, four-car electric units that can be extended to five B70 carriages or hooked together to form doubled trains. Don't confuse them with GermanRail's InterCity Express train, which is based on an entirely different concept. NSB's IC runs up to 100 mph, but with stops you average 56 mph, which is about the same as if you drove a car. It saves 45 minutes between Oslo and Gothenburg compared to the

InterNord train it replaced, which traveled at a maximum speed of 75 mph and averaged 30 to 40 mph.

NSB based these trains on marketing research which showed that business travelers demand on-time departures, short journey times, good service, and clean working areas. IC passengers can choose between three classes. You need only second-class tickets, but pay different supplements depending on seating quality.

• InterCity Office is the top section, with seats facing tables, designed for working business travelers. These travelers pay a surcharge of about $19 within Norway or about $31 to or from Sweden. They receive either a breakfast brunch or an evening meal, including wine and beer (according to the menu they find in their seats), served at their seats in specially designed airline-style trays. There is no restaurant car.

• InterCity Office plain covers a smaller section for those who want to relax, without tables. Passengers pay about $8 ($12.50 to Sweden) and receive no meal.

• InterCity Economy corresponds to first class on most European trains. It seats Eurailpass and ScanRail Pass holders in larger compartments without surcharge, but you require seat reservations costing about $3 within Norway and to Sweden. Snacks are available from a food trolley.

Two-carriage Type 93 diesel-powered Talent Railcars are used on the Roros line between Trondheim and Hamar. The 87-mph railcars went into operation in 2000 under the condition that they did not operate in deep snow until further testing. They differ from other versions of the Talent Railcar because of extra insulation for temperatures as low as minus 40 degrees Fahrenheit and snowplows set higher than usual to give track clearance when tilting and deflect any animals such as elk. Each unit seats 88 and up to three units may be connected together.

Danish Trains

DSB (*www.dsb.dk*, click on "journey planner") and a few private railroads make traveling easy in Denmark by covering the country with a dense network of modern services supplemented with buses on quieter sections. Trains are classified InterCity (IC), InterRegional (IR), Regional (Re), and InterCity "Lyn," meaning "lightning." EuroCity (EC) trains run to and from Hamburg and a EuroNight (EN) train runs to Munich, Innsbruck, and Stuttgart. The rapid-transit S-bane (suburban train) network carries you through greater Copenhagen. IC trains are the backbone of Denmark's national railroad service. They call at most main city stations hourly. Generally, IC trains link Zealand, Funen, and Jutland, starting and ending in Copenhagen or Copenhagen's airport. You can use IC trains for short trips all over Denmark but not for local trips in the greater Copenhagen area. Lyn is a special service that links most Danish provinces during the day, Monday through Friday. This service is designed for business travelers and requires a first-class Eurailpass or ScanRail Pass. Re trains link local and rural stations all over Denmark. You cannot reserve seats on Re trains, but you can bring your bicycle, baby carriage, or wheelchair. "S-tog" is the Copenhagen rail service. Trains run every five to 10 minutes during the day and at longer intervals at night. The Copenhagen Card (see below), a 24-hour ticket, or a 10-trip ticket is useful for bus and train throughout greater Copenhagen.

IC trains offer Standard (second) class and Business (first) class. Standard includes only your trip. Business gives you a complimentary buffet with coffee, tea, and soft drinks. Lyn trains carry no standard class seats, but offer Business and Business Plus, which includes a welcome drink and a menu.

DSB provides no-smoking sections on all trains and allows no smoking at all for Business passengers traveling on certain IC trains. Baby carriages are allowed on all trains, but you need to book a space in advance on an IC train. Bicycles are allowed on all trains except Lyn and rush-hour S-trains. On some IC trains you need to make advance reservations for your bicycle. Most Re trains have space for six to eight bicycles. Pets may travel on all trains but are restricted to special areas. Mobile telephones are welcome except in the reservable resting area of IC and Lyn trains. Seats on most IC and Lyn trains have plugs for earphones and 220-volt electrical outlets.

DSB's greatest achievement of the past decade are the modular, 125-mph, IC3 diesel and IR4 electric trains, the white slivers with recessed drivers' cabins that you see racing on DSB's mainlines. The IC3 units are designed for long-distance work, and the IR4 units for suburban, local, and middle-distance work. They are the world's most computerized—they sniff the temperature outside and decide how early to turn themselves on in the morning. First-class sections are marked with yellow stripes on the outside. Passengers rely on their seat reservation numbers to find their carriage, which is indicated above the carriage doorway.

The interiors are divided in "Salon" (first class), "Hvidepladser" (quiet area), "Familieplatser," and "ICpladser." All seating is in open salons. The seats themselves are arranged facing across tables in IC3s, and mostly airline style in IC4s. Opening the interior doors is tricky because a beam from the ceiling triggers them. Merely touch the center of the door to activate the mechanism.

Adapted to the Danish countryside, where there is less than 14 miles on average between cities, these trains accelerate and brake rapidly, slashing journey times and increasing convenience. Both the IC3 and IR4 have the same aluminum bodywork, articulate, and employ the same microprocessor control system. These factors allow DSB to join them together to form a single train for peak-hour service.

Along the great crescent mainline taking you from Copenhagen to the northern tip of Denmark, electrified IR4 trains and new double-decked trains on hire from Switzerland dive beneath Danish waters through the East tunnel of the bridge-and-tunnel Fixed Link across the Great Belt waterway project connecting the Danish capital on the main island of Zeeland with the peninsula of Jutland. From Zeeland to the tiny island of Sprogo, you travel for five miles, up to 255 feet beneath sea level, in the 1996 two-tube tunnel with 38 miles of new track, including approaches.

In contrast to your train's route which includes combined tunnel and bridge, the automobile path crosses the waters of the Great Belt entirely on bridges including the East bridge, the world's longest suspension bridge at 4.2 miles, suspended between two pylons, each 833 feet high (about six times the height of the Statue of Liberty) and 5,327 feet apart. Automobile drivers view the waters 213 feet below.

Train tunnel and bridge construction was a mammoth job. They reduce your crossing time from 70 to seven minutes and tie Denmark's capital city with the Jutland peninsula economically, socially, and politically. Traffic is expected to increase from four to 10 million per year.

Rising to sea level from the Great Belt tube, your train now crosses the western expanse of the Great Belt 1993 from the island of Sprogo to Funen on the 4.1-mile low bridge delivered in 1994. It carries two train lines and the parallel four-lane superhighway.

On Funen, your train calls at Odense where many passengers disembark to visit the Hans Christian Andersen city. Others continue to

Fredericia, the junction for international trains from Hamburg. Past Fredericia travelers continue on the mainline trains north on the Jutland peninsula to Aarhus, Aalborg, and finally to Hjorring. There, travelers take the connecting second-class-only private train for the 12-mile trip to Hirtshals (20 to 25 minutes), for a Color Line's crossing to Kristiansand, Norway, (where they receive a rail pass discount) or Oslo on the M/S *Color Festival.* They might also continue a half-hour more to Frederikshavn for the Stena Line crossing to Gothenburg, Sweden, or Oslo, Norway, the Larvik Line crossing to Larvik, Norway, or the DA-NO Linjen crossing to Oslo.

Finnish Trains

1996's S220 Pendolino electric tilting express trains are the pride of VR (*www.vr.fi*). They are so named because they speed up to 220 km/hr (137 mph) on conventional track and chop your travel time on the south coastal route between Turku and Helsinki.

S220 is unique as the world's first wide-gauge and the most spacious tilting train. They are Fiat adaptations of Italy's ETR460. While the ETR460 has a luxurious dining car suitable for long travel times, the short travel time between Helsinki and Turku allowed VR to substitute a snack and refreshments kiosk, with no seating, and insert standard seating into the remainder of the carriage.

Travel time between Turku and Helsinki, which for years had been 158 minutes, fell to 114 minutes in 1995, and shrank to 108 minutes in 1996 when the S220 trains were permitted full-speed operation because of track improvements. VR claims the improvements were not just due to the arrival of the Pendolino, but were simply the repair of old and worn track. The upgrading allowed 100 mph on nontilting trains compared with 135 mph for the Pendolino.

The tracks were electrified throughout, level crossings were removed, and modern safety and access control equipment installed. This allowed the Pendolino's running to be extended to Pori, Seinajoki, Tampere, Kuopio, Kouvola, Joensuu, and to the Russian border.

Every weekday you ride the S220 Pendolino round-trip between Turku and Helsinki four times, three times on Saturdays and Sundays. It makes intermediate stops at Kupitaa, Salo, Karjaa, Espoo, and Pasila. The Pendolino's interior was designed by Giugiaro, like Italy's ETR460, and the comfortable blue-gray seats and carpeting were made in Finland. All seats are arranged one-opposite-two, giving you great space, even in second class, and the arrangement makes traveling second class on these trains a great bargain.

Each tilting train has six carriages, including a seven-seat smoking compartment and lounge at one end and an office compartment equipped with a telephone, fax, and overhead projector at the other. S220 Pendolino seats 264 passengers in all. The trains can be hooked together to form a doubled train. You have plenty of room because Finland's broader gauge allows these trains to be wider by almost 16 inches, and higher by 10.6 inches, than their counterparts running in Italy (see "Italy" chapter).

The S220 Bistro kiosk offers a full range of refreshments, but you won't need a full meal for such a short run, and the Mini-Bistro serving cart brings drinks and snacks to your seat. Overhead monitors display the layouts of the main arrival stations.

S220 Pendolino trains alternate service between Helsinki and Turku with Intercity 2 (IC2) trains of four to six double-deck, totally nonsmoking carriages made in 2000. You can use the Mini-Buffet no matter on which deck you sit. In business class, you can reserve two adjoining seats in order to spread out. There are compartments for travelers with allergies, as well as for families and the handicapped. You can bring your pet along, and there are spaces for three bicycles.

New (1996-1999) Sr2 locomotives that set the Nordic speed record for locomotives (141 mph) are painted red and white to match the red-and-white InterCity ("IC") trains with flashing LED displays on the outside showing their destinations and times of arrival. Fast trains (*P*) consist of blue-gray 1980s carriages of older fashion and run with slightly less velocity. "Lokal" electrified railcars providing frequent commuter service to and from Helsinki's outlying suburbs are being refurbished in and out and their color transformed from brown to red and white.

VR times InterCity and Pendolino trains primarily to suit business travelers who want to reach Helsinki in the morning and depart in the afternoon. When you ride an InterCity or Pendolino train, a staff member offers you a Finnish newspaper. First-class reservations cost about $5. You also must reserve second-class seats on IC and Pendolino trains.

InterCity first-class carriages consist of compartments with fixed seats and an end salon with fixed seats at the ends and swivel chairs around red plastic tables.

VR's diesel-hauled trains usually consist of older carriages, sometimes outfitted with video monitors showing American movies with Finnish subtitles. They require no reservations. You usually will ride them on secondary lines.

VR uses nearly the same wide gauge (five feet) as in the Soviet Union because the lines were laid before Finland became independent of Russia. VR's wide-gauge electric locomotives were manufactured in former East Germany; the diesels and carriages in Finland.

Airport Trains

Planners located the new airport train stations in Copenhagen, Stockholm, and Oslo so that mainline, long-distance trains call to discharge and board passengers. The stations also are served by dedicated airport trains from the respective city centers. As such, they are all mainline train stations.

Three times an hour, since September 27, 1998, when DSB ran its Air Rail Train, these trains depart from the surprisingly elegant, subterranean terminal beneath the delta-wing-shaped Copenhagen Kastrup International Airport for their 10-minute run to Copenhagen. Your ride costs about $2.50.

The distance from the platforms to Terminal 3 airport check-in is the shortest in the world, only 200 feet. Free luggage carts await you on the platform. You ride an escalator or elevator to check-in counters, ticketing offices, information desks, restaurants, and fast-food outlets. The DSB ticketing office, for travel to Copenhagen, Malmo, and points beyond, and for rail pass validation is on train level.

Passengers not only take the Oresund Link trains and X2000 trains to Sweden, but on weekdays those heading west across the Great Belt bridge can reach destinations such as Odense with no need to change trains at Copenhagen. This arrangement makes Kastrup one of the most versatile of Europe's many airport train stations. You reach Odense in one hour, 45 minutes, and Aarhus in Eastern Jutland in three hours and two minutes.

The first international hotel to be built in Copenhagen, the Copenhagen Airport Hilton, is adjacent to the new Air Rail Terminal within walking distance of the air terminals, ground transportation, parking, and car rental companies.

Your 11-mile trip to the airport from Copenhagen begins through a one-mile tunnel, completed in 1996 to protect a densely populated urban area with many businesses. You then cross the harbor on a new bridge to Amager Island. The island is mainly flat, very marshy land.

Past the new station at Orestad, the center of a new town, and Tarnby station, which is 20 feet below ground level, you dip underground approaching Kastrup Airport and tunnel below a two-story car park, and then head into the station, which is located as close as possible to the airport terminal building.

Threatening, with dragon eyes, Stockholm's other-worldly Arlanda Express (*www.arlandaexpress.com*) airport train with yellow face and gray livery occupies its own special terminus at platforms 1 and 2 in Stockholm's Central Station. It has its own platforms, its own lounge, and its own tickets, although Eurailpasses, ScanRail Passes, and Sweden Railpasses are valid.

In the reception area you have a private waiting room, a counter for check-in by British Airways, Finnair, and Iberia passengers and SAS passengers with hand luggage only. There is also a Forex money change counter, but the ATMs are located in Central Station's main hall. You will not find any luggage carts, but the platforms are smooth, and everything is on street level, so there are no stairs.

King Carl Gustaf and Queen Silvia officially inaugurated the 124-mph Arlanda Express from Stockholm to Arlanda Airport on November 24, 1999. The trains take 19 minutes for the 25-mile trip. You ride seven four-carriage electrical units carrying 190 passengers each. Alsthom in Birmingham, England, built them.

Your train runs above ground from the Stockholm Central Station terminus to Arlanda Airport. All seats are arranged 2+2 facing the generous luggage storage racks. Announcements are in Swedish and English. It speeds so fast the signs on the SL train platforms seem a blue streak. The train is handicapped accessible. Service is from 4:35 A.M. to 12:35 A.M., every 10 minutes, except half-hourly on Saturdays and Sunday mornings.

Tickets cost about $13.50 for an adult and $6.75 for ages eight to 17. Those under eight ride free. Seniors and students pay $9; full families $27. Taxis charge $39 from Arlanda to Stockholm and $49 from Stockholm to Arlanda.

At Arlanda Airport, the train dips below the airport, making two stops. Its first stop serves airport Terminals 2, 3, and 4. Its second stop is for Terminal 5 and Skycity. Among the larger airlines, American Airlines, British Airways, Finnair, Iberia, and Swissair serve Terminal 2. SAS (domestic) serves Terminal 3. Air France, KLM, Lufthansa, and

SAS (international) are located in Terminal 5. Luggage carts are available at the airport stations, and you will use the elevators ("Hiss"), not the escalators.

In addition to the Arlanda Express train, all SJ mainline trains north of Stockholm detour onto the new branch to call at Arlanda, making it convenient for all passengers two hours north, which at 125 mph is 250 miles. It also is convenient for travelers to and from Uppsala, Gavle, Borlange, and Sundsvall. From the south, trains take passengers to and from Eskilstuna and Sodertalje to Arlanda, 25 miles north of Stockholm, via Stockholm Central Station.

The new 30-mile-long link connecting Oslo's Gardermoen Airport train station and Sentral station takes you through the Romeriksporten tunnel, Norway's longest, which opened on August 22, 2000. Oslo's rather ugly, tilting "Flytoget" (Airport Express trains), which officially debuted on October 8, 1998, depart every 10 minutes between the airport and Oslo like gray bullets, reaching 130 mph and averaging 94 mph. Every second one continues to Asker, southwest of Oslo. The trains are similar to Signatur units, but the interiors of the air-conditioned, three-car electric units feature flight information displays. Travel time is 19 minutes. Punctuality has been good. Passenger satisfaction is excellent. NSB provides in Oslo Sentral Station a separate check-in area for the Flytoget at the head of platform 13/14.

One child up to the age of 15 can ride free for each adult. Rail passes are not valid on Oslo's Flytoget. Those with rail passes may prefer to ride InterCity trains between Skien in the south and Lillehammer in the north (via Oslo Sentral Station). Also, the day and night trains to and from Trondheim stop at Gardermoen, but at separate platforms from the Airport Express Trains. Your rail pass is valid on these trains, allowing you to save the Airport Express Train fare.

Stations and Subways

Plan to use the centrally located train stations in all of Scandinavia's capital cities as your bases. They all contain tourist offices/hotel booking services and are hubs for subways leading throughout their cities. Their frequently running suburban rapid transit systems are a convenience for everyone. When you book a hotel room at a hotel reservations counter in or near a station, ask whether your chosen hotel is near a rapid-transit station. Using these trains saves you time, struggling with luggage, and is free with a rail pass.

Copenhagen's clean and safe, red-brick train station, Copenhagen

338 TRAVELING EUROPE'S TRAINS

(for "Hovedbanegard," or "head train station"), comfortable as an old shoe, is a busy antique dating from 1911. Take a glance at the interior. The structure was renovated in 1994 to expose the original roof beams and the original lamps were duplicated. It is small, but very charming, accommodating 100,000 passengers a day. Twenty-five shops and restaurants are housed in the central hall with a post office at one end. Escalators run parallel to the ramp to the InterCity platform and elevators marked "Spor" (for track) located in the center of the main hall descend to each of the platforms. The "InterRail Center" (open daily from May to October, 6:30 to 10:30 A.M. and 4 to 10 P.M.) is a young traveler's haven open to holders of Eurail Youthpasses. It has a room to hang out in, toilets, showers, bulletin board covered with lodging notices and personal messages, and soft-drink machines. It is basic and funky, but perhaps more attractive to those under 26 because of the casual exchange of information with their peers.

Lockers located downstairs with the entrance at the west end of the hall past track 12, where they are electronically monitored, are safer and out of the way to prevent theft, and also provide more commercial space in the main hall.

The large, modern international travel center ("DSB Rejsecenter") is located at the north entrance across from the information center. Here you find free information leaflets for various international destinations and a free timetable for international connections. You can validate your Eurailpass or ScanRail Pass, and Danish residents may buy the various passes available to them (take a number for service).

Copenhagen has a bank inside the station. After 8 P.M. closing, you may still use the ATMs ("KontantService" or "Kontantnen") on the wall. Outside, in the same block as the station, facing the Tourist Office is also a full-service bank with ATMs on the street.

The Tourist Information Office (open daily 9 A.M. to 8 P.M. during the summer) and accommodations service/hotel reservations bureau (open daily 9 A.M. to midnight during the summer) are located across the street from the station's east entrance at Bernstoffsgade 1, next to the Tivoli Gardens. There are several good hotels in front of the station and many cheaper hotels to the left of the station in a seedier area.

You may use "City Bike" bicycles free within the Copenhagen city area by depositing a 20 DKK coin at any City Bike stand. Your coin is returned when you return the bike to any stand. There is one stand on Tietgensgade on the street bridge over the back of the station platforms, and two on Vesterbrogade, the main street across the train plaza in front of the station—one near the 7-11 Market and one near Hotel Astoria. If all bikes are in use, there are maps showing other City Bike stands. Failing this, visit the Cycling Center rent-a-bike with entrance outside the station. Use the left station exit.

InterCity platforms are divided into sectors with video monitors to advise you at which sector to find your carriage ("Vogn") according to your destination. The kiosk at the center of the platform between InterCity tracks 5 and 6 selling optional InterCity seat reservations opens 30 minutes before train departures (and you are asked to be in your seat two minutes before departure). Oresund trains leave from a special terminal at the end of platform 5/6.

The electric S-bane trains depart from nearby platforms along corridors through Copenhagen with stops at Vesterport, Norreport, and Osterport. The 1996 fleet differs radically from the former S-bane trains. The trains are comprised of six short cars that are two feet wider to allow a 30 percent increase in seating capacity to 330.

When you arrive on an international ticket marked "Kobenhavn," and not for any particular station, your ticket is valid on an S-bane train to wherever you choose. When you book a room at the tourist office across the street from Copenhagen station, ask whether your hotel is convenient to an S-train station.

Odense train station is brand new and surprisingly large. It has everything for you: fast-food restaurants, shopping, a library, lockers, and center for reservations and train information. Luggage carts are available for a 10 or 20 DKK deposit. The escalators taking you to and from the platforms help make the station passenger-friendly, and you may exit to the "Centrum" or to the regional bus station.

Odense is Hans Christian Andersen's "Fairy Tale City," home to the Danish Railroad Museum, the Viking Ship Museum, and well worth an excursion.

Oslo Sentral Station, christened by King Olav V in February 1987, underwent a complete rebuilding of the main hall completed in 2001. You find everything you need, bank, post office, tourist office in the station (open 8 A.M. to 11 P.M.), fast food and not-so-fast food, and more, because part of the complex is a virtual shopping mall as well as supermarket. Luggage carts are available on mainline platforms for a 20 NOK deposit. Ramps and moving walkways take you throughout the complex station.

In Oslo, twice-an-hour local train service tunnels from the outdoor platforms take you through the heart of the city. Use stops such as

340 TRAVELING EUROPE'S TRAINS

"National Theater" to get around. An entrance to the subway ("T-Bane") taking you throughout the Oslo area is within Sentral station. Connected by walkway/overpass is the "Bussterminalen" for regional buses and also the airport buses, "Flybussen."

You may arrive from Sweden on platforms 14-19 in the Ostbanehalle, the former Oslo East station remodeled in 1994 into a light and airy annex adjoining the Sentral station. The Ostbanehalle contains lockers, kiosks, cafes, flower shops, a grocery for travelers' provisions, and a fast-food outlet.

The Oslo Transport Museum in Vognhall 5 (open Sun.-Mon. noon to 3 P.M.,) built in 1913 on Majorstuen, contains a horse-drawn tram from 1875, streetcars, and Oslo's last trolleybus.

Trondheim Sentral Station sports a shining 1999 annex with ATM ("Minibank"), and ticketing for train, boat, and bus. The international reservation office is separate, in the earlier structure. Luggage carts are available (10 NOK deposit); ramps connect the platforms.

The famous Hell Train Station is within walking distance of Vaernes, the Trondheim airport stop on the mainline, but you can reach Hell by the TronderBanen network of rapid transit trains from Trondheim Sentral Station, if you like.

Stockholm Central Station is an expanded multilevel complex with all services and many entrances. Look in the elegant Orient Express Restaurant on the street level, south end, next to McDonald's, or enter from the street. As you would hope by its name, the Orient Express is decorated with original Wagons-Lits memorabilia. The Central Hotel Booking Service is on the street level (open daily 9 A.M. to 6 P.M.). The Tagkompaniet Office, "Rese Centralen," is located next to the Forex money change counter at the main entrance. Hosts in the "Citysalong" first-class lounge (open weekdays 7 A.M. to 9 P.M.) invite those holding first-class reservations on X2000 trains to wait for their train in comfort.

Stockholm's Central station is well connected to the region with regional trains (SL) and subways. SL accepts rail passes; show them to the guard at the entrance gate. The subway is marked by a *T* ("Tunnelbana") in Stockholm.

Malmo Central Station is a bright, cheerful station with a central hall brightened by sunlight through the glass skylight cascading onto comfortable wooden benches. The station is dominated by Forex money change (open daily 7 A.M. to 9 P.M.) and Malmo City Tourist Office (open Mon.-Fri. 9 A.M. to 8 P.M., Sat.-Sun. 10 A.M. to 5 P.M.) at one end, and a fast-food outlet at the other. A single ATM faces Forex in the central hall. Malmo C is an easy station because it is on one level with no stairs to climb. Luggage carts are available on the platform for a deposit of a 5 or 10 SEK or a 5 or 10 FIM coin. Oresund trains depart from platform 5/6.

Gothenburg Central Station, remodeled in 1993, impresses with extensive wooden paneling and judicious use of glass to make it bright and comfortable. Hosts at the "Citysalong" lounge opposite platform 2 welcome first-class ticket and pass holders. Free coffee and cookies are available.

Helsinki's red-granite, 1919 station is a wonder. On both sides of the main entrance you see granite figures holding lanterns in their hands. Its 156-foot-tall clock tower is still one of the highest in Helsinki.

The Helsinki ticketing/reservations room chimes with bells calling customers to the windows. Take a number: green button for Finnish trains; white for international trains including trains to Russia, which agents handle in the back of the hall. For information, visit the small office to the right at the entrance to save time.

When you arrive by train seeking a hotel, do not go into the arrivals hall. Pass directly to the entrance next to track 11 for "Hotelcentralen" (open Mon.-Sat. 9 A.M. to 7 P.M., Sun, 10 A.M. to 6 P.M.). Agents make reservations for you and give you all information about Helsinki as well as other Finnish towns you may want to visit. There is also a hotel console for you to make reservations by telephone. The post office/Postal Museum (free admission) faces the station. Look for the subway entrance, an *M* for "Metroon/Metron," down an escalator in a busy shopping center.

The small Turku Station has a restaurant upstairs, ticketing, and tourist kiosk where you can buy your Turku Card (see below) and receive information, but not make hotel reservations—just telephone numbers. The electronic departures board shows trains for Helsinki, IC departures for Kuopio, and *P* train departures for Pieksamaki and Tampere. There is also a Turku satama station to convey passengers arriving and departing on the great Baltic ferries.

Midnight Sun Travel

The long distances you travel, especially in Norway and Sweden, and the long summer daylight hours make you want to seriously consider traveling around the clock because you can cover long distances without sacrificing your views of the untouched and wild natural scenery.

All the Nordic railroads own their domestic couchettes or sleeperettes and sleeping cars. Prices for three-bedded sleeping cars compare favorably with those of six-bunk couchettes in the south. Reserve them as early as possible.

NSB's 1987 red-and-black (to match NSB's "B7" carriages) pairs of WLAB-2 sleeping cars are the longest (too long for international traffic) and quietest in Norway, and the widest in Europe (which means the corridor accommodates jump seats and tables, and still has room for refreshment trolleys to pass).

NSB's night fleet on the Dovre Line between Oslo and Trondheim includes two redecorated lounge cars with restaurant, bar, reception, and library corner; BC3 sleeperette cars with reclining seats, earphone jacks, and blankets available; and refurbished WLAB-2 sleeping cars for one or two persons.

On NSB's night trains, you can ride in sleeper cars with one, two, or three beds per compartment. On INN trains between Oslo and Stockholm and Oslo and Copenhagen, sleeper cars with showers are available. When starting from a large city, you may check in from 9 P.M. until the train leaves, usually around 11 P.M. After arrival you may use your compartment until 8 A.M. You can order your breakfast from the conductor to be served at the station restaurant or nearby hotel.

On the older NSB three-berth compartments, you pay about $62 to $78 for single occupancy (only a second-class ticket or pass is required), $31 to $39 for double occupancy, and $12.50 for a bed. In the newer NSB two-berth compartments, a bed will cost about $31. Normal seats require the usual $3 reservation fee. The sleeperette seats between Oslo and Trondheim and the couchettes between Oslo and Stavanger require only a $3 reservation for first-class rail pass holders, but second-class rail pass and ticket holders pay $8.

SJ's sleeping cars are of two basic types with a range of supplements. The older sleeping cars have one berth in first class, two or three berths in second class. SJ's new, blue sleeping cars with the shower logo on the exterior (including those acquired by Svenska Tagkompaniet) offer one- or two-berthed first-class compartments with shower and WC, and one- or two-berthed first- and second-class carriages with a quasi-shower-cum-toilet cubicle next to the entrance. You can make do with the shower when necessary, but don't expect it to be relaxing. Couchettes are second class only and have six berths. Reservations are obligatory.

VR has no couchettes, but large, very inexpensive sleeping cars—single and double-bedded in first class; double and three-bedded in second. They run north all the way to Rovaniemi from Helsinki; four sleeping cars depart from Turku. Second-class prices are lower when you depart Mondays through Thursdays.

Your Gateway to Russia

Your Eurailpass, ScanRail Pass, or FinnRail Pass is valid to Finland's Russian border so you save nearly half on your ticket from Helsinki to St. Petersburg by showing your pass at the international ticketing section in Helsinki's station. If you don't plan to return to Helsinki, time your trip to coincide with the expiration of your Eurailpass or FinnRail Pass. Pass holders entering Finland from Russia may have their passes validated by the Finnish train conductor on board.

Sibelius is the crack FinnRail morning express train to St. Petersburg with first-class compartments and special office suite, second-class seats (2+2), and restaurant car (credit cards and U.S., Finnish, and Swedish currencies accepted). Customs formalities take place on the train. Repin is the Russian railroads' afternoon train to St. Petersburg with second-class seats, sleeping compartments, and restaurant car from the Russian border. The Tolstoi is the Russian overnight train to Moscow with sleeping compartments and restaurant car from the Russian border only.

The Russian Connection
from Helsinki

Sibelius	Repin	Tolstoi				Tolstoi	Repin	Sibelius
0630	1534	173	dep.	HELSINKI	arr.	1130	1230	2128
0714	1625	1825	dep.	Riihimaki	arr.	1032	1134	2040
0716	1704	1904	dep.	Lahti	arr.	0952	1954	2007
0821	1745	1948	dep.	Kouvola	arr.	0910	1012	1932
0910	1842	2042	arr.	Vainikkala	dep.	0814	0915	1842
0932	1902	2102	dep.	Vainikkala	arr.	0754	0852	1822
1108	2038	2245	arr.	Vyborg *	dep.	0811	0915	1845
1128	2058	2315	dep.	Vyborg	arr.	0741	0855	1825
1307	2237	|	arr.	ST. PETERSBURG (Finland Station)	dep.	|	0718	1648
|	|	0838	arr.	MOSCOW (Oktyabrskaya Station)	dep.	2217	|	|

* note time change
| = does not travel this route

Using Eurailpass Bonuses

Eurailpasses are valid on the national railroads of all four Nordic countries, on the railroad buses in Finland, and on the railroad ferries in Denmark. In addition to the popular ferry crossing between Puttgarden and Rodby, Eurailpass holders have other options to travel to Scandinavia. Eurailpasses give you a direct route between Berlin and Leipzig and Scandinavia via free Scandline ferry services between Trelleborg, Sweden, and Sassnitz, Germany. In addition, TT-Line (*www.ttline.de*) gives Eurailpass holders a 50 percent reduction on normal fares for the ferry crossings between Trelleborg, Sweden, and Lubeck-Travemunde, Germany, and TR Line gives a 50 percent reduction between Trelleborg and Rostock, Germany. Finally, Silja Line (*silja.com/english*) offers Eurailpass holders the student rate discount on its GTS Finnjet crossings between Helsinki, Finland, and Lubeck-Travemunde and Rostock.

You receive a 50 percent discount on steamer crossings between Frederikshavn, Denmark, and Gothenburg, Sweden's second city, operated by Stena Lines (*www.stenaline.com*) and it is a good way to reach Gothenburg to begin your trip to Narvik. Unfortunately, the steamer landing is far from the train station and to get there you must carry your luggage through crowded public transportation or take a taxi.

Stena Lines also gives a 50 percent reduction from Frederikshavn to Oslo, Norway. The Color Line (*www.colorline.no*) gives Eurailpass holders a 30 percent reduction on day crossings between Hirtshals near the northern tip of Denmark's Jutland peninsula and Kristiansand and Moss in Norway. To reach Hirtshals, change at Hjorring from DSB's Frederikshavn mainline to the 12-mile-long private railroad that gives a 50 percent discount to Eurailpass holders. In Kristiansand, board NSB's Sorlands mainline trains to Oslo or Stavanger.

You receive a 25 percent reduction for travel on the Scandlines Flyvebadene hydrofoil between Copenhagen and Malmo, Sweden. This will be the only fare you pay for a "Round the Sound" trip—one of the most interesting one-day excursions from Copenhagen. Either take an Oresund train to Malmo, or board the hydrofoil at Havngade in Copenhagen for the half-hour trip across the Oresund to Malmo. In the brick station house across the street from the landing in Malmo, change to a local train for the 40-mile run through Skane, Sweden's chateau country. Break your trip to enjoy historical sights and the pastoral scenery. On return, board a Eurailpass-covered Scandlines ferry from Helsingborg to Helsingor and then continue by DSB train to Copenhagen H.

Also use your Eurailpass to make several other excellent one-day excursions. Make a round trip to Odense to see the house where Hans Christian Andersen grew up (historians agree that no one knows the house where he was born) and the 1988-remodeled Railroad Museum (25 percent discount), to Roskilde to see the Viking Ship Museum, to Hillerod to see Frederiksborg Castle, and to Humlebaek to visit the Louisiana Art Museum.

You receive free deck transportation for the day crossing between Stockholm and Turku and substantial discounts on Tourist II Class four-berth cabins between Stockholm and Helsinki and Turku aboard Silja Line's great blue-and-white ferries (see "Crossing the Bothnia," below).

Finally, you may ride free the ferries crossing the Samso Belt via Kalundborg between Copenhagen and Aarhus and train ferries between Kundshoved and Halskov or Bojden and Fynshav (for Sonderborg Castle on the island of Als). You receive a 20 percent reduction on the normal fares of the Scandinavian Seaways Co. between Copenhagen and Oslo.

ScanRail Pass

The railroads of Denmark, Norway, Sweden, and Finland together offer first- and second-class ScanRail Passes for unlimited travel on either a flexipass or consecutive-day basis on northern Europe's four networks and include the buses connecting the networks of Sweden and Finland north of the Gulf of Bothnia. Buy them for five or 10 travel days in two months or 21 days of consecutive travel. They save big compared to Eurailpasses and Eurail Flexipasses of the same durations. Adults over 60 receive a 12 percent discount buying a ScanRail 60 Pass. Children four-11 pay half the adult fare. Youth passes, available first- and second-class, cost about 25 percent less than adult passes.

ScanRail Passes are available from agents in North America and Britain; in North America through Rail Europe, DER Rail, BritRail (see Appendix A), and Scantours, 1535 Sixth Street, Santa Monica, CA 90401 (Tel. 800-223-7226, Fax 310-395-2013). They are also available in Scandinavia with the restrictions that the five-day Flexipass is limited to 15 days' validity, the 10-day Flexipass is not available, and only three days travel are allowed in the country of purchase. ScanRail Passes issued in North America consist of a single ticket for your name, signature, and validity limits that the agent inks in when you present it for validation and stamping in Scandinavia or Finland. You also see a network of day boxes for you to complete sequentially when you travel.

With a ScanRail Pass, you receive more than the bonuses listed for Eurailpass, including discounts on youth hostels and Oslo cards.

Not included are supplements for the Flam railroad (about $6), DSB IC trains, SJ X2000 trains, VR IC and S220 Pendolino trains, seating in NSB's Signatur trains' premium sections, and reservation fees.

A ScanRail Pass includes 50 percent discounts on
• Silja Line ferries between Stockholm and Helsinki, Stockholm and Turku, and Umea and Vaasa,
• Color and Stena Line ferries between Frederikshavn and Gothenburg,
• Stena Line ferries between Frederikshavn and Oslo, Frederikshavn and Moss,
• Bornholmstrafikken between Copenhagen and Ronne and between Ystad and Ronne,
• DFDS ferries between Copenhagen and Oslo,
• Color Line ferries between Hirtshals and Kristiansand,
• TT Line ferries between Travemunde and Trelleborg,
• Larvik Line ferries between Frederikshavn and Larvik, Nynashamn and Visby, and Oskarshamn and Visby,
• Ferries between Sandefjord, Norway, and Stromstad, Sweden.
Cabin reservations are obligatory on most of the longer-distance ferries.

In addition, you receive 25 percent reductions on
• High-speed catamarans ("Flaggruten") between Stavanger and Bergen,
• OSO between Copenhagen and Malmo, and
• HSD Hardanger Fjord ferry routes.
Also, you receive half off
• Inlandsbana railroad between Mora and Gallivare in Sweden,
• Hjorring Railroad between Hjorring and Hirtshals,
• Skagen Railroad between Frederikshavn and Skagen,
• Most of the buses operated in North-Norway and from Andalsnes.
The card entitles the holder to free entrance to the Railroad Museums at Gavle, where SJ 4-6-2 steam loco is SJ's "parade loco" and is resplendent on the Gavle roundhouse; Hamar and Hyvinge Railroad

Museums, plus a 50 percent discount at the Odense Railroad Museum. It allows a discount in more than 160 Nordic hotels of the Best Western chain.

National Rail Passes

Norway Rail Passes giving unlimited travel on NSB only are available for either three, four, or five days' travel within one month. Passengers 60 and over receive a 20 percent discount. Children under 16 pay half adult fare. The four- and five-day versions are only available outside Scandinavia. Within Norway, you can purchase the pass also for seven or 14 consecutive days. NSB automatically gives half off to travelers over 67 for travel on any train. Buy passes and tickets at any train station in Norway. Norwegian students receive discounts, but foreign students with foreign student cards are out of luck.

The Norway Rail Pass is not valid on the Flam Railroad. Passholders receive a 30 percent discount. First-class Norway Rail Passholders pay 50 percent of the supplement required on Signatur Express Trains, and they receive a 50 percent reduction on the hydrofoils of the HSD boat *Bergen-Haugesund-Stavanger* (Flaggruten).

On "green departures" (off-peak departures are marked with a green point in the timetable), you can purchase a special one-way, low-priced ticket for point-to-point travel with no stopovers allowed. You must purchase these tickets one day in advance at any train station in Norway.

A Sweden Railpass is similar to the Norway Rail Pass, but prices are a little higher, except that in 2001, travelers receive one extra travel day at no extra charge, which makes it less expensive than a Norway Rail Pass. Up to two children travel free with each adult. In Sweden, travelers over 65 receive a 50 percent discount without having to show a separate pass—only their passport.

Unlimited-travel FinnRail Passes are available for first- or second-class travel for three, five or 10 travel days within a month. They are distributed in the U.S. by Rail Europe, DER Travel, Scantours (Tel. 800-223-7226), and Sea'N Air Travel (Tel. 800-848-6444), or you can buy them (or Senior Passes) in Finnish marks at VR's major stations or when you step off the Silja Line ferries in the Silja Line terminals.

Travelers 65 and over receive half off trips covering at least 48 miles one way. All trains in Finland give a 20 percent discount for three or more adults traveling together. When you travel with a group of 10 or more, you are eligible for a 25-50 percent discount. These discounts are only available at train stations in Finland.

Over 700 clean and modern express buses leave Helsinki every day for all parts of the country. Traveling by bus is especially practical in Lapland, where buses are the main form of public transportation. You can buy a Coach Holiday Ticket, which allows you to travel up to 525 miles during any two-week period, at any bus station or travel agency in Finland.

In Denmark you can buy a "Pendlerskort" for 30 days unlimited travel on all DSB services. It costs about $480, first-class; $330, second. Second-class seat reservations cost about $2; business class reservations are included in the price. A photo card is required.

DSB discounts fares for groups of eight adults traveling together, and offers discount tickets to those over 65. You can buy 10-ride passes for about a 20 percent discount. Children under nine travel free. Those aged 10 to 15 pay about half adult fare.

City Travel Cards

In larger cities in the Nordic countries you can usually buy city travel cards to save money on local trains, buses, subways, and sometimes ferries. Buy them valid for one, two, or three days at train stations, tourist offices, hotels, and kiosks in their areas. These cards are especially economical for local transportation when you are traveling with a Eurailpass or ScanRail Flexipass, so that you can save your daybox validations for long trips.

The Copenhagen Card, with half price for children aged five to 11, inclusive, gives you free transportation on the S-train network and buses in the entire metropolitan region including all of North Zealand, Roskilde, and Koge; discounts to Sweden; and free admission to more than 70 surprisingly varied museums and castles, such as the Tivoli Gardens, HT Museum for streetcars and buses in Rodovre, and the Classic Automobile Museum. When you show the card, more than 20 restaurants offer two drinks for the price of one. The helpful booklet that comes with the card lists admission prices for adults and children, open hours, buses and trains, and a reference map. The booklet alone is worth the card price. You can buy it valid for 24 (about $24), 48 (about $39), or 72 (about $49) hours. For information, access *www.visitcopenhagen.dk.*

All trains and buses in the Greater Copenhagen area are part of a common fare and ticket system. You use the same tickets on trains and buses and fares are calculated the same way. Greater Copenhagen is divided into 95 zones and you pay to enter every one. It's a bewildering system. If you have trouble programming your VCR, a glance at the color-coded maps in stations and at bus stops will show you that it is hopeless. Luckily, downtown Copenhagen is all in one zone and the minimum fare covers two zones, which is just about anywhere a typical traveler will go. The Copenhagen transit authority (HT) sells a twenty-four-hour ticket for unlimited bus or train travel in the Greater Copenhagen area. All you have to do is validate it in the bus or at the station before starting. Then you can get on and off as you please. You don't have to worry about zones.

Oslo Cards provide free admission to most Oslo museums and sights plus you receive unlimited free travel by streetcar, bus, train, boat, and subway within Oslo, including NSB commuter trains within Oslo, free car parking, and more. The three-day card gives you 30 percent off round trips from Oslo to anywhere in Norway. The Oslo Package consists of discounted hotel accommodations, breakfast, and the Oslo Card. Apply at the tourist office in Oslo's Sentral train station.

In Norway you can buy similar Stavanger and Bergen cards and packages. In addition to the perks included in the Oslo card, the Stavanger card provides a 50 percent discount on the catamarans between Stavanger and Lysebotn and a 25 percent discount on the catamaran to Bergen.

Stockholm Cards include unlimited free travel by bus, metro, and local trains (except airport buses), fee parking, free sightseeing by boat with Stockholm Sightseeing, free one-hour bus sightseeing with City Sightseeing, free admission at 70 attractions and museums, a round trip by boat to Drottningholm for the price of a one-way ticket, and many more discounts on cruises, shopping, and dining.

When you need only a discount card to get around Stockholm, buy a "SL Tourist Card" at subway station entrances for one-third the price of a Stockholm Card. It is valid for a day (choose between either the inner city only or the whole network) or three days on the networks of suburban trains, subways, and buses in the county of Stockholm (except the SAS airport bus), on Djurgarden ferries, and at the Tram Museum. A three-day card also includes admission to Skansen, Grona Lund, and Kaknas Tower. When you stay longer, a monthly (or yearly) card is your most cost-efficient way to get around. A 15-trip strip card saves you 30 percent. Buy all tickets at kiosks called "Pressbyran" and at the central station, "T-Centralen."

Gothenburg, the capital of Sweden's West Coast, promotes the Goteborg Card covering free travel on buses, trams, Paddan Canal sightseeing, and free entry to Liseberg amusement park (Sweden's most popular visitor attraction) plus dozens of other places of interest, museums, and sports and recreation facilities. It includes a free day's excursion on the Stena Line to Frederikshavn in Denmark that alone would cost more than the card. Be sure to ride the vintage tram to Liseberg that is covered by the card. The Goteborg Card is included free in the "Goteborg Package" for hotels during the summer—one of the cheapest ways of staying in Gothenburg. The Gothenburg tourist office is located a short walk from the train station in the Nordstan shopping center (open Monday to Friday, 9:30 A.M. to 6 P.M.; Saturday to 3 P.M.).

Helsinki Cards give you an 80 percent reduction on Helsinki sightseeing, unlimited free travel on public transportation, ferry and waterbus to Suomenlinna and Korkeasaari, a guided city walk, admission to nearly 50 museums, discounts on guided tours out of Helsinki, and opera, theater, and concerts. You also get a 100-page guidebook. You can buy the card for 24, 48, or 72 hours at the Hotel Book Center in the train station before you book a hotel, at travel agencies, ferry terminals, and the Helsinki City Tourist Office (*www.hol.fi*) located at Pohjoisesplanadi 19 (open Monday to Friday, 9 A.M. to 7 P.M., Saturday to 3 P.M.).

For one-third off, you can buy a Helsinki-region "Tourist Ticket," a pass for one, three, or five days limited to subway trains, trams, and buses, or you can buy a 10-trip ticket giving one-sixth off the single fare price. Buy them in the subway station below the train terminus or you can buy the "Tourist Ticket" before you leave (contact the Finnish Tourist Board, Appendix A).

The Turku Card for 24 or 48 hours is valid for free entrance to most museums in Turku, discounts in many shops and restaurants, free bus within the city limits, and telephone calls up to FIM 5. A similar card is available in Tampere, Finland's second city.

Ready yourself for fresh clean air and sparkling fjords as you travel through Lapland and the land of the Midnight Sun on the following adventures: Norway's Bergen and Flam lines, a trip across the Arctic Circle, Norway's Rauma Train, a crossing by deluxe ferry from Stockholm to Finland, and a circle trip through Finland's natural lakelands.

Norway in a Nutshell
Complete Travel with the Trolls

The plateau is a vast stretch of mountaintop, uninhabited, treeless, flat. You see no spiked Matterhorns here, just featureless mountains with tops swept away by glaciers—a frozen, crystalline surface, polished by howling wind. It is Arctic, remote, lonely, and only your powerful train keeps you from feeling stranded at the top of the world.

You are well above the timberline so far north, running along the stark, clear-aired, snow-pocked edge of the Hardanger Plateau. It is so white that any speck of color seems to be out of place. Just before you stop at Myrdal, you look to your right and see the browns and greens of the mountain walls of a grand canyon of a rift. You gasp at the sight so many hundred feet down of the temperate Flam valley. The Oslo-Bergen route—free on a Eurailpass or ScanRail Pass—is NSB's important flagship route. Without it, Bergen would be isolated by land from the rest of the country, because behind Bergen, the wall of the Hardanger Plateau forms a dead end.

When you look at a topographic map of Norway, you can appreciate that this route is an engineering triumph. Engineers successfully designed the line to climb and descend safely from sea level to 4,267 feet in inaccessible, hostile Arctic country.

Your early morning departure hurried punctually out of Oslo Sentral station through built-up Oslo and past the suburbs. Climbing alongside a broad river, you first pass flowery meadows, placid lakes, and foliage brightened by red rowanberries. Then you hear the whine of sawmills at work and see tractors idling beside red farmhouses in patchwork fields close by the rails.

You cross through meager and noticeably thinning farmland, past natural, untouched emerald valleys, and finally out of pine groves and woods of ringed silver birch trees, away from the temperate environment of the Oslo Fjord and up into the mountains.

Thirty minutes past Drammen, dramatic scenery unfolds. You see the waters run faster. The trees thin. Patches of snow appear. The country is mantled in white by the time you arrive in Geilo. At 2,650 feet, you are only miles short of the timberline.

Geilo, known as the St. Moritz of Norway for its excellent skiing, is also a good base for mountaineering in summer. The small yellow stationhouse is comfortable, with heated waiting room and lockers outside.

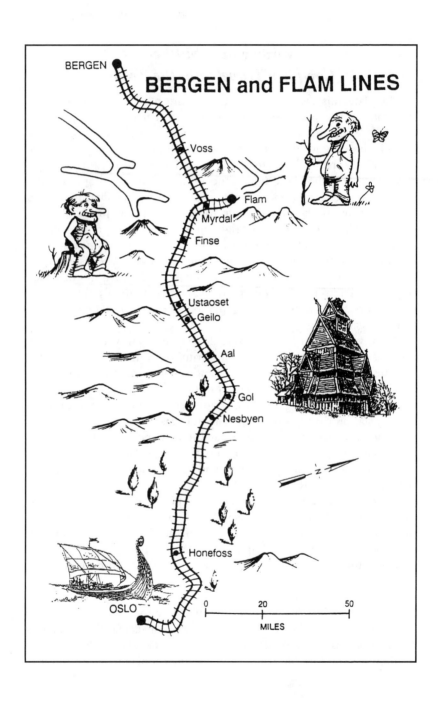

BERGEN and FLAM LINES

BERGEN

Voss

Flam

Myrdal

Finse

Ustaoset

Geilo

Aal

Gol

Nesbyen

Honefoss

OSLO

0   20   50

MILES

The post office and modern tourist office with helpful ladies are just below the station and below that is the "Geilojordet," which is an interesting assembly of seven preserved wooden, historic houses moved from farms in Hol and arranged on the site to create a farmyard typical for the period and the district.

In Geilo you can hire bicycles to follow northern Europe's most popular biking route, the Rallarvegen (Raller Road), the Bergen line's construction road, which is now closed to automobiles for most of its length, and return your bicycle in Flam or even Voss.

As you continue to climb, the scenery changes from ski resort to glacier. You leave the last of the trees at Ustaoset.

At Storodi, about six miles east of Finse, your train accelerates to nearly 105 mph. A nine-mile segment of new line, built on a low embankment to ease snow clearance problems, was put into service in 1999. The landscape glares whitely. It is dominated by the frigid Hardanger glacier looming in the south higher by 2,000 feet than Finse (4,010 feet). George Lucas filmed here the bitterly cold opening sequences of *The Empire Strikes Back*.

Finse is the highest stop on the line—the entire NSB network, in fact. The train station was closed in 2000, although train tickets are sold in Finse Hotel, when it is open during the summer. You might like to tramp into the snowbanks to take spectacular photos of the glacier and visit the Finse Rallarmuseum (open daily during summer, 10 A.M. to 10 P.M.), which shows the history of the Bergen Railroad, from the early preparation starting in 1871 until it was officially opened in 1909. It shows how it was kept open during the winter, and you see different snowplow equipment. The museum is situated in the locomotive stable, with the Documentation Center for the Bergen Railroad. See *www.rallarmuseet.no*

West of Finse you enter the 1993, 6.4-mile Finse tunnel which prevents line closings due to avalanches. The tunnel to Myrdal, which cut 2.7 miles from the length of your trip, is unfortunate from a scenic point of view, but no tragedy, because views from this section were obscured by snowsheds. Curiously, the highest point of the line, 4,123 feet, is in this tunnel. Before the tunnel was built, the highest point was at 4,267 feet.

Flam Railroad

At Myrdal station, dominated by a mountain with icy whiskers of frozen waterfalls, you don your parka and bundle into the coaches of the waiting apple-green Flam train. You leave behind a high, bleak, and contrary glacial plateau for the green and serene beauty of one of Norway's sweetest valleys. Your trip doesn't take long, but minute by minute, as your train inches down Europe's steepest adhesion route and turns surprising corners, you are rewarded by one of the most breathtaking of Norway's adventurous trains. The conductors also make it Norway's friendliest.

The Flam valley you see is an immense opening through the mountains, similar to the Grand Canyon in the sheer inclination of its mountain walls. Its upper railhead, Myrdal, is 2,845 feet above sea level. The lower terminus, Flam, near the ferry landing on the Aurlandsfjord, is an hour and 12 miles down the valley. This section is the steepest of any NSB line. In one stretch you drop one foot for every 18 you travel, quite brave for an adhesion train without cogwheels. The five braking systems give your cautious engineer more sureness than a Norwegian mountain goat. Any one system is enough to halt the train safely.

This line was not built for passenger traffic. Perhaps that is why it is so unspoiled. It was built in the wilds, connecting fjord and glacier, to carry construction materials and heavy machinery for completing the central section of the Bergen line. They were ferried up the fjord to Flam and then carted by horses up to Myrdal. You see the surviving horse trail of 1895-96 still paralleling the line. The line was originally designed to carry 24,000 a year. In 1999, it carried around 370,000, mostly tourists.

You follow a tortuous path of 21 hairpin curves, in and out of tunnels. On the most scenic sections, your engineer thoughtfully slows or stops, so you can linger and absorb the impact of views more dazzling than you have imagined. You see sturdy wild mountain goats peering curiously at the train from granite boulders only a few feet from your window.

At first descent, your Flam train moves roughly parallel to the Bergen line, between snow fences, but after Vatnahalsen, splendid panoramas quickly begin to unfold. You soon reach the highlight of your trip. Your train trudges across a sturdy embankment and the engineer brakes politely.

Beside the line, so close you can feel the pressure of the roaring action filling cameras' viewfinders, a fury of foam plunges over a cliff, raging down at you in a smoking torrent. It is not so much a waterfall as rapids out of nowhere. At your feet it vanishes safely into a natural channel beneath the trestle supporting your train. This is Kjosfoss, "foss" meaning "waterfall."

You appreciate the announcements, in English, over the loudspeaker by the conductor. These men take a sincere interest in the well-being and pleasure of travelers who come to visit their proud little valley.

If they feel a certain affinity for Americans, it is because more than a third of the population left this valley during the hard years of 1845-65 to settle in the New World, mostly in the Midwest. More than 1,000 emigrated. More than a century later, 2,000 live here, mostly making their living from farming, and English is widely spoken.

The conductors actually encourage passengers to scatter off the train onto the wooden-plank platform and soggy turf at Kjosfoss, to gawk and admire and pose for photographs before the powerful, raging waterfall/rapids less than a stone's toss away. Its fury easily drowns out the accumulated sounds of shutters clicking.

Farther down, you cross lesser wild rivers without benefit of bridges. (There are no bridges on this line.) Here again, the viaducts were blasted out of the mountains just as the construction engineers blasted the looping tunnels. When you enter the longest tunnel, Nali (1,476 yards), you look back and see the extraordinary sight of the rail bed cutting four ledges of the mountainside, one almost above the other.

When you leave the tunnel, you have a brief glimpse of the highest Flam valley farm, where 3,000 goats are kept to produce orange-colored Norwegian goat cheese. Another waterfall, Fjoandfoss, drops 400 feet down the mountainside in the afternoon shade.

At Hareina (158 feet), a timid village beside the prospering Flam River where anglers make their catches at the break of day, your views from between tunnels and cuttings disappear, the valley widens, and you see the panorama of the highest toylike farms below. The fields here seem more vividly green than possible because your eyes are still adjusting from the white glare above. Looking ahead, you see the 300-year-old Flam Church, flowering fruit orchards, the blue of the fjord coming near, and the brown of the mountains behind.

The formerly remote village of Flam has blossomed into a significant tourist minihub. The lonesome station house, Fretheim Hotel catering to proper English ladies, and camping grounds have been supplemented by a larger station house, a sweater "factory," restaurants (one in historic railroad carriages), a cafeteria, the Flam Line Museum (15 NKR admission), a vast car and tour bus parking lot, souvenir shops, and a supermarket.

Norway's newest craze is bicycling the Flam line. Since a feature appeared on Norwegian television and was then picked up by *The New York Times*, the number of visitors renting a bicycle in Geilo or Myrdal (no deposit required), bicycling to Flam, and returning to Myrdal by train has doubled and redoubled to 800 bicycles a day.

With cafeteria open until 8 P.M., Flam's Hotel Fretheim Touristhotell is white with wooden lace and seems more like a romantic summer cottage or guesthouse than a dignified vacation hotel with mostly British visitors. You know before you enter that everything will be spotless, the waitresses will wear dirndls, and all guests will be snoring by 10:30 P.M. but will be up at the crow of the cock and the glimmer of dawn—except that in summer, day breaks at 2 A.M. and roosters crow all night.

Norway in a Nutshell Program

Your descent along the Flam Line is your first leg of "Norway in a Nutshell," the three-stage excursion to reveal the essence of this beautiful country. For the second leg, board Kaptain Lid Kjell's *Skagastol* at Flam's pier, located at the end of the rail line, to begin a tranquil cruise of both the Aurlandsfjord and the Naeroyfjord, which are branches of the larger Sognefjord.

Kaptain Kjell is proud of his vessel and of his country's beauty. He is proud that so many foreigners come such long distances to admire the loveliness of his surroundings and he does his best to make their visit a happy one.

"But," he says, "the *Skagastol* is a boat. In our country, a ferry carries automobiles." Try to tell him that it is a passenger ferry. He shrugs.

In fact, the *Skagastol* is a ferry converted with the extensive addition of glass to make it convenient from most of the boat to see high to the crests of the steep walls surrounding the fjords. It cruises at 12 knots and carries up to 500 passengers (during bad weather it carries 300 inside).

It was named for the tallest mountain on the Sognefjord.

After 20 minutes, you make your first landing at Aurland (pop. 1,900), the county seat. Farther along the fjord you pass Undredal (pop. 100) on your left. Undredal boasts Scandinavia's smallest stave church still in use. It dates from 1147.

On the steep and rugged mountainside you see the two farms of

Stigen (elevation 980 feet). Stigen was settled continuously until 1949, but now it is farmed only during the summer.

As you approach the mouth of the Naeroyfjord at Beitelen, Kaptain Kjell swings your boat left and you enter the narrowest and wildest arm of the Sognefjord. Snowcapped peaks reach to 4,500 feet. Small and peaceful farms and villages nestle beside the fjord.

Norway's fjords look and feel like mountain lakes rather than labyrinthian arms of the sea. The water is calm, slightly saline, and cold from the melting snow.

Passengers constantly exclaim about the filmy waterfalls cascading down those steep walls. There are no beaches, swimmers, sailboats, or water skiers. It is just you and nature together. On a good day you may see a seal diving to avoid the boat.

As the color of the fjord lightens and the fjord becomes shallower, Kaptain Kjell orders the motor stopped and you cruise the final stretch up the Naeroyfjord to the landing at Gudvangen.

Gudvangen grew into a small tourist center at the end of the nineteenth century. It is your assembly point for the low-gear, one-hour bus climb up the steep Stalheims kleivane road to Voss through the narrow Naeroy Valley.

Here is a "Kafeteria-Souvenirs" shop and a small green space below birch trees to relax. More importantly, in the parking area passengers are already boarding a fleet of blue-and-white Volvo and Mercedes buses ready to take you up the mountainside through Stalheim to Voss.

The drivers shift into low gear and the several buses crawl in caravan up the narrow, corkscrew highway. Your windows expose views of valleys, rivers and farmhouses far below and bring you face to face with many a roaring waterfall.

You are rolling merrily along when a sign demands: "Change to Low Gear." Obediently, your driver complies as his bus crosses a stretch of road cantilevered over a precipice. Swinging wide on a hairpin turn, you look back on the waterfall you just passed.

Finally, the driver slips his bus into second gear and your bus seems to dart along a level stretch and pulls into the parking lot of the Stalheim Hotel.

"Ten minutes," says the driver.

Most buses stop in Stalheim—lunch is on the itinerary of some tour groups. It has a grand and spectacular outdoor veranda and glassed indoor lounge for rainy days.

The ice-cream-cone peak of Mt. Jondal is the centerpiece of the marvelous panorama from the veranda and you realize, tossing a pebble from the stone balcony, what a long, long way it is down to the floor of the Naeroy Valley.

Your bus' final stretch carries you past a high mountain lake with rowboats at the ready. Yellow fields of hay stretch down to the water's edge.

When your bus pulls up in front of the Voss train station, you have completed the third and final leg of "Norway in a Nutshell." You can join a train to Bergen or Oslo or use Voss as your base for further exploration of Norway's rugged mountains.

NSB offers Norway in a Nutshell day tickets from Bergen or Oslo and one way between Oslo and Bergen. Those holding Eurailpass, ScanRail Pass or Norwegian rail passes pay only for the boat and bus tickets plus the small supplement to ride the Flam railroad.

Norway in a Nutshell

dep.	Oslo	0631	0811	Reserve Train
arr.	Myrdal	1152	1248	
dep.	Myrdal	1200	1255	Flam Line
arr.	Flam	1257	1346	
dep.	Flam	1315	1500	Boat
arr.	Gudvangen	1515	1650	
dep.	Gudvangen	1520	1715	Bus
arr.	Voss	1645	1830	
dep.	Voss	1650	1900	Reserve Train
arr.	Oslo	2214		
arr.	Bergen		2018	

Bergen Railroad

Returning to Myrdal and continuing west toward Bergen, leaden-looking, chilling, and forbidding lakes surround you. Reindeer race between boulders and leap over patches of snow. Afternoon sun on granite boulders seems to shiver against icy, rushing rivers. Tattered tunnels burrow like snow snakes. You catch glimpses of brown, purple, and flaky yellow mosses through gapes in the drifts.

Then you suddenly realize the snow is melting and the water is running west instead of east, and you know your train is descending to Bergen and the North Sea's warm Gulf Stream.

You pass giant waterfalls, leaving bleak and wind-scoured snowland

and entering valleys with dazzling, purple rhododendrons blooming all around you. No sooner do you clear your ears from the increasing air pressure than you are rolling along the shores of Sorfjorden and then through the five-mile Ulriken tunnel into Bergen's end-of-the-line train terminal, where the glass arches were restored in 1992 to the classical style of the thirties when steam locomotives were used.

Bergen's end-of-the-line graystone train station is small—only four platforms—but convenient. The tourist office (*i*) (open 7:15 A.M. to 11 P.M. daily) is well marked at your left as you arrive. You can arrange accommodations and change money as well as pick up useful literature. An extensive array of lockers ("Oppbevaring"), opposite, was installed in 1994.

You still see evidence of Bergen's former isolation. Hansa merchants came to Bergen in the Middle Ages, making it their trade center for dried fish. Even now new buildings are patterned after Hanseatic architecture. Houses have a red- and black-brick look similar to northern Germany's Hansa cities. But this architecture is deceiving, because the Bergenese soon reveal the city is fiercely Norwegian.

The Bergenese are particularly friendly to Americans, sophisticated, and many speak English. Named a "Cultural Capital of Europe" for 2000, Bergen is a vital city, a major gateway opening on the West, the former home of Edvard Grieg and the center of an international music festival. It has reputedly the finest youth hostel in the North.

For a fine overview and orientation of Bergen and its harbor setting, make your first project the five-minute funicular ride to the top of Mount Floien.

Daily Bergen Railroad Service

61	601	63				62	602	64
0748	1043	1543	dep.	OSLO (Sentral)	arr.	1426	1758	2214
0848	1124	1625	dep.	Drammen	dep.	1349	1717	2131
0939	1221	1722	dep.	Honefoss	dep.	1259	1610	2041
1058	1347	1843	dep.	Gol	dep.	1137	1450	1920
1116	1408	1902	dep.	Aal	dep.	1118	1431	1901
1137	1428	1922	dep.	Geilo	dep.	1056	1406	1839
1148	1439	1933	dep.	Ustaoset	dep.	1045	1353	1827
1216	1512	1959	dep.	Finse	dep.	1018	1320	1800
1240	1541	2024	arr.	MYRDAL*	dep.	0953	1248	1734
1243	1545	2025	dep.	MYRDAL*	arr.	0952	1243	1730
1327	1626	2109	dep.	Voss	arr.	0912	1204	1650

| 1422 1741 2208 | dep. | Arna | dep. | 0814 1104 1553 |
| 1430 1752 2215 | arr. | BERGEN | dep. | 0805 1055 1544 |

* Change at Myrdal to/from Flam

Trains 61/64 carry first- and second-class carriages, Bistro Car, bicycles, children's carriage. Reservations required.
Trains 601/602 carry first- and second-class carriages, snacks. Reservations required.
Signatur Trains 62/63 carry first- and second-class carriages, Bistro Car, children's carriage. Reservations required.

Lapland Excursion
Midnight Sun to Narvik

Your steep descent into Narvik on the northernmost train in Western Europe is heady stuff. Each bend of your Ofot train opens up the quintessence of Norwegian travel. You see new vistas of unspoiled mountain, sea, and sky. While your Iron-Ore Railroad train passes through stands of spruce, wild reindeer leap between snowbanks. You lean forward to better watch—on your right—your climactic, precipitous descent down to the Ofot Fjord.

The direct descent from the summit is 27 miles, but your zigzagging descent on this stretch of the Lapland train takes nearly a full hour.

As you descend, surroundings change from bleak, icy lakes and the snow remnants of winter. You feel the green embrace of the warming Gulf Stream. Looking down 350 feet you see the silvery surface of the Romsdalfjord creeping in an arc under the distant Skjombrua (bridge) from the Norwegian Sea, and you begin to make out the waves of the Norwegian Sea breaking on the shores. Then you see Narvik's wooden houses. Brick shops form a patchwork pattern of color against black conveyor belts and iron-ore loading facilities.

Setting off in Stockholm or Gothenburg, your train takes you through the remote top of the Scandinavian Peninsula, across the Arctic Circle and finally to Norway's end-of-the-line train station on the Ofot Fjord. You see it all while it is light in the domain of the Midnight Sun.

You travel north through fir forests. Blue placid lakes mirror the serene beauty of the sturdy, rounded mountains. Puffy clouds are made golden from the sun deep on the horizon at midnight. The lonesome clickety-clack of your train tattoos over and over because of

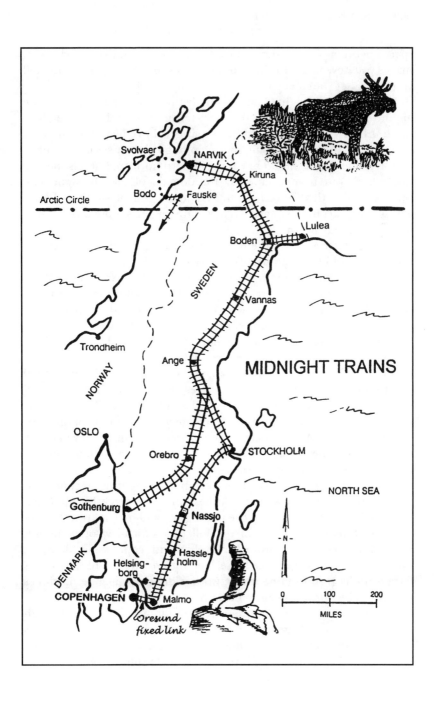

Svolvaer
NARVIK
Kiruna
Arctic Circle
Bodo · Fauske
Lulea
Boden
SWEDEN
Vannas
Trondheim
Ange
MIDNIGHT TRAINS
NORWAY
OSLO
Orebro
STOCKHOLM
NORTH SEA
Gothenburg
Nassjo
-N-
DENMARK
Helsing-
borg
Hassle-
holm
COPENHAGEN
Malmo
0   100   200
Oresund
fixed link
MILES

spaces between the northern rails. You see sights unlike anywhere. It makes you never want to close your eyes to sleep. Northern Swedes tell you not to set your sleep by the sun, but by the clock.

In the eerie midnight glow, you inhale the sweet scent of pine in the air and gaze at foggy mists in the rocky terrain and in the birches, leafless until early summer. Clouds in the silvery sky reflect in the remote, silent lakes. And then the shimmering orange globe rises in the northeast. It seems like it should be on the eastern horizon, but it is the wee hours and your train is entering the domain of the Midnight Sun. Birds chirp at this unlikely hour. Then the red of sunrise spreads across the peaceful lakes and creates a fragile, glassy pink, beginning your second day north.

It is an experience for the intrepid, romantic traveler who admires the green and blue (and white) outdoors. Sweden has the most lakes of all nations. When you travel by train beyond the Arctic Circle, there is only you, your chugging, solitary diesel locomotive, moonlit freshwater lakes, wild moose, reindeer, cackling birds, and the rich, sweet smells of pine forest and mossy brook.

In Boden you find a pretty frontier city set along a blue lake. From Boden you can take the train service that was reopened to Haparanda on June 13, 2000 (until mid-August), and from there walk about 2,500 feet to the Finnish bus station. Carriages are detached in Boden, and your section for Narvik rolls on. About 1 1/4 hours out of Boden, your train slows for photographs. Have your camera ready for the large, neat sign on your left: "Arctic Circle." Even the Swedes admit that while they were children, they visualized the Arctic Circle as a green line running around the earth. You are in the land of the Midnight Sun.

From here you pass through barren and remote tundra, climb past scraggly trees and then scrubby bushes, until you reach Kiruna (pop. 27,000), the preeminent iron-ore-mining city and most northerly commune in Sweden. You see on the hill the colorful wooden houses painted rust-red, green, brown, and yellow with copper and tile roofs, but you can only imagine the huge, labyrinthine tunnels of the world's largest underground mine where work is done by gigantic machines that could be out of a George Lucas movie.

You thread your way northwest from the mines of Kiruna through green spruce and clean earth damp with melting snow. White stripes of birch trunks pattern the blanket of deep, green grass. Lovers of the outdoors and mountaineers leave your train at primitive outposts. This is one big national park north of the Arctic Circle.

From Kiruna, you are traveling along the route of the Iron-Ore Railroad built specifically to carry ore from Kiruna in Sweden to Narvik, Norway, the all-year port kept free of ice by the Gulf Stream. Swedish politicians would have preferred to use a port in Sweden for export of their ore, but the freezing of the Gulf of Bothnia in winter left them no choice.

Swedish train experts insist the so-called Ofotbanen, carrying 20 million tons of ore annually through Norway, is the most exciting piece of track in the Swedish system. Iron-ore trains runs frequently, except from mid-June to mid-July, when everyone in Sweden is on vacation. The line was electrified in 1923, just 20 years after being opened. For years, this was the world's most northerly railroad, but the line reaching Murmansk in Russia has now taken this distinction. When conditions allow, you can see the complete disk of the sun at midnight from May 26 to July 19.

You cross the border into Norway at Riksgransen. Over the crest, you enter Norway slowly, through steel-and-wood snowsheds. You descend along the 68-mile segment from 1,700 feet to 20 feet at the port of Narvik. The gradient is one in 59.

The Goteborg/Stockholm-Umea-Kiruna/Narvik route was considered unprofitable by SJ and put out for bid. Svenska Tagkompaniet AB (literally, Swedish Train Company, Inc.) (*www.tagkompaniet.se/ tag_eng.html*) assumed operation on January 10, 2000. The private company, with headquarters at Lulea, likes to think of itself as being pure northern Swedish, with its own simple fares system, and to cooperate with other private companies, such as the bus company, Swebus.

To enable you to see the stunning northern scenery, ST returned to service five panorama carriages that were originally part of the German Trans Europe Express (TEE) Rheingold before passing to Switzerland's Mittel Thurgau Bahn (railroad) for a showcase carriage on the Gotthard route between Zurich and Milano.

The panorama coaches now sport the new apple-green-and-white livery of the ST and are decorated with lynx decals because of the ability of lynx to see well in dim light. Each panorama coach is equipped with a bar, two first-class compartments, and a double-deck section where a roof of glass arches over you.

In addition, for the 19-hour journey, ST acquired five former Wagons-Lits sleeping cars from the Swiss Railroads and leased 93 passenger cars from SJ. Every other wall between the nostalgic sleeping compartments folds away to create a suite with up to six berths.

The former SJ carriages are comfortable, and the doors open with a nudge on a bar. The brown second-class seats in the nonsleeping carriages are comfortable, arranged 2+2 or 3+1 with seats facing. This curious arrangement allows passengers to fold the arm rests into the seat backs and to lie, and sleep, across three seats if the train is not crowded. Alternately, passengers may recline facing seats by pulling cushions forward and stretch out parallel to the direction of travel.

A cinema car, which include the bistro, is fitted like a tiny movie theater, with rows of seats. ST prides itself on showing current films and changing them regularly. Children watch free in the morning. Buy your movie tickets on the train.

Nordserve, Tagkompaniet's caterer, staffs ST's bistro. The menus are typical northern Swedish, prepared in Lulea. Are you ready for reindeer meat in a cream sauce, or pancakes served with jam made from berries from the northern wilderness? In the morning, get up early for fresh-brewed coffee, fresh bread, juice, and yogurt.

ST accepts Eurailpasses, ScanRail Passes, and Sweden Rail Passes. Reservations are required, and you should make them well in advance, but because Tagkompaniet is a private company, you must telephone them in Sweden at (46) 690-691-045 or book online at *www.tagkompaniet.se.*

Narvik (pop. 20,000) is a pup among cities. In 1880, there were but one or two isolated farms and a few not-so-contented-cows grazing here. Narvik grew out of the railway construction town of Rombaksbotn, which burned to the ground in 1903. It was here that the "rallarne" lived—the migrant construction workers who built the Ofoten Line. The "rallar," with his broad-brimmed hat, became a symbol of the town and the railway. At the train station, look for the statue of the workers' cook, known as "Svarta Bjorn" (Black Bear).

The low but constant angle of the sun on the horizon causes very little temperature change between day and night. It is already warm when you awake and still pleasant late into the evening.

The Narvik train station is cozy, with attached cafeteria. Up the hill from the station on the corner of Kongens Gt. ("Kings' Street"), you find a small shopping mall, which includes an ATM ("MiniBank"). Across from the prizewinning city hall, a small, thought-provoking museum (open during the summer 10 A.M. to 10 P.M. Mon.-Sat., and 11 A.M. to 5 P.M. Sun.) records Narvik's place in history. In May 1940, the

British sank 10 Nazi destroyers in Narvik Fjord and temporarily recaptured the city, the first Allied victory of World War II.

The Narvik Tourist Office (*www.Narvikinfo.no,* open 9 A.M. to 4:30 P.M.) is about a 20-minute walk from the train station down Kongens Gt. to 26, past the museum. The cableway 10 minutes from the city center, at the head of Kongens Gt., lifts you 2,000 feet to the very top of Mount Fagernesfjell in only 13 minutes. When you rise in the aerial gondola above the city, your perspective adjusts. First you see the iron-ore loading facilities open up and then the fjords gradually surrounding and then dwarfing the village while snow-covered mountains appear to rise in the distance.

From the top of the lift, the sun warms the terrace of the restaurant and you see the "Sleeping Queen," a panorama resembling Queen Victoria reposed, 5,191 feet high. The official name of Narvik at the turn of the century was "Victoriahamn," meaning "Victoria's Harbor."

Midnight Trains to Narvik

		1700						
		1700	dep.	Gothenburg	arr.	1050		
1727	2013		dep.	STOCKHOLM C.	arr.		0740	1040
1752	2035		dep.	Arlanda	arr.		0705	1005
1817	2106		dep.	Uppsala	arr.		0653	0944
2218	0142	0142	dep.	Ange	dep.	0300	0220	0553
0304	0622	0622	arr.	Vannas	dep.	2226	2140	0102
0625	1050	1050	arr.	Boden C.	dep.	1753	1720	2155
0842	1316	1316	dep.	Gallivare	dep.	1521	1521	1945
0948	1417	1417	arr.	Kiruna C.	dep.	1417	1417	1839
1230	1720	1720	arr.	NARVIK	dep.	1120	1120	1550

You can return by train directly to Stockholm, take the buses north to Kirkenes near the Russian border, or take the nearly five-hour, red, white, and blue NOR-WAY bus trip (*www.nor-way.no*) south across fjords to Fauske to join NSB's network south to Trondheim. You may purchase tickets in the Narvik train station or on the bus (about $30, no reduction for Eurailpass, 50 percent for ScanRail Pass holders and seniors).

From Fauske or Bodo, you ride NSB's Nordland line, the longest line in Norway. The "Journey that's worth every penny" takes 10 hours to Trondheim. You start at sea level and end at sea level, but you wend your way between fjords and hills, cross two mountain ranges, and pass the Arctic Circle at 67.2 degrees north. The summer stop at the Arctic Circle delights the groups of children enjoying the special children's carriage playroom. Have your cameras ready for the pyramid on the west side of the train. This is the highest point of the Nordlands line at 1620 feet.

Curiously, although Trondheim Airport handles about one and a half million passengers a year, your train stops at Vaernes Station, 36 minutes north of Trondheim, only on request.

Your diesel train carries classic first-class 1980 carriages. During the day, passengers enjoy leg rests, curtains, blankets, overhead luggage space, and free coffee or tea. Second-class is more conventional, with open 2+2 seating. For the night service, NSB markets them as "Hvilevogn," reclining seats, with curtains to close, or you can reserve sleeping compartments with one, two, or three berths. Smokers use a special glassed-in smoking room next to the wooden-panel Bistro Carriage. Breakfast is included for those in one- or two-berth compartments. Bistro Cars serve all others.

Instead of the NOR-WAY bus, a more adventurous way south from Narvik to Bodo, and worth the additional cost, are the steamers operated by the Ofotens S.S. Co. to connect with coastal steamers north and south. You can sit snugly in the cafeteria of the 30-knot m.v. *Skogoy*, built in 1985, or go on deck to watch the landings and deliveries of cargo at the tiny hamlets along the way. You reach the codfish city of Svolvaer for a change to the much larger cruise ships of the Coastal Express Service. This gives you a few hours in Svolvaer to explore the interesting codfishing harbor.

Train and NOR-WAY Bus Service
between Narvik and Trondheim

1615	0700	dep.	NARVIK (bus)	arr.		1420	2300
2120	1150	arr.	FAUSKE	dep.		0930	1815

(2)	(1)					(2)	(1)
2100	1130	dep.	Bodo (train)	arr.		0955	1830
2140	1208	arr.	FAUSKE Station	dep.		0905	1750
2148	1211	dep.	FAUSKE Station	arr.		0913	1747
N/A	1328	dep.	Arctic Circle*	dep		N/A	1630
0657	2056	arr.	Vaernes	dep.		2340	0904
0740	2128	arr.	TRONDHEIM	dep.		2310	0832

* Time approximate. Mid-June to mid-August only.

Bus, Narvik to Fauske/Bodo. Change at Fauske to NSB train to/from Trondheim.

(1) Day trains carry first- and second-class carriages, children's carriage, Bistro Car, bicycles. Reservations required.

(2) Night trains carry sleeping cars, children's carriage, Bistro Car, bicycles. Reservations required.

The Rauma Train
Marvels per Minute

You look down the valley and see three railroad lines. You are twisting along one, there's another farther on, on the edge of a cliff, and still farther, below a cascading waterfall on the other side of the valley, you see a third. All three belong to the Rauma Railroad, carrying you in a huge double spiral to reach the valley floor through two circular tunnels in the Norwegian mountainsides.

Halfway down the 71-mile Rauma Railroad to Andalsnes, you are still nearly 1,700 feet above sea level, the best scenery is yet to come, and you have to get down somehow. Your train must circle to lose altitude. You pass wild mountains, soaring peaks, and crashing waterfalls and then you enter mountains cored by internal twists and spirals.

The first tunnel you enter, the Stavem, is 4,650 feet long. In the heart of the mountain, you retrace your path. When you return to daylight, you are running on the second segment, opposite to your direction a few minutes ago. You are several levels farther down the valley and see the Vermafoss falls straight ahead plummeting in misty cascades about 1,250 feet down the mountain ridge opposite.

The mint-green Rauma River below you dashes with all the gusto of a Norwegian hare, tumbling down over steep precipices and slabs of rock.

Entering the Kylling tunnel, you sweep through the mountain and under the highway in a long shallow curve, 1,500 feet long and so gentle you don't feel it. Back into daylight, you cross Kylling Bridge over a narrow gorge and see again the Rauma River, now frothing and foaming untamed only 200 feet below. As though to make itself most beautiful, the river snakes around pebbly white islets and sandbars of white granite powder and jumps across rapids, trailing glorious white bubbly wakes.

You have reached the third and lowest track and finally you can look back on this ingeniously engineered line from below. The complex double curve made the Rauma Railroad about five miles longer, but allowed you to descend 330 feet safely.

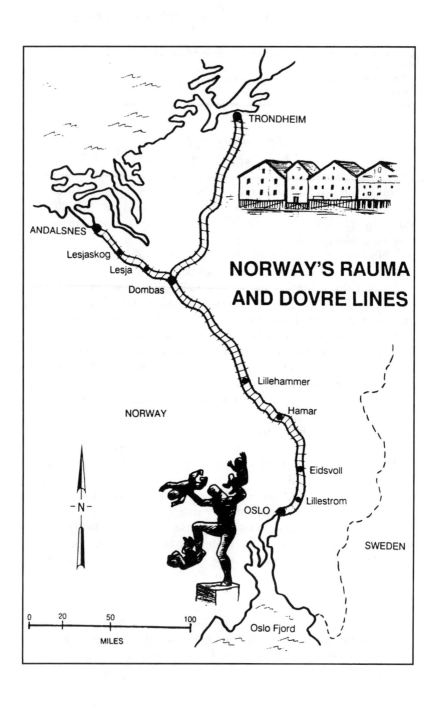

TRONDHEIM

ANDALSNES

Lesjaskog

Lesja

Dombas

**NORWAY'S RAUMA
AND DOVRE LINES**

Lillehammer

Hamar

NORWAY

Eidsvoll

Lillestrom

OSLO

-N-

SWEDEN

| 0 | 20 | 50 | 100 |

MILES

Oslo Fjord

While the Rauma River gradually tires and meanders more calmly through wide gentle bends, the mountain scenery by contrast turns starker and more rugged and you are entering a new episode in the adventure of the Rauma Railroad. You are now traveling at the foot of towering rocky precipices and looking up at triple-tongued, monstrous waterfalls crashing down at you.

This is what makes train travel exciting. You have passed from one spectacular phase into one differently wondrous. Passengers run from side to side of your class BM93 diesel unit—which tilts—pointing and shouting to each other with delight. One rider shouts, "This is the most beautiful ride in the world."

This 1 1/2-hour jaunt, unfolding rich detail and color, justifies you making a single memorable trip to Norway, and is, happily, completely covered by Eurail, Norwegian, and ScanRail Passes, like most NSB travel.

The morning departure of your Signatur No. 43 tilting train north from Oslo Sentral first passes through the severe architecture, and Star-Wars designs, and the tunnel under Olso's 1998 Gardermoen Airport, before continuing through rich farmlands and then up the eastern shore of Lake Mjosa, Norway's largest and deeper than the North Sea. On the lake you see the one-funnel steamship, the P. S. *Skibladner* (say "Shebladner"), the world's oldest paddle steamer still in regular service, built in 1854, in Sweden. You pass red-and-brown wooden summer cottages, and wild flowers dancing like yellow fire— dandelions, buttercups, mustard, and rapeseed (Canola) for monounsaturated oil.

Your first stop on Lake Mjosa is in the important hub of Hamar, at the widest point. Inhale deeply here. The air is fresh and pure, reputedly the most healthful in Scandinavia. The 1896 Norwegian State Railroad Museum in Hamar (*www.jernbaneverket.no*, open daily during the summer, 10 A.M. to 4 P.M.) is one of the oldest train museums in the world. Visit the outdoor museum park with tracks, signals, and engine sheds. A narrow-gauge steam train operates during the summer.

At your second stop on Lake Mjosa, the vacation center of Lillehammer, you see the improvements the Norwegian government invested ($370 million) for the 1994 Winter Olympic Games. Past Lillehammer, you enter Gudbrandsdal, the "Valley of Valleys" ("dal" means "valley"). Farmers here still maintain the old building styles. You pass lined-up farmhouses climbing the mountainsides like soldiers.

At Dombas' brown plaster station house with warm interior, you change to the Rauma Railroad down the Romsdal. Now, looking forward as you wind down toward Andalsnes on the Ice Fjord, the sheer face of unscalable Trollveggen, meaning Troll Wall, stands in front of you. You must crane your neck to see the summits of the huge mountains soaring heavenward on either side, one after another. From a terrible height, famous waterfalls drop from the mountainside like countless silver fingers.

When you approach Marstein, where the mountains stand so high the stationmaster only sees the sun seven months of the year, your ride has settled down to merely splendid. You watch capricious mists of cloud dancing midway up sturdy cliffs nearly barren of trees.

You wind around the wedge-shaped, 4,250-foot high Mongegjura Mountain and the weird range of peaks resembling a row of trolls squatting menacingly over the valley. Its gray walls, scarred and stained, rise sheer from the valley floor to 6,000 feet.

Trolls reputedly set up camp here to gain an advantage over their enemies, gnomes on the valley floor. In one battle, they hid until the gnomes appeared at the foot of the mountains and then hurled down a terrible avalanche to bury them in rock and stone. But the gnomes triumphed in the end, for they had tricked the trolls, who are permitted to roam only at night. For their foolish midday attack, the trolls fossilized into these jagged blue-gray mountain massifs, so steep the snow will not lie on their slopes and no vegetation will grow.

The valley is almost entirely surrounded by the peaks above you. You cannot see the top of the Romsdalshorn. Finally, you look up at the 6,300-foot Trollveggen, the highest vertical rock face in northern Europe.

Now you descend. You have always been dropping, of course, following a course above the mint-green river, but now you sense it by the multiplication of the flowering wild plants and the passing of the terrible, high mountains.

You see the river joining the fjord and rows of pleasant homes along ordered streets. This is the tidy township of Andalsnes, where you come to a halt beside the modern, 1991 station house with cafe.

Andalsnes (pop. 2,500) is one of the loveliest settings along the coast of Norway. Situated on the Ice Fjord, the head of the Romsdalsfjord, at the foot of the Romsdal, it is framed by the Setnefjell mountain on the west and Mount Nesaksla on the east.

You won't find much to do in Andalsnes but admire the scenery and hike the mountains. That is more than enough. Buses (not covered by rail pass) stand by the train station to take you to Alesund and Molde, which is a stopping place for the coastal steamers, a superb 2 1/2-hour mail-boat trip across the fjord.

You can return up the mountainside to connect with Signatur No. 45 from Oslo to continue from Dombas to Trondheim, Norway's third city, with a population of 145,000. About 25 minutes north of Dombas, you pass the highest point of the line, about 3,360 feet, and see the snow-capped, highest mountain in Norway (7,500 feet) to the west.

Trondheim, under its former name of Nidaros, was Norway's first capital. There is much for you to see here, including numerous colorful wharf houses and Nidaros Cathedral, where Norway's kings are crowned. It is the largest medieval building in Scandinavia. Since Trondheim's Sentral Station was redeveloped with a stunning 1999 annex, with ATM ("MiniBank"), taxi stand, bus station and sales counters for train, bus, and express boat tickets, there has been a large increase in suburban traffic, attracting many away from their autos. Luggage carts are available for a deposit and ramps connect the platforms. The InterRail Center in the train station is open 7 A.M. to 11 P.M. during July and August.

When you wish to go to Hell simply to have your photograph taken below the famous ochre Hell train station's signboard, you can reach Hell by the TronderBanen network of rapid transit trains.

Dovre Line Signature Train Service
Oslo to Trondheim

		41	43	45	47
dep.	OSLO (Sent.)	0729	0848	1448	1649
dep.	Oslo Airport	0745	0913	1513	1713
dep.	Hamar	0845	0959	1600	1800
dep.	Lillehammer	0932	1043	1643	1844
dep.	Ringebu	1009	1125	1740	1922
dep.	Vinstra	1025	1141	1736	1938
dep.	Otta	1045	1205	1756	1958
arr.	DOMBAS *	1116	1232	1823	2025
dep.	DOMBAS	1116	1245	1840	2035
arr.	Oppdal	1205	1325	1916	2119
arr.	Heimdal	1319	1439	2027	2233
arr.	TRONDHEIM (S)	1330	1450	2038	2245

Connections to/from Andalsnes

dep.	DOMBAS	N/A	1245	1840	2035*
arr.	Andalsnes	N/A	1411	2005	2220

dep.	Andalsnes	0925	N/A	1630	N/A
arr.	Dombas	1055	N/A	1800	N/A

Trondheim to Oslo

		40	42	44	46
dep.	TRONDHEIM (S)	0700	0858	1452	1605
dep.	Heimdal	0712	0910	1504	1620
dep.	Oppdal	0825	1026	1617	1737
arr.	DOMBAS	0913	1116	1705	1827
dep.	DOMBAS	0915	1119	1707	1829
dep.	Otta	0943	1148	1736	1857
dep.	Vinstra	1002	1207	1759	1915
dep.	Ringebu	1023	1223	1815	1936
arr.	Lillehammer	1059	1259	1858	2012
arr.	Hamar	1140	1340	1940	2055
arr.	Oslo Airport	1228	1428	2028	2146
arr.	OSLO (Sent.)	1253	1453	2053	2212

Connections to/from Andalsnes

dep.	DOMBAS	N/A	1245	N/A	1840
arr.	Andalsnes	N/A	1411	N/A	2220

dep.	Andalsnes	N/A	0925	1500*	1630
arr.	Dombas	N/A	1055	1645	1800

N/A = Not available
* bus service
All Signatur trains carry first- and second-class carriages, Bistro Car, children's carriage. Reservations Required. Nos. 40 and 41 do not run Sundays; Nos. 44 and 47 do not run Saturdays.

Crossing the Bothnia Free Deck to Finland

"Tervetuloa. Welcome aboard the Silja Line." The veteran captain speaks from the bridge of your ship crossing from Stockholm to Finland—Turku or Helsinki—a vantage point some 100 feet and 12 stories above the water.

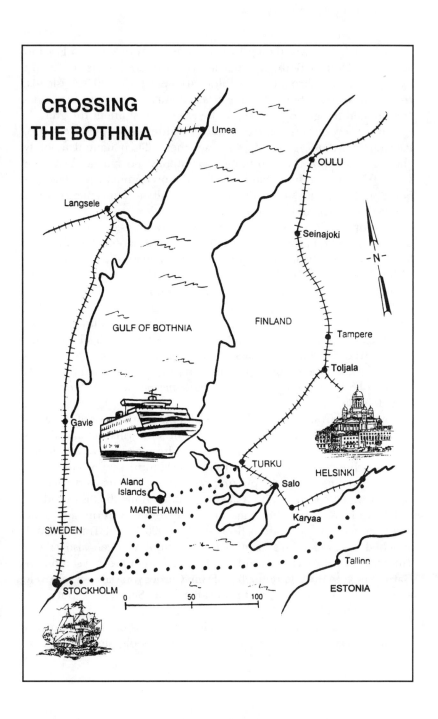

CROSSING
THE BOTHNIA

Umea

OULU

Langsele

Seinajoki

-N-

GULF OF BOTHNIA

FINLAND

Tampere

Toljala

Gavle

TURKU

HELSINKI

Aland
Islands

Salo

MARIEHAMN

Karyaa

SWEDEN

Tallinn

STOCKHOLM

0   50   100

ESTONIA

You watch fir trees gliding by your window. Your entry to Finland across the Gulf of Bothnia is not as absent of scenery as you might expect. You sail through an endless archipelago of 80,000 islands, rocks, and skerries. Some are tree-covered. All are remnants of the glacier era and the geologic rising of the earth's crust under the gulf.

Almost everything is fresh aboard ship—and well kept up. Passengers are doing whatever pleases them. Their natural mobility aboard ship allows them to mingle, or not, as they please. Everyone seems friendly. You hear that Finnish is the predominate language on board, but everyone speaks English to you. All announcements are in Swedish, Finnish, and English.

Most of the travelers seem to be in their twenties, but Nordic children seem to be having the best of it. Northern parents know how to look after their offspring. Children frolic in a glassed playroom filled with colored plastic bubbles. You can see that they are returning from a family excursion to the "big city" of Stockholm.

The Silja Line is the premier line carrying passengers across the Gulf of Bothnia from Stockholm to Turku or Helsinki. Eurailpass and ScanRail Pass holders are particularly interested in the Silja Line. They receive free daytime deck passage on the M.S. *Silja Europa* or *Silja Scandinavia* between Stockholm and Turku and substantial discounts on the M.S. *Silja Serenade* or M.S. *Silja Symphony* between Stockholm and Helsinki.

You depart from Silja Line's Stockholm pier in the port of Vartan—in the northeastern part of town. Silja Line's information and ticketing offices are located there and you can also make use of a self-service cafe, children's playroom, souvenir kiosk, tourist information (for arrivals), waiting room, telephones, rest rooms, lockers, and check-in counter which opens two hours before sailing. A mailbox is outside.

Pickup is free by a white Silja Line bus from City Terminalen, the bus terminal on the bottom floor of the 1990 World Trade Center attached to Stockholm's Central train station. You can also take a Tunnelbana (subway) train to Ropsten, the end-of-the-line station, or Gardet, next to the end of the line. From Gardet you walk—a relatively easy, 10-minute hike. Signs to Vartahamnen, Silja Line's port, are posted in the subway.

The attraction is irresistible on Silja Line ships offering a tropical Sunflower Oasis with water slides, swimming pools, steam bath and bars; a play area for children; a promenade, teak-covered atrium, lined with reasonably priced restaurants and shops and overlooked by cabins above; a casino with Las Vegas-style slot machines; the Neon Disco and a romantic dance floor; duty-free shopping; gourmet restaurants sprinkled throughout the ship . . . .

Silja Line's 1993, 55,000-ton, M.S. *Europa* is the world's biggest cruise liner, with 3,000 berths. Her 765,000 square feet of glass opens up vast seascapes to travelers. Enormous windows cover the prow, giving you unobstructed views from the buffet restaurant and nightclub. Below, a 90-seat McDonald's restaurant is open late for Big Mac attacks and a 500-seat theater mounts musicals such as Rodgers and Hammerstein's *Oklahoma!*

The *Europa* is joined on the Stockholm-Turku run by 1992's m.s. *Silja Scandinavia*, which can accommodate 2,400 passengers and has 673 furnished cabins.

The 1991 M.S. *Silja Symphony*, Silja Line's 23-knot, 58,400-ton luxury liner, carries up to 2,500 passengers and incorporates cruise vessel luxuries never before seen in the industry. It is paired with her identical sister ship, the 1990, M.S. *Silja Serenade*, for daily service all year round from Helsinki and Stockholm with departures from each port in the evening and arrivals the next morning.

Silja Line's ships were designed for service between Finland and Sweden, but they also comply with rules of construction for long international voyages and meet the requirements for ice navigation without the help of icebreakers. Due to dense traffic and narrow routes in the archipelagoes, the bottoms of the hulls are designed for minimal wave generation and minimal response to heavy seas.

The fare structure for Silja Line makes little sense. Between Helsinki and Stockholm, the new ships have no available deck space, but reservations are mandatory. Twenty categories of cabins all require reservations. The 141 listed prices don't even include the fare for Eurailpass holders, which is $30 in a Tourist II Class 4-Berth cabin (less than half regular adult fare). ScanRail Pass holders pay the same, but it is calculated differently.

Aboard the M.S. *Silja Serenade* and M.S. *Scandinavia* between Turku and Stockholm, deck passage is free for daytime sailings, which makes it most attractive. On the night sailings, Eurailpass holders pay $20 for a Tourist II Class 4-berth cabin.

ScanRail Pass holders receive a 50 percent discount (to $10) on passage without cabin on both day and night sailings. During the night sailings, you will find that the free Pullman chairs ("Sittsalong") are surprisingly comfortable with spacious washrooms nearby. You stow your small bags in nearby lockers. Leave your large luggage in the luggage room.

The cabins are a good value when you are receiving a deep discount. A bunk in a four-person cabin costs about the same price as a second-class couchette on a train. The ships' cabins give you many comforts: shower, bunk beds, mirror, toilet, wash basin, and open closet. (Advance reservations: Silja Line, 505 Fifth Avenue, New York, NY 10017, Tel. 212-986-2711).

Choose between two daily departures from Stockholm to Turku (morning and evening) and one only at 6 P.M. to Helsinki. Note that the time in Finland is an hour earlier than in Sweden.

When the captain announces your ship will be docking in Helsinki in half an hour, look to your left entering Helsinki's harbor. Your ship's only possible navigable channel takes you through Suomenlinna, Finland's Seafortress, a complex of six islands fortified in 1748. Once the greatest fortress of the Swedish empire, it was surrendered to the Russians in 1808 and then bombarded by the British fleet in 1855 during the Crimean War. It finally became Finnish in 1917 when it was renamed "Finland's Seafortress."

The first building you spot in Helsinki will probably be the white capitol-like dome of the 1852 Uspensky Lutheran Cathedral. On debarking, pass through the customs hall and you will see an office to change money and a tourist office where you can buy Helsinki Cards for transportation or book a hotel room in the city for a small service charge. Tram 3T goes to Market Square a few blocks away and Tram 3B (which runs the opposite direction of Tram 3T) takes you to the train station.

Travelers sailing into Turku see an unmatched view of high Turku Castle, a medieval bastion (but now a museum) guarding the harbor. Turku's Harbor train station is separate from the main Turku station. Trains wait side-by-side at the Harbor station to take you onto the VR network to Helsinki, Tampere, and Joensuu. These conventional trains, which do not require reservations, carry cafeteria cars with snacks and coffee, but are not the S 220 Pendolino. You can buy train tickets in the Silja Line terminal.

Summer Silja Line and VR Train Service
between Stockholm and Turku or Helsinki

0800	1700	2015	dep.	STOCKHOLM				
				(Vartahamn.)	arr.	1915	0700	0830
1450	2359	|	dep.	Mariehamn	dep.	1450	|	0400
|	|	0350	dep.	Langnas*	dep.		| 0130	|
2020	|	0800	arr.	TURKU (Harbor)	dep.	0915	2115	|
2110t	|	0844t	dep.	Turku (Harbor)	arr.	0823	2032	|
2122	|	0854	dep.	Turku (City)	arr.	0810	2007	|
2334	0930	1102	arr.	HELSINKI (Etelasatama)	dep.	0550t	1804t	1800

* Langnas is 16 miles from Mariehamn.
t—Train connection to/from Helsinki train station. VR also provides Silja Line connections at Turku Harbor to and from Tampere and Joensuu.
\|—Does not travel this route

Round Finland by Train
Lakeland and Nature

You suddenly come within inches of a granite sculpture. The powerful figure sitting on the ground cradles its head with one arm and peers steadily down upon you at the window of your train. Then you enter a black tunnel, and when you emerge, on your left, the medieval towers and ramparts of Olavinlinna castle, the best-preserved in the Nordic countries, unravel doubly, one vision straight ahead, and one image dancing in the calm waters of Kyronsalmi Straits.

Nature becomes redefined: quiet waters, towering firs, singing birds, pine needles on forest floor filtered by magical light. About 180 endangered Saimaa fresh-water seals frolic in the lake, their last refuge. It is said that trout fight among themselves to be the first to take anglers' lures in Kyronsalmi Straits.

The lakeside village of Savonlinna is your heart of Finland's Saimaa Lakeland. The community grew around Olavinlinna castle, and together with the captivating countryside has become Finland's most magnetic place. The granite sculpture that greeted you marked the entrance to the Retretti Art Center at Punkaharju, the largest art center in the Nordic countries. Curators fill its subterranean grottoes with outstanding exhibits of modern and traditional international art.

The diesel-hauled train that brought you to Savonlinna's

Olavinlinna castle connected with the electric IC train from Helsinki at Parikkala. If VR maintains this 37-mile spur from Parikkala, visitors flock throughout July to attend the Savonlinna Opera Festival, which is held on the stage magnificently located within the walls of Olavinlinna. Unfortunately, VR threatens to replace trains on the Parikkala-Savonlinna line with buses, which nevertheless will honor rail passes.

Finland does not end with Helsinki. The beauty and serenity of Finland lies in the lake districts. Luckily for visitors, the geography of Finland dictates that rail lines originally built for lumber transport must link lakeside villages and reveal Finland's secrets to train travelers.

Like the limbs of a pear tree, with Helsinki at its root, VR's Ostrobothnian line shoots to the north beside the Gulf of Bothnia, VR's Karelian line branches north beside the Russian border, and the Savo line shoots straight north between lakes. At Joensuu a VR bus honoring rail passes takes you to Kontiomaki for a connection to the Ostrobothnian line at Oulu and thus completes a pear-shaped ring around Finland's two magnificent lakelands and makes a circle trip not only feasible, but essential to absorb the grandness, greatness, and captivation of the Finnish enchanting lakeland.

Ten percent of Europe's fifth-largest country is water—lakes and rapids. In Finland, the rivers flow garnet, tinted with soluble iron ores. The Saimaa Lakeland runs from Lappeenranta in the south to Nurmes in the north. The Western Lakeland is bounded by Tampere on the west and Hameenlinna on the south.

Varieties of trees commingle on the flat Finnish countryside as happily and thickly as birds on their limbs. Pines prefer dryer land and make up more than half of Finland's forests. Spruce make up about one-third; birch about one-tenth. In the south occasional oak, lime, ash, and maple join the forests.

Starting your trip from Helsinki's startling, red-granite Central train station, where you ask for the free pocket timetable, "Taskuaikataulu" (English is the first foreign language in Finland), you leave from a central train yard with all departures marked by electronic signs.

The preserved wooden station houses you come upon in the Finnish countryside are kept in mint condition. Count on them being painted either ocher or rust red and trimmed with white. And almost always, you see an ancient, black steam locomotive standing nearby on a pedestal.

When your train branches onto the Karelian line north toward Lappeenranta, away from the route leading into the Soviet Union, the land by the tracks looks marshy but the trees look sturdy. Looking north, you see your first lake. Now your adventure begins.

Reaching Parikkala, only two miles from the present border of Russia, birders pull out their color booklets. Parikkala is a lure for birders. Siberian birds nest and fly over the Siikalahti Conservation Area, as far west as they venture.

You continue north to Joensuu, the provincial capital meaning "river mouth," where the branches of Finnish State Railroads thin. Out of Joensuu, you pass through rolling hills with stands primarily of spruce. You see lakes everywhere, but no one using the waters. Occasionally you see an abandoned canoe pulled up onto turf or a quiet outboard motorboat with its motor lying beside it.

At Lieksa station the black steam locomotive that usually stands on display outside every Finnish train station is not present. Instead you see a tiny railroad cart loaded with a single, cut commemorative segment of tree trunk, honoring the origins of this railroad as a lumber-hauling operation.

You travel up the east shore of 60-mile-long Lake Pielinen, the biggest lake in Karelia, until you halt on the northern tip of the lake at Nurmes, center of ski and hiking trails. Nearby is the touristy Karelian settlement of Bomba. You recognize Karelian architecture by its log houses with wide balconies, pillars, balustrades, overhanging eaves, and ornate "pretty" window frames giving them a cutesy charm.

Trains have been replaced by VR buses to Kontiomaki. At Nurmes, you have reached the top branch of the tree of electrified lines. Your bus runs 68 miles to Kontiomaki, where you can choose to return south to Helsinki via the Savo line, but adventurers making the great loop north change to the train to Oulu on the Gulf of Bothnia. You travel your last 101 miles, Kontiomaki to Oulu (Uleaborg in Swedish), at 50 mph.

After passing through solitude, Oulu surprises you. Dynamic and progressive, happy and prosperous, 100,000-population Oulu claims to be the Silicon Valley of northern Scandinavia. You find astonishingly modern hotels such as the Rivoli and the Eden at half the price of Helsinki hotels on weekends and in June and July, a university town, a marvelous Science Museum, a magnificent Lutheran cathedral, and preserved neo-Renaissance architecture. Oulu is your natural jumping-off point to see Lapland or travel by bus north of the Gulf of Bothnia to Sweden and Norway.

South from Oulu, you join the fully electrified Ostrobothnian line. Trains run faster. IC trains are the fastest way to return to Helsinki. As your InterCity approaches Tampere, you see that you are entering the Western Lakeland—and welcome it is to see—as Lake Nasijarvi opens to your east. Crossing the long bridge across Tampere's Tammerkoski Rapids, you stop in the city center.

One glance at Tampere's brick stacks and you see that Tampere is industrialized—in fact it is the most heavily industrialized city in Finland, but here industry does not look like the dirty word that travelers fear. Tampere charms you as you walk wide boulevards past quiet green parks and see the plentiful hotels, art nouveau architecture from which Finland adopted its national Romantic style, rolling hills, and blissful lakes. Those quiet stacks give vertical thrusts to Tampere's beautiful setting like exclamation points.

Situated as Tampere is, the hub of the electrified Ostrobothnian line and the east-west spoke from Puri to Pieksamaki and Joensuu, Tampere is your natural home for the Western Lakeland. To reach Tampere's Tourist Office, head four blocks straight down Hameenkatu from in front of the station and then turn left at Verkatehtaankatu, 2.

As your train approaches Hameenlinna, look for one of the most impressive sights you can see from a mainline train. While you feel your train braking for the station house, look across the narrow lake to the brick Hameenlinna ("linna" means "castle"), dating from the 1260s. It was built by the Swedes to link the Hame region with the mother country and—you guessed it—to collect taxes from the relatively wealthy area.

Hameenlinna was the northern terminus of Finland's first railroad line from Helsinki in 1862, when goods were transloaded between railroad and lake steamer for further shipment along the lake system to and from the north. Rapid progress soon connected Hameenlinna station to St. Petersburg before it was named Leningrad. The present station building was erected in 1920 following the old one's demolition during the Finnish revolution when Germans, who were supporting "White" Finns in their battles with the "Red" Finns, exploded a railroad carriage filled with gunpowder.

Helsinki-Joensuu
via Karelian Railroad

IC 1				IC10
0702	dep.	HELSINKI	arr.	1902
0753	dep.	Riihimaki	arr.	1812
0827	dep.	Lahti	arr.	1736
0902	dep.	Kouvola	dep.	1700
0940	arr.	Lappeenranta	dep.	1613
1013	dep.	Imatra	dep.	1542
2059	arr.	Parikkala	dep.	1500
1203	arr.	JOENSUU	dep.	1337
1405	arr.	Nurmes	dep.		

IC1 and IC10 trains carry first- and second-class carriages and dining car.

Joensuu-Oulu bus service

1405	dep.	JOENSUU (bus)	arr.	1540
1605	dep.	Nurmes	dep.	1335
1835	arr.	Kajaani (bus)	dep.	1125
1220	arr.	OULU	dep.	0830

Monday to Saturday service only.

Helsinki-Oulu
via Ostrobothnian Railroad

(1)				(2)
1458	dep.	HELSINKI	arr.	1356
1546	dep.	Riihimaki	arr.	1308
——	dep.	Hameenlinna	dep.	1245
1648	arr.	TAMPERE	dep.	1202
1650	dep.	TAMPERE	arr.	1159
1816	dep.	Seinajoki	dep.	1030
1946	dep.	Kokkola	dep.	0913
2146	arr.	OULU	dep.	0710

(1) First- and second-class carriages, dining car. Runs daily except Saturdays to/from Kokkola, Fridays and Sundays to/from Oulu.
(2) First- and second-class carriages, snacks available. Runs daily.

Germany

Smart Traveling on the Trains
of Germany

InterCity trains—InterRegio trains—Tilting railcars—Domestic night trains—S-Bahn trains—Metropolitan trains Cologne-Hamburg—Airport trains—Using rail pass bonuses—German Railpass

Starting in 2000, Germany's Deutsche Bahn (DB—also called DBAG, where "AG" is the equivalent of "Inc.," *www.bahn.de*), prefers to be known as "Die Bahn," (DB, "The Railroad"). It is the combination of the former Deutsche Bundesbahn (DB) of West Germany and Deutsche Reichsbahn (DR) of the East. DB takes you everywhere you want to go. Overall, DB spans 24,800 miles, of which 10,500 miles are electrified. More than 33,000 trains, including 1,200 long-distance trains, transport more than four million passengers per day, and serve nearly 8,000 cities and villages in unified Germany. Trains take you to the Alps, North Sea beaches, along the Rhine River, and through the Black Forest. Many conductors and staff speak English.

ICE, IC, IR, and EC trains crisscross Germany one after another, with fast, on-time connections. Each has a very precise definition: IC trains link principal cities between which there is an established travel flow and do not normally stop in towns with a population less than 100,000. IR trains take you to towns of 40,000 or more every two hours. RegionalExpress (RE) trains provide services up to 100 mph on trips averaging up to 31 miles at a minimum frequency of two hourly. They provide fast, limited-stop regional services and consist of locomotive-hauled trains with older carriages repainted in IR sea-green livery. RegionalBahn (RB) trains are slower and cost less to ride. They cover local services with an average length of 18.5 miles, speeds of up to 62 mph, and at least two-hourly frequency. StadtExpress (SE) is the name given outer suburban trains with an average journey of 15 to 31 miles, speeds up to 87 mph and at least hourly frequency. SE trains call only at key stations and thus offer a fast way to get from city center to outer, suburban centers. S-Bahn trains give you extensive urban transportation.

GermanRail EC and ICE trains link practically all of the major cities in Europe, e.g., Paris, Prague, Budapest, Vienna, Zurich, Copenhagen, Milan, and Venice, and connect with the Thalys network at Cologne. You receive an on-board timetable called "Ihr Reiseplan" ("Your travel schedule") on every high-speed ICE, IC, EC, and even many slower trains, showing not only your time of arrival and departure at every stop along your way, but—more useful—telling you where to change for your ultimate destination.

DB's ICE, EC, IC, and IR trains run punctually at least every other hour, usually hourly, and depart at the same minute after the hour. If you miss a train, it is usually wiser to wait for the next train of the same class than to take a local train that departs sooner. Even then, check the yellow departure sheets to make sure the train stops where you want to go.

To price riding on ICE trains, DB introduced a so-called Loco-Price concept whereby passengers' fares take into account the commercial benefits of the time saved in addition to distance traveled. These point-to-point prices do not affect rail pass holders, who do not pay surcharges.

Reservations are not required on German trains, but if you desire, it is easy to make reservations in Germany (and you save money by not making them from the U.S.). DB charges a reservation fee of three DM to travelers who show their rail pass. You pay the same when you buy a ticket and reserve at the same time, but nine DM if buy a ticket and then you come back later for a reservation.

GermanRail accepts Visa credit cards in 155 major train stations, and waiters in BordRestaurants accept MasterCard (Eurocard), Visa, Diners Club, and traveler's checks in U.S. dollars, German Marks, and British pounds sterling.

Larger GermanRail stations have escalators to the platforms (Berlin's Zoo, Friedrichstasse, and Alexanderplatz, Dusseldorf, Koblenz, Hamburg, Hanover, Heidelberg, Mainz, Mannheim, etc.) and some 130 smaller ones such as Freiburg have automatic conveyer belts to lift your luggage. In most DB platforms you find racks of luggage carts ("Kofferkulis") so that you can unlock one for a deposit of a one- or two-Mark coin. You get your coin back if you return your cart, but you won't find abandoned carts because DB employees are instructed to round up stray carts to prevent them from rolling onto the tracks.

DB posts porters at Hamburg, Leipzig, Dresden, Frankfurt/Main, Stuttgart and Munich main stations. The charge is about $3.50 for the first two pieces of luggage and $1.75 for each additional piece. DB encourages bicycle rentals, and you can find "Bahn & Bike" programs in most German states. Almost 60 percent of all long-distance trains allow you to take along your bike.

Nearly all DB stations have lockers for you to store your luggage in a safe place. There are four sizes of lockers, with rentals ranging from about $1 to $3 for 24 hours, depending on size. Maximum storage time is 72 hours. If you do not remove your luggage on time, attendants remove your belongings and charge you a $7.50 service charge. Long-term rentals are also available for $30 to $60 a month, depending on locker size.

In Frankfurt/Main Hauptbahnhof, Frankfurt/Main Airport Train Station, Cologne Hauptbahnhof, Leipzig, and Hanover Hauptbahnhof, DB maintains first-class lounges (open daily 6:30 A.M. to 11 P.M., and some later). Show your first-class pass or ticket and enjoy a quiet atmosphere, comfortable seats, free drinks and snacks, functional laptop workplaces, and access to a conference room. Those without first-class passes or tickets can pay about $7.50 for admission.

DB's primary claim to greatness comes from its magnificent network of ICE trains running hourly along long high-speed lines through the West (see "ICE Generation," below).

InterCity Trains

DB has no central hub, such as FrenchRail's Paris or SpanishRail's Madrid, but rather a spread of key cities with equal commercial status. DB has cunningly interlaced hourly IC service between them so that it is possible for you to board at any of the 60 IC-network cities and, by following the on-board timetable, arrive with all speed in any other station you might choose by making only one split-second across-the-platform change or two at most. GermanRail's trains and platforms are designed to simplify connections. First-class carriages are in front of the train, then BordRestaurant, then second-class ones in the rear. Travelers need only cross the platform to find equivalent accommodation on the connecting train. Travelers boarding for the first time know where to stand by consulting the "Wagenstandanzeiger" train composition boards on the platforms or the digital signs overhead, which in addition to the usual departure information also show you where the first- and second-class sections come to rest.

In addition to the frequent nodes where IC trains interchange passengers, the IC system synchronizes with the ICE network at Mannheim, Nuremberg, Fulda, and Kassel-Wilhelmshohe, where you can change from 125-mph trains to trains running up to 174 mph.

GermanRail's IC carriages were refurbished in 1999-2000 with a second generation interior refurbishment known as "Redesign 2," with new seats, extensive light wood and brushed aluminum trim, family compartments, and an improved catering area. The exteriors stand out with fire-red liveries, lavender stripes down the sides, and leaf push-button doors. Don't look for a yellow stripe denoting first class. Rely instead on the bold *1* and *2* numerals on the shiny exteriors. Restaurant carriages are lettered "BordRestaurant" on the red exteriors.

Most of GermanRail's IC and EC trains carry one or two salon carriages while the rest of the train consists of compartment carriages. Dining cars are located between the first- and second-class sections.

InterRegio Trains

For medium-range travel you ride GermanRail's InterRegio (IR) trains. The IR network offers you express service within Germany on 18 routes carrying 1,760 trains weekly. You find infinitely variable mini-salons and haphazard rows of light-green seats mixed in every carriage, jump seats for children, and high chairs that convert to tables. Parents with children find special compartments; one per train is for handicapped in wheelchairs. Second-class carriages on many IR routes accommodate bicycles.

GermanRail timed its IR carriages (sky blue, sea blue, and white livery for second; white, lavender, and red livery for first class) to arrive and depart at regular two-hour intervals, so you know in advance at what minute to expect IRs. They average at least 56 mph, but reach 125 mph.

Tilting Railcars

Standing behind the driver, peering through the glass partitions, you have a panoramic view of the road ahead, although standing means that you notice the tilt more than when you sit in the back. You might never realize you are riding aboard one of GermanRail's tilting trains ("NeiTec" is the German acronym for tilting train) until your train tilts eight degrees. They look conventional when you see their standard profiles and GermanRail's light-gray-and-mint-green liveries. Their aluminum bodies are only slightly tapered from the waist up so that the interiors are roomy, light, and comfortable. Travelers in second-class use an imaginative mix of salon-type seats and groups of four seats around tables. All line up perfectly with the windows to give you an exhilarating ride with beautiful views. But underneath, mechanisms tilt the trains on curves and increase speed on winding stretches of track in order to decrease your travel time and increase your riding comfort.

The trains were unique in being the first European diesel units to be equipped with active tilt systems (previous examples were electric trains). With a maximum speed of 100 mph, they are genuinely exciting to ride as you blast straight ahead, see a major bend ahead, and realize you are not going to brake.

Second-generation, two-carriage units with Mercedes-Benz electric-drive tilt systems run on regional routes Halle-Hildesheim, Mainz-Karlsruhe, Hof-Zwickau, and Gottingen-Gera. The tilt equipment, which was derived from the mechanism, which keeps the gun barrel of a tank stable while the machine moves up and down, is entirely below the floorboards so the carriages carry up to 12 more passengers. Earlier tilting units carry you on the Stuttgart-Tubingen-Ebingen route. These are DB's first diesel units to be cooled by air-conditioning.

Domestic Night Trains

GermanRail's Nachtzuge trains (NZ) are excellent. On four routes they actually consist of Spanish-designed Tren Hotel tilting carriages painted in GermanRail's night blue livery with GermanRail embellishments.

The routes of these tilting NZ are
- Berlin (Lichtenberg)-Berlin (Zoo)-Berlin (Wannsee)-Halle-Augsburg-Munich,
- Berlin (Lichtenberg)-Berlin (Zoo) - Berlin (Wannsee)-Dortmund-Essen-Duisburg-Dusseldorf-Cologne-Bonn,
- Hamburg-Bremen-Hanover-Augsburg-Munich, and
- Hamburg-Bremen-Frankfurt/Main-Heidelberg-Stuttgart.

These Talgo night trains are so low-slung that GermanRail's standard locomotives rise high above them. The trains tilt rounding curves and include a lavish dining room for first-class passengers and a Bistro for those less affluent, with the exception of the Berlin-Bonn train, which provides only the Bistro.

The first-class, air-conditioned cabins contain their own private shower, wash basin and toilet. You can book them either as a single or a double. The beds are aligned in the direction of travel. You lock your compartment with your key card.

In addition to carriages, which each contain five deluxe single and double sleeping compartments, you can ride in second-class carriages fitted with 1996-designed couchettes, which, on the Berlin-Bonn train, are aligned in the direction of travel and separated by curtains. Traditional DB couchette carriages sleep 60, the new ones, 48. In the middle are 12, two-person compartments with curtains. In addition there are two compartments with sliding doors designed for four adults and a child and two compartments designed for two adults and two children.

The GermanRail first: sleeperette seats, which recline deeply, are the equivalent of business class in air travel. Caterers provide food service from a trolley. The luggage car also carries bicycles for a nominal charge.

When you hold a rail pass, you pay less than half for cabins, and the equivalent of $3 for a sleeperette seat or couchette when you make your reservation in Germany.

In addition to the tilting NZ you can ride traditional NZ on the routes between Binz and Munich, Binz and Stuttgart, and Munich and Dortmund. These carry couchettes, sleeping cars and second-class compartments for six, and provide a Bistro.

S-Bahn Trains

Use GermanRail's rapid-transit, frequent-service "S-Bahn" trains in seven independent regions of intense train travel in and around Berlin, Frankfurt/Main, Hamburg, Munich, Nuremberg, the Ruhr, Cologne, Stuttgart, and Leipzig. Hamburg's system is the oldest; Nuremberg's the newest. Berlin's will take you to Potsdam for Sanssouci. You will especially appreciate them in Berlin, where they are a vital link between East and West, and in Munich, where S-Bahn trains parallel Munich's subways and use the same underground station entrances along the Hauptbahnhof-Marienplatz-Ostbahnhof corridor. Look for the green-and-white *S* signs marking station entrances, and remember that rail passes are valid on S-Bahn trains, but not on U-Bahn trains.

Metropolitan Trains Cologne-Hamburg

Silver-livery "Metropolitan" business trains between Cologne and Hamburg began running on August 1, 1999, with stops only in Dusseldorf and Essen. The Metropolitan is an elite train, operated by Metropolitan Express Train GmbH, Hewlett-Packard Strasse 4, 61352 Bad Homburg, *www.met.de*, which is 63 percent owned by DB, and 37 percent by the company's employees. Rail passes are not honored. Trains have 350 seats, all upholstered in black leather. Interior finish is largely of light wood. Business travelers can sit in three areas: "Office," which is like working in an office; "Silence," where they find blankets, pillows, earphones, and cellular phones are banned; and "Club," where they find a choice of film or DVD. You can make a reservation costing DM 30 (about $15) through the usual DB channels. Although you receive a discount with a rail pass, you need a first-class, full-fare DB ticket.

Metropolitan Train Service

0619 1119 1519 1919	dep.	Cologne (Hbf.)	arr.	0617 0852 0916 0942
0641 1141 1541 1941	dep.	Dusseldorf	arr.	1118 1352 1416 1442
0704 1204 1604 2004	dep.	Essen	arr.	1517 1752 1816 1842
0949 1443 1845 2243	arr.	Hamburg (Hbf.)	dep.	1922 2154 2216 2242

Airport Trains

The $220 million Frankfurt/Main Airport high-speed train station ("Fernbahnhof") opened on May 31, 1999. At the underground station, which is 2,300 feet long and 200 feet wide, you can board 84 daily mainline ICE and IC trains (from 5:30 A.M. to midnight) on four tracks to take you directly to and from the airport on two ICE and two IC lines using the first, short, completed section of the new high-speed Cologne-Frankfurt/Main line that will be opened completely on May, 2002.

Two levels above the station you can buy train tickets and validate your rail pass at the Reisezentrum, you can relax in the DB first-class lounge, and departing passengers can check in for some flights. On the roof level, agents will give you hotel and other service information, and you can patronize restaurants.

S-Bahn line S8 trains leave the separate Frankfurt/Main Airport S-Bahn station four or five times per hour for the 11-minute, six-mile trip to Frankfurt/Main's Hauptbahnhof and three other city stops. Other S-Bahn trains take you westward to Mainz and Wiesbaden. Rail passes cover all of these trains.

To board your train, simply follow the blue-and-white signs illustrating a GermanRail locomotive. Push your luggage on the airport's escalator-friendly carts right to the doors of your train at the train station below.

In 2000, Dusseldorf Airport became the third German airport (after Frankfurt/Main Airport and Berlin Schonefeld) to provide ICE connections. German Chancellor Gerhard Schroeder, President Wolfgang Clement, and the head of DB opened the station, which will be served by 270 ICE, IC, IR, local, and S-Bahn trains daily. You transfer between the airport and ICE station by shuttle bus, although a modern people-mover is planned for 2002.

The separate S-Bahn terminal remains directly under the airport and is now named "Dusseldorf Flughafen Terminal." Since 1990, you have been able to use regular-interval S-Bahn trains to Dortmund and Duisberg as well as to Cologne and Dusseldorf's main train station. Passengers on the line to Ohligs will ride in 2000 trains. Use the escalator right from the airport's main hall. Line S7 S-Bahn trains run every 20 minutes to the Dusseldorf Hauptbahnhof, 13 minutes away.

Munich's 1992 Franz-Joseph Strauss Airport in Erding is locked into the Munich S-Bahn system by line two lines, S-1 and S-8. S-8 takes you along the new 13-mile S-Bahn stretch from the 1992 underground station below the airport terminal to the trunk S- and U-Bahn corridor at Ostbahnhof, where you may change to the DB network. S-8 continues through Rosenheimer Platz station, Isartor, Marienplatz (where you find the nouveau-Gothic city hall with its Glockenspiel and can change to U-Bahn line 6 for Schwabing, the student quarter, and the university), Karlsplatz, and the Hauptbahnhof (for ICE departures, Romantic Highway Europabuses, and the hotel-reservations office). Line S-8 then continues to Pasing in the west, where four more S-Bahn lines continue north- and southwestward.

Line S-1, which was connected with the airport in 1998, takes you through stops at Neufahrn and Ingolstadt before approaching the Hauptbahnhof from the west. Line S-8's three-carriage S-Bahn trains run every 20 minutes starting at 3:13 A.M. from Pasing and finishing with their 12:55 A.M. departure from Munich's airport station. Traveling the 23 miles from the airport terminal to Munich's Hauptbahnhof takes 41 minutes. Figure 32 minutes to the Ostbahnhof and 37 minutes to Marienplatz. Travelers north should check the bus shuttle via Freising.

Berlin's Schonefeld Airport, opened on October 6, 1960, with a 2.1-mile runway, is so far in the outskirts of Berlin that it adds another unwanted leg to your long journey. Luckily, few travelers from the West will have occasion to use it, unless after visiting Berlin they continue to the East. Mainline trains, including the ICE, stop here on their long runs between Berlin and Dresden, and it also is served by GermanRail's frequent regional "Airport Express" line RB24 trains, which will carry you with few stops to the center of Berlin— Ostbahnhof, Friedrichstrasse, Alexanderplatz, and Zoo train stations. S-Bahn trains serve additional stops along the way and therefore take longer. Tickets for both regional and S-Bahn trains are sold at the airport. Rail passes are valid on both. Alternately, you may take bus 171 from the airport to U-Bhf Rudow to join the U-Bahn network—and this will be your fastest way to the southern part of Berlin, Kreuzberg, and Tempelhof. Your Berlin Transit Authority bus ticket will also put you aboard Berlin's U-Bahn system.

Berlin's busy Tegel Airport is not a mega-airport like Frankfurt/ Main's. It is constructed like a hexagonal doughnut. International pictographs are used (the same as in the train stations) so finding your way around is not difficult. The "Service Center" will make hotel bookings for you. Several bus lines, both express and local, have stops in front of the station at the curb. These require normal bus tickets, which are available from the machines facing the curb.

The Stuttgart airport is connected to Stuttgart Hauptbahnhof by

1993 S-Bahn lines S2 and S3 on the lower level of the train station. S-Bahn departures every 10 minutes carry you the 13 miles in 25 minutes. Rail passes cover the S-Bahn.

From Hamburg's Fuhlsbuttel Airport, the "Airport Express" bus shuttle waits by the Kirchenallee/Hachmannplatz exit. Running every 10 minutes, they take you to the main train station in 30 minutes. Or you may take bus line 110 to Ohlsdorf rapid transit station where you cross the highway and board S-Bahn train line 1 or U-Bahn train line 1. Both lines take you to the Hauptbahnhof in 30 minutes, but via different routes. Only the S-Bahn line is covered by rail pass.

Using Rail Pass Bonuses

Eurailpasses, Europasses, and Eurail Selectpasses take you over the entire network of GermanRail, both Eastern and Western Germany. They also give you two of the most pleasant excursions in Europe: 75 percent off Romantic Highway and Castle Road Europabus (Lines 190 and 189) trips, and the famous Rhine Cruise from Cologne to Mainz, absolutely free.

In addition, you receive free Moselle River cruises provided by the KD German Rhine Line between Koblenz and Cochem. Rail-pass holders must pay extra to travel by hydrofoil ("Tragflugelboot") on the Rhine River. Specifically excluded are the tourist cruise ships making multiple stops between Basel and Rotterdam and between Trier and Koblenz.

Travelers to Sweden travel free on TT Line between Sassnitz and Trelleborg and receive half off from TT-Line's Travemunde Skandinavienkai pier to Trelleborg and half off the full fare of TR-Line's ferries between Rostock and Trelleborg. A group/student rate is applicable for the ferry crossing Travemunde-Helsinki on the Finnjet (earliest reservations seven days before departure).

Fringe benefits allow half off the fares of the regular steamer services on Lake Constance and the Rhine River to Schaffhausen; a reduced fare on the Freiburg (Breisgau)/Schauinsland rack railroad; half off the Wurm & Kock Danube cruises from Passau to Linz, Austria; and one-quarter off the Zugspitze ("Schneefernerhaus") rack railroad from Garmish-Partenkirchen and some aerial gondolas in the summit area.

German Railpass

Buy German Railpasses in one-day increments from four to 10 days of travel within one month, either first or second class. DB gives an additional bargain to two adults traveling together, either first or second class. The second person pays about one-quarter less than the first German Railpass for what GermanRail calls a "Twinpass." German Railpasses give you the national travel bonuses mentioned above, and even better, the Europabuses mentioned are entirely free when you hold a German Railpass.

The German Rail 'n Drive Pass gives travelers two days of unlimited train travel and two days of an unlimited-mileage Avis rental car within a one month period, using either first- or second-class train and a choice of economy, compact, intermediate, or compact automatic vehicles. You may add additional rail days (up to three) and additional auto days.

The Schones Wochenende ("Happy Weekend") ticket is for any five people traveling together or parents with any number of children. It is valid for unlimited second-class travel on all DB regio S-Bahn, SE, RB, and RE trains and most public transportation throughout Germany from midnight Saturday or Sunday until 3 A.M. the following day. Conductors note the size of the group and it cannot be changed. It is available from most automatic ticket machines for about $17 per day.

Many regions offer regional tickets for travel Mon. to Fri., 9 A.M. to 4 P.M. and then 6 P.M. to 3 A.M. Tickets cost about $20 for up to five people traveling together, and are valid only on S-Bahn, SE, RB, and RE local trains, except in Bavaria where D and IR services also can be used for a supplement.

In Germany you can buy a GermanRail BahnCard valid for half-fare travel on all regularly scheduled GermanRail trains throughout Germany. It is highly recommended for anyone visiting Germany more than once a year, especially seniors over 60. It will pay for itself with two long round trips and give 50 percent off all future fares. It is valid for one year from date of validation.

The basic ("Basiskarte") BahnCard, costing about $120, is for persons aged 23-59. First-class ("BahnCard First") cards cost double.

There are six pricing variations for the basic BahnCard. BahnCards cost half for those over 60, for Juniors aged 18-22, and for spouses of basic BahnCard holders. Teens (12-17) and children (4-11) pay about $30 and double for BahnCards First. In addition there is a family card. For about $15 extra on top of the national half-price card, you may buy "Railplus" to give you 25 percent off the international legs of trips to or from Germany. It's valid for travel in all European countries except former Soviet Union states, Bosnia, and Yugoslavia. In Italy and the Irish Republic, it applies to seniors only; in France, Norway, and Sweden, it applies only to seniors and youth. The "DB Citibank Visa BahnCard" serves also as a Visa credit card with no Citibank service charge. Visitors who don't want a full Visa card can still buy the rail-only BahnCard or a DB Citibank Electron BahnCard which only allows the use of Visa ATMs.

Discoverers in Germany ride Europe's most expensive and extensive high-speed train network, cruise aboard laid-back steamers on the Rhine, tramp through the Black Forest, uncover well-preserved medieval towns by Europabuses, and discover Germany's new metropolis.

The ICE Generation
Wide, White, and Whizzing

Both German children are behaving like such lambs with their earphones plugged in, watching the video, that their parents leave them to themselves and repair to the bar car. The American teenager is glued to the German-language-dubbed video even though he can't understand a word of German. "I've already seen it."

The business traveler has spread his papers across the table and is tapping his analysis into his laptop. You are in the vestibule watching the digital speedometer readout inch toward 280 km/hr (174 mph) as you head south from Hanover toward Wurzburg aboard GermanRail's spacious ICE 1 train.

For more than 20 years DB planned new high-speed trains, laid extensive new track and upgraded existing lines to support a record-breaking domestic high-speed network. Along the way the ICE experimental unit set a short-lived world speed record of 253 mph. The enormous, well-synchronized, integrated ICE network takes you from Kiel and Hamburg and Berlin to Munich and Interlaken and Zurich and throughout the entire transportation infrastructure of most of Germany. It is thus the world's largest, most complex, and most expensive high-speed network. ICE trains surpass everything running in travel comfort and service. They are environmentally friendly, fast, and safe.

For the first time on June 2, 1991, travelers rode ICE1 trains in regular high-speed service on new track between Munich—popular travelers' destination, home of Fasching and the Oktoberfest, the "World

City with Heart," capital of Bavaria in the south—and the Hanseatic city of Hamburg in the north.

By making the ICE1 slightly wider than conventional trains, GermanRail could allow travelers to ride more comfortably. Instead of 111.2 inches, the width of GermanRail's early '90s InterCity carriages, GermanRail made the ICE1 118.9 inches wide. Couple that with a more generous salon seat area than in a French TGV (12.9 square feet versus 9.7 square feet in first class; 9.7 square feet compared to 6.5 square feet in second class)—and passengers are elated. Also, dining cars, toilets, and compartments are larger and more comfortable.

Ironically, this widening and lengthening subjected GermanRail to great criticism within Germany when the German public realized that their expensive ($30 million each) new domestic ICE1s were just that: domestic. The trains were too wide, too long, and not equipped to cope with differing electrical power supplies in neighboring countries. ICE1's range beyond Germany was limited to Switzerland.

The ICE1 trains are a great success. Frankfurt/Main and Stuttgart became 90 minutes apart by ICE; Hanover and Munich, a little more than four hours. ICE trains via Fulda between Hamburg and Munich take only five and a half hours. But ICE1's overhead cost is high and for some connections the train is too long. Therefore the 368-seat, 1996 second-generation ICE2 trains were made shorter and lighter, but remain wide and limited to domestic electrical supplies. ICE2s consist of one locomotive and seven carriages instead of two locomotives and up to 14 carriages. When DB needs high capacity, it couples two ICE2s, which are like half ICE1s, together with an automatic coupler but separates the two halves quickly at a station and sends them to different destinations. They make DB's timetable more flexible. ICE2 went into service in September, 1996, on the line between Hamburg and Frankfurt/Main.

The 1999-2000 member of the ICE family, the ICE T, and the 2001 ICE TD, use tilting technology to gain higher speeds over the old tracks, which have frequent curves. This technical innovation allowed DB to offer faster speed and greater comfort where laying entirely new tracks was not economic. Taking charge of the IC routes, these tilting trains take you along the slower lines that the DB has no funds to upgrade. You ride five-carriage IC Ts Stuttgart-Zurich and Berlin-Leipzig-Munich, and seven-carriage IC Ts Frankfurt/Main-Dresden. Both five- and seven-carriage IC Ts serve Dusseldorf-Berlin. From

2001, ICE TDs take you Hamburg-Copenhagen-Malmo and Munich-Zurich. They are able to maintain their speed around curves by using the same Fiat tilting system as the Italian Pendolino trains ETR 460 and ETR 470 (see "Italy" and "Switzerland" chapters).

By 2000, DB had increased the ICE network to seven lines stretching about 3,100 miles at ICE speeds and frequencies. The new ICE T improved Berlin-Leipzig-Munich and Stuttgart-Zurich travel. This radically changed ICE version, which has a regular top speed of 143 mph, is an electrical unit with five to seven carriages and no locomotive. The traction equipment is spread over the entire train. To comply with international restrictions, the shorter carriages are narrower than ICE1 and ICE2 by 2.8 inches, which is still wider than the early '90s InterCity carriages. ICE T and ICE TD have more pointed noses with a new window arrangement so that the passengers in the first and last carriages can look out through the cabin. Like the ICE2, two trains can be coupled together.

You will ride the ICE3 on the new high-speed line between Cologne and Rhein/Main that began construction in 1995, and between Amsterdam and Frankfurt/Main, and Paris and Frankfurt/Main. Thirteen ICE3 trains are equipped with multivoltage power equipment to allow them to range internationally throughout Europe.

While ICE high-speed lines were being financed and laboriously constructed, GermanRail engineers approached the design of their first-generation high-speed trains with admirable scientific method. First, engineers built a full-size "InterCity Experimental" train, a research and demonstration tool; loaded it with sensors and recorders; tested it under various conditions of speed, track condition, weather, and loading; and evaluated every significant variable.

These tests led to two important developments in train design technology and provided a firm basis for ICE1's final design and cosmetic appearance.

• Depressurization caused by high speeds in tunnels had to be considered unacceptable.

Depressurization of the InterCity Experimental train while racing through tunnels caused riders to complain. (Engineers recognize the Bernoulli effect at work.) GermanRail's new trains had to be made pressure tight. It was a blow, especially because the Landrucken tunnel lies on the line chosen for ICE1's inaugural run. It meant not only sealing ICE1's windows, doors, and ventilation, but redesigning its closed toilet systems.

• A wider train would ride more efficiently.

Serendipitously, engineers found they could increase ICE1's width.

• Cosmetic changes would increase the marketing appeal of the train.

The rounding of the nose of the power car was given a sharper radius to reduce its drag coefficient and improve its appearance. A grill introduced between the headlights ventilates the drivers' compartment.

The drivers' cabin is celebrated as a haven for railfans and government ministers making publicity trips. It was redesigned to make it more photogenic and functional.

Sensationalism fell from the ICE1 when FrenchRail's TGV Atlantique began setting new world speed records one after another (the last was 320 mph on May 18, 1990), surpassing the earlier ICE speed record of 253 mph. It became apparent that first running of a 155-mph ICE1 in Germany two years after implementation of 186-mph TGV Atlantique service in France would no longer be considered by the world as a breakthrough, but rather the heart of Europe catching up.

A funny thing happened on the opening of the 60-mile segment between Wurzburg and Fulda that cut a half-hour off the normal travel time between Munich and Hamburg and set the tone for GermanRail's ICE network. The train paused and the rear vestibule became packed with German travelers peering out the exposed rear window, chattering all together and repeating details they had just read in GermanRail's on-board magazine.

It pulled up the ramp specially built with two parallel pairs of strong rails and concrete sleepers onto an overpass and into the Rossberg tunnel. Suddenly, it seemed to spring over the southern segment of the Wurzburg-Hanover high-speed stretch past new fences and flourishing saplings bordering the route. It didn't seem as though it were traveling so fast—there were no roads or houses and very few cows to stare at it—until it passed another train flying in the opposite direction that disappeared into a speck before a cow could swish its tail.

The high-speed section north of Wurzburg, where GermanRail set the former world rail travel speed record with important ministers aboard, shoots you from tunnel to tunnel—from the Rossberg to the Muhlberg to the new Landrucken, now GermanRail's longest (6.7 miles). Above the tunnels the gracious thick forests do not appear to mind the velocity beneath. In the tunnels, you just see lights flying through the blackness.

Construction of these tunnels and placing rails between gently sloping embankments helped DB solve troubling environmental issues, particularly noise pollution, a major concern of German environmentalists.

German landscape architects also planted grasses and trees alongside the new tracks, not only to protect the earth from erosion, but also to provide habitats for birds and small wildlife. Native hazelnut, rowanberry, and fragrant wild roses require little care and complement the existing ecological system.

All ICEs have a quickly identifiable look because of the continuous level of reflecting windows. They look streamlined even when standing still. All conform to the color codes of the GermanRail: GermanRail-red and pink with a gray-white background. Lavender horizontal striping below the noses of the power cars at each end make them appear more streamlined. Prominent gray "ICE" letters identify each side.

ICE1's 12 aluminum-body middle carriages include four first- and six second-class cars, a specially fitted carriage, and a dual-service dining car called a "BordRestaurant." Riding first class reminds you of riding in a modern, five-star hotel, because of the spaciousness and deluxe furnishings, but riding second class is a significant step down because the carriages are so popular that you lose the chance to wander about, admiring this and that, such as the vacuum-emptied WCs; the elaborate telephone booths with portable telephones designed to work without interruption even in the many tunnels punctuating the lines; 30 seats featuring small, flat, LCD color screens; individual jacks and controls for earphones; the computer readouts in the vestibules alternately announcing your route, carriage and train number, coming stop, your current speed in kilometers per hour, and the time of day; the free private lockers for purses, briefcases, cameras, and day packs (take the key with you); the coat closets breaking the potential monotony of large interiors; and above all the marvelous BordRestaurant.

Push the buttons to enter. The doors close automatically behind you. The LCD display shows you whether you are in second or first class. The tinted windows give a cool appearance, but you see that what appears to be a continuous, mirrored window line from the outside is merely a clever cosmetic touch. In reality, the extraordinarily long windows corresponding to two rows of seats are indeed separated and provide spaces to hang coats. It strikes you immediately that you are in a *big* train. As you walk through the wide aisle, the doors open and close automatically and crossing between the carriages is as safe as a baby's crib.

ICE1's BordRestaurant is a revelation. Waiters from a central kitchen crammed with stainless-steel, high-tech equipment and microwave ovens serve a selection of German and European meals, with wine selection, to the travelers in the sit-down, white-tablecloth dining room on the end adjacent to the first-class carriage. In the other dining room, adjacent to the second-class carriage, travelers gather in the "BordTreff" at formica tables, bunching around a German Stehbar. Draft beer is the product of choice (as you can tell by the laughter), but snacks are also available to eat at benches around the side in the casual, self-service bistro-style cafe. Bright modern pink, blue, and white interiors with beechwood fittings and large semi-panoramic windows have recessed lighting, and—almost like an atrium—raised ceilings with futuristic latticework to shield direct sunlight. With rooflines higher than the rest of the train, ICE's BordRestaurants recall the panorama of the former TEE Rheingold observation cars, and give you an airy, spacious feeling. You cannot smoke in either the dining room or "BordTreff." More than 77 percent of those surveyed preferred no smoking.

The ICE2s are shorter and lighter than ICE1s, but remain wide and limited to friendly electrical supplies. They consist of one power car, seven carriages, and a driving trailer instead of two power cars and up to 14 carriages.

Riding ICE2s, you realize they are an efficient, swift way to get you from place to place at the fastest-feasible speed. ICE2 is clearly the more cost-effective train that accountants prefer and yet comfortable to ride. They are like half ICE1s. When DB needs high capacity, it couples two together. While you sit in your seat, ICE2's automatic couplers separate the two halves quickly and send you to your desired destination.

Except for the couplers, ICE2's power cars are otherwise interchangeable with the ICE1's so as to give DB complete fleet flexibility. Their length (67.5 feet), operating power (4,800 kW) and maximum speed (174 mph) are the same, while the weight is slightly less (86 tons). Most mechanical and electrical components are also the same.

You probably won't realize you have boarded one of GermanRail's ICE2 trains instead of an ICE1 until you take your seat. Both ICE1 and second-generation ICE2 have the same red-striped white livery and the same distinctive semicontinuous line of reflective windows.

In addition to the ICE 2 being shorter, a careful observer will see that the new generation's front headlights rise much higher, changing the appearance noticeably. Under nose doors you can detect the automatic couplers that make ICE2 special.

You won't need a seat reservation ticket, so when you board, be sure to check the electronic destination indicators outside. These indicators are essential for a train that splits. You don't want to suddenly find you are on the train to Dusseldorf when your friends are waiting in Cologne.

Once you find your seat (reserved seats are indicated by electronic displays which replace the paper reservation slips in most trains—rail pass holders don't need reservations, but you don't want to sit in someone's reserved seat), you are disappointed when the first thing you notice is that the newly designed seats are less substantial than those of the ICE1.

DB figured out a diabolical way to arrange seats more closely together without crimping your leg- or elbow-room. This way they can pack more paying passengers into an ICE2.

Although the seats are clearly less substantial, DB's spin doctors explain eight ways the new seats are more comfortable, including the fact that you can manually recline the first-class seats (but not the second). Console yourself that at least you have a footrest.

ICE2's designers squeezed out even more places to sit by minimizing ICE1's gracious wardrobe/luggage locker spaces and eliminating the popular six-person compartments. Both first- and second-class ICE2 sections are arranged around a wide central aisle, partly in rows, partly around tables.

At all fixed tables, you can plug your laptop computer into European two-pronged electrical outlets mounted below the windows. Many passengers take this opportunity to work en route. All other seats have outlets for earphones to hear audio music. At 72 seats, you can also watch video programs. You can pull down the sunscreens in the windows.

There are two restaurants in two ICE 2s coupled together, and your walk to a restaurant is shorter, so you won't object to their smaller size.

Seating is limited in the restaurant section. Eight tables seat 23, but the gray, polka-dot decor is quite pleasant and the ceiling, although lacking the striking atrium roof of the ICE1, is attractively contoured.

The Bistro sections are separated from the restaurants by a kitchen, as in ICE1s. ICE2 tried Zeolith-based, ecologically friendly refrigerators, but they didn't take long to break down. DB had to replace them with old-fashioned technology.

The new Bistros will disappoint you. You have no place to sit and only two stand-up counters at which to snack. DB expects second-class passengers to take their food to their seats. The space went to the relocated conductor's compartment and a toilet for the disabled.

The ICE T, DB's third-generation ICE train, made a highly successful debut over the curving tracks between Zurich and Stuttgart on May 30, 1999. It tilts.

DB's tilting mechanism is not the only thing that makes the ICE T radically different than earlier ICE trains. DB distributed the power equipment throughout the train rather than having a locomotive/power car as in the conventional trains.

ICE T's new exterior design is much more sleek and stylish than the previous generations and interiors are some of the most luxurious seen in trains in recent years.

The Zurich-Stuttgart ICE T consists of five carriages, one first-class with lounge, three second class, and one with a cafe plus second-class seating. The ICE T is exciting to ride because lounges in front for first-class passengers and in back for second-class passengers allow you to look over the driver's shoulder at the views he sees ahead. This new perspective is possible because there is no locomotive.

Your impression of the interior of the ICE T is compelling. The lounges front and back are the most startling innovation of the ICE T, but the reclining bucket seats of black leather in first-class will catch your eye. They give you the impression you are racing in an expensive sports car and make your speed seem faster.

In the lounge area there are six seats behind the driver, who is separated by a glass panel, so that you not only have views to the sides, but straight ahead through the wraparound driver's window. You also have the view of the driver who sits in the center of the cockpit because in Switzerland the trains run on the left, while in Germany they run on the right.

The flooring is matching gray carpet. The doors fly open on approach, triggered by sensors in the carpet. The foldout tables are handsome wood veneer. The windows of the ICE T are large, and make the train seem more airy. Sunscreens pull down manually.

Those first-class seats without tables are arranged in rows with video screens facing the passenger for German-language movies. In the center of the carriage are three four-person compartments with glass doors that may be closed. Electrical outlets for notebook computers are located at every seat.

ICE T's high-tech extends even to the reservations markings. Paper slips have been replaced with electronic indicators. LCD screens in the vestibules display not only the next stop, but on which side to exit.

ICE T has a children's play area. It's not large, but it is large enough for children to romp and do what children do. The advantage for other passengers is that it has a glass door that shuts to shield passengers from the inevitable screams and shouts.

Second-class is of course more conventional. Seats are dark blue moquette arranged two-opposite-two; the flooring is carpeted.

In both classes you have no trouble finding a place for your luggage. In addition to the usual above-seat shelves, there are coin-operated lockers at the ends of carriages. In one carriage you can use an open luggage rack with devices to attach to your luggage to prevent its theft.

Every ICE T has either a cafe (*BordBistro*) or restaurant (*BordRestaurant*), and where the five-carriage ICE T fails is the quality of the dining facility. Whereas Cisalpino devotes a full carriage to the best and most tasteful dining area to be found on the trains of Europe, the five-carriage ICE T has only a token cafe with no seats. It provides only places to lean while using four oval stand-alone tables.

Some carriages in the ICE T have been fitted with repeaters to enhance cellular telephone communication. Use of cellular telephones in the other carriages is discouraged. The cellular-friendly carriages are No. 28 (first-class) and Nos. 21 and 23 (second-class).

Certain ICE Ts have a bicycle room, but because of limited space, bicycle take-along should be reserved in advance at phone 01803-194-194.

ICE3 debuted on November 5, 2000, when DB's multivoltage, third-generation InterCity Express Train, dubbed "ICE International," began to take you between Amsterdam and Frankfurt/Main every two hours. The trains are staffed by combined German and Dutch teams.

ICE3 is the latest, and crown, of the evolution of high-speed and comfortable ICE trains DB offers visitors. It is rated at 205 mph maximum speed, but running at normal line speeds between Amsterdam and Frankfurt/Main, it isn't permitted to go full throttle. It won't show its full power until it debuts on the new high-speed line between Frankfurt/Main and Cologne in 2002.

ICE3 is a complete break from the design of ICE1 and ICE2. Power equipment is distributed throughout train. The driving cars are powered, but do not have pantographs, which are placed on intermediate carriages to accommodate the roller-coaster running of the high-speed line through the Taunus hills with steep gradients. ICE3 appears similar to ICE T, but with a sharper front end. Its posh interior, with 136 leather seats in first class and 244 dark blue moquette seats in second, light woods, and brushed metal fittings, is almost identical to ICE T's interior.

The ICE Generation

	ICE 1	ICE 2	ICE 3	ICE T	ICE TD
Year	1991	1996	2000-2001	1999-2000	2001
Number of Trains	59	44	50	43	20
Carriages	12	7	8	5-7	4
Power Cars	2	1	0*	0*	0*
	Electric	Electric	Electric	Electric	Diesel
Length, feet	1,174	672	656	436-607	351
Seats	673	391	404/415	250-381	195
Top speed	174 mph	174 mph	205 mph	143 mph	125 mph
Power	9600 KW	4800 KW	8000 KW	3000-4000 KW	1700 KW
Extra			13 multi-voltage	Tilting	Tilting
Routes	Hanover-Wurzburg	Berlin-Hanover	Cologne-Rhein/Main	Curving	Curving

* Power distributed below carriages.

Rollin' on the Rhine
Lured by a Siren's Song

The Rhine River is squeezed down to one-third its width. The Lorelei towers 430 feet above you. You feel the rock's magnetism and almost hear the beautiful Lorelei's singing attracting fishermen and causing their deaths on those rocks and cliffs close to the prow of your white steamer.

The quiet of your waterway's west bank is constantly pierced by shrieks of trains racing along GermanRail's west bank line below castles and above barges. On the east bank freight trains and passenger trains rumble between the wine villages dotting that shore.

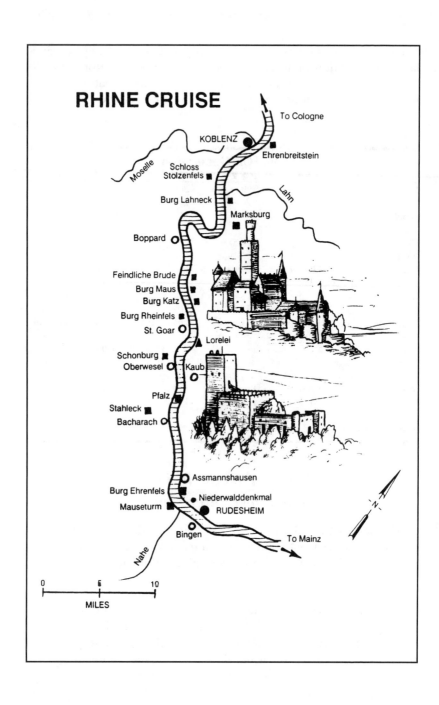

RHINE CRUISE

To Cologne

KOBLENZ

Ehrenbreitstein

Moselle

Schloss
Stolzenfels

Burg Lahneck

Lahn

Marksburg

Boppard

Feindliche Brude

Burg Maus

Burg Katz

Burg Rheinfels

St. Goar

Lorelei

Schonburg

Oberwesel

Kaub

Pfalz

Stahleck

Bacharach

Assmannshausen

Burg Ehrenfels

Niederwalddenkmal

Mauseturm

RUDESHEIM

Bingen

Nahe

To Mainz

N

0   5   10

MILES

Traveling by train along the west bank of the Rhine, studying the scenery from above the river, epitomizes relaxing train travel at its finest. Every once in a while a hilltop jewel sparkles into view, but trains will be rerouted and you will not be able to do this conveniently when DB opens its new high-speed line between Cologne and Rhein/Main in 2002.

Luckily for you, your cruise from Koblenz to Mainz is even better. It gives you time to savor the beauty of this river. Vater Rhein, Europe's busiest waterway, carries a constant stream of barges and passenger ships, including the KD German Rhine Line steamer you are riding without charge courtesy of your rail pass.

You are participating in Eurailpass's most beloved bonus, also available to holders of Europasses, Eurail Selectpasses, and GermanRail Passes. Rail-pass holders ride free on the KD German Rhine Line (Koln-Dusseldorfer Deutsche Rheinschiffahrt) making regular runs between Cologne and Frankfurt/Main. Just show your pass when boarding. No boarding pass is required.

Dusseldorf and Mainz are the end stations, and the complete run downstream takes 10 hours, but you see the most scenic parts making a 5 1/2-hour trip upstream (or 3 1/2 hours downstream) from Koblenz to Rudesheim. You sail past the Lorelei, the Rhine gorge, dozens of world-famous castles, and through the Rhine's most scenic region.

You have little trouble making train connections on either end.

It is best to make the cruise on a sunny day. In the morning the west bank presents portraits for your camera and in the afternoon the east bank puts its historic castles in the right light.

When you commence this stretch filled with castles, it is useful to remember that the English word "castle" has two equivalents in the German language. You pass both "Burg," a fortified castle built for defensive purposes, and "Schloss," a palace which may or may not have been fortified and was usually the seat of royalty.

A good place to begin a trip upstream is in Koblenz, where the Moselle (Mosel) River flows into the Rhine. In front of the Koblenz Hauptbahnhof is a signboard/map illustrating the location of the various bus stops. You want to take bus line No. 1 to "Rheinfahre" stop, which shows an outline of a ferry. The bus runs every 20 minutes from across the street in front of the station (the round Tourist Office side) to the Deutsches Eck monument. The ferry dock is on Konrad Adenauer Ufer ("river bank") on the river below. Only when you are sailing upstream ("Rheinaufwarts"), walk 10 to 15 minutes directly east down the Markenbildchenweg to the "Rheinanlagen," KD's second landing on the Rhine. Ships sailing upstream call here five minutes after casting off from KD's main Koblenz landing.

Seamen release the ropes and your ship bound upstream steams against the current of the Rhine. Passengers scramble for chairs.

Huge Festung Ehrenbreitstein, atop the hill overlooking your vessel, is one of the strongest fortresses in Europe. The French captured it in 1799 only by starving out its defenders. The neoclassical architecture that you see today was added between 1817 and 1828.

Below the railroad bridge, you see orange-brown Schloss Stolzenfels with crenelated turrets and walls high on the west bank. Once a customs point for the city of Trier, Friedrich Wilhelm IV of Prussia had it reconstructed in 1825-45 for a summer residence.

At the confluence of the Lahn and the Rhine, you dock in Oberlahnstein, formerly a rich and important center because of its toll station and local silver mining. Burg Lahneck was built to protect it. Over the centuries this castle has collapsed into ruin, thus becoming an inspiration for Rhine Romanticists.

The best-kept castle on the Rhine, high above Oberlahnstein, is the Marksburg on a steep slate cliff 490 feet over the Rhine. It contains cannons, weapons, chastity belts, and a good castle inn. Nowhere else on the Rhine are the Middle Ages so well preserved as in the Marksburg. Now it is the seat of the German Castles Association and houses the largest collection of castle-related literature in Europe.

All high castles have one aspect in common: a lovely view. Long sight lines on the river were necessary to supervise the collection of tolls from passing ships and an overview of the surrounding lands and forests was necessary for protection from enemies.

A big curve in the Rhine takes you past Osterspay which is famous due to Schloss Liebeneck, high above on the east bank, erected around 1700 as a hunting and summer castle. You still see the original baroque forms despite the numerous subsequent alterations.

The barren hills are interrupted by lovely Boppard, a popular stopoff. Shortly, you see on top of the hills the castles of the Feindliche Brude. Legend has it that two arguing brothers erected ramparts between their castles. Since then the castles have been referred to as "The Hostile Brothers."

Passing Bad Salzig on the west bank in springtime is unforgettable because of its flowering cherry orchards. You sail back to the west bank below Burg Maus ("Mouse Castle"), one of the technically outstanding structures of its time. It was built in 1356 by the Archbishop of Trier. In 1806, it was partially destroyed and rebuilt between 1900 and 1909. St. Goarshausen, with partly intact city walls, on the east bank, is hemmed tightly below Burg Katz on a jutting cliff. The castle was built in 1393 by the Counts of Katzeneinbogen, one of the richest families in medieval Germany.

St. Goar back on the west bank is a pilgrim's center for the grave of St. Goar, who died in 611, below the Rheinfels ruins.

Burg Rheinfels is so close it seems you could reach up and rub the dust off the walls of its rambling terraces. This mighty ruin used to be the greatest castle on the Rhine. It was destroyed by the French in 1797.

Now you are below the Lorelei rock. When you pass the cliff, your captain plays a tape of Heinrich Heine's poem about the Lorelei virgin combing her golden hair and singing to lure sailors to the rocks. Now the song of the beautiful Lorelei is the best-known folk song of the Rhine. This is the narrowest spot of the river. In the water you see the rocks of the "Sieben Jungfrauen" (Seven Virgins) turned to stone.

In Oberwesel, on the west bank, you pass the homes of fishermen and Rhine sailors. It is a tiny and romantic place dominated by its fourteenth-century, red-brick Gothic Liebfrauenkirche (church), narrow and steep like a ship.

Schonburg castle is situated above Oberwesel. It was built in the twelfth century. At one time it served as an imperial castle. Today parts of it are used as an international youth hostel.

The five-sided customs fortress in the center of the Rhine upstream from Kaub, the "Pfalz," was completed in its current form in the seventeenth and eighteenth centuries. Its many pinnacles and little towers contain a naval museum. From water level it looks like a stone barge on the swirling Rhine. Following its restoration it was repainted in the old Gothic colors.

Above Kaub on the east bank, a friendly city profiting from slate quarrying, you see Burg Gutenfels (1200), one of the most important examples of defensive and living structures in the period of the Hohenstaufer. It is now used as a hotel.

Crossing again to the west bank you arrive in Bacharach, a village with 16 watchtowers and black-slate-roofed Burg Stahleck above. Burg

Stahleck, built in 1134, was destroyed in 1689. Beautifully rebuilt between 1925 and 1967, it serves as a youth hostel.

Eleventh-century Burg Nollig was erected upstream of Lorch as part of Lorchhausen's main fortifications. Ships which had to avoid the Bingerloch, the whirlpool on the Rhine, docked here for reloading of their cargoes onto smaller ships or for transportation overland.

You sail past the Mauseturm ("Mice Tower") on an island near the west bank. Since the rise of Rhine Romanticism, Mice Tower on a rock in the Rhine has become Bingen's emblem although it actually once was a customs house belonging to Burg Ehrenfels, the magnificent tower on the opposite bank. Later Mice Tower served as a signal tower for this once perilous stretch of the Rhine. Now that the danger of the Bingerloch, the whirlpool, has been alleviated, the tower merely serves to remind you of the story that Bishop Hatto, who fled here after burning starving farmers' barns, was eaten alive by thousands of rats who swam the Rhine and scaled the tower's walls to reach him. Since its renovation in 1972, you again see the Mauseturm in its medieval hues.

Where the Nahe River flows from the west into the Rhine, you stop in the wine village of Bingen, below Burg Klopp. The large KD Rhine Line landing at Bingen lies a quarter mile downstream from the Bingen Stadt train station and 0.6 miles upstream from the Bingen Hauptbahnhof/Bingerbruck train station. InterCity trains skim right past these stations but local trains take you leisurely to Mainz and Koblenz. Do not confuse Bingen Hauptbahnhof and Bingen Stadt stations. Use the latter.

Famous Rudesheim is an excellent village to stop over or to conclude your trip on the Rhine with a glass of wine on the famous Drosselgasse, a street only about 10 feet wide and 200 yards long, but resounding with the constant percussion of bands playing traditional oompah to modern music. Enjoy a free wine-tasting session at a celebrated winery. You will feel the Rhineland's "Frohsinn," gaiety, everywhere.

Be sure to top off your trip with a gondola ride up over Rudesheim's vineyards to the colossal Niederwalddenkmal, the neoclassical memorial on an outlook plateau 980 feet above the city, commemorating the unification of the German Empire after the 1870 defeat of the French. Born of national enthusiasm in an era fond of monuments, the proportions of the lady are equally optimistic. She is about 125 feet tall and weighs some 700 pounds. From her feet you see one of the top 10 panoramas in Germany.

Rudesheim's train station is well situated below the village near the east bank of the Rhine. From here the KD Rhine Line's landing is a 12-minute walk upstream on the path between the railroad tracks and the Rhine. You make train connections on the secondary line running along the east bank of the Rhine and into Mainz. Mainz is an excellent place to stay overnight. It is only 18 minutes to the Frankfurt/Main airport, it lies on mainlines served by InterCity and EuroCity trains, and you push your luggage carts to the hotels across the Bahnhofplatz from the station with no stairs to climb.

KD German Rhine Line sails frequently during July and August, less often in the spring and fall, and not at all between late October and late March.

KD German Rhine Line Summer Service
Upstream, Cologne to Mainz

COLOGNE (Rheingarten)	dep.						0930
Bonn	dep.	0945					1220
Konigswinter	dep.	1045					1320
Bad Honnef	dep.	1105					1340
Remagen	dep.	1135					1410
Linz am Rhein	dep.	1205					1440
Bad Breisig	dep.	1235	0815				1510
Bad Honningen	dep.	1240	0820				1515
Andernach	dep.	1325	0905				
Neuwied	dep.	1345	0925				
KOBLENZ	arr.		1055				
KOBLENZ	dep.		0900	1100		1400	1800
Niederlahnstein	dep.		0925	1125		1425	1825
Braubach	dep.		1000	1200		1500	1900
Boppard	dep.	0900	1050	1250	1410	1550	1950
St. Goarshausen	dep.	1005	1155	1355	1520	1655	
St. Goar	dep.	1015	1205	1405	1535	1705	
Bacharach	dep.	1130	1315	1515	1645	1815	
Bingen	dep.	1300	1440	1640	1810	1940	
RUDESHEIM	arr.	1315	1450	1650	1820	1950	
Wiesbaden-Biebrich	arr.			1840	2015		
MAINZ (Am Rathaus)	arr.			1915	2035		

Downstream, Mainz to Cologne

MAINZ (Am Rathaus)	dep.		0900	1000		
Wiesbaden-Biebrich	dep.		0920	1020		
RUDESHEIM	dep.	0900	1030	1130	1400	1620
Bingen	dep.	0915	1045	1145	1415	1635

Bacharach	dep.	1000	1130	1230	1500	1720
St. Goar	dep.	1045	1215	1315	1545	1800
St. Goarshausen	dep.	1055	1225	1325	1555	1810
Boppard	dep.	1140	1310	1400	1640	1850
Braubach	dep.	1210	1335	|	1710	1920
Niederlahnstein	dep.	|	1355	|	1740	1940
KOBLENZ	arr.	1300	1420	|	|	2000
KOBLENZ	dep.	|	1430	|	|	|
Neuwied	dep.	1410	1510	|	|	|
Andernach	dep.	1430	1530	|	|	|
Bad Honningen	dep.	1505	1605	|	|	|
Bad Breisig	dep.	1515	1615	|	|	|
Linz am Rhein	dep.	1540	1640	|	|	|
Remagen	dep.	1550	1650	|	|	|
Bad Honnef	dep.	1615	1715	|	|	|
Konigswinter	dep.	1635	1735	|	|	|
Bonn	arr.	1705	1805	|	|	|
COLOGNE (Rheingarten)	arr.	|	1945	|	|	|

Through the Valley of Hell
Cuckoo Clocks and Characteristic Houses

Your ride through Hell's Valley ("Hollental") is romantic enough for an archduchess on her way to her wedding. Marie Antoinette's advisors planned her carriage trip through this scenic valley in 1770, on her way from Vienna to Paris to marry the future King Louis XVI. She was 14 1/2 years old at the time. She was beheaded 23 years later.

When you travel on the Black Forest Railroad, you see the famous Black Forest houses, onion-dome churches, and even occasional cuckoo clocks. Its 62 miles from Offenburg to Donaueschingen take you over the crest of the Black Forest in an unusual series of loops. In the heart of the Black Forest you change to your connecting Hell's Valley ("Hollental") train, which justifies its name in only a few spots. Rail passes cover both.

When German railroad construction from Paris reached Freiburg, now the western terminus of the Hell's Valley train, dreamers talked of linking Paris to Vienna by train through Hell's Valley. On May 23, 1887, the Hell's Valley Railroad was opened—the first German State railroad with mixed cogwheel and adhesion traction.

It remained that way until 1933 when the cogwheels were taken out and special locomotives put into service on the steep stretch. The line

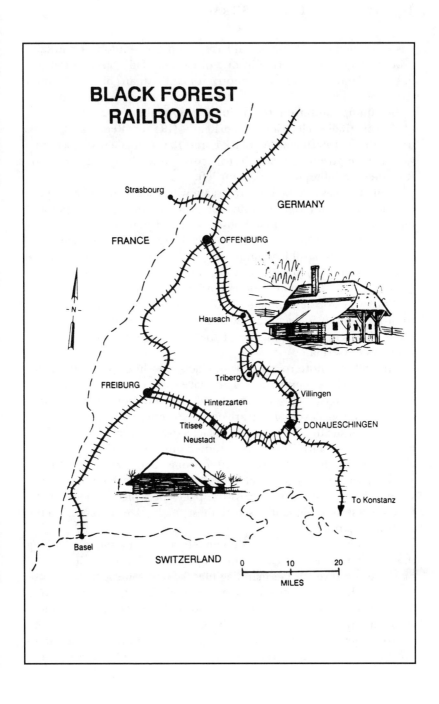

BLACK FOREST RAILROADS

Strasbourg

GERMANY

FRANCE

OFFENBURG

Hausach

Triberg

FREIBURG

Villingen

Hinterzarten

DONAUESCHINGEN

Titisee

Neustadt

To Konstanz

Basel

SWITZERLAND

0   10   20

MILES

- N -

was electrified in 1936 on a trial basis and patched into GermanRail's grid in 1960. Now you ride in one of GermanRail's Spartan railcars, but the landscape remains more romantic than on most other stretches.

Beginning south from the mainline at Offenburg (522 feet) in one of GermanRail's electrified InterRegio (IR) or Regional Express trains, the first stretch of the Black Forest Railroad takes you past vineyards, fruit trees, wheat, hops, corn, and below a dramatic Romanesque hilltop castle on your left.

While you pass along a pretty stream with fishermen in green jackets and hats on the right of your train, the hillsides grow steeper and more wooded and the first houses with red geraniums in window boxes appear. This is a sure sign the Black Forest is not far away.

The eye-catching gilded minute and hour hands and numerals on the brown-and-tan clock tower give Gengenbach (564 feet) a Black Forest gateway feeling. The newer houses tend to have long sloping roofs.

When you stop at Hausach (790 feet), the Black Forest store across from the station is decorated with multicolored baskets on a rope. From Hausach, you begin one of the most rugged and picturesque stretches in Germany.

The valley is more romantic with black-and-white cows in the fields and houses with gigantic roofs. They have eaves on four sides and balconies of hand-carved wood, front and back, but not the sides where the tentlike roofs overhang nearly to the ground.

Soon you see thatched, wooden Black Forest houses to your right— just like in the tourist literature—and an onion-shaped church belfry, also on your right. Some houses offer rooms to let: "Zimmer Frei."

The farms get bigger, the trees get bigger, and your climb gets steeper. You are traveling across the pages of a picture book of the Black Forest. It is pleasant to see all these textbook examples from the comfort of a train.

At Hornberg (1,260 feet), you come to a stop at a site overlooking the village and below a castle amazingly perched atop a hill. A small black, red, and yellow German flag flies from its tower.

Across the valley you see a cuckoo clock factory. Hikers wearing leather shorts and green knee socks and carrying walking sticks tramp through forests down the mountainsides.

Now it gets wilder suddenly. You pass through tunnel after tunnel— every one punctuated by screeches from the train's whistle. Read their conveniently placed names as you enter. Between tunnels, you have picture-postcard views of farms and forests.

Triberg's modern, new train station (2,020 feet) centers this watch- and clockmaking hub, which is the highlight of this stretch, smack in the heart of the Black Forest, and this is a good place to break your trip. Walk directly to the Black Forest Museum to enjoy quietly (except for the blasting mechanical organ) old local costumes, watch- and clock-making exhibits, and a working model of your Black Forest Railroad.

Back on your train, you continue to climb. You emerge from a long tunnel into a thick forest.

The Black Forest is more attractive than other woods not because the trees grow close together, but because they are evenly spaced, not wild. They are uniform, almost tailored, so they don't allow much light to fall except for a few spots of sunlight on the flooring of pine needles.

After you cross the summit you pick up speed. Although you aren't rushing, your pace seems breakneck compared to your slow ascent.

Past Sommerau (2,729 feet), the hills below you still have their wild look. Exiting the tunnel before St. Georgen brings a whole new experience. The surroundings are mundane, more developed, and modestly industrialized. The excitement and enchantment is over. By the time you descend to the large brown-brick, tile-roofed Villingen station house (2,309 feet), industry has sadly triumphed over the Black Forest.

In Donaueschingen (2,221 feet), change from your Black Forest train, which continues to Lake Constance, for the Hell's Valley train, beginning with GermanRail's sea-green Regional Express diesel railcar (direction: Neustadt) which takes you west again. You reenter the Black Forest. The trees grow stronger and stronger and surround your slick railcar as you glide downhill toward Hufingen (2,220 feet) in Hell's Valley. You are making a charming if not spectacular journey through forests, fields, and meadows to give you a second impression of a quieter Black Forest.

At Neustadt you join once more an electrified line to Freiburg and change from your diesel railcar to an electrified train to Freiburg. Your next stop, Titisee (2,814 feet), is your major stop on the Hell's Valley line. Titisee ("See" means "lake," although it's not visible from here) is the premier resort of the Black Forest. It is a hiker's and vacationer's paradise. On your right stand vacation homes; on your left forests trail down to the valley.

The segment between Hollsteig and Hinterzarten takes you up at a gradient of one foot for every 18 you pass. This is the third steepest segment in Germany using adhesion traction.

Hinterzarten (2,903 feet), a stylish mountain resort, is the highest point of the Hell's Valley Railroad, higher even than the summit of the Black Forest Railroad. You are surrounded by trees of every sort, leaves rustling in the breezes, hiking trails, and timbered houses. The air feels woodsy.

Downhill you travel through the thick of the Black Forest. It must be idyllic if Marie Antoinette passed here. You see trees, mountains, and many autos. Then you see nothing. You are passing through a tunnel. The conductor checks your pass. You enter two tunnels and pass Posthalde station without stopping. Then you reach another tunnel.

There are supposed to be nine tunnels between Posthalde and Freiburg, but it seems you pass at least a dozen. Many are very short and are possibly counted as underpasses. In GermanRail's list the shortest tunnel, Ravenna Tunnel, is 157 feet long, third from the crest. Maybe 150 or 125 feet is too short for DB's tunnel census.

By the time you reach Himmelreich (1,493 feet), you have left behind most of the heavy forest.

When you stop in Kirchzarten (1,286 feet), across from Gasthaus Alte Post, the kilometer markers show you have 11 km (6.8 miles) left to travel.

You travel through a broad valley; mountains surround you, rye and corn flourish, and you near Freiburg-Littenweller stop (1,040 feet) on the outskirts of Freiburg. Still in the Black Forest, you see red-tile roofs, gardens for pensioners, picnic grounds, and a sports stadium on your right.

Now you have 5.6 km to the main train station. But that didn't used to be true because the train ran through the middle of Freiburg. In 1934, the track was moved and the line rerouted in a loop around the city, thus adding another 1.4 kilometers to your trip. This meant all kilometer markers had to be changed, but the administration of the time skimped. It changed only the markers near its offices in Freiburg. When you reach Freiburg-Wiehre's green station house (918 feet), you come to kilometer marker "0."

By the time you arrive in Freiburg's Hauptbahnhof you have entered the "Twilight Zone." You have traveled on a line with a negative length. Look for the enameled, black-on-white kilometer marker: "-1.4," with numbers arranged vertically.

Freiburg (pop. 200,000), which is more fully known as "Freiburg im Breisgau" to identify it geographically, is a jewel of southern Germany. It was founded in the twelfth century by the Dukes of Zahringer. Its Gothic cathedral, octagonal tower, and dazzling market square make your visit here unforgettable.

The tourist office (Schwarzwald-und Freiburg-Informationen) is at Rotteneckring 14, a five-minute walk straight ahead from the station. It is open Mon.-Fri. 9:30 A.M. to 8 P.M., Sat. to 5 P.M., and Sun. 10 A.M. to noon. Go inside; there is also hotel information outside.

It was in Freiburg on May 4 or 5, 1770, that Archduchess Marie Antoinette said goodbye to Austria and entered France at Strasbourg.

Black Forest Railroad Service

IR	RE				IR	RE
0757	0836	dep.	OFFENBURG	arr.	0801	0917
0816	0904	dep.	Hausach	dep.	0741	0851
0825	0815	dep.	Hornberg	dep.	0732	0841
0839	0932	dep.	TRIBERG	dep.	0719	0826
0854	0948	dep.	St. Georgen	dep.	0704	0811
0903	1000	dep.	Villingen	arr.	0654	0750
0913	1013	arr.	DONAUESCHINGEN	dep.	0645	0743

IR trains and RE trains alternate departures every two hours approximately on the minute until 9 P.M.

Hell's Valley Train Service

0847	dep.	DONAUESCHINGEN	arr.	1010
0926	arr.	Neustadt (Schwarzwald)	dep.	0931
0931	dep.	Neustadt (Schwarzwald)	arr.	0925
0938	dep.	TITISEE	arr.	0919
1018	arr.	FREIBURG (Breisgau)	dep.	0841

Trains depart hourly approximately on the minute until 7 P.M. Change trains in Neustadt.

Medieval Germany by Europabus Castles, Romance, and Rococo

In the 1890s the city fathers decided never to build a train station. They expected iron horses to corrupt the ambience of their fair city.

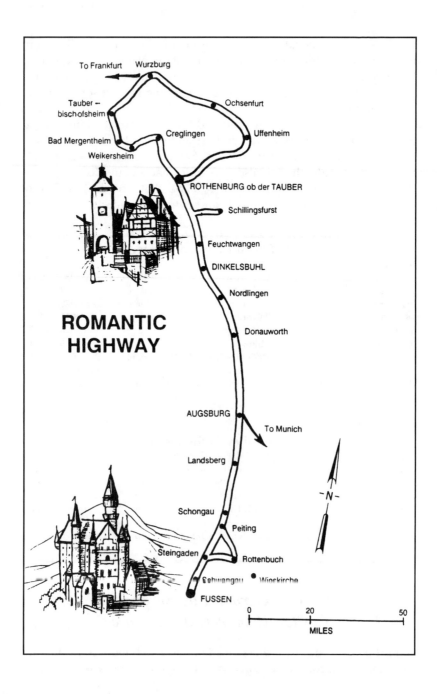

To Frankfurt   Wurzburg

Tauber –
bischofsheim

Ochsenfurt

Bad Mergentheim

Creglingen

Uffenheim

Weikersheim

ROTHENBURG ob der TAUBER

Schillingsfurst

Feuchtwangen

DINKELSBUHL

Nordlingen

Donauworth

**ROMANTIC
HIGHWAY**

AUGSBURG

To Munich

Landsberg

~ N ~

Schongau

Peiting

Steingaden

Rottenbuch

Schwangau   Wieskirche

FUSSEN

0   20   50

MILES

They wanted Rothenburg ob der Tauber (on the Tauber River) to remain the finest surviving medieval town.

This city, by law, remains as it was in the seventeenth century, after the Thirty Years War. The city council regulates progress so carefully that even house colors are set out in official government rule books. The householder with the prettiest window-box flower display wins a cash prize.

Travelers with even the slightest curiosity in seeing old gabled houses, Gothic roofs, oriel windows, fortress walls, fairy-tale watchtowers, cobbled streets, and graceful, flowing fountains make discovering Rothenburg top priority.

Take a local train to a small branch station outside the city walls, or better, travel to Rothenburg aboard a sea-green Europabus along the Romantic Highway or Castle Road. It is a cheap way when you hold a rail pass. You ride 75 percent off with a Eurailpass, Europass, or Eurail Selectpass. You ride free with a GermanRail Pass.

Romantic Highway and Castle Road Europabuses converge on Rothenburg after passing along the most scenic coach routes in Germany. Europabus is the network of long-distance motor coaches throughout most of Europe operated in association with the national railroad administrations. Their vehicles are Mercedes coaches with continuous windows and ample luggage space below. Passengers on the scenic routes are assisted by exemplary recorded announcements in English, German, and Japanese and by English-speaking guides giving personal directions.

Sorry, "Romantic" does not necessarily refer to boy meets girl. Instead, you feel a special romance—a nostalgic pleasure in half-timbered houses, restored ramparts, town gates, baroque cherubs, palace gardens, arching stone bridges over rivers, and royal castles implanted on steep, rocky slopes.

The Romantic Highway gives you the essence and spirit of picture-book Germany. It seems like the founders of the medieval villages deliberately lined up all the worthwhile sights of the region in order to show you everything without making you detour. They could not have done it better.

Your big, smooth-riding coach takes you through one charming village after another. Discovering Dinkelsbuhl makes the whole trip memorable. Nordlingen and Donauworth are wonderful surprises with their carefully preserved and colorfully painted Romantic structures.

The Romantic Highway and the Castle Road meet at Rothenburg ob der Tauber, giving you the option there of changing from one to the other there and starting or ending at popular cities on the octopus network.

You board southbound Europabuses in Frankfurt/Main, Wurzburg, Mannheim, or Heidelberg. Northbound, you travel from Fussen or Munich, where there is a Europabus office in the Hauptbahnhof. When your Europabus lets you off at Rothenburg's train station, don't be tempted to jump aboard the first departing train like most of the Asian tourists, their noses buried in their guide books.

Depending on your connection, you have one to one and three-quarters hour in Rothenburg to climb the Town Hall belfry, dating from the fourteenth century, and to walk along the wide city wall. First, head directly down the Schmiedgasse to see the Plonlein, the most photographed scene in Germany (and every photo is a gem).

Traveling south from Rothenburg, your bus gives you a 50-minute break in Dinkelsbuhl where renovators are multiplying the number of preserved medieval gems faster than a Pentium processor. On a good day you arrive at the Schweinemarkt, but alternately stop at the Stauffer Wall. Ask your guide for directions to the Deutsches Haus. You do not want to miss photographing this admired fifteenth-century gabled building which you see on the "Visit Germany" travel posters. In Dinkelsbuhl you choose either a Europabus to Fussen in the Allgauer Alps or one to Munich, the beer-hall city and bright spot of Bavaria.

Both routes pass Nordlingen, where the Bavarian Train Museum is open on Sundays from noon to 4 P.M. during the summer.

Your Europabus driver to Munich pulls onto the Autobahn at Augsburg, bringing you into Munich's Starnberger station next to Munich's Hauptbahnhof, but if you plan to change to a train, save time by getting off at the Augsburg train station.

The driver of the second Europabus south from Rothenburg continues through Bavaria to Fussen with distant views of King Ludwig's fantasy Neuschwanstein Castle. You pass the astonishing church in the Wies going south, but stop there northbound. Its breathtaking rococo interior makes it often mentioned as Germany's finest church. From Fussen, there are hourly Regional Express train departures to Augsburg or Munich until 11:05 P.M. Fussen's principal welcome is a nearby youth hostel.

The Castle Road between Rothenburg and Heidelberg is so-called because it connects red-sandstone Heidelberg Castle, heart of Romanticism, on one end, with the gray-granite Neuschwanstein Castle on the other, and features castles, large and small, around every curve of the Neckar valley (Heidelberg to Rothenburg). Board either in Mannheim or the "Student-Prince" university town, spend your lunch hours in Rothenburg, explore Dinkelsbuhl, and then join a Romantic Highway bus to Fussen or Munich.

When you want to tempt the rage of Rothenburg's city fathers, use the small, local railroad that is, in fact, outside of Rothenburg's city walls. Thirteen trains a day on weekdays (fewer on weekends) connect to Steinach, seven miles away, where you change for Wurzburg to join the ICE network. Bus service is sometimes substituted (covered by rail passes), especially on weekends. Be sure you check the timetable for the day you will be traveling, because bus connections are usually a few minutes different from train connections.

Make reservations at a Europabus office in Germany or by postcard or fax (to arrive at least three days before departure) to Deutsche Touring GmbH, Am Romerhof 17, D-60486 Frankfurt/Main (Tel. 069 790-3235, Fax 069 790-3219, *www.deutschetouring.de*). Indicate date, route, and number of seats you require. Seat reservations are free of charge, but you must pay a nominal registration and baggage checking fee for luggage. It includes insurance up to about $1,200.

Romantic Highway Summer Europabus Service between Frankfurt/Main and Wurzburg and Augsburg, Munich, and Fussen

0800		dep.	FRANKFURT/M (Hbf./Sud)	arr.		2030
1000		dep.	WURZBURG (Omnibusbf.)	arr.		1845
1035		dep.	Tauberbischofsheim	dep.		1755
1045		dep.	Lauda-Konigshofen (Rat.)	dep.		1745
1100		dep.	Bad Mergentheim (Bf.)	dep.		1730
1245		arr.	ROTHENBURG o.d.T. (Bf.)	dep.		1615
1430		dep.	ROTHENBURG o.d.T. (Bf.)	arr.		1450
1510		dep.	Feuchtwangen (Omnibusbf.)	dep.		1415
1525		arr.	DINKELSBUHL (Schweine.)	dep.		1400
1615	1530	dep.	DINKELSBUHL (Schweine.)	arr.	1245	1245
1657	1615	dep.	Nordlingen (Rathaus)	dep.	1205	1215
1730	1645	dep.	Donauworth (Kirche)	dep.	1115	1115

1835	1800	dep.	AUGSBURG (Hbf.)	dep.	1000	1035
1850			arr.	MUNICH (Starnberger Bf.)	dep.			0900
	1950	arr.	Schwangau (Verkehrsburo)	dep.	0810		
	1955	arr.	Hohenschwangau	dep.	0807		
	2005	arr.	FUSSEN (Bf.)	dep.	0800		

| —Does not travel this route

Castle Road Summer Europabus Service
Mannheim-Heidelberg-Rothenburg

0730	dep.	MANNHEIM (Hbf.)	arr.	2110
0800	dep.	HEIDELBERG (Hbf.)	arr.	2040
0822	dep.	Neckargemund (Bf.)	dep.	2018
0845	dep.	Eberbach (Neckaranlagen)	dep.	1955
1045	dep.	Heilbrunn (Marktplatz)	dep.	1835
1145	dep.	Schwabisch Hall (Busbf.)	dep.	1725
1330	arr.	ROTHENBURG o.d.T. (Bf.)	dep.	1615

Berlin
High-speed Metropolis

DB honors Europasses, Eurailpasses, Eurail Selectpasses, and German Railpasses, so that you can get to and from Berlin without trouble using either a regular train ticket or a rail pass. Further, passes and train tickets are also valid for travel on Berlin's S-Bahn (but not on the U-Bahn). You won't find it economic to validate a day box for inexpensive S-Bahn trips but you can use the S-Bahn during the days of your arrival and departure to travel from east to west or vice versa and/or to reach a residential quarter.

You ride DB's newest high-speed line, open in May, 1997, between Berlin and Hanover. Don't be disappointed at first in the key link in the European high-speed rail superhighway London/Paris-Brussels-Cologne-Hanover-Berlin-Warsaw-Moscow. Leaving Hanover's Hauptbahnhof, you're not yet on the high-speed line. Your ICE first travels 48 miles to Wolfsburg over merely upgraded line. Leaving urban Hanover at Hanover Berliner Allee, your ICE reaches 100 mph over the 10-mile stretch to the outskirts of Lehrte, but then cuts back to 75 mph to traverse a complicated junction. From Lehrte through Gifhorn to the outskirts of Wolfsburg, you peak at 124 mph. At last you enter the flat, 98-mile stretch

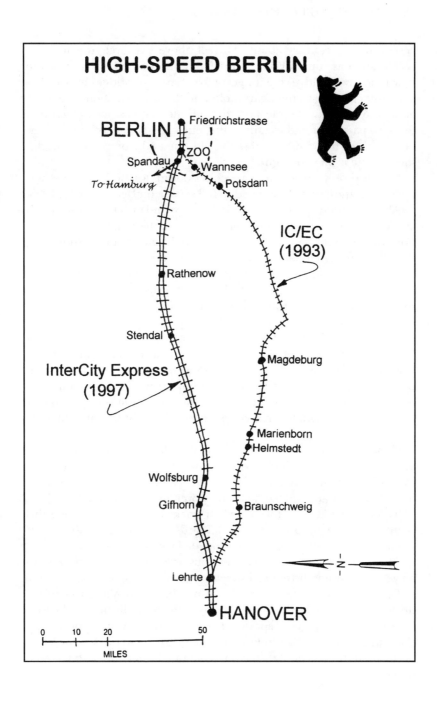

HIGH-SPEED BERLIN

BERLIN
Friedrichstrasse
ZOO
Spandau
Wannsee
To Hamburg
Potsdam

IC/EC
(1993)

Rathenow

Stendal

InterCity Express
(1997)

Magdeburg

Marienborn
Helmstedt

Wolfsburg

Gifhorn
Braunschweig

Lehrte

HANOVER

N

0   10   20   50
MILES

across marshy country about 180 feet above sea level. You feel the acceleration as your ICE bursts to 155 mph. At Stendal you cross the new Elbe River bridge, the longest of the series of bridges over canals and rivers parallel to the nearby, old line that you see about two miles away on your left. The old line through Stendal has been electrified for local passenger and freight traffic, but a link connects it to the new line south of the city. You cross the old line and from here to Berlin the old line is on your right.

You stop only once before reaching downtown Berlin, at the new Spandau station that DB opened to full service on December 14, 1998.

About 12 minutes before you arrive in Spandau (check your watch and your on-board timetable), now east of Rathenow, be sure to take note of the expensive, high, weed-covered embankments squeezing your line through a flat, particularly marshy area.

This marks the Buckow Conservation Area and the habitat of a colony of great bustards, one of the rarest birds in Europe. They are so rare you will be hard-pressed to see one, and the embankments mean you seldom see birds of any kind.

Great bustards (Otis tarda) are one of the largest land birds in Europe, over three feet long. They are related to cranes and vaguely resemble skinny, flying turkeys. Citizens were concerned that 155-mph trains straight through the last breeding grounds of the bustards might offend the flying creatures and cause them some danger; in particular, environmentalists feared that bustards might be tempted to fly smack in front of speedy ICEs.

To shield the rare birds, DB and the Brandenburg state government agreed to build 10-foot-high earthen banks alongside the three-mile critical path in question with the idea that the banks would divert the birds' flight trajectory and induce them to fly over, not in front of, the ICEs.

The first banks were formed when track construction reached this point, in fall 1995, to protect the bustards from heavy equipment. It was agreed to build them higher as needed when the trains began running, depending on reactions of the bustards, and even then to probably run the trains at reduced speeds.

Construction of the banks was suspended from May to October, during the bashful birds' breeding season, to avoid disturbing the love habits of the endangered species. The German government picked up the additional cost, $45 million, or about $1.3 million per bird. DB pointed out that it could fly the birds out one by one to save taxpayers' money.

In a 2000 announcement, DB reported that the population of the large birds had increased from 16 to 37 since the beginning of work on the line. Evidently, bustards are prevailing over the multiplying foxes in the area, which have been vaccinated against rabies and pose a threat to the bustard population.

By Dallgow you feel Berlin growing close, as you gradually slow and enter the greater Berlin metropolitan complex. After stopping at Spandau's new station, you cruise through Westend at 62 mph and meet Berlin's red S-Bahn trains running beside you. Now you wind your way along Berlin's Stadtbahn at 37 mph through Charlottenburg, Zoo, Friedrichstrasse, and Alexanderplatz stations to Ostbahnhof.

You complete your trip in one hour, 45 minutes, which is considerably better than the four hours that former InterCity trains required with stops along the way.

Before the Wall fell in 1989, there were 18 regularly scheduled trains and three seasonal trains between East and West. In 1990, there were about 200. Passenger traffic increased 600 percent. Earlier international trains were permitted to cross the border at three places. Now travelers cross at nine. May, 1991, marked the first publishing since the Second World War of a timetable combining all the states of Germany.

Travelers entering the Railroad Museum in Dresden couldn't miss the splendid map showing train connections as they were before the First World War. Berlin was the center of the German Railroad network. Links radiated like spokes across the entire empire as far as Konigsberg, which is now Kaliningrad in Russia.

After the Second World War, east-west connections withered, crossings were closed, Soviets tore down catenaries, weeds overgrew rails, and the West German Bundesbahn had to realign along new north-south routes.

At 8:48 A.M. on May 27, 1990, officials welcomed the "Johann Sebastian Bach" at Bebra and the first unified German InterCity train crossed the border to join both halves together with speedier, quality service. The second IC, the "Max Liebermann," connected Berlin and Hamburg in fall 1990 with nostalgic TEE equipment. The "Flying Hamburger" train began operation on May 29, 1997, between Hamburg and Berlin along mainline tracks GermanRail rebuilt at a cost of DM3.5 billion. It took six years to complete. (It is not appropriate to joke that the Flying Hamburger is the name of a fast-food outlet. Citizens of Hamburg, who are rightly called Hamburgers, have become thin-skinned with the jokes of their friends from Bremen and Lubeck and now often prefer to be called "Hanseats," after the Hanseatic League heritage of their city.)

The upgraded line between Hamburg and Berlin was project No. 2 of the transport infrastructure program for Germany dubbed "German unity." Conversion of the line to twin track and full electrification began in 1991 following the reunification of Germany even while the line continued to carry passengers. Engineers installed a modern signaling system to guarantee traffic safety at 100 mph.

German railfans anticipated at last beating the 1934 timing achieved by the legendary Fliegender Hamburger streamlined diesel train. The original Flying Hamburger was powered by Maybeck diesel engines that took it between cities in two hours, 18 minutes, which was the fastest service in the world in 1933. It is supposed that the Flying Hamburger's development at that time was used to subversively make and test engines for submarines because armaments had been prohibited by the Versailles Treaty at the end of the First World War.

Presently your fastest way to Berlin is aboard one of the high-speed ICE trains that made their first runnings to Berlin on May 23, 1993. These mesh with the integrated ICE network in West Germany, allowing you to reach any German city of size (and Switzerland, too) in record time (see ICE section, above).

Berlin Train Stations

The first railroad company in Berlin (to Potsdam, in 1838) built Berlin's first terminal, the Potsdamer Bahnhof. Until 1877 each new railroad company entering Berlin built its separate terminus. In 1882, the kaiser ordered 11 stations connected by an east-west line across the city center on a still-standing, elevated brick viaduct and this was known as the Stadtbahn. From west to east, these stations were Charlottenburg, Savignyplatz, Zoologischer Garten, Tiergarten, Bellevue, Lehrter, Friedrichstrasse, Borse (renamed Marx-Engels-Platz and now Hackescher Markt), Alexanderplatz, Jannowitzbrucke, and Schlesischer Bahnhof (renamed Hauptbahnhof in 1882, then Ostbahnhof, then again Hauptbahnhof under the communists, and now again Ostbahnhof).

As one of the federal government's reunification projects following the "Wende," Berlin's major trains stations were rebuilt and regional and mainline train traffic was reorganized. Mainline trains call at Zoo, Ostbahnhof, and Spandau mainline stations, while regional trains call additionally at Alexanderplatz and Friedrichstrasse regional train stations.

The Berlin Transit Authority called it "rejuvenation." Commuters used harder words. GermanRail and the Berlin Transit Authority spent about one billion U.S. dollars to modernize the 5.5-mile, two-track S-Bahn and parallel mainline stretches. Key S-Bahn stations were open to traffic over the "rejuvenated" tracks, but closed to long-distance travel. Workers installed escalators. Stations Friedrichstrasse and Alexanderplatz were realigned into regional train hubs. The original, estimated completion date was May, 1997. That was before workers discovered the unexploded World War II bomb embedded in the brick Stadtbahn foundation and specialists from the bomb squad had to be called in to search the whole length for more. Then engineers discovered during renovation that the 1882 bridge across the Spree River next to Friedrichstrasse station and the Bode Museum was not salvageable, and they had to completely tear it down and build a new one for $20 million. Meanwhile, electricians completely electrified the stretch between Zoo and Hauptbahnhof and engineers widened the track area and platforms. Friedrichstrasse station reopened in May 1999; Alexanderplatz station in spring 1998.

Bahnhof Zoo, which handles both mainline and S-Bahn trains, and S-Bahn trains in an underneath annex, was remodeled with DM 40 million. The structure was cleaned, relighted, and modernized stage by stage. Escalators and a travel center were installed.

Because Zoo Station is the center of the Zoo complex, you can't fail to find any possible service or shop in the station itself or nearby. In the station itself you find a bookstore, a restaurant, and snack opportunities of every sort. On the mezzanine there is a private hotel booking service, and look for the hotel reservations display of some 42 hotels with an accompanying map showing their locations. Inserts show pictures of the hotels, their prices for single and double rooms, what services they offer, and other details. Adjacent is a cluster of buttons that are either red or green depending on whether they are full or have rooms available. Using this information you can choose one suiting your location and financial requirements and call the telephone number shown in the insert rather than walk over to the tourist office and stand in line and pay their DM 5 service fee. The attached coin telephone takes three 10-pfennig coins.

Lockers in back of the station require DM 2 for 24 hours. Luggage carts standing on the platform require you to insert either a DM 1 or DM 2 coin to release them. There are elevators in back that you will have to search for. You get your coin back when you return your cart to a stand, but of course you can't make any money by inserting a one-Mark coin and hoping for a two-Mark coin to be returned.

The DB agent in the service center in the middle of the hall is available to answer quick questions only. The Reisezentrum is the place to go for reservations and ticket purchases, where you stand in lines, which move *very* slowly. For first-class ticket holders, including holders of Eurailpasses, Europasses and first-class GermanRail Passes, a special counter is open.

The toilets are called "McClean" and the troop of ladies responsible for the cleaning tries to live up to its reputation. To use McClean you will pay DM 1.50, except that men using only the urinals pay DM 1, and children relieve themselves without charge. Sooner or later in Berlin, probably sooner, you will be confronted by one of Berlin's take-no-prisoners Toilettenfrauen ("toilet women") who will demand 50 Pfennige or a Mark. Grin and bear it. It's their profession and they should be paid handsomely for working in such disgusting surroundings It's also cheaper than in some neighboring countries.

Euraide, an American-run operation, has a neat office in the rear of Zoo train station. Look for the Euraide Office down the corridor past the stairs to McClean toilets. Not only will they book your reservations and issue you train tickets in colloquial English, they will give you free information on getting where you want to go by train in Germany and guide you through the rail pass jungle (German Railpass, Eurailpass, Europass, Eurail Selectpass and InterRailpass). Further they will help you with low-cost accommodations in Berlin and steer you onto the right "Berlin Walks" tours in English. They are open daily during the summer 8 A.M. to noon and 1 to 6 P.M..

A five-minute walk out of the front of Zoo station leads you across the Kurfurstendamm to the Berlin Tourist Office in the Europa Center on Budapesterstrasse. (open Monday to Saturday, 8 A.M. to 11:30 P.M., and Sunday, 9 A.M. to 9 P.M.). Its branch is located at the Brandenburg Gate. The post office is across the street.

Despite extensive reconstruction, which was begun by the East German Railways before unification and not completed until 1992, Berlin's Ostbahnhof lacks charm. It is the terminus of the high-speed line to the west. Most long-distance trains originate here, and call at

Bahnhof Zoo and Bahnhof Spandau before branching to their destination. The station contains all facilities, with up-only escalators. S-Bahn trains use platforms 8, 9, and 10.

Mainline Train Station Bahnhof Spandau was inaugurated in September 1998, when the great, long ICE trains began make their first Berlin stops approaching the center of the city as they slowed from their high-speed rush along their new high-speed line. Bahnhof Spandau platforms were lengthened to accommodate the long trains and covered with glass arches to protect arriving and departing passengers from the weather. Inside you find all the functions you expect in a mainline train station—new ticketing counters and an information center. Regional trains supplement the high-speed trains and S-Bahn connections to Berlin neighborhoods.

Regional Bahnhof Alexanderplatz was built in 1880-82 out of glazed yellow-brown brick as a station for the new Stadtbahn ("City Railroad"), but you are hard put to see the early structure because of its 1994-98 reconstruction. After nearly four years of reconstruction from the ground up, politicians finally got their opportunity to make their speeches at the reopening of Berlin's historic Alexanderplatz train station on March 12, 1998.

Berlin Mayor Eberhard Diepgen said, "Alexanderplatz is the pulsating heart of Berlin. The new station is a symbol of the growing together of the city." The reconstruction was such a success that the station is easy and comfortable to use. Automatic doors fly open so wide that they seem to know you are towing a fully packed suitcase. The arch-covered through station is used by both S-Bahn and regional trains on elevated tracks. From this level you have interesting views through the windows on the south side on the close-by Television Tower and the activities on Alexanderplatz.

Underground, far removed from the elevated Alexanderplatz train station, U-Bhf Alexanderplatz is a junction of three S-Bahn lines. It is a complete, sprawling complex below Alex S-Bahn station.

Regional Bahnhof Friedrichstrasse has been completely rebuilt from the ground up into a regional train station. Opened May 1999, it shines. Alive with trains rumbling, it is a hub of huge activity. Passengers scamper freely back and forth, jumping aboard elevated regional trains and east-west S-Bahn lines, or up and down escalators to north-south S-Bahn and S-Bahn trains below ground. On the ground level autos and streetcars on busy Friedrichstrasse bisect the station.

Now that it's a beautiful station with every modern convenience, you have to use your imagination to visualize what it was like before the unification and Friedrichstrasse Station was the only possible rail crossing point between East and West. Visitors from the West had to pass a solid iron wall right in the station and undergo heavy scrutiny and painstaking security inspections to visit East Berlin. You got out of the train, clutching your passport, climbed down into an underground cavern, and took a number to await clearance by the Grepo, who manned the barrier. If you didn't understand German when your number was called, you were out of luck. You sat on a bench for a half-hour or more. You had to pass gray-faced border guards sitting behind bulletproof glass at several observation posts and surrender your passport to a succession of guards who studied it as if they were learning to read. They looked at it, looked at you, looked at the mirror in back of you, consulted a computer, took some mysterious notes, and eventually waved you on, always expressionless, without exchanging any talk. You had to have your film-loaded camera X-rayed. If you had a suitcase, guards passed it through a curtain to a back room for inspection. If you carried any Western books or newspapers, you had to leave them behind. You also had to exchange DM 25 at the official rate of one to one when you could get five times more on Alexanderplatz, but you could never find anything worthwhile to buy with them, so it didn't matter. And just when at last you thought you were finished with the inspecting and registering, you might be pulled out of line and taken to a small room for further interrogation.

Now you can't figure out where the labyrinth of guard posts and interrogation rooms might have existed. Everything is pastel.

Regional Bahnhof Lichtenberg's brick station building with glass front has been enlarged. You can transfer between S- and S-Bahn trains, but it is not convenient. The station has a bright interior and is large enough and well enough organized that right in the station you can make reservations and buy tickets to foreign countries and within Germany in the efficient "Reisezentrum." There are telephones ("Fernsprecher"), lockers, a drugstore, a McDonald's, and a traveler's shop. Train departures are printed on yellow posters; arrivals on white. Lichtenberg's upstairs Bistro cafe is nicely located in the "Galerie" mezzanine. Tip: It is most convenient to board DB's night trains here because you have time to settle in before the crowds board at Zoo Station.

Lehrter Bahnhof will be rebuilt into the largest train station in Europe by 2003. Platforms 50 feet below ground will be crowded with passengers on the new north-south traffic route that will run in tunnels below the Spree River, the new federal chancellor's office, the Tiergarten Park, and the new city quarter at Potsdamer Platz. New platforms rising 30 feet over the street will continue to carry mainline, regional, and S-Bahn trains in the usual east-west direction. An estimated 240,000 travelers daily will pass through the new crossing.

With trains newly routed on the north-south tunnel through Berlin's center, the mammoth new Berlin station at the site of the present Lehrter Bahnhof (the name of a city nearby) was widely believed to be renamed "Central Bahnhof." Not so, its name will be (drum roll, please) Lehrter Bahnhof.

Passengers boarding at the new train station will cross through the new two-mile-long north-south tunnel ending south of the Landwehr Canal. While the tunnel was being built, a 660-foot (200 meters) stretch of the Spree River had to be moved 230 feet (70 meters) north because the river bed was only three feet (one meter) above the new tunnel, making it too difficult to dig from below. The new tunnel will allow passengers to get on and off at stations along a nearly 5.5 mile (9 kilometer) travel corridor through Berlin's new Potsdamer Platz central area.

DB maintains ticketing offices in all mainline and regional stations such as Zoo, Friedrichstrasse, Alexanderplatz, and Ostbahnhof. Those under 26 should head for Wasteels Reisen (Pestalozzistr. 106, Tel. 312-4061) for single train trips. They sell young people round-trip and one-way tickets from Berlin to more than 100 destinations in West Germany and 4,000 destinations in Europe and North Africa at rock-bottom prices. Round-trip tickets are valid for two months while one-way tickets are valid for four days. You can make as many stopovers en route as you please within the time limits.

Getting around Berlin

In Berlin you are able to ride an extensive, integrated system of S-Bahn ("Subway") trains, S-Bahn, single- and double-decker buses and streetcars reaching from the East into the West. One ticket, valid for two hours, covers all.

Most of the U- and S-Bahn stops have escalators and/or elevators. Too many visitors tote heavy suitcases up flights of stairs because they don't take the time to look for the signs indicating the location of an escalator or elevator. There are usually local street maps in stations to help you find your way in the neighborhood. Look at the information *i*) bulletin board.

The transportation authority, BVG, operates the largest public transportation system in Germany. Anyone who has mastered getting around London or Paris will have no trouble in Berlin. By referring to the charts posted in all U- and S-Bahn stations, pasted to the walls of the trains themselves, available free from the BVG kiosk in front of station Zoo, and included in dozens of kinds of advertising material, you can move seamlessly from one line to another.

Berlin's public transportation has an amazingly simple ticketing system. There are three zones: *A*, *B*, and *C*. Forget all this and buy a Day Card, a Welcome (3-day) Card, or a 7-Day Ticket. They are remarkably cheap compared to single tickets.

Zone A covers everything you probably want to see, and includes all of the main train stations. Zone B gets you to the two outer airports, Tegel and Schonefeld. You can get as far as Potsdam in zone C.

With any ticket, you can take, without extra charge, up to three children under seven years with you. Bicycles are allowed on S-Bahn trains from 9 A.M. to 2 P.M., after 5:30 P.M., and all day Saturdays, Sundays, and holidays. There is a fare for bicycles, but buyers of some of the multiday cards below take their bicycles without additional charge.

A "Kurzstrecke" ("short-distance") ticket covers only three stations by U- or S-Bahn or six stops with bus or streetcar. A "Langstrecke" ("long-distance") ticket is valid for up to two hours in two zones so that you can change trains or buses in any direction, even run an errand and return to your starting point. A "Ganzstrecke" ("network") ticket is valid for two hours in all three zones.

A "Tageskarte" ("Day Card"), valid until 3 A.M. the following day, is a bargain. With your three children you can also take along a bicycle, a baby buggy and a dog. If you want to add a third zone, add DM 1,00.

The so-called Berlin Potsdam WelcomeCard is valid for 72 hours, covers all zones, three children, bicycle, baby buggy, happy pooch, and museum discounts and costs DM 29.00. Included with your Welcome Card is a booklet allowing you sightseeing discounts. Note that these discounts duplicate some of those granted by the Culture Card, so you may not want to have both cards at the same time.

Best transportation value of all is the "7-Tage-Karte" ("7-day ticket") valid up to midnight on the seventh calendar day. Lend it to your companion when you aren't using it.

The Welcome Card is available at U- and S-Bahn ticket counters, tourist offices, the Service Office at Tegel Airport, and many hotels. The rest are dispensed by the blue machines at the entrances of all stations and bus stops, including that at the Tegel Airport. A single two-hour ticket ("Fahrschein") is delivered already time-stamped. Insert all others for time-stamping into one of the orange automatic date/time/location validators at platform entrances.

Those visiting Berlin for extended periods can take advantage of a month- or year-"Umweltkarte" ("Environmental Ticket"), either standard or premium (so you can take your bicycle with you). Environmental tickets start at DM93/month. The similar month- and year-"Schulertickets" and "Ausbildungstickets" apply to those taking courses of study in Berlin or Brandenburg. Month- and year-"Seniorenkarten" apply to those over 65. Take your passport and one passport photo to BVG-Kundenzentrum (open Mon.-Fri. 8 A.M. to 6 P.M., Sat. 7 A.M. to 2 P.M.), at the top of the escalator at U-Bhf Turmstrasse. Those applying for student rates should also take their student I.D. The large, yellow BVG card is valid for 6 months, but each month you must affix a new stamp available from any ticket counter.

S-Bahn lines form an interwoven fabric so that by changing from line to line at interchange stations you can get anywhere in Berlin. Superimposed on this is the S-Bahn system. Getting from one place in Berlin to another takes more time than you expect. Berlin is big, but you can get to your destination with just one transfer from an S-Bahn train to an S-Bahn train and then to a bus or streetcar. Still, it takes a lot of time.

The Berlin S-Bahn network is one of the longest in the world. The first lines were opened in 1902 and included an elevated line on viaduct (now part of Line U1). The initial system was completed in 1930, and construction did not start again until 1953. Since then, several lines have been newly built or extended in West Berlin, and all of the lines in the West were modernized and therefore have been more efficient than the older S-Bahn lines. For visitors, the S-Bahn network in the West is centered on Zoo station, but you may change between S-Bahn trains at any of the many hubs throughout the city. Use the maps posted in the trains. In the East, Alexanderplatz and Friedrichstrasse are often used for changing.

The term S-Bahn used for Berlin's suburban electric railroad system is an abbreviation of "Schnellbahn" and not of "Stadtbahn." It's not true that all S-Bahn trains are old and rickety and run on square wheels. Some might seem that way, but there are beautiful new trains that coast into the stations with doors that open with a press of the button instead of having to tear them apart like Hercules breaking chains. The DR decided in 1921 to electrify its Berlin suburban lines. The first opened in 1924 and most were complete by 1930, replacing the steam trains. The badge was a white *S* on a green background, still used today. Further lines were electrified in 1933 and a north-south connection across the city, mainly in a tunnel, was completed in 1939. Several lines were interrupted by bombing raids in 1943, but most were repaired until the Red Army brought the system to a halt in April 1945.

The building of the Berlin Wall in 1961 sealed the system's fate as a crosstown transportation system. West Berliners boycotted the S-Bahn in their part of the city because it was run by the DR. References to the S-Bahn were deleted from signs at S-Bahn stations and bus stops. Only 5 percent of West Berliners used it for transportation. It became an issue in the Berlin 1981 elections. On January 9, 1984, operation of the S-Bahn in the West was purchased by West Berlin transit authorities and the number of travelers tripled from 50,000 to 150,000 daily.

At the Wende there were 239 miles (385 kilometers) of trains. The S-Bahn was split into 45 miles (72 km) in the West; 107 miles (173 km) in the East. The S-Bahn stretched 71 miles (114 km) in the West; 16 miles (26 km) in the East. Before the Wende it was only possible to interchange at the Friedrichstrasse train station.

Regional trains supplement the S-Bahn trains and take you into Berlin's suburbs. A transportation ticket or pass covering zone *C* will cover the entire local network, although only zone *B* coverage is required to Potsdam. Regional train departure times from Zoo station are shown on the mechanical departures board in the main hall.

The sea-green Regional Express (RE) trains between Potsdam's Hauptbahnhof, which opened on May 28, 2000, and Zoo station consist of well-used carriages that once did InterRegio service. Regional Express trains provide services up to 100 mph on trips averaging up to 31 miles at a minimum of two-hourly frequency. They provide fast, limited-stop regional services and consist of locomotive-hauled trains with older carriages repainted in IR sea-green livery.

Regional Bahn (RB) trains are also sea green and locomotive hauled, but are shorter trains. They are slower and cost less to ride. They cover local services with an average length of 18.5 miles, speeds of up to 62 mph, and at least two-hourly frequency. They contain space for bicycles. Traveling in either a RE or RB train, although far short of riding in an ICE, is faster and more comfortable than traveling aboard an S-Bahn, but the trains call at far fewer stations.

Berliners take their far-reaching, on-time and reliable bus network for granted. West Berlin is one of the few places in the world outside the British Isles where a large number of the buses are double-decked. Given the time, you see more while traveling by bus than S-Bahn, and in fact many routes save you time by not requiring you to make S-Bahn changes. On glassed-in bus stop walls and in most S-Bahn stations you find large Berlin maps showing the bus routes.

The 1997 Mannesman double-deckers have three side doors with the stairs in the far back. They are rarely so full that you can't sit in front upstairs and watch Berlin unfold before you.

Streetcars fill out the transportation network in the East the same way that buses do in the West. They are an effective way of getting to places located between S- and S-Bahn stations.

Electric streetcar history began in Berlin in 1879 when Dr. Werner von Siemens introduced the first electric streetcar at a trade show. The world's first electric streetcar went into service in Berlin on May 16, 1881. The line, about 1.2 miles (2 kilometers) long, ran from today's Lichterfelde-Ost station to the Kadettenanstalt. The 26 passengers sped through the city streets at 12 mph (20 km/hr). After 1896, electrification gradually replaced horses and the last horse-drawn streetcar was withdrawn on December 14, 1902. Streetcar traffic in West Berlin hit a low on October 2, 1967, when Line 55 ran for the last time to Zoo station. In the East, well-maintained, clean electric streetcars continue racing down the median strips through East Berlin on an extensive network of 30 lines getting you from Prenzlauer Berg to Kopenick. In the housing areas northeast of the center the services are provided by articulated vehicles built by Tatra in Czechoslovakia and are referred to locally as the "Tatra-Bahn."

Most subway and regular streetcar and bus lines stop running about 1-1:30 A.M. and don't start again until 4-5 A.M. (except Lines U12 and U9, which run 24 hours during the weekends). During this downtime the night bus system in the West and the night streetcar system in the East provide excellent half-hourly service from about 1 A.M. to 4 A.M.

Great Train Attractions

Through Anhalter Bahnhof, Europe's largest covered train station building, Sally Bowles made her grand entry into Berlin in Isherwood's *Goodbye to Berlin*. Built from 1875 to 1880, it could have contained Berlin's mammoth Congress Center with room to spare. The rail yards stretched for three miles through Kreuzberg. Each day saw 120 trains speeding to destinations like Constantinople, Brindisi, and Nice.

The station was severely damaged during World War II, but despite gaping holes in the roof, the walls remained sound and it was thought at the time that it would make an excellent museum. Despite the damage, trains continued running until May 18, 1952, when the surviving remains were destroyed by a surprise terrorist bombing for unknown reasons.

Except for the portico, which luckily survived the explosion, the station was razed in 1960-61. A trip via Anhalter S-Bahn station shows you merely the preserved brown-brick facade consisting of four columns and four circular windows, but it is worth seeing because of such decoration and detail as Corinthian columns, and you can try to imagine the station.

After you have seen the demolished Anhalter train station, visit the delightful jewel-box Wittenbergplatz S-Bahn station, Germany's first and finest. It has been brightly restored in Jugendstil as a historical monument.

The Deutsches Technikmuseum Berlin ("German Technical Museum in Berlin") is housed in a great, brand-new structure on the site of the former the Museum fur Verkehr und Technik ("Transportation and Technical Museum"), Trebbiner Strasse 9, Tel. 254-84-0 (open Tue.-Fri. 9 A.M. to 5:30 P.M., Sat.-Sun. 10 A.M. to 6 P.M.). The cornerstone was laid on March 27, 1996, but it wasn't completed until the year 2000. Berlin architects Helga Pitz and Ulrich Wolf have devised a low-energy building in which daylight and solar energy are used to optimum effect.

The museum is a favorite for Berliners and a delight for the technically minded, but those in search of art treasures or political history can better spend their time elsewhere. Partially set in the converted, overgrown freight yard of the former Anhalter Bahnhof, in the courtyard you see an original round table and a steam-driven snowplow locomotive. Included is an original arch salvaged from the Anhalter Bahnhof after its destruction.

The museum is crowded with families with children on Sundays, so it is a good idea to avoid going on this day. The signs are in German and occasionally English. Use U-Bhf Mockernbrucke, U-Bhf Gleisdreieck, which means "Rail Triangle," bus 129 or 248. U-Bhf Gleisdreieck is unusual because two S-Bahn lines are linked together by ramps. As you exit an S-Bahn station, look for the direction sign.

Inside the museum you see many classic automobiles; the copper-and-cast-iron 1904 fire engine; a 1922 Brennabor automobile, which could reach 45 mph (70 km/hr); a bizarre, finned 1921 Rumpler; and Germany's best-selling small car in 1924, the Grattawagen. There are radial air-cooled, six-cylinder in-line, water-cooled, and all designs of motors including a room-sized V-12 liquid-cooled motor used on a seaplane.

On the first floor is a technical exhibit of computers and calculators. The ancient bicycle exhibit featuring a wooden 1820 model will amuse anyone who has ever ridden a bicycle: two-wheelers with leather seats and carvings of horses on the front; bicycles made out of wood with removable, candlelit headlights; a Wanderhochrad ("touring high bicycle") from 1886; and an original 1818 hobbyhorse.

Filling the main hall is the greatest steam locomotive display of Prussian locomotives of various kinds, small and large, in the world. Side-by-side examples include a mammoth freight steam locomotive of the Austrian Sudbahn built in 1860, small 1903 colonial field locomotives, and an enormous ("gigantic" is not too tame a word) 1914 Prussian traffic locomotive P-8. All show years of hard usage. A Prussian S-10 Schnellzug ("Fast Train") has been arc-torch-separated away to display the steam-driven inner workings with each part marked in German explaining its function. You can walk in a clean trench below one train to study the undercarriage to get a feeling for the oil and grease that accumulates during service.

July 31, 1991, was the end of the line for Berlin's Magnetbahn after carrying 2.5 million passengers over 71,400 miles in two years. "End of the line. Station Gleisdreieck. Everybody out," a woman's voice announced over the loudspeaker.

Not far from the Technical Museum, S-Bahn station Gleisdreieck was the former terminus for the one-mile demonstration Maglev (magnetic levitation) line M-1 to Kemperplatz that was built by the German electrical firm AEG. The smooth-riding cars were outfitted like any U- or S-Bahn train; engineering interest was in the propulsion (although brake failures sometimes smashed up the realigned stations). The stations were dismantled at a cost of DM 10 million to allow reconstruction of the S-Bahn line connecting East and West Berlin.

The Museum fur Gegenwart Berlin ("Museum for Contemporary

Art"), Invalidenstrasse 50-51, Tel. 39-78-34-0, Fax 39-78-34-13 (open Tue.-Fri. 10 A.M. to 5 P.M., Sat.-Sun. from 11 A.M.) was opened on November 3, 1996, north of the Spree River and beside the Schifffahrtskanal ("Shipping Canal") in the Hamburger Bahnhof ("Hamburg Train Station"). The building, the oldest existing train station in Berlin, had been the terminus of the 180-mile (300-kilometers) stretch connecting industrial Berlin with port-city Hamburg. When traffic dwindled at the end of the nineteenth century, a new Traffic and Building Museum moved in. Hamburger Bahnhof was restored for Berlin's 750th anniversary in 1987 after it came to the West as part of the DM 3 million package that the West Berlin transport authority paid to take over the rundown S-Bahn system in 1984. The Hamburger Bahnhof, like the S-Bahn, had been owned by the East German railroads despite being situated in the West's Tiergarten District. The original purpose of the building is quickly revealed when you enter and see the high, glassed roof designed for steam engines and the slightly elevated areas that were boarding platforms.

The museum's international collection of Erich Marx is a multimedia artistic knockout. You are treated to dynamic art; specifically, art completed after the Second World War. There are wonderful exhibits, paintings, and multimedia, but nothing traditional. You see Andy Warhol's classic *Mao* and hear/watch *The audiovisual Joseph Beuys archive* contributed by the National Gallery. In addition to Warhol, representative work from Anselm Kiefer, Lichtenberg, Joseph Beuys, Robert Rauschenberg, and Cy Twombly enliven the walls and floor space. You find collections of Italian Transavanguardia and Minimal Art. Pride of show is Beuy's *The secret block for a secret person in Ireland*, which comprises 450 drawings.

Austria, Hungary, Slovenia, and Croatia

Smart Traveling on the Trains of Austria, Hungary, Slovenia, and Croatia

Austrian trains—Hungarian trains—Slovenian trains—Croatian trains—Vienna to Budapest—Austria's private lines and steam trains—Vienna's train stations—Getting around Vienna—Vienna's airport train—Budapest's train stations—Steam Railroad Museum—Using Eurailpass and Europass bonuses—Austrian Railpass—Hungarian Railpass—European East Railpass

Many of the trains serving Budapest and Vienna reflect the musical heritage of the Hungarian and Austrian capitals. When you board one of the five trains named after a Hungarian or Austrian composer, you hear a musical accompaniment in stations and on the trains themselves. While you watch the Bela Bartok arriving, you hear the charming "Evening in the Village." The Franz Lehar is greeted with the more up-tempo "Gold and Silver." The Franz Liszt leaves Budapest and Vienna to the strains of the "Hungarian Fantasy" and the Kalman Imre elicits music from the composer's "Gypsy Princess."

You reach Austria, one of the world's most beautiful countries, with a choice of 34 EuroCity and five EuroNight trains, including a EuroNight, to and from Austria's neighboring countries, plus Benelux. However some EuroCity trains call only in Innsbruck, not in the heart of the Austrian Federal Railroads (Osterreichischen Bundesbahnen, OBB, *www.oebb.at*) and several travel between Munich and Switzerland, picking up passengers only in Bregenz en route. OBB's flagship EC Transalpin with the first-class Swiss panoramic carriage takes you between Vienna, Linz, Salzburg, Innsbruck, Zurich, and Basel. It has been the fastest connection between Switzerland and Austria since 1958. Transalpin's carriage with the Teddy bear drawing is the children's play carriage.

Most travelers discover Vienna before Budapest, but you can reach Budapest directly aboard the Berlin-Prague-Bratislava-Budapest main line as well as through trains that continue from Vienna's Westbahnhof en route. GermanRail's EC Franz Liszt is a fast way to Budapest from Cologne, Frankfurt/Main Airport and Frankfurt/Main. The Kalman Imre comes from Munich.

Austrian Trains

The most sweeping change and massive investment program that OBB has experienced since its 1923/24 creation is gathering momentum year by year. The Vienna-Salzburg route, the "Westbahn," has been quadrupled and upgraded to 125 mph. You speed across new bridges, through new tunnels, over newly electrified stretches and stop in new stations in new air-conditioned carriages with at-seat drinks and snacks from a restaurant car, and sleep in the most modern trains.

The 27-mile stretch of the "Sudbahn" between Gloggnitz in Lower Austria and Murzzuschlag in Styria ranks as a classic example of railroad construction. It was Europe's first railroad to traverse a mountain chain and was constructed between 1848 and 1854. The Semmering Railroad (*www.noe.co.at*) contains 16 viaducts, some which are multilevel, and 15 tunnels.

This stretch of track was laid by some 20,000 workers, more than 750 of whom died of cholera and typhus. Opened on July 17, 1854, this railroad was electrified in 1959. In 1998, it became the first property belonging to OBB to be honored as a World Heritage Site.

OBB's red-and-white InterCity trains are the heart of fast and comfortable travel in Austria. First-class salon carriages have facing 2+1 seating, plush upholstery, air-conditioning, curtains, and matting on floor. The ICs are especially convenient to ride because OBB follows GermanRail's excellent concept of connecting InterCity trains with across-the-platform connections into matching carriages as closely as its network allows.

The trademark "InterCity" provides high standards of quality, with no surcharge, by:
* Running up to 87 mph,
* Serving 60 InterCity train stations,
* Predictable composition with second- and first-class cars in back and a train restaurant or "Bistro" car catered by the Austrian company, Trainristo, in the center with meals according to the time of day and length of the trip,
* Preferential treatment by staff, and
* A "Reisebegleiter/Travel Guide" timetable on the seats.

You may ride InterCity trains on seven lines: 1) Vienna-Salzburg-Bregenz (via Rosenheim, Germany); 2) Vienna-Salzburg (via Bischofshofen); 3) Vienna-Graz; 4) Vienna-Villach-(Salzburg); 5) Bruck an der Mer-Villach; 6) Linz-Selzthal-(Graz); and 7) Graz-Salzburg/Innsbruck.

In addition to using the IC trains, which you spot instantly by their IC symbol (no yellow stripe indicating first class) and familiar alignment with the restaurant or Bistro between first- and second-class sections, business travelers pay a supplement to ride the domestic trains designated "EuroCity" (!) supposedly because of their international standard. They run morning and evening between the most important business centers in Austria. Riders make free reservations, are greeted by a host on the platform, and read free newspapers.

Further, OBB provides excellent, punctual service with a full complement of fast trains (*D*), intermediate-speed trains (*E*), regional (no letters), and S-Bahn (rapid-transit suburban trains) on a regular-interval timetable with departures either hourly or two-hourly on all main routes.

Hungarian Trains

Hungary is very proud of its railroads ("Magyar Allamvasutak," known as MAV). 1996 marked the 150th anniversary of railroads in Hungary. MAV's gray-blue and white fleet of modern carriages are the cornerstone of the EC network serving eastern Europe. The Gyor-Sopron line is operated by Gyor-Sopron-Edbenfurthi Vasut (GySEV). MAV plays a central role in the nation's economy, carrying a far higher percentage of travelers than do most other European railroads; even so, MAV has suffered drastic passenger losses since the beginning of the free-market economy.

Budapest, with three large train stations, is the hub. Diesel and electric local, fast, express, InterCity, and EuroCity trains serve the country well. Most of the main network is electrified. MAV's domestic trains are reliable and travel is very cheap. Yellow stripes mark first class. MAV's international carriages travel far, to Frankfurt/Main and Berlin. The carriages are fine, but with fewer comforts than their Western counterparts. The gauge throughout Hungary is the same as in Western Europe. At Zahony, on the Ukraine frontier, a change from European to wide gauge takes place.

Hungarian train stations are all well posted with arrival and departure signs. Trains to the countryside are pulled by red diesel locomotives.

Reservations are compulsory on EC, IC, and InterPici (IP) trains, except for international EC trains to or from Austria or Germany, where you may make reservations, but they are not compulsory. A small supplement, which includes the reservation fee, is added for travel aboard EC and IC trains. Passengers with rail passes pay only the reservation fee, which is negligible.

Hungarian InterCity trains use modern equipment, fares are higher, and reservations are required. There are five InterCity lines: 1) trains every three hours travel Budapest-Miskolc averaging 61 mph; 2) trains every three hours travel Budapest Nyugati-Nyiregyhaza averaging 58 mph; 3) trains every four hours travel Budapest Nyugati-Szeged averaging 55 mph; 4) trains every four hours travel Budapest Deli-Pecs averaging 57 mph; and 5) trains every four hours travel Budapest-Gyor-Sopron-Szombathely averaging 49 mph.

Although train fares are cheap in Hungary, a Eurail, Eurail Select, European East, or Hungarian Railpass really pays for itself in the time and hassle you save trying to buy a correct ticket. You thank your lucky stars for a rail pass that allows you to escape the incredible confusion of the complex and unmarked ticketing windows.

Budapest is as dazzling a city as you will find in Europe, but sightseeing in the flat Hungarian countryside is disappointing. Hungary is a breadbasket. You imagine Batu Khan's Mongol army sweeping south of the Carpathian Mountains across the plain; horsemen with no barriers to hinder them; the run of the country by horseback—yet from the train you see no horses.

Do not expect the same comfort as you find aboard Western European trains. The Hungarian language barrier is difficult to break. Some of those with connections to tourism speak English; more speak German, so go prepared. Excursions into the countryside are not as scenic as those in the West. Each little train station in the countryside is alive with flowers and boasts a showpiece black steam locomotive on a pedestal in front, but you don't see charming villages or church spires, no thatched roofs or typical architecture.

Slovenian Trains

Following a 10-day war after the proclamation of independence from Yugoslavia, on June 26, 1991, the nation of two million people became independent and, in 1992, a new railroad company appeared. Slovenia's national railroad, Slovenske Zeleznice (SZ, *www.slozeleznice.si*) is not affiliated with any of the rail-pass programs.

The best way to Slovenia is aboard the EC Mimara day train, which runs Zagreb-Ljubljana-Salzburg-Munich. In addition to the EC, SZ operates IC, ICS, Zeleni vlak, International, and Regional trains.

The sky-blue and white, 124-mph Slovenian tilting train, the ETR 310, which is based on the Italian ETR 470, is known as ICS (Inter City Special, or sometimes Inter City Slovenia) It began operation on September 24, 2000, between Ljubljana and Maribor, Slovenia's two largest cities, with only two intermediate stops, cutting half an hour off previous schedules. Passengers in all three levels of seating (second class, second class plus, and first class plus) are offered free parking or the option of a taxi for a flat fee. Future dual-voltage sets will allow operation into Croatia and Hungary.

Zeleni vlak ("Green Train," for the livery) are InterCity diesel railcars purchased in 1970 from Germany. Vivid, sun-colored (red, orange, and yellow) SZ electric railcars serve domestic routes. International carriages are brightly repainted carriages of Austrian origin. Those inherited from the Yugoslavian Railroads are drab green with repainted logos.

The IC Kras runs to Trieste, and the IC Drava to Venice. You may arrive or depart on the overnight Lisinski to Munich or Venezia Express to Venice. Visas are issued aboard trains at the border without fees, forms, or photos. Slovenian conductors generally speak English.

The best crossing from the West to Slovenia is via Jesenice on the Austrian border because it is the closest to Ljubljana and thus holders of rail passes, valid in Austria but not Slovenia, only pay extra for the shorter distance.

Although Slovenia has 36 miles of Adriatic coastline, it is essentially an Alpine country "on the sunny side of the Alps," and solicits visitors in cooperation with the Alpine Tourist Commission. Ljubljana (meaning "my loved one") is known as the Salzburg of the Slovenes, with river, castle, and baroque architecture. In its thrown-together train station, currently being remodeled, all functions are conveniently located in one room: International Ticketing, Money Change, Train Information, and Tourist Information, making it as easy as possible for you first to request your ticket to the border at the International Ticketing counter, ask the price, change the right number of dollars or other hard currency into Slovenian tolar at the Change counter, and return to International Ticketing to pay for your ticket. It is very smooth. All signs have English-language subtitles. An underground passage connects platforms.

Traditionally, however, Ljubljana has been primarily an important stop for the mainline trains along the Balkan mainline from Switzerland and Germany to Zagreb, which is now across a second border to Croatia.

The timetable "Vozni Red" is helpful. It costs about $4 at main train stations. "Zahod" means departures, and "Vzhod" means arrivals. "Cas" means time and "tir" refers to track number. A word of caution is appropriate: be very careful when boarding. Many of the international trains split departing Ljubljana so that you must double-check to board the correct section of the poorly marked trains.

Within Slovenia, you can take the train to Lesce-Bled station, but it is about three miles from Bled, the exquisite Julian Alps resort on glacial lake Bled, so you'll need to take a bus into the city itself. Most prefer the hourly 90-minute bus trip directly to Bled from the bus terminal in front of the Ljubljana train station.

Trains between Ljubljana and Postojna, taking about an hour, bring you a half-hour's walk from the entrance to one of the world's great natural wonders, the Postojna Caves. Again, a bus may be more convenient because it cuts about 10 minutes from your walking time. A narrow-gauge train takes you about a mile into the cave.

The Slovenian Railroad Museum at Kolodvorska 11, Ljubljana (open Mon.-Thur. 9 A.M. to 1 P.M., Fax +38 61 131 50 77), housed in low buildings beside the Ljubljana-Villach mainline, has a remarkable collection including an 1861 Sudbahn locomotive.

Getting to Ljubljana and Zagreb from Vienna*

(1)	(2)				(2)	(1)
0834	1604	dep.	VIENNA (Sudbf.)	arr.	1356	2158
1038	1844	dep.	Graz (Hbf.)	arr.	1122	1920
1139	1930	arr.	Maribor	dep.	1022	1820
1405	2230	arr.	LJUBLJANA	dep.	0740	1600
1457	2235	arr.	ZAGREB	dep.	0730	1520

(1) INTERCITY EMONA: First- and second-class compartments between Vienna and Ljubljana and Vienna and Zagreb and dining car between Vienna and Ljubljana.
(2) INTERCITY CROATIA: First- and second-class compartments between Vienna and Ljubljana and between Vienna and Zagreb and dining car between Vienna and Zagreb

* Trains split/combine at Maribor.

Getting to Ljubljana and Zagreb from Munich*

(1)	(2)	(3)				(3)	(2)	(1)
0725	1525	2320	dep.	MUNICH (Hbf.)	arr.	0622	1436	2234
0913	1713	0115	dep.	Salzburg (Hbf.)	arr.	0415	1244	2044
1200	1956	0357	dep.	Villach	arr.	0134	0950	1758
1236	2032	0435	arr.	Jesenice	dep.	0057	0923	1723
1352	2143	0555	arr.	LJUBLJANA	dep.	2335	0814	1605
1636	2359	0836	arr.	ZAGREB	dep.	2100	0555	1305

(1) EUROCITY: First- and second-class compartments and dining car Munich-Zagreb
(2) EUROCITY MIMARA: First- and second-class compartments and dining car Munich-Zagreb
(3) LISINSKI: First- and second-class sleeping cars, second-class couchettes, and second-class compartments Munich-Zagreb

ICE and night train connections to/from Berlin exist.

Getting to Ljubljana and Zagreb on the Budapest-Venice route

		(1)	(2)	(3)	(4)	(5)
BUDAPEST	dep.	0750	0640	1505	1735	1005
Szekesfehervar	dep.	0852	N/A	1611	1839	1118
Nagykanizga	dep.	1104	N/A	1856	2110	1403
ZAGREB	arr.	N/A	1147	2214	2326	1605
LJUBLJANA	arr.	1550	N/A	N/A	0310	N/A
Trieste (Centrale)	arr.	1915	N/A	N/A	0657	N/A
VENICE (S.Lucia)	arr.	2138	N/A	N/A	0918	N/A

		(1)	(2)	(3)	(4)	(5)
VENICE (S.Lucia)	dep.	0814	N/A	N/A	2122	N/A
Trieste (Centrale)	dep.	1035	N/A	N/A	2339	N/A
LJUBLJANA	dep.	1350	N/A	N/A	0250	N/A
ZAGREB	dep.	N/A	1550	0705	0537	1320
Nagykanizga	arr.	1820	N/A	1031	0814	1539
Szekesfehervar	arr.	2028	N/A	1320	1049	1820
BUDAPEST	arr.	2143	2053	1438	1208	1943

(1) DRAVA: First- and second-class compartments and dining car between Budapest and Venice

(2) KVARNER: First- and second-class compartments and dining car between Budapest and Zagreb/Rijeka

(3) MAESTRAL: First- and second-class compartments, first- and second-class sleeping cars, and (during the summer only) second-class couchettes between Budapest and Zagreb/Split

(4) VENEZIA EXPRESS: First- and second-class compartments, first- and second-class sleeping cars, and second-class couchettes between Budapest and Venice

(5) AVAS: First- and second-class compartments between Zagreb and Budapest/Nyiregyhaza

(6) ADRIATICA: First- and second-class compartments, first- and second-class sleeping cars between Budapest and Zagreb/Rijeka

Croatian Trains

Zagreb, Croatia's capital city, formerly the Austrian Empire city of Agram, has become the dead end of the Balkan mainline. Zagreb's through station, where all trains stopped, was used by suffering merrymakers complaining about their crowded trains as they flocked from Germany and Scandinavia through Zagreb to Athens, Istanbul, and sunny Aegean beaches. Former Yugoslavia's defunct finest train, an InterCity, used to run between Zagreb and Belgrade. At the height of the Yugoslav War, traffic had to be withdrawn from 35 percent of the new Croatian Railroads' ("HZ," for "Hrvatske Zeljeznice") 1,809-mile network. Bridges were destroyed or damaged, stations were in shambles, and locomotives and carriages were stolen, destroyed, and seized. As a result, HZ is truncated—all travel south of Zagreb is difficult. Travel is better north of Zagreb. Service was resumed in August 1995, on the important Zagreb-Split line, with a morning and an overnight train, each carrying first- and second-class passengers. In 1996, HZ took delivery from the Swedish Railroads of 20 second-hand, Fiat diesel railcars that had been built in 1979-81. Zagreb is connected via

Ljubljana to West Europe's EuroCity network by the EC Mimara to Munich and Berlin.

A "vozna karta" is a ticket; "potvrda" is reservation; "kola" is carriage; and "sjedalo" is seat.

Life is normal in Zagreb, but prices are very high. The city was last bombed in May 1995. Zagreb's Glavni Kolodvor station is long, poor, and mostly in need of refurbishing, but with some modern touches such as its snappy electronic departure signs. It provides all the normal services, including money changing, but note that first- and second-class ticketing windows are in separate rooms. You won't have trouble finding your way around because international pictographs are used throughout. If you look sufficiently lost, a friendly conductor will point your way. Although staff have undergone special training to be proficient in German, someone will speak English. Nevertheless, save time and error by writing out your ticketing requests beforehand. Arrivals are listed on white-paper posters; departures on yellow.

"Croatia Express" is the name of the ticketing and train reservations service. They also have an office facing the green square in front of the station at Trg Tomislava 17.

Worth noting is the short funicular from Tomiceva Street in the lower city to Gradec in the upper town. It is very inexpensive, with departures every 15 minutes, but hardly worth waiting long for because the walk down the stairs is easy.

In addition to the trunk line through Ljubljana to Western European capitals, there are international lines that serve as back doors to Budapest and Vienna. Buy your tickets at the "international" ticket counter, even if you have a rail pass valid in Austria, Hungary, or Italy and only need a domestic ticket to the border. The segment of Croatia connecting at the border is subject to international rates, which are astronomically higher than internal Croatian ones. The line to Budapest runs for a long distance along Hungary's Lake Balaton, the mass-tourism vacation area, but there is an interminable wait at the border crossing for customs inspections on board the train and while the locomotive is changed to a Hungarian one. Your 219-mile trip to Budapest takes some six hours, about the same as the 286-mile trip to Vienna. You need not leave the train to have a Eurailpass, Europass, or European East Railpass validated. Austrian or Hungarian conductors are responsible for this task.

Vienna to Budapest

You may choose between four express trains a day along the 156-mile Vienna-Budapest train corridor. The EuroCity Lehar leaves Vienna's Sudbahnhof at 6:46 A.M. The EuroCity Bela Bartok leaves Vienna's Westbahnhof at 2:35 P.M.. The German EuroCity Franz Liszt leaves the Westbahnhof at 4:03 P.M., followed by the overnight Dacia Express train to Bucharest at 8:05 P.M. and the Beograd Express to Belgrade at 11:30 P.M. Further, during the wee hours, the Kalman Imre calls at Vienna's suburban Hutteldorf station en route to Budapest.

Because of the change of line voltage between Austria and Hungary, most trains change locomotives at Hegyeshalom, but OBB's dual-voltage electric locomotives compatible with the networks of both OBB and MAV carry without change EuroCity trains between Vienna and Budapest. The Kalman Imre overnight train changes locomotive at Vienna Hutteldorf. The ECs take you between Vienna and Budapest in two hours, 45 minutes. For the first time since 1932 (when the legendary Hungarian train "Arpad" raced along this route), you can travel between Budapest and Vienna in less than three hours, in part due to MAV's recent upgrade of the Hegyeshalom-Budapest line. This fast turnaround makes it possible for you to make a quick one-day excursion from Vienna to Budapest and back.

The flagship EuroCity Lehar consists of a first-class 1993 blue-and-gray MAV salon-type car (with yellow first-class stripes), one similar-livery restaurant car, and six bright, newly painted, red-and-black OBB cars for passengers with standard compartments in second-class coaches. The gray-and-white MAV restaurant car features Magyar specialties. On your seat you find the timetable, "Ihr Zug/Your Train/Az on Vonata." Austrian and Hungarian newspapers are offered en route.

Your border crossing at Hegyeshalom is shortened to three minutes, barely enough time for Hungarian border guards to scramble aboard. Border passport, visa, and customs inspections are performed aboard the Lehar.

Austria's Private Lines and Steam Trains

Step off your OBB mainline train at its first stop traveling east, 18 minutes from Innsbruck, and you step into a special railroading world—a world where you see steam rising from locomotives warming up; well-greased cogwheel tracks leading up sharp inclines, and the promise of secluded Alpine lakes criss-crossed by steamers. Groups of Germans are singing drinking songs on this bright morning.

In Jenbach, the Achensee (Lake Achen) Railroad (*www.tiscover.com/ achensee*) the Zillertal (Ziller valley) Railroad, and the OBB share the same station and present their departure times on the same yellow, timetable sheets, but they leave from different tracks with different gauges.

Over a century ago, engineers opened the meter-gauge, 4.2-mile Achensee Railroad that carries you up an incline reaching 160 o/oo with the help of Riggenbach-system cogwheels. From Jenbach these cogwheels help you ascend over the summit to the high Achensee, rightly known as "Tyrol's fjord." The Achensee Railroad runs May to October.

Find your place in one of the 55-seat, antique carriages. During the first part of your ascent you pass stretches of wildflowers beside the track plus berry bushes, forests of beech, spruce and fir, and sights of green valleys and grazing cows.

Motorists standing in the woods hiding the railroad have parked their cars and crossed to shoot photos of your passing train. Climbing at only five to six mph gives you the chance to relax and savor the mountains and valleys.

Pushing from the rear of your train to prevent possible breakaway, the world's oldest cogwheel steam locomotive in regular service was built in the Vienna Locomotive factory in Floridasdorf. It is nose down into the earth. This odd-looking design keeps the boiler tubes horizontal to maintain heat transfer and holds the firebox level to prevent firebrands from tumbling onto the footplate. For each round trip, workers load 770 pounds of hard coal and pump 800 gallons of water into the 18-foot-long machine.

When your train slows to a crawl, you see Eben's pilgrim church, the restaurant and clusters of houses. The church, a jewel of baroque architecture, contains the chalice of St. Notburga, whom locals in the Tyrol and Bavaria venerate as the patroness of servants. Make a visit to the church to be astonished by the remarkable legend. At the summit (3,182 feet) at Eben, you have a 10-minute break as workers exchange the steam locomotive pushing you from behind for another in front to pull you downhill, without cogs, into the valley and to the ships' landing at Seespitz.

During your stop at Maurach, a few mountaineers in hiking boots disembark to walk to the valley station of the white Rofan aerial gondolas (Seilbahnen). In five minutes the aerial gondolas lift them from the valley floor at 3,215 feet to the mountain station, 6,037 feet high in the Rofan Alpine range. They can hike along 90 miles of carefully tended and well-marked walking trails among rare Alpine flowers, chamois, and marmots. Ascent costs about $12; round-trip costs about $15.

Your train steams to a final halt at the lakeside terminus of Seespitz, 3117 feet. The steam swirling about you, the merriment at the snack bar created by schnapps sippers, the pier beckoning you aboard the Achensee steamers and, above all, the serene turquoise lake nestling between the Karwendel and Rofan Alpine mountain ranges give new meaning to the word "idyllic."

The Achensee is the largest lake in Tyrol, with an altitude of 3,025 feet, almost 1,300 feet above the Inn valley. Schedulers coordinated the railroad timetable with the ship's timetable. The well-outfitted passenger ships crisscrossing the Achensee vary in capacity from 40 to 400 persons. Sooner or later you will pass the historic St. Josef, the St. Benedikt, and the Stadt Innsbruck. The flagship of the Achensee fleet, the 15-mph, 600-passenger ship *Tirol*, was built in 1994 by Oswag Werft Linz under contract to Innsbruck's Tiroler Wasserkraftwerke (Power Station), owner of the lake (!).

The Tyrolean power station itself is in Jenbach. Against all geologic theory, the Achensee empties towards the north through the Achenbach River, which carries the water out of Austria into a tributary of the German river, Isar. Nevertheless, when Austrians laid out the hydroelectric scheme, they directed the water for Tyrol's benefit by cascading it to the Austrian power station about 350 yards below.

Visitors have been navigating Lake Achen since 1887. It is every bit as exciting today as it was then. The lake is 5.5 miles long and 0.6 miles wide. At night, brightly lighted ships cruising the serene waters provide a beautiful spectacle.

You can't help but enjoy yourself on a round trip on the magic Achensee. Get on and off as you please. Join the 15-mile path around the lake, hike, or just sit yourself down for a beverage in a lakeside village and rejoin a later ferry.

Past Buchau your ship calls at the lakeside resort of Pertisau on the only flat ground surrounding the lake. It was created by convergence of the valleys coming down from the Karwendel limestone massif. Your next landing is Gaisalm. An "Alm" is an Alpine pasture. Gaisalm is famous as Europe's only one that is accessible by lake.

Leave your ship at Scholastika landing for the mandatory 10-minute walk through the village of Achenkirch to visit the "Sixenhof," a preserved Tyrolean residence. It stands today on its original site that goes back to 1361. After a fire it was rebuilt in 1810. A preservation society has maintained the farmhouse as accurately as possible in its original state, except for modern sanitation. Visiting it gives you an insight how these mountain residents once lived and worked. With forests so close at hand, you won't be surprised to see that most of the working equipment was made of wood.

Austria, filled with high Alps and rolling countryside dotted with spectacularly beautiful lakes, offers you many chances to leave mainline trains for very special local and private lines. Steam locomotives still operate on a scheduled basis, steam rack railroads climb steep inclines to lofty mountaintops, trains on standard- and narrow-gauge short lines make frequent steam excursions, and numerous museum trains welcome railfans.

The Achensee Railroad is only one of the truly enjoyable private lines in Austria. Others you will long remember visiting include the following:

• The nearby narrow-gauge (30 inches) Zillertal Railroad travels from Jenbach 20 miles into the Ziller Valley (*www.tiscover.com/zillertal*) at speeds up to 22 mph. The Zillertal Railroad's historic locomotives are not tilted because the Ziller Valley route is flatter than the Achensee Railroad's. It is one of Austria's broadest and richest north-south valleys. You see grazing cows. Their milk yields famous cheese. The very popular Zillertal beer is made in Zell am Ziller. The valley terminates at a glacier and the train goes three-fourths of that distance.

• The 11.3-mile Stubaital (*www.tiscover.com/stubai*) Railroad running hourly to Fulpmes is the most amazing city tram in Europe. Once your No. 6 tram leaves Innsbruck's city limits it climbs into the mountains and follows the slope of the green and fertile Stubai Valley. Along the route you cross above Innsbruck's Olympic ice rink, Ambras castle, and the Europa bridge, Europe's highest highway bridge on pillars.

• The eight-mile Montafon Railroad opened December 18, 1905, as Austria's westernmost private railroad and the first standard-gauge local electric railroad in the Austro-Hungarian empire. It now is carried by a Swiss-made, 1992 electric railcar between Bludenz and

Schruns connecting villages in the Montafon mountain valley and serving as a lifeline to the areas of Aussermontafon and Ausserfratte.

• Linz' Postlingberg Railroad is proud to be in the Guinness Book of Records as the world's steepest adhesion railroad. It runs every 20 minutes from its lower terminus along an 18-minute route to the lovely pilgrim's church crowning the Postlingberg summit. The railroad was laid out by Emile Zola's father to allow convenient access for the devout.

One of Austria's provinces is a railroad operator in its own right. Styria runs both standard and 2 1/2-foot gauge lines under the banner of the Steiermarkische Landesbahnen with headquarters in Graz. Its longest line, the 48-mile Murtalbahn, runs from Unzmarkt to Mauterndorf. On Tuesdays and Wednesdays during the summer you ride steam along half of this line.

You are welcome to call numerous train enthusiast groups in Austria. For more details, contact the Austrian National Tourist Office (see Appendix A).

Vienna's Train Stations

The heart of Austria—and the OBB—is Vienna. Vienna has three train stations with high-speed train service. You usually arrive at the West train station, the "Westbahnhof." Vienna's West station handles most traffic from Switzerland and Germany. Vienna's South train station, the "Sudbahnhof," connects with Italy, Slovenia, and the eastern countries.

Travelers arriving from the west or south must use surface transportation to change from the Westbahnhof to the Sudbahnhof or vice versa. This inconvenience makes Vienna an obvious place to break your journey, but here's a tip: you can shave at least an hour off your travel time by getting off your train from the west in Vienna-Hutteldorf, where all international trains stop, before it reaches Vienna-Westbahnhof. In Hutteldorf, change to S-Bahn Line 3, where you make direct connections to the Sudbahnhof.

Vienna Nord train station connects the airport, the city, the small area north of the Danube, and Slovakia. Vienna Mitte train station is a sprawling nonmainline hub consisting of four S-Bahn platforms (which also accommodate E trains), a U-Bahn connection of several lines, buses stopping in front, and a streetcar stop on the corner (line 0 to the Sudbahnhof).

The highly glassed Westbahnhof is a big, well-organized structure rebuilt in 1953 to handle all electrified train traffic in the direction of Western Europe. It was renovated in 1990 to provide access to the new Line 6 U-Bahn facilities. Information for hotels and trains is available in one office in the middle of the hall. The tourist information office opens early (6:15 A.M.) to accommodate travelers arriving on the first international trains, and remains open late (11 P.M.).

Luggage carts fitted for the escalators are available.

The South Train Station (Sudbahnhof) is a graceful station because of the moving walkways leading to two upper levels, which make it easy for you to convey carts and luggage with wheels. One flight up takes you to the second floor ("Ostbahn") for departures to Hungary, Slovakia, the Czech Republic, and Poland; two flights up takes you to the "Sudbahn" for Italy, Slovenia, and Croatia. There are separate smoking and nonsmoking waiting rooms and kiosks selling travel provisions ("Reiseproviant"), as well as sit-down coffee shops on these levels.

On the expansive ground floor, you find nearly every service you need, including money changing (open 6:30 A.M. to 10 P.M. during the summer), tourist information (open 6:30 A.M. to 10 P.M. daily), train information, reservations and ticketing, lockers, a barbershop, and shower. Escalators take you down to the S-Bahn station out the south face. Platform numbers are shown on the electric departure boards.

Vienna's third station is the striking glass-fronted Franz-Josefs-Bahnhof, a model for the modern trend toward integrating train facilities with commercial shopping centers. Most of its traffic is the commuter service along the southern bank of the Danube and north of the Danube, including double-decked trains to Krems, which you use to connect to the Danube River steamers. Electrification of the final 50-mile stretch of the Franz-Josefs line to Gmund, in Lower Austria on the Czech Republic's border, means that OBB no longer has to change locomotives en route and permits faster, through running of the Waldviertel -Kurier and the Waldvietel Express.

Getting around Vienna

Plan to use Vienna's public transportation from the train stations, including the surface streetcar and bus network, S-Bahn, and U-Bahn. They interchange at Karlsplatz on the Ring. A ticket for one is good for unlimited transfers to all. You can change from metro to tram to bus without having to buy another ticket. Tickets are valid in one direction only for 1 1/2 hours.

Franz Josef I of Austria-Hungary, the dour emperor with mutton-chop whiskers, disapproved of citizens traveling underground like moles and lower animals. He refused to allow engineers to cover the first sunken railroads of Vienna and went to great pains to avoid offi-cially opening the new stations.

The master of Vienna's art nouveau movement, Otto Wagner, created the splendid Hofpavilon Hietzing train station close by Schonbrunn Palace, the emperor's summer residence, specifically for the emperor's use. However, the emperor traveled only twice in his beautifully appointed personal carriage along Vienna's newfangled Stadtbahn, or "city rail system"—once on June 16, 1899, to open the Vienna River Line, and once on April 12, 1902, for the Danube Canal Line.

Steam-hauled trains of the Stadtbahn, working with a frequency of three minutes, are gone now, the historic segments of the Viennese present subway (U-Bahn) network are uncovered still, and futuristic silver subway trains race past Schonbrunn Palace, but you still see the gilded traces of the nineteenth-century Stadtbahn preserved as muse-ums in the heart of Vienna.

Vienna's integrated city transportation system is arguably the most convenient in Europe (and improvements are still continuing), but you still see a few of Otto Wagner's 40 art nouveau stations from Vienna's glamorous heyday at the turn of the century (1895-1902) like tiny jewel boxes along the routes of the old Stadtbahn.

After 1969, the former Danube Canal and Vienna Valley Stadtbahn lines were converted into subway Line U-4. In the process, old station buildings at Schonbrunn, Kettenbruckgasse, Stadtpark, and Rossauer Lande were restored. The centerpiece intersection at Karlsplatz was so extensively enlarged in 1978 that the two Stadtbahn pavilions, partic-ularly elegant with their gilded marble, had to be dismantled, rebuilt, and restored.

One of them now serves as one of the entrances to the Karlsplatz subway station and as the home of small exhibitions on specialized themes; the other as a summer cafe.

South of Vienna's present Hietzing U-4 subway station, look for the Otto Wagner Hofpavilon Hietzing, "Kaiser Franz Josef I Stadtbahnstation." This emperor's train station was never intended for use by the public—it was reserved for the use of Franz Josef, members of his court, and distinguished guests. Now you view a precious museum that is open daily except Mondays, 9 A.M. to 12:15 P.M. and 1 to 4:30 P.M. (except January 1, May 1, and December 25). Inside you see a mural of old Vienna, gilding, flocked wallpaper, and lush carpeting.

Unlimited-mileage rail passes such as Austrian Railpasses, Eurailpasses, Europasses with the Austria add-on, and European East Passes cover the blue-and-cream S-Bahn trains of the Austrian Railroads as well as the railroad's more familiar long-distance trains. The futuristic silver U-Bahn trains, however, are covered only by city passes and not rail passes.

Children under the age of seven travel free on Vienna's public transportation network all year round. Youth under the age of 16 may travel free on Sundays and holidays, including the Christmas holidays from December 23 to January 6 and school holidays during the second week of February. Carry a photo I.D. at all times.

For adults, the Viennese city transport system has just the pass, card, or ticket for you to ride U-Bahn trains, S-Bahn trains, streetcars, and buses. Select one to best fit your itinerary at the kiosk below Vienna's Schwechat Airport or visit the Transit Authority's information office in the subway station below St. Stephans' Square (Stephansplatz). You can buy single city transportation tickets (about $1.60 for adults, 85 cents for children) in any U-Bahn station by automat or aboard a tram or bus for about 30 cents more. The automats take 1, 5, and 10 Schilling coins and 100 Schilling bank notes. Four- and eight-trip strip cards are also available from machines for about $6.50 and $13, respectively. You can use a strip ticket for any number of travelers—just punch the same number of strips as there are people in your group. Unlimited 24-hour (about $4.80) and 72-hour ($12.50) tickets are designed so you can let a friend or spouse use them when you are not. The eight-day network ticket is a bargain for those spending any eight days in Vienna because it can be used on nonconsecutive days even years apart and never expires. Buy your tickets at Vienna Transport Authority ticket offices such as the one at the airport or from any of the tobacco kiosks around the city. Validate them in the automatic canceling machines aboard the trams.

The Vienna Card, costing about $18, offers you 72 hours unrestricted travel on Vienna's underground, streetcar, and bus network as well as various benefits at around 60 museums, shops and restaurants. It is available from most hotels, Vienna's Tourist Office, Karntner Strasse 38 (open daily 9 A.M. to 7 P.M.) and the major Transport Authority ticket offices.

Reach the Sudbahnhof from Vienna's West station by U-Bahn Line 6 to Meidling station, changing to S-Bahn Line 1, 2, or 3. From Franz-Josefs-Bahnhof to the Westbahnhof, it is easiest to walk a block toward the Danube Canal to the Friedensbrucke U-Bahn station where U6 takes you to the Westbahnhof.

Vienna's Airport Train

The best way between downtown Vienna and the local train station directly below Schwechat Airport is on the line Vienna (Nord)-Vienna (Mitte)-Vienna (Schwechat)-Wolfsthal, which runs every half hour during the day and approximately hourly during the early and late hours. It passes from Praterstern/Wien Nord station (which also serves Line U-1) along track 3 of Wien Mitte/Landstrasse station (in turn connected to Lines U-3 and U-4). Look for the signs: "Richtung Flughafen" and the electric departure sign reading "Wolfsthal" and displaying an airplane profile. Do not follow the sign: "City Air Terminal/Hilton," up the stairs; that will take you to a bus for the airport. Bus fare is two-thirds higher than riding the trains, which are free in any event to holders of rail passes. Trains take 35 minutes to the airport.

Visitors arriving by plane at Schwechat should follow the pictographs illustrating a train to the station below. Escalators are up only. At the ticket office on the platform below you can buy a single ticket for downtown Vienna, validate your European East, Eurailpass, Europass with Austria add-on or Austrian Railpass, or buy a city transportation pass.

Your train reaches the airport station only after you enter a tunnel beyond Klein and Gross Schwechat stops and the plastics factory stop, so don't fret you will pass it. The tunnel is the underpass for the train station below the landing field. You see the sign: "Flughafen Wien-Schwechat."

Alternately, it may be more convenient for you to use one of OBB's "Vienna Airport Lines" bus services, which serve Vienna Airport from the West Train Station, with a pick-up at the South Train Station daily between 5:30 A.M. and 12:15 A.M. They take 35 minutes to the airport from the West station. In addition, OBB runs a Vienna Airport bus line from the City Air Terminal to the airport every 20-30 minutes from 5 A.M. to 12:30 A.M. and hourly during the small hours. Transit time takes 20 minutes.

Budapest's Train Stations

Budapest has four mainline termini, three of which ("Nyugati" or

West; "Deli" or South; and "Delete" or East) are named after directions
and the other (Jozsefvaros) is named for the district in which it lies.
The first three train stations are connected with each other and within
the city with three ("yellow," "blue," and "red") no-graffiti subway lines
that are the world's second-oldest (after London's). The subways and
subway stations are excellent. You travel directly between Deli station
and Keleti station on the "red" line (M2), but to reach Nyugati (West)
train station you change at Deak subway station to Line M3 (blue). Be
sure to go to the correct station for departure. You can also use blue
line M3 to reach Ferihegy Airport by traveling south to the end of the
line, Kobanya Kispest, and transferring there to bus No. 93, which
stops at both airport terminals. Reaching the airport takes about an
hour and requires two metro tickets (70 cents). Single metro tickets
costing about thirty-five cents are valid for 30 minutes. Validate them
in the punching machines. Guards are especially zealous checking foreigners for valid tickets.

The most convenient place for you to buy train tickets in Hungary
is at Hungarian Travel Bureau offices. Someone there usually speaks
English. There is an office of the Budapest Tourist Information Office
in Nyugati station, but the main office, Hungarian Tourism Service at
Margit korut 85 (Tel. (36 1) 155-1691; Fax (36 1) 175-3819) provides
a wide range of tourist information about Budapest's sights and
accommodations and sells sightseeing tours, tourist guides, and maps.
MAV requires that you reserve express trains ("gyorsvonat") a day in
advance, but local trains ("szemelyvonat") need no booking.

You can buy a subway/streetcar/bus map at a metro station ticket
office, but the metro stations are so well posted you will not need one
when you confine yourself to metro travel.

The three train stations of Budapest have much in common. They
are large, sprawling, and bewildering. All have electronic departure
signboards in the departure hall and at the heads of platforms. The
escalators all work and all have attached, well-marked metro (*M*) stations. Signing is by international pictographs that you may be hard
pressed to find because they are not displayed prominently, and the
agents will never speak English. Moreover they all give you a hard time
and can be extremely difficult to deal with.

Only Hungarians read Hungarian ("the devil's tongue") so the written signs ring no bells for you. Follow arrows. Search for pictographs.
And trust to common sense.

Keleti (East train station), loosely modeled on Berlin's former

Lehrter train station, as the main international terminal, is usually the terminus for two lines you will be most likely to travel, the link to Vienna and the Bratislava-Prague-Berlin route, but for summer 2001, MAV has abolished most passenger train movements on the circular line in Budapest. In addition, here you board trains to Venice, Belgrade, Ljubljana, Bucharest, and Warsaw. Keleti is a large, ranging station on the Pest side of Budapest. Statues of George Stephenson, inventor of the locomotive, and James Watt, creator of the steam engine, grace the front of the eclectic, charming exterior of the tremendous nineteenth-century structure.

Keleti's arrival hall has 13 tracks, but only 6 through 9 stretch to the front. The front entrance is closed, but it is not necessary to descend the stairs. Exit on the side next to platform 6 where you find a wing containing three or four accommodations offices, an Ibusz agency (open Monday to Saturday, 8 A.M. to 7 P.M.), an "Express" youth travel office (open Monday to Saturday, 8 A.M. to 6 P.M.), 24-hour luggage storage, train information (English not spoken), and a couchette and sleeping car reservations counter. Find ticketing at Window 20, which is not identified in English. Currency change (look for the German-language "Geld Wechsel" sign) is everywhere.

Keleti's metro station below is crowded with shops, more ticketing windows, vending machines, and a hot dog/pizza/pretzel kiosk. You can purchase a cup of espresso coffee on the terrace. Frequent metro service takes you to the city center and under the Danube to Deli station.

Nyugati (West) train station, which was designed and built by the French Eiffel company, is usually the terminus for the InterCity trains. This Pest-side, sprawling, but spic-and-span station at the head of Lenin Street just before it reaches Marx Square is quite handsome with its Victorian-looking red- and brown-brick facade and blue-gray latticework.

You find all the facilities, luggage check, water, barber, traveler's sleeping facilities, the Budapest Tourist Information Office, (open Monday to Saturday, 8 A.M. to 7 P.M.; Sunday to 6 P.M.), money change, etc., beside platform 10 so walk alongside platform 10 for the escalator exit to this complex.

A car park above the station connects with a massive shopping center next to the station. Below is a complex subterranean metro station on the blue line.

McDonald's has refurbished the former restaurant building, beautifully recalling Belle Epoque railroading. Take a look at the shining furnishings. It was voted the best McDonald's in the world. Enter on street level.

The outdated wooden hall of Deli (South station) in the west (!) was completely destroyed during World War II, and the current modern station was built in stages. Most of the traffic departs on the lines for the Lake Balaton region and nonstop InterCity trains to Pecs. Deli is Budapest's most modern station, with an exterior of aluminum, glass, and concrete. Inside you find a post office, Ibusz (open Monday to Saturday, 8 A.M. to 7 P.M.), money change, souvenirs (hard currency only), shops of every nature, coin-operated lockers, and sweeping staircases. The station is also the farthest from the center of town, lying in the Buda side of the Danube (Duna) at the terminus of line M2. You find various foods in the stalls scattered about. Deli's platforms have pushcarts and drinking water from fountains with spigots.

Steam Railroad Museum

Hungary's national railroad preservation site, opened on July 14, 2000, in the northern suburbs of Budapest, is located in the former Eszaki roundhouse, also known as the Tatai ut shed. The museum is also given the nickname "Fusti," which means "Steamy."

Using Eurailpass and Europass Bonuses

Eurailpasses are valid in both Austria and Hungary , including the small GySEV network, (but not in Slovenia or Croatia) and because they are Eurail countries, you may choose to select them for a Eurail Selectpass, e.g., Switzerland-Austria-Hungary. When you enter Austria or Hungary via train from a country that doesn't honor Eurailpasses (such as Slovenia or Poland), you need not prevalidate your pass at a train station; the Austrian or Hungarian conductor assumes the responsibility. You need to purchase the Austria option at the same time you purchase your Europass, but both Austria and Hungary may be chosen with a Eurail Selectpass.

The Puchberg am Schneeberg-Hochschneeberg rack railroad described below gives a 10 percent discount to Eurailpass and Europass holders. The ships of Wurm & Kock give a 50 percent reduction for trips on the Danube between Linz and Passau and the ships of the DDSG Blue Danube Line allow a 15 percent discount on trips between Melk, Krems, and Vienna.

Travelers south of Salzburg in the beautiful Salzkammergut should take advantage of the 15 percent discount on the St. Wolfgang-

Schafbergspitze rack railroad and the 20 percent discount on the steamers on idyllic Lake Wolfgang leading to it. Not advertised by Eurailpass, the Steiermarkische Landesbahnen grants a 50 percent reduction to Eurailpass holders. Use the Austrian port of Bregenz (site of the summer lake festival) to begin journeys on Lake Constance, for which Eurailpass and Europass allow you a 50 percent reduction.

Austrian Railpass

OBB's Austrian Railpass is a flexipass valid for three to eight travel days in 15 of first- or second-class unlimited travel on the OBB network (except between the Austrian border and Hegyeshalom, Hungary), a special price on the Schneeberg rack railroad and a discount on bicycle rentals at over 160 Austrian train stations. You may choose the exact number of days you wish to use your flexipass. Minimum is three; maximum is eight.

Buy Austrian Railpasses from your travel agent through DER and Rail Europe offices in the United States or (in Austrian Schillings) OBB offices in Austria. Children six through 12 pay half. Children under six ride free.

In Austria you can buy the "VorteilsCard" (Advantage Card) introduced in 1996 by producing a photo at any train station. This credit-card-size piece of plastic allowing you to travel for half price over the OBB network for one year is available in 12 variations ranging from Classic ($89), Senior (men over 65, women over 60, $23), Family ($16), and Students ($16). You also receive discounts on bicycle rentals at train stations , the Schneeberg Rack Railroad, and the Austrian timetable. Further, you receive half off automobile rentals with Europcar, Hertz, ARAC and Avis plus discounts on Best Western and Steigenburger hotels in Austria, Germany, Switzerland, the Netherlands and Spain. Seniors also get half off buses and Lake Constance steamers.

On April, 1995, public transport in Austria became more attractive when the buses operated by the Austrian Railroads, the post office, private companies, and the Innsbruck transit authority were united under a common flag and a standard fare structure. Visitors now buying one single ticket are able to use all the "Verkehrsverbund" routes. Prices for a day ticket increase according to increasing distance, with a maximum at about 60 miles. The maximum applies to any distance over 60 miles regardless of actual distance.

Vorarlberg was Austria's first federal state to introduce a grid system for its entire public transportation network covering both bus and train. The Grid Ticket gets you where you want to go at reduced prices. A one-day ticket costs about $6.50; a one-week ticket, $14; and a family day-ticket, $9.50. At least 12 regions now provide such regional bus and train passes. Area passes are available as well. Be sure to check at your local train station.

Hungarian Railpass

First-class Flexible Railpasses valid for five days in 15 or 10 in one month are available from travel agents through Rail Europe. Because travel in Hungary is covered by Eurailpass, Eurail Saverpass, and European East Railpass, few travelers will have occasion to take advantage of their cheap price, but for those not purchasing any of these, buying a Hungarian Railpass will give them a tremendous convenience skirting the language problem.

In Hungary you buy a MAV "Turistaberlet," which is a rail pass giving unlimited travel on domestic MAV trains for seven or 10 consecutive days, first or second class. The pass is not valid on international trains except on MAV carriages attached for domestic service. It also does not cover the much smaller GySEV network, which sells its separate GySEV Turistaberlet, but if you buy either rail pass, you receive a 20 percent discount on tickets for the alternate railroad.

Public transportation fares are very inexpensive in Budapest and you can buy tickets in your hotel, but day passes give you the convenience of unlimited travel on the trams, electric buses, metro, and the four suburban train lines called HEV. For an additional charge, buy one including city bus travel as well.

European East Railpass

The five-country European East Railpass lets you travel as you please over the OBB and MAV networks and through Poland, the Czech Republic, and Slovakia. These passes are your most convenient way to travel about these Eastern nations, which, like Hungary, present language difficulties. Good international train connections take you from Vienna and Budapest to Bratislava, Prague, and Warsaw.

European East Railpasses are flexible. You buy them for any five or 10 days travel in a month, for first-class travel only. Their price is based on the one-way Salzburg/Vienna/Budapest/Prague/Warsaw Eurail

Tariff price, so when you travel more than this stretch, you save money, especially when you make Vienna your gateway to Eastern Europe.

The great cruise ships on the Austrian Danube and the great train described in this chapter, Austria's Schneeberg Rack Railroad, make your traveling exciting in Austria. Travelers receive half off the Passau-Linz cruise and discounts on the rack railroad with Eurailpasses, Europasses with Austria add-on, Austrian Railpasses, and European East Passes.

Cruising the Mellow Danube
Off with Your Shoes

Passengers pull their deck chairs closer to the railings. Their maps, guidebooks, camcorders and digital cameras threaten to fall into the Danube. They read their texts aloud, compare notes, chatter excitedly, and pan their cameras over the sights in front of them.

You see the castle where his enemy, Leopold V, Duke of Austria, imprisoned Richard the Lionhearted, King of England.

The sights of castles, abbeys, and picture-book villages and the warmth of the wine- and fruit-bearing slopes makes experiencing the Wachau district in Austria from the deck of a Danube River steamer one of the great river adventures. To show it off, proud Austrian hosts take their foreign visitors on the deck of a river steamer for that "special occasion."

Europe's second river (after the Volga) flows through Austria only 224 miles, but this one-eighth segment of the river is wholly navigable so you see commercial vessels, even Russian ones, all along its length, some traveling all the way from West Germany to the Black Sea. Your principal landings are at Linz, Melk, Krems, and of course Vienna.

Commerce pays your freight, so to speak. It keeps the river navigable so you can see the most picturesque sections of the Danube valley right from the surface of the river itself.

A series of three Danube River cruise lines make it all possible. You can make a trip in either direction, but there is something more rhythmic and restful about the throbbing of your ship going downstream from Passau to Linz to Krems to Vienna. Three river steamer firms combine to offer cruises of connecting segments of the Danube. Their Danube ships are all one class and shipshape in every respect. You could spend an excellent week exploring the length of the

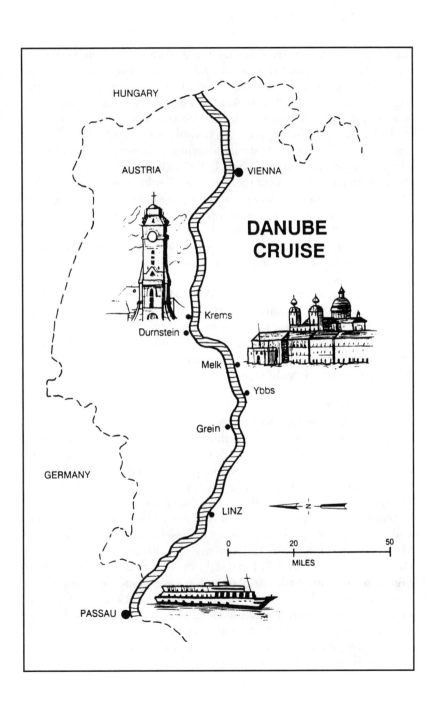

Austrian Danube by river steamer and visiting such highlights as Passau, Linz, Melk, and Durnstein. Only one day a week can you cram it all into a getaway: depart Passau 1:10 P.M. on Saturday, enjoy the night in Linz, depart 9 A.M. Sunday, change ships at Durnstein or Krems and arrive Vienna at 8:45 P.M. You won't need reservations.

Along the way, you may see signs pointing to "DDSG." Follow those signs. DDSG was the Austrian-government-owned forerunner of today's cruise ship system. When DDSG collapsed—Austrians blame their politicians—all nine of their ships were sold to private enterprise. Many of the presently active shipping companies bought eight of them. The ninth, a steam-powered paddlewheeler, was sold to OGEG, the Austrian Railroad Preservation Society headquartered in Linz, for one Schilling (about 10 cents) plus tax because the ship had been deemed a national treasure. OGEG shows it off by scheduling occasional excursions.

The Danube is a good river. Its color is always changing, depending on the time of day, weather conditions, time of year, whether the sun is rising and lightening it, whether it is overcast and gloomy, and whether it is carrying the spring glacier runoff or sediment. It is lined by castles, sparkles like an emerald in bright sunlight, and remains joyful for you to travel by ship.

Passau to Linz

Passau, the German port at the very head of the stretch of the Austrian Danube, occupies a beautiful site on the peninsula formed by the Inn and Danube rivers. Passau's Wurm + Kock Danube cruise ships (*www.donauschiffahrt.de*) depart from piers 11 and 12 at the Untere Donaulande at the Hotel Konig. Wurm + Kock gives Eurailpass and Europass holders half off their full fare ($21) between Passau and Linz.

Wurm + Kock operates two ships based in Linz, the M.S. *Johanna* and the M.S. *Anton Bruckner*. The latter vessel was formerly named the M.S. *Germania*, but it was rechristened in 1996 to honor the noted composer who was born in Linz and now is buried there beneath an organ, as was his wish. The name, *Germania*, did not appeal to Austrians. The *Johanna* seats 146 on the upper deck and 228 on the lower in bright, restrained ambience. The five- to 13-knot *Bruckner* seats 141 above and 154 on the entrance deck.

After the junction of the Inn River with the Danube below Passau (the Inn is the larger at this point), the Danube is wide and majestic and bordered with wooded, rocky slopes. Gravel plains along the valley were formed when glaciers receded. You sail past green meadows, marshes, and evergreen forests now covering the hills. After your ship stops at Engelhartszell, you see the river open out into a magnificent lake. This is the reservoir of the Jochenstein Dam. The rocky island in the river was supposedly the dwelling of a water fairy called Isa, the sister of the more infamous Lorelei of Rhine River notoriety.

Past Wesenufer, a pretty village with flowers on the balconies, you reach the highlight of this segment, which is an amazing quirk of nature, a wide, sunken loop called the "Schloegener Schlinge," meaning "Sling of Schloegen." At the outermost point of your great U-turn, a Roman castle of the second century has been excavated. It guarded communications between Castra Batava (Passau) and Lentia (Linz).

After stopping at Aschach, where you see the surprising brown, blue, and orange colors used to decorate the villages in this area, you continue to Linz for a stopover in "The Excursion Center on the Danube."

Wurm + Kock Passau - Linz Summer Service
Daily except Wednesday

1310	dep.	PASSAU	arr.	1510
1415	dep.	Obernzell	dep.	1450
1500	dep.	Engelhartszell	dep.	1300
1515	dep.	Niederranna	dep.	1230
1520	dep.	Wesenufer	dep.	1220
1540	dep.	Schlogen	dep.	1200
1620	dep.	Obermuhl	dep.	1130
1650	dep.	Neuhaus-Untermuhl	dep.	1050
1735	dep.	Aschach	dep.	0955
1745	dep.	Brandstatt-Eferding	dep.	0935
1910	arr.	LINZ	dep.	0800

Linz

Linz's (*www.linz.au*) location on the Switzerland to Vienna "Westbahn" line makes Linz an ideal and picturesque site to begin your cruise on the Danube. At the very end of the Linz Hauptbahnhof departure hall you find the Sparda Bank, a "Bankomat" ATM, a banknote changing machine, and a tourist information video which gives you choices of location, with maps, and prices of all categories of hotels. The staffed Linz tourist office is located on the Hauptplatz, but you may telephone for a hotel from the train station.

Before you sail from Linz in the morning, visit Linz's showpiece main square, the Hauptplatz, which was renovated in 1990. Note particularly the Old Town Hall which was finally restored in spring 1997. From the Hauptplatz, it is only a block to the Niebelungen Bridge over the Danube from where you see the embarkation station for the cruise ships. It is an easy walk.

You see a striking ensemble of diverse buildings on the Hauptplatz. The fascinating baroque Trinity column dominates the center of the square. Emperor Charles VI directed that it be erected in 1723 to celebrate the escape of the city from the plague, fire, and Turkish invasion. You see baroque columns of this type in many towns of Austria and Bavaria, but this is the best example. Nearby is the Old Town with narrow, cobbled streets and lined with preserved facades. This is Linz's "Bermuda Triangle" nightlife section (young Austrians go in to have fun. They have so much fun that they *never* come out).

If you arrive early at the train station you find a warm waiting room (open 6:30 A.M. to 12:30 A.M.) in the station giving you the comfortable feeling of Austrian Gemutlichkeit.

Streetcar line No. 3 in the direction "Bergbahn" takes you from in front of the train station to the Hauptplatz and the ferry landing along the river nearby. To reach the Hauptplatz, you will need to buy a "Midi" streetcar ticket costing about $1.70 for more than six stops. One-day unlimited-travel streetcar tickets cost about $3.25. Two-day ($7.40) and three-day ($9.25) tickets are also available from tobacco kiosks and the tourist office and in addition include access to the Postlingberg Railroad (see "Austria's Private Lines," above).

Linz to Krems

You depart downstream from Linz to Krems aboard Ardagger Danube Shipping's beige-colored, 1996 *Ostarichi*. Access the Ardagger Web site through *www.linz.at*, click "tourismus," click "Donau-Schiffahrt," click "Ardagger," click "Englisch version." Ostarichi is the old name for Austria (Osterreich). Two hundred passengers ride in the air-conditioned lounge and 200 in the half-sheltered deck area. The Ostarichi was built at a cost of $2.2 million in Linz shipyards. Immediately downstream, you sail past the largest steel mill in Austria and a booming chemical industry, but when you see the hills grow green and wooded and the houses and barns become picturesque and when you find yourself peeping into the lives of dwellers by the river, washing and boating and threshing and piling hay into yellow haystacks, your cruise begins to unroll like a continuous reel of travelogue color adventure. You have well begun the singing, guitar strumming, cooling swing down the Danube.

Your cruise is a marvelously soothing change from the helter-skelter madness of rush-around sightseeing, cathedrals that all look alike after a while, fortresses perched at the ends of dusty climbs, endless museums, crowded palaces, and bumpy cobblestone streets in the summer sun which finally make you believe your feet will burst into flames any minute. Your Danube cruise is fun.

Shortly after leaving Linz at 9 A.M., the youthful aboard shed their shirts, shoes, and socks and gather to play guitars. Even more reserved passengers take this opportunity to slip off their shoes and socks and wriggle their toes from the ship's deck in the fresh, cooling breezes above the river.

Passengers scrape their deck chairs to the railings and compare their geography texts with the highlights of the passing countryside. You overhear no English. You are adventuring off the common tourist path, but all the deck personnel cheerfully answer your questions in English.

Downstream, about noon, you are hemmed between rocky, wooded slopes. Your approach to Grein is beautiful. This pleasant little town, guarded by its castle, lies ideally at the foot of a wooded bluff watching over the entrance to the Strudengau gorges.

Below Grein begins the most dramatic section of the Austrian Danube. At one time river passengers feared the infamous rapids of Strudel and Wirbel. Now with the dangerous rocks blasted away, you pass around willow-covered islands, past the ruins of the castles of Struden and Sarmingstein, and soon find yourself on a placid lake nearing the Ybbs-Persenbeug dam, a major power station.

The crew members are excited and rushed. They scurry passengers below and rope off the upper deck while the locks of the power station loom larger and larger. When the Danube is high, the clearance between your steamer and the locks is so slim that anyone poking his head above the ship's railings will be seriously injured.

When you pass Persenbeug, look for the castle where the last

Austrian emperor, Charles I, was born. From Persenbeug, at the head of a well-tilled plain where the river bends to Melk, you pass through the valley you know from episodes in The Nibelungenlied. You may hear echoes of Brunhild and Kriemhild, Gunther and Siegfried.

Pochlarn, on the right bank, was settled in the tenth century by the Babenbergs, who began the vigorous growth of the Austrian monarchy. When you next land at Melk, with its spectacular Benedictine abbey perched above you, you enter the Wachau.

Ardagger Danube Shipping Service Linz - Krems
Sun., Tue., Thurs., from Linz*;
Mon., Wed., Fri. from Krems (summer only)

0900	dep.	LINZ	arr.	1820
1025	dep.	Mauthausen	dep.	1745
1200	dep.	Ardagger	dep.	1535
1220	dep.	Grein	dep.	1525
1340	dep.	Ybbs	dep.	1345
1405	dep.	Marbach/M.-Taferl	dep.	1305
1420	dep.	Pochlarn	dep.	1240
1515	dep.	MELK (Altarm)	dep.	1150
1605	dep.	Spitz	dep.	1020
1615	dep.	Weissenkirchen	dep.	0955
1625	dep.	Durnstein	dep.	0930
1645	dep.	KREMS	dep.	0900

* with summer connections to Vienna (arrive 8:15 P.M.) on Sundays.

The Wachau

Competition is keen through the Wachau. In addition to Ardagger service, DDSG Blue Danube Shipping (*www.ddsg-blue-danube.at*) has three round trips a day, and gives 15 percent off for rail-pass holders aboard the M.S. *Prinz Eugen* and M.S. *Wachau*.

The stretch of the Danube from Melk to Krems, the Wachau, is considered the most interesting stretch of river landscape in Europe. You see charming villages lining the river, the ruins of fortified castles crowning the crests, and onion-shaped belfries adding notes of fantasy to the countryside.

The Wachau is a beautiful sight regardless of whether the trees are in blossom, apricots are bright on trees, or grapes are heavy on vines and every wine village is celebrating the harvest.

You are making one of the premier excursions from Vienna. Frau Vera Kreisky, wife of the president of Austria at the time, took Rosalynn Carter on this trip on June 16, 1979, while the Austrian and American heads of state were in Vienna attending to business.

The Wachau makes a splendid debut at Melk where the buff-and-gold, 1726 Benedictine abbey rises like a vision above fine middle-class houses. You pass below the abbey's south wall, nearly a quarter-mile long, overlooking the Danube from a 150-foot rocky bluff.

Melk's Donauarm landing is directly below the abbey, a 15- to 20-minute walk from the mainline Melk train station served by expresses from Vienna and Linz.

As you cruise out to the main Danube current, the chords of the "Blue Danube" waltz strike a romantic and unforgettable note. Soon you see Schonbuhel Castle, which has guarded entry to the Wachau since the ninth century.

After passing the yellow-painted village of Aggsbach, your steamer proceeds five minutes past Aggstein, precipitously below the castle, one of the largest and most formidable of the towers high on the mountain. This castle is notorious as a robber baron's haunt where prisoners were forced to jump to their deaths.

Passing Willendorf is especially interesting because the famous "Venus of Willendorf" prehistoric limestone statuette found here proved that man lived in the hills surrounding you since the dawn of civilization.

Spitz is almost the center of the Wachau, and its largest village. You see houses clustering below a hill, graceless but prosperous. The rows after rows of vines flowing over the rocky hillsides make it famous as "Thousand Pail Hill," known for the staggering amount of wine it produces in a good year. There are only 3,580 acres planted in the Wachau and yet it is Austria's premier white wine region.

Past Spitz on the left, fifteenth-century St. Michael appears—the oldest church in the Wachau. Thriving vineyards continue to cover the hillsides with spectacular riesling and gruner veltliner plantings terraced in parallel rows. This region has the mildest climate in Austria.

The next picturesque stop is the village, marked by the fortified steep red-tiled roof, of Weissenkirchen, the center of the region known as "Wahowa" that gave its name to the entire Wachau.

Then, after sweeping past a broad bend in the Danube, you see the most famous scene in the Wachau—Durnstein—a historical, fortified town. As you near, you can feel its almost completely preserved medieval and baroque character.

Richard the Lionhearted in disguise was seized on his way back to his native England at the end of the Third Crusade. His faithful troubadour/detective, Blondel, discovered his master here in Durnstein by strumming his mandolin and singing Richard's favorite ballad while searching through the castle.

Your next landing marks the end of the Wachau. You pass under a 500-year-old bridge at Krems, the historic city (not village) on the left bank. At the foot of loam hills covered with prominent, terraced vineyards rivaling those upstream, you cross the famous "Iron Route," an ancient trade artery. Now a simple city, Krems was once an imperial fortress, more important than Vienna because of Danube trade.

DDSG Blue Danube Service
through the Wachau
Daily during summer

1100 1350 1615	dep.	MELK (Altarm)	arr.	1315	1540 1840	
1150 1440 1720*	dep.	Spitz	dep.	1145	1420 1725*	
1210 1510 1740	dep.	Durnstein	dep.	1050	1330 1620	
1240 1530 1800	arr.	KREMS	dep.	1015	1300 1545	

* change ships

Krems-Vienna

You have completed the exciting part of your trip. Wachau steamers debark in Krems, where you can take OBB's hourly, second-class-only double-decked electric train into Vienna's Franz-Josefs-Bahnhof (*E* trains run every two hours). The Krems station is far from your ship's landing, but there is more. For about $18, on Sundays, you can change from Ardagger's *Ostarichi* at Krems or Durnstein for a downstream cruise all the way to Vienna aboard DDSG Blue Danube Shipping's M.S. *Admiral Tegetthoff*, although Ardagger, also, makes Sunday-only connections to Vienna.

From Krems, the Danube spreads broadly over a wide plain. It does not narrow until just above Vienna, where you pass solid, stone embankments. It will be darkening as your ship from Krems nears the Vienna Woods at Greifenstein.

You ship docks first in Vienna at the Nussdorf landing, but you continue to the Schiffahrtszentrum, sailing beneath the reinforced-concrete Reichsbrucke, meaning "empire bridge" (the former one suddenly collapsed one morning in 1971 and fell into the river). At Vienna/Reichsbrucke landing you find taxi stops, but you have only an eight-minute walk to the Vorgartenstrasse U-1 subway station.

DDSG Blue Danube Service
Durnstein - Vienna
Sundays during summer

1630	dep.	Durnstein	arr.	1430
1650	dep.	KREMS	dep.	1355
1845	dep.	Tulln	dep.	1120
1952	dep.	Korneuberg	dep.	0945
2045	arr.	VIENNA (Reichsbrucke)	dep.	0845

Puffing up the Schneeberg Wieder Kaputt!

The first thing you feel is the chattering of the cogwheels. While your comic steam train pulls you slowly out of the Austrian village of Puchberg, your glimpse ahead does not promise as much as your creaky train finally delivers. The Schneeberg Rack Railroad may be your slowest, steamiest, jerkiest discovery, but it may be the most fun. This diverting day's excursion through 21 tunnels and across 15 long viaducts takes you to Austria's highest train station (5,888 feet).

Then you hear the nasty hissing of the tough steam engine and see the black clouds swirling behind you. The Schneeberg Railroad has enough antique and functional features to turn a railfan's heart into Apfel Strudel.

What the Austrians call a "schmalspurige dampfbetriebene Zahnradbahn" is a narrow gauge, steam-driven, cogwheel railroad. It is fired by coal from Poland and belches fumes as black as a loan manager's heart.

When you leave Puchberg am Schneeberg, south of Vienna, each chug of the steam-driven pistons shoves your little engine inches more across the highway and up onto the mountain. Chagrined, you have no doubt you can walk faster than the train can climb, but as your train

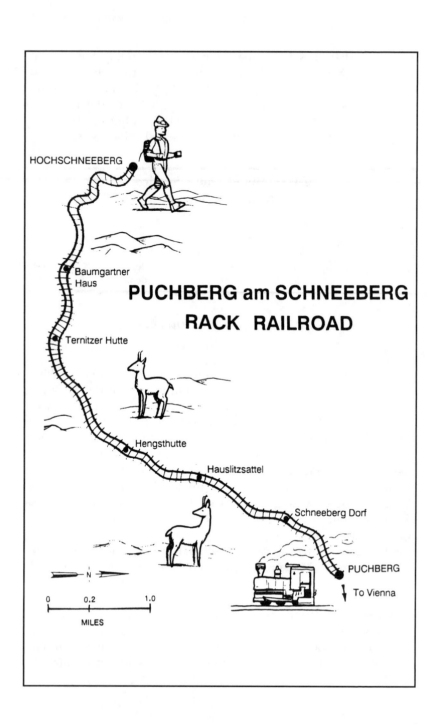

HOCHSCHNEEBERG

Baumgartner
Haus

PUCHBERG am SCHNEEBERG

RACK RAILROAD

Ternitzer Hutte

Hengsthutte

Hauslitzsattel

Schneeberg Dorf

PUCHBERG

To Vienna

N

0   0.2   1.0

MILES

tilts upward through wild ground, the engine seems to leap ahead and virtually races past the perspiring mountaineers struggling up the nearby trails.

To reach Puchberg from Vienna, you use the Sudbahnhof (South train station). An hourly IC service—covered by rail pass—runs to the city of Wiener Neustadt. Puchberg is a local stop bypassed by express trains, so change in the city of Wiener Neustadt unless you start your trip on a local. It takes just over 1 1/2 hours for the complete journey to Puchberg.

When your OBB train from Wiener Neustadt reaches Puchberg, you file down the platform a few feet to the carved wooden sign: "Zahnradbahn." The Puchberg terminal of the narrow-gauge Schneeberg (meaning "Snow Mountain") cogwheel railroad lies about 50 miles southwest of Vienna.

At Puchberg, show your rail pass at the counter and take a "Zahlkarte," a number for boarding one of the little wooden cars to the summit of the Schneeberg. Without a rail pass buy a "Wanderticket" valid for OBB transportation to Puchberg and the rack railroad's climb to the summit. Attached is a coupon ("Gutschein") for a luncheon meal at any one of the station restaurants. Buy these tickets at the "Inland" ticket counters in Vienna's South train station or stops en route.

Try to sit on the left going up. Your car is crammed five abreast with so many passengers the interior seems like Noah's ark. The Viennese consider Schneeberg their home in the mountains. The fascination of your trip is the little, black steam locomotive with tilted fireboxes.

Passengers complain about the hard seats and crowded conditions. They give thanks for small favors: at least the north wind is blowing the steam locomotive's noxious fumes away from them.

Pushing from the rear of your train to prevent possible breakaway, the four steam locos built by Krauss and Company in Linz in 1896/7 (plus an even older one, built in 1893) are nose-down into the earth like Viennese professors peering over their spectacles. They look as though their front axles have collapsed and they are grubbing for worms. The Schneeberg railroad was offered new oil-burning locomotives but it declined, saying their beloved antiques were good enough. Further, the Schneeberg is the aquifer for Vienna's drinking water. Three large pipelines carry fresh water to Austria's capital and pollution restrictions are severe. Authorities feared oil spillage from oil-burning locomotives might contaminate the precious water supply.

While your train scales the steep mountainsides, this odd-looking design keeps the boiler tubes horizontal to maintain heat transfer and holds the firebox level to prevent firebrands from tumbling onto the footplate.

You climb immediately from the station and curve around the village of Schneebergdorfl (2,007 feet). After about 25 minutes you reach Hauslitzsattel (2,717 feet); your engine brakes. You see blue cornflowers, red poppies, and a dozen delicate Alpine blooms—and, for the first time, smell forest odors. This is the first of a vast system of mountain huts constructed throughout the Austrian Alps for the benefit of mountaineers.

Eleven minutes later you are high enough to see the majesty of the green valley floor below when you reach Hengsthutte (3,323 feet), the halfway point, surrounded by pines. Hikers are stepping downhill with bouquets of wild flowers, sweaters tied around their waists.

You make a stop at Ternitzer Hutte. It is considerably cooler here. Your angle of ascent is so steep, and because you perceive the interior of the carriage as being horizontal, the fir trees outside appear to be growing diagonally out of the mountainside. Passengers disembark but watch their seats so as not to lose them. They are restless.

This is an escapist trip. Few carry a camera to burden them. They are ready for the freedom of the hiking trails above.

A 10-minute halt is scheduled at Baumgartner's station house (4,582 feet). Your locomotive is watered and recoaled while you go inside for refreshment or a snack. Try the prune bread loaf for a pleasant treat.

Now comes your real climb! For a short while, at least, you drive uphill on the cog-tracks through forests, wild valleys, mountain huts, and brooks gurgling down the mountainside. Then you make another unexplained stop. "Wieder kaputt!" ("Broken again!") maintains a stout Bavarian visitor wearing Lederhosen.

Suddenly, the person in front of you sees wild chamois ("Gemse") near your train. As one, 50 passengers stand, point to these small antelope, and shout, "Gemse!" The Gemse are near the first patches of snow and fleeing uphill.

Now you enter a 390-foot tunnel. Passengers sitting next to the windows hurry to shut them tightly to prevent steam locomotive fumes and soot from flooding the carriage. Smoke billows between carriages.

When you exit the tunnel, soot has covered the train windows. Passengers lower them immediately.

Shortly you enter a second, 500-foot tunnel. People close the windows once again, but the train stops and sits and they reopen them. "Wieder kaputt!" shouts the Bavarian. Finally under way, the train's lights come on in the tunnel. Emerging, you are above the timberline. You see swathes of tightly bunched, gold and blue wildflowers blooming through the snow. A pinelike shrub grows in patches. To your right is the green-copper-topped stone chapel, the Elizabeth Kirche. Down the rail line to your left is the Berghaus Hochschneeberg (5,889 feet)—but eager hikers are already well on the winding way up the path in the opposite direction. The summit is Enzian paradise. This tiny, much-admired, blue flower (the gentian) is used for Alpine schnapps. Go immediately into the station house to select your "Zahlkarte" for your choice of return times.

You can cash in the "Wanderticket" coupon for a meal at the Berghaus Hochschneeberg, where they also serve a "Kaisermenu" duplicating that of the Kaiser when he visited in 1901—or use your coupon at other locations. The mountain hotel contains a sauna and solarium.

In addition to experiencing the novel train, this excursion gives you a choice opportunity to hike high in the northern limestone spur of the Austrian Alps. The Schneeberg retains a covering of snow throughout the summer.

Trails take you around the Waxriegel peak (6,193 feet) to the Dambockhaus, where serious hikers buy inexpensive meals and sleeping accommodations.

Top off your excursion by walking (2 1/2 hours round trip) up to the Kaiserstein peak (6,762 feet) for the Alpine panorama north as far as the Vienna Woods. Or climb to the Klosterwappen summit (6,808 feet) for the view south across the ravine called "Hell's Valley" (Hollental) to the Rex Plateau, the geologic twin of the Schneeberg.

Your ride down is rocking, swaying, and squeaking like a rusty spring. It takes less time going down, about an hour, but it is more subdued because passengers are tired.

Across the street from the Puchberg train station, an idyllic lakefront promenade is perfect for picnicking. The Puchberg station has a buffet serving meals.

In 1997, OBB and the provincial government of Lower Austria formed the Niederosterreichische Schneebergbahn (NOSBB, Lower Austria Schneeberg Railroad) and introduced motor units with the very odd livery of dark green with orange spots. The design is named "Feuersalamander" (spotted salamander) because it resembles the small amphibian abiding on the slopes of the Schneeberg. The shape of the coaches is rounded to pass through the tunnel at the top of the line, which is located on a curve. The motor units are narrower than the passenger carriages to allow passengers to leave easily in case of an emergency inside one of the tunnels.

Steam service varies with season and demand. There are daily steam locomotive departures at 9:45 A.M. and 10:45 A.M. from Puchberg during the summer, with returns at 12:40 P.M. and 2:45 P.M. Other steam locomotive departures are added as required. On most hours at 40 minutes past the hour, there are also departures of the Spotted Salamander trains.

Italy
and Greece

Smart Traveling on the Trains
of Italy and Greece

Italian trains—Crossing between Italy and Greece—Greek trains—Athens train stations—Getting around Athens—Airport trains—Domestic Italian overnight trains—Traveling in Sicily—Compelling Sardinia—Using rail pass bonuses

Italy is a flashy and artistic country. Expect no less of the showpiece Italian State Railroads, "Ferrovie dello Stado" (FS). FS's 10,000-mile network has touches of a maestro.

Greece is a country of great history. It's curious how trains mirror the nature of the countries. Don't expect the trains of "Organismos Siderodromon Ellados (OSE)," the Greek Railroads Organization, to provide you with great comfort, speed, or convenience. Greek trains are timeless—without regard to time (so always have a backup plan ready). The best travel experience in Greece is on the Aegean ferries.

Italian Trains

The trains of Italy are as long as a Roman's nose, and just as full of character. A full complement of Eurostar Italia (ERT), EuroCity (EC), Intercity (IC), and Interregionale (iR) trains blanket the country. Below the top-level Eurostar Italia services, there are InterCity trains and Interregionale trains. You ride one of Europe's most modern and speediest fleets from the Italian Alps to the newly electrified stretch to Palermo on the tip of Sicily. The rest of FS's fleet takes you to villages and the seaside in an eclectic set of Espressos (*E*), Trenos Diretto (*D*), and Trenos Locale (*L*), of less speed and desirability.

Your fastest ride is the ETR 500, 186-mph train running along the Milan-Florence-Rome-Naples corridor. Next speediest are the 155-mph Pendolino ETR 450 and ETR 460 trains, which tilt. (More about riding these trains in the "Italian Eurostar" chapter to follow.) IC and EC trains can run up to 125 mph while IR trains peak at 87, 94, 99, or 112 mph, depending on equipment.

Reservation requirements are strictly enforced in Italy (except when the computer people are on strike and making reservations is impossible). With few exceptions, all Eurostar Italia trains must be reserved in advance. Eurostar Italia passengers must pay a fee that covers both reservation and supplement, which varies according to destination and type of train. Check the timetables. An *R* in a box indicates that a reservation is obligatory. A *PG* in a box shows that you may make seat reservations, but they are not required. If you board and find an unreserved seat in a train requiring reservations, the conductor will charge you for the seat, plus a penalty!

Connecting Milan and northern Europe you can ride Cisalpino's trains to/from Geneva, Basel, and Zurich; Artesia's TGV-R service to/from Paris; tilting ETR 480 trains from to/from Lyon; and conventional FS Eurocity trains. FS's EuroCity trains to northern Europe are gray-livery, with blue piping. Some use the same deluxe coaches dating from 1975-90 that comprised former Trans Europ Express trains. They retain their superior ambience and convenience with features such as behind-the-seats coat closets. The first-class open salons with 2+1 seating are especially comfortable. The trains carry white-linen "Chef Express" restaurant carriages or "Self Service" cafeteria cars staffed by Wagons-Lits.

The food selection and cashier stool of the FS's "Self Service" or "Snack Bar/Ristorante" (they have borrowed the English words) cafeteria cars are conventional, but the facilities for eating your meal are unusual. Your dining area consists of orange formica saw-tooth spaces with swivel stools placed along the windows and separated with orange dividers. Diners on one side of the train look forward; the other half looks backwards. Perhaps this is to minimize dawdling.

At smaller stops in Italy, trackside vendors with fully loaded push-carts are eager to sell you cold drinks, sandwiches, and candy, but they are increasingly discouraged by FS's conversion to sealed-window, air-conditioned carriages. Listen for their persistently tinkling bells. If you can, open your window and make your orders from the train; other-wise, join the clusters at the steps to the train.

In addition to FS, there are numerous private railroads in Italy such as the Transvesuviano between Naples and Sorento (for Pompeii) and the Circumetna in Sicily. Some provide commuter service and some serve rural districts and reach villages not connected to FS. None honor rail passes.

For travel in Italy, the yellow "Pozzorario Generale" timetable is much more valuable than others are. It gives you such useful addi-tional information as the type of Italian Eurostar train being used on a specific route and departure time, which overnight trains carry sleep-erettes in addition to couchettes, and the schedules of private lines. The Pozzorario Generale is for sale in station bookstores and maga-zine stalls. It also gives you the correct FS timetable in a country where you get three different answers to the same question asked at three dif-ferent information desks.

Signboards on the trains use Italian shorthand, so for Naples Centrale, expect to read "Napoli C.le," and for Rome Termini station, read "Roma T.ni." The trains are clean inside and out. Train and win-dow washing is performed in Rome Termini, Florence Santa Maria Novella, and Venice Santa Lucia stations by motorized machines that are steered past the trains.

Crossing between Italy and Greece

Greece is a magnet to Eurail Pass holders with validity in Greece because of the promise of free deck-class ferry transportation—except that you must pay a high-season surcharge between June 10 and September 30—and the carefree stopover on Corfu's beaches. You may sail between Brindisi, Italy, and Patras, Igoumenitsa or Corfu, Greece, aboard the Greek Hellenic Mediterranean Lines (HML) and the Blue Star Ferries. The large, white ferries of Attika Superfast (*www.attika.com*), a German company, began offering rail pass service on July 1, 2000, between Ancona-Patras-Ancona, Bari-Patras-Brindisi, Igoumenitsa-Bari, and Brindisi-Patras-Brindisi (in cooperation with HML).

To reach the harbor from the train station in Brindisi, walk straight downhill past the white fountain (it's about a half-hour all the way to the harbor). A few minutes past the white fountain, you see on your right the shipping office across from McDonald's.

Sailings are scrambled from Brindisi to Patras and vice versa. Some stop in Corfu en route and some take you without stop. Others take you between Brindisi and Corfu and the northern Greek port of Igoumenitsa, but don't continue to Patras. Igoumenitsa has no train service, but you can take a bus from Igoumenitsa through the rugged mountains of the Epirus Region to Kalambaka with a second-class-only, narrow-gauge train connection to Karditsa, where you can take a standard-gauge IC train via Paleofarsalos to Athens.

At Patras' landing you board either a train or bus. Buses park near the ship's landing. Trains are a short walk away. From your ferry, you will generally walk to your right, staying within the port fence to gate 3 entrance. The train station, with snack bar and open-air snack restaurant attached, is across the tracks. A Citibank with ATM is across the street. Buses are not covered by Eurailpasses; the trains of the Peloponnesian Line are.

When you talk with others about this crossing, you hear horror stories. This is the least comfortable of European ferry crossings. The ships are crowded; backpackers cover the deck entirely with their mats; the seating room is stuffy and smells like those sleeping; the cabins are primitive; the crews are hostile. It is sensible to approach this journey with careful planning.

• Make train reservations to Brindisi and also from Brindisi if you know in advance when you will return. Allow extra time for possible train delays en route. Trains run to Brindisi down Italy's Adriatic coast from Rome and Bologna. Station timetables indicate these trains are for "Lecce." Brindisi's Centrale station is the stop before Lecce.

• Dress coolly. It is sometimes stiflingly hot waiting for the ferry.

• Take your own food aboard the ships. Food served on the ships is unreliable.

• Take a cabin for the crossing. Although it is not covered by Eurailpass, you will avoid inconveniences. Make your arrangements when you board.

• Allow extra days. When you lay out your overall itinerary, allow several days for unexpected developments.

• Make hotel arrangements in Athens in advance. There is no hotel service at the station in Athens. Especially when you arrive late in Athens, the unfamiliar alphabet and the location of Athens' remote train station can cause difficulties for the unprepared.

• You arrive in Athens' Peloponnesian Station. Follow the directions below ("Athens Train Stations") to reach the new Athens metro rather than being hassled by gouging taxi drivers.

• Stop over in Corfu. Anyone who has read about Corfu or is interested in casual beach life will not miss this opportunity.

• Allow extra time in Brindisi before boarding. You pass through customs, passport, port tax payments, ticketing, and boarding bureaucracies.

Greek Trains

All OSE trains honor rail passes. There are reduced rates for travelers under 26, and for foreign students presenting an I.D. card.

The Peloponnesian trains are modern InterCity red-and-white railcars or falling-apart traditional trains with a diesel locomotive that appears Neolithic. OSE's 1992 InterCity, German-built diesel railcars between Patras and Athens have a maximum speed of 75 mph. In trials it achieved a speed record on the meter-gauge line of 83.3 mph. You will be lucky to catch it in Patras, so don't delay boarding, because Europe's only meter-gauge InterCity train allows you to reach Athens at a decent hour. If your ferry is late, you will take a local train getting you to the Hellenic capital two hours later. Eurailpass, Eurail Selectpass, and Europass holders with Greek add-on have an advantage here because they can board before the crowd and don't have to stand in a long line to buy a ticket (by which time it may have left).

Greece has two train networks. The 550-mile long, meter-gauge line circles the Peloponnesian Peninsula through Patras and Athens, while the 970-mile long, standard-gauge northern network connects Athens to Thessaloniki (Salonika) and supports the trains to the Balkans and central Europe.

Traveling with a top speed capability of 100 mph (which set speed records in Greece), OSE's flagship nonstop InterCity trains began in 1996 connections between Athens and Thessaloniki, cutting 20 minutes from the timetable. They take five hours, 50 minutes, averaging

54 mph over the 318 miles between Athens and Thessaloniki. OSE's 12 air-conditioned red-and-white railcars of East German origin carry 180 passengers without standing in four carriages including driver's cars. Second-class salons are front and back of two middle carriages. The 36-seat first-class middle carriage includes a bar and a kitchen.

These are being supplemented, between late 2000 and 2005, with a new generation of modular, low-floor articulated railcars built by Adtranz but assembled at Hellenic Shipyards. The new units consist of two passenger cars plus the short central motor unit.

OSE's Kalavryta Railroad in the Peloponnesus, originally built for mining by an Italian company between 1885 and 1895, is usually considered Greece's most scenic train ride. Rail passes are accepted. Travelers leave from Diakofto, near Patras on the line from Athens, so it is possible to make the excursion as a 14-hour day trip from Athens. The lines of the 14-mile-long, 750-mm-gauge, cogwheel railroad begin across the plaza adjacent to the OSE tracks where a little black steam locomotive retired in the late '50s stands proudly as the centerpiece. A two-carriage diesel-electric unit was joined on August 31, 1996, by the line's first steam locomotive (1891) that was restored to working order at the OSE workshops in Piraeus. The line climbs 2,300 feet in one and a half hours, taking you through tunnels and along rocky ledges through the mouth of the granite Vouraikos River gorge that has never been pierced by more than your little railroad to Kalavryta with a stop at Zahlorou, at 2,086 feet, about half-way to the southern terminus at Kalavryta, 14 miles from the Gulf of Corinth. Three-quarters of an hour by foot or on donkey from Zahlorou, the 362 A.D., Orthodox Byzantine monastery of Mega Spileon on the side of a vertical granite peak attracts many pilgrims but only men may overnight there. The pleasant mountain resort of Kalavryta contains the graveyard of over 1,500 males murdered by the Nazis on December 13, 1943. You may visit the Holocaust Museum, graveyard, and village church.

The port of Athens is Piraeus, just five miles south of the Hellenic capital. This is your gateway for the ferries to Greece's Aegean islands. Although OSE's Peloponnesus trains originate here, and you can take a train from Athens' Peloponnesus station, it is easier to take the subway from Athens' Omonia Square.

The Athens Train Museum at 4, Siokou Street opposite 301 Liossion Avenue, (open 9 A.M. to 1 P.M. Fri.-Sun, and 5 to 8 P.M. Wed., admission free) contains actual carriages from a 1884 train as well as preserved fixtures.

Athens Train Stations

Because of OSE's two gauges, Athens—which is the hub of both networks—has two train stations in the city's northwest section. There are no through trains. When you take the train from Patras, you arrive in the Peloponnese station. When you arrive via the Balkans or from Thessaloniki, you arrive in Larissa station.

Small Larissa Station has a waiting room, ticketing, an information window, baggage checking, an adjoining snack bar and potted trees on the platforms. You won't find luggage carts or hotel assistance. The timetables on the walls are last year's, updated with changes in felt pen. There is an ATM ("Telebank") inside and out outside. The Larissa subway entrance to Red No. 2 line is directly in front of the station. The elevator access is across the street.

Peloponnesia Station is nearly useless except for ticketing and the snack bars. To reach Peloponnesia Station from Larissa Station, exit, turn right, cross the steel bridge, walk about 350 feet left. It takes about five minutes. From Peloponnesia Station, you need to go to Larissa to access the subway. Cross the street from Peloponnesia Station, walk left past the bus station, three minutes to the steel steps and cross the bridge to Larissa.

Tourist information is unavailable in either train station. The Greek National Tourist Office personnel provide information and free maps plus money conversion at their Infodesk at 2, Amerikis Str., on the ground floor next to the Aliki Theater (open Mon.-Fri. 9 A.M. to 7 P.M., Tel. 331-0561). An Internet cafe is nearby, at 5, Stadiou Street.

Athens' OSE office is located at Filleilion 18, which is short blocks (five minutes) from Syntagma Square. Pick up a timetable and ask the agent to translate the Greek names for you. Here you can make the required train reservations for international trains to the north and validate rail passes.

Getting Around Athens

Athens metro system, opened with much publicity on January 28, 2000, is an ultramodern, $2.5 billion network, with two additional lines, new stations, new rolling stock, and the latest technology. The largest, most complex project ever undertaken in Greece, the new metro makes getting around Athens remarkably efficient and pleasant. Some stations display replicas and photos of archaeological artifacts uncovered during construction.

Athens' enlarged metro system is perhaps the cleanest and spiffiest in all Europe. Look for the new stations marked by the stylized blue *M* on an illuminated white background, which is the distinctive metro sign. Designed and built by a Greek, French, and German consortium, the new system increased capacity to 780,000 from 330,000 passengers daily, with 168 new subway carriages and a policeman around every corner. The two new red (No. 2) and blue (No. 3) lines added more than 12 miles and 21 new stations to the existing green line (No. 1) that runs between the port of Piraeus in southwest Athens to Kifissia in the northeast. The east-west blue line connects Monastiraki in Plaka, the old town, to Ethniki Amyna, where a future extension is planned to the new international airport due in 2001. The red line extension in October, 2000, connects the southwest suburb of Daphni with Athens' northwest reaches. Both lines intersect at the new two-level station on Constitution (Syntagma) Square, or you can transfer at Monastiraki (green and blue lines), Omonia, or Attiki (red and green lines).

The graffiti-free, six-carriage trains, although criticized as being out-of-date, unattractive, and not air-conditioned, run every three minutes at rush hours, five to 10 minutes apart at nonpeak hours, and cost roughly $0.70 per ride. A day card costs about $2.80. Car floors are level with platforms. Special lighting and signs in Greek and Roman letters make getting around easy. Persons with special needs find ramps, escalators, and elevators. Exits have escalators, but going down long stairways can be a problem with luggage. Always look for the elevator.

The new metro is not only Greece's largest construction project to date, it is also the country's largest archaeological dig. More than 750,000 square feet were excavated at a cost of $20 million to $30 million. Because five of the new stations lie in ancient Athens within the shadow of the Acropolis, the project intrudes on one of the world's richest classical sites. Archaeologists took care to remove all significant finds and avoid damage to existing monuments. Tunnel boring machines dug 7.5 miles through solid rock to avoid cultural treasures. Underground tunneling techniques, used in preference to surface excavation, were also used at several stations near know archaeological sites. Discoveries included a bathhouse, metalworking shops, aqueducts, cisterns, drains, ancient roads, city walls, and cemeteries. One intriguing discovery turned up a room filled with oil lamps and decorated with erotic scenes.

Other surprises included a sarcophagus at Ethniki Amyna Station, and large Roman drains at Larissa Station. Photos and replicas of the most interesting finds decorate several stations in the area of the dig. The Syntagma Station is like a minimuseum. When the Acropolis metro station opened in November 2000, it was more phenomenal than the one in Syntagma Square. In addition, they discovered Artistotle's ancient Lyceum while digging for the metro in Athens' outskirts. If it were not for the subway, this fantastic find might have remained buried forever.

Larissa Station stop is your gateway to OSE trains. At the Akropoli Station stands the Acropolis itself, the Temple of Olympian Zeus, and Hadrian's Arch, which marked the city limits in 132 A.D. At Thissio Station you can view the ancient Agora and the Temple of Hephaestus, the best-preserved temple in Greece.

Airport Trains

Arriving by air in Rome's Leonardo da Vince Airport at Fiumicino, you start out saving money with your rail pass, because the airport train, which FS decided in 2000 to name the Leonardo Express, to Rome's Termini station is fully covered, although one-way fare is about $8, so you might not want to use up a day box of a flexipass. The Fiumicino-Rome Termini airport bus was discontinued when the train service began.

Take the escalator or elevator up from the Arrivals level on the ground floor to the second-floor "Stazione FS," shown by international train pictographs. Air arrivals validate their pass at the airport train station and then use it for the 20-mile run to Rome's Termini station in the center of the Eternal City, or they can purchase their tickets at the entrance to the platforms. The machines accept credit cards. Validate your ticket in an orange validating machine before boarding.

Rome's Leonardo Express connects Fiumicino Airport with Rome Termini Station every half hour from 6:51 A.M. to 9:51 P.M., taking a half hour, nonstop. The trains are comprised of a loco and four refurbished one-class carriages. Three Leonardos operate this line, and one is kept on stand-by.

The Leonardo drops you in 2000 reconstructed Terminal Giubileo track ("binario") 25, which falls short of extending into the large Termini Station complex. Terminal Giubileo's impressive spaces, brightly colored and precious marbles, a towering roof, big arches and brick vaults contain a travel agency for train, ferry, and air tickets; Alitalia check-in (for those with hand luggage only); tourist information, and money exchange. Lockers for luggage storage are adjacent to track 24. Taxis await outside Terminal Giubileo.

A second Rome's Fiumicino Airport service using electric double-decked IR trains leaves from platforms parallel to the Leonardo's at the airport train station. They take you every 15-30 minutes to Orte, with intermediate stops at Rome's Tiburtina, Tuscolana, Ostiense, and Trastevere stations (but not Termini).

It is a 40-minute ride to Rome Tiburtina Station, where an island platform on the important north-south bypass of Rome allows you to change to some IR and overnight trains running the Milan-Florence-Naples-Sicily service.

Milan's double-decked Malpensa Express trains, in Malpensa Express livery, white with Bordeaux red front ends, debuted on May 30, 1999, connecting Milan's Malpensa International Airport with Cadorna Ferrovie Nord Milano (FNM, Northern Railroads) Station in the center of Milan every 30 minutes. Travel time is 40 minutes over the 6.92-mile double track at 87 mph peak speed with stops at the following FNM stations: Milan Bovisa, Politechnico, and Saronno Central. Bus services are substituted for the first two morning runs and the last three night runs. They have no intermediate stops.

Board the Malpensa Express on the lower ground floor in Malpensa Airport Terminal One or at the Cadorna FNM Station, platforms one and two. The trains carry 415 passengers, who enjoy air conditioning, electronic display boards, a public announcement system, low entry platforms, and access for the disabled.

You can buy tickets in every Malpensa Express station: Cadorna, Bovisa, Politechnico, Saronno, Malpensa and in all FNM stations. A single ticket costs about $7.50 for adults, $4 for children 4-15. If you purchase the ticket aboard the train, the charge is $10 and $6.50 for children. Day return, monthly, and year tickets are also available. Rail passes are not valid. Your ticket is valid for the Milan Railroad Link ("Passante Ferroviaria"), so you may begin or end your journey at any Milan railroad station, whether it belongs to FNM or FS, and use your ticket on bus 82 or trolley bus 92.

At Cadorna you can connect to metro lines MR1 and MG2, bus, trolley, and taxis at the exit. Or you can change trains departing from Cadorna for Meda-Canzo-Asso, Saronno-Novara, and Saronno-Lake Como.

Cadorna Station is the heart of the city's historic center and very close to many of its most important monuments, including Milan Cathedral, and Castello Sforzesco, Leonardo's Last Supper, and the Scala Opera.

Half-hourly Air Pullman buses from bus platforms 3-4 (use exit 6) take you to the piazza beside the Centrale Station. Air Pullman buses also run to Milan's Linate Airport from bus platforms 19-20 (use exit 4). To reach Linate Airport from Milan, take Metro Line MR1 (see "Milan Centrale" below) to San Babila, then bus No. 73.

Pisa's San Giusto Airport, served by both national and international airlines such as Lufthansa, Air France, Alitalia, and British Airways, is about 50 miles from Florence. It is served by train from Florence S.M.N. station, with check-in at S.M.N.'s Air Terminal, Track 5.

Domestic Italian Overnight Trains

Because of the long travel distances within Italy between Milan or Rome and Sicily or Brindisi, FS's overnight trains are frequently crowded and stuffy (because of the warm climate). Rather than hoping for space to stretch out in sitting compartments, first-class rail-pass holders are more comfortable booking FS's domestic first-class couchettes. These contain only four bunks instead of the six you find in second class. When you don't have time for an advance reservation, you can go directly to the couchette cars and ask the porter. Italian couchette cars have an illuminated sign in three languages (Italian, French, and German) indicating couchette availability.

FS's blue, orange, and white "Sleeperette" carriages contain deeply reclining seats arranged in a salon, so you will avoid paying for a sleeping car. Look for the reclined seat symbol in FS's timetable and departure billboards in the train station.

For upscale comfort (as discussed in "International" chapter above) you ride the EN Pablo Casals between Milan and Barcelona in unprecedented luxury. This is your best connection between Italy and Spain. From Paris, take Artesia's Galilei to Florence, Palatino to Rome, Rialto to Venice, or EN Stendhal to Milan. From Vienna, use the EN San Marco to Venice and the EN Remus to Rome.

Traveling in Sicily

A circuit of Sicily by train gives you a perspective of the sun-toasted island that has been ruled for centuries by foreigners from abroad (meaning Rome in the present case). You see magisterial mountains and farming regulated by water and sun. For 25 centuries Sicilians have accepted Byzantine tax gatherers, Berber emirs, Spanish viceroys, and, since Garibaldi set foot on shore in 1860, the Italian kings and the Italian Republic's governments.

Sicily is by and large a beautiful island, but not well laid-out for an independent traveler by train even though renovation of many Sicilian train stations was completed in 1996. The sights are in the countryside. Local trains are second-string. There are few tourist offices for finding hotels and these are seldom located near the train stations.

This means that to get the best from Sicily you should
• arrange your sleeping accommodations in advance, and
• use a Rail 'n'Drive pass or car-rental arrangement.

Mainline connections to Sicily are to Palermo on the north coast and Siracusa on the east. Stops along the east coast include Messina, Taormina, and Catania (for the city and Mt. Etna). Agrigento lies on the south coast. You can take day trains to/from Rome or Naples, or overnight trains to/from Milan, Rome, or Naples (but be sure to check because some of the Rome trains bypass Rome's Termini station and instead use the suburban Ostiense or Tiburtina stations). For those trains that don't serve Naples Centrale, Naples Piazza Garibaldi station is underground and connected to Centrale with escalators.

Messina Centrale is where the trains from the peninsula split. Half of the carriages go through a 2000 tunnel under Peloritani mountains to Palermo (saving 20 minutes), half to Siracusa. The opposite is true in reverse. The segments are joined together and travel as one up to Naples, Rome, and Milan.

Messina Centrale is good sized, the threshold for all Sicily. It has a very pleasant bar (in the Italian sense, meaning sandwiches, limited hot plates, and of course espresso), but no restaurant. The tourist information office is across the street. In the brown-marble waiting room you can see the arrivals and departures information on color monitors. "Ritardo" means minutes late.

You will be disappointed in Palermo Centrale station. The entrance hall has a shiny marble floor and looks splendid, but train departures' posting is hard to find. You find them in the entrance hall and on the platforms. The direction pictographs are well organized and easy to see.

There is no restaurant, but the bar has a "Tavalo Caldo" (hot table) with fine pasta and some of the biggest sandwiches you will find. If you happen to find someone in the tourist office, the agent will give you an excellent map of Palermo and the region. Good hotels are in the city center, about a mile away, but there is a clutter of two-star hotels straight across Piazza Giulio Cesare down Via Roma.

The limited subway (Metropolitana) connects Centrale station to the port for sailings to Genoa, Leghorn, Naples, Cagliari (Sardinia), Ustica, and Tunis.

Directly to the right as you enter the station from Piazza Giulio Cesare is the train information office. There is an English-/French-language window that is also the Eurail Aid office for Sicily (see Appendix B). Nearby is a small chapel and a day hotel for a shower or haircut. Reservations and ticketing windows line the ticket hall. The waiting room is next to platform 4.

The first thing you see upon arrival in Agrigento is the chapel, but Agrigento Centrale is built on a hillside and is a split-level station. It was renovated in 1996. Departures are on the lower level. Escalators are up only and it is a long way down the steps with bulky luggage. Outside the station, where the city buses stop, is a large map of the Commune of Agrigento and the addresses of the tourist offices. Unfortunately the Greek treasures of the Agrigento region are too far from town to be seen by the use of train. You will need to rent a car or take a sightseeing tour to the Valley of the Temples and the National Archaeological Museum of San Nicola.

Catania Centrale station sits in a beautiful setting, facing the sea. Foaming breakers crash on the black lava rocks below. Most of the facilities line platform 1, including first- and second-class waiting rooms, but you have to use an underground passage ("Sottopassagio") with no escalator to reach the platforms. There is no cafeteria, but there is the usual bar. There are no tourist office or city maps to be found, as well as a dearth of hotels near the train station.

The Circumetnea (FCE) train circles the foot of Mt. Etna and does not climb it. Opened on June 27, 1999, FCE's electrified metro serves a stop beside Catania Centrale FS Station, and the port, and runs on the surface past the scenic sea wall to Borso, where you change to the diesel railcars of the FCE's 68-mile, narrow-gauge line. Rail passes are not accepted.

Taormina Giardini station, which was renovated in 1996, doesn't live up to its beautiful reputation, although taxis waiting in front are ready to take you to dozens of villas and resorts. The small station is cramped on a level above the sea and below the mountain ridges. There is no cafeteria or tourist office.

Siracusa station, renovated in 1996, is arranged along platform 1 with an underpass connecting platforms. There are first- and second-class waiting rooms. There is no cafeteria, but an average bar. On platform 1 you find a large map of Siracusa with red spots indicating the locations of tourist offices within walking distance.

Compelling Sardinia

Italy's green and rocky island of Sardinia is 112 miles from the Italian mainland smack in the center of the western Mediterranean. Getting there by train: very difficult.

Neither Romans nor Phoenicians, Greeks nor Arabs ever subdued Sardinia, the second-largest island in the Mediterranean after Sicily. The uncompromised integrity of the Sardo way of life makes travel through the island personal and compelling.

Nevertheless, rail passes make it possible for you to use without extra charge the fleet of ferries of the Italian State Railroads (FS) which take you to Golfo Aranci, a town at the foot of Capo Figari and gateway to the stupendous Emerald Coast.

Depart from Civitavecchia, 50 minutes by train from Rome. At the FS pier, board one of five FS ferries ready to take you directly to Golfo Aranci in eight hours. FS's newest ferry, the *Logudoro*, was put into service in 1990.

Golfo Aranci is midway between Olbia and the Costa Smeralda. Connecting FS trains take you to Olbia and, via Ozieri Chilirani, to Sassari and Cagliari.

You can also reach Sardinia by Tirrenia Lines ferries from Genoa (Genova), Leghorn (Livorno), La Spezia, Naples (Napoli), and Palermo, Sicily, but these routes are not covered free by your rail pass.

Your rail pass entitles you to free passage aboard the FS ferries using the deck spaces on the verandas, in the salons, and in the bars. For a small supplement you may book reclining chairs for overnight sailings departing both ports at 0:30 p.m. For a greater supplement you can reserve single or double cabins. Cabin reservations are obligatory. Make them at any Italian train station with a reservations terminal.

The FS network honoring your rail pass connects major cities. Decent, cheap private trains and buses take you past sweeping, high-altitude panoramas and surprising stone outcroppings and through countryside known to harbor notorious sheep-nappers. Rome's Forestation Bureau keeps planting fast-growing Canadian pines; shepherds keep burning them down.

You see rocks sculpted like elephants and bears, visit prehistoric nuraghe structures, walk through jewel-box Argonese Alghero and relax on beaches named for the unique color of their waters. No one can do "dolce farniente," sweet nothingness, with more elegance than Italians.

Sardinia's most distinctive finds are the 7,000 nuraghi, which are Bronze Age temples, dwellings, and tombs. They remind you of beehive-shaped cones with large stones laid one over another without the use of mortar. Openings in the domes let in the light.

The nuraghe center is at Barumini, where the ruins are grouped around a central three-story nuraghe. But several are within easy touring distance of the Costa Smeralda.

Sardinia's extensive bus system connects the island's towns and villages, and buses run frequently among the coastal tourist centers. They give the lie to the notion that getting around Sardinia is difficult or dull.

Rome is sending diesel Pendolino trains to Sardinia to scamper through Sardinia's easy central valley. They skirt the wilds that make Sardinia so special. Stop-and-go local trains take you to out-of-the-way, wonderful corners and backwoods. You may miss convenience and luxury, but there is no finer way for you to discover the gracious, proud feel of Sardinia.

Railcars take you from Sassari's busy train station, which is seemingly lost in the center of Sassari's sea of red roofs rolling over graceful hills. But looks are deceiving, for Sassari is a bustling commercial city, the second town in Sardinia, and its train station is crowded.

Sassari's faded, Roman gold-colored terminus serves both FS (some visitors come by train the whole length of the island from Sardinia's capital city, Cagliari) and the private railroad to Alghero, which has its headquarters here.

Alghero lies on a small peninsula surrounded by Aragonese fortifications. Until 1848 the town was locked tightly at night. The former entrance, at the stubby tower of the Porta Terra, is still a good place to begin your walking tour through the narrow streets. The tourist office is nearby, so pick up free color maps for your explorations.

In a sense, Alghero isn't a Sardinian town at all. It started as one, in the early Middle Ages, but Spaniards from Aragon began their Sardinian conquest by annexing Alghero in 1355. The Algherese did not prove to be docile subjects; after two fierce rebellions the Aragonese solved their problem by deporting the entire population to the interior and replacing them with Catalans from the Iberian peninsula.

Everyone enjoys the friendly Catalan atmosphere here—Alghero is now known as "Little Barcelona." Strolling through the narrow streets of the old town gives you a sense of quiet adventure and colorful leisure protected by Aragonese fortifications. You soon discover the busy quay. Photograph scenes along the dock showing a way of life you don't find at home. Green and blue fishing boats tie up to unload crawling, creeping, and leaping Mediterranean marine-life catches. Fishermen mend orange-colored nets on the beaches. You admire the raw pink coral destined for the exquisite cameos.

In 1962, the Aga Khan and his well-heeled friends comprising the Consorzio Costa Smeralda shoveled into Sardinia's northeast coast more than $35 million 1960s dollars to convert the 35-mile strip into a jet-set heaven. They named it Costa Smeralda, the Emerald Coast, for the unparalleled clarity of its waters.

When the Aga Khan arrived, the pastures on the cliffs by the sea were almost uninhabited. The shepherds considered them less valuable than other pieces of land. Think of the Costa Smeralda as an ecological development before ecology became trendy. The consorzio designed and built its dwellings resolving not to impose construction on the environment. The hotels were built to blend into the wild landscape. Tall buildings were forbidden. Construction followed the natural contours of the land. Buildings were earth-colored.

Rail Pass Bonuses

Eurailpass, Europass, Eurail Selectpass, Italy Railcard, and Italy Flexi Rail Card are valid over the entire FS 10,000-mile network, but not private train operators, and include the ferry crossings between Civitavecchia and Golfo Aranci, Sardinia, and Villa S. Giovanni and Messina, Sicily. They include all supplements usually payable for use of high-speed trains except Eurostar Italia.

Eurailpass, Eurail Selectpass, and Greek Flexipass are valid for all OSE travel in Greece, but you must purchase a Greece add-on when you purchase a Europass.

The deck-class crossing to Greece covered free with these passes is a great bargain; otherwise, deck passage would cost about $162, first class; $138, second (plus the charges discussed below). Consecutive-day Eurailpasses in Greece are a great waste, however, because the Greek network is so limited and you will watch your Eurailpass days flitting away unused if you head to the Aegean Islands. With a flexipass, you can enjoy your days on sunny beaches without fretting over lost paid-in-advance Eurailpass days.

Using the free ferry crossings between Brindisi and Patras requires that you pay a high-season surcharge from June 10 to September 30, inclusive. You must pay port taxes in local currencies. Sleeping accommodations such as cabins or airline-type seats cost extra. Before boarding, you must check in at the shipping line's office at the pier. If you wish to stop over in Corfu or Igoumenitsa, you must so state when you receive your ferry ticket. When you ticket only to Corfu, you cannot change your mind and continue to Patras. Clearly, there is much bureaucracy involved.

Italian Railpasses and Italy Flexi Railcards are valid for unlimited travel on FS's network, including the train ferries between Reggio Calabria and Messina.

Second-class travel on Pendolino and ETR 500 trains where comfort is built in and reservations are required is an excellent value; otherwise you will be more comfortable traveling first class in Italy. Second-class trains are sometimes crowded and the Italian habit of lining the corridors can make it hard to move around.

Italy Railcards give you a choice of any eight, 15, 21, or 30 consecutive days of unlimited train travel, either first or second class. Italy Flexi Railcards in both classes are also available for four, eight or 12 travel days in one month. An Italy Rail'n'Drive Pass gives you any three days unlimited train travel in either first or second class with one month to complete your travel, plus two days Hertz car rental in a choice of four car categories.

You may buy your Italian Railcards before you leave or at 16 main train stations in Italy. You validate rail passes at a FS ticket counter before you begin your travel. Make sure the agent enters the first date and last date of validity at the same time. You are not permitted to enter the validity dates yourself. Italian Flexi Railcards issued in Europe must be validated within two months after the date of issue; all others must be validated within six months. Before starting your journey with a flexipass, enter your date of travel in an appropriate box on

492   TRAVELING EUROPE'S TRAINS

your flexipass. Your flexipass is then valid from midnight to midnight. If you are traveling at midnight, your validation is good until the next scheduled stop. When your journey begins after 7 P.M. on an overnight train, enter the following day's date. When using your flexipass on a sea section (Civitavecchia-Sardinia), enter either the date of departure or the date of arrival. Passes are nonrefundable and you don't receive a refund in case of a railroad strike.

First- and second-class Italian Kilometric Tickets (KM) are valid for 20 trips on the entire FS network, but limited to 1,875 miles (3,000 kilometers) within two months. As many as five travelers may participate, even if not related. Each trip is calculated by multiplying the distance traveled by the number of travelers. It only covers the mileage component of the fare.

Travelers 60 and older can purchase a Silver Card allowing a 30 percent reduction on first- and second-class tickets. It is available for one year, five years, and for life. Travelers between 12 and 26 can buy a $20 Green Card valid for one year giving them 30 percent discounts on all first- and second-class tickets (20 percent in high season). A Carta Prima, costing about $20, gives you a 30 percent discount on first-class tickets. For $40 to $75 they join Club Eurostar to also give them access to FS's first-class Eurostar lounges. These cards must be purchased in Italy.

For travel in Greece, you may purchase a Greek Flexipass Rail or a Greek Flexipass Rail & Fly, which gives you to additional option of a one-way flight between Athens and any Greek Island served by Olympic Airlines. The adult rail flexipass is available for three, four, five, or six days travel within a month. The youth rail flexipass is available for three or five days. With the fly option, adults have a choice of three or four days rail, while youth has only the three-day option.

Only at the international ticketing window in Thessaloniki or at the main OSE office at 1 Karolou Street, Athens (open 8 A.M. to 3 P.M., about a five-minute walk from Athens Larissa Station, near Omonia Square, Tel. 529-7001), can you buy very inexpensive Greek Tourist Cards (Carte de Tourisme) valid for 10, 20, or 30 consecutive days travel for one to five people. The 10-day card costs about $40. It does not include supplements payable for travel on IC trains. Senior cards allowing five single trips free (dates restricted) and 50 percent reduction thereafter are granted to travelers over 60.

Traveling in Italy takes you aboard sleek Eurostar Italia trains and gives you five great train stations to serve as your bases.

Eurostar Italian Style
Will the Real Eurostar Please Stand Up?

Try to imagine the looks on the faces of the Eurostar executives in London, Paris, and Brussels when they first heard that FS was going to label their ETR services "Eurostar."
Despite their howls, FS did adopt the name Eurostar for its domestic network of high-speed trains. The use of the Eurostar name was agony to operators of the cross-Channel services, but Fiat, the builder of the train, had "protected" the name before cross-Channel Eurostar services were inaugurated and thus was entitled to use it to promote its new, high-quality ETR 460 and ETR 500 services and to solve the marketing problem created when the nontilt ETR 500 went into commercial service. Previously, FS had designated its high-speed services *P*, for its tilting trains, Pendolinos. To encompass also their super-high-speed, nontilting train, they had to find a snappy, new designation and the cross-Channel services had created name recognition. The bright, new, right-raked-star logo that FS has emblazoned on their ETRs does not infringe on the "real" Eurostar symbol.

The ETR Eurostar Italia
Success Story

1988 ETR 450	1st generation Pendolino	155 mph/Tilting Italy
1995 ETR 460	2nd generation Pendolino	155 mph/Tilting Italy
1996 ETR 470	Cisalpino	124 mph/Tilting To Switzerland
1996 ETR 480	Dual-voltage ETR 460	155 mph/Tilting To France
1996 ETR 500	High-speed train	186 mph/No tilt Italy
2000 ETR 500	Second generation	186 mph/Dual voltage

Italy's modern, high-speed trains are known as ETRs, for "Elettro Treni Rapidi," or rapid electric trains.
Board one of the hourly Eurostar Italia ETR 500 trains from Milan. You pick up speed and streak across the flat Po Valley along the 58-mile Milano-Bologna line, which is one of the most congested in Italy, also carrying IC and IR trains. A new high-speed line, costing about $5.7 million, will open in 2006. On the straightaway, the fertile, green Po Valley's fields of grain, corn, and produce whiz past your graceful train, following the first chord of the Milan-Rome ("MI-RO") segment of the Milan-Bologna-Florence-Rome-Naples-Reggio de Calabria spinal chord which carries about one-third of all FS traffic.

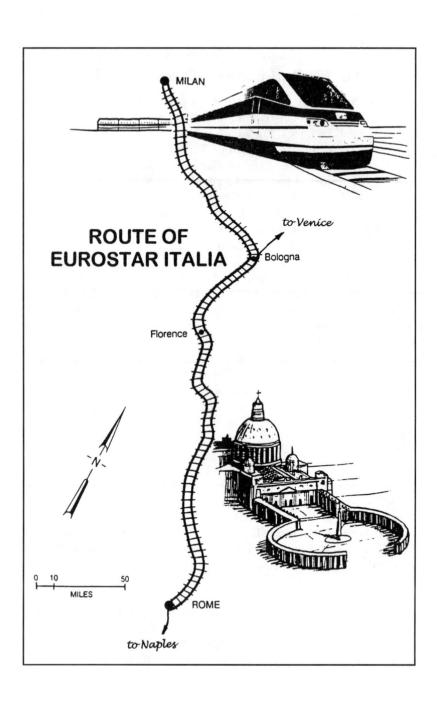

MILAN

**ROUTE OF
EUROSTAR ITALIA**

to Venice

Bologna

Florence

N

0 10   50
    MILES

ROME

to Naples

After your four-minute stop in Bologna Centrale Station, you run at 125 mph about 45 percent of the time along the sinuous route to Florence. The Bologna-Florence chord of the new high-speed line will open in 2004. After an eight-minute halt at Florence S.M.N. Station, you negotiate the main ranges of the Apennines over the already completed double-tracked direttissima high-speed line to Rome through tunnels one after another built in the 1920s, rebuilt to 186-mph capability in the 1990s, and accelerate along an almost straight swath across Latium, Umbria, and Tuscany. Tunnels, including the 8.7-mile Adriana tunnel, eliminate all road-level crossings, and connect FS's older, more wandering route to the new direttissima at various points. In effect, FS created a four-track system between Florence and Rome that successfully handles mixed ETRs, ICs, IRs, and freight, each traveling at a different speed.

Check your watch: Your trip between Italy's two largest cities, 393 miles, takes you four hours, 30 minutes, at an average speed of over 87 mph, with hourly departures. Compare these times to flying between Rome and Milan. You would spend an hour and five minutes in the air, but by the time you add an hour and a half at each end to get to and from the airports and then allow time to check in before your flight and collect your luggage afterwards, the time you spend traveling from city center to city center is about the same. Yet, you spend it more restfully on your luxurious Eurostar Italia, and you can do your work, socialize aboard, and arrive more relaxed.

Perhaps you would rather drive a Lamborghini and pay the tolls on the Autostrada, but you will arrive earlier with the Eurostar Italia at a fraction of the cost. Eurostar Italia gives you more comfort than flying and more speed than a red Lamborghini racing down the Autostrada. ETR 500 competes with the speed of French TGVs, and takes you in great luxury and gives you more time to study the details of the Vatican, the Uffizi, and the Brera museums.

Tilting ETR Pendolino trains have been a success ever since the bullet-nosed, first-generation ETR 450 hit the rails in May 1988. "Si, si," the captain of your train says, nodding to the conductor beside him when you ask about his Pendolino. He volunteers that indeed Pendolino means "little pendulum," because its body tilts gently whenever it rounds a curve, thus minimizing the forces of gravity, but he laughs when he compares the train to a banana, calling the first generation "bananalino" to describe its long and thin profile. Pendolinos' crews are congenial. They are not direct employees of the Italian State Railroads, but hand-picked employees of FS's subsidiary, "Ristofer," hired to staff these beautiful trains.

FS's network of high-speed Eurostar trains includes ETR 500 service Turin-Milan-Verona-Venice, Milan-Bologna-Florence-Rome-Naples (the Rome-Naples high-speed line opens in 2002), and Milan-Bologna-Ancona. ETR 450 and 460 trains take you along the routes Turin/Milan-Genoa-Pisa-Rome-Naples-Foggia-Bari,   Rome-Lecce, Ancona-Rome, Turin-Cuneo-Ventimiglia, Trento-Venice, Florence-Siena-Chiusi, Rome-Campobasso, and Bari-Taranto-Reggio di Calabria via Cosenza or Catanzero.

As ETR 500 units were delivered to FS from the manufacturer, they displaced ETR 460 trains. The ETR 460s then displaced ETR 450 trains with the result that FS continually cascaded modern equipment from prime routes onto offbeat routes, such as to and from Ancona, Palermo, and Taranto.

Like French TGVs (although the concept was not original with them) sleek integral power cars front and back propel the Eurostar Italia trains. The fabrics, materials, and designs remind you so much of airplane interiors that you can't help comparing them to first-class travel on an airplane.

ETR 500

The ETR 500 is a beefy train of two locomotives plus 11 carriages in striking green-and-white livery by Pininfarina. Its first production units began regular service on June 2, 1996. A second generation, dual-voltage ETR went into service on May 28, 2000, traveling the Milan-Rome route. Three carriages are first class with 2+1 seating, and six are second class with 2+2 seating.

The first-generation ETR 500's power cars are somewhat ominous looking and vaguely recall a hooded cobra, with a two-piece windshield, but they were designed also by the Pininfarina company, better known for its design of flashy sports cars. The dual-voltage ETRs appear more benign because the front end has been completely redesigned with a central windshield. The second-generation power cars can operate off 25,000 volts A.C. on the high-speed line, and at 3,000 volts D.C. on the older Italian systems. It can also operate under reduced power at 1,500 volts D.C., and FS hopes to run an eight-carriage ETR 500 between Milan and Paris over the French high-speed lines.

When you board you see the carriage number displayed on the digital display. "FUM" stands for "fumatori," or smoking. "NFM" is nonsmoking. Your first reaction is surprise. It is not like any train you have seen. Perhaps your emotions are heightened by the red color. Flashy red upholstery covers the bucket seats and headrests and extends up the walls to the roofline. It appears big and the carriages long. FS didn't skimp on the furnishings, first class. It's a snazzy train.

The first-class carriages are broken into 2+1 units with facing seats separated by a magazine-rack/trash-receptacle/fold-out-lap-table console. The table is ideal for laptop computers. These console dividers add a degree of privacy. It is a tie-and-briefcase train. You are startled occasionally by the sounds of cellular telephones ringing. The seats recline electrically by the press of a button; push buttons in the armrest control your reading light intensity; and sun screens which you electrically raise and lower between double-paned windows filter the sun's rays to your comfort level. The corridor connections are pressure sealed, which is a help, because there are many tunnels on the Italian high-speed lines.

Make your way to the art deco cafe with 30 yellow-tablecloth restaurant seats arranged 2+1, a stainless steel galley with hot plates and microwave ovens. The stand-up bar of the kind that is familiar on high-speed trains is equipped with an overwhelming coffee machine. Finally, there is a "special-service" carriage with 23 first-class seats, facilities for the handicapped, and two, four-passenger business compartments.

Although ETR 500s do not tilt, the manufacturers claim that the 500 can corner 10-15 percent faster than conventional trains because of its low center of gravity. Even so, you will observe that the ETR 500's ride is not as smooth as a Pendolino at 125 mph over the Milan-Florence stretch, and over the 186-mph Florence-Rome stretch it is not as smooth as a French TGV at the same speed.

ETR 450

FS's ETR 450 train with the Buck Rogers' bullet nose and the "FIAT" nameplate was the leader of the Pendolino generation. It is long, lean, and was at first all first class. Racing like an antelope, it gives you a taste of speed, service, and extravagance. These tilting maroon-and-red Pendolino trains that took you between Rome and Milan with unprecedented speed still provide you quality accommodation, ride, and speed over FS' branch lines.

The 450's luxurious interiors allow you to fold down tables and stretch out in the 22-inch wide, fresh-smelling aquamarine and slate-green plush seats, which are lined up 2+1, with a 39-inch pitch. Wall-to-wall carpeting is blue; cooling and heating originates at baseboards. Coach bodies are tapered from the waist up so that when the 450 tilts it does not protrude beyond the travel envelope. The windows are streamlined, longer, but not nearly so high as on older trains. You pass through fearless gangways between carriages so you don't feel terrified crossing from car to car while purring along up to 155 mph. Leave your luggage in the luggage racks near the door when you enter.

The environmentally correct closed-cycle toilets in front are also similar to those on airlines, except the Pendolino's are larger and have a rubber mat flooring.

ETR 460

FS' second-generation ETR 460 Eurostar Pendolino train is the utilitarian workhorse of Italy's mainline network. The 40 ETR 460 trains (there are 15 ETR 450s) entered service in May 1995, and now carry you over nearly all the main routes of FS, serving routes to and from Genoa, Venice, Bari, Lecce, and Sicily.

You look ahead and see you are approaching a considerable curve: watch to see how your Eurostar Italia ETR 460 Pendolino performs. You are seriously startled to observe one side of your carriage physically rising. Pendolini overcome curves magnificently. They tilt positively, hold their stance through the arc and return you comfortably to the horizontal without delay.

This second-generation Pendolino differs from the ETR 450 in several significant features.

• The exterior by Giugiaro design replaces the ETR 450's bullet nose, which was considered old-fashioned, but which made a statement. The ETR 460's more functional and less dramatic profile gives better vision and more room in the driver's cabin.

• Wider body width makes it less of a "Bananalino" and allows second-class seats to be positioned 2+2 without crowding.

• Higher-powered motors allow the number of individual carriages that are powered to be reduced from eight to six.

• Full pressure-sealing permits maximum-speed transit through the many tunnels on the direttissima high-speed line between Florence and Rome and the other associated lines served by Pendolinos.

- The tilt system is located entirely beneath the carriages instead of taking up passenger space.
- Improved interiors equipped with earphone jacks for taped music at every seat.
- Higher-strength coach body aluminum extrusions and positioning of pantographs.

You find the 460's ride excellent, like gliding on velvet. The interiors are respectable, but not extravagant. The 460s have the same short windows as the 450s and some interior design similarities to the ETR 500s of the same age. The 460's seats recline mechanically. Consoles separate facing seats, which happens seldom in first class, but occurs at every second set of rows in second class. These smaller consoles accommodate fold-out tables only.

Grand Train Stations
Islands of Order

Italian train stations are islands of order in seas of confusion. Travelers in Italy find sustenance in five of Europe's best stations. Use Milan's, Rome's, and Florence's centrally located stations as your bases for luxuries and good cafeterias. Venice's remarkably located Santa Lucia station is a scenic vaporetto ride away from the Piazza San Marco. You'll pass through Naples Centrale on your way to the beautiful Amalfi coast.

Milan Centrale

This is the grand station of Europe, a cyclopean complex opened in 1931. The station itself is a tourist sight. Its grandiose, eclectic style has been characterized as "Assyrian-Babylonian," or "Mussolini Modern." Over the arriving trains a set of five glassed arches ascending in size make this a magnificent construction. Its waiting room is enormous, and its staircases between street and train levels—humanely equipped with up and down escalators—sweeping. If you pause on one of the beautiful landings midway on the stairs, take a long look at the expanse of the lower hall.

When you enter the upper hall you see a feature so gracious it is unique. A bubbling water fountain—its sounds fighting the cacophony of the trains—shoots above a polished rose-colored marble floor surrounded by wire-web jump seats and warm pastel mosaics.

ISLANDS OF ORDER

MILAN

VENICE

ITALY

FLORENCE

Mediterranean Sea

-N-

0   20   100

MILES

ROME

The long hall itself is highlighted by the creatively positioned "Gran Bar" at one end and "Informazioni" (for train information) at the other. FS's Informazioni is where you validate your rail passes. It also contains a money change counter. In fact, you find three places to change your money in Milan Centrale: in the bank located on the long wall next to the "APT Tourist Information" sign indicating the city information office on the train level (open 8 A.M. to 7 P.M., Monday-Saturday; 9:30 A.M. to 12:30 P.M. and 1:30 to 6 P.M., Sunday), in the FS Informazioni office, and a glitzy money change operation right next to the tracks. The bank gives the best rate, the change operator the poorest. There is an ATM machine between the bar in the center and track entrance numbered 3. Outside the bank is a bank-note change machine working (hopefully) 24 hours. Instructions are in four languages—press "English." You simply slip in American greenbacks and out come paper lire. It takes most European and overseas currencies, so it is a quick way to change stray leftover francs, marks, or pounds sterling. Exchange rates are superior to the money change office in the platform area.

The tourist information office has a back room filled with free brochures and booklets to answer your questions. Be sure to pick up a monthly "What's on in Milan," a good map, and (in English) a comprehensive "Museums in Milan."

Luggage checking is deviously located down a hall near the information office. Look for the illuminated suitcase sign. Also along the corridor you won't miss the "Free Shop." This name must be some kind of a Milanese joke considering the substantial prices, but it is a highlight walk-through to see the most devastatingly complete "travelers' provisions" store in Europe. You find everything that you considered packing but left behind because you didn't have space. Get items ranging from take-out pizza to alarm clocks and blank video tapes. Use it as your source of take-along liter bottles of water.

Near the center of the long wall upstairs is the entrance to the waiting room, "Sala Attesa." The classic second-class room is filled with banks of antique, varnished wooden benches. You would hear echoes from its marble walls except that modernization has introduced an emergency fire exit, a children's play area, and a false ceiling with indirect lighting.

The architectural counterpoint to the Free Shop is the glass and chrome stand-up bar next to the "Gran Bar" at the end of the station. Here you can enjoy coffee, cakes, and sandwiches.

In a station so enormous it is lucky that ticketing and reservations, domestic and foreign have been organized on street level into four sections in three halls ("Biglietteria") with towering ceilings. To give it some kind of order, the windows are all numbered. Biglietteria Est (east) windows 49-60 (open 7 A.M. to 8:30 P.M.) are available for seat reservations and couchettes. Take a waiting number from the machine as you enter. Credit cards are not accepted here. In Biglietteria Ovest (west), window 14 is for local lines, window 16 is for resident rail passes, and windows 20 and 22 are for international tickets. In the center you buy domestic tickets at windows 27-46 (credit cards accepted).

The "Self Service" is a dimly lit cafeteria next to the "Gran Bar," down from a place for freshening up called the "Hour Hotel." Food is relatively good, and the lighting fixture looks as though it hopped right out of a thirties movie.

The entrance to the post office is outside on the ground level, conveniently tucked into the same edifice.

You must produce a ticket or rail pass to enter the train area, a good idea that keeps the platform relatively negotiable. Luggage carts that fit the escalators to street level rent for 1,000 lire, which is not returnable.

You can't have much respect for a Metro system when the ticketing machines are broken and you must buy your ticket from a newsstand, but Milan has three Metro lines. Line 1 (red line) with its sober Italian design dates from the sixties; Line 2 (green line) was opened second; and Line 3 (yellow line) was opened in 1990. Shorthand designations for the lines are MR1, MG2, and MY3.

Milan's transportation network includes surface lines as well as the three underground lines. A ticket costing 1500 lire is valid for 75 minutes in any combination of surface and metro, but for only one metro stretch (up to the limits of Cascina Gobba and Sesto Marelli), so be sure to save your ticket when you leave the subway for the free transfers. You may also buy one- or two-day tickets at about 3.5 and 6 times, respectively, the cost of a single-fare ticket. A booklet of 11 tickets is sold for the price of 10, and more than one person may use them provided one of the group holds the serial number of the ticket booklet. This is a good deal for groups or families visiting Milan for more than one or two days. A day or two-day ticket is better for single travelers zipping back and forth on public transportation. Write your name and passport number on the ticket.

Enter the subway stations at signs with the white letter *M*

(Metropolitana) in a red field. Surface stops for streetcars, etc., are marked by orange signposts bearing the emblem of the transit authority (ATM) and showing the stops on the route. Milan's two subway lines from the outlying areas in the western and northeastern sections of the city intersect near the Sforza Castle and Piazzale Loreto. One of Milan's great pleasures is rising on the escalator from the subway and seeing Milan's wedding-cake Duomo (cathedral) revealed before you.

Obtain a free system map and helpful guide (in English) at the office of the transit authority in the Duomo station, the Provincial Tourist Authority in Cathedral Square, or the Municipal Information Office in the nearby Galleria.

Line MY3 takes you from in front of Centrale station to the Duomo, the center of town with adjacent arcade and nearby opera house. The subway corridors are serpentine but decently signed. For the Duomo on Line 3 use direction "S. Donato" from Centrale. To return, use direction "Zara."

Milan's train stations include Porta Garibaldi, which is slightly closer to the center than Centrale, on metro Line MG2, for suburban train service; Porta Genova, on the southwest edge of the city; Lambrate for trains not intended to serve Milan; Rogoredo; and Porta Romana, mainly used for freight. Cadorna Northern Railroads Station at the junction of MR1 and MG2 lines (near Sforza Castle, and only two subway stops from the Duomo) is the terminus for the Malpensa Express airport train and Northern Railroads' connection to Como, Erba, Varese, etc. Porta Genova on Line MG2 connects Milan to the west. Line MG2 connects Lambrate with Centrale, Cadorna, and Piazza Genova train stations.

Reaching Milan's Centrale station from Milan's Porta Garibaldi station is quite simple. Follow the signs to the subway, buy your subway ticket, and take Line MG2 (direction: "Gessate") two stops to "Centrale F.S."

Rome Termini

On January 29, 2000, the Italian prime minister inaugurated the refurbished Rome Termini Station, which after a long and thorough restyling, became the largest train station in Europe, according to the prime minister, but he didn't give any basis. In fact, it is 2.37 million square feet large.

Architects designed the enlarged complex to serve not only as a transit point for visitors, but to also to be a service complex for Romans. Pathways were cleared for access to trains, including the Fiumicino Airport train, buses, taxis, and the Metropolitano subway. New elevators, escalators, a main staircase, and a moving walkway make it easier for you to get around the expanded station and to the Metropolitano below.

The electric signs are the most modern, and a closed-circuit surveillance system connects with a control room to alert police. You find 40 automatic ticketing machines, 240 electronic information points, and 100 shops. Free luggage carts, with no deposit, are aligned in front of the station, but you will be lucky to find one on a platform when you arrive.

On the street level, in the so-called "Dinosaur," the famous glassed-over outer hall built in the fifties by architect Montouri, you find ticketing for the day of travel, an enormous book store, and office for making your reservations and advance ticketing. Take a number, and be prepared for a long wait. If you know your train and date of travel, it is easier to use one of the ticketing machines, which accept debit cards but not credit cards, but rail pass holders seeking a reservation without a ticket have no choice but to wait in the reservations/ticketing office.

In the expanded inner hall, adjacent to the train platforms, you find the Eurail Aid office (take a number), Club Eurostar (open only to members), the fine cafeteria "Self Serve," a storefront McDonald's so you can carry food onto the trains, money change, "Bancomat" ATMs, and a tourist information office with friendly interns. Adjacent to track one are lockers costing about $1.50 or $2, depending on size (press the "English" button), a pleasant waiting room, and a WC costing about $.50. Adjacent to track 24 you find more lockers, the terminal for the Leonardo Express airport train, a second information office, and a taxi row.

"Self Service" cafeteria is now the best train station cafeteria in Europe and recommendable anywhere. Management has taken a formerly very good cafeteria, added a live piano player at mealtimes, and beautified it with marble, flowers, and modular service centers to make it a pleasure to use. It even has a mezzanine and an outdoor patio with umbrella-shaded tables. Service is good. Selection is excellent.

On the underground level, you find a new 130,000-square-foot center containing Rome's largest bookshop, with many travel titles, an

Internet Cafe, a second, sit-down McDonald's, and "Drug Store," which is really a supermarket. Follow the signs *M* to the Metropolitano. Rome has two subway lines: *A* (red) and *B* (blue). One wonders what color the subway trains were originally, because they are so completely covered by graffiti it is impossible to tell. Fares are about $1.25 within Rome, valid for 75 minutes, and about $4 to Fiumicino Airport by subway.

Metro line *A*'s cars take you between Anagnina Station and Ottaviano Station near the Vatican City with stops at Roma Nord train station; Spagna for the Spanish Steps; Vittorio E, and Barberini. Metro line *B*'s cars run south to the EUR Center, where some hotels are located. Deposit the correct change in the ticket-vending machines on the walls of the entrance hall or buy metro tickets individually or in booklets of 10 for a 14 percent discount in one of the station's several tobacco shops.

Rome has five train stations. When you ride a through train scheduled to connect two cities other than Rome, the trains stop at Rome's Tiburtina or Ostiense station in Rome's outskirts. Some 12 FS trains a day depart from Termini via Ostiense, but it is easier to reach Ostiense via subway. Tuscolana and Trastevere serve trains in the direction of Pisa. But your prime destination is Rome's Termini, in the throbbing heart of the Eternal City.

Florence S.M.N.

The tile-roofed Tuscan town on the Arno River doesn't quite center on Florence S.M.N. (Santa Maria Novella) station, but the whole area between the station and the Pitti Palace across the Arno is crowded year round with European tourists. Congregation areas include in front of the Duomo (cathedral), Piazza della Signorina, Piazza della Republica, and the Ponte Vecchio.

Florence's station is similar to Rome's Termini. Probably the same architectural firm was employed. It is one of the most pleasing Italian train stations because of its long architectural lines and modern layout, and is airy with its inner and outer halls and parking garage below. Because there is no metro to complicate getting around, it is easy to find your way, and luggage carts are available.

Facing the spacious track area are money change counters and waiting rooms ("Sala di Attesa") opposite track 5. Next to the waiting rooms go to "Informazioni Treni," open 7 A.M. to 9 P.M., for train information.

Take a number slip from the machine. "Ufficio Turismo," tourist information, where patient agents make your hotel reservations is opposite track 16.

As you exit the platform area into the enclosed hall you pass "Composizione Treni Principali" boards. In the enclosed hall you probably won't use windows 9-20 for domestic ticketing, but enter the side room to find reservations ("prenotazioni") counters, open 7 A.M. to 9 P.M.; international ticketing ("Biglietti Internazionali"), open 6:30 A.M. to 10 P.M.; and window 7 for boat tickets to Sardinia. Take a number from the machine on the wall for your turn to be announced.

S.M.N.'s "Self Service" restaurant is the equal of those in other grand Italian stations. It is managed well and offers excellent selections.

Florence S.M.N. is conveniently located near the center of Florence. Hotels surround it, and more hotels are located in the direction of the Arno River, the Duomo, and the Piazza della Signorina, but the city nearly cracks at the seams with travelers during the summer so it is best to get there early and to rely on arrangements by the Tourist Office.

Other train stations in Florence include Castello, Rifredi (where FS's Pendolinos call), Fiesole Caldine, and Campo di Marte, but S.M.N. is your base. Train calls are made in Italian and English.

Venice's Santa Lucia

Leaving Santa Lucia is like stepping into a dream. The Grand Canal stretches right before you, crammed with gondolas and busy with vaporetti (water buses) ready to take you through a wondrous world.

Travelers lured to the City of the Doges will be pleased with their welcome at Venice's beautifully situated Santa Lucia station. Although not a hub like the other grand stations, it provides an appropriate terminal for excellent trains such as Pendolinos and InterCities.

At the head of the tracks you find palm trees and blooming red flowers. Facing the platforms is a restaurant, a sweet shop for take-out items, and a self-service cafeteria area extending to an open-air awning-covered verandah facing the canal where you enjoy dining in one of the most gracious train terminal surroundings. Inside you find a Tourist Office, FS change office, bank, reservations counter open until 10 P.M., ticketing, luggage storage, and post office.

Venice has two stations. Mestre is the stop for your express trains between Italy and Slovenia and Croatia. Santa Lucia is your stop to meet the vaporetti to St. Marks Square. In style it recalls Florence

S.M.N. with long marble steps covered with young and old idlers. Across the Grand Canal, visitors lounge on the steps of green-domed Fondamente S. Simeon Piccolo and on the Ponte degli Scalzi soaring over the canal in picture-book Venetian style. Gondoliere mooring their black gondolas across the canal do a brisk business.

Vaporetti require two floating terminuses. On the left as you exit Santa Lucia, line 2 (Diretto) takes a shortcut through a side canal to reach San Marco. Line 34 (Tourist) takes the scenic route.

Naples Centrale

Naples is a teeming, busy, littered city—Europe's most densely populated. There are almost no green or parks in the center. But it is not threatening either, as you may have heard. Naples is not a tourist destination, but it is a jumping-off point for the beautiful Amalfi coast and Capri, which are some of your best holiday choices. You can visit Sorrento, Pompeii, Herculaneum, and Mt. Vesuvius by use of the private Circumvesuviana railroad with a station below the Centrale station. It does not accept Eurailpass, Europass, or Italian Railpass, but fares are inexpensive.

Naples Centrale train terminus is complex. It consists of four train stations. On the surface you see the glass and steel shell of Naples Centrale, a dead-end station where trains refuse to end. Sharing the level below are FS's Naples Piazza Garibaldi station (which is a through station), the Metropolitana, and the second station of the Circumvesuviana, the private commuter-cum-tourist-mininetwork between Naples and Sorrento. The first Circumvesuviana station is Stazioni Termine. In the bowels of the earth, down a second set of escalators, the trains themselves burrow their separate ways like moles determined to reach the Amalfi Coast (with a stop at Pompeii).

Naples Centrale has all the facilities of the great Italian stations. In particular, the snack bar serves the best pizza from a wood-fired pizza oven. Pizza is one of the few things less expensive in Italy than the U.S.

The ticketing windows in the main entry, "Biglietteria," are marked electronically from 1 to 24. Window 17 is for rail passes. Window 18 is for automobile and ship transportation and sleeping car reservations. Windows 19-23 are for couchette and seat reservations. The tourist office opposite window 1 ("Ente Provinciale per il Turismo di Napoli") is small, with limited brochures. train information and money change are by window 24.

Naples Centrale is the major station of Naples, but the line through Piazza Garibaldi station also connects Naples Piazza Cavour, Naples Montesanto, Naples Mergellina, and Naples Campi Flegrei stations, east to west.

Eastern Europe
and Russia

Most train travelers prefer to travel no farther east than the limits of the EuroCity network, i.e., the guarantee of decent service (which is Warsaw, Prague, Bratislava, Budapest, and Zagreb), but for the hearty and stalwart, traveling east is not difficult once you have your papers in order. It is just arduous and irksome.

Traveling farther east into Russia requires that you be as hardy as a bear. Travel is an endless exercise in problem solving. When you enjoy this exercise, you'll be at home. For relaxation, travel the trains in the West. As you travel east, trains become slow and dirty, service is rude, reservations are difficult or impossible, and getting as far as Moscow or St. Petersburg from central Europe takes days. The farther you travel from your jumping-off place, Berlin or Vienna, the more difficult trains become. Take with you a deck of cards, map(s), pages photocopied from the Thomas Cook European Timetable, meals to eat, and liquids to drink. When you travel with determination and a hide of steel, you'll get to your destination knowing you got a good price.

Trains are improving as the Eastern countries get their economic noses above water. You can buy Polrailpasses, Czech Flexipasses and Prague Excursion Passes, Hungarian Flexipasses, Bulgarian Flexipasses, European East Flexipasses, and Balkan Flexipasses for excellent prices.

One of the woes of traveling in the East is the non- or partial convertibility of the national currencies. Polish and Czech currencies are accepted nowhere else, but they may be reconverted to hard currency (at a substantial penalty) before leaving. If you have Russian rubles, you are stuck. No one will change rubles into hard currency.

Take as many dollar notes as you feel you may need, and then take 50 percent more. Take lots of $1, $5, and $20 bank notes, crisp from your bank, and you will be surprised how much difficulty this saves you. In Russia, you can get a taxi ride when you say "dollars." Dollar notes are accepted—and given priority—everywhere.

Smart Traveling on the Trains of Poland, the Czech Republic, and Slovakia

Trains of Poland—Polrailpass—Trains of the Czech Republic—Czech Rail Passes—Trains of Slovakia

Although Poland, the Czech Republic, and Slovakia were closely associated with the Soviet Union for many years, the trains of these countries run on standard European gauge, boast nearly Western standards, and look Western rather than Russian. They do however share a concession from the Russian Railways—they are the only national railroads that are allowed to run carriages into Russia.

You can get around quite easily provided you don't mind waiting in line for reservations, which makes a rail pass, issued before you leave, even more attractive. Reservations are required on many of the better trains, but when you carry a first-class rail pass, you will find the first-class sections relatively empty, compared with the often-crowded second-class sections. Travelers who enjoy leaning out windows and cursing air-conditioning will love these trains. The windows can be lowered after you locate the push button in the stainless-steel grip at the top.

When you plan to travel in Poland, the Czech Republic, and Slovakia plus Austria and Hungary, a European East Pass (valid for unlimited travel in these countries) works wonders. The European East Pass is available for first-class (your only option) travel for five days plus optional additional days bringing your total to 10 days travel within a month. Children four-11 pay half adult fare; those under four travel free.

Trains of Poland

The Polish Railroads (PKP, for Polskie Koleje Panstwowe, *www.pkp.pl*, and click "Europe Online") runs a full complement of first- and second-class trains over its 14,438-mile network. The Polish-built carriages are Western in nature, with compartments on the long-distance trains. Trains are classified

- Pociag osobowy (local), which are uncomfortable and slow, characterized by crowding and generally poor standards of maintenance and cleaning.
- Pociag pospieszny (fast), which stop at moderately sized stations, and usually have a first-class carriage,
- Pociag expresowy (express), which run between major cities, charge a higher fare, carry a buffet car, and require seat reservations except for pass holders, and
- Pociag InterCity/Eurocity, which are top-quality expresses, with full service restaurant car, and require a higher supplement. Seat reservations are advisable even for pass holders, and may be easier to make at Orbis offices than train stations. You may receive a complimentary snack at your seat. InterCity trains linking Warsaw with Poznan, Katowice, Krakow, and Gdansk are well appointed.

Tickets are sold at most stations. Credit cards are usually accepted, but be sure to use a counter displaying a credit card logo. If you board from a station without an open ticket counter, go immediately upon boarding to the conductor's office in the first carriage to buy one. An *R* inside a box means that reservations are mandatory, an *R* without a box means that seat reservations are required on part of the train, and an *RF* means that you can make reservations if you desire. They are free.

First-class carriages are red-and-white, seat 3+3, and have carpeting. Green-and-white second-class carriages seat 4+4 and have linoleum on the floor. Couchettes, with six bunks per compartment, are blue-and-white. The red WARS ("Przedsiebiorstwa Wagonow Sypialnych i Restauracyjnych") restaurant cars have kitchen and white-tablecloth covered tables. For short domestic routes, PKP hooks together three-unit, second-class-only, yellow-and-blue electric railcars to form nine-car trains. The domestic timetable shows departures for 20 destinations. ECs, ICs, IRs and Expresses (Ex) comprise about two-thirds of the total.

Warsaw is the hub of the Polish Railroads' domestic network. PKP radiates from Warsaw along a 201-mile mainline to the Baltic coast at Gdansk; east through Brest to Moscow; south to Krakow; southwest to Vienna with connections to Prague; northeast to St. Petersburg via Vilnius; and west to Berlin via Poznan.

Leave your train at Centralna station on Al. Jerozolimskie for your
visit to Warsaw. Trains continue underground until approximately
three long blocks west of the Vistula and cross the Vistula rail bridge
to Wschodnia station at Ul. Kijowska, but Wschodnia is primarily platforms with little else. Warsaw-Gdanska (located at ul. M. Buczka) lies
on the north side of the Polish capital. It primarily serves Gdansk, but
is also used by Russian trains to and from Berlin running through
Warsaw. The Warsaw Railroad Museum is located at the Warsaw
Glowna train station near Zawiszy Square, where you see dozens of
model trains from around the world, and its outdoor yard has steam
locomotives of all types and sizes.

You approach Centralna on ground level and pass into a large, dark
platform area with the four-level station building constructed over the
tracks. The aluminum-and-glass structure is spattered with posters and
grit to make it appears as unattractive as possible, yet it is located in the
midst of a new generation of modern hotels with many of the internationally known names represented. It's a convenient arrangement for
you, although it is a good mile from Warsaw's beautiful Old City.

The centerpiece of Centralna is the soaring main hall with domestic reservations windows consuming an entire wall. On the opposite
side, you find money change ("Kasa Walutowa," open 8 A.M. to 10 P.M.)
located in the domestic information ("Informacja") side room. The
tourist information office (open 9 A.M. to 7 P.M.) provides information
in English, including information on train connections, public transportation in Warsaw, hotel prices, and sightseeing in Warsaw.
Sandwich counters, open 24 hours, are located on facing side of the
hall. You want international reservations, which are entered at counters 1-11 on the mezzanine level upstairs (open 24 hours, with breaks).
The mezzanine level also contains waiting rooms.

In the main hall, clacking arrivals ("Przyjazdy") and departures
("Odjazdy") signboards direct you to the correct platform ("Peron")
below. Train composition charts are posted in the center of the departure platforms.

Centralna is connected underground to an extensive shopping center and the adjacent Srodmiescie station for local trains.

The best train south from Warsaw is the Polish EuroCity Sobieski,
departing at 10:17 A.M., to Vienna's South train station, arriving at 4:33
P.M. The Sobieski cuts about 50 minutes from the former timetable,
running along the along on the Polish CMK (Central Main Line) line

through quiet farm country. The line, which is an inverted *Y* with Warsaw at the top, Krakow at the southeast, and Katowice at the southwest, also hosted French TGV-R trains, where they ran at 100 mph, and provided a venue for testing Italian ETR 460 trains, where they established the Polish speed record of 155 mph. To Prague, ride the Polish IC Praha. To Berlin, use the EuroCity Varsovia or the Polish EuroCity Berolina. The direct Warsaw-Krakow Express Malopolska rips right along the CMK reaching Krakow (178 miles) at 68 mph.

The new platforms at Krakow's Glowny station are very good and well arranged and the station house has been brightly touched up to be very pleasant and efficient, but here's the problem: they didn't build the platforms near the station (no Polish jokes, please). The solution is not to descend and then climb the platforms' stairs, which will lead you to the street, but to look for the yellow station house across the tracks and then walk to the very end of the platform where there is a makeshift ground-level walkway directly to the station house. You avoid the stairs and enter the main doorway to the station. The station is orderly. Without difficulty you find a money change office (no ATM), ticketing, information, a bright waiting room with blond wooden benches, and taxis and streetcars outside. There's a pizzeria and a very nice WARS cafeteria ("Restauracja"). The train compositions ("Plan Zestawienia Wagonow") are given in the tunnel beneath the tracks. Departure posters include the departure platform number ("Peron").

Connections to Minsk and Moscow use Polish carriages attached to Russian trains. To reach Krakow from the West, you travel either southeast on the Polish IC Wawel, using the border crossing at Frankfurt/Oder, from Berlin, or from Prague (with changes at Prerov and Katowice). To reach Krakow from Vienna, use the EuroCity Sobieski and change at Katowice.

Before you go, write the Polish National Tourist Office. They will send you a fine packet containing a good road map of Poland, a good Poland brochure as well as Warsaw and Krakow brochures, Orbis and American Travel Abroad brochures, a LOT brochure of nonstop flights to Warsaw from New York and Chicago, a hotel list, and—if you ask—a list of domestic trains.

Polrailpass

With a rail pass, at a moment's notice, you can hop on a train and be on your way. A Polrailpass is available from Orbis in North America (see Appendix A, *www.orbis-usa.com*), Europe, or Poland, and at PKP stations within Poland. It may not be readily recognized, but it allows unlimited travel on most trains (including expresses) without prior seat reservation (subject to availability). It is advisable to make reservations for seats on EC and IC trains, and these reservations are free. Reserved sleepers and couchettes require an extra charge. To order a Polrailpass in the U.S., send to Orbis your passport number and date of travel. If you are unsure of your date of travel, Orbis can issue an open pass for you to validate at any railway station in Poland before your trip. On the other hand, if you are entering Poland by train, it will be wise to have it validated when it is issued so that you merely show it to the Polish conductor when he checks.

Adult passes are available, first- and second-class, for eight, 15, and 21 days and one month. Juniors under 26, having the same choices, receive 30 percent off. Children four-10 pay half. You can refund unused fixed-date passes, less a $10 service charge, provided they are returned before you depart. Open (undated) passes can be refunded, less $10, within six months after date of issue. No refunds are granted for lost or stolen passes.

EuroCity trains between Berlin and Warsaw

(1)	(2)	(3)				(3)	(2)	(1)
0655	1255	1655	dep.	BERLIN (Zoo)	arr.	1301	1702	2302
0815	1415	1815	dep.	Frankfurt/Oder	arr.	1145	1545	2345
0834	1434	1834	arr.	Rzepin	dep.	1120	1520	2120
1012	1612	2012	arr.	Poznan (Glowny)	dep.	0945	1345	1945
1301	1901	2301	arr.	WARSAW (Centralna)	dep.	0700	1100	1700
1312	1915	2315	arr.	WARSAW (Wschodnia)	dep.	0645	1045	1645

(1) EUROCITY VARSOVIA: First- and second-class compartments and dining car between Berlin and Warsaw
(2) EUROCITY PADEREWSKI: First- and second-class compartments and dining car between Berlin and Warsaw
(3) EUROCITY BEROLINA: First- and second-class compartments and dining car between Berlin and Warsaw

---

Trains of the Czech Republic

Americans don't need a visa to visit the Czech Republic for up to 30 days, and British and Irish citizens can stay for up to 180 days, but

Canadians, New Zealanders and Australians must obtain a visit for a stay of up to 30 days. Immigration checks and customs inspections take place aboard your train without its having to stop at the border.

On the sides of musty green Czech carriages and worn locomotives that deserve service stripes for their many years of hard usage, you used to see "C S D" for the CzechoSlovakian Railroads (the former Ceskoslovenske Statni Drahy). Often the *S* was erased, leaving "C...D," for Ceske Drahy (*http://idos.datis.cdrail.cz*), now the Czech Republic's railroads. The newer carriages and locomotives of course now bear only "CD."

CD operates 7,238 passenger trains daily, of which 32 are EuroCity (EC), two are SuperCity (SC), 11 InterCity (IC), 16 Expres (Ex), 257 fast trains (R = Rychlik), 208 semifast trains (Sp = Spesny vlak), and 617 local trains (Os = Osobni vlak). First-class costs 50 percent more than second. Visa and MasterCard are accepted.

In 2000, CD speeded up operation on the mainline between Prague and Brno, permitting 100-mph operation for the first time in history. Running via Pardubice and Ceska Trebova, the Brnensky Drak Express (meaning "Brno Dragon") and EC trains cover the 160-mile line in two hours, 42 minutes, which is 19 minutes faster than before, at an average speed of 59 mph, which is the fastest ever train connection between these cities. You will see further time savings with the full completion in 2002.

You save 30 minutes along whole 282-mile corridor between Decin and Breclav. Between Prague and Brno, the republic's largest cities, there are seven pairs of EC trains, including the EC Johann Gregor Mendel to Vienna, which runs in July and August only.

On the northern corridor Prague-Berlin, six EC trains run daily, with departures every two hours during most of the day. EC Jan Hus runs between Prague and Dresden. EC Alois Negrelli runs between Prague and Hamburg. An overnight train takes you Prague-Amsterdam via Dresden.

CD hopes in 2003 to put into service seven 143-mph tri-voltage tilting trains based on the Italian Pendolino for running on the Berlin-Prague-Vienna corridor. Production is taking place in the Fiat Ferrovaria plant in Savigliano, Italy. Each seven-carriage set will offer 102 first-class and 220 second-class seats. The sets will be equipped for the D.C. and A.C. systems used in the Czech Republic and the power supplies in Germany and Austria.

The green-and-white Czech EC and IC train carriages are of good quality, and stop only at major stations. Some have dining cars. Overnight trains have couchettes and sleeping compartments. You can reserve your seat; reservations are obligatory on some fast trains. Semifast trains run over longer routes and stop only at stations judged to be significant. They bypass smaller stations most of the time but may stop at every station in a mountain region. They carry both first- and second-class carriages. Local trains generally stop at every station and provide second-class service only.

EuroCity and InterCity trains cross into the Czech Republic from all its neighbors. Your best train between Prague and Munich and Zurich is the Swiss EuroCity Albert Einstein. At Ceska Kubice, shortly after the border crossing, the German locomotive is changed to a CD diesel, and uniformed Czech customs officials walk through the train, joking among themselves. They merely glance at American passports. No visa is required. It seems no one even notices your luggage. The CD on-board timetables are in Czech, but the times and city names are clear.

The EC Vindobona and EC Hungaria provide service from Berlin in the morning. The Hungarian EC Hungaria then continues through to Bratislava and Budapest. The EC Vindobona continues to Vienna. The EC Antonin Dvorak connects Vienna and Prague.

Take the German EuroCity Karlstein from Dortmund-Cologne-Frankfurt/Main-Nuremberg. The Russian train Vltava leaves Prague's Hlavni station with three CD sleeping cars for a two-day, two-night trip through Poland and Belarus for Moscow.

JLV (Jidelni a Luzkove Vozy), the Czech Restaurant and Sleeping Car company, caters service in sleeping cars, in couchettes, in restaurant cars, and in station facilities. You can ride blue Czech sleeping cars and couchettes arranged the same as those of the Western European railroads and travel over many routes, including the Dukla between Prague and Moscow, and to and from destinations as far away as Malmo, Berlin, Paris, Venice, Athens, and Bucharest. Their restaurant cars travel as far as Zurich, Vienna, Warnemunde, and Budapest. The restaurant cars on these trains are valiantly fighting decay, but it is a losing battle. Nevertheless the meals are very good. The menu is in Czech, German, and English. Although prices are quoted in Czech crowns, Swiss Francs, German Marks, and Austrian Schillings are equally welcome. The price level is about the same as in Germany.

Prague has four train stations, but only Hlavni nadrazi (Main station) and Nadrazi Holesovice handle mainline and international traffic.

Trains terminating in the Czech capital favor Hlavni, while Holesovice, north of Prague's center, is preferred by trains en route between north and south. Hlavni is a through station beneath two glass arches. It is large, modern, dirty, busy, rambling, poorly organized, and puzzling, with dozens of money-change ("Wechselstuben," in German) and accommodations counters and kiosks. Signs are in Czech, sometimes Cyrillic, often German, and only occasionally English, but boarding announcements are given in Czech, German, and English with such a strong British accent that they sound as though they are generated by computer. Allow extra time to make your way around. Also be careful of your wallet or purse. Departures ("Odjezo," which you see also in German: "Abfahrt") are grouped by destinations. Compositions of trains ("Rodeni") are meticulously shown in stainless-steel showcases adjacent to complete timetables mounted on turntables (the CD information office is so crowded that it is hopeless). On your way to your train's platform ("Nastupiste"), take a look up at the interior of Hlavni's marvelous cupola.

The Prague Tourist Office has a location in Hlavni as well as at Na Prikope 20, Staromestska radnice (Old City Hall), and Malostranska Mostecka Vez (the Charles Bridge).

For international tickets, go to the small "CD Travel Office" located with an outside door on the south face of Hlavni between the entrance marked "Metro" and the "Cargo" office. Tickets may be issued just as easily by Cedok's downtown office at Na Prikope 18 (Tel. 42-2-212-7359). Domestic tickets for distances up to 60 miles are sold in ticket machines as well as at the cash desks. If you arrive late for your train, you can buy your ticket from the conductor for a surcharge of about 35 cents, but be sure to report to him because if he finds you without a ticket, the surcharge is about $3.50.

Hlavni is served by one of Prague's three interconnecting metro lines, which allows you to move around the city easily. The Prague metro is simple. Lines *A, B,* and *C* interconnect at strategic points. The best way to get around town is by metro. It is fast, cheap, and reliable. Tickets are available from machines perched just outside the ticket validating machines. Directions are in English. The machines take correct change only in multiples of ticket prices. All Czech coins are accepted. Tickets are valid for one hour and are spot-checked by plainclothes inspectors who seem to think that foreigners are likely "black travelers." The bus and clacking, busy streetcar system is one of the best existing in Europe. In Prague buses and trams run from 4:30 A.M. to 11:30 P.M. Buy your tickets costing about 36 cents at your hotel or at newsstands. Tourist tickets valid for one, two, three, four, or five days costing about $3.25 to $10.30 are available in some metro stations. Hlavni and Holesovice station are connected on metro Line C. Holesovice station is the end of the line.

Prague's second station, Holesovice, is in need of a good scrubbing, inside and out, yet the large number of change and hotel reservation counters will dazzle you. It is a smaller, more approachable station than Hlavni. In Holesovice, EC trains arrive and depart to and from Hamburg, Budapest, Berlin, and Vienna in order to avoid the dead end downtown station. For example, the Austrian EuroCity Vindobona (with Czech dining car) runs between Vienna and Berlin, the Hungarian EuroCity Antonin Dvorak travels to Vienna's South train station, the Czech EC Comenius goes to Berlin, the IC Csardas from Budapest takes you through to Dresden and Malmo, GermanRail's EC Porta Bohemica goes to Hamburg, and the Hungarian EC Hungaria connects Budapest and Hamburg. These are your second choices (after the EC from Munich/Zurich) for getting to and from Prague.

Seat and sleeping reservations counters are clearly marked by international pictographs. Near the display case you can find the composition of express and fast trains ("Radeni Expresnich") and the display of arrival and departure times. Holesovice reminds you of a small airport terminus partly because of its arrangement and partly because of the clacking departure signs.

Accommodations and money-changing agencies abound as well as food kiosks and a Czech Railroads' restaurant above. Access to the trains (in German: "Zu der Zuge") is through a tunnel with both stairs and ramps (which are good for luggage with wheels) to the Holesovice's three platforms. Like those at Hlavni, departure announcements are in three languages.

The new connections of the EC Vindobona, which ran on the old route for decades, between Prague and Vienna shave nearly an hour and a half off your trip by using the longer, but faster, fully electrified "Nordbahn" via Brno and Breclav into Vienna's South train station instead of the shorter route from Prague's main train station (Hlavni) via Tabor and Gmund to Vienna's Franz-Josefs-Bahnhof. Austrians strongly criticized this change because of the nine-mile additional length (and increased ticket price, which is based on distance) to Prague's less centrally located Holesovice station. You save 85 minutes traveling north and 88 minutes traveling south and have the advantage of using better Austrian carriages.

Pilsen's (the Czech Republic's second city) repainted Hlavni station looks beautifully baroque outside and conventionally modern inside. The city celebrated its 750th anniversary in 1995.

Czech Rail Passes

The Europe East Pass is valid in the Czech Republic, and Rail Europe also sells a Czech Flexipass valid on the trains of the republic only. The Czech Flexipass is available for five days of travel in 15, first class only. Children four-11 pay half; those under four travel free.

Since Prague has become so popular with German and foreign visitors, GermanRail makes available a Prague Excursion Pass which is valid for seven days and allows round-trip travel (including all supplements) to Prague from Czech Republic borders with Germany, Austria, Poland, and Slovakia. You don't have to use the same border crossing when departing the Czech Republic which means you can use the Excursion Pass to travel the full length of the republic from Germany to Slovakia.

Prague Excursion Passes are available in first and second classes for adults, youths, and children. You can buy them in Europe at the offices of Euraide in the Munich Hauptbahnhof (room 3, along track 11) and Berlin Zoo stations. In the U.S., DER Rail sells the Prague Excursion Pass, so when you plan to buy an Excursion Pass, it is convenient to buy it at the same time you buy a GermanRail Pass or Eurailpass from DER Rail. Note that the Czech Republic is not included in the Eurail system, so that Europasses or Eurail Selectpasses can not be applied.

Trains connecting Prague and Bratislava
with Vienna/Budapest and Berlin/Hamburg

(1)	(2)	(3)				(3)	(2)	(1)
N/A	N/A	1020	dep.	Budapest (Kel.)	arr.	1942	N/A	N/A
N/A	N/A	1300	arr.	BRATISLAVA (Hl.)	dep.	1703	N/A	N/A
0655	1055	N/A	dep.	Vienna (Sud.)	arr.	N/A	1903	2303
0803	1155	1403	dep.	Breclav	dep.	1600	1755	2155
0838	1238	1438	dep.	Brno (Hlavni)	dep.	1523	1723	2123
1121	1531	1731	arr.	PRAGUE (Holes.)	dep.	1239	1439	1839

N/A	1804	2004	arr.	Dresden (Hbf.)	dep.	0955 1155 N/A
N/A	2026	2226	arr.	Berlin (Zoo)	dep.	0730 0930 N/A
N/A	2312	N/A	arr.	Hamburg (Hbf.)	dep.	N/A 0658 N/A

N/A—Does not travel this route

(1) EUROCITY ANTONIN DVORAK: First- and second-class compartments and dining car Vienna-Prague
(2) EUROCITY VINDOBONA: First- and second-class compartments and dining car Vienna-Prague-Berlin-Hamburg
(3) EUROCITY HUNGARIA: First- and second-class compartments and dining car Berlin-Prague-Bratislava-Budapest

Best Trains to and from Prague

(1)	(2)				(2)	(1)
N/A	0933	dep.	ZURICH (Hbf.)	arr.	1827	N/A
N/A	1449	dep.	MUNICH (Hbf.)	arr.	1303	N/A
0538	N/A	dep.	DORTMUND (Hbf.)	arr.	N/A	0022
0700	N/A	dep.	Cologne (Hbf.)	arr.	N/A	2306
0845	N/A	dep.	Mainz	arr.	N/A	2113
0903	N/A	dep.	Frankfurt/Main	arr.	N/A	2055
1036	N/A	dep.	Wurzburg (Hbf.)	arr.	N/A	1929
1147	N/A	dep.	Nuremberg (Hbf.)	arr.	N/A	1817
1329	N/A	arr.	Cheb	dep.	N/A	1635
1643	2058	arr.	PRAGUE (Hlavni)	dep.	0659	1309

N/A—Does not travel this route

(1) EUROCITY KARLSTEIN: German Railroads' first- and second-class compartments and dining car between Dortmund and Prague
(2) EUROCITY ALBERT EINSTEIN: Swiss Railroads' first- and second-class compartments and dining car between Bern and Prague

Trains of Slovakia

The Slovakian Republic Railroads, Zeleznice Slovenskej Republiky (ZSR, www.zsr.sk), is responsible for the trains running on the 2,276-mile network of the republic. The main long-distance service within Slovakia runs Bratislava-Zilina-Kosice.

Bratislava's nicely remodeled and well-kept Hlavna (Main) train station is modest. It gives you a favorable first impression of Slovakia's capital. Directions are in Slovakian, but well-placed international pictographs make it easy for you to make your way around. Track numbers are marked "K Nastupistiam." Train compositions are given in the "Radenie Expresnych Vlakova Rychlikov" displays. Departures ("Odchod") are shown on the usual European yellow-paper departure posters and arrivals ("Prichod") on white. The Bratislava Tourist Office ("Informacie") is to the left as you enter the main hall from the tracks (do not use the bypass tunnel). Money change ("Zmenaren") is in a separate, glassed-in room farther to the left with a "Bankomat" ATM machine outside. The reservations counters 17 and 18 face it. Find ticketing on street level. The Meridian Bistro Cafe is in the mezzanine.

The new station at Bratislava Petrzalka is the most modern in Slovakia, and was rebuilt for the reopening of the cross-border line to Vienna, but it also improves links with urban transport. Of the station's 13 tracks, two are designed for passenger trains to Vienna via Kittsee, Austria. The electrified Vienna-Bratislava line opened on December 15, 1998, allows 100 mph running, but joint customs authorities and border police demand 15 minutes at Petrzalka because they are unable to provide checks en route.

Getting to Bratislava is not difficult because it is a major stop for trains on the (Hamburg)-Berlin-Prague-Budapest-Belgrade-(Sofia) mainline. The best train to Bratislava is the ZSR's flagship, first-class-only, EC Slovenska Strela, one of the many trains from Prague. The Slovenska Strela runs up to 100 mph over upgraded portions of the line in the Czech Republic. Also good are the Hungarian EuroCity trains Comenius, between Prague and Budapest, and Hungaria, between Berlin and Budapest. Bratislava is served also by the IC Csardas between Prague and Budapest. You can also reach Bratislava in one hour by Danube cruise ships from Vienna.

ZSR's best domestic train is the first-class-only IC Dunaj between Bratislava and Kosice. It carries a refurbished dining carriage and covers the route in four hours, 48 minutes at an average speed of almost 59 mph, calling only at Zilina and Poprad. Unfortunately, the remainder of the domestic connections are carried aboard drab green trains with dirty windows or seedy diesel red-and-yellow railcars with dirty windows.

The Tatra Electric Railroad (TEZ) operates the most scenic lines in Slovakia. Meter-gauge, electric mountain railcars climb into the High Tatra Mountains, the most beautiful part of Slovakia, on the 1908 line from Poprad Tatry to Stary Smokovec. The eight-mile climb takes some 40 minutes. There is an electric rack and pinion line between Strba and Strbske Pleso in the Tatras that takes 13 minutes to climb three miles. Unfortunately, the frequent departures from Bratislava's

Hlavni station take about five hours to Poprad Tatry, so it isn't feasible for you to plan a day excursion to the mountains.

Smart Traveling on the Trains of the Balkans

Trains of Romania—Trains of Bulgaria—Trains of Yugoslavia— Trains of Macedonia—Rail Passes—Trains of Bosnia- Herzegovina—Trains of Albania

Balkan trains have the reputation of being unpleasant and uncomfortable. One encounters shoddy trains, broken seats, disgusting toilets, failed heating, and unspeakably awful experiences without a bite to eat.

Even the domestic trains, primarily used by locals, are daunting because of the language difficulties and crowding. Yet it is possible to get around by train and, once aboard, you have a good chance to meet and talk with residents, for trains are the most popularly used form of transportation.

The railroads of these countries use standard European gauge, which makes it possible for you to board any one of the omnibus, long-distance overnight trains originating in Western Europe and travel without change to the capital cities of the Balkan countries. Travel is slow, long, time-consuming, and crowded, but you can book from the U.S. or Western Europe. You reach Belgrade and Bucharest directly from the West by trains on separate lines from Budapest (Vienna, Prague, and Munich make good starting points). Although Belgrade used to be reached by the Balkan mainline through Zagreb, now trains are routed via Budapest. Belgrade in turn is the hub for through trains to the other Balkan countries, although no Yugoslavian carriages can be connected. Skopje and Sofia trains pass through Belgrade and on to Athens and Istanbul. Albania remains without train connections from its neighbors.

Be aware that once you settle into your bed or bunk, you should never leave your carriage. The porters lock the doors between carriages, disappear into their compartments, and under no circumstance will allow you back into your paid-for berth or bunk.

Trains of Romania

Radiating from Bucharest (Bucuresti), CFR (Caile Ferate Romane, *www.cfr.ro*), the Romanian Railroads, provides a 6,210-mile network serving all parts of this Latin-language land. Although the British built Romania's 37-mile, first railroad in the late 1860s from Bucharest to the Danube, you can see the French influence on later construction. Taking a train is the best way to see Romania's countryside, although it requires resolve. Eleven trains a day on the popular, 140-mile line from Bucharest to Constanza, on the Black Sea, cross the 1890-95 Saligny Bridge and causeway system. On three of them, you can remain aboard for the Black Sea resorts of Eforie and Mangalia.

Birders can travel by four trains a day 143 miles northeastward to Galati, where they can take boats downstream through the Danube delta, famous for its bird life. Dracula freaks will take the tourist line into the Transylvanian Mountains, which is also the mainline to Budapest.

You can ride overnight trains to and from Bucharest, including the Pannonia Express from Prague, the Dacia Express from Vienna, the Kalman Imre from Munich, and the EuroNight Ister from Budapest. The EC Traianus provides day service from Budapest. The night trains carry various combinations of first- and second-class sleeping cars and compartments, couchettes, and dining cars.

Try to buy a CFR timetable ("Mersul Trenurillor"). The keyed map will make it simple for you to get around. Many cities and towns have two stations. One is called "Nord." Bucharest Nord is the main station for the capital although it is at least a mile distant from the heart of Bucharest. Buses and streetcars serve the station.

CFR's best trains are "rapid" ("accelerat") because they make the fewest stops. Train schedules are posted in railway CFR stations. "Sosire" means "arrival" and "Plecare" means "departure." Book your reservations for seats on long-distance trains and couchettes at a CFR Agentia or in Carpati's central office (generally open Monday to Friday, 7:30 A.M. to 3:30 P.M., and Saturday 8:30 A.M. to 1:30 P.M.), where you will usually find someone who speaks English.

Getting to and from Bucharest

(1)	(2)				(2)	(1)
	1359	dep.	Hamburg (Hbf.)	arr.	1412	
0625	1625	dep.	BERLIN (Zoo)	arr.	1131	2331
0853	1853	dep.	Dresden (Hbf.)	arr.	1102	2102
1143	2133	dep.	PRAGUE (Holesovice)	dep.	0822	1822
	2148	arr.	PRAGUE (Hlavni)	dep.	0807	
	2310	dep.	PRAGUE (Hlavni)	arr.	0531	

1630	0412	dep.	Bratislava (Hlavni)	arr.	2353	1331
1903	0812	arr.	Budapest	dep.	2025	1050
1025	2257	arr.	BUCHAREST (Nord)	dep.	0720	2046

|—Does not travel this route

(1) EC HUNGARIA/OVIDUS: First- and second-class sleeping cars between Budapest and Bucharest; first- and second-class carriages and dining carriage between Budapest and Berlin. Change in Budapest between EC HUNGARIA and OVIDUS.
(2) PANNONIA EXPRESS: First- and second-class sleeping cars, second-class couchettes, and first- and second-class compartments between Prague and Bucharest. Change in Prague to/from EC CARL MARIA VON WEBER for Dresden/Berlin/Hamburg.

(1)	(2)				(2)	(1)
	2319	dep.	MUNICH (Hbf.)	arr.	0603		
	0116	dep.	Salzburg	dep.	0352		
	0233	dep.	Linz	dep.	0229		
2005			dep.	Vienna (Wbf.)	arr.		0900
2102	0528	arr.	Hegyeshalom	dep.	2335	0802
2303	0723	arr.	Budapest	dep.	2140	0600
1354	2257	arr.	BUCHAREST(Nord)	dep.	0745	1655

|—Does not travel this route

(1) DACIA EXPRESS: First- and second-class sleeping cars, second-class couchettes, and second-class compartments between Vienna and Bucharest
(2) KALMAN IMRE: First- and second-class sleeping cars, second-class couchettes, and second-class compartments between Munich and Budapest; second-class compartments between Munich and Bucharest; and first- and second-class compartments between Budapest and Bucharest.

Trains of Bulgaria

The 2,696-mile Bulgarian State Railroads (Bulgarski Durzhavni Zheleznitsi, or "BDZ," www.bg400.bg/bdz) network fans eastwards from the capital, Sofia (Sofija), to the Black Sea at Varna and through European Turkey to Istanbul. The mainline route used by international trains between the West was cancelled during the NATO attacks on Yugoslavia because it passed through Belgrade. Alternative routes were initiated but these were never satisfactory because of the increased travel times. The line to Belgrade passes through Dimitovgrad, the border station to Yugoslavia, and you cross though to the wild and dramatic Dragoman Pass. Trains from the Eastern countries and Russia pass through Bucharest, entering at Ruse, before reaching Sofia.

The president of the premier Bulgarian tour operator has been quoted as saying, "Nothing works in Bulgaria. There is the normal mess that comes from destroying an old system and not having enough time to build a new system. We are in a transition period, and even this doesn't work."

BDZ's fastest trains are not the international trains, but the domestic ones (average express train speeds in Bulgaria reach 50-55 mph) between Sofia and Varna, Bulgaria's leading port and recreation area.

Sofia's main station has complete information (if you can speak Bulgarian or German—train information on the station boards is almost always shown in the Cyrillic script). There are cafes and restaurants, and hotels nearby. Contact the Bulgarian Tourist Information Center (Balkan Holidays, Appendix A) in advance for Bulgarian tourist information, and insist on train information.

Trains of Yugoslavia

The Yugoslavian Railroads (JZ) are headquartered in Belgrade's (Beograd) unroofed main train station, where all express trains back up.

When NATO bombing closed the Belgrade station, it put a halt to train traffic between Western Europe, Macedonia, and Greece. In winter 1999 trains began running again on most lines, although the number of services was reduced compared with the situation before the NATO air strikes, primarily due to the poor availability of trains. Some stations remain closed and no progress has been made repairing the bridge across the Danube. JZ cancels or terminates short of destination up to 20 trains each day. Locomotives are in poor condition and unreliable. Local trains between Sobotica and Belgrade consist of one or two carriages and passengers are packed like sardines There are three trains a day in each direction between Budapest and Novi Sad and overnight service between Vienna and Novi Sad with a sleeping carriage and one carrying couchettes. There is also one sleeping car each from Kiev and Moscow to Novi Sad.

Europe's most spectacular line, with Eastern Europe's finest scenery, reopened in November 1999 between Belgrade and the seaport of Bar on the Adriatic coast. Due to political tensions between Serbia and Montenegro, trains change locomotives at the border station of Vrbnica as the Belgrade and Podgorica divisions of JZ are unwilling to let their locos leave their administrative areas. Two trains a day make the full trip, but the second arrives in Bar after darkness falls while you are traveling over the breathtaking viaducts except during the longest days of June.

Train connections from Serbia into Kosovo remain closed as Serbia is not interested in repairing the bridges at present, although Britain, France, and Germany have each supplied diesel locomotives to Kosovo.

Overnight Service Belgrade-Venice

1500	dep.	Belgrade	arr.	2122
1858	dep.	Vinkovci	arr.	0550
2217	arr.	Zagreb	dep.	0857
0918	arr.	Venice (S.L.)	dep.	1212

Train carries through carriages including a couchette.

Trains of Macedonia

Skopje, the capital of this remote country nestled between Yugoslavia and Greece, is a stop on the line from Western Europe to Salonika and Athens that was closed during the NATO bombing of Belgrade. It became relatively isolated from the Western European network but remained accessible from Greece. The Macedonian railroads (Macedonskih Zeleznica, MZ) escaped damage from the Yugoslav war. There are two express trains a day linking Belgrade and Skopje.

Getting to and from Skopje

391	395		390	394
1350	2115	Belgrade	0701	2257
1757	0141	Nis	0245	1900
2306	0656	Skopje	2200	1420

Trains 394 and 395 carry couchettes and sleeping cars.

Rail Passes

Rail Europe sells rail passes valid on the national networks of Romania and Bulgaria. The Romanian Pass and the Bulgarian Flexipass are valid each for first-class for any three days out of one month. The Balkan Flexipass covers both countries plus Greece, Macedonia, and Turkey. It is available for five, 10, or 15 days of travel within one month, either as an adult first-class flexipass, or a special discounted first-class youth flexipass for those under 26. All of these passes offer you the freedom of the trains and an excellent way of escaping the bureaucracy of the train stations. Children four to 11 pay half adult fare; those under four travel free.

Trains of Bosnia-Herzegovina

From 1991 to 1993, there were two railroad companies in the territory of the present Federation of Bosnia-Herzegovina. One operated in the Muslim areas between Sarajevo and Kakanj and Sarajevo and Zenica, while the second railroad operated in the Croatian areas with local trains between Mostar and Capljina. In 1998 the two merged into one company with operating name Zeljeznice Bosne I Hercegovine (ZBH, www.geocities.com/CapeCanaveral/3976/zbh.html). A two-car train made a four-mile journey through Sarajevo's northwestern suburbs from the main station on February 8, 1995. Because all locomotives were in Yugoslavian hands outside the city, the train was pulled by a Mercedes truck fitted with train wheels. The last previous train left Sarajevo's main station in May 1992, one month after the Bosnian War erupted.

Sarajevo station is largely intact, although the main building was burned out and the large square in front, with its streetcar loop, was scattered with wrecks. The "Bosna Ekspres" passenger service between Sarajevo and Ploce, Croatia, was reopened on July 30, 1996, but requires a lengthy change of train at Caplijina, the border crossing. Ploce is the port for Bosnia. GermanRail has given the Bosnian-Herzogovinan railways (ZBH) 25 diesel locomotives. Train service has been restored over many short lines, but service is irregular due to electrical breakdowns.

Trains of Albania

Albania was a latecomer to the European railroad system. All of Albanian Railroads' (Hekurudhae e Shqiperise, HSH) passenger system was built by "volunteer" labor gangs after the Second World War, with Chinese help. Tirana (Tirane) is the capital, but the port of Durres is the focal point of HSH's 234-mile system.

During the past decade, vandalism and open thievery paralyzed most of HSH's system, but 1.1 million passengers traveled by train over the first six months of 2000, which was an increase of 8.4 percent over 1999. The increasing number of riders is due to service improvements as well as the use of "new" Austrian and Italian carriages. In 2000, the Japanese government provided $1.9 million to buy spare parts for Czech-built locomotives and to help rebuild the system. The lines from Durres to Tirana and Pogradec are operational and the line connecting Fier and Ballsh was restored in 2000. The 22-mile line to Tirana carries six, one-class trains a day, taking nearly an hour.

A line from Shkoder to Podgorica (formerly Titograd, in Montenegro) was opened in 1984, for freight only. The only known passenger-carrying train was the line's inaugural one, which only took passengers from Podgorica as far as the Albanian border at Hani-Hotit. The Bajza international freight train station, which connects Albania's railroad system to Europe through Montenegro, resumed work in February 1996, after three and a half years of interruption because of the international embargo to Yugoslavia.

Italy's Adriatica Line ferries serve Durres, with sailings from Trieste and Bari (rail passes not valid); you also can cross from Corfu. These boats from Italy are the easiest route to Albania, but shipping was greatly dislocated by the Kosovo War and the financial insolvency of the Adriatica Line. The longest, but most spectacular, way to Tirana is by the winding, nine-hour bus ride from Skopje, Macedonia, along sheer mountain roads and past Lake Ohrid.

Smart Traveling on the Trains of the C.I.S. and Baltic States

Moscow—St. Petersburg—Trains of the Ukraine—Trains of the Baltic States—Trains of Belarus—Trains of Moldova

When you arrive in Moscow's Kiev train station and there is not one sign that you can read or understand—don't worry. If you could read them and understand them they wouldn't help you. There is no place to make hotel arrangements, no place to change money (not that you would want to), and it is very difficult to make train reservations or legally buy train tickets in Russia.

A Russian timetable is not available—it would be too expensive to produce. The clerks at the windows speak no foreign language and reservations are completely sold out 45 days in advance, anyway.

The director of the Russian Ministry of Transportation noted that Russia's trains are often crowded because train travel is much less expensive than flying, but it is not cheap when booked by a foreigner. For example, the one-way fare between Moscow and St. Petersburg is $146 for soft class and $82 for hard class (plus a hefty booking fee), but foreigners are expected to pay more than Russians do. Prices of Aeroflot tickets increased five- to sevenfold when Aeroflot began to compete internationally. Passengers who formerly traveled by air now can't afford it, and take trains. Only business and emergency travelers fly-or those going to places where it is possible only to fly. "It's practically impossible for an American to go up and buy a train ticket" in the C.I.S., the director said.

It's also difficult for a Russian to buy a ticket. A line forms when tickets go on sale, and the tickets are sold out in two or three days except for the quota set aside for foreign tourists, VIPs, and essential business travelers. This special allocation is released an hour before train departure.

There is a black market for railroad tickets. You can find scalpers outside most train stations asking you (in Russian) whether you need a ticket. Don't worry about finding a scalper—he will find you. Most of them are probably reliable, but you can never be sure.

Visitors to Moscow will look in vain for a Russian Railroads (Rossiyskie Zeleznue Dorogi, RZD) office. They have no staff that can speak English. If you wish to brave long lines and take a gamble, you can visit the Central Railway Agency at Griboedova Str. 6. There you can wait two to three hours and still not be certain of getting tickets, even when you pay in dollars. "Buying a ticket in the U.S. is the only proper way to make a trip in my country," the spokesman said. Tickets and reservations for Russian carriages from Western European cities to Russia and return can also be made at the International Ticketing Office of major European train stations, although reservations must be made before 9 A.M. on the day of departure. For tickets within Russia, agents in Western European train stations can also telex Russia, but they need a four-day minimum lead time.

There are 19 railroad districts in Russia. They include

• the Moscow Railroad, which spreads over the territory of almost all European Central Russia, from Moscow in the north to Kursk in the south.

• the October Railroad, which links St. Petersburg with Moscow, Novgorod, Pskov, Murmansk, Petrozavodsk, and Helsinki. Its headquarters is in St. Petersburg. This was the first Russian passenger railroad. Its construction began in 1836, and the first segment from St. Petersburg to the czar's residence (now, Pushkin) was completed in 1837.

• the Northern Railroad, including the Yaroslav Division with more than 39 pairs of daily commuter trains, the Moscow-Aleksandrov Division, the Kostroma Division, and the Vologda Division.

When the former Soviet Union dissolved, all states of the C.I.S., including the Ukraine and Belarus, agreed to maintain the status of the railroad network without change. Thus when you travel between (now independent) republics you will see no difference in the railroads.

The most interesting and most important lines include Moscow to St. Petersburg ($146, soft class), to the Baltic States (about $200), to Kiev ($185), to Minsk ($172), to Warsaw ($306), Prague ($363), and Helsinki ($240), plus the Trans-Siberian. It is convenient to ride these routes because you can reserve them in advance and not have to struggle for tickets and reservations.

The secret is to make your reservation as early as possible. Tickets are only sold with reservations for a carriage ("vagon") and seat ("mesto"). Dealing with the Russians takes time. Try to make reservations 45 in advance if possible; seven to 10 days is dicey.

The Russian Railroads' European routes are extensive. Along the eastern margin you can travel from Helsinki to St. Petersburg, St. Petersburg to Moscow, and from Moscow's Kurskiy station via Kharkhov in the Ukraine to Sevastopol. A southwestern mainline will take you from Moscow's Kievskiy station through Kiev to Odessa (Ukraine), Kishinev (Moldova), and Lvov for Hungary, Slovakia, and southern Poland. The westward route from Moscow takes you through Minsk (Belarus) to Warsaw. The mainline from St. Petersburg takes you through Vilnius (Lithuania) to Warsaw.

The prestige/name trains are the most comfortable. The Red Arrow is Russia's most famous, but all prestige trains are quality trains and are almost the same. They run to practically every major city of the former Soviet Union, 160 trains a day.

When you first see them, the intimidating Russian cars look straight from Dr. Zhivago: high, formidable, and military green. Except for the prestige cars, they all look the same, with no markings on the outside. The only difference is the number of layers of paint covering the rust of the Russian winters. The prestige trains to Kiev, named the Kiev and the Ukrania, are blue. The six Red Arrow trains to St. Petersburg are red. The prestige trains to the Volga region and to the north are dark yellow. The Trans-Siberian is Bordeaux red.

Russian trains are different than those in the West. When you board you see how difficult the large size of the Russian carriages makes it to hoist luggage aboard. Russian trains generally carry bunks instead of seats. In the West, the sleeping cars have one, two, or three bunks on one wall within about a four-foot-by-six-foot space with wash basin and hangers on the facing wall. Russian compartments have four bunks (two on each side, one above another) per compartment in second class ("hard") and two bunks (one on each side, with no empty bunk hanging above) per compartment in first class ("soft"). Neither have a wash basin within a five-foot-by-six-foot space, and therefore offer more room.

Each bunk is provided with a pillow; a thin, but sufficient, mattress pad; linen consisting of a bottom sheet, clean pillowcase, and either a fresh blanket cover (better) in which you insert your blanket, or a top sheet, plus the blanket; and towel (sometimes there is a small charge for linen). Berths are sold without sex distinction. WCs are at the end of every car. An attendant ("provodnik," if male; "provodnitsa," if female) for every car furnishes tea and hot water from an iron samovar (if you want coffee, take instant with you), but has absolutely no other snack or refreshment.

When the smaller Western European Czech and Polish sleeping carriages are hooked together with Russian ones, their unequal heights make crossing/jumping between them at 40 mph something out of an action movie.

Russian trains carry very basic restaurant cars ("Pectopah") located somewhere in the middle, but the menus are limited. The waiter won't speak English. Don't expect breakfast, lunch, and dinner. Don't expect breakfast at all. Breakfast is the same as dinner. Eggs are available midafternoon when a waiter pulls an aluminum basket of hard-boiled eggs through the train. The menus you receive (in Russian) are the same for any and every meal: an excellent soup, a salad, a meat you may or may not be able to identify, lots of potatoes, Coca-Cola (not water), and tea or instant coffee from Israel. Beer is the most readily available item.

You should do what the Russians do: bring with you all the food and drink (except beer, which you buy aboard) you may need—salami, cheese, fruit, bread, etc. At mealtimes you will offer your spread to your neighbors. Don't count on finding food in the stations or from vendors along the track.

The Russian carriages were made in the Republic of Georgia, the locomotives in former East Germany and Czechoslovakia. Some 1500 vehicles were modernized by a joint venture of Russian and Spanish companies overseen by RENFE, the Spanish Railroads. Why RZD runs on wider gauge (5 feet) than the rest of Europe, which is 4 feet 8 1/2 inches (except in Iberia, which is 5 feet, 6 inches), is not clear, but the notion that it was built differently to protect Russia from military invasion has been discredited. It is possible that, as in England, engineers determined the width between wheels from the horse-drawn postal coaches of the time, which were wider spaced in Russia than in England. Alternately, the English—where the first locomotive was ordered—measured the width between the inside of the rails and the Russians from the outside. Many historians prefer the report that when the czar received the news that the English had built the first railroad, the czar replied, "Why then, we must have one—but ours will be bigger."

All other things being equal, wide gauge is safer than standard gauge, but all other things are never equal, and in fact maintenance of the railbed is usually considered the most important safety factor.

For travelers, the wider gauge is a major disadvantage. You must suffer the time wasted entering and leaving the C.I.S. in order to adjust the wheel spacing to the different gauge. It's interesting to watch—but it makes for almost three hours of lost time. First your carriage, with you in it, is hauled to a special facility beside mechanical screw jacks; your carriage is lifted with much banging, great bumping, and violent slamming; the old bogies are rolled away; new ones are rolled below; and your carriage is lowered onto them and pinned through a hole in the floor of the WC. The mechanics are generally pleased with their work when your carriage finally rolls successfully away.

There's real interest in traveling by train to Russia, but a train of paperwork follows you.

First you will need a visa, which will be valid in Russia and Belarus, but not in the Ukraine. You can try for three kinds of visa to Russia—tourist, business, or private (homestay). For a Russian tourist visa you will need

• A visa support invitation and confirmed reservations for every night of your stay in Russia, which means you must supply a cover letter from a travel agent arranging your visit with dates of entry and exit, places to be visited in Russia, index and reference number of the incoming Russian travel agency;

• A photocopy of the vital pages of a valid passport containing the personal data of the traveler;

• A filled-in application form in English or Russian, which you can download at *www.russia-travel.com/visas_regulations.htm*;

• Three identical color or black-and-white passport photos; and

• Fee in money order or company check amounting to $70 for visa delivery in two weeks. When you need it sooner, a higher fee is charged.

Alternately, you may apply for a business visa with an official invitation from a Russian host organization, a private visa with an invitation from relatives or friends, or a transit visa with copies of confirmed tickets in the country of destination.

You may obtain visas at the Russian consular posts in Washington, D.C., New York, San Francisco, and Seattle (see Appendix A). Your Russian visa is a separate, three-part paper. It is not attached to your passport. Unless you read Cyrillic, you cannot even read your name. When you book hotels or tours through a travel agency, the agency will obtain your visa for you, for an additional fee, and this is the most practical way to go. Your local travel agent will arrange it for you, or you go directly to a Russia specialist such as Monomax (*www.2russia.com*) or Intourist (*www.intourist.com*). Young travelers should make arrangements with Sindbad (*www.sindbad.ru/en*) for student discounts and hostel arrangements.

The best way to Moscow by train from the West is via St. Petersburg from Helsinki. From Central Europe, it is easier to travel from Berlin via Warsaw so that you pass through Belarus rather than the Ukraine and do not need to buy a Ukrainian visa in addition to your Russian one.

Moscow

On the preferred route from the West to Moscow via Belarus you will travel two days and two nights. The EuroNight Jan Kiepura carries first- and second-class carriages between Cologne and Moscow, and a dining carriage between Brest and Moscow. The Chopin carries first- and second-class carriages between Vienna and Moscow. The Moskva

Express carries first- and second-class sleeping cars between Berlin and Moscow, and the Vltava carries first- and second-class sleeping cars between Prague and Moscow. There are also second-class sleeping cars between Moscow and Budapest and first- and second-class sleeping cars between Moscow and Venice (journey of three nights).

In Moscow you will find nine train stations (called "Vokzal," from London's Vauxhall Gardens, where the czar first saw a train in the 1830s), but Westerners usually use only four or five. Trains from Byelorussi station, which is also known as Smolenski station, serve the line to Belarus and Warsaw; trains from Kiev station ("Kievskiy Vokzal") serve Kiev, the Ukraine, and the Balkans; Oktyabrskaya station serves St. Petersburg; and Yaroslavl station ("Yaroslavskiy Vokzal") is the terminus for the Trans-Siberian train. The others are named Kazan, Kursk, Paveletskiy, Rizhski, and Savelovskiy.

The Oktyabrskaya station, next to the Yaroslavl station, has remarkable, arching eaves and almost whimsical architecture of grand design and magnificent presence. Its interior is Moscow's best kept. It is accessible, with clean lines, counters selling magazines, etc., and windows for ticketing in the outer hall. There is a striking alabaster bust of Lenin dominating the center. The spaces leading to the platforms, which are outside in back of the station, are filled with a wonderful mingling of life. Kiosks and glassed stalls stand in irregular, makeshift rows, their occupants selling anything and everything at very low ruble prices. Passersby crowd to see what is for sale and at what price.

At adjacent Yaroslavl some platforms are covered with galvanized iron; the rest are open. Boarding occurs outdoors. Inside Yaroslavl is a large railroad map of the stations of the former Soviet Union served by Yaroslavl which extend to Vladivostok and Murmansk. Above the ticket counters, a long schematic drawing divides the Trans-Siberian route into eight different time zones. The hall is marked with columns and an escalator, shops, chairs for waiting, and a bank of telephones. Across the street is the gingerbready configuration of Kazanskiy station with trains to Rostov-on-Don, Kazan, Volgograd, and Central Asian republics.

If Oktyabrskaya station is Moscow's best, Kiev station is the worst. It is crowded, cheap, and stifling.

Between Yaroslavl and Oktyabrskaya stations is a gray building that reminds you of an Orthodox church. It is the Komsomolskaya metro station, which you can use to get there. Smolensk train station is beside the metro stop of the same name. Kiev station is by Kievskaya metro. All three metro stations are on the Circle Line (Koltsevaya Linia), but you will need time to master the Cyrillic complexity of the highly acclaimed and highly bewildering Moscow metro system. Despite rumor to the contrary, taxis are available at the train stations, usually from in front, but not necessarily where the station signs indicate, and they don't all have yellow lights on the roof. The sign to look for is a double row of checkered squares. In Moscow and St. Petersburg, the taxi drivers seem to be more decent than in many large cities—which is something you can't say for the condition of their cabs or their driving safety. Just tell them you are paying in dollars and they become lambs. Then you can agree on the fare before you put your luggage in the trunk.

St. Petersburg

When you arrive from Moscow in St. Petersburg's Moscow ("Moskovskiy Vokzal") station, you will be stunned. Deja vu. Could you have taken the wrong train and returned to where you started? The interior of St. Petersburg's Moscow station is identical to the interior of Moscow's Oktyabrskaya station where you departed. Lenin's alabaster bust stands in St. Petersburg just as it did in Moscow. The rectangular hall and the high ceiling of geometric shapes came from the same workshop.

St. Petersburg has four mainline stations. Three of them, Warsaw, Vitebsk, and Finland, share the same metro line. Small Varshavskiy Vokzal (meaning Warsaw station) is peeling yellow plaster with an enormous statue of Lenin facing the highway. Ticket scalpers gathered on the side will approach you in Russian as you pass. Arrivals see the sign that reads, not "St. Petersburg," but "Leningrad," in large Roman letters. Most people, especially in Moscow, by habit often refer to the city by its former name. At No. 2 window you will find someone for international traffic. It will save you trouble if you have your train ticket validated here. St. Petersburg's peeling and run-down Baltic ("Baltiskiy Vokzal") train station is a 10-minute walk from the Warsaw station, but only local trains leave from here in the direction of the Baltic States. The adjacent Baltic metro station is the closest one to Warsaw station as well.

Vitebsk ("Vitebskiy Vokzal") station, with a green patina roof and tile floors, is named for the Belarussian city of the same name. It is the terminus for trains due south to Kiev and Odessa. Follow the signs showing an old-fashioned locomotive to the platforms. A metro station is adjacent.

The Finland station ("Finlyandskiy Vokzal") is St. Petersburg's best—certainly the most modern—to welcome hard-currency visitors from Helsinki. Each year 150,000 Finns visit Russia. You won't have trouble paying with finnmarks. On the platform you see the train preserved under glass in which Lenin arrived in Petrograd, as it was known then, on October 7, 1917 (the October revolution was on October 25, but a change in calendar makes it now November 7). The train was a gift of the Finnish people to the Russian people. Finland station's large hall contains a marble floor that is broken in many places.

With the shortages in Russia, kiosk after kiosk has sprung up on the main streets and especially beside the train stations. What you see is what you can get, which encourages window-shopping but not one-stop shopping.

From the West, trains to St. Petersburg via Warsaw, a segment of Belarus, and then Vilnius (Lithuania) leave Cologne (Hbf.) at 7:16 P.M. twice a week and Berlin at 11:02 P.M. nightly, but clearly the easiest way to St. Petersburg is to take a Finnish day train or Russian night train from Helsinki (see "Scandinavia and Finland" chapter).

Trains of the Ukraine

A Russian visa is not sufficient to enter the Ukraine, but you may buy a Ukrainian visa at the border. There are no photos required, but the procedure is not as simple as it might be.

When you reach the Ukraine, literally a small army of customs officers and border guards is waiting for the train. You fill out a Cyrillic-script customs declaration form. Two uniformed border guards march you into a dingy back room. You fill out a second form (with directions in English and Ukrainian) and eventually receive an odd strip of paper, which you take to an obscurely located bank in a back building and pay $15—only crisp notes are accepted. Returning, guards take your bank receipt, return your passport, now with an "emergency" Ukrainian visa stamp, and your Russian visa, and you rush to rejoin your train.

Your train isn't there.

It is early in the morning. As well as you can make out, the Cyrillic departure board says a train to Moscow leaves at 10:30 A.M. You are stranded, without breakfast, in a station with no restaurant and nothing to eat. Finally your train pulls in. Your porters are genuinely happy to see you. They were wondering what to do with your possessions.

Trains of the Ukrainian Railroads (Ukrainska Zaliznitsa, UZ) are indistinguishable from those of the Russian Railroads. Kiev (Kyiv) is the capital of the Ukraine. People like to walk below the gleaming domes of ancient churches in Kiev. To stroll along Khreshchatyk, the main street, past buildings painted in pastels and shaded by chestnuts is to feel an Old World softness that Moscow seldom matches. The Ukraine has a well-developed transportation network. With a total length of 14,500 miles, UZ is divided into six regions: Donetsk Railroads (Donetsk), L'vov Railroads (L'vov), Odessa Railroads (Odessa), By-Dnieper Railroads (Dniepropetrovsk), South Railroads (Kharkov), and Southwest Railroads (Kiev).

The trains for Moscow generally pass through Kiev in the middle of the night, but on Tuesdays, Thursdays, and Saturdays, first- and second-class carriages from Cologne arrive at 12:32 P.M. and the Kiev Express, departing from Berlin daily at 11:02 P.M., carrying second-class Russian carriages, arrives in Kiev at 6:06 A.M. the next day.

Trains of the Baltic States

Train travel in the Baltic States is not unlike travel in Russia because the same trains, same gauge, and same overnight travel scheme are used except on local routes, where you will find yourself sitting on benches, three across on both sides of the aisle. The Estonian (EVR, Eesti Raudtee, *www.evr.ee*), Latvian (LVD, Ladvijas Dzelzcels), and Lithuanian Railroads (LG, Valstybine Imone Lietuvos Gelezinkeliai, *www.randberg.com/li/lithrailways.html*), which are under separate managements, connect the three capitals, Tallinn, Riga, and Vilnius, along a snaking Baltic mainline.

You may buy tickets for immediate departures in Riga's Central Station ("Centrala Stacija") in the main departure hall on the right of the entrance, counters 3 to 9. Buy tickets for the electric commuter trains in the smaller departure hall on the right of the station. For advance bookings, go into the smaller local train departure hall, on your right.

Avoid the so-called "obshti" and "platzkart" carriages, which are very crowded. For overnight trips choose the "coupe," four-bunk compartments or, on the Latvijas Ekspresis to Moscow, the first class, "SV," two-bunk compartments with video.

Vilnius' train station is quite acceptable by Western standards. Signs are written in English. Change your money in the office in the waiting hall on the left or at the 24-hour change counter to the left as you exit. Leave your luggage at the storage in the basement (open 24 hours). Find its entrance on the right as you face the station. Electric bus lines 2, 5, and 7 take you from in front of the station to the center of town. Buy your bus tickets at the newsstand in the main hall.

U.S. and U.K. citizens require no visa to enter any of the Baltic states; a 90-day stay is permitted. For multiple-entry visas or longer stays, contact the consulate or embassy of the state in question (Appendix A). Canadian citizens require a visa for any one of the Baltic states to enter the others at will.

To avoid having to get a Belarus or Russian visa, enter the Baltic states via Sestokai, which is the only border crossing point between Poland and Lithuania. Take the two-class Balti Ekspress departing Warsaw's Centralna station in the morning. You pass through the Polish border station at Trakiszki, and continue on standard-gauge rails to Mackawa, where Lithuanian border checks are made, to Sestokai, which is the end of the line for standard gauge. Across the border stands a second-class-only train that reaches Vilnius in the evening. With the Balti, you must change trains at the border, but this eliminates waiting for the time-consuming change-of-gauge ritual required of Russian trains. All other travel to the Baltic States by train from Western Europe or Finland takes you through Russia or Belarus. In this case you will need also a one- or two-entry Russian transit visa, which you should obtain before you leave. Trains run to St. Petersburg from Tallinn and to Moscow from Riga, and Vilnius's key location controlling the mainline between St. Petersburg and Warsaw makes Vilnius of great importance to the Russian Railroads. Mainline Russian Railroads' train from St. Petersburg to the West passes through Vilnius, Belarus, and then Warsaw on its way to Berlin's Lichtenberg Station. Yet, LG would like to establish a viable freight route to Poland bypassing Belarus.

It is possible to reach the Baltic States by air, and very attractive to board a ship from Scandinavia or Finland.

Trains of Belarus

Political ties are very close between Belarus and Russia. There are no customs checks at their common border. The trains of the

Belarussian Railroads (Bielorusse Zeleznue Dorogi, BCZ) are generally a legacy of Soviet rule. Minsk, the capital of Belarus, is located on the Moscow-Warsaw mainline, so many passengers will pass through Minsk in the middle of the night, except for the Moskva Express, which arrives at 12:28 P.M., having left Berlin Lichtenberg station at 6:12 P.M., and the EN Jan Kiepura, which arrives at 9:28 P.M. Day and night prestige trains connect Minsk with Moscow.

Buy your tickets for C.I.S. and Western European destinations in the main international ticket hall on the first floor of Minsk train station and tickets for local trains in the smaller ticket hall on the ground floor. Only Russian is spoken. An "obshchy" is a single seat and a "mezhoblastnoy" is one that reclines. "Platskartny" carriages are divided into six-bunk compartments with no doors. "Coupes" are four-bunk compartments with doors.

Trains of Moldova

Visas for Moldova are issued only upon authorization of the Moldovan Foreign Ministry. Refer to the Russian visa information above. A Moldovan visa is valid for transit through Russia.

The trains of the Russian Railroads serve Moldova. You reach Kishinev (Chisinau) by trains from Kiev or Odessa. The overnight Prietenia and Romania Express trains serve Kishinev from Bucharest.

Appendix A

Train Information, Tourist Offices, Consulates, and Embassies

U.S.

Austrian National Tourist Office
P.O. Box 1142
New York, NY 10108-1142
Tel. 212-944-6880
Fax 212-730-4568
www.anto.com

Austrian National
    Tourist Office
11601 Wilshire Blvd., Suite 2480
Los Angeles, CA 90025
Tel. 310-477-2038
www.anto.com

Balkan Holidays (for Bulgaria)
41 East 42nd Street
New York, NY 10017
Tel. 212-573-5530

Belarus Embassy
1511 K Street N.W.
Suite 619
Washington, DC 20005
Tel. 202-638-2954

Belgian Tourist Office
780 Third Avenue, #1501
New York, NY 10017
Tel. 212-758-8130
Fax 212-355-7675
www.visitbelgium.com

British Tourist Authority
551 Fifth Avenue, 7th Floor
New York, NY 10176-0799
Tel. 800-GO2-BRIT
Fax 212-986-1188
www.visitbritain.com

British Tourist Authority
625 N. Michigan Avenue,
    Suite 1001
Chicago, IL 60611
Tel. 800-462-2748
Fax 312-787-9641
www.visitbritain.com

British Tourist Authority
10880 Wilshire Blvd.,
    Suite 570
Los Angeles, CA 90024
Tel. 310-470-2782
Fax 310-470-8549
www.visitbritain.com

BritRail
Tel. 877-677-1066
Fax 877-477-1066
www.britrail.net

CIE Tours International
100 Hanover Avenue
P.O. Box 501
Cedar Knolls, NJ 07927-0501
Fax 800-338-3964
www.cietours.com

CIT Rail
9501 West Devon Ave.,
    Suite 1
Rosemont, IL 60018
Tel. 800-CIT-RAIL

Czech Republic Tourist Office
1109-1111 Madison Avenue
New York, NY 10028
Tel. 212-288-0830

Danish Tourist Board
655 Third Avenue,
    18th Floor
New York, NY 10017
Tel. 212-885-9700
Fax 212-885-9726
www.visitdenmark.com

DER Travel
9501 West Devon Avenue
Rosemont, IL 60018-4832
Tel. 888-337-7350
Fax 800-282-7474
www.dertravel.com

Estonian Embassy
630 Fifth Avenue, Suite 2415
New York, NY 10111
Tel. 212-247-7634

EurAide, Inc.
P. O. Box 2375
Naperville, IL 60567
Tel. 708-420-2343
Fax 708-420-2369
www.euraide.de

Forsyth Travel Library
Tel. 800-FORSYTH
www.forsyth.com

French Government Tourist Office
444 Madison Avenue, 16th Floor
New York, NY 10022-6903
Tel. 900-990-0040
    (95 cents a minute)
Fax 212-838-7855
www.francetourism.com

French Government Tourist Office
9454 Wilshire Boulevard, Suite 715
Beverly Hills, CA 90212-2967
Tel. 900-990-0040
    (95 cents a minute)
Fax 310-276-2835
www.francetourism.com

French Government Tourist Office
676 N. Michigan Avenue
Chicago, IL 60611-2819
Tel. 900-990-0040
    (95 cents a minute)
Fax 312-337-6339
www.francetourism.com

FrenchRail. See Rail Europe.

German National Tourist Office
122 E. 42nd Street,
    52nd Floor
New York, NY 10168-0072
Tel. 212-661-7200
Fax 212-661-7174
www.germany-tourism.de

German National Tourist Office
401 North Michigan Avenue
Chicago, IL 60611-4212
Tel. 312-644-4212
Fax 312-644-0724
www.germany-tourism.de

German National Tourist Office
P. O. Box 641009
Los Angeles, CA 90064
Tel. 310-234-0250
Fax 310-474-1604
www.germany-tourism.de

GermanRail. See DER Rail.

Greek National Tourist Org.
645 Fifth Avenue, 5th floor
New York, NY 10022
Tel. 212-421-5777
Fax 212-826-6940
www.gnto.gr

Hungarian Tourist Board
c/o Embassy of the Republic
    of Hungary
Office of the Commercial
    Counsellor
150 East 58th Street,
    33rd Floor
New York, NY 10155-3398
Tel. 212-355-0240
Fax 212-207-4103
www.hungary.com/tourinform/

Irish Railroads. See CIE Tours.

Irish Tourist Board
345 Park Avenue
New York, NY 10154
Tel. 212-418-0800
Fax 212-371-9052
www.ireland.travel.ie

Italian Government Tourist Board
630 Fifth Avenue, Suite 1565
New York, NY 10111
Tel. 212-245-4822

Italian Government Tourist Board
401 N. Michigan Avenue
Chicago, IL 60611
Tel. 312-644-0990
Fax 312-644-3019

Italian Government Tourist Board
12400 Wilshire Boulevard,
    Suite 550
Los Angeles, CA 90025
Tel. 310-820-0098
Fax 310-820-6357

Italian State Railroads.
    See CIT Tours.

Latvian Embassy
4325 17th Street, NW
Washington, DC 20011
Tel. 202-726-8213
Fax 202-726-6785

Lithuanian Consulate
420 Fifth Avenue
New York, NY 10118
Tel. 212-354 7849
Fax 212-354-7911

Luxembourg National Tourist Office
17 Beekman Place
New York, NY 10022
Tel. 212-935-3589
Fax 212-935-5896
www.visitluxembourg.com

Monaco Government Tourist Office
845 Third Avenue
New York, NY 10022
Tel. 212-759-5227

Netherlands Board of Tourism
355 Lexington Avenue, 21st Floor
New York, NY 10017
Tel. 212-370-7367
www.goholland.com

Netherlands Board of
Tourism
225 N. Michigan Avenue, Suite 1854
Chicago, IL 60601
Tel. 800-GO-HOLLAND
www.goholland.com

Northern Ireland Tourist Board
551 Fifth Avenue
New York, NY
10176-0799
Tel. 212-922-0101
www.ni-tourism.com

Norwegian Tourist Board
www.norway.org

Orbis Polish Travel Bureau
342 Madison Avenue, Suite 1512
New York, NY 10173
Tel. 800-223-6037
Fax 212-682-4715
www.orbis-usa.com

Polish National Tourist Office
275 Madison Avenue, Suite 1711
New York, NY 10016
Tel. 212-338-9412
Fax 212-338-9283
www.polandtour.org

Portuguese National Tourist
Office
590 Fifth Avenue, 4th Floor
New York, NY 10036-4704
Tel. 212-354-4403
Fax 212-764-6137

Rail Europe (French/SwissRail)
500 Mamaronech Avenue, Suite 314
Harrison, NY 10528
Tel. 888-382-7245
Fax. 800-432-1329

Russian Federation Embassy
1825 Phelps Place, N.W.
Washington, DC 20008
Tel. 202-939-8907
Fax 202-483-7579

Russian National Tourist Office
13 West 42nd Street, Suite 412
New York, NY 10036
Tel. 212-575-3431
Fax 212-575-3434
www.interknowledge.com/russia

Slovakia: See Victor International.

Slovenia Tourist Office
345 East 12th Street
New York, NY 10003
Tel. 212-358-9686

Spain, Tourist Office of
666 Fifth Avenue, 35th Floor
New York, NY 10103
Tel. 212-759-8822
Fax 212-265-8864
www.okspain.org

Spain, Tourist Office of
San Vicente Plaza Building
8383 Wilshire Boulevard, Suite 956
Beverly Hills, CA 90211
Tel. 323-658-7188
Fax 323-658-1061
www.okspain.org

Spain, Tourist Office of
845 North Michigan Avenue, Suite
915-E
Chicago, IL 60611
Tel. 312-642-1992
Fax 312-642-9817
www.okspain.org

Spain, Tourist Office of
1221 Brickell Ave.,
    Suite 1850
Miami, FL 33131
Tel. 305-358-1992
Fax 305-358-8223
www.okspain.org

Swedish Tourist Board
P. O. Box 4649
Grand Central Station
New York, NY 10163-4649
Tel. 212-885-4649
Fax 212-885-9726
www.gosweden.org

Swiss Federal Railroads. See Rail
    Europe

Switzerland Tourism
608 Fifth Avenue
New York, NY 10020
Tel. 1-877-SWITZERLAND (Toll-free
    USA only)
Tel. 011-800-100-200-30 (Mon.-Fri.
    from 9 A.M. to 9 P.M. EST;
    International Toll-free)
www.myswiterland.com

Ukrainian Embassy
2001 L Street, N.W.
Suite 200
Washington, DC 20036
Tel. 202-452-0939

Victor International Travel
10 East 40th Street
New York, NY 10016
Tel. 212-680-0730

CANADA

Austrian National Tourist Office
2 Bloor Street E., Suite 3330
Toronto, Ont M4W 1A8
Tel. 416-967-3381
Fax 416-967-4101
www.anto.com

Belgian Tourist Office
P.O. Box 760
Succursale N.D.G.
Montreal, P.Q. H4A 3S2
Tel. 514-484-3594
Fax 514-489-8965
visitbelgium.com

British Tourist Authority
111 Avenue Road, Suite 450
Toronto, Ont M5R 3J8
Tel. 416-925-6326
Fax 416-961-2175
www.visitbritain.com

BritRail
Tel. 877-677-1066
Fax 877-477-1066
www.britrail.net

CIT Tours
80 Tiverton Court, Suite 401
Markham, Ont L3R 0G4
Tel. 800-387-0711
www.cit-tours.com

CIT Tours
1450 Councillors Street, Suite 750
Montreal, P.Q. H3A 2E6
Tel. 800-361-7799
www.cit-tours.com

Czech Republic
P. O. Box 198
Exchange Tower
2 First Canadian Place, 14th Floor
Toronto, Ont. M5X 1A6

DER Rail
904 The East Mall
Etobicoke, Ont M9B 6K2
Tel. 416-695-1211
Fax 416-695-4700

Estonian Consulate
958 Broadview Avenue
Toronto, Ont M4K 2R6
Tel. 416-461-0764

French Government Tourist Office
30 St. Patrick Street, Suite 700
Toronto, Ont M5T 3A3
Tel. 416-593-6427

GermanRail. See DER Rail.

Greek National Tourist Org.
Main Level, 1300 Bay Street
Toronto, Ont M5R 3K8
Tel. 416-968-2220
Fax 416-968-6533
www.gnto.gr

Irish Tourist Board
160 Bloor Street E., Suite 1150
Toronto, Ont M4W 1B9
Tel. 416-929-2777
Fax 416-929-6783

Italian Government Tourist Board
1 Place Ville Marie, Suite 1914
Montreal, P.Q. H3B 3M9
Tel. 514-866-7667

Italian State Railroads: see CIT
   Tours.

Latvian Embassy
112 Kont Street
Place de Ville, Tower B,
   Suite 208
Ottawa, Ont
Tel. 613-238-6868

Netherlands Board of Tourism
25 Adelaide Street E.,
   Suite 710
Toronto, Ont M5C 1Y2
Tel. 1-800-GOHOLLAND
www.goholland.com

Northern Ireland Tourist Board
2 Bloor Street West,
   Suite 1501
Toronto, Ont M4W 3E2
Tel. 416-925-6368/800-576-8174
www.discovernorthernireland.com

Portuguese Trade and
   Tourism Commission
60 Bloor St. W., Suite 1005
Toronto, Ont M4W 3B8
Tel. 416-921-7376
Fax 416-921-1353

Rail Europe
Tel. 800-361-RAIL

Spain, Tourist Office of
2 Bloor Street West, Suite 3402
Toronto, Ont M6W 1A1
Tel. 416-961-3131
Fax 416-961-1992
www.okspain.org

Switzerland Tourism
926 The East Mall
Etobicoke, Toronto, Ont M9B 6K1
Tel. 011-800-100-200-30
(Mon.-Fri. from 9 A.M. to 9 P.M. EST;
International Toll-free)
www.myswiterland.com

AUSTRALIA

British Tourist Authority
Level 16, Gateway
1 Macquarie Place
Sydney NSW 2000
Tel. (02) 9377-4400
Fax (02) 9377-4499
www.visitbritain.com/au

CIT World Travel
263 Clarence Street
Sydney, NSW 2000
Tel. (02) 9267-1255
Fax. (02) 9261-4664
www.cittravel.com.au

Eden Travel
Shop 626, Royal Arcade
255 Pitt Street
Sydney, NSW 2000
Tel. (02) 9264-8302
Fax (02) 9261-3274

Mid City Travel
Level 4, 541 George Street
Sydney, NSW 2000
Tel. (02) 9283-5818
Fax (02) 9284-5898

CIT World Travel
Level 4, 227 Collins Street
Melbourne, VIC 3000
Tel. (03) 9650-5510
Fax (03) 9654-2490
www.cittravel.com.au

Concorde International Travel
9th Floor, 510 King Street
Melbourne, VIC 3003
Tel. (03) 9920-3833
Fax (02) 9920-3822
www.concorde.com.au

Plain Flying
495 Collins Street
Melbourne, VIC 3000
Tel. (03) 9629-5302
Fax (03) 9629-1047

Rail Plus
Level 3, 459 Little Collins Street
Melbourne, VIC 3000
Tel. (09) 9642-8644
Fax (09) 9642-8403
www.railplus.com.au

Angas Travel
303 Angas Street
Adelaide South, SA 5000
Tel. (08) 8223-1690
Fax (08) 82244-0984

Dunsborough Travel
Shop 2, Naturalliste Forum
Dunsborough, WA 6281
Tel. (08) 9755-3122
Fax (08) 9756-8009

Peregrine Travel
1st Floor, 132 Wickham Street
Fortitude Valley, QLD 4006
Tel. (07) 3854-1022
Fax (07) 3854-1079

Raine Square Travel
Shop 30B, Raine Square
Perth, WA 6000
Tel. (08) 9322-5155
Fax (08) 9322-1310

World Wide Travel
15 Toorak Road
South Yarra, VIC 3181
Tel. (03) 9510-6077
Fax (03) 9510-6145

NEW ZEALAND

Budget Travel
(over 50 branches)
Tel. 0800 80-80-40
www.budgettravel.co.nz

Holiday Shoppe
(over 80 branches)
Tel. 0800 80-84-80
holidayshoppe.co.nz

Appendix B

European Eurail Aid Offices

Austria

Innsbruck Hauptbahnhof
Sudtiroler Platz 7
Tel. (0512) 503-5460
Open Mon.-Sun.
  6 A.M. to 9 P.M.

Salzburg Hauptbahnhof
Sudtiroler Platz 1
Tel. (0662) 8887-5428
Open Mon.-Sun.
  8. A.M. to 8 P.M.

Vienna Westbahnhof
Europaplatz 1
Tel. (01) 58800-33598
Open Mon.-Fri.
  9 A.M. to 4 P.M.

Belgium

Brussels South (Midi/Sud)
  Train Station
Travel Center/Service
  International
Tel. (02) 0900-10366
Open Mon.-Fri.
  9 A.M. to 7:30 P.M.;
Sat. 9 A.M. to 5 P.M.

Denmark

Copenhagen Central
  Station
DSB Travel Office
Tel. (033)-150-400-21742
Open Mon.-Sun.
  8 A.M. to 7 P.M.

Finland

Helsinki Central Train Station
Ticket Office/International Services
Tel. (09) 707-5703
Open Mon.-Fri.
    8:30 A.M. to 5:15 P.M.;
Sat.-Sun. 10 A.M. to 5:15 P.M.

France

Paris Lyon Station
International Window
Galerie des Fresques
Tel. (01) 53-33-11-67
Open Mon.-Fri.
    6 A.M. to 10 P.M.

Paris St. Lazare Station
Service International
Tel. (01) 53-42-27-62
Open Mon.-Fri.
    10 A.M. to 7 P.M.;
Sat. 9:30 A.M. to Noon and 1 to 6 P.M.

Paris Nord Station
Bureau Information
Espace Grandes Lignes
Tel. (01) 55-31-52-02
Open Mon.-Sat
    9 A.M. to 8 P.M.

Paris Orly Airport SNCF Office
Tel. (01) 48-84-26-74
Open Mon.-Sat. 8 A.M. to 8 P.M.;
Sun. 9:45 A.M. to 1 P.M. and
    2:45 to 6:30 P.M.

Paris Charles de Gaulle Airport
    SNCF Station
Terminal 1 - Arrivals Floor/Gate 22
Tel. (01) 48-16-10-16
Open Mon.-Sun.
    8 A.M. to 8 P.M.
Terminal 2
Tel. (01) 48-79-61-39
Open Mon.-Sun. 8 A.M. to 7 P.M.

Marseille St. Charles Train Station
Tel. (04) 95-04-14-03
Open Mon.-Sun.
    6 A.M. to 10 P.M.

Nice Ville (SNCF) Train Station
Bureau Information/Reservation
Tel. (04) 92-14-82-65
Open Mon.-Sat. 8 to 11 A.M. and
    2 to 6:30 P.M.

Germany

Berlin Zoo Train Station
ReiseZentrum
Hardenburgplatz 11
Tel. (030) 2974-9277
Open Mon.-Sun.
    4:45 A.M. to 11 P.M.

Cologne Hauptbahnhof
ReiseZentrum
Trankgasse 11
Tel. (0221)-141-2658
Open Mon.-Fri.
    5:30 A.M. to 11 P.M.;
Sat.-Sun. 5:30 A.M. to 10:30 P.M.

Dresden Hauptbahnhof
ReiseZentrum
Am Hauptbahnhof 4
Tel. (0351) 461-4183
Open Mon.-Sun. 7 A.M. to 10 P.M.

Frankfurt/Main Hauptbahnhof
ReiseZentrum
Tel. (069) 265-34581
Open Mon.-Sun.
    6 A.M. to 10:30 P.M.

Frankfurt/Main Airport
ReiseZentrum
Hugo-Ecker-Ring
Tel. (069) 265-15522 or
    265-37950
Open Mon.-Sun.
    6 A.M. to 10:30 P.M.

Hamburg Hauptbahnhof
ReiseZentrum
Hochmannplatz 10
Tel. (040) 39-18-43-13
Open Mon.-Fri.
7:30 A.M. to 8 P.M.;
Sat.-Sun. 10 A.M. to 1 P.M.
and 2 to 5 P.M.

Hanover Hauptbahnhof
ReiseZentrum
Tel. (0511) 286-5464
Open Mon.-Sun.
6 A.M. to 10 P.M.

Heidelberg Hauptbahnhof
ReiseZentrum
Tel. (06221) 525-341
Open Mon.-Fri.
5:45 A.M. to 8:45 P.M.;
Sat.-Sun. 6:30 A.M. to 8:45 P.M.

Leipzig Hauptbahnhof
ReiseZentrum
Willy-Brandt-Platz 5
Tel. (0341) 968-11661
Open Mon.-Sun.
5:30 A.M. to 10 P.M.

Munich Hauptbahnhof
ReiseZentrum,
Windows 19/20
Bahnhofplatz 2
Tel. (089) 130-85-890
Open Mon.-Fri.
7 A.M. to 8 P.M.;
Sat.-Sun. 8 A.M. to 5 P.M.

Stuttgart Hauptbahnhof
ReiseZentrum/
Bahn Touristik
Arnulf-Klett-Platz 2
Tel. (0711)-2092-24-64
Open Mon.-Fri.
7:30 A.M. to 8 P.M.;
Sat. 7:30 A.M. to 1:30 P.M.;
Sun. closed.

Great Britain

Rail Europe Travel Shop
179 Picadilly
London
Tel. (0990) 848-848
Open Mon.-Fri.
10 A.M. to 6 P.M.;
Sat. 10 A.M. to 5 P.M.

Rail Europe Ltd.
10, Leake Street
London
Tel. (08705) 848-848
Open Mon.-Fri.
8 A.M. to 8 P.M.;
Sat. 9 A.M. to 4 P.M.

German Rail UK
18 Conduit Street
London
Tel. (44171) 317-0919
Open Mon.-Fri. 9 A.M. to 5 P.M.
Sat. 9:30 A.M. to 1 P.M.

Greece

Athens Greek Railroads Office
Bureau des Voyages et du Tourisme
No. 2
1, rue Karolou
Tel. (01) 522-4563
Open Mon.-Sat. 8 A.M. to 3 P.M.

Athens Greek Railroads Office
Bureau des Voyages et du Tourisme
No. 7
17, rue Filellinon -
Syntagma Square
Tel. (01) 323-67-47 and 323-62-73
Open Mon.-Fri. 8 A.M. to 3 P.M.

Patras Central Station
Tel. (061) 221-311 or 273-694
Open summer Mon.-Sun.
8 A.M. to 8 P.M.;
winter 8 A.M. to 2 P.M.

Thessaloniki Central Station
Tel. (031) 599-033
Open Mon.-Sun. 5:30 A.M. to
1 P.M. and 2 to 8 P.M.

Hungary

Menetjegyuiroda
(Customer Service Office)
Andrassy Ut 35
Budapest
Tel. (1) 322-9082
Apr.-Sept. open Mon.-Fri.
9 A.M. to 6 P.M.;
Oct.-Mar. open Mon.-Fri.
9 A.M. to 5 P.M.

Ireland

Dublin International Rail
Travel Center
35 Lower Abbey Street
Tel. (01) 703-4127
Open Mon.-Fri. 9 A.M. to 5 P.M.

Italy

Bari Centrale Station
Ticket Office
Tel. (080) 573-2003 or 521-2202
Open Mon.-Sat. 9 A.M. to
1 P.M. and 4 to 8 P.M.

Florence Santa Maria Novella
Station
Information Office
Tel. (055) 235-2595
Open Mon.-Sat. 9 to 11 A.M.

Milan Centrale Station
Information Office
Tel. (02) 6371-2565
Open Mon.-Sun. 7:30 A.M. to 9:40 P.M.

Naples Centrale Station
Information Office
Tel. (081) 567-4700
Open Mon.-Sun. 7 A.M. to 9 P.M.

Palermo Centrale Station
Information Office
Tel. (091) 603-3558
Open Mon.-Sun. 8 A.M. to 8 P.M.

Rome Termini Station
Information Office
Tel. (06) 4730-6385
Open Mon.-Sun.
7 A.M. to 9 P.M.

Venice Santa Lucia Station
Ticket Office
Tel. (041) 715-555
Open Mon.-Sun. 8 A.M. to 8 P.M.

Luxembourg

Luxembourg Train Station
Information and Sales Center
Tel. 492-424
Open Mon.-Fri. 8 A.M. to noon and 1
to 5 P.M.

Netherlands

Amsterdam Central Station
International Ticket Counter
Tel. (020) 557-8088
Open Mon.-Sun. 8 A.M. to 8 P.M.

Amsterdam Schiphol Airport
NS International Ticket Office
Schiphol Plaza
Fax (020) 601-9424
Open Mon.-Sun.
8 A.M. to 9 P.M.

Rotterdam Central Station
International Ticket Office
Tel. (010) 282-4401
Open Mon.-Fri. 8 A.M. to 7 pm.

Utrecht Central Station
NS International Ticket Office
Tel. (030) 235-4171
Open Mon.-Fri.
8:30 A.M. to 9 P.M.

Norway

Oslo Sentral Station
International Ticket Office
Tel. (02) 315-2448
Open Mon.-Sun.
7 A.M. to 11 P.M.

Portugal

Faro Train Station
Largo de estacao
Tel. (089) 23815
Open Mon.-Sun. 10 A.M. to 6 P.M.

Lisbon Santa Apolonia Station
International Ticket Office
Avenida Infante D. Henrique
Tel. (01) 888-4181 x189
Open Mon.-Sun. 9 A.M. to 6 P.M.

Porto Sao Bento Station
Praca Almeida Garret
Tel. (02) 2002-722 ext. 28
Open Mon.-Sun.
6:30 A.M. to 4 P.M.
(to 6 P.M. weekdays during July and
August)

Spain

Barcelona Franca Train Station
Avda. Marques de Argentera s/n
Tel. (093) 919-6567
Open Mon.-Fri. 9 A.M. to 2 P.M. and 4
to 6:30 P.M.

Barcelona Sants Train Station
Tel. (093) 490-3851
Open Mon.-Sun.
9 A.M. to 8 P.M.

Madrid RENFE Downtown Office
Alcala, 44
Tel. (091) 531-4707
Open Mon.-Sat.
9:30 A.M. to 8 P.M.

Madrid Bajaras Airport
RENFE office
Tel. (091)-305-8544
Open Mon.-Sun. 8 A.M. to 9 P.M.

Madrid Chamartin Station
Travel Office
Tel. (91) 314-0829
Open Mon.-Sun. 9 A.M. to 10 P.M.

Seville RENFE Office
Calle Zaragoza 29
Tel. (0954) 222-693
Open Mon.-Fri. 9 A.M. to 1:15 P.M.
and 4 to 7 P.M.
Sat. 9 to 12:30

Seville Train Station
Calle Zaragoza 29
Tel. (954) 222-693
Open Mon.-Fri.
9 A.M. to 1 P.M. and
4 to 7 P.M.;
Sat. 9 A.M. to 12:30 P.M.

Sweden

Stockholm Central Station
Ticket Office
Tel. (08) 762-4855
Open Mon.-Fri. 8 A.M. to 6 P.M.;
Sat. 9 A.M. to 5 P.M.
Sun. 9 A.M. to 4 P.M.

Switzerland

Basel SBB Station
Tel. (0512) 292-484
Open Mon.-Fri. 7 A.M. to 8 P.M.;
Sat. 7 A.M. to 5 P.M.
Sun. 8 A.M. to 5 P.M.

Bern Main Train Station
Train Information Office
Tel. (0512) 201-451
Open Mon.-Fri. 8 A.M. to 7 P.M.;
Sat. 8 A.M. to 5 P.M.

Geneva Train Station
Train Information Office
Tel. (0512) 251-410
Open Mon.-Fri.
  8 A.M. to 7 P.M.
Sat. 9 A.M. to 5:30 P.M.

Geneva Airport Train Station
Train Information Office
Tel. (022) 7910-250
Open Mon.-Fri.
  9:15 A.M. to 5:45 P.M.;
Sat. 9 A.M. to 5:45 P.M.

Interlaken West Train Station
Tel. (033) 826-4750
Open Mon.-Sun.
  8 A.M. to noon and
  2 to 6 P.M.

Lucerne Train Station
Train Travel Office
Tel. (0512) 271-350
Open Mon.-Fri.
  8 A.M. to 7:45 P.M.;
Sat. 8 A.M. to 6 P.M.
Sun. 9 A.M. to 6 P.M.

Zurich Hauptbahnhof
Train Information Office
Tel. (0512) 223-364
Open Mon.-Fri. 6:45 A.M. to 8:30 P.M.
Sat.-Sun. 6:45 A.M. to 7:30 P.M.

Zurich Airport Train Station
Train Travel Center
Tel. (0512) 227-376
Open Mon.-Sun. 7 A.M. to 7 P.M.

Index